THE
NAME
BOOK

DOROTHY
ASTORIA

THE
NAME
BOOK

OVER 10,000 NAMES–
THEIR MEANINGS,
ORIGINS, AND
SPIRITUAL
SIGNIFICANCE

DOROTHY
ASTORIA

BETHANY HOUSE PUBLISHERS
MINNEAPOLIS, MINNESOTA 55438

The Name Book
Copyright © 1982, 1997
Bethany House Publishers

Revised and updated by Christopher J. Soderstrom

Cover design by Eric Walljasper

Published by Bethany House Publishers
A Ministry of Bethany Fellowship International
11400 Hampshire Avenue South
Minneapolis, Minnesota 55438
www.bethanyhouse.com

Printed in the United States of America by
Bethany Press International, Minneapolis, Minnesota 55438

Library of Congress Cataloging-in-Publication Data

Astoria, Dorothy.
    The name book / by Dorothy Astoria.
        p.   cm.
    ISBN 1–55661–982–0 (pbk.)
    Names, Personal—Dictionaries.   I. Title.
CS2367.A95   1997
929.4'03—dc21   97–21023
                                                         CIP

CONTENTS

WHAT'S IN A NAME? – 7

THE DECIDING FACTORS – 11

GUIDE TO USING NAME LISTINGS – 17

ALPHABETICAL LISTINGS OF NAMES – 19

LIST OF BIBLE NAMES – 291

BIRTHSTONES AND FLOWERS – 299

HERITAGE OF NAMES – 300

OUR FAVORITE GIRL NAMES – 302

OUR FAVORITE BOY NAMES – 303

WHAT'S IN A NAME?

Names have been in existence as long as humanity. God created a timeless tradition when he gave Adam the first name, meaning "formed of earth." In the same manner, humans have been handing out names since the beginning of recorded time.

But why names? Why not labels, symbols, or codes? Part of the answer is found in Genesis 1:27. "So God created human beings in his image. In the image of God he created them. He created them male and female" (NCV). If we were merely another species of God's creation, we would all have one name, such as "lion," "sparrow," or "mole." But because we are a special and unparalleled creation— individuals—we each have a name.

Names are an integral part of who we are. While we are all intrinsically unique, names bestow upon us a tangible way to distinguish one another. God reveals this individuality in Isaiah 43:1 in saying, "I have redeemed you; I have called you by name, you are mine" (NRSV). The names we now bear have meaning to the Lord! Not only this, but in Revelation 2:17 He tells his children that He will give us "a new name that no one knows except the one who receives it" (NLT).

The evolution of names has been shaped by both religious and cultural influences. In ancient times people were generally given one name (called a "given name"). This name often related to a circumstance surrounding a child's birth ("Moses," meaning "drawn from the water") or a trait that parents hoped a child would possess ("Salome," meaning "peaceful"). Also, the name could be connected with a promise or an aspiration ("Isaac," meaning "laughter") or possibly a simple object ("Esther," meaning "star").

In latter ancient history, some utilization of second names (and third, and fourth, et al.) can be observed. These names were usually given to demonstrate a person's identification with a particular family and/or clan (Gaius Julius Caesar) or with a father (Simon bar-Jonah, with "bar" meaning "son of"). This practice was carried into modern times through various tribal societies.

These additional names, however, were not commonplace in Western civilization until about 900 years ago (around A.D. 1100). At first, added names were taken only by the nobility. They became known as "surnames," derived from the the literal words "sir names." This practice was gradually embraced by the common people over the centuries until, in 1465, King Edward V of England delivered an edict requiring that surnames be adopted universally for identification purposes. He ordered that the names taken reflect the individual's identity, representing either a town, color, art, or office. Therefore, many new surnames came into being, such as Black, Smith, Miller, and Baker.

Over time, the means by which names were chosen and/or acquired broadened significantly. Some came from physical characteristics. For example, dark-haired Elizabeth became Elizabeth Browne, and blond James became James White. Some also were formed by adding "son" to the father's name (Wilson, Carlson, Johnson, and Anderson). Others came about by adding prefixes meaning "son" to the father's name (Fitzpatrick, Fitzgerald, MacMurray, MacDonald, O'Bannon, and O'Shea). There were also many other means of deriving and obtaining surnames.

The Church had an unparalled influence over the choosing of names in medieval times. In the twelfth century, it decreed that only children named after saints and martyrs could be baptized. This was an attempt to stop the practice of naming children after pagan gods and entities. It was rather effective, for a priest of the Church had to be present to officiate at a child's baptism and confirmation. Since these practices were generally believed to be integral to salvation, most people honored the edicts. Statistics show that the great majority of women at that time were named Mary, Ann, Elizabeth, or Catherine, while most men were named John, James, William, Charles, or George.

For the most part, additional titles, known to us as "middle names," were not utilized until the eighteenth century. At this time, these new names became a way of further distinguishing an individual and also of honoring deceased relatives or admired persons. These, along with surnames, have emerged with ever-increasing importance as the earth's population has continued to geometrically increase.

While all names have both denotative (inherent) and connotative (implied) meaning(s), this is no longer as important to many parents who are choosing names for their child. Often a child is still named for a characteristic or place, but in many cases names are now selected for the way in which they commemorate someone or something, or simply on the basis of their own various asthetic qualities.

When inherent meaning is important to prospective parents, names are normally chosen on the merits of their positive implications. Parents naming their daughter "Cady" often do so in the expectation and hope that she will be pure. In the same way, parents who choose "Matthew" for their son most likely consider him a gift of God.

So, what's in a name? Names are a celebration not only of our humanity, but also a reminder of our individuality—that we are uniquely made in the image of God. They are wonderful gifts, given second only to the gift of life itself—lasting testimonies to the beauty of personhood. Best of all, *you* now have the opportunity to make these choices for your child. Enjoy your quest.

THE DECIDING
FACTORS

Associations

While particular names are given for many different reasons, three associations are of primary importance to most people. One, most children are in some way named after at least one relative. Two, they are often named in honor of historical figures and celebrities. Three, the majority of people in the Western hemisphere is named for biblical characters. Naturally, there is a great amount of overlap between these areas. For example, a baby named "Joseph Lincoln Johnson" could be named after both his grandfather Joseph and the Joseph of biblical renown, while also commemorating Abraham Lincoln.

Gender

While there seems to be a vast discrepancy in the ratio of male and female biblical names, since there are over 3,000 men listed in the Bible and less than 200 women, it's not as "unequal" as it might appear. Many of the male names recorded in the Scriptures are now used frequently for females, such as Ariel, Dara, Jada, Neriah, Reba, Susi, and Zina. In the same way, there are many names which were once considered to be exclusively for boys or girls that now are commonly used and considered appropriate for both sexes. Pay attention to name usage around you—you may have more options than you realized! Examples of "gender-neutral" monikers are: Adrian, Audrey, Courtney, Dana, Greer, Jamie, Kelly, Kevin, Lee, Lindsay, Madison, Robin, Sydney, Taylor, Terry, Tierney, and Tony. Even so, it is important to be mindful of the consequences of choosing a traditionally gender-specific name for a child of the opposite sex. Innovation is fun, but try to envision any possible disadvantages as well.

Characteristics

Children are frequently named in celebration of treasured ideals, or given names that intrinsically represent these characteristics (Charity,

Hope, or Grace, for example). Also, some are named after commemorative circumstances surrounding the child's birth, such as Spring, Noel, or Joy. In addition, parents often give names which represent elements of character that it is hoped the child will possess. For instance, Ryan (meaning "little ruler"), Alexis (meaning "defender of mankind"), Katrina (meaning "pure"), or Caleb (meaning "bold").

Nicknames

There are two important factors to consider regarding the use of shortened names. One, don't use a longer name that will likely be shortened to a name that is undesirable to you. That is to say, if you cringe at the thought of Josh or Ash, don't name your baby Joshua or Ashleigh. Other people *will* shorten it. Two, in most cases it's preferable to give your child the "long version" of the chosen name. "Allison" and "Jacob" can always be abbreviated by merely using "Allie" and "Jake," if those are the names you happen to prefer. However, if you choose the nickname as the given name, you impose unnecessary limits. As your child matures he or she may desire to put aside the nickname in favor of the full name. This may be difficult if the legality of the situation hinders such change (like altering a birth certificate).

Acronyms

An acronym is a word formed from letters of a set of words that stands for the group of words as a whole (usually the first letter or letters). Some common examples are *S.C.U.B.A.* (Self-Contained Underwater Breathing Apparatus), *R.A.D.A.R.* (RAdio Detection And Ranging), and *P.A.N.I.C.* (Parents Attempting to Name Imminent Children). What is not commonly realized, however, is that often the set of names given to a person will lend itself to an acronym. This can be a wonderful thing. For instance, you may want to give your child names which will spell out *L.U.V.* (Lexi Umaya Vanderberg) or *T.R.U.* (Tyler Robinson Ulrich). Another enjoyable option has been to create a set of names that will match the standard nickname of the given name. Megan Elizabeth Gander brings out *Meg,* and Nicholas Ian Cortese emits *Nic.*

There are elements of acronyms which are, perhaps, less desirable. First, the gender of the child should be taken into account. *H.U.G.* might seem adorable for a child, but a young man might see it differently, as did one great military officer. Hiram Ulysses Grant (who also became our eighteenth president) was so mortified by the hazing he received at West Point for his acronym that he changed his name to the more commonly recognized Ulysses Simpson Grant. Likewise, *B.I.G.* could be both fun and appropriate for a baby boy who weighs in at 10 lbs., 4 oz., but Brianna Ingrid Gates certainly will someday object.

Second, there are many acronyms which should be avoided altogether.

Don't combine names that invite merciless teasing. Most of these can be spotted as soon as they are spelled out. Avoid, for instance, Ferris Alastair Tannen, Zachery Isaac Thatcher, and (for those who prefer longer titles) Brittaney Ariel Rhiannon Frazier.

Humor

Often parents give their children names that evoke concrete images of one thing or another. *Every* name carries connotations, just as every word does. However, if humor is involved, in each case it must be decided how far this will be carried. This is especially true when it comes to rhymes. Conventional wisdom says to forgo combinations that are "overly harmonious." Mild examples are "Sarah Barah" or "Jason Mason." Sometimes these can be fun, although it might not be fun for your child.

Even more consideration should be given to those names which could bring further ridicule. Real-life demonstrations are offered by Robin Banks, Wayne Dwopp, Cinder Eller, Krystal Ball, Flip Side, Otto Graph, Ann Cuff, Iona Mink, Paul Bearer, Candy Barr, and Constance Noring.

Spelling

There are some other points to mull and muse. It's always enjoyable and challenging to look for ways to make the names that you select "stand out." If you're thinking about utilizing a notably unique name or a considerably variant spelling of a name, remember: your child will need to write it out each and every time a full signature is required throughout his or her life. Your darling baby might someday come to resent your creativity if you invent a "Ghennyphur Kolleene" or a "Qristaphir Writcherd."

Pronunciation

No matter what languages underlie the root of the name you choose, there is a fair chance that you have many options available to you in terms of pronunciation. Frequently, notably ethnic and exotic names bring new zest to communication. Sometimes variety is refreshing. Bring to mind, however, this simple maxim: People tend to pronounce a name the way it looks. Ask yourself honestly whether having to repeatedly correct the name's pronunciation and/or spelling will at some point become burdensome to your child (or you!).

Trends

Many people opt for trendy names. This is often regarded as a means to ensure that as children grow up they will "fit in" with others of or near their age. But first consider: which is more important to you—commonality or exclusivity? Tradition or authenticity? Harmony or distinction?

In many cases both can be had. Most of us are given at least three names. Ponder this with special consideration in regard to the first name.

Do you want your child to have six others in her class/office/sandbox/ committee who share the same name? Or would you rather give him one which will set him apart in one or more ways?

A pair of asides might be examined here. First, you can label your child with an exact era if a name is a falling star (beautiful and thrilling, yes, but burned up in the atmosphere in a flash). Second, while a name's denotative, or official, meaning probably won't change quickly, it's connotative, or implied, meanings often do. It usually takes the passing of three generations for a name to be regenerated from its previously imagined meanings. This is not altogether bad—all names will change to a degree in this sense over the course of a lifetime. Do try to evaluate possible names with the big-picture timeline in mind.

Flow

It has been said that names are either the best or worst presents a child can be given. That is to say, the implications of a child's given names should be thoroughly considered. In so doing, picture your child having these particular names all of his or her life. One of the most effective means of carrying this out is by saying, out loud, the prospective full name(s) of the child. Also, you might try writing the information out, in index card form. For example:

Name: Danelle Marie Soderstrom
Initials: DMS
First and Middle: Danelle Marie
First and Last: Danelle Soderstrom
Possible Nicknames: Dani, Dee, Nell, Nelly

By working this out, you may possibly avoid an unforeseen disaster. If you don't, you might end up with an Anna Graham or an Evan Gelical.

Surnames

Surnames can be a determining element in deciding first and middle names. The standard factors are how long and how distinguished surnames appear to be. First, if you have a short, easily recognized surname (Chang or Jones), you can be somewhat more "adventurous" in selecting the other names. You might choose longer or more unique names such as Jacqueline, Payton, Savanah, or Madison. Second, if your surname is uncommon or extra long, you may want to choose a simpler or shorter first name to provide contrast.

Phonetics

In many cases you'll want to avoid choosing a given name that ends with the same letter or sound with which the middle or surname begins. If this is not observed, it can be difficult to know where one name ends and the other begins. Some examples are Lauren Newall, Janelle Leeden,

Caleb Billings, Joseph Foston, Phillip Pryors, and Bob Block. It would take some thought to process these names. This is particularly noticeable with vowels: Joshua Aling, Cori Easter, or Kayla Underman.

Hyphenation

Many parents today give their child a hyphenated surname in order that the maiden surname of the mother is preserved, e.g., Caitlyn Paige Larsen-Wilder, or Austin Cole Jennings-Thurston. Another option would be to use the mother's maiden name as the child's middle name, shortening the surname. In this case, your child might be Haley McDonald Fair or Alexander Brown Hastings.

TO USING
NAME LISTINGS

AARON, Aaran, Aaren, Aarin, Aaronn, Aarron, Aron, Arran, Arron
(see also Aran, Aren)
Language/Cultural Origin: Hebrew
Inherent Meaning: Light Bringer
Spiritual Connotation: Radiating God's Light
Scripture: Isaiah 60:1 KJV
Arise, shine; for thy light is come, and the glory of the LORD is risen upon thee.

Primary Name (example: Aaron):

In most cases, this is the form of the name that is most commonly used. Sometimes a more secondary form will be listed first. This is done when, for instance, this form was used in the Bible or in classical literature (i.e., original rendering).

Alternative Spellings (examples: Aaran, Aaren, . . .):

These are other ways in which the name has been used. These lists are not meant to be exhaustive. There are many additional possible spellings, renderings, and combinations of names.

(See also . . .):

This indicates that another name which is quite similar to the one listed has its own entry in the book and can be cross-referenced.

This symbol indicates that the primary name listed appears (in form) in the Bible.

Language/Cultural Origin:

This is the primary cultural and lingual setting from which the name is derived. In most cases, the origin is quite apparent. There are instances, however, in which a word (name) has legitimate roots in two or more languages. In these cases, the focus has been to determine the most common usage of the name and follow it in this book. Bear in mind, as well, that names evolve in form as they cross lingual barriers. Consequently, there may exist several forms of the same name.

Inherent Meaning:

This is the literal, or *denotative*, meaning of the name. Here, also, most of the names listed have a clear heritage. As a result, most of the inherent meanings are readily discoverable. Even so, some may have more than one meaning (again, having crossed languages). In addition, many of the words originate in ancient tongues and have notably changed in meaning. The greatest efforts have been made to ensure that the meaning listed is that which is derived from the original language of the name.

Spiritual Connotation:

This is an implied, or *connotative*, meaning of the name. The goal has been to take connotative meanings and interpret them in a spiritual (or abstract) sense. There is a subjective element here, for almost every name has more than one connotative meaning. However, the goal here is not to exhaustively list the traits or characteristics implied by a given name. Instead, one or two are listed to give a general idea of what are often seen as intrinsic qualities of a particular name, such as would be desired, thought, or hoped for a child given the name to possess.

Scripture:

This is a reference from God's Word which is intended to shed light upon the inherent and implied meanings of the name. Attention has been centered especially upon the promises, encouragements, and exhortations the heavenly Father has given.

AARON, Aaran, Aaren, Aarin, Aaronn, Aarron, Aron, Arran, Arron (see also Aran, Aren)
Language/Cultural Origin: Hebrew
Inherent Meaning: Light Bringer
Spiritual Connotation: Radiating God's Light
Scripture: Isaiah 60:1 KJV
Arise, shine; for thy light is come, and the glory of the LORD is risen upon thee.

ABBOT, Abbott
Language/Cultural Origin: Aramaic
Inherent Meaning: Spiritual Leader
Spiritual Connotation: Walks in Truth
Scripture: 2 Kings 20:3 NKJV
Remember now, O LORD, I pray, how I have walked before You in truth and with a loyal heart, and have done what was good in Your sight.

ABDIEL, Abdeel, Abdeil
Language/Cultural Origin: Hebrew
Inherent Meaning: Servant of God
Spiritual Connotation: Worshiper
Scripture: Psalm 2:11 TLB
Serve the Lord with reverent fear; rejoice with trembling.

ABDUL, Abdoul
Language/Cultural Origin: Middle Eastern
Inherent Meaning: Servant
Spiritual Connotation: Humble
Scripture: Matthew 23:12 RSV
Whoever exalts himself will be humbled, and whoever humbles himself will be exalted.

ABEL, Abell
Language/Cultural Origin: Hebrew
Inherent Meaning: Breath
Spiritual Connotation: Life of God
Scripture: Ephesians 5:2 NLT
Live a life filled with love for others, following the example of Christ, who loved you and gave himself as a sacrifice to take away your sins.

ABI, Abbey, Abbi, Abby (see also Abigail)
Language/Cultural Origin: Anglo-Saxon
Inherent Meaning: God's Will
Spiritual Connotation: Secure in God
Scripture: Psalm 91:2 NKJV
I will say of the LORD, He is my refuge and my fortress; my God, in Him I will trust.

ABIA, Abiah (see also Habaiah)
Language/Cultural Origin: Hebrew
Inherent Meaning: God Is My Father
Spiritual Connotation: Child of God
Scripture: Galatians 4:7 NKJV
Therefore you are no longer a slave but a son, and if a son, then an heir of God through Christ.

ABIEL, Abielle (see also Aviel)
Language/Cultural Origin: Hebrew
Inherent Meaning: Child of God
Spiritual Connotation: Heir of the Kingdom
Scripture: Luke 18:16 NASB
Permit the children to come to Me, and do not hinder them, for the kingdom of God belongs to such as these.

ABIGAIL, Abbigayle, Abbigail, Abbygayle, Abigael, Abigale
Language/Cultural Origin: Hebrew
Inherent Meaning: My Father Rejoices
Spiritual Connotation: Cherished of God
Scripture: Zephaniah 3:17 NKJV
The LORD your God in your midst, the Mighty One, will save; He will rejoice over you with gladness, He will quiet you with His love, He will rejoice over you with singing.

ABIJAH, Abija, Abiya, Abiyah
Language/Cultural Origin: Hebrew
Inherent Meaning: Will of God
Spiritual Connotation: Eternal

Scripture: 1 John 2:17 NRSV
And the world and its desire are passing away, but those who do the will of God live forever.

ABNER, Ab, Avner
☞ Language/Cultural Origin: Hebrew
Inherent Meaning: Enlightener
Spiritual Connotation: Believer of Truth
Scripture: Ephesians 1:18 NASB
I pray that the eyes of your heart may be enlightened, so that you may know what is the hope of His calling, what are the riches of the glory of His inheritance in the saints.

ABRAHAM, Abe, Abrahim, Abram
☞ Language/Cultural Origin: Hebrew
Inherent Meaning: Father of the Nations
Spiritual Connotation: Founder
Scripture: Genesis 12:2 TLB
I will cause you to become the father of a great nation; I will bless you and make your name famous, and you will be a blessing to many others.

ABRIEL, Abrielle
Language/Cultural Origin: French
Inherent Meaning: Innocent
Spiritual Connotation: Tenderhearted
Scripture: Ephesians 4:32 RSV
Be kind to one another, tenderhearted, forgiving one another, as God in Christ forgave you.

ACE, Acey, Acie
Language/Cultural Origin: Latin
Inherent Meaning: Unity
Spiritual Connotation: One With the Father
Scripture: John 6:44 TLB
For no one can come to me unless the Father who sent me draws him to me, and at the Last Day I will cause all such to rise again from the dead.

ACTON, Akton
Language/Cultural Origin: Old English
Inherent Meaning: Oak-Tree Settlement
Spiritual Connotation: Agreeable
Scripture: Matthew 18:20 NASB
For where two or three have gathered together in My name, there I am in their midst.

ADA, Adah, Adalee, Aida
☞ Language/Cultural Origin: Hebrew

Inherent Meaning: Ornament
Spiritual Connotation: One Who Adorns
Scripture: 1 Peter 3:4 NKJV
Let [your adornment] be the hidden person of the heart, with the incorruptible beauty of a gentle and quiet spirit, which is very precious in the sight of God.

ADAEL, Adayel (see also Adiel)
Language/Cultural Origin: Hebrew
Inherent Meaning: God Is Witness
Spiritual Connotation: Vindicated
Scripture: Job 16:19 TLB
Yet even now the Witness to my innocence is there in heaven; my Advocate is there on high.

ADALIA, Adala, Adalin, Adelyn
☞ (see also Adeline)
Language/Cultural Origin: Hebrew
Inherent Meaning: Honor
Spiritual Connotation: Courageous
Scripture: Joshua 1:9 NKJV
Be strong and of good courage; do not be afraid, nor be dismayed, for the LORD your God is with you wherever you go.

ADAM, Addam, Adem
☞ Language/Cultural Origin: Hebrew
Inherent Meaning: Formed of Earth
Spiritual Connotation: In God's Image
Scripture: Genesis 1:27 KJV
So God created man in his own image, in the image of God created he him; male and female created he them.

ADARA, Adair, Adaira
☞ Language/Cultural Origin: Hebrew
Inherent Meaning: Exalted
Spiritual Connotation: Worthy of Praise
Scripture: Luke 14:11 NASB
For everyone who exalts himself will be humbled, and he who humbles himself will be exalted.

ADAYA, Adaiah
☞ Language/Cultural Origin: Hebrew
Inherent Meaning: God's Jewel
Spiritual Connotation: Valuable
Scripture: Matthew 6:26 TLB
Look at the birds! They don't worry about what to eat . . . for your heavenly Father feeds them. And you are far more valuable to him than they are.

ADDI, Addy (see also Adelaide)

Language/Cultural Origin: Hebrew
Inherent Meaning: My Witness
Spiritual Connotation: Chosen
Scripture: Acts 1:8 NRSV

But you will receive power when the Holy Spirit has come upon you; and you will be my witnesses.

ADDISON, Adison, Adisson

Language/Cultural Origin: Old English
Inherent Meaning: Son of Adam
Spiritual Connotation: In God's Image
Scripture: Ezekiel 36:27 RSV

And I will put my spirit within you, and cause you to walk in my statutes and be careful to observe my ordinances.

ADELAIDE, Addey, Addie (see also Addi)

Language/Cultural Origin: Old German
Inherent Meaning: Joyful
Spiritual Connotation: Spirit of Joy
Scripture: Psalm 5:11 NKJV

But let all those rejoice who put their trust in You; Let them ever shout for joy.

ADELINE, Adalina, Adella, Adelle, Adelynn (see also Adalia)

Language/Cultural Origin: Old German
Inherent Meaning: Noble
Spiritual Connotation: Under God's Guidance
Scripture: Psalm 31:3 NKJV

For You are my rock and my fortress; therefore, for Your name's sake, lead me and guide me.

ADIA, Adiah

Language/Cultural Origin: African
Inherent Meaning: Gift
Spiritual Connotation: Gift of Glory
Scripture: John 17:22 NASB

And the glory which Thou hast given Me I have given to them; that they may be one, just as We are one.

ADIEL, Addiel, Addielle (see also Adael)

Language/Cultural Origin: Hebrew
Inherent Meaning: Ornament of God
Spiritual Connotation: Lovely
Scripture: 1 Peter 3:4 NLT

You should be known for the beauty that comes from within . . . which is so precious to God.

ADINA, Adena, Adeena

Language/Cultural Origin: Hebrew
Inherent Meaning: Adorned
Spiritual Connotation: Clothed With Praise
Scripture: Jeremiah 31:4 RSV

Again I will build you. . . . Again you shall adorn yourself with timbrels, and shall go forth in the dance of the merrymakers.

ADLAI, Adley (see also Hadlai)

Language/Cultural Origin: Hebrew
Inherent Meaning: Justice of God
Spiritual Connotation: Truthful
Scripture: Zechariah 8:16 NKJV

Speak each man the truth to his neighbor; Give judgment in your gates for truth, justice, and peace.

ADLAR, Addler, Adler

Language/Cultural Origin: Old German
Inherent Meaning: Eagle
Spiritual Connotation: Youthful
Scripture: Psalm 103:2, 5 NKJV

Bless the LORD, O my soul, and forget not all His benefits . . So that your youth is renewed like the eagle's.

ADONIJAH, Adonia, Adoniah, Adonija, Adoniya, Adoniyah

Language/Cultural Origin: Hebrew
Inherent Meaning: God Is My Lord
Spiritual Connotation: Reverent
Scripture: Exodus 3:5 NCV

Then God said, "Do not come any closer. Take off your sandals, because you are standing on holy ground."

ADORA, Adoree

Language/Cultural Origin: Latin
Inherent Meaning: Beloved
Spiritual Connotation: Gift of God
Scripture: Malachi 1:2 NKJV

I have loved you, says the LORD.

ADRIA, Adría, Adriah

Language/Cultural Origin: Latin
Inherent Meaning: Love of Life
Spiritual Connotation: Filled With Life
Scripture: Psalm 36:7 TLB

How precious is your constant love, O God! All humanity takes refuge in the shadow of your wings.

ADRIAN, Adreian, Adreyan, Adriaan, Adrien, Adrion, Adryan, Adryon
Language/Cultural Origin: Greek
Inherent Meaning: Rich
Spiritual Connotation: Prosperous
Scripture: Deuteronomy 8:18 RSV
You shall remember the LORD your God, for it is he who gives you power to get wealth; that he may confirm his covenant which he swore to your fathers, as at this day.

ADRIANNA, Adriana
Language/Cultural Origin: Italian
Inherent Meaning: Dark
Spiritual Connotation: Guarded of God
Scripture: Psalm 121:7–8 NASB
The LORD will protect you from all evil; He will keep your soul. The LORD will guard your going out and your coming in from this time forth and forever.

ADRIEL, Adrial
Language/Cultural Origin: Hebrew
Inherent Meaning: Member of God's Flock
Spiritual Connotation: Nurtured of God
Scripture: John 10:11 NKJV
I am the good shepherd. The good shepherd gives His life for the sheep.

ADRIENNE, Adriane, Adriann, Adrianne, Adrien, Adriene
Language/Cultural Origin: Greek
Inherent Meaning: Confident
Spiritual Connotation: Faith in God
Scripture: Mark 9:23 NCV
Jesus said to the father, "All things are possible for the one who believes."

AENEAS, Eneas
Language/Cultural Origin: Greek
Inherent Meaning: Praised
Spiritual Connotation: Honored
Scripture: Proverbs 12:8 NKJV
A man will be commended according to his wisdom, but he who is of a perverse heart will be despised.

AFONYA, Afonja
Language/Cultural Origin: Russian

Inherent Meaning: Immortal
Spiritual Connotation: Eternal
Scripture: 1 Corinthians 15:54 RSV
When the perishable puts on the imperishable, and the mortal puts on immortality, then shall come to pass the saying that is written: Death is swallowed up in victory.

AFTON, Affton, Aftan, Aftyn
Language/Cultural Origin: Old English
Inherent Meaning: From Afton, England
Spiritual Connotation: Righteous
Scripture: Matthew 5:10 RSV
Blessed are those who are persecuted for righteousness' sake, for theirs is the kingdom of heaven.

AGATHA, Agata, Aggie
Language/Cultural Origin: Greek
Inherent Meaning: Benevolent
Spiritual Connotation: Kind
Scripture: Proverbs 21:21 NRSV
Whoever pursues righteousness and kindness will find life and honor.

AGRIPPA
Language/Cultural Origin: Latin
Inherent Meaning: Pain of Childbirth
Spiritual Connotation: Promise
Scripture: Genesis 17:16 NASB
And I will bless her ... and she shall be a mother of nations; kings of peoples shall come from her.

AGNES, Agness, Agnessa, Agniya
Language/Cultural Origin: Greek
Inherent Meaning: Pure
Spiritual Connotation: Innocent
Scripture: Matthew 5:8 KJV
Blessed are the pure in heart: for they shall see God.

AHAB, Ahabb
Language/Cultural Origin: Hebrew
Inherent Meaning: My Father's Brother
Spiritual Connotation: Learned
Scripture: Proverbs 2:10 TLB
For wisdom and truth will enter the very center of your being, filling your life with joy.

AHARAH, Aharra, Aharhel, ☞Aharia, Aharya

Language/Cultural Origin: Hebrew
Inherent Meaning: Brother of Rachel
Spiritual Connotation: Loyal
Scripture: Proverbs 18:24 NLT

There are friends who destroy each other, but a real friend sticks closer than a brother.

AHMAD, Ahamad, Ahmaad, Amaud

Language/Cultural Origin: Middle Eastern
Inherent Meaning: Most Highly Praised
Spiritual Connotation: Servant
Scripture: Mark 10:43 NLT

Whoever wants to be a leader among you must be your servant, and whoever wants to be first must be the slave of all.

AHMED, Ahamed, Amed

Language/Cultural Origin: Swahili
Inherent Meaning: Praiseworthy
Spiritual Connotation: Sincere
Scripture: Matthew 10:32 NKJV

Therefore whoever confesses Me before men, him I will also confess before My Father who is in heaven.

AHSAN, Ahsahn, Ahsán (see also Hasani, Ihsan)

Language/Cultural Origin: Middle Eastern
Inherent Meaning: Charitable
Spiritual Connotation: Generous
Scripture: 2 Corinthians 9:7 NRSV

Each of you must give as you have made up your mind, not reluctantly or under compulsion, for God loves a cheerful giver.

AIAH, Aija, Aijah, Aiya, Aiyah, ☞Aja, Ajah (see also Aya)

Language/Cultural Origin: Hebrew
Inherent Meaning: Bird of Prey
Spiritual Connotation: Strength of God
Scripture: Psalm 132:8 NKJV

Arise, O LORD, to Your resting place, You and the ark of Your strength.

AILEEN, Ailean, Ailene, Ailina, Aleene (see also Eileen)

Language/Cultural Origin: English
Inherent Meaning: Light Bearer
Spiritual Connotation: Messenger of Truth

Scripture: Matthew 5:14 NKJV

You are the light of the world. A city that is set on a hill cannot be hidden.

AINSLEY, Ainslee, Anslea, Anslee, Ansleigh, Ansley, Aynslee, Aynsley

Language/Cultural Origin: Scottish
Inherent Meaning: My Own Meadow
Spiritual Connotation: Bringer of the Word of Life
Scripture: Philippians 2:16 KJV

Holding forth the word of life; that I may rejoice in the day of Christ, that I have not run in vain, neither laboured in vain.

AIESHA, Aesha, Aisha, Aishah, Ayashah, Ayishah, Ayshea (see also Asia, Iesha)

Language/Cultural Origin: Middle Eastern
Inherent Meaning: Woman
Spiritual Connotation: Companion
Scripture: Genesis 2:18 NLT

And the LORD God said, It is not good for the man to be alone, I will make a companion who will help him.

AJANI, Ayani

Language/Cultural Origin: Yoruba
Inherent Meaning: Victorious in the Struggle
Spiritual Connotation: Overcomer
Scripture: 2 Thessalonians 2:15 NRSV

So then, brothers and sisters, stand firm and hold fast to the traditions that you were taught by us.

AJAY, Aja, Ajai

Language/Cultural Origin: Indo-Pakistani
Inherent Meaning: Immovable
Spiritual Connotation: Stable
Scripture: 1 Corinthians 15:58 NCV

So my dear brothers and sisters, stand strong. Do not let anything change you. Always give yourselves fully to the work of the Lord.

AKIL, Ahkeel, Akeel, Akhil, Akiel

Language/Cultural Origin: Middle Eastern
Inherent Meaning: Intelligent
Spiritual Connotation: Wise
Scripture: Proverbs 2:6 NKJV

For the LORD gives wisdom; from His mouth come knowledge and understanding.

AKIM, Ackeem, Akeam, Akeem (see also Hakim, Joachim)
Language/Cultural Origin: Russian
Inherent Meaning: God Will Establish
Spiritual Connotation: Obedient
Scripture: Deuteronomy 28:9 RSV
The LORD will establish you as a people holy to himself . . . if you keep the commandments of the LORD your God, and walk in his ways.

AKSEL, Acksel (see also Axel)
Language/Cultural Origin: Norwegian
Inherent Meaning: Father of Peace
Spiritual Connotation: Pleasant
Scripture: Proverbs 16:7 NKJV
When a man's ways please the LORD, He makes even his enemies to be at peace with him.

ALADDIN, Alaaddin
Language/Cultural Origin: Middle Eastern
Inherent Meaning: Pinnacle of Faith
Spiritual Connotation: Righteous
Scripture: Luke 7:9, 50 TLB
Jesus was amazed. . . . He said, "Never among all the Jews in Israel have I met . . . with faith like this." And Jesus said . . . "Your faith has saved you; go in peace."

ALAN, Al, Alen, Allan, Allen, Allin, Allon, Allyn
Language/Cultural Origin: Irish
Inherent Meaning: Harmonious
Spiritual Connotation: At One With Creation
Scripture: 2 Corinthians 13:11 NKJV
Be of good comfort, be of one mind, live in peace; and the God of love and peace will be with you.

ALANNA, Alaina, Alainna, Alainnah, Alana, Alanis, Alannah, Alayna, Allana, Allanah, Allanis, Allayna
Language/Cultural Origin: Gaelic
Inherent Meaning: Cheerful
Spiritual Connotation: Effective Witness
Scripture: John 13:35 NKJV
By this all will know that you are My disciples, if you have love for one another.

ALASTAIR, Alistair, Alister, Allastair, Allaster, Allastir, Allister, Allyster
Language/Cultural Origin: Scottish

Inherent Meaning: Defender
Spiritual Connotation: Courage
Scripture: Psalm 27:14 NKJV
Wait on the LORD; be of good courage, and He shall strengthen your heart; wait, I say, on the LORD!

ALBEN, Albain, Alban, Albany, Albein
Language/Cultural Origin: Latin
Inherent Meaning: Of the City on a White Hill
Spiritual Connotation: Secure in God's Love
Scripture: Isaiah 41:13 KJV
For I the LORD thy God will hold thy right hand, saying unto thee, Fear not; I will help thee.

ALBERT, Al, Alberto, Elbert
Language/Cultural Origin: Old English
Inherent Meaning: Noble
Spiritual Connotation: Brilliant
Scripture: Psalm 18:28 NKJV
For You will light my lamp; the LORD my God will enlighten my darkness.

ALDA
Language/Cultural Origin: Old German
Inherent Meaning: Prosperous
Spiritual Connotation: Under God's Direction
Scripture: Joshua 1:8 NKJV
This Book of the Law shall not depart from your mouth, but you shall meditate in it day and night. . . . For then you will make your way prosperous, and then you will have good success.

ALDEN, Aldin, Aldis, Aldous, Aldwin
Language/Cultural Origin: Anglo-Saxon
Inherent Meaning: Wise Protector
Spiritual Connotation: Guided of God
Scripture: Psalm 73:24 NKJV
You will guide me with Your counsel, and afterward receive me to glory.

ALDRICH, Aldric, Aldrick, Aldridge
Language/Cultural Origin: Old English
Inherent Meaning: Wise Counselor
Spiritual Connotation: Strong of Mind
Scripture: 2 Timothy 1:7 NKJV
For God has not given us a spirit of fear, but of power and of love and of a sound mind.

ALEA, Aleah, Aleea, Aleeah, Alia, Allia (see also Aliah)
Language/Cultural Origin: Middle Eastern

Inherent Meaning: Exalted
Spiritual Connotation: Servant
Scripture: Luke 14:11 RSV
For every one who exalts himself will be humbled, and he who humbles himself will be exalted.

ALEJANDRO, Alejándra, Alesandra, Alesandro, Alessandra, Alessandro
Language/Cultural Origin: Spanish/Italian
Inherent Meaning: Defender of Mankind
Spiritual Connotation: Sincere
Scripture: James 1:27 NCV
Religion that God accepts as pure and without fault is this: caring for orphans or widows who need help, and keeping yourself free from the world's evil influence.

ALETHA, Alathea, Aleta, Aletha, Alethea, Alithea (see also Althea)
Language/Cultural Origin: Greek
Inherent Meaning: Truthful
Spiritual Connotation: Wise
Scripture: Luke 7:35 NASB
Yet wisdom is vindicated by all her children.

ALEXANDER, Alax, Alec, Aleck, ☞Aleksandar, Aleksander, Alexandar, Alexandrus, Alexius, Alexxander, Alic, Alixander, Allax, Allex
Language/Cultural Origin: Greek
Inherent Meaning: Defender of Mankind
Spiritual Connotation: Brave Protector
Scripture: Jeremiah 22:3 TLB
The Lord says: Be fair-minded. Do what is right! Help those in need of justice!

ALEXA, Aleksa, Aleksia, Alex, Alexia, Allex, Allix, Alyx, Allyx
Language/Cultural Origin: Hungarian
Inherent Meaning: Defender of Mankind
Spiritual Connotation: Benefactor
Scripture: Isaiah 1:17 RSV
Learn to do good; seek justice, correct oppression; defend the fatherless, plead for the widow.

ALEXANDRA, Aleksandra, Alexandria, Lexandra
Language/Cultural Origin: Greek
Inherent Meaning: Defender of Mankind
Spiritual Connotation: Generous

Scripture: Jeremiah 7:7 NASB
I will let you dwell in this place, in the land that I gave to your fathers forever and ever.

ALEXIS, Aleksei, Aleksey, Aleksi, Alexes, Alexi, Alexis, Alexus, Alexys
Language/Cultural Origin: English
Inherent Meaning: Defender of Mankind
Spiritual Connotation: Intercessor
Scripture: Jeremiah 27:18 NKJV
But if they are prophets, and if the word of the LORD is with them, let them now make intercession to the LORD of hosts.

ALFONSO, see Alphonso

ALFRED, Alf, Alfredo
Language/Cultural Origin: Old English
Inherent Meaning: Benevolent Ruler
Spiritual Connotation: Obedient
Scripture: Luke 10:27 NKJV
So he answered and said, "You shall love the LORD your God with all your heart, with all your soul, with all your strength, and with all your mind, and your neighbor as yourself."

ALI, Aly (see also Allie)
Language/Cultural Origin: Swahili
Inherent Meaning: Exalted
Spiritual Connotation: Greatest
Scripture: Luke 13:30 NCV
There are those who have the lowest place in life now who will have the highest place in the future.

ALIAH, Alia, Aliya, Aliyah ☞(see also Alea)
Language/Cultural Origin: Hebrew
Inherent Meaning: Exalted
Spiritual Connotation: Humble
Scripture: 1 Peter 5:6 NCV
Be humble under God's powerful hand so he will lift you up when the right time comes.

ALIANNA, Aliana
Language/Cultural Origin: Scottish
Inherent Meaning: Bearer of Light
Spiritual Connotation: Ambassador of Truth
Scripture: Isaiah 49:6 NASB
I will also make You a light of the nations So that My salvation may reach to the end of the earth.

ALICE, Alis, Allis, Alysse
Language/Cultural Origin: Greek
Inherent Meaning: One of Integrity
Spiritual Connotation: Truthful
Scripture: Proverbs 11:3, 5 RSV
*The integrity of the upright guides them. . . .
The righteousness of the blameless keeps his
way straight.*

**ALICIA, Alica, Alicea, Alicya,
Aliecia, Alycia, Elicia, Ellicia**
Language/Cultural Origin: Hispanic
Inherent Meaning: Truthful
Spiritual Connotation: Child of Truth
Scripture: 1 John 3:18–19 NRSV
*Little children, let us love, not in word or
speech, but in truth and action. And by this
we will know that we are from the truth.*

ALIKA, Alikah
Language/Cultural Origin: Nigerian
Inherent Meaning: Most Beautiful
Spiritual Connotation: Beauty of God
Scripture: Psalm 27:4 RSV
*One thing have I asked of the LORD. . . . That I
may dwell in the house of the LORD all the
days of my life, to behold the beauty of the
LORD, and to inquire in his temple.*

ALIM, Aleem
Language/Cultural Origin: Middle Eastern
Inherent Meaning: Scholar
Spiritual Connotation: Wise
Scripture: Proverbs 8:11 NKJV
*For wisdom is better than rubies, and all the
things one may desire cannot be compared
with her.*

ALINE, Alene
Language/Cultural Origin: Old German
Inherent Meaning: Noble
Spiritual Connotation: Righteous
Scripture: 2 Chronicles 16:9 TLB
*For the eyes of the Lord search back and
forth across the whole earth, looking for
people whose hearts are perfect toward him,
so that he can show his great power in
helping them.*

**ALISA, Alissa, Allissa, Allysa,
Alysa, Alyssa, Allyssa
(see also Elissa, Elysia, Lissa)**
Language/Cultural Origin: English

Inherent Meaning: Noble
Spiritual Connotation: Bold
Scripture: Hebrews 13:6 NRSV
*So we can say with confidence, The Lord is
my helper; I will not be afraid. What can
anyone do to me?*

**ALISHA, Aleasha, Aleesha, Aleisha,
Alesha, Aliesha, Alishah, Alishia,
Alysha, Alyshia, Alyssha**
Language/Cultural Origin: English
Inherent Meaning: Highborn
Spiritual Connotation: Victorious
Scripture: Isaiah 25:8 KJV
*He will swallow up death in victory; and the
Lord GOD will wipe away tears from off all
faces.*

ALLIE, Alley, Alli (see also Ali)
Language/Cultural Origin: Anglo-Saxon
Inherent Meaning: Brilliant
Spiritual Connotation: Illuminated
Scripture: Psalm 18:28 TLB
*You have turned on my light! The Lord my
God has made my darkness turn to light.*

**ALLISON, Alicen, Alicyn, Alison,
Alisson, Alisyn, Allyson**
Language/Cultural Origin: Old German
Inherent Meaning: Truthful
Spiritual Connotation: Holy
Scripture: 1 Chronicles 16:29 KJV
*Give unto the LORD the glory due unto his
name . . . worship the LORD in the beauty of
holiness.*

ALLARD, Alard (see also Ellard)
Language/Cultural Origin: Old English
Inherent Meaning: Brave
Spiritual Connotation: Dedicated
Scripture: Psalm 119:38 NKJV
*Establish Your word to Your servant, Who is
devoted to fearing You.*

ALLEGRA, Alegrea, Allegréa, Allegria
Language/Cultural Origin: Latin
Inherent Meaning: Cheerful
Spiritual Connotation: Eager to Live
Scripture: Psalm 37:4 NRSV
*Take delight in the LORD, and he will give you
the desires of your heart.*

ALLEN, see Alan

ALMA, Almah

Language/Cultural Origin: Latin
Inherent Meaning: Loving
Spiritual Connotation: Patient
Scripture: 2 Thessalonians 3:5 NKJV

Now may the Lord direct your hearts into the love of God and into the patience of Christ.

ALMIRA, Allmira, Almeera, Almeira

Language/Cultural Origin: Middle Eastern
Inherent Meaning: Princess
Spiritual Connotation: Fulfillment of Truth
Scripture: Psalm 25:10 KJV

All the paths of the LORD are mercy and truth unto such as keep his covenant and his testimonies.

ALONZO, Alanzo, Almanzo, Alonso

Language/Cultural Origin: Old German
Inherent Meaning: Ready for Battle
Spiritual Connotation: Prepared
Scripture: Luke 1:17 NKJV

He will also go before Him in the spirit and power of Elijah . . . to make ready a people prepared for the Lord.

ALOYSIUS

Language/Cultural Origin: Old German
Inherent Meaning: Noble
Spiritual Connotation: Great
Scripture: John 14:12 NCV

I tell you the truth, whoever believes in me will do the same things that I do. Those who believe will do even greater things than these, because I am going to the Father.

ALPHA

Language/Cultural Origin: Phoenician
Inherent Meaning: Ox
Spiritual Connotation: Restful
Scripture: Matthew 11:29 NKJV

Take My yoke upon you and learn from Me, for I am gentle and lowly in heart, and you will find rest for your souls.

ALPHAEUS

☞ Language/Cultural Origin: Greek
Inherent Meaning: Traveler
Spiritual Connotation: Nourished
Scripture: Exodus 33:14 NRSV

My presence will go with you, and I will give you rest.

ALPHONSO, Alfonso, Alfonzo, Alphanso, Alphonzo

Language/Cultural Origin: Italian
Inherent Meaning: Noble
Spiritual Connotation: Mighty Protector
Scripture: Jeremiah 33:3 KJV

Call unto me, and I will answer thee, and show thee great and mighty things, which thou knowest not.

ALTHEA, Altheya, Althia (see also Aletha)

Language/Cultural Origin: Greek
Inherent Meaning: Healer
Spiritual Connotation: Wholesome
Scripture: Philippians 4:8 NRSV

Finally, beloved, whatever is true, . . . honorable, . . . just, . . . pure, . . . pleasing, . . . [and] commendable, if there is any excellence and if there is anything worthy of praise, think about these things.

ALTON, see Elton

ALVA (see also Elva)

Language/Cultural Origin: Latin
Inherent Meaning: Brightness
Spiritual Connotation: Alive
Scripture: Job 33:4 NASB

The Spirit of God has made me, and the breath of the Almighty gives me life.

ALVIN, Al, Alvan, Alven, Alvyn (see also Elvin)

Language/Cultural Origin: German
Inherent Meaning: Friend of All
Spiritual Connotation: Sincere
Scripture: Proverbs 18:24 RSV

There are friends who pretend to be friends, but there is a friend who sticks closer than a brother.

ALVIS (see also Elvis)

Language/Cultural Origin: Scandinavian
Inherent Meaning: All-Knowing
Spiritual Connotation: Conqueror
Scripture: Romans 8:37 NKJV

Yet in all these things we are more than conquerors through Him who loved us.

ALYSSA, see Alisa

AMADA, Amadea, Amadia
Language/Cultural Origin: Spanish
Inherent Meaning: Beloved
Spiritual Connotation: Cherished
Scripture: Ephesians 5:29–30 NRSV
For no one ever hates his own body, but he nourishes and tenderly cares for it, just as Christ does for the church, because we are members of his body.

AMADEUS, Amadeaus, Amado, Amador, Amadeo
Language/Cultural Origin: Latin
Inherent Meaning: Lover of God
Spiritual Connotation: Obedient
Scripture: Joshua 22:5 TLB
Be sure to continue to obey all of the commandments Moses gave you. Love the Lord and follow his plan for your lives. Cling to him and serve him enthusiastically.

AMADIKA, Amadikah
Language/Cultural Origin: Rhodesian
Inherent Meaning: Beloved
Spiritual Connotation: Close to God
Scripture: 1 John 2:5 RSV
But whoever keeps his word, in him truly love for God is perfected. By this we may be sure that we are in him.

AMAL, Amaal
☞Language/Cultural Origin: Hebrew
Inherent Meaning: Sorrowful
Spiritual Connotation: Productive
Scripture: Exodus 35:2 NASB
For six days work may be done, but on the seventh day you shall have a holy day, a sabbath of complete rest to the LORD.

AMANDA, Amandah, Amandalyn, Amandi (see also Mandie)
Language/Cultural Origin: Latin
Inherent Meaning: Worthy of Love
Spiritual Connotation: Virtuous
Scripture: Ephesians 5:25 NCV
Husbands, love your wives as Christ loved the church and gave himself for it.

AMAR, Amarr
Language/Cultural Origin: Punjabi
Inherent Meaning: Immortal
Spiritual Connotation: Unending
Scripture: Psalm 121:8 RSV
The LORD will keep your going out and your coming in from this time forth and for evermore.

AMARA, Amarah
Language/Cultural Origin: Greek
Inherent Meaning: Wished-for Child
Spiritual Connotation: Precious Gift
Scripture: Proverbs 17:6 KJV
Children's children are the crown of old men; and the glory of children are their fathers.

AMARANTHA, Amaranda, Amiranda, Amiranté, Amirantha
Language/Cultural Origin: Greek
Inherent Meaning: Immortal
Spiritual Connotation: Everlasting
Scripture: Revelation 22:5 NCV
There will never be night again. They will not need the light of a lamp or the light of the sun, because the Lord God will give them light.

AMARIAH, Amaria, Amariya, ☞Amariyah, Amarya, Amaryah
Language/Cultural Origin: Hebrew
Inherent Meaning: Covenant of God
Spiritual Connotation: Preserved
Scripture: Exodus 23:22 RSV
But if you hearken attentively to his voice and do all that I say, then I will be an enemy to your enemies and an adversary to your adversaries.

AMARIS, Amarissa
Language/Cultural Origin: Hebrew
Inherent Meaning: Promise of God
Spiritual Connotation: Promise fulfilled
Scripture: Lamentations 3:23 KJV
[His compassions] are new every morning: great is thy faithfulness.

AMASIAH, Amaziah
☞Language/Cultural Origin: Hebrew
Inherent Meaning: My God Has Strength
Spiritual Connotation: Reverent
Scripture: Psalm 54:1 NKJV
Save me, O God, by Your name, And vindicate me by Your strength.

AMAYA, Amayah
Language/Cultural Origin: Japanese

Inherent Meaning: Night Rain
Spiritual Connotation: Gentle
Scripture: 2 Timothy 2:24 TLB
*God's people must not be quarrelsome;
they must be gentle, patient teachers of
those who are wrong.*

AMBER, Ambur (see also Ember)
Language/Cultural Origin: Latin
Inherent Meaning: Like a Jewel
Spiritual Connotation: Cherished
Scripture: Psalm 143:8 KJV
*Cause me to hear thy lovingkindness in the
morning; for in thee do I trust: cause me to
know the way wherein I should walk; for I
lift up my soul unto thee.*

AMBROSE, Ambros, Ambrus
Language/Cultural Origin: Greek
Inherent Meaning: Divine
Spiritual Connotation: Immortal
Scripture: 1 Corinthians 15:54 NKJV
*So when . . . this mortal has put on
immortality, then shall be brought to pass the
saying that is written: Death is swallowed up
in victory.*

AMELIA, Amaley, Amalia, Amalie, Amaliya, Amallia, Amelee, Amélie (see also Emelia, Emily)
Language/Cultural Origin: Latin
Inherent Meaning: Industrious
Spiritual Connotation: Independent
Scripture: 1 Thessalonians 4:11–12 NASB
*Make it your ambition to lead a quiet life
and attend to your own business and work
with your hands, . . . so that you may behave
properly toward outsiders and not be in any
need.*

AMERY, Aimery, Ameri, Ammerie, Ammery, Amory (see also Emery)
Language/Cultural Origin: German
Inherent Meaning: Divine
Spiritual Connotation: Shows the Way
Scripture: Job 32:8 KJV
*But there is a spirit in man: and the
inspiration of the Almighty giveth them
understanding.*

AMES, Aimes
Language/Cultural Origin: French
Inherent Meaning: Friend

Spiritual Connotation: Faithful
Scripture: Amos 3:3 KJV
Can two walk together, except they be agreed?

AMICA, Amicah
Language/Cultural Origin: Italian
Inherent Meaning: Beloved Friend
Spiritual Connotation: Valuable
Scripture: Proverbs 27:17 NRSV
*Iron sharpens iron, and one person sharpens
the wits of another.*

AMIN, Ameen
Language/Cultural Origin: Hebrew
Inherent Meaning: Trustworthy
Spiritual Connotation: Obedient
Scripture: Ecclesiastes 12:13 NKJV
*Fear God and keep his commandments, for
this is man's all.*

AMINA, Aminah, Aminda, Amindah
Language/Cultural Origin: Middle Eastern
Inherent Meaning: Peaceful
Spiritual Connotation: Secure in Christ
Scripture: John 10:28 NLT
*I give [my sheep] eternal life, and they will
never perish. No one will snatch them away
from me.*

AMIR, Ameir
Language/Cultural Origin: Hebrew
Inherent Meaning: Proclaimed
Spiritual Connotation: Known of God
Scripture: Romans 8:29 NASB
*For whom He foreknew, He also predestined
to become conformed to the image of His
Son, that He might be the first-born among
many brethren.*

AMIRA, Ameira
Language/Cultural Origin: Hebrew
Inherent Meaning: Speech
Spiritual Connotation: Unhidden
Scripture: Luke 12:3 RSV
*Therefore whatever you have said in the dark
shall be heard in the light, and what you
have whispered in private rooms shall be
proclaimed upon the housetops.*

AMIRAN, Ameiran, Ameiren
Language/Cultural Origin: Hebrew
Inherent Meaning: My Nation Is Joyful
Spiritual Connotation: Chosen of God

Scripture: **Deuteronomy 28:7** RSV

The LORD will cause your enemies who rise against you to be defeated before you; they shall come out against you one way, and flee before you seven ways.

AMITTAI, Ahmitay, Amitai, Amitei

Language/Cultural Origin: Hebrew
Inherent Meaning: Friend
Spiritual Connotation: Friend of God
Scripture: **John 15:15** NRSV

I have called you friends, because I have made known to you everything that I have heard from my Father.

AMITY, Amitee, Amitie

Language/Cultural Origin: French
Inherent Meaning: Bound by Friendship
Spiritual Connotation: Faithful Friend
Scripture: **Ecclesiastes 4:12** KJV

A threefold cord is not quickly broken.

AMMIEL, Amiel

Language/Cultural Origin: Hebrew
Inherent Meaning: God of My People
Spiritual Connotation: My Nation Is God's
Scripture: **Deuteronomy 32:9** NCV

The LORD took his people as his share, the people of Jacob as his very own.

AMMON, Amon, Amonn

Language/Cultural Origin: Hebrew
Inherent Meaning: Of My Nation
Spiritual Connotation: Chosen
Scripture: **Leviticus 26:12** NKJV

I will walk among you and be your God, and you shall be My people.

AMOS

Language/Cultural Origin: Hebrew
Inherent Meaning: Bearer of a Burden
Spiritual Connotation: Compassionate
Scripture: **Galatians 6:2** RSV

Bear one another's burdens, and so fulfil the law of Christ.

AMY, Aimée, Aimey, Aimi, Aimie, Aimmie, Aimy, Amey, Amie, Ammy

Language/Cultural Origin: Latin
Inherent Meaning: Beloved
Spiritual Connotation: Serene Spirit
Scripture: **Psalm 4:8** NASB

In peace I will both lie down and sleep, For Thou alone, O LORD, dost make me to dwell in safety.

AMYAS, Amias

Language/Cultural Origin: Latin
Inherent Meaning: Beloved
Spiritual Connotation: Tenderhearted
Scripture: **Galatians 5:22–23** RSV

But the fruit of the Spirit is love, joy, peace, patience, kindness, goodness, faithfulness, gentleness, self-control; against such there is no law.

ANAIAH, Anaiya, Aniah, Anijah, Aniya, Aniyah

Language/Cultural Origin: Hebrew
Inherent Meaning: God Has Answered Me
Spiritual Connotation: Restored
Scripture: **Psalm 39:12** NLT

Hear my prayer, O LORD! Listen to my cries for help!

ANANI, Annani, Ananni

Language/Cultural Origin: Hebrew
Inherent Meaning: Covered With God
Spiritual Connotation: Guarded
Scripture: **Psalm 3:3** RSV

But thou, O LORD, art a shield about me, my glory, and the lifter of my head.

ANANIAS, Ananiah

Language/Cultural Origin: Hebrew
Inherent Meaning: God Is Gracious
Spiritual Connotation: Witness
Scripture: **2 Corinthians 6:1** NLT

As God's partners, we beg you not to reject this marvelous message of God's great kindness.

ANASTASIA, Anastasha, Anastashia, Anastassia, Anastassya (see also Tasia)

Language/Cultural Origin: Greek
Inherent Meaning: Resurrection
Spiritual Connotation: Awakening
Scripture: **Romans 8:11** NLT

The Spirit of God, who raised Jesus from the dead, lives in you. And just as he raised Christ from the dead, he will give life to your mortal body by this same Spirit living within you.

ANDREA, Andee, Andi, Andraia, Andraya, Andreah, Andreea, Andreia, Andreya, Andria
Language/Cultural Origin: Greek
Inherent Meaning: Womanly
Spiritual Connotation: Filled With Grace
Scripture: Proverbs 31:28 NKJV
Her children rise up and call her blessed; her husband also, and he praises her:

ANDREW, Anders, Anderson, Andrae, ☞Andras, Andre, André, Andreas, Andrei, Andrés, Andy, Aundré (see also Drew)
Language/Cultural Origin: Greek
Inherent Meaning: Courageous
Spiritual Connotation: Enduring
Scripture: Psalm 27:1 KJV
The LORD is my light and my salvation; whom shall I fear? The LORD is the strength of my life; of whom shall I be afraid?

ANEMONE, Anemonee, Anémonie
Language/Cultural Origin: Greek
Inherent Meaning: Breath
Spiritual Connotation: Life of God
Scripture: Psalm 150:6 KJV
Let every thing that hath breath praise the LORD. Praise ye the LORD.

ANESKA, Aneshka
Language/Cultural Origin: Czech
Inherent Meaning: Pure
Spiritual Connotation: Likeness of Christ
Scripture: 1 John 3:2–3 NRSV
For we will see him as he is. And all who have this hope in him purify themselves, just as he is pure.

ANGELA, Angee, Angel, Angelea, Angelee, Angeleigh, Angelica, Angelíca, Angie, Angelena, Angeliana, Angelina, Angeline, Angelique, Angi, Anjelíka, Anjelina
Language/Cultural Origin: Greek
Inherent Meaning: Angel/Messenger
Spiritual Connotation: Bringer of Glad Tidings
Scripture: Revelation 22:16 RSV
I Jesus have sent my angel to you with this testimony for the churches. I am the root and the offspring of David, the bright morning star.

ANGELO, Angelos
Language/Cultural Origin: Italian
Inherent Meaning: Angel/Messenger
Spiritual Connotation: Bringer of Glad Tidings
Scripture: Luke 2:10–11 NKJV
I bring you good tidings of great joy which will be to all people. For there is born to you this day in the city of David a Savior, who is Christ the Lord.

ANGUS
Language/Cultural Origin: Scottish
Inherent Meaning: Unique Strength
Spiritual Connotation: Creative Spirit
Scripture: Luke 10:7 KJV
And in the same house remain, eating and drinking such things as they give: for the labourer is worthy of his hire. Go not from house to house.

ANI, Anii (see also Ann)
Language/Cultural Origin: Hawaiian
Inherent Meaning: Beautiful
Spiritual Connotation: Lovely in Spirit
Scripture: Isaiah 52:7 NRSV
How beautiful upon the mountains are the feet of the messenger who announces peace . . . who says to Zion, your God reigns.

ANIA, Aniah (see also Anya)
Language/Cultural Origin: Polish
Inherent Meaning: Compassion
Spiritual Connotation: Merciful
Scripture: Proverbs 21:21 NASB
He who pursues righteousness and loyalty finds life, righteousness and honor.

ANIKA, Aneka, Anekah, Anica, Anicka, Anikka, Annika
Language/Cultural Origin: Czech
Inherent Meaning: Favor
Spiritual Connotation: Grace of God
Scripture: 1 Samuel 2:26 KJV
And the child Samuel grew on, and was in favour both with the LORD, and also with men.

ANITA, Aneeta, Anetra, Anitra (see also Nita)
Language/Cultural Origin: Hispanic
Inherent Meaning: Gracious
Spiritual Connotation: Kindness

Scripture: 1 Corinthians 13:4 NRSV
Love is patient; love is kind; love is not envious or boastful or arrogant.

ANN, Anne, Annette, Anni, Annie, Anny (see also Ani)
Language/Cultural Origin: English
Inherent Meaning: Graceful
Spiritual Connotation: Understanding
Scripture: Psalms 111:10 KJV
The fear of the LORD is the beginning of wisdom: a good understanding have all they that do his commandments: his praise endureth for ever.

ANNA, Ana, Anah, Anka
☞ Language/Cultural Origin: German
Inherent Meaning: Gracious
Spiritual Connotation: Full of Grace
Scripture: Luke 1:28 NKJV
And having come in, the angel said to her, Rejoice, highly favored one, the Lord is with you; blessed are you among women!

ANNABELL, Annabelle
Language/Cultural Origin: Latin
Inherent Meaning: Graceful
Spiritual Connotation: Beloved
Scripture: Psalm 89:1 KJV
I will sing of the mercies of the LORD for ever: with my mouth will I make known thy faithfulness to all generations.

ANNELISA, Annalisa, Annalise, Annelise
Language/Cultural Origin: English
Inherent Meaning: Oath of God
Spiritual Connotation: Gracious Promise
Scripture: Genesis 9:9, 11 RSV
Behold, I establish my covenant with you and your descendants after you, . . . and never again shall there be a flood to destroy the earth.

ANNEMARIE, Annamaria, Anna-Maria, Annamarie, Anne-Marie, Annmaria, Annmarie
Language/Cultural Origin: American
Inherent Meaning: Bitter Grace
Spiritual Connotation: Faithfulness of God
Scripture: Hebrews 13:5 NRSV
Keep your lives free from the love of money,

and be content with what you have; for he has said, I will never leave you or forsake you.

ANSON, Ansun
Language/Cultural Origin: Old German
Inherent Meaning: Divine
Spiritual Connotation: Partaker in Glory
Scripture: 1 Peter 5:10 RSV
And after you have suffered a little while, the God of all grace, who has called you to his eternal glory in Christ, will himself restore, establish, and strengthen you.

ANSEL, Ancell, Ansell
Language/Cultural Origin: Middle English
Inherent Meaning: Noble
Spiritual Connotation: Follower of Truth
Scripture: Jeremiah 33:6 KJV
Behold, I will bring it health and cure, and I will cure them, and will reveal unto them the abundance of peace and truth.

ANTHONY, Anfernee, Anthoney, Anthonie, Antoiné, Antony (see also Antonio, Tony)
Language/Cultural Origin: Latin
Inherent Meaning: Praiseworthy
Spiritual Connotation: Prosperous
Scripture: Psalm 122:7, 9 KJV
Peace be within thy walls, and prosperity within thy palaces. Because of the house of the LORD our God I will seek thy good.

ANTON, Antonn
Language/Cultural Origin: Slavic
Inherent Meaning: One of Value
Spiritual Connotation: Eloquent
Scripture: Proverbs 25:11 KJV
A word fitly spoken is like apples of gold in pictures of silver.

ANTONIA, Antoinette, Antonette, Antoñia (see also Tania, Toni)
Language/Cultural Origin: Latin
Inherent Meaning: Priceless
Spiritual Connotation: Jewel of Light
Scripture: Matthew 5:16 KJV
Let your light so shine before men, that they may see your good works, and glorify your Father which is in heaven.

ANTONIO, Antoñio, Antonius
Language/Cultural Origin: Italian

Inherent Meaning: Priceless
Spiritual Connotation: Righteous
Scripture: Isaiah 54:14 KJV

> In righteousness shalt thou be established: thou shalt be far from oppression; for thou shalt not fear: and from terror; for it shall not come near thee.

ANYA, Annya (see also Ania)
Language/Cultural Origin: Russian
Inherent Meaning: Favor of God
Spiritual Connotation: Peace
Scripture: Proverbs 16:7 RSV

> When a man's ways please the LORD, he makes even his enemies to be at peace with him.

APOLLOS, Apollo
Language/Cultural Origin: Greek
Inherent Meaning: Youthful God of Music
Spiritual Connotation: Joyful
Scripture: Psalm 33:2 NCV

> Praise the LORD on the harp; make music for him on a ten-stringed lyre.

APRIL, Aprill, Apryl
Language/Cultural Origin: Latin
Inherent Meaning: New in Faith
Spiritual Connotation: Awakened
Scripture: Ezekiel 37:14 KJV

> And [I] shall put my spirit in you, and ye shall live.

AQUILLA, Aquila
Language/Cultural Origin: Latin
Inherent Meaning: Eagle
Spiritual Connotation: Strong
Scripture: Isaiah 40:31 NCV

> But the people who trust the LORD will become strong again. They will rise up as an eagle in the sky; they will run and not need rest; they will walk and not become tired.

ARAM, Aramia
Language/Cultural Origin: Syrian
Inherent Meaning: Exalted
Spiritual Connotation: Humble
Scripture: 1 Corinthians 1:28–29 NLT

> God chose things despised by the world ... and used them to bring to nothing what the world considers important, so that no one can ever boast in the presence of God.

ARAN, Aranne, Aronne
(see also Aaron, Aren)
Language/Cultural Origin: Hebrew
Inherent Meaning: Firm
Spiritual Connotation: Gifted
Scripture: Ephesians 4:11 NLT

> He is the one who gave these gifts to the church.... Their responsibility is to equip God's people to do his work and build up the church, the body of Christ.

ARCHER, Arch, Archie
Language/Cultural Origin: Latin
Inherent Meaning: Bowman
Spiritual Connotation: Steadfast
Scripture: Isaiah 40:31 KJV

> But they that wait upon the LORD shall renew their strength; they shall mount up with wings as eagles; they shall run, and not be weary; and they shall walk, and not faint.

ARDEL, Ardell
Language/Cultural Origin: Latin
Inherent Meaning: Industrious
Spiritual Connotation: Creative
Scripture: Exodus 23:12 NKJV

> Six days you shall do your work, and on the seventh day you shall rest.

ARDELLE, Ardella
Language/Cultural Origin: Latin
Inherent Meaning: Eager
Spiritual Connotation: Spirit of Praise
Scripture: Psalm 67:5–6 NKJV

> Let the peoples praise You, O God; Let all the peoples praise You. Then the earth shall yield her increase; God, our own God, shall bless us.

ARDITH, Ardath, Ardeth, Ardyth
Language/Cultural Origin: Hebrew
Inherent Meaning: Faithful
Spiritual Connotation: Dependent Upon God
Scripture: Psalm 28:7 KJV

> The LORD is my strength and my shield; my heart trusted in him, and I am helped: therefore my heart greatly rejoiceth; and with my song will I praise him.

ARDON, Ardan, Arden, Ardyn
Language/Cultural Origin: Hebrew
Inherent Meaning: Descendant
Spiritual Connotation: Promise

Scripture: 1 Chronicles 16:15 NKJV

Remember His covenant forever, the word which He commanded, for a thousand generations.

ARELI, Arilee, Arileigh, Ariley

☞ Language/Cultural Origin: Hebrew

Inherent Meaning: Heroic

Spiritual Connotation: Miraculous

Scripture: 2 Thessalonians 1:10 NCV

This will happen on the day when the Lord Jesus comes to receive glory because of his holy people. And all the people who have believed will be amazed at Jesus.

AREN, Arenn (see also Aaron, Aran)

Language/Cultural Origin: Danish

Inherent Meaning: Eagle

Spiritual Connotation: Perseverance

Scripture: Hosea 12:6 NRSV

But as for you, return to your God, hold fast to love and justice, and wait continually for your God.

ARETAS, Areetas, Aritas

☞ Language/Cultural Origin: Greek

Inherent Meaning: Pleasing

Spiritual Connotation: Wise

Scripture: Proverbs 3:17 NCV

Wisdom will make your life pleasant and will bring you peace.

ARETHA, Areatha, Areetha

Language/Cultural Origin: American

Inherent Meaning: Virtuous

Spiritual Connotation: Pure

Scripture: Matthew 5:8 NASB

Blessed are the pure in heart, for they shall see God.

ARIADNE, Ari, Ariane, Ariann, Arianne, Arien, Arienne

Language/Cultural Origin: Greek

Inherent Meaning: Holy

Spiritual Connotation: Presented to God

Scripture: Romans 6:13 TLB

Do not let any part of your bodies ... to be used for sinning; but give yourselves completely to God.

ARIANA, Aeriana, Arianna, Arieana, Aryanna (see also Irina)

Language/Cultural Origin: Italian

Inherent Meaning: Holy

Spiritual Connotation: Pure in Heart

Scripture: 2 Corinthians 7:1 NIV

Let us purify ourselves from everything that contaminates body and spirit, perfecting holiness out of reverence for God.

ARIC, Aaric, Arick, Arik, Arric, Arrick, Arrik (see also Eric)

Language/Cultural Origin: Old English

Inherent Meaning: Holy Ruler

Spiritual Connotation: Just

Scripture: Colossians 4:1 NCV

Masters, give what is good and fair to your slaves. Remember that you have a Master in heaven.

ARIEL, Aerial, Aeriell, Arial, Ariale, Arielle, Ariyel, Arrial, Arriel (see also Uriel)

☞ Language/Cultural Origin: Hebrew

Inherent Meaning: Lion or Lioness of God

Spiritual Connotation: Royal Servant

Scripture: 1 Peter 2:18 RSV

Servants, be submissive to your masters with all respect. ... For one is approved if, mindful of God, he endures pain while suffering unjustly.

ARIN, Arinn, Aryn (see also Erin)

Language/Cultural Origin: Hebrew

Inherent Meaning: Enlightened

Spiritual Connotation: Filled With Light

Scripture: Ephesians 1:18–19 NRSV

So that, with the eyes of your heart enlightened, you may know what is the hope to which he has called you ... and what is the immeasurable greatness of his power for us who believe.

ARINA, Areena

Language/Cultural Origin: Russian

Inherent Meaning: Peace

Spiritual Connotation: Encourager

Scripture: Romans 14:19 NKJV

Therefore let us pursue the things which make for peace and the things by which one may edify another.

ARIOCH, Arioc, Arriok

☞ Language/Cultural Origin: Hebrew

Inherent Meaning: Lionlike

Spiritual Connotation: Dependent Upon God

Scripture: Psalm 34:10 NLT
Even strong young lions sometimes go hungry, but those who trust in the LORD will never lack any good thing.

ARION, Arian, Ariane, Arien, Arrian (see also Ariadne)
Language/Cultural Origin: Greek
Inherent Meaning: Charming
Spiritual Connotation: Captivating
Scripture: Song of Songs 4:1 NASB
How beautiful you are, my darling, how beautiful you are!

ARISTOTLE, Ari, Arias, Arie, Aris, Arri
Language/Cultural Origin: Greek
Inherent Meaning: Greatest Achievement
Spiritual Connotation: Intelligent
Scripture: Proverbs 8:10 NCV
Choose my teachings instead of silver, and knowledge rather than the finest gold.

ARLEN, Arlan, Arland, Arlend, Arlin, Arlyn, Arlynn
Language/Cultural Origin: Irish
Inherent Meaning: Pledge
Spiritual Connotation: Truthful
Scripture: Psalm 34:1 NRSV
I will bless the LORD at all times; his praise shall continually be in my mouth.

ARLENE, Arlana, Arleen, Arleyne, Arline, Arlis, Arliss, Arlyss
Language/Cultural Origin: Old English
Inherent Meaning: Pledge
Spiritual Connotation: Truthful
Scripture: Luke 8:15 NASB
But the seed in the good soil, these are the ones who have heard the word in an honest and good heart, and hold it fast, and bear fruit with perseverance.

ARLEY, Arleigh, Arlie, Arly
Language/Cultural Origin: Old English
Inherent Meaning: Hunter
Spiritual Connotation: Pledge
Scripture: Genesis 1:28 NKJV
Then God blessed them, and God said to them, Be fruitful and multiply; fill the earth and subdue it; have dominion . . . over every living thing that moves on the earth.

ARMAND, Armando, Armond
Language/Cultural Origin: Old German
Inherent Meaning: Army Man
Spiritual Connotation: Strong
Scripture: Psalm 37:39 NASB
But the salvation of the righteous is from the LORD; He is their strength in time of trouble.

ARMON, Arman, Armen, Armin
Language/Cultural Origin: Hebrew
Inherent Meaning: Fortress
Spiritual Connotation: Guarded
Scripture: Psalm 5:12 TLB
For you bless the godly man, O Lord; you protect him with your shield of love.

ARMONI, Armani, Armonni
☞ Language/Cultural Origin: Hebrew
Inherent Meaning: From the Palace
Spiritual Connotation: Blessed
Scripture: 1 Timothy 6:6 NCV
Serving God does make us very rich, if we are satisfied with what we have.

ARNOLD, Arne, Arney, Arni, Arnie
Language/Cultural Origin: Old German
Inherent Meaning: Strong as an Eagle
Spiritual Connotation: Brave
Scripture: Psalm 103:1, 5 KJV
Bless the LORD, O my soul . . . Who satisfieth thy mouth with good things; so that thy youth is renewed like the eagle's.

ARRIO, Ario
Language/Cultural Origin: Hispanic
Inherent Meaning: Warlike
Spiritual Connotation: Protector
Scripture: Psalm 82:3 NKJV
Defend the poor and fatherless; Do justice to the afflicted and needy.

ARSENIO, Arsenius, Arsinio
Language/Cultural Origin: Greek
Inherent Meaning: Masculine
Spiritual Connotation: One of Integrity
Scripture: Psalm 119:9 NIV
How can a young man keep his way pure? By living according to your word.

ARSLAN, Aslan
Language/Cultural Origin: Turkish
Inherent Meaning: Lion
Spiritual Connotation: Symbol of Christ
Scripture: Revelation 10:3 NRSV

He gave a great shout, like a lion roaring. And when he shouted, the seven thunders sounded.

ARTHUR, Art, Arte, Arther, Arthor, Artie, Artis, Arturo, Artur

Language/Cultural Origin: Irish
Inherent Meaning: Bold
Spiritual Connotation: Gracious Ruler
Scripture: Exodus 34:6 NLT
I am the LORD, I am the LORD, the merciful and gracious God. I am slow to anger and rich in unfailing love and faithfulness.

ASA, Asah

Language/Cultural Origin: Hebrew
Inherent Meaning: Healer
Spiritual Connotation: Healer of the Mind and of the Body
Scripture: Isaiah 33:6 KJV
And wisdom and knowledge shall be the stability of thy times, and strength of salvation: the fear of the LORD is his treasure.

ASAD, Asaad, Asád, Assad (see also Hasad)

Language/Cultural Origin: Middle Eastern
Inherent Meaning: Lion
Spiritual Connotation: Strength of God
Scripture: Chronicles 29:12 NKJV
In Your hand is power and might; in Your hand it is to make great and to give strength to all.

ASAPH

Language/Cultural Origin: Hebrew
Inherent Meaning: Remover of Reproach
Spiritual Connotation: Gentle
Scripture: Proverbs 15:1 NKJV
A soft answer turns away wrath, but a harsh word stirs up anger.

ASAREL, Ahsarel, Azarael, Azareel (see also Asriel, Azarel, Azriel)

Language/Cultural Origin: Hebrew
Inherent Meaning: Upright
Spiritual Connotation: Exalted
Scripture: Genesis 41:43 NASB
And he had him ride in his second chariot; and they proclaimed before him, "Bow the knee!" And he set him over all the land of Egypt.

ASENATH, Asennath

Language/Cultural Origin: Egyptian
Inherent Meaning: Belonging to the Goddess
Spiritual Connotation: Honored
Scripture: Genesis 41:50 NKJV
And to Joseph were born two sons . . . whom Asenath . . . bore to him.

ASHA, Ashia

Language/Cultural Origin: Middle Eastern
Inherent Meaning: Vitality
Spiritual Connotation: Humble Strength
Scripture: Genesis 49:15 TLB
When he saw how good the countryside was, how pleasant the land, he willingly bent his shoulder to the task and served his masters with vigor.

ASHBY, Ashbey

Language/Cultural Origin: English
Inherent Meaning: From the Ash-Tree Farm
Spiritual Connotation: Fear of God
Scripture: 2 Corinthians 7:1 NKJV
Let us cleanse ourselves from all filthiness of the flesh and spirit, perfecting holiness in the fear of God.

ASHER, Ashor, Ashur

Language/Cultural Origin: Hebrew
Inherent Meaning: Blessed
Spiritual Connotation: Fortunate
Scripture: Psalm 16:11 NKJV
You will show me the path of life; In Your presence is fullness of joy; At Your right hand are pleasures forevermore.

ASHFORD, Ash

Language/Cultural Origin: English
Inherent Meaning: From the Ash-Tree Ford
Spiritual Connotation: Victorious
Scripture: Revelation 2:7 NKJV
To him who overcomes I will give to eat from the tree of life, which is in the midst of the Paradise of God.

ASHLEY, Ashelee, Asheleigh, Asheley, Ashlea, Ashleah, Ashleay, Ashlee, Ashleigh, Ashly

Language/Cultural Origin: Old English
Inherent Meaning: Of the Ash-Tree Meadow
Spiritual Connotation: Harmony
Scripture: Psalm 133:1 NRSV
How very good and pleasant it is when kindred live together in unity!

ASHLYNN, Ashlan, Ashlen, Ashlin, Ashling, Ashlyn, Ashlyne, Ashlynne
Language/Cultural Origin: Irish
Inherent Meaning: Dream
Spiritual Connotation: Vision of God
Scripture: Ezekiel 12:23 NKJV
The days are at hand, and the fulfillment of every vision.

ASHTON, Ashtin
Language/Cultural Origin: English
Inherent Meaning: From the Ash-Tree Farm
Spiritual Connotation: Supplicant
Scripture: Psalm 57:2 NLT
I cry out to God Most High, to God who will fulfill his purpose for me.

ASIA, Aisia, Asya, Aysia
Language/Cultural Origin: English
Inherent Meaning: Eastern Sunrise
Spiritual Connotation: God Is Sovereign
Scripture: 2 Samuel 7:22 NKJV
For there is none like You, nor is there any God besides You, according to all that we have heard with our ears.

ASRIEL, Ashrael, Ashreel, Ashrayel, Ashriel, Asrael, Asreel, Asreyel (see also Asarel, Azarel, Azriel)
Language/Cultural Origin: Hebrew
Inherent Meaning: God Is Joined
Spiritual Connotation: Unity
Scripture: Psalm 133:1 NRSV
How very good and pleasant it is when kindred live together in unity!

ASTHER, Aster (see also Esther)
Language/Cultural Origin: English
Inherent Meaning: Flower
Spiritual Connotation: Righteous
Scripture: Isaiah 58:8 NKJV
Then your light shall break forth like the morning, Your healing shall spring forth speedily, and your righteousness shall go before you; The glory of the LORD shall be your rear guard.

ATARAH, Atara, Atarra
Language/Cultural Origin: Hebrew
Inherent Meaning: Crown
Spiritual Connotation: Faithful
Scripture: Revelation 2:10 NCV

Do not be afraid of what you are about to suffer. . . . Be faithful, even if you have to die, and I will give you the crown of life.

ATHALIA, Atalya, Athalya
Language/Cultural Origin: Hebrew
Inherent Meaning: Afflicted
Spiritual Connotation: Honor
Scripture: Isaiah 38:19 TLB
The living, only the living, can praise you as I do today. One generation makes known your faithfulness to the next.

ATHENA, Athina
Language/Cultural Origin: Greek
Inherent Meaning: Wise
Spiritual Connotation: Mind of God
Scripture: 1 Corinthians 2:16 NKJV
For who has known the mind of the LORD that he may instruct Him? But we have the mind of Christ.

ATHERTON
Language/Cultural Origin: Middle English
Inherent Meaning: Of the Town by the Spring
Spiritual Connotation: Abundant Life
Scripture: John 10:10 NASB
The thief comes only to steal and kill and destroy; I came that they may have life, and have it abundantly.

ATLEY, Atlea, Atlee, Atleigh, Attley
Language/Cultural Origin: English
Inherent Meaning: From the Meadow
Spiritual Connotation: Purchased
Scripture: Corinthians 7:23 NLT
God purchased you at a high price. Don't be enslaved by the world.

ATWELL, Attwell
Language/Cultural Origin: English
Inherent Meaning: From the Well
Spiritual Connotation: Refreshing
Scripture: Song of Songs 4:15 TLB
You are a garden fountain, a well of living water, refreshing as the streams from the Lebanon mountains.

AUBREY, Aubray, Aubreigh, Aubrie
Language/Cultural Origin: Old German
Inherent Meaning: Noble
Spiritual Connotation: Compassionate

Scripture: Proverbs 31:26 NASB
She opens her mouth in wisdom, and the teaching of kindness is on her tongue.

AUBURN, Auburne
Language/Cultural Origin: English
Inherent Meaning: Reddish-Brown
Spiritual Connotation: Released
Scripture: Isaiah 35:5 NKJV
Then the eyes of the blind shall be opened, and the ears of the deaf shall be unstopped.

AUDIE, Audi
Language/Cultural Origin: Old English
Inherent Meaning: Property Guardian
Spiritual Connotation: Strong of Heart
Scripture: John 16:33 NASB
These things I have spoken to you, so that in Me you may have peace. In the world you have tribulation, but take courage; I have overcome the world.

AUDREY, Audra, Audray, Audree, Audri, Audrianna, Audrie, Audry
Language/Cultural Origin: Old English
Inherent Meaning: Noble Strength
Spiritual Connotation: Overcomer of Many Difficulties
Scripture: 1 John 2:14 NKJV
I have written to you, young men, because you are strong, and the word of God abides in you, and you have overcome the wicked one.

AUDRIC, Audrich (see also Aldrich)
Language/Cultural Origin: French
Inherent Meaning: Wise Ruler
Spiritual Connotation: Chosen
Scripture: Revelation 2:10 NKJV
Be faithful until death, and I will give you the crown of life.

AUGUSTUS, August, Augustine
☞ Language/Cultural Origin: Latin
Inherent Meaning: Venerable
Spiritual Connotation: Exalted
Scripture: Proverbs 27:18 NCV
Whoever takes care of his master will receive honor.

AUGUSTA, Agusta, Augustina
Language/Cultural Origin: Latin
Inherent Meaning: Majestic

Spiritual Connotation: Queenly
Scripture: Proverbs 31:25 NLT
She is clothed with strength and dignity, and she laughs with no fear of the future.

AUREL, Aurèle, Aurelio
Language/Cultural Origin: Czech
Inherent Meaning: From Aurek
Spiritual Connotation: Reverent
Scripture: Malachi 4:2 TLB
But for you who fear my name, the Sun of Righteousness will rise with healing in his wings.

AURELIA, Auralia, Aurelea, Aureliana, Aurielle, Aurilia
Language/Cultural Origin: Latin
Inherent Meaning: Golden
Spiritual Connotation: Sealed
Scripture: Hebrews 5:9 NKJV
And having been perfected, He became the author of eternal salvation to all who obey Him.

AURORA, Auroré
Language/Cultural Origin: Latin
Inherent Meaning: Dawn
Spiritual Connotation: Mouthpiece of God
Scripture: Psalm 50:1 NKJV
The Mighty One, God the LORD, has spoken and called the earth from the rising of the sun to its going down.

AUSTIN, Austan, Austen, Austyn
Language/Cultural Origin: Latin
Inherent Meaning: Renowned
Spiritual Connotation: Guided of God
Scripture: Isaiah 58:11 KJV
And the LORD shall guide thee continually, and satisfy thy soul in drought . . . and thou shalt be like a watered garden.

AVA, Avae, Ave (see also Eva)
Language/Cultural Origin: English
Inherent Meaning: Filled With Life
Spiritual Connotation: Filled With Praise
Scripture: Psalm 106:1 KJV
Praise ye the LORD. O give thanks unto the LORD; for he is good: for his mercy endureth for ever.

AVERY, Averey, Averie
Language/Cultural Origin: Middle English

Inherent Meaning: Ruler
Spiritual Connotation: Wise Counselor
Scripture: Proverbs 20:5 TLB
Though good advice lies deep within a counselor's heart, the wise man will draw it out.

AVIEL, Avi, Avian, Avion (see also Abiel)
Language/Cultural Origin: Hebrew
Inherent Meaning: God Is My Father
Spiritual Connotation: Child of God
Scripture: 1 John 5:1 NCV
Everyone who believes that Jesus is the Christ is God's child, and whoever loves the Father also loves the Father's children.

AVIS, Avia, Aviana
Language/Cultural Origin: Latin
Inherent Meaning: Refuge
Spiritual Connotation: Place of Freedom
Scripture: Galatians 5:1 NASB
It was for freedom that Christ set us free; therefore keep standing firm and do not be subject again to a yoke of slavery.

AXEL, Axell, Axil, Axill (see also Aksel)
Language/Cultural Origin: Scandinavian
Inherent Meaning: My Father Is Peace
Spiritual Connotation: Victory
Scripture: Romans 16:20 NASB
And the God of peace will soon crush Satan under your feet. The grace of our Lord Jesus be with you.

AYA, Ayah (see also Aiah)
Language/Cultural Origin: Hebrew
Inherent Meaning: Bird
Spiritual Connotation: Committed
Scripture: Proverbs 27:8 NASB
Like a bird that wanders from her nest, so is a man who wanders from his home.

AYANNA, Aiyana, Ayana, Ayania, Ayannah
Language/Cultural Origin: Cherokee
Inherent Meaning: Everlasting Bloom
Spiritual Connotation: Blessed
Scripture: Genesis 13:15 NKJV
All the land which you see I give to you and your descendants forever.

AYASHA, Ayashah
Language/Cultural Origin: Middle Eastern
Inherent Meaning: Life
Spiritual Connotation: Eternal
Scripture: John 6:27 NLT
But you shouldn't be so concerned about perishable things like food. Spend your energy seeking the eternal life that I, the Son of Man, can give you.

AZAREL, Ahzarel, Azarael, Azareel (see also Asarel, Asriel, Azriel)
Language/Cultural Origin: Hebrew
Inherent Meaning: God Helped
Spiritual Connotation: Delivered
Scripture: Psalm 34:4 NKJV
I sought the LORD, and He heard me, And delivered me from all my fears.

AZARIAH, Azariyah
Language/Cultural Origin: Hebrew
Inherent Meaning: The Lord Will Keep Us
Spiritual Connotation: Preserved
Scripture: Numbers 6:24 NASB
The LORD bless you, and keep you.

AZEEM, Aseem
Language/Cultural Origin: Middle Eastern
Inherent Meaning: Defender
Spiritual Connotation: God's Warrior
Scripture: Zechariah 12:8 NASB
In that day the LORD will defend the inhabitants of Jerusalem.

AZRIEL, Azrayel, Azriela, Azrielle (see also Asarel, Asriel, Azarel)
Language/Cultural Origin: Hebrew
Inherent Meaning: God Is My Help
Spiritual Connotation: Prayerful
Scripture: Psalm 77:2 NCV
I look for the Lord on the day of trouble. All night long I reach out my hands, but I cannot be comforted.

AZZAN, Azzán
Language/Cultural Origin: Hebrew
Inherent Meaning: Sharp
Spiritual Connotation: Devout
Scripture: Proverbs 27:17 NASB
Iron sharpens iron, So one man sharpens another.

BAARA, Bara, Baarah
☞Language/Cultural Origin: Hebrew
Inherent Meaning: Burning
Spiritual Connotation: Flame of God
Scripture: Hebrews 12:29 NKJV
Our God is a consuming fire.

BAASHA, Basha
☞Language/Cultural Origin: Hebrew
Inherent Meaning: Boldness
Spiritual Connotation: Empowered
Scripture: Acts 4:29 NCV
*And now, Lord, listen to their threats.
Lord, help us, your servants, to speak your
word without fear.*

BABBIE, Bab, Babb, Babs
Language/Cultural Origin: American
Inherent Meaning: Stranger
Spiritual Connotation: Foreigner
Scripture: Philippians 3:20 TLB
*But our homeland is in heaven, where our
Savior, the Lord Jesus Christ, is; and we are
looking forward to his return from there.*

**BADEN, Bayden, Baydon, Beyden,
Beydon (see also Bedan)**
Language/Cultural Origin: Old English
Inherent Meaning: Bather
Spiritual Connotation: Cleansed
Scripture: Psalm 51:2 NKJV
*Wash me thoroughly from my iniquity, and
cleanse me from my sin.*

**BAILEY, Bailee, Bailey, Bailie,
Bali, Baylee, Bayley, Baylie**
Language/Cultural Origin: Old French
Inherent Meaning: Stewardship
Spiritual Connotation: Protector
Scripture: 1 Peter 4:10 NASB
*As each one has received a special gift,
employ it in serving one another, as good
stewards of the manifold grace of God.*

BAIN, Baine (see also Bane)
Language/Cultural Origin: Gaelic
Inherent Meaning: Fair
Spiritual Connotation: Cleansed
Scripture: 1 Corinthians 6:11 TLB
*Now your sins are washed away, and you are
set apart for God; and he has accepted you
because of what the Lord Jesus Christ and the
Spirit of our God have done for you.*

BAIRD, Bairde, Bard
Language/Cultural Origin: Irish
Inherent Meaning: Traveling Singer of Ballads
Spiritual Connotation: Song of Harmony
Scripture: Psalm 81:1 NLT
*Sing praises to God, our strength. Sing to the
God of Israel.*

BAKER, see Baxter

BALAAM, Balam, Balám
☞Language/Cultural Origin: Hebrew
Inherent Meaning: Lord of the People
Spiritual Connotation: Vessel of God
Scripture: Numbers 23:8 NASB
*How shall I curse, whom God has not cursed?
And how can I denounce, whom the LORD has
not denounced?*

BALDWIN, Baldwyn
Language/Cultural Origin: Old German
Inherent Meaning: Bold Friend
Spiritual Connotation: Courageous
Scripture: 1 Chronicles 28:20 NASB
*Be strong and courageous, and act; do not
fear nor be dismayed, for the LORD God, my
God, is with you. He will not fail you nor
forsake you.*

BALIN, Baylin (see also Valin)
Language/Cultural Origin: Indo-Pakistani
Inherent Meaning: Mighty Warrior
Spiritual Connotation: Successful

Scripture: Jeremiah 50:9 NKJV

And they shall array themselves against her; from there she shall be captured. Their arrows shall be like those of an expert warrior; none shall return in vain.

BAMBI, Bambee, Bambie

Language/Cultural Origin: Italian
Inherent Meaning: Child
Spiritual Connotation: Innocent
Scripture: Mark 9:37 NKJV

Whoever receives one of these little children in My name receives Me; and whoever receives Me, receives not Me but Him who sent Me.

BANE, Bayne (see also Bain)

Language/Cultural Origin: Hawaiian
Inherent Meaning: Child of Exhortation
Spiritual Connotation: Heir
Scripture: Hebrews 12:5 NRSV

My child, do not regard lightly the discipline of the Lord, or lose heart when you are punished by him.

BANI, Baani, Banni, Bannie

Language/Cultural Origin: Hebrew
Inherent Meaning: Built
Spiritual Connotation: Honorable
Scripture: Psalms 127:1 NKJV

Unless the LORD builds the house, they labor in vain who build it.

BANNER, Bannor

Language/Cultural Origin: Scottish
Inherent Meaning: Flag Follower
Spiritual Connotation: God's Soldier
Scripture: Isaiah 31:9 NCV

They will panic, and their protection will be destroyed. Their commanders will be terrified when they see God's battle flag.

BANNING, Baning

Language/Cultural Origin: Irish
Inherent Meaning: Small and Fair
Spiritual Connotation: Cleansed of God
Scripture: John 17:19 KJV

And for their sakes I sanctify myself, that they also might be sanctified through the truth.

BARBARA, Barb, Barbe, Barbie, Barbora, Barbra, Barby

Language/Cultural Origin: Greek

Inherent Meaning: Stranger
Spiritual Connotation: Purchased
Scripture: Ephesians 2:19 NKJV

Now, therefore, you are no longer strangers and foreigners, but fellow citizens with the saints and members of the household of God.

BARCLAY, Barkley, Berkeley, Berkley

Language/Cultural Origin: Scottish
Inherent Meaning: From the Meadow of the Birch Trees
Spiritual Connotation: Renewed in Spirit
Scripture: John 6:63 NASB

It is the Spirit who gives life; the flesh profits nothing; the words that I have spoken to you are spirit and are life.

BARIAH, Bariya, Bariyah, Barriah (see also Beraiah)

Language/Cultural Origin: Hebrew
Inherent Meaning: Fugitive
Spiritual Connotation: Seeker of Truth
Scripture: Psalms 39:12 NLT

Hear my prayer, O LORD! Listen to my cries for help! Don't ignore my tears. For I am your guest—a traveler passing through.

BARKER, Barcker

Language/Cultural Origin: Old English
Inherent Meaning: Shepherd
Spiritual Connotation: Guide
Scripture: Ecclesiastes 12:11 NLT

A wise teacher's words spur students to action and emphasize important truths. The collected sayings of the wise are like guidance from a shepherd.

BARNABAS, Barnaby, Barney, Barnie

Language/Cultural Origin: Hebrew
Inherent Meaning: Son of Exhortation
Spiritual Connotation: Praise to God
Scripture: Psalm 25:1 KJV

Unto thee, O LORD, do I lift up my soul.

BARRIE, Bari, Barri

Language/Cultural Origin: Old English
Inherent Meaning: Markswoman
Spiritual Connotation: Brave
Scripture: Judges 4:9 NKJV

There will be no glory for you in the journey you are taking, for the LORD will sell Sisera into the hand of a woman.

BARRY, Barrey, Bary

Language/Cultural Origin: Irish
Inherent Meaning: Marksman
Spiritual Connotation: Strong
Scripture: Luke 10:27 NKJV

You shall love the LORD your God with all your heart, with all your soul, with all your strength, and with all your mind, and your neighbor as yourself.

BARTHOLOMEW, Bart, Bartlet

Language/Cultural Origin: Aramaic
Inherent Meaning: Son of Tolmai
Spiritual Connotation: Heir
Scripture: Colossians 1:12 NASB

Giving thanks to the Father, who has qualified us to share in the inheritance of the saints in light.

BARUCH, Boruch

Language/Cultural Origin: Hebrew
Inherent Meaning: Blessed
Spiritual Connotation: Righteous
Scripture: James 1:12 NRSV

Blessed is anyone who endures temptation. Such a one has stood the test and will receive the crown of life that the Lord has promised to those who love him.

BARUSHKA, Baruska

Language/Cultural Origin: Czech
Inherent Meaning: Stranger
Spiritual Connotation: Approved
Scripture: Proverbs 27:2 NKJV

Let another man praise you, and not your own mouth; a stranger, and not your own lips.

BASIA, Basha, Basya, Batia, Batya

Language/Cultural Origin: Hebrew
Inherent Meaning: Daughter of God
Spiritual Connotation: Valued
Scripture: Matthew 21:5 NRSV

Tell the daughter of Zion, Look, your king is coming to you.

BASIL, Bazil

Language/Cultural Origin: Greek
Inherent Meaning: Kingly
Spiritual Connotation: Magnificent
Scripture: 1 Chronicles 29:12 NASB

Both riches and honor come from You, and You rule over all, and in Your hand is power and might.

BAXTER, Baker

Language/Cultural Origin: Middle English
Inherent Meaning: Provider
Spiritual Connotation: Industrious
Scripture: 2 Corinthians 9:10 NASB

Now He who supplies seed to the sower and bread for food, will supply and multiply your seed for sowing and increase the harvest of your righteousness.

BAY, Baye

Language/Cultural Origin: Vietnamese
Inherent Meaning: Born on Saturday/Born in the Month of July
Spiritual Connotation: Forgiven
Scripture: Romans 4:8 TLB

Yes, what joy there is for anyone whose sins are no longer counted against him by the Lord.

BEATRICE, Bea, Beatricia, Bee

Language/Cultural Origin: Italian
Inherent Meaning: Bringer of Joy
Spiritual Connotation: Love of Life
Scripture: Deuteronomy 27:7 KJV

And thou shalt offer peace offerings, and shalt eat there, and rejoice before the LORD thy God.

BEAU (see also Bo)

Language/Cultural Origin: French
Inherent Meaning: Handsome
Spiritual Connotation: Peacemaker
Scripture: Psalm 133:1 NASB

Behold, how good and how pleasant it is for brothers to dwell together in unity!

BEBE, Babe (see also Bibi)

Language/Cultural Origin: Spanish
Inherent Meaning: Baby
Spiritual Connotation: Faith
Scripture: Luke 18:17 NASB

Truly I say to you, whoever does not receive the kingdom of God like a child shall not enter it at all.

BECK, Beckett

Language/Cultural Origin: Middle English
Inherent Meaning: From the Stream
Spiritual Connotation: Satisfied
Scripture: Psalm 36:8 NLT

You feed them from the abundance of your own house, letting them drink from your rivers of delight.

BECKY, Becca, Becka, Becki, Beckie, Beka, Bekka, Bekki, Bekkie (see also Rebecca)

Language/Cultural Origin: English
Inherent Meaning: Bound by Love
Spiritual Connotation: Loving
Scripture: 1 Corinthians 13:4 NCV

Love is patient and kind. Love is not jealous, it does not brag, and it is not proud.

BEDAN, Baedan, Baedán, Bédan, ☞Bedán (see also Baden)

Language/Cultural Origin: Hebrew
Inherent Meaning: Son of Judgment
Spiritual Connotation: Encourager
Scripture: James 5:9 NLT

Don't grumble about each other, my brothers and sisters, or God will judge you. For look! The great Judge is coming. He is standing at the door!

BELA, Béla, Belah

Language/Cultural Origin: Hebrew
Inherent Meaning: Devouring
Spiritual Connotation: Godly Example
Scripture: Isaiah 60:3 NRSV

Nations shall come to your light, and kings to the brightness of your dawn.

BELDON, Belden

Language/Cultural Origin: Old English
Inherent Meaning: From the Beautiful Valley
Spiritual Connotation: Sanctified
Scripture: Isaiah 40:4 NKJV

Every valley shall be exalted and every mountain and hill brought low.

BELINDA, Belynda

Language/Cultural Origin: Spanish
Inherent Meaning: Lovely
Spiritual Connotation: Beauty of Soul
Scripture: Ephesians 4:7 NASB

But to each one of us grace was given according to the measure of Christ's gift.

BELLE, Bell, Bellina

Language/Cultural Origin: French
Inherent Meaning: Beautiful
Spiritual Connotation: Blessed
Scripture: Psalm 104:33 NCV

I will sing to the LORD all my life; I will sing praises to my God as long as I live.

BENAIAH, Benaiya, Beniyah

Language/Cultural Origin: Hebrew
Inherent Meaning: The Lord Has Built
Spiritual Connotation: Foundation
Scripture: 1 Samuel 12:24 NKJV

Only fear the LORD, and serve Him in truth with all your heart; for consider what great things He has done for you.

BEN-AMMI, Ben Ami, BenAmi, ☞Ben-Ami, Benn-Ami

Language/Cultural Origin: Hebrew
Inherent Meaning: Son of My People
Spiritual Connotation: Ancestor
Scripture: Genesis 17:6 NKJV

I will make you exceedingly fruitful; and I will make nations of you, and kings shall come from you.

BEN-HANAN, BenHanan, ☞Ben-Hannan, Benn-Hanan

Language/Cultural Origin: Hebrew
Inherent Meaning: Son of Kindness
Spiritual Connotation: Loving
Scripture: Ephesians 4:32 NKJV

And be kind to one another, tenderhearted, forgiving one another, just as God in Christ forgave you.

BENITA, Benitta

Language/Cultural Origin: Spanish
Inherent Meaning: Blessed
Spiritual Connotation: Cherished
Scripture: Numbers 6:25 NRSV

The LORD make his face to shine upon you, and be gracious to you.

BENJAMIN, Ben, Benjaman, ☞Benjamen, Benji, Benjie, Benn, Bennie, Benny, Benyamin

Language/Cultural Origin: Hebrew
Inherent Meaning: Son of My Right Hand
Spiritual Connotation: Mighty
Scripture: Psalm 18:35 NKJV

You have also given me the shield of Your salvation; Your right hand has held me up, Your gentleness has made me great.

BENNET, Bennett

Language/Cultural Origin: English
Inherent Meaning: Blessed
Spiritual Connotation: Walks With God

Scripture: Romans 8:14 NASB
For all who are being led by the Spirit of God, these are sons of God.

BENOIT, Benoîte
Language/Cultural Origin: French
Inherent Meaning: Blessed
Spiritual Connotation: Received
Scripture: Exodus 20:24 NKJV
In every place where I record My name I will come to you, and I will bless you.

BENSON, Bensen
Language/Cultural Origin: English
Inherent Meaning: Son of Ben
Spiritual Connotation: Honor of God
Scripture: Psalm 127:1 NCV
If the LORD doesn't build the house, the builders are working for nothing. If the LORD doesn't guard the city, the guards are watching for nothing.

BENTLEY, Bentlea, Bentlee
Language/Cultural Origin: Old English
Inherent Meaning: From the Grassy Meadow
Spiritual Connotation: Peaceful
Scripture: Psalm 121:8 NLT
The LORD keeps watch over you as you come and go, both now and forever.

BERAIAH, Beraiyah (see also Bariah)
Language/Cultural Origin: Hebrew
Inherent Meaning: The Lord Has Created
Spiritual Connotation: Joyful
Scripture: Job 1:21 NASB
The LORD gave and the LORD has taken away. Blessed be the name of the LORD.

BERGEN, Bergan, Bergin
Language/Cultural Origin: Scandinavian
Inherent Meaning: From the Hill
Spiritual Connotation: Made Righteous
Scripture: Psalm 15:1–2 NKJV
LORD . . . Who may dwell in Your holy hill? He who walks uprightly, and works righteousness, and speaks the truth in his heart.

BERNADETTE, Bernadine
Language/Cultural Origin: French
Inherent Meaning: Courageous
Spiritual Connotation: Valiant

Scripture: 1 Corinthians 15:57 NKJV
But thanks be to God, who gives us the victory through our Lord Jesus Christ.

BERNARD, Barnard, Bernardo, Berndt, Berney, Bernhard, Berni, Bernie, Birnee, Birney, Burney
Language/Cultural Origin: Old German
Inherent Meaning: Brave as a Bear
Spiritual Connotation: Wise
Scripture: Proverbs 17:12 NCV
It is better to meet a bear robbed of her cubs than to meet a fool doing foolish things.

BERNICE, Berenice, Berni, Bernise
Language/Cultural Origin: Greek
Inherent Meaning: Bringer of Victory
Spiritual Connotation: Victorious
Scripture: Mark 9:23 NLT
Anything is possible if a person believes.

BERTRAM, Bartram, Bert
Language/Cultural Origin: Old English
Inherent Meaning: Brilliant
Spiritual Connotation: Magnificent
Scripture: Isaiah 62:3 RSV
You shall be a crown of beauty in the hand of the LORD, and a royal diadem in the hand of your God.

BERTRAND, Bertran
Language/Cultural Origin: French
Inherent Meaning: Bright Shield
Spiritual Connotation: Protected of God
Scripture: 2 Samuel 22:31 NKJV
As for God, His way is perfect; the word of the LORD is proven; He is a shield to all who trust in Him.

BESSIE, Bess, Bessi, Bessy
Language/Cultural Origin: English
Inherent Meaning: Oath of God
Spiritual Connotation: Loyal
Scripture: Isaiah 30:29 NRSV
You shall have a song as in the night when a holy festival is kept; and gladness of heart.

BETH, Bethe, Bethel, Bethell
(see also Bethany, Elizabeth)
Language/Cultural Origin: Hebrew
Inherent Meaning: Oath of God
Spiritual Connotation: Wise

Scripture: Isaiah 48:17 TLB

I am the Lord your God, who punishes you for your own good and leads you along the paths that you should follow.

BETH ANN, Bethann, Beth-Ann, Beth Anne, Beth-Anne

Language/Cultural Origin: English
Inherent Meaning: Gracious Oath of God
Spiritual Connotation: Promise
Scripture: Acts 2:39 NASB

For the promise is for you and your children, and for all who are far off, as many as the Lord our God shall call to Himself.

BETHANY, Bethanney, Bethani, Bethanie, Bethanney, Betheny

Language/Cultural Origin: Aramaic
Inherent Meaning: House of Figs
Spiritual Connotation: Productive
Scripture: Matthew 7:16 NASB

You will know them by their fruits. Grapes are not gathered from thorn bushes nor figs from thistles, are they?

BETHUEL, Bethuelle

Language/Cultural Origin: Hebrew
Inherent Meaning: Dwells in God
Spiritual Connotation: Secure
Scripture: Psalm 23:6 RSV

Surely goodness and mercy shall follow me all the days of my life; and I shall dwell in the house of the LORD for ever.

BETSY, Betsey, Betsi, Betsie

Language/Cultural Origin: English
Inherent Meaning: Oath of God
Spiritual Connotation: Confirmed
Scripture: Hebrews 7:21 RSV

The Lord has sworn and will not change his mind, "Thou art a priest forever."

BETTY, Bett, Bette, Betti, Bettie

Language/Cultural Origin: English
Inherent Meaning: Oath of God
Spiritual Connotation: Reverent
Scripture: Psalm 119:39 NRSV

Turn away the disgrace that I dread, for your ordinances are good.

BEVAN, Bevann, Beven, Bevin, Bevon

Language/Cultural Origin: Welsh
Inherent Meaning: Son of the Young Warrior

Spiritual Connotation: Youthful
Scripture: Psalm 71:17 NKJV

O God, You have taught me from my youth; and to this day I declare Your wondrous works.

BEVERLY, Bev, Beverlee, Beverley

Language/Cultural Origin: English
Inherent Meaning: Peace and Harmony
Spiritual Connotation: Enlightened
Scripture: James 1:17 KJV

Every good gift and every perfect gift is from above, and cometh down from the Father of lights, with whom is no variableness, neither shadow of turning.

BEVIS, Bevys

Language/Cultural Origin: Old French
Inherent Meaning: Bull
Spiritual Connotation: Powerful
Scripture: Isaiah 10:13 NRSV

I have removed the boundaries of peoples, and have plundered their treasures; like a bull I have brought down those who sat on thrones.

BIANCA, Biancha, Bionca, Bioncha

Language/Cultural Origin: Italian
Inherent Meaning: Fair
Spiritual Connotation: Wisdom
Scripture: Job 5:8–9 NASB

But as for me, I would seek God, and I would place my cause before God; Who does great and unsearchable things, wonders without number.

BIBI, Beebee (see also Bebe)

Language/Cultural Origin: Middle Eastern
Inherent Meaning: Honored
Spiritual Connotation: Praised
Scripture: Mark 10:43 NCV

But it should not be that way among you. Whoever wants to become great among you must serve the rest of you like a servant.

BILL, see William

BING

Language/Cultural Origin: German
Inherent Meaning: From the Kettle-Shaped Hollow
Spiritual Connotation: Blessed
Scripture: Luke 3:5 RSV

Every valley shall be filled, and every mountain and hill shall be brought low, and the crooked shall be made straight, and the rough ways shall be made smooth.

BIRDIE, see Roberta

BIRNEY, Birnie, Birny
Language/Cultural Origin: Middle English
Inherent Meaning: From the Island With the Stream
Spiritual Connotation: One of Integrity
Scripture: Romans 8:28 NKJV
And we know that all things work together for good to those who love God, to those who are the called according to His purpose.

BJORN, Bjarn, Bjarne, Bjorne
Language/Cultural Origin: Scandinavian
Inherent Meaning: Bear
Spiritual Connotation: Voice of God
Scripture: Joel 2:11 RSV
The LORD utters his voice before his army, for his host is exceedingly great.

BLADE, Blayde
Language/Cultural Origin: Middle English
Inherent Meaning: Knife
Spiritual Connotation: Weapon
Scripture: Matthew 10:34 NKJV
Do not think that I came to bring peace on earth. I did not come to bring peace but a sword.

BLAINE, Blain, Blane, Blayne
Language/Cultural Origin: Gaelic
Inherent Meaning: Lean
Spiritual Connotation: Trusting
Scripture: Isaiah 42:16 NRSV
I will turn the darkness before them into light, the rough places into level ground. . . . I will not forsake them.

BLAIR, Blaire
Language/Cultural Origin: Irish
Inherent Meaning: Field Worker
Spiritual Connotation: Diligent
Scripture: Ephesians 6:7 NLT
Work with enthusiasm, as though you were working for the Lord rather than for people.

BLAISE, Blaize, Blayze, Blaze
Language/Cultural Origin: French

Inherent Meaning: Flame/One Who Stammers
Spiritual Connotation: Flame of God
Scripture: Hebrews 12:29 NRSV
Indeed our God is a consuming fire.

BLAKE, Blakelee, Blakeleigh, Blakeley, Blakely
Language/Cultural Origin: English
Inherent Meaning: Attractive
Spiritual Connotation: Forgiven
Scripture: Ephesians 2:4–5 NASB
But God, being rich in mercy, because of His great love with which He loved us . . . made us alive together with Christ.

BLANCHE, Blanch
Language/Cultural Origin: French
Inherent Meaning: Pure
Spiritual Connotation: Gentle
Scripture: Psalm 49:3 RSV
My mouth shall speak wisdom; the meditation of my heart shall be understanding.

BLOSSOM, Blossum
Language/Cultural Origin: Old English
Inherent Meaning: Flower
Spiritual Connotation: Joyful
Scripture: Isaiah 35:1–2 NKJV
And the desert shall rejoice and blossom as the rose; it shall blossom abundantly and rejoice, even with joy and singing. . . .

BLYTHE, Blithe, Blyth
Language/Cultural Origin: English
Inherent Meaning: Joyful
Spiritual Connotation: Cheerful
Scripture: John 16:33 NKJV
These things I have spoken to you, that in Me you may have peace. In the world you will have tribulation; but be of good cheer, I have overcome the world.

BO, Boe (see also Beau)
Language/Cultural Origin: Chinese
Inherent Meaning: Precious
Spiritual Connotation: Honored
Scripture: Isaiah 43:4 TLB
Others died that you might live; I traded their lives for yours because you are precious to me and honored, and I love you.

BOAZ, Boas, Boz
Language/Cultural Origin: Hebrew

Inherent Meaning: Swift
Spiritual Connotation: Bearer of the Covenant
Scripture: Isaiah 16:5 NRSV
A throne shall be established in steadfast love in the tent of David, and on it shall sit in faithfulness a ruler who seeks justice and is swift to do what is right.

BOB, see Robert

BOBBIE, Bobbi
Language/Cultural Origin: American
Inherent Meaning: Foreigner
Spiritual Connotation: Stranger
Scripture: 1 Peter 2:11 NASB
Beloved, I urge you as aliens and strangers to abstain from fleshly lusts, which wage war against the soul.

BODAN, Bohdan
Language/Cultural Origin: Ukranian
Inherent Meaning: World Leader
Spiritual Connotation: Orchestrator of Peace
Scripture: Isaiah 60:17 NIV
I will make peace your governor and righteousness your ruler.

BODANA, Bodanna, Bogdana, Bohdana
Language/Cultural Origin: Polish
Inherent Meaning: Heavenly Presence
Spiritual Connotation: Keenly Aware
Scripture: Psalm 89:7 TLB
The highest of angelic powers stand in dread and awe of him. Who is as revered as he by those surrounding him?

BODEN, Bodee, Bodie, Bodin
Language/Cultural Origin: French
Inherent Meaning: Messenger/Herald
Spiritual Connotation: Ready for Service
Scripture: Isaiah 6:8 NLT
Then I heard the Lord asking, Whom should I send as a messenger to my people? Who will go for us? And I said, Lord, I'll go! Send me.

BODHAN, Bodhun
Language/Cultural Origin: Russian
Inherent Meaning: Mighty
Spiritual Connotation: Devoted
Scripture: Deuteronomy 6:5 NKJV
You shall love the LORD your God with all your heart, with all your soul, and with all your strength.

BONNIE, Bonita, Bonne, Bonni, Bonnita, Bonny
Language/Cultural Origin: French
Inherent Meaning: Beautiful
Spiritual Connotation: Pure in Heart
Scripture: Matthew 5:8 NKJV
Blessed are the pure in heart, for they shall see God.

BOONE, Boon, Boonie
Language/Cultural Origin: French
Inherent Meaning: Good
Spiritual Connotation: Obedient
Scripture: Psalm 119:2 RSV
Blessed are those who keep his testimonies, who seek him with their whole heart.

BORDEN, Bordan
Language/Cultural Origin: French
Inherent Meaning: From the Cottage
Spiritual Connotation: Righteous
Scripture: Proverbs 3:33 NASB
The curse of the LORD is on the house of the wicked, but He blesses the dwelling of the righteous.

BORIS, Boriss, Borris
Language/Cultural Origin: Slavic
Inherent Meaning: Warrior
Spiritual Connotation: Trusting
Scripture: Psalm 36:7 NRSV
How precious is your steadfast love, O God! All people may take refuge in the shadow of your wings.

BOTAN, Botán
Language/Cultural Origin: Japanese
Inherent Meaning: Blossom
Spiritual Connotation: Youthful
Scripture: Ezekiel 16:7 NKJV
I made you thrive like a plant in the field; and you grew, matured, and became very beautiful.

BOWEN, Bowie
Language/Cultural Origin: Gaelic
Inherent Meaning: Small
Spiritual Connotation: Victorious
Scripture: Psalm 20:5 NASB
We will sing for joy over your victory, and in the name of our God we will set up our banners. May the LORD fulfill all your petitions.

BOYCE, Boice, Boise, Boycee, Boycie
Language/Cultural Origin: French
Inherent Meaning: From the Forest
Spiritual Connotation: Joyful
Scripture: Psalm 96:12 TLB
> Praise him for the growing fields, for they display his greatness. Let the trees of the forest rustle with praise.

BOYD, Boid
Language/Cultural Origin: Scottish
Inherent Meaning: Golden-Haired
Spiritual Connotation: Quiet Spirit
Scripture: Proverbs 15:33 NCV
> Respect for the LORD will teach you wisdom. If you want to be honored, you must be humble.

BRADEN, Bradan, Bradin, Braeden, Brayden (see also Bradon)
Language/Cultural Origin: English
Inherent Meaning: From the Broad Clearing
Spiritual Connotation: Redeemed
Scripture: Romans 5:9 NLT
> And since we have been made right in God's sight by the blood of Christ, he will certainly save us from God's judgment.

BRADFORD, Brad, Braddford
Language/Cultural Origin: English
Inherent Meaning: From the Water Crossing
Spiritual Connotation: Delivered of God
Scripture: Mark 14:24 NKJV
> And He said to them, "This is My blood of the new covenant, which is shed for many."

BRADLEY, Brad, Bradd, Braddlee, Bradlay, Bradlee
Language/Cultural Origin: Old English
Inherent Meaning: From the Broad Meadow
Spiritual Connotation: Joyful
Scripture: Proverbs 15:13 NASB
> A joyful heart makes a cheerful face.

BRADON, Braedon, Braydon (see also Braden)
Language/Cultural Origin: English
Inherent Meaning: From the Broad Hill
Spiritual Connotation: Called of God
Scripture: John 15:16 NRSV
> You did not choose me but I chose you. And I appointed you to go and bear fruit.

BRADY, Bradey (see also Brede)
Language/Cultural Origin: Irish
Inherent Meaning: Spirited
Spiritual Connotation: Gentle
Scripture: Galatians 5:22–23 NASB
> But the fruit of the Spirit is love, joy, peace, patience, kindness, goodness, faithfulness, gentleness, self-control; against such things there is no law.

BRANDON, Brandan, Branddon, Branden, Brandin, Brandyn, Brannan, Brannon
Language/Cultural Origin: Old English
Inherent Meaning: From the Flaming Hill
Spiritual Connotation: Fervent
Scripture: Romans 12:11 NLT
> Never be lazy in your work, but serve the Lord enthusiastically.

BRANDY, Brandee, Brandi, Brandie
Language/Cultural Origin: Middle Dutch
Inherent Meaning: Distilled Wine
Spiritual Connotation: Filled With Joy
Scripture: Psalms 4:7 NKJV
> You have put gladness in my heart, more than in the season that their grain and wine increased.

BRANT, Brandt, Brannt, Brantley
Language/Cultural Origin: Czech
Inherent Meaning: Proud
Spiritual Connotation: Focused
Scripture: 2 Timothy 2:4 TLB
> And as Christ's soldier, do not let yourself become tied up in worldly affairs, for then you cannot satisfy the one who has enlisted you in his army.

BRAXTON, Braxtun
Language/Cultural Origin: Old English
Inherent Meaning: From Brock's Town
Spiritual Connotation: Faithful
Scripture: 1 Corinthians 7:20 NKJV
> Let each one remain in the same calling in which he was called.

BREANNE, Breann, Bre-Ann, Bre-Anne, Breeann, Breeanne, Breighann, Briann, Brianne, Brieann, Briene, Brienne, Bryanne (see also Brenna, Brianna)
Language/Cultural Origin: Celtic

Inherent Meaning: Strong
Spiritual Connotation: Dependent
Scripture: Psalm 68:34 NRSV

Ascribe power to God, whose majesty is over Israel; and whose power is in the skies.

BRECK, Brec, Brek, Brekk
Language/Cultural Origin: Irish
Inherent Meaning: Freckled
Spiritual Connotation: Approved
Scripture: Job 5:17 NKJV

Behold, happy is the man whom God corrects; therefore do not despise the chastening of the Almighty.

BREDE, Braede, Bréde
(see also Brady)
Language/Cultural Origin: Scandinavian
Inherent Meaning: Glacier
Spiritual Connotation: Immovable
Scripture: Job 38:29–30 NLT

Who is the mother of the ice? Who gives birth to the frost from the heavens? For the water turns to ice as hard as rock, and the surface of the water freezes.

BRENDA, Brendie
Language/Cultural Origin: Old Norse
Inherent Meaning: Sword
Spiritual Connotation: Glory of God
Scripture: Psalms 70:4 NASB

Let all who seek You rejoice and be glad in You; and let those who love Your salvation say continually, let God be magnified.

BRENDAN, Brenden, Brendin,
Brendon, Brenndan
Language/Cultural Origin: Irish
Inherent Meaning: Stinking Hair
Spiritual Connotation: Devout
Scripture: 1 Timothy 1:5 NASB

But the goal of our instruction is love from a pure heart and a good conscience and a sincere faith.

BRENNA, Brena, Brenin, Brennah,
Brennaugh, Brynna
Language/Cultural Origin: Irish
Inherent Meaning: Little Raven
Spiritual Connotation: Faithful Friend
Scripture: Philippians 2:13 NCV

God is working in you to help you want to do and be able to do what pleases him.

BRENNAN, Brennen, Brennon
Language/Cultural Origin: Irish
Inherent Meaning: Little Raven
Spiritual Connotation: Gift of God
Scripture: Romans 6:23 NKJV

For the wages of sin is death, but the gift of God is eternal life in Christ Jesus our Lord.

BRENTON, Brendt, Brent, Brentan,
Brenten, Brentin, Brentton, Brentyn
Language/Cultural Origin: English
Inherent Meaning: From the Steep Hill
Spiritual Connotation: Wise
Scripture: Ecclesiastes 4:13 RSV

Better is a poor and wise youth than an old and foolish king, who will no longer take advice.

BRETT, Bret, Brette
Language/Cultural Origin: Scottish
Inherent Meaning: Gifted
Spiritual Connotation: Blessed
Scripture: Proverbs 18:16 NRSV

A gift opens doors; it gives access to the great.

BRIAN, Briant, Brien, Brient, Brion,
Bryan, Bryant, Bryen, Bryent, Bryon
Language/Cultural Origin: Celtic
Inherent Meaning: Virtue and Honor
Spiritual Connotation: Follower of God
Scripture: Isaiah 48:17 NRSV

I am the LORD your God, who teaches you for your own good, who leads you in the way you should go.

BRIANNA, Breana, Breanna, Breeana,
Breeanna, Bria, Brianda, Briana,
Briannah, Briannon, Briannon,
Bryana, Bryanna, Bryannah
(see also Breanne, Brenna)
Language/Cultural Origin: Celtic
Inherent Meaning: Honorable
Spiritual Connotation: Virtuous
Scripture: Ruth 3:11 NASB

And now, my daughter, do not fear. I will do for you whatever you ask, for all my people in the city know that you are a woman of excellence.

BRIAR, Brear, Brier, Briet,
Brietta, Bryar, Bryer
Language/Cultural Origin: French

Inherent Meaning: Heather
Spiritual Connotation: Child of God
Scripture: Job 29:12 NLT
> For I helped the poor in their need and the orphans who had no one to help them.

BRIDGET, Bridgete, Bridgett, Bridgette, Bridgot, Briget, Brigette, Brigitte, Brigitta
Language/Cultural Origin: Irish
Inherent Meaning: Strength
Spiritual Connotation: Enduring Spirit
Scripture: Psalm 27:1 NKJV
> The LORD is my light and my salvation; whom shall I fear? The LORD is the strength of my life; of whom shall I be afraid?

BRIGHAM, Briggs
Language/Cultural Origin: English
Inherent Meaning: From the Covered Bridge
Spiritual Connotation: Challenger of Apostasy
Scripture: Ecclesiastes 12:1 NRSV
> Remember your creator in the days of your youth, before the days of trouble come.

BRINA, Breena, Breina, Brin, Brinan, Brindy, Brinn, Brinnan, Bryn, Brynan, Brynn, Brynne
Language/Cultural Origin: Irish
Inherent Meaning: From the Fairy Palace
Spiritual Connotation: God's Salvation
Scripture: Psalm 9:14 NCV
> Then, at the gates of Jerusalem, I will praise you; I will rejoice because you saved me.

BRINLEY, Brindlee, Brindley, Brinlee, Brinly, Brynley
Language/Cultural Origin: Old English
Inherent Meaning: Burnt Wood
Spiritual Connotation: Sacrifice
Scripture: Psalms 54:6 NRSV
> With a freewill offering I will sacrifice to you; I will give thanks to your name, O LORD, for it is good.

BRIONA, Breeon, Breona, Briele, Brielle, Brieon, Brieona, Brione, Brionne, Briony, Bryoni
Language/Cultural Origin: Irish
Inherent Meaning: Mighty
Spiritual Connotation: God's Power

Scripture: Exodus 9:1 NKJV
> Thus says the LORD God of the Hebrews: "Let My people go, that they may serve Me."

BRIT, Brita, Britt, Britte
Language/Cultural Origin: Swedish
Inherent Meaning: Strong
Spiritual Connotation: Prayerful
Scripture: Numbers 14:17 NASB
> But now, I pray, let the power of the Lord be great, just as You have declared.

BRITTANY, Britain, Britane, Britaney, Britani, Britanny, Britlee, Britley, Britlyn, Britlynn, Britnee, Britney, Britni, Britnie, Britny, Brityn, Brittain, Brittanee, Brittaney, Brittani, Brittania, Britteney, Brittiney, Brittiny, Brittnay, Brittnee, Brittneigh, Brittney, Brittni, Brittnie, Brittoni, Brittony, Bryttani, Bryttany, Bryttney, Bryttni, Bryttny
Language/Cultural Origin: English
Inherent Meaning: From Britain
Spiritual Connotation: Stranger
Scripture: Ruth 2:10 NKJV
> Why have I found favor in your eyes, that you should take notice of me, since I am a foreigner?

BROCK, Broc, Brocke, Brok, Broque
Language/Cultural Origin: Old English
Inherent Meaning: Badger
Spiritual Connotation: Full of Praise
Scripture: Psalm 3:4 NKJV
> I cried to the LORD with my voice, and He heard me from His holy hill.

BRODERICK, Broderic, Brodric, Broadrick (see also Roderick)
Language/Cultural Origin: Norse
Inherent Meaning: Brother
Spiritual Connotation: True Friend
Scripture: Psalm 18:24 NASB
> Therefore the LORD has recompensed me according to my righteousness, according to the cleanness of my hands in His eyes.

BRODIE, Brodee, Brodey, Brodi
Language/Cultural Origin: Irish
Inherent Meaning: Canal Builder
Spiritual Connotation: God Is My Foundation

Scripture: Psalm 127:1 NKJV
Unless the LORD builds the house, they labor in vain who build it; unless the LORD guards the city, the watchman stays awake in vain.

BROÑA, Bronja, Bronya
Language/Cultural Origin: Czech
Inherent Meaning: Bringer of Victory
Spiritual Connotation: Revered
Scripture: 1 Corinthians 15:55 TLB
O death, where then your victory? Where then your sting?

BRONSON, Bronnson, Bronsen, Bronsin, Bronsson
Language/Cultural Origin: English
Inherent Meaning: Son of the Dark-Skinned
Spiritual Connotation: Great Ruler
Scripture: Psalm 100:2 NRSV
Worship the LORD with gladness; come into his presence with singing.

BROOK, Brooke, Brooks, Broox
Language/Cultural Origin: Old English
Inherent Meaning: Peaceful
Spiritual Connotation: Refreshed
Scripture: Zechariah 2:10 NASB
Sing for joy and be glad, O daughter of Zion; for behold I am coming and I will dwell in your midst.

BROOKLYN, Brooklin, Brooklynn
Language/Cultural Origin: American
Inherent Meaning: Stream of the Waterfall
Spiritual Connotation: Praise
Scripture: Psalm 74:15 NLT
You caused the springs and streams to gush forth, and you dried up rivers that never run dry.

BROWNING, Brownyn, Bronwyn
Language/Cultural Origin: Middle English
Inherent Meaning: Dark
Spiritual Connotation: Enlightened
Scripture: Matthew 4:16 NKJV
The people who sat in darkness have seen a great light, and upon those who sat in the region and shadow of death Light has dawned.

BRUCE, Bruse
Language/Cultural Origin: Scottish
Inherent Meaning: From the Woods

Spiritual Connotation: Dignity
Scripture: Ephesians 2:10 NASB
For we are His workmanship, created in Christ Jesus for good works, which God prepared beforehand, that we should walk in them.

BRUNO, Brûno
Language/Cultural Origin: Old German
Inherent Meaning: Brown
Spiritual Connotation: Rich in God's Grace
Scripture: Philippians 4:19 KJV
But my God shall supply all your need according to his riches in glory by Christ Jesus.

BRYAN, see Brian

BRYCE, Brice
Language/Cultural Origin: Welsh
Inherent Meaning: Responsive
Spiritual Connotation: Ambitious
Scripture: Ecclesiastes 9:1 NKJV
For I considered all this in my heart . . . that the righteous and the wise and their works are in the hand of God.

BRYNA, BRYNN, see Brina

BUCKLEY, Bucklea, Bucklee
Language/Cultural Origin: Middle English
Inherent Meaning: From the Deer Meadow
Spiritual Connotation: Worshiper
Scripture: Psalm 111:1 NKJV
Praise the LORD! I will praise the LORD with my whole heart, in the assembly of the upright and in the congregation.

BUDDY, Bud, Budd, Buddie
Language/Cultural Origin: Old English
Inherent Meaning: Companion
Spiritual Connotation: Godly
Scripture: Psalm 119:63 NKJV
I am a companion of all who fear You, and of those who keep Your precepts.

BURGESS, Burges, Burgiss
Language/Cultural Origin: English
Inherent Meaning: From the Town
Spiritual Connotation: Steadfast
Scripture: 1 John 2:10 TLB
But whoever loves his fellow man is walking in the light and can see his way without stumbling around in darkness and sin.

BURKE, Berke, Birk, Burk
Language/Cultural Origin: Old French
Inherent Meaning: From the Fortress
Spiritual Connotation: Courageous
Scripture: Deuteronomy 31:6 NKJV
Be strong and of good courage, do not fear nor be afraid of them; for the LORD your God, He is the One who goes with you. He will not leave you nor forsake you.

BURTON, Berton, Burt
Language/Cultural Origin: Middle English
Inherent Meaning: From the Fortified Town
Spiritual Connotation: Amply Supplied
Scripture: Psalm 23:1–2 NKJV
The LORD is my shepherd; I shall not want. He makes me to lie down in green pastures; He leads me beside the still waters.

BYRAM, Byramm
Language/Cultural Origin: Middle English
Inherent Meaning: From the Fields
Spiritual Connotation: Freedom
Scripture: Psalm 146:7 NCV
He does what is fair for those who have been wronged. He gives food to the hungry. The LORD sets the prisoners free.

BYRON, Bieran, Biran, Biren, Biron, Byran, Byrann, Byren
Language/Cultural Origin: Old English
Inherent Meaning: From the Barn
Spiritual Connotation: Forgiving
Scripture: Mark 11:25 NKJV
And whenever you stand praying, if you have anything against anyone, forgive him, that your Father in heaven may also forgive you your trespasses.

CACHET, Cache, Cachea, Cachée
Language/Cultural Origin: French
Inherent Meaning: Prestigious
Spiritual Connotation: Blessed
Scripture: Matthew 25:34 NASB
> Come, you who are blessed of My Father,
> inherit the kingdom prepared for you from
> the foundation of the world.

CADELL, Cadel, Cadelle
Language/Cultural Origin: Welsh
Inherent Meaning: Battler
Spiritual Connotation: Attentive
Scripture: 1 Corinthians 14:8 RSV
> And if the bugle gives an indistinct sound,
> who will get ready for battle?

CADENCE, Cadenze, Kadence
Language/Cultural Origin: Latin
Inherent Meaning: Rhythmic Flow
Spiritual Connotation: Symphony
Scripture: Psalm 98:5–6 NLT
> Sing your praise to the LORD with the
> harp . . . and trumpets and the sound of
> the ram's horn. Make a joyful symphony
> before the LORD, the King!

**CADY, Cadee, Cadey, Cadi, Cadie
(see also Kadee, Katy)**
Language/Cultural Origin: English
Inherent Meaning: Pure
Spiritual Connotation: Blameless
Scripture: Proverbs 2:21 NASB
> For the upright will live in the land,
> and the blameless will remain in it.

**CAELAN, Caelin, Cailan, Cailean,
Cailen, Cailin, Caillin, Calan, Calin,
Calon, Callan, Callen, Callon, Caylan
(see also Cailin, Kaylyn)**
Language/Cultural Origin: Scottish
Inherent Meaning: Victorious
Spiritual Connotation: Defended of God
Scripture: Isaiah 54:17 NKJV
> No weapon formed against you shall prosper,
> And every tongue which rises against you in
> judgment You shall condemn.

**CAELEY, Caelee, Caelie, Cailee,
Cailey, Cailie, Caley, Caylee, Cayley,
Caylie (see also Kaylee)**
Language/Cultural Origin: American
Inherent Meaning: Crowned
Spiritual Connotation: Temperate
Scripture: 1 Corinthians 9:25 NLT
> All athletes practice strict self-control. They
> do it to win a prize that will fade away, but
> we do it for an eternal prize.

**CAESAR, Ceasar, César, Cesare,
☞Cesareo, Cesario, Cesearc,
Cezar, Czar, Kaiser, Sezare**
Language/Cultural Origin: Latin
Inherent Meaning: Long-Haired
Spiritual Connotation: Friend of Many
Scripture: Matthew 7:12 NKJV
> Therefore, whatever you want men to do to
> you, do also to them, for this is the Law and
> the Prophets.

**CAILIN, Caelyn, Caelynn, Cailyn,
Cailynn, Cailynne, Caylin, Caylyn
(see also Caelan, Kaylyn)**
Language/Cultural Origin: American
Inherent Meaning: Genuine
Spiritual Connotation: Godly
Scripture: 2 Peter 1:7 NLT
> Godliness leads to love for other Christians,
> and finally you will grow to have genuine
> love for everyone.

CAIN, Caine (see also Kane)
☞Language/Cultural Origin: Hebrew
Inherent Meaning: Spear
Spiritual Connotation: Weapon
Scripture: 2 Corinthians 6:7 TLB
> We have been truthful, with God's power
> helping us in all we do. All of the godly man's
> arsenal . . . have been ours.

CAITLIN, Caitlan, Caitland, Caitlen, Caitlinn, Caitlyn, Caitlynn, Catlin (see also Kaitlin)
Language/Cultural Origin: Irish
Inherent Meaning: Pure
Spiritual Connotation: Innocent
Scripture: Daniel 6:22 NKJV
My God sent His angel and shut the lions mouths, so that they have not hurt me, because I was found innocent before Him.

CALA, Calah, Calla, Callah (see also Kala)
Language/Cultural Origin: Middle Eastern
Inherent Meaning: Fortress
Spiritual Connotation: Protected
Scripture: Psalm 59:9 NCV
God, my strength, I am looking to you, because God is my defender.

CALANDRA, Calandria, Calendra, Kalandra, Kalandria
Language/Cultural Origin: Greek
Inherent Meaning: Lark
Spiritual Connotation: Created of God
Scripture: Genesis 1:21 TLB
So God created great sea animals, and every sort of fish and every kind of bird.

CALEB, Caeleb, Cale, Kaleb
Language/Cultural Origin: Hebrew
Inherent Meaning: Faithful
Spiritual Connotation: Great Spiritual Potential
Scripture: Numbers 13:30 NKJV
Then Caleb quieted the people before Moses, and said, "Let us go up at once and take possession, for we are well able to overcome it."

CALHOUN, Colhoun
Language/Cultural Origin: Scottish
Inherent Meaning: Strong Warrior
Spiritual Connotation: Great in Spirit
Scripture: Psalm 33:16 NKJV
No king is saved by the multitude of an army; a mighty man is not delivered by great strength.

CALLAHAN, Calahan, Callaghan
Language/Cultural Origin: Irish
Inherent Meaning: Saint
Spiritual Connotation: Faithful

Scripture: 1 Samuel 2:9 NRSV
He will guard the feet of his faithful ones, but the wicked shall be cut off in darkness; for not by might does one prevail.

CALLIE, Caleigh, Cali, Callee, Calleigh, Calli, Cally (see also Kalei, Kali, Kalli)
Language/Cultural Origin: Middle Eastern
Inherent Meaning: Fortress
Spiritual Connotation: Guarded of God
Scripture: Psalm 46:7 NLT
The LORD Almighty is here among us; the God of Israel is our fortress.

CALLISTA, Calesta, Calista, Calysta, Kalesta, Kalista, Kallista, Kalysta
Language/Cultural Origin: Greek
Inherent Meaning: Most Beautiful
Spiritual Connotation: Lovely
Scripture: Song of Songs 2:14 NKJV
O my dove ... Let me see your face, let me hear your voice; for your voice is sweet, and your face is lovely.

CALLON, see Caelen

CALLUM, Callam, Calum
Language/Cultural Origin: Irish
Inherent Meaning: Dove
Spiritual Connotation: Free
Scripture: Psalm 55:6 NKJV
So I said, "Oh, that I had wings like a dove! I would fly away and be at rest."

CALVERT
Language/Cultural Origin: Old English
Inherent Meaning: Cattle Herder
Spiritual Connotation: Lover of All Creatures
Scripture: Psalm 9:2 NKJV
I will be glad and rejoice in You; I will sing praise to Your name, O Most High.

CALVIN, Cal
Language/Cultural Origin: Latin
Inherent Meaning: Bald
Spiritual Connotation: Favored
Scripture: Proverbs 22:20–21 NKJV
Have I not written to you excellent things of counsels and knowledge ... that you may answer words of truth to those who send to you?

CAMBRIA, Camberlee, Camberleigh, Camberly, Cambrea, Cambrya, Kamberly, Kambria, Kambriea
Language/Cultural Origin: Latin
Inherent Meaning: From Wales
Spiritual Connotation: Delivered
Scripture: Colossians 1:13 NRSV
He has rescued us from the power of darkness and transferred us into the kingdom of his beloved Son.

CAMDEN, Camdan
Language/Cultural Origin: Old English
Inherent Meaning: From the Winding Valley
Spiritual Connotation: Freedom
Scripture: John 8:32 NKJV
And you shall know the truth, and the truth shall make you free.

CAMELLIA, Camala, Camalia, Camelia, Camella, Kamalia, Kamelia, Kamellia
Language/Cultural Origin: Italian
Inherent Meaning: Evergreen
Spiritual Connotation: Persistent
Scripture: 1 Thessalonians 2:8 NRSV
So deeply do we care for you that we are determined to share with you not only the gospel of God but also our own selves, because you have become very dear to us.

CAMERON, Cam, Cameran, Camren, Camron, Kam, Kameron, Kamron
Language/Cultural Origin: Scottish
Inherent Meaning: From the Crooked Stream
Spiritual Connotation: Spiritual Potential
Scripture: Psalm 36:9 NKJV
For with You is the fountain of life; in Your light we see light.

CAMI, Cammi, Cammie, Cammy (see also Kami)
Language/Cultural Origin: French
Inherent Meaning: Ceremonial Attendant
Spiritual Connotation: Helper
Scripture: Hebrews 13:6 NKJV
So we may boldly say: The LORD is my helper; I will not fear. What can man do to me?

CAMILLE, Camila, Camill, Camilla, Cammille, Chamelle, Chamille
Language/Cultural Origin: Latin

Inherent Meaning: Devoted
Spiritual Connotation: Loving
Scripture: 1 John 4:7 NCV
Dear friends, we should love each other, because love comes from God. Everyone who loves has become God's child and knows God.

CAMPBELL, Cambell
Language/Cultural Origin: French
Inherent Meaning: Beautiful Field
Spiritual Connotation: Consistent
Scripture: Proverbs 24:21 NRSV
My child, fear the LORD and the king, and do not disobey either of them.

CANAAN, Caenan, Caynon
Language/Cultural Origin: Hebrew
Inherent Meaning: Lowland
Spiritual Connotation: Covenant
Scripture: Hebrews 11:9 NCV
It was by faith that he lived like a foreigner in the country God promised to give him.

CANDACE, Candice, Candy, Candyce, Kandace, Kandise, Kandy
Language/Cultural Origin: Greek
Inherent Meaning: Unblemished
Spiritual Connotation: Shining
Scripture: Isaiah 62:3 NKJV
You shall also be a crown of glory In the hand of the LORD, and a royal diadem in the hand of your God.

CANDRA, Candrea, Candria, Kandra
Language/Cultural Origin: Latin
Inherent Meaning: Incandescent
Spiritual Connotation: Reflection of Christ
Scripture: Matthew 5:15 NRSV
No one after lighting a lamp puts it under the bushel basket, but on the lampstand, and it gives light to all in the house.

CANNON, Cannan, Cannen, Canning, Canon (see also Kannon)
Language/Cultural Origin: French
Inherent Meaning: Church Official
Spiritual Connotation: Esteemed
Scripture: 1 Timothy 5:17 NASB
Let the elders who rule well be considered worthy of double honor, especially those who work hard at preaching and teaching.

CANUTE, see Knute

CARA, Caragh, Carah, Carra
(see also Kara, Kerani)
Language/Cultural Origin: Latin
Inherent Meaning: Beloved
Spiritual Connotation: Chosen
Scripture: Matthew 25:34 NKJV
Come, you blessed of My Father, inherit the kingdom prepared for you from the foundation of the world.

CAREY, Caray, Carrey
(see also Caryn, Kerry)
Language/Cultural Origin: Welsh
Inherent Meaning: Castle
Spiritual Connotation: Dependent
Scripture: Psalm 91:2 NKJV
I will say of the LORD, He is my refuge and my fortress; My God, in Him I will trust.

CARI, Carie, Carii
(see also Carrie, Kari)
Language/Cultural Origin: Turkish
Inherent Meaning: Flowing Like Water
Spiritual Connotation: Filled With Life
Scripture: Psalm 104:10 TLB
He placed springs in the valleys and streams that gush from the mountains.

CARIANNE, Karianne

CARINA, Carena (see also Corina, Kaarina, Karena, Karina, Korina)
Language/Cultural Origin: Italian
Inherent Meaning: Dear Little One
Spiritual Connotation: Precious
Scripture: Mark 9:37 NKJV
Whoever receives one of these little children in My name receives Me; and whoever receives Me, receives not Me but Him who sent Me.

CARISSA, Cariisa, Carisa, Carrissa, Charisa, Charissa, Kariisa, Karisa, Karissa, Karrisa, Karrissa, Karyssa (see also Corissa)
Language/Cultural Origin: Latin
Inherent Meaning: Ingenious
Spiritual Connotation: Creative
Scripture: Hebrews 13:20 NCV
I pray that the God of peace will give you every good thing you need so you can do what he wants.

CARITA, Caritta, Karita, Karitta
Language/Cultural Origin: Latin
Inherent Meaning: Loving
Spiritual Connotation: Preserved
Scripture: Isaiah 42:6 NASB
I am the LORD, I have called you in righteousness, I will also hold you by the hand and watch over you.

CARL, Carel, Carle, Carlis, Karal, Karel, Karl, Karle, Karlis
Language/Cultural Origin: German
Inherent Meaning: Tiller of the Soil
Spiritual Connotation: Strong in Spirit
Scripture: Isaiah 40:31 NKJV
But those who wait on the LORD shall renew their strength; they shall mount up with wings like eagles, they shall run and not be weary, they shall walk and not faint.

CARLA, Carlia, Karla, Karlia
Language/Cultural Origin: Italian
Inherent Meaning: Endearing
Spiritual Connotation: Ransomed
Scripture: Isaiah 49:15 NKJV
Can a woman forget her nursing child, and not have compassion on the son of her womb? Surely they may forget, yet I will not forget you.

CARLANA, Carlæna, Karlana
Language/Cultural Origin: Irish
Inherent Meaning: Little Heroine
Spiritual Connotation: Conscientious
Scripture: Judges 4:9 NLT
The Lord's victory over Sisera will be at the hands of a woman.

CARLENE, Carleen, Karlene, Karleen
Language/Cultural Origin: Old English
Inherent Meaning: Womanly
Spiritual Connotation: Respectful
Scripture: Titus 2:3 NASB
Older women likewise are to be reverent in their behavior.

CARLIN, Carlan, Carlen, Carlii, Carling, Carlyn, Karlan, Karleigh, Karlen, Karlii, Karling (see also Carly)
Language/Cultural Origin: Irish
Inherent Meaning: Champion
Spiritual Connotation: Protected

Scripture: Isaiah 42:6 NKJV
I, the LORD, have called you in righteousness, and will hold your hand; I will keep you and give you as a covenant to the people, as a light to the Gentiles.

CARLINA, Carleena, Carliana, Karleena, Karlina, Karliana (see also Carlana)
Language/Cultural Origin: English
Inherent Meaning: Little Champion
Spiritual Connotation: Victor
Scripture: Romans 8:37 NKJV
Yet in all these things we are more than conquerors through Him who loved us.

CARLISLE, Carlyle, Carlysle
Language/Cultural Origin: Old English
Inherent Meaning: Brave
Spiritual Connotation: Defender of Wisdom
Scripture: Proverbs 4:7 NKJV
Wisdom is the principal thing; therefore get wisdom. And in all your getting, get understanding.

CARLISSA, Carlisa, Carlise, Carlisha, Carlissia, Karlisa, Karlissa, Karlise, Karlisha, Karlissia
Language/Cultural Origin: American
Inherent Meaning: Endeared
Spiritual Connotation: Consecrated to God
Scripture: Romans 8:33 NCV
Who can accuse the people God has chosen? No one, because God is the One who makes them right.

CARLOS, Carlo, Karlo, Karlos
Language/Cultural Origin: Spanish
Inherent Meaning: Noble Spirit
Spiritual Connotation: Spiritual Discernment
Scripture: Hebrews 5:14 NASB
But solid food is for the mature, who because of practice have their senses trained to discern good and evil.

CARLOTTA, Karlotta
Language/Cultural Origin: Italian
Inherent Meaning: Womanly
Spiritual Connotation: Godly Heroine
Scripture: 1 Peter 3:4 NCV
No, your beauty should come from within you—the beauty of a gentle and quiet spirit that will never be destroyed and is very precious to God.

CARLTON, Carleton, Carltonn (see also Charlton)
Language/Cultural Origin: Middle English
Inherent Meaning: From the Gathering of the Farmers
Spiritual Connotation: Industrious
Scripture: Ezekiel 34:27 NKJV
Then the trees of the field shall yield their fruit, and the earth shall yield her increase. They shall be safe in their land; and they shall know that I am the LORD.

CARLY, Carlee, Carley, Carli, Carlie, Karlee, Karley, Karli, Karlie, Karly (see also Carlin)
Language/Cultural Origin: English
Inherent Meaning: Little Woman/Little Man
Spiritual Connotation: Innocent
Scripture: Matthew 11:25 NLT
O Father, Lord of heaven and earth, thank you for hiding the truth from those who think themselves so wise and clever, and for revealing it to the childlike.

CARMELA, Carmalla, Carmelia, Carmella, Carmellina, Carmelita
Language/Cultural Origin: Italian
Inherent Meaning: Garden
Spiritual Connotation: Nurtured of God
Scripture: Isaiah 58:11 TLB
And the Lord will guide you continually, and satisfy you with all good things, and keep you healthy too; and you will be like a well-watered garden, like an ever-flowing spring.

CARMEN, Carmaine, Carman, Carmene, Carmon, Karman, Karmen, Karmin, Karmon
Language/Cultural Origin: Latin
Inherent Meaning: Voice Like Soft Music
Spiritual Connotation: Joyful
Scripture: Psalm 149:1 NRSV
Praise the LORD! Sing to the LORD a new song, his praise in the assembly of the faithful.

CARMI, Carmee, Carmey, Carmie, Karmey, Karmie
Language/Cultural Origin: Hebrew
Inherent Meaning: My Vineyard
Spiritual Connotation: Responsible
Scripture: Proverbs 31:16 NKJV
She considers a field and buys it; from her profits she plants a vineyard.

CARMICHAEL, Charmikael
Language/Cultural Origin: Latin
Inherent Meaning: Follower of Michael
Spiritual Connotation: Abundant Power
Scripture: Philippians 4:13 KJV
I can do all things through Christ which strengtheneth me.

CARMIEL, Carmiah, Carmiela, Carmielle, Carmiya, Karmiah, Karmiel, Karmiela, Karmielle
Language/Cultural Origin: Hebrew
Inherent Meaning: God Is My Wisdom
Spiritual Connotation: Secure
Scripture: Proverbs 28:26 TLB
A man is a fool to trust himself! But those who use God's wisdom are safe.

CARNEY, Karney
Language/Cultural Origin: Irish
Inherent Meaning: Victorious
Spiritual Connotation: Preserved
Scripture: Psalm 32:7 NASB
You are my hiding place; You preserve me from trouble; You surround me with songs of deliverance.

CAROL, Carel, Carole, Karole, Karrole (see also Carrol)
Language/Cultural Origin: French
Inherent Meaning: Song of Joy
Spiritual Connotation: Joy of God
Scripture: John 15:11 KJV
These things have I spoken unto you, that my joy might remain in you, and that your joy might be full.

CAROLEE, Carolea, Caroleigh
Language/Cultural Origin: American
Inherent Meaning: Little Beloved
Spiritual Connotation: Just
Scripture: John 7:24 NCV
Stop judging by the way things look, but judge by what is really right.

CAROLINE, Caralin, Caraline, Carolin, Carolina, Carolyn, Carrolin, Carroline (see also Carlin, Karilynn, Karolyn)
Language/Cultural Origin: French
Inherent Meaning: Womanly
Spiritual Connotation: Filled With Praise

Scripture: Psalm 150:6 NKJV
Let everything that has breath praise the LORD. Praise the LORD!

CARON, Carron, Carrone
Language/Cultural Origin: Welsh
Inherent Meaning: Loving
Spiritual Connotation: Witness
Scripture: John 13:34 NASB
A new commandment I give to you, that you love one another.

CARRICK, Karrick (see also Garrick)
Language/Cultural Origin: Irish
Inherent Meaning: Surrounded by Sea
Spiritual Connotation: Child of God
Scripture: Jeremiah 31:33 NKJV
But this is the covenant that I will make with the house of Israel after those days, says the LORD. . . . I will be their God, and they shall be My people.

CARRIE, Carree, Carri, Karrie, Karry (see also Cari, Kari)
Language/Cultural Origin: English
Inherent Meaning: Beloved
Spiritual Connotation: Redeemed
Scripture: Romans 5:8 NKJV
But God demonstrates His own love toward us, in that while we were still sinners, Christ died for us.

CARROL, Carell, Caroll, Carroll (see also Carol)
Language/Cultural Origin: Gaelic
Inherent Meaning: Champion
Spiritual Connotation: Steadfast
Scripture: Hebrews 12:1 NRSV
Therefore . . . let us also lay aside every weight and the sin that clings so closely, and let us run with perseverance the race that is set before us.

CARSON, Carrson
Language/Cultural Origin: English
Inherent Meaning: Diligent
Spiritual Connotation: Loyal
Scripture: John 15:16 NKJV
You did not choose Me, but I chose you and appointed you that you should go and bear fruit, and that your fruit should remain.

CARTER, Cartar
Language/Cultural Origin: Old English

Inherent Meaning: Driver of a Cart
Spiritual Connotation: Privileged
Scripture: Revelation 3:8 NASB
I know your deeds. Behold, I have put before you an open door which no one can shut.

CARY, Caree, Carree, Carry (see also Carey, Kerry)
Language/Cultural Origin: Latin
Inherent Meaning: Beloved
Spiritual Connotation: Divine
Scripture: 2 Peter 1:4 NRSV
Thus he has given us . . . his precious and very great promises, so that through them you may . . . become participants of the divine nature.

CARYN, Caren, Carin, Carran, Carren, Carrin, Carynn (see also Karen, Karin)
Language/Cultural Origin: Danish
Inherent Meaning: Unblemished
Spiritual Connotation: Blameless
Scripture: Job 8:20 NKJV
Behold, God will not cast away the blameless, Nor will He uphold the evildoers.

CARYS, Caris, Carris, Caryss (see also Karis)
Language/Cultural Origin: Welsh
Inherent Meaning: Loving
Spiritual Connotation: Respectful
Scripture: Matthew 19:19 NKJV
Honor your father and your mother, and, you shall love your neighbor as yourself.

CASEY, Cacey, Cacy, Case, Casie, Casy, Caysee, Caysey, Caysie, K.C., Kace, Kacee, Kacey, Kaci, Kacie, Kacy, Kaicey, Kasee, Kasey, Kasie, Kaycee, Kaycie, Kaysea, Kaysee, Kaysey
Language/Cultural Origin: Irish
Inherent Meaning: Valorous
Spiritual Connotation: Leader
Scripture: 1 John 5:4 NKJV
For whatever is born of God overcomes the world. And this is the victory that has overcome the world; our faith.

CASIMIR, Cachie, Cash, Cashmere, Cashmir, Kashmere, Kasimir, Kasmir, Kasmira, Kazmir, Kazmira
Language/Cultural Origin: Old Slavic

Inherent Meaning: Peacemaker
Spiritual Connotation: Flexible
Scripture: Matthew 5:9 NRSV
Blessed are the peacemakers, for they will be called children of God.

CASPER, Caspar
Language/Cultural Origin: Persian
Inherent Meaning: Treasurer
Spiritual Connotation: Watchful
Scripture: Matthew 25:21 NKJV
I will make you ruler over many things. Enter into the joy of your lord.

CASSANDRA, Casandera, Casandra, Casandria, Casaundra, Casaundria, Casondra, Cassaundra, Cassey, Cassi, Cassie, Cassondra, Cassondria, Cassundra, Cassy, Kasandra, Kasaundra, Kasondra, Kasoundra, Kassandra, Kassaundra, Kassey, Kassi, Kassie, Kassy, Krisandra, Krissandra
Language/Cultural Origin: Greek
Inherent Meaning: Helper of Mankind
Spiritual Connotation: Hostess
Scripture: Hebrews 13:2 NASB
Do not neglect to show hospitality to strangers, for by this some have entertained angels without knowing it.

CASSIA, Casia, Casiya, Cassya, Casya, Kasia, Kassia, Kasiya, Kasya
Language/Cultural Origin: Greek
Inherent Meaning: Spicy Cinnamon
Spiritual Connotation: Treasured
Scripture: Song of Songs 4:10 NCV
Your love is so sweet, my sister, my bride. Your love is better than wine, and your perfume smells better than any spice.

CASSIDY, Cass, Cassady, Kass, Kassady, Kassidy
Language/Cultural Origin: Irish
Inherent Meaning: Clever
Spiritual Connotation: Wise
Scripture: 1 Corinthians 10:15 TLB
You are intelligent people. Look now and see for yourselves whether what I am about to say is true.

CASSIUS, Caz, Cazzie
Language/Cultural Origin: Latin

Inherent Meaning: Protective Cover
Spiritual Connotation: Guarded
Scripture: Psalm 3:3 NASB
But You, O LORD, are a shield about me, My glory, and the One who lifts my head.

CASSON, Cassón, Kasson
Language/Cultural Origin: English
Inherent Meaning: Helper of Mankind
Spiritual Connotation: Protected of God
Scripture: Proverbs 30:5 NKJV
Every word of God is pure; He is a shield to those who put their trust in Him.

CATALINA, Catalena, Katalena, Katalina
Language/Cultural Origin: Spanish
Inherent Meaning: Unblemished
Spiritual Connotation: Refined
Scripture: Daniel 12:10 NASB
Many will be purged, purified and refined, but the wicked will act wickedly; and none of the wicked will understand, but those who have insight will understand.

CATAVA, Catavah, Katava, Katava
Language/Cultural Origin: African
Inherent Meaning: Restful
Spiritual Connotation: Bringer of Peace
Scripture: Zechariah 1:11 NRSV
We have patrolled the earth, and lo, the whole earth remains at peace.

CATERINA, see Katerina

CATHERINE, Cat, Catharina, Catharine, Catheren, Catherin, Catherina, Catheryn, Cathrine, Cathryn (see also Katherine)
Language/Cultural Origin: Greek
Inherent Meaning: Pure
Spiritual Connotation: Accountable
Scripture: Psalm 119:15–16 NKJV
I will meditate on Your precepts, and contemplate Your ways. I will delight myself in Your statutes; I will not forget Your word.

CATHLEEN, Cathaleen, Cathlene (see also Kathleen)
Language/Cultural Origin: Irish
Inherent Meaning: Unblemished
Spiritual Connotation: Spotless

Scripture: Romans 6:16 NASB
You are slaves of the one whom you obey, either of sin resulting in death, or of obedience resulting in righteousness.

CATHY, Cathee, Cathey, Cathi, Cathie, Kathee, Kathey, Kathi, Kathie, Kathy
Language/Cultural Origin: English
Inherent Meaning: Spotless
Spiritual Connotation: Sanctified
Scripture: Philippians 1:6 NASB
For I am confident of this very thing, that He who began a good work in you will perfect it until the day of Christ Jesus.

CATO, Catón (see also Kato)
Language/Cultural Origin: Latin
Inherent Meaning: Wise
Spiritual Connotation: Servant
Scripture: Romans 12:16 NRSV
Live in harmony with one another; do not be haughty, but associate with the lowly; do not claim to be wiser than you are.

CATRINA, see Katrina

CATRIONA, Katriona
Language/Cultural Origin: Irish
Inherent Meaning: Flawless
Spiritual Connotation: Perfect
Scripture: Matthew 5:48 NKJV
Therefore you shall be perfect, just as your Father in heaven is perfect.

CAVAN, Caven, Cavin, Kavan (see also Kevin)
Language/Cultural Origin: Irish
Inherent Meaning: Handsome
Spiritual Connotation: Blessed
Scripture: Psalm 45:2 TLB
You are the fairest of all; your words are filled with grace; God himself is blessing you forever.

CAVANAUGH
Language/Cultural Origin: Irish
Inherent Meaning: Caring
Spiritual Connotation: Discerning
Scripture: Galatians 6:2 NKJV
Bear one another's burdens, and so fulfill the law of Christ.

CAYLA, Caela, Caila, Cailah, Caylah (see also Kaela, Kaila, Kayla, Kyla)
Language/Cultural Origin: Hebrew
Inherent Meaning: Empowered
Spiritual Connotation: Spirit-Filled
Scripture: Acts 1:8 NKJV
But you shall receive power when the Holy Spirit has come upon you; and you shall be witnesses to Me in Jerusalem, and in all Judea and Samaria, and to the end of the earth.

CECIL, Cecile, Cécile, Cecill
Language/Cultural Origin: Latin
Inherent Meaning: Blind
Spiritual Connotation: Illuminated
Scripture: Ephesians 5:8 NKJV
For you were once darkness, but now you are light in the Lord. Walk as children of light.

CECILIA, Cacelia, Caecilia, Cece, Cecelia, Cecilea, Cecillia, CeeCee
Language/Cultural Origin: Latin
Inherent Meaning: Blind
Spiritual Connotation: Of the Spirit
Scripture: 1 Corinthians 2:12 NCV
Now we did not receive the spirit of the world, but we received the Spirit that is from God so that we can know all that God has given us.

CEDRIC, Cedrec, Cédric, Cedrik
Language/Cultural Origin: English
Inherent Meaning: Battle Chieftain
Spiritual Connotation: Courageous Defender
Scripture: Galatians 6:4 NKJV
But let each one examine his own work, and then he will have rejoicing in himself alone, and not in another.

CEELEY, Ceelee, Ceeleigh, Ceelie, Ceely, Seelee, Seeleigh, Seelie, Seely
Language/Cultural Origin: Old English
Inherent Meaning: Blessed
Spiritual Connotation: Favored
Scripture: Hebrews 13:9 NLT
So do not be attracted by strange, new ideas. Your spiritual strength comes from God's special favor.

CELENA, see Selena

CELESTE, Celesta, Celestia, Celestial, Celestine
Language/Cultural Origin: French
Inherent Meaning: Heavenly
Spiritual Connotation: Blessed
Scripture: Ephesians 1:3 NKJV
Blessed be the God and Father of our Lord Jesus Christ, who has blessed us with every spiritual blessing in the heavenly places in Christ.

CELINE, Celene, Celinda, Céline
Language/Cultural Origin: English
Inherent Meaning: Fair as the Moon
Spiritual Connotation: Lovely
Scripture: Song of Songs 5:9 NKJV
What is your beloved more than another beloved, O fairest among women? What is your beloved more than another beloved, that you so charge us?

CEPHAS, Cephus
☞ Language/Cultural Origin: Aramaic
Inherent Meaning: Rock
Spiritual Connotation: Foundation
Scripture: Matthew 16:18 NLT
Now I say to you that you are Peter, and upon this rock I will build my church, and all the powers of hell will not conquer it.

CERELLA, Cerelisa
Language/Cultural Origin: Latin
Inherent Meaning: Springtime
Spiritual Connotation: Gentle
Scripture: Psalm 72:6 TLB
May the reign of this son of mine be as gentle and fruitful as the springtime rains upon the grass—like showers that water the earth!

CÉRISE, Cerese, Ceri, Cerice, Cerissa, Cerrice, Cerrina, Ceryce (see also Cherise)
Language/Cultural Origin: French
Inherent Meaning: Cherry
Spiritual Connotation: Ageless
Scripture: Psalm 92:14 NCV
When they are old, they will still produce fruit; they will be healthy and fresh.

CHADWICK, Chad, Chadd, Chadley, Chadrick, Chadron, Chadwyck
Language/Cultural Origin: Middle English
Inherent Meaning: From the Warrior's Town
Spiritual Connotation: Privileged
Scripture: Revelation 22:1 RSV

Then he showed me the river of the water of life, bright as crystal, flowing from the throne of God and of the Lamb.

CHAI, Chae (see also Chay)
Language/Cultural Origin: Hebrew
Inherent Meaning: Healthy
Spiritual Connotation: Eternal
Scripture: John 6:27 NKJV
Do not labor for the food which perishes, but for the food which endures to everlasting life.

CHAIM, Khaim
Language/Cultural Origin: Hebrew
Inherent Meaning: Life
Spiritual Connotation: Discerning
Scripture: John 12:25 NLT
Those who love their life in this world will lose it. Those who despise their life in this world will keep it for eternal life.

CHALICE, Chalace, Chalcie, Chalise, Chalissa, Challis, Challisse, Chalsey
Language/Cultural Origin: French
Inherent Meaning: Goblet
Spiritual Connotation: Cheerful
Scripture: Proverbs 15:15 NRSV
All the days of the poor are hard, but a cheerful heart has a continual feast.

CHALINA, Chaleena, Chara, Charah
Language/Cultural Origin: Hispanic
Inherent Meaning: Rose
Spiritual Connotation: Joy
Scripture: Isaiah 35:1 NKJV
The wilderness and the wasteland shall be glad for them, And the desert shall rejoice and blossom as the rose.

CHALMERS, Chalmer, Chamar
Language/Cultural Origin: Scottish
Inherent Meaning: Head of the Household
Spiritual Connotation: Prosperous Protector
Scripture: Isaiah 55:11 NKJV
So shall My word be that goes forth from My mouth; It shall not return to Me void.

CHAMADYA, Chamadaea, Chamadia
Language/Cultural Origin: Hebrew
Inherent Meaning: Desired
Spiritual Connotation: Blessed
Scripture: Psalm 45:2 TLB

You are the fairest of all; Your words are filled with grace; God himself is blessing you forever.

CHAN, Chanae, Chann, Chayo
Language/Cultural Origin: Cambodian
Inherent Meaning: Sweet-Smelling Tree
Spiritual Connotation: Image of God
Scripture: Ephesians 5:2 NCV
Live a life of love just as Christ loved us and gave himself for us as a sweet-smelling offering and sacrifice to God.

CHANAH, Chana, Channa
Language/Cultural Origin: Hebrew
Inherent Meaning: Favor of God
Spiritual Connotation: Prayerful
Scripture: Malachi 1:9 NKJV
But now entreat God's favor, that He may be gracious to us.

CHANAN, Chanen
Language/Cultural Origin: Hebrew
Inherent Meaning: Cloud
Spiritual Connotation: Provision
Scripture: Exodus 13:22 NKJV
He did not take away the pillar of cloud by day or the pillar of fire by night from before the people.

CHANDELLE Chandal, Chandel, Shandal, Shandel, Shandelle
Language/Cultural Origin: French
Inherent Meaning: Candle
Spiritual Connotation: Witness
Scripture: Matthew 5:14 NCV
You are the light that gives light to the world. A city that is built on a hill cannot be hidden.

CHANDLER, Chandan, Chandlan, Chanlan, Chandon
Language/Cultural Origin: English
Inherent Meaning: Candle Maker
Spiritual Connotation: Bearer of Light
Scripture: John 8:12 NKJV
I am the light of the world. He who follows Me shall not walk in darkness, but have the light of life.

CHANDRA, Chanda, Chandea, Chandee, Chandre, Chandrelle, Chandria, Shandra, Shandee, Shandrelle, Shandria
Language/Cultural Origin: Indo-Pakistani

Inherent Meaning: Fair as the Moon
Spiritual Connotation: Lovely
Scripture: Song of Songs 1:8 NCV
You are the most beautiful of women.

CHANEL, Chanell, Chanelle, Channel, Shanel, Shanell, Shanelle, Shannel
Language/Cultural Origin: English
Inherent Meaning: Channel
Spiritual Connotation: Abundance
Scripture: Psalm 78:16 RSV
He made streams come out of the rock, and caused waters to flow down like rivers.

CHANEY, Chayne, Chayney, Cheney, Cheyne, Cheyney
Language/Cultural Origin: Old French
Inherent Meaning: Oak Wood
Spiritual Connotation: Sealed
Scripture: 1 Chronicles 16:33 NASB
Then the trees of the forest will sing for joy before the LORD; for He is coming to judge the earth.

CHANNING, Chane, Chaning, Chann
Language/Cultural Origin: English
Inherent Meaning: Wise
Spiritual Connotation: Obedient
Scripture: Deuteronomy 4:6 NCV
Obey these laws carefully, in order to show the other nations that you have wisdom and understanding.

CHANTAL, Chantael, Chantalle, Chantara, Chantay, Chantée, Chantel, Chantell, Chantiel, Chantielle, Chantil, Chantill, Chantoya, Chantrel, Chantrell, Chauntay, Chauntell, Chauntelle, Chauntel (see also Shantel)
Language/Cultural Origin: French
Inherent Meaning: Song
Spiritual Connotation: Healed
Scripture: Isaiah 49:13 NKJV
Sing, O heavens! Be joyful, O earth! And break out in singing, O mountains! For the LORD has comforted His people, and will have mercy on His afflicted.

CHANTE, Chánte, Chanté, Chantha, Chantra (see also Shantae)
Language/Cultural Origin: French

Inherent Meaning: Singer
Spiritual Connotation: Treasured
Scripture: Zephaniah 3:17 NKJV
The LORD your God in your midst, the Mighty One, will save; He will rejoice over you with gladness, He will quiet you with His love, He will rejoice over you with singing.

CHANTREA, Chantria
Language/Cultural Origin: Cambodian
Inherent Meaning: Moonbeam
Spiritual Connotation: Symbol
Scripture: Psalm 136:9 NCV
He made the moon and stars to rule the night. His love continues forever.

CHANTRICE, Chantreese, Shantreece, Shantrice
Language/Cultural Origin: French
Inherent Meaning: Singer
Spiritual Connotation: Joyful
Scripture: Psalm 126:2 NKJV
Then our mouth was filled with laughter, and our tongue with singing. Then they said among the nations, the LORD has done great things for them.

CHAPMAN, Chapmann
Language/Cultural Origin: English
Inherent Meaning: Merchant
Spiritual Connotation: Wise
Scripture: Matthew 13:45–46 NKJV
Again, the kingdom of heaven is like a merchant seeking beautiful pearls, who, when he had found one pearl of great price, went and sold all that he had and bought it.

CHARISSA, Charesa, Charis, Charisa, Charisse, Charista, Sharesa, Sharese, Sharis, Sharisa, Sharissa, Sharisse, Sharista, Sheresa, Sherisa, Sherise, Sherissa, Sherisse, Sherista
Language/Cultural Origin: English
Inherent Meaning: Kindness
Spiritual Connotation: Virtuous
Scripture: Proverbs 31:26 NKJV
She opens her mouth with wisdom, and on her tongue is the law of kindness.

CHARITY, Charitee, Chariti
Language/Cultural Origin: English
Inherent Meaning: Benevolent
Spiritual Connotation: Compassionate

Scripture: Psalm 23:6 KJV
Surely goodness and mercy shall follow me all the days of my life: and I will dwell in the house of the LORD for ever.

CHARLEEN, Charlaine, Charlanna, Charlena, Charlene, Charline, Sharlaina, Sharlanna, Sharlena, Sharlene, Sharleen
Language/Cultural Origin: English
Inherent Meaning: Valiant
Spiritual Connotation: Courageous
Scripture: 1 Chronicles 28:20 NKJV
Be strong and of good courage, and do it; do not fear nor be dismayed, for the LORD God; my God; will be with you.

CHARLES, Charle, Charley, Charlie
Language/Cultural Origin: English
Inherent Meaning: Manly
Spiritual Connotation: Valiant
Scripture: Joshua 1:9 NKJV
Be strong and of good courage; do not be afraid, nor be dismayed, for the LORD your God is with you wherever you go.

CHARLOTTE, Charlette, Sharlotte
Language/Cultural Origin: French
Inherent Meaning: Womanly
Spiritual Connotation: Joy to the Lord
Scripture: Zephaniah 3:17 RSV
The LORD, your God, is in your midst, a warrior who gives victory; he will rejoice over you with gladness.

CHARLTON, Charleton, Charltonn (see also Carlton)
Language/Cultural Origin: English
Inherent Meaning: From the Dwelling of the Free Peasants
Spiritual Connotation: Servant
Scripture: Matthew 23:11 NKJV
But he who is greatest among you shall be your servant. . . . He who humbles himself will be exalted.

CHARMAIN, Charmaine, Charmane, Charmayne, Charmian, Sharmain
Language/Cultural Origin: Latin
Inherent Meaning: Singer
Spiritual Connotation: Joyful
Scripture: Jeremiah 15:16 NKJV

Your word was to me the joy and rejoicing of my heart; for I am called by Your name, O LORD God of hosts.

CHASADYA, Chasádia, Chasádya
Language/Cultural Origin: Hebrew
Inherent Meaning: Mercy of God
Spiritual Connotation: Chosen
Scripture: Romans 9:16 NLT
So receiving God's promise is not up to us. We can't get it by choosing it or working hard for it. God will show mercy to anyone he chooses.

CHASE, Chaise
Language/Cultural Origin: Old French
Inherent Meaning: Hunter
Spiritual Connotation: Pursuer of Truth
Scripture: Amos 5:8 TLB
Seek him who . . . turns darkness into morning and day into night, who calls forth the water from the ocean and pours it out as rain upon the land..

CHASTITY, Chasady, Chasiti, Chassady, Chassey, Chassidy, Chassie, Chassity, Chastady, Chastidy, Chastin, Chastney
Language/Cultural Origin: Latin
Inherent Meaning: Pure
Spiritual Connotation: Virtuous
Scripture: Luke 11:34 NLT
Your eye is a lamp for your body. A pure eye lets sunshine into your soul.

CHASYA, Châsia
Language/Cultural Origin: Hebrew
Inherent Meaning: Shield
Spiritual Connotation: Protected by God
Scripture: Psalm 2:12 NKJV
Blessed are all those who put their trust in Him.

CHAUNCEY, Chancey, Chauncy
Language/Cultural Origin: Middle English
Inherent Meaning: Chancellor
Spiritual Connotation: Worthy of Trust
Scripture: Romans 8:16 NKJV
The Spirit Himself bears witness with our spirit that we are children of God.

CHAVA, Chavah, Chavalah, Chavarra, Chavé, Chavel, Chavvis, Kava
Language/Cultural Origin: Yiddish

Inherent Meaning: Bird
Spiritual Connotation: Joyful
Scripture: Psalm 50:11 NASB
I know every bird of the mountains, and everything that moves in the field is Mine.

CHAVON, Chavonn, Chavonna, Chavonne, Chevon, Chevonn, Chevonna, Shavon, Shavón
Language/Cultural Origin: Hebrew
Inherent Meaning: God Is Gracious
Spiritual Connotation: Cherished
Scripture: Psalm 103:8 NKJV
The LORD is merciful and gracious, slow to anger, and abounding in mercy.

CHAY, Cháy, Ché (see also Chai)
Language/Cultural Origin: Spanish
Inherent Meaning: God Will Add
Spiritual Connotation: Dependent
Scripture: Philippians 4:19 NASB
And my God shall supply all your needs according to His riches in glory in Christ Jesus.

CHAYA, Chayka, Chayla, Chaylah, Chaylea, Chayley, Chayra
Language/Cultural Origin: Hebrew
Inherent Meaning: Alive
Spiritual Connotation: Heavenly Treasure
Scripture: Matthew 19:29 NKJV
And everyone who has left houses or brothers or sisters or father or mother or wife or children or lands, for My name's sake, shall . . . inherit everlasting life.

CHAYANNA, Chaeanna, Chayana
Language/Cultural Origin: American
Inherent Meaning: Alive
Spiritual Connotation: Childlike
Scripture: John 1:4 TLB
Eternal life is in him, and this life gives light to all mankind.

CHAZ, Chazz
Language/Cultural Origin: English
Inherent Meaning: Strong
Spiritual Connotation: Reverent
Scripture: Luke 12:5 NKJV
But I will show you whom you should fear: Fear Him who, after He has killed, has power to cast into hell.

CHAZAYA, Chazaia, Chazial, Chaziel, Chazielle
Language/Cultural Origin: Hebrew
Inherent Meaning: God Has Seen
Spiritual Connotation: Remembered
Scripture: Genesis 31:42 NKJV
Unless the God of my father . . . had been with me, surely now you would have sent me away empty-handed.

CHAZON, Chazón
Language/Cultural Origin: Hebrew
Inherent Meaning: Revelation
Spiritual Connotation: Disciple
Scripture: Galatians 1:12 NLT
For my message came by a direct revelation from Jesus Christ himself. No one else taught me.

CHELSEA, Chelcie, Chelcy, Chellsie, Chelsa, Chelsae, Chelsay, Chelsee, Chelsey, Chelsia, Chelsie, Chelsy, Cheslee, Chesley, Cheslie, Shelsea, Shelsee, Shelsie, Shelsey
Language/Cultural Origin: Old English
Inherent Meaning: Seaport
Spiritual Connotation: Shield
Scripture: Psalm 65:5 NRSV
By awesome deeds you answer us with deliverance, O God of our salvation; you are the hope of all the ends of the earth and of the farthest seas.

CHELUB, Chélub, Cheylub
Language/Cultural Origin: Hebrew
Inherent Meaning: Wicker Basket
Spiritual Connotation: Creative
Scripture: Exodus 31:3 NLT
I have filled him with the Spirit of God, giving him great wisdom, intelligence, and skill in all kinds of crafts.

CHERAN, Cherran, Cheranne (see also Sharon)
Language/Cultural Origin: Hebrew
Inherent Meaning: Union
Spiritual Connotation: Harmonious
Scripture: Psalm 133:1 NRSV
How very good and pleasant it is when kindred live together in unity!

CHERIE, Cheri, Cherí, Chérie (see also Shari)
Language/Cultural Origin: French

Inherent Meaning: Sweetheart
Spiritual Connotation: Valuable
Scripture: Proverbs 20:15 RSV

There is gold, and abundance of costly stones; but the lips of knowledge are a precious jewel.

CHERISE, Chareese, Charese, Charice, Charise, Cher, Cherice, Cherrise, Shareese, Sharese, Sharice, Sharise, Sher, Shereece, Sherese, Sherice, Sherrice (see also Cerise, Charissa)
Language/Cultural Origin: French
Inherent Meaning: Treasured
Spiritual Connotation: Beloved
Scripture: Psalm 62:5 NKJV

My soul, wait silently for God alone, for my expectation is from Him.

CHERISH
Language/Cultural Origin: English
Inherent Meaning: Precious
Spiritual Connotation: Inestimable
Scripture: Proverbs 31:10 NASB

An excellent wife, who can find? For her worth is far above jewels.

CHEROKEE, Cherika, Sherokee
Language/Cultural Origin: Native American
Inherent Meaning: Tribe
Spiritual Connotation: Worshiper
Scripture: 2 Chronicles 20:6 NLT

He prayed, O LORD, God of our ancestors, you alone are the God who is in heaven.

CHERYL, Chereen, Chereena, Charrell, Charelle, Charil, Charyl, Cherelle, Cherrelle, Cheryle (see also Sheryl)
Language/Cultural Origin: French
Inherent Meaning: Filled With Grace
Spiritual Connotation: Beloved
Scripture: Zephaniah 3:17 RSV

The LORD, your God, is in your midst, a warrior who gives victory; he will rejoice over you with gladness.

CHESNA, Chesnee, Chesney, Chesnie
Language/Cultural Origin: Slavic
Inherent Meaning: Peaceful
Spiritual Connotation: Regal Servant

Scripture: Isaiah 9:7 NASB

There will be no end to the increase of His government or of peace, on the throne of David and over his kingdom.

CHESTER, Ches, Cheston, Chet
Language/Cultural Origin: Old English
Inherent Meaning: From the Campsite
Spiritual Connotation: Valiant Defender
Scripture: Psalm 31:3 NKJV

For You are my rock and my fortress; therefore, for Your name's sake, lead me and guide me.

CHEVY, Chev, Chevi, Chevie, Chevvy
Language/Cultural Origin: American
Inherent Meaning: Knight
Spiritual Connotation: Victor
Scripture: Isaiah 9:3 NLT

Israel will again be great, and its people will rejoice.... They will shout with joy like warriors dividing the plunder.

CHEYENNE, Cheyan, Cheyana, Cheyann, Cheyanne, Cheyene, Cheyenna, Chi-Anna, Chyann, Chyanna, Chyanne, Sheyenne, Shiana, Shiane, Shianna, Shianne, Shyana, Shyanne, Shyenna
Language/Cultural Origin: Native American
Inherent Meaning: Tribe
Spiritual Connotation: Creative
Scripture: Exodus 35:10 NKJV

All who are gifted artisans among you shall come and make all that the LORD has commanded.

CHIARA, Chiarah
Language/Cultural Origin: Italian
Inherent Meaning: Clear
Spiritual Connotation: Sealed
Scripture: Revelation 21:21 NKJV

And the street of the city was pure gold, like transparent glass.

CHICKARA, Chickarra, Chikona
Language/Cultural Origin: Japanese
Inherent Meaning: Near and Dear
Spiritual Connotation: Loving
Scripture: Romans 13:10 NLT

Love does no wrong to anyone, so love satisfies all of God's requirements.

CHIKO, Chikora

Language/Cultural Origin: Japanese
Inherent Meaning: Pledge
Spiritual Connotation: Promise
Scripture: Acts 2:39 NKJV

For the promise is to you and to your children, and to all who are afar off, as many as the Lord our God will call.

CHILTON, Chiltonn

Language/Cultural Origin: English
Inherent Meaning: From the Farm by the Spring
Spiritual Connotation: Refreshed
Scripture: Psalm 104:10 NKJV

He sends the springs into the valleys, they flow among the hills.

CHINARAH, Chinara, Chinika

Language/Cultural Origin: Swahili
Inherent Meaning: God Receives
Spiritual Connotation: Offering to God
Scripture: Hebrews 7:8 NKJV

Here mortal men receive tithes, but there he receives them, of whom it is witnessed that he lives.

CHIP, Chipper

Language/Cultural Origin: English
Inherent Meaning: Strong
Spiritual Connotation: Power of God
Scripture: Exodus 10:2 NLT

You will be able to tell wonderful stories to your children and grandchildren about the marvelous things I am doing . . . to prove that I am the LORD.

CHISLON, Cheslin, Cheslon, ☞Cheslyn, Chislan, Chislyn

Language/Cultural Origin: Hebrew
Inherent Meaning: Trust
Spiritual Connotation: Dependent
Scripture: Proverbs 3:5–6 NASB

Trust in the LORD with all your heart, and do not lean on your own understanding. In all your ways acknowledge Him, and He will make your paths straight.

CHLOE, Chloé, Chlöe, Chloee, ☞Cloe, Cloey, Kloe, Klöe

Language/Cultural Origin: Greek
Inherent Meaning: Vibrant
Spiritual Connotation: One Who Searches

Scripture: Psalm 105:4 NKJV

Seek the LORD and His strength; seek His face evermore!

CHLORIS, Cloris, Clorissa

Language/Cultural Origin: Greek
Inherent Meaning: Pale
Spiritual Connotation: Fair
Scripture: Psalm 45:2 NASB

You are fairer than the sons of men; grace is poured upon Your lips; therefore God has blessed You forever.

CHONI, Chonee, Choney, Chonia, Chonie, Choniya, Chonya

Language/Cultural Origin: Hebrew
Inherent Meaning: Gracious
Spiritual Connotation: Mercy of God
Scripture: Deuteronomy 4:31 RSV

The LORD your God is a merciful God; he will not fail you or destroy you or forget the covenant with your fathers which he swore to them.

CHORESH, Choresch

Language/Cultural Origin: Hebrew
Inherent Meaning: Thicket
Spiritual Connotation: God's Sacrifice
Scripture: Genesis 22:14 NASB

And Abraham called the name of that place The LORD Will Provide.

CHOSEN, Chosan, Chósen

Language/Cultural Origin: Hebrew
Inherent Meaning: Power
Spiritual Connotation: Immunity
Scripture: Mark 16:18 TLB

They will be able to place their hands on the sick and heal them.

CHRISTA, Chris, Chrisa, Chrisie, Chrissey, Chrissi, Chrissie, Chrissy, Christi, Christie, Christy, Chrys, Chryssa, Chrysta, Chrysti, Chrystie, Chrysty, Cris, Crissa, Crissie, Crista, Cristee, Cristey, Cristi, Cristie, Cryssa, Crysta, Crysti, Crystie (see also Kirsty, Krista)

Language/Cultural Origin: German
Inherent Meaning: Follower of Christ
Spiritual Connotation: God's Reflection

Scripture: John 13:35 NKJV
By this all will know that you are My disciples, if you have love for one another.

CHRISTEN, Christan, Christin, Christyn, Chrystan, Chrysten, Chrystin, Cristan, Cristen, Cristin, Cristyn, Crystan, Crysten, Crystin (see also Kristen)
Language/Cultural Origin: English
Inherent Meaning: Follower of Christ
Spiritual Connotation: Obedient
Scripture: John 8:31 NCV
If you continue to obey my teaching, you are truly my followers.

CHRISTIAN, Christiaan, Christianos, Christion, Christon, Christos, Christyan, Chrystian, Cristian, Cristiano, Cristón, Khristian, Kristar, Krister, Kristjan, Krystian
Language/Cultural Origin: Greek
Inherent Meaning: Follower of Christ
Spiritual Connotation: Anointed
Scripture: Acts 10:38 NASB
You know of Jesus of Nazareth, how God anointed Him with the Holy Spirit and with power, and how He went about doing good.

CHRISTINA, Christeena, Christena, Christiana, Christiane, Christiann, Christianna, Christinna, Christy-Anna, Cristeena, Cristina, Cristiona Crystina (see also Kristina)
Language/Cultural Origin: Greek
Inherent Meaning: Follower of Christ
Spiritual Connotation: Awareness of Christ
Scripture: 2 Corinthians 4:5 NRSV
For we do not proclaim ourselves; we proclaim Jesus Christ as Lord and ourselves as your slaves for Jesus' sake.

CHRISTINE, Christeen, Christene, Chrystine, Cristeen, Cristine, Crystine (see also Kristine)
Language/Cultural Origin: French
Inherent Meaning: Follower of Christ
Spiritual Connotation: True Disciple
Scripture: Luke 9:23 NLT
If any of you wants to be my follower, you must put aside your selfish ambition, shoulder your cross daily, and follow me.

CHRISTOPHER, Chris, Chriss, Christepher, Christobal, Christofer, Christoff, Christoffer, Christophe, Christopherr, Christophor, Chrys, Cris, Cristóbal, Cristofer, Cristopher, Khris, Khriss, Khristofer, Khristoffer, Khristopher, Kris, Kriss, Kristofer, Kristophe, Kristopher, Kristophor, Krys
Language/Cultural Origin: Greek
Inherent Meaning: Bearer/Carrier of Christ
Spiritual Connotation: Anointed
Scripture: Galatians 6:17 NIV
Finally, let no one cause me trouble, for I bear on my body the marks of Jesus.

CHUCK, Chuckie, Chucky
Language/Cultural Origin: American
Inherent Meaning: Strong
Spiritual Connotation: Genuine
Scripture: Mark 12:30 NKJV
And you shall love the LORD your God with all your heart, with all your soul, with all your mind, and with all your strength.

CHUMA, Chumah
Language/Cultural Origin: Rhodesian
Inherent Meaning: Wealthy
Spiritual Connotation: Heavenly Treasure
Scripture: Luke 6:20 NASB
Blessed are you who are poor, for yours is the kingdom of God.

CIAN, Cianán, Ciannan
Language/Cultural Origin: Irish
Inherent Meaning: Ancient
Spiritual Connotation: Persistent Faith
Scripture: Mark 11:22 NKJV
Have faith in God.

CID, Cyd (see also Sidney)
Language/Cultural Origin: Spanish
Inherent Meaning: Master
Spiritual Connotation: Discreet
Scripture: Romans 14:4 NASB
Who are you to judge the servant of another? To his own master he stands or falls; and stand he will, for the Lord is able to make him stand.

CIERRA, see Sierra

CINDY, see Cynthia

CIPRIANNA, Cipriana, Cypriana, Cyprianna, Cyprianne
Language/Cultural Origin: Greek
Inherent Meaning: From Cyprus
Spiritual Connotation: Bold Witness
Scripture: Romans 1:16 NIV
I am not ashamed of the gospel, because it is the power of God for the salvation of everyone who believes: first for the Jew, then for the Gentile.

CISSY, Cissee
Language/Cultural Origin: American
Inherent Meaning: Blind
Spiritual Connotation: Discerning
Scripture: Ephesians 5:17 RSV
Therefore do not be foolish, but understand what the will of the Lord is.

CLAIRE, Clair, Clara, Clarette, Clarina, Clarinda, Clarita
Language/Cultural Origin: French
Inherent Meaning: Brilliant
Spiritual Connotation: Shining Light
Scripture: Psalm 36:9 NKJV
For with You is the fountain of life; in Your light we see light.

CLANCY, Clancey
Language/Cultural Origin: Irish
Inherent Meaning: Red-Haired Fighter
Spiritual Connotation: Christlike
Scripture: Philippians 2:3 NKJV
Let nothing be done through selfish ambition or conceit, but in lowliness of mind let each esteem others better than himself.

CLARENCE, Clare, Clarance, Clarrance, Clarrence
Language/Cultural Origin: Latin
Inherent Meaning: Victorious
Spiritual Connotation: Pure
Scripture: Philippians 4:8 NKJV
Finally, brethren, whatever things are true, . . . noble, . . . just, . . . pure, . . . lovely, . . . [or] praiseworthy; meditate on these things.

CLARISSA, Claresa, Claressa, Clarice, Clarisa, Clarisse, Clarrisa, Clarrissa, Clerissa (see also Klarissa)
Language/Cultural Origin: Italian
Inherent Meaning: Brilliant
Spiritual Connotation: Wise Discerner
Scripture: Hosea 14:9 NKJV
Who is wise? Let him understand these things. Who is prudent? Let him know them.

CLARK, Clarke
Language/Cultural Origin: Old French
Inherent Meaning: Scholar
Spiritual Connotation: Enlightened Spirit
Scripture: James 3:17 NKJV
But the wisdom that is from above is first pure, then peaceable, gentle, willing to yield, full of mercy and good fruits, without partiality and without hypocrisy.

CLAUDIUS, Claude, Claudell, Claudio
Language/Cultural Origin: Latin
Inherent Meaning: Lame
Spiritual Connotation: Strong in Victory
Scripture: Isaiah 40:29 NKJV
He gives power to the weak, and to those who have no might He increases strength.

CLAUDIA, Claudeen, Claudette
Language/Cultural Origin: Latin
Inherent Meaning: Lame
Spiritual Connotation: Loved
Scripture: 1 Peter 5:7 NKJV
[Cast] all your care upon Him, for He cares for you.

CLAUS, see Klaus

CLAY, Clae
Language/Cultural Origin: English
Inherent Meaning: Malleable Earth
Spiritual Connotation: Adaptable
Scripture: 2 Corinthians 4:7 NKJV
But we have this treasure in earthen vessels, that the excellence of the power may be of God and not of us.

CLAYBORNE, Claeborne
Language/Cultural Origin: Middle English
Inherent Meaning: From the Clay Brook
Spiritual Connotation: Molded by God
Scripture: Jeremiah 18:6 NKJV
Look, as the clay is in the potter's hand, so are you in My hand, O house of Israel!

CLAYTON, Clayten
Language/Cultural Origin: Old English
Inherent Meaning: From the Clay Estate
Spiritual Connotation: Molded by God
Scripture: Isaiah 64:8 NKJV
> But now, O LORD, You are our Father; we are the clay, and You our potter; and all we are the work of Your hand.

CLEMENT, Clem, Clemens, Clément, ☞ Clemente, Klem, Klemens, Klement
Language/Cultural Origin: Latin
Inherent Meaning: Mild, Merciful
Spiritual Connotation: Benevolent
Scripture: Leviticus 19:34 NKJV
> You shall love [the stranger who lives among you] as yourself; for you were strangers in the land of Egypt: I am the LORD your God.

CLEMENTINE, Clementia, Clementina, Clemette
Language/Cultural Origin: English
Inherent Meaning: Merciful
Spiritual Connotation: Charitable
Scripture: John 13:34 NKJV
> A new commandment I give to you, that you love one another.

CLEO, Clio
Language/Cultural Origin: English
Inherent Meaning: One of Eminence
Spiritual Connotation: Understanding Spirit
Scripture: Psalm 36:9 NKJV
> For with You is the fountain of life; In Your light we see light.

CLEON, Kleon
Language/Cultural Origin: Greek
Inherent Meaning: Famous
Spiritual Connotation: Bold
Scripture: Philippians 1:20 NRSV
> I will not be put to shame in any way, but that by my speaking with all boldness, Christ will be exalted now as always in my body, whether by life or by death.

CLEOPATRA, Cliopatra
Language/Cultural Origin: Greek
Inherent Meaning: Fame of Her Father
Spiritual Connotation: Cherished
Scripture: Zephaniah 3:17 RSV
> The LORD, your God, is in your midst, a warrior who gives victory; he will rejoice over you with gladness.

CLIFFORD, Cliff, Cliford, Clyff
Language/Cultural Origin: Old English
Inherent Meaning: From the River's Heights
Spiritual Connotation: Vigilant
Scripture: Psalm 18:32 NKJV
> It is God who arms me with strength, and makes my way perfect.

CLIFTON, Cliffton, Clift
Language/Cultural Origin: Old English
Inherent Meaning: From the Cliff Estate
Spiritual Connotation: Prosperous
Scripture: Psalm 91:11 NKJV
> For He shall give His angels charge over you, to keep you in all your ways.

CLINTON, Clint, Clinten
Language/Cultural Origin: Old English
Inherent Meaning: From the Hill Town
Spiritual Connotation: Honorable
Scripture: Malachi 3:10 NKJV
> I will . . . open for you the windows of heaven and pour out for you such blessing that there will not be room enough to receive it.

CLIVE, Cleve, Clyve
Language/Cultural Origin: English
Inherent Meaning: From Upon the Cliff
Spiritual Connotation: Enduring
Scripture: Jeremiah 33:11 NKJV
> Praise the LORD of hosts, for the LORD is good, for His mercy endures forever.

CLUNY, Clooney
Language/Cultural Origin: Irish
Inherent Meaning: Meadow
Spiritual Connotation: Restful
Scripture: John 10:9 NRSV
> I am the gate. Whoever enters by me will be saved, and will come in and go out and find pasture.

CLYDE, Clide
Language/Cultural Origin: Welsh
Inherent Meaning: Loving
Spiritual Connotation: Rewarded
Scripture: Luke 12:32 NKJV
> Do not fear, little flock, for it is your Father's good pleasure to give you the kingdom.

COBY, Cobe, Cobey, Cobi, Cobie, Kobe, Kobee, Kobi, Kobie, Koby
Language/Cultural Origin: American

Inherent Meaning: Successor
Spiritual Connotation: Wise
Scripture: Hebrews 6:12 NLT
You will follow the example of those who are going to inherit God's promises because of their faith and patience.

COCO, Cocco, Coccoa (see also Koko)

Language/Cultural Origin: Spanish
Inherent Meaning: Coconut
Spiritual Connotation: Sacrifice
Scripture: Ephesians 5:2 NKJV
And walk in love, as Christ also has loved us and given Himself for us, an offering and a sacrifice to God for a sweet smelling aroma.

CODY, Codee, Codey, Codi, Codie, Kodee, Kodey, Kodi, Kodie, Kody

Language/Cultural Origin: English
Inherent Meaning: Cushion
Spiritual Connotation: Joyful Witness
Scripture: Mark 5:19 NASB
Go home to your people and report to them what great things the Lord has done for you, and how He had mercy on you.

COLBERT, Culbert

Language/Cultural Origin: English
Inherent Meaning: Brilliant Seafarer
Spiritual Connotation: Anchored in God
Scripture: Psalm 46:1 NKJV
God is our refuge and strength, a very present help in trouble.

COLBY, Colbey, Colbi, Colby, Collby, Kolby, Kollby

Language/Cultural Origin: Old English
Inherent Meaning: From the Coal Farm
Spiritual Connotation: Dependent
Scripture: 1 Peter 5:7 NKJV
[Cast] all your care upon Him, for He cares for you.

COLE, Kole

Language/Cultural Origin: English
Inherent Meaning: Victory of the People
Spiritual Connotation: Granted Success
Scripture: 1 Thessalonians 4:16 NKJV
For the Lord Himself will descend from heaven . . . and the dead in Christ will rise first.

COLETTE, Coletta, Collette, Kolette, Kollette (see also Nicole)

Language/Cultural Origin: French
Inherent Meaning: Victorious
Spiritual Connotation: Faithful
Scripture: Galatians 5:22–23 NKJV
But the fruit of the Spirit is love, joy, peace, longsuffering, kindness, goodness, faithfulness, gentleness, self-control.

COLEY, Colee, Coleigh, Koley

Language/Cultural Origin: English
Inherent Meaning: Victorious
Spiritual Connotation: Bold
Scripture: 1 Corinthians 15:57 NKJV
But thanks be to God, who gives us the victory through our Lord Jesus Christ.

COLIN, Colan, Colen, Colyn

Language/Cultural Origin: Irish
Inherent Meaning: Victorious
Spiritual Connotation: Destined
Scripture: 1 Corinthians 2:9 NKJV
Eye has not seen, nor ear heard, nor have entered into the heart of man the things which God has prepared for those who love Him.

COLLEEN, Coleen, Colene, Colleene, Collene, Colline, Koleen, Kolleen

Language/Cultural Origin: Gaelic
Inherent Meaning: Maiden
Spiritual Connotation: Excellent Virtue
Scripture: Psalm 107:9 NKJV
For He satisfies the longing soul, and fills the hungry soul with goodness.

COLLIN, Collen, Collins, Collyn

Language/Cultural Origin: Scottish
Inherent Meaning: Victorious
Spiritual Connotation: Pressured
Scripture: Matthew 12:20–21 NKJV
A bruised reed He will not break, and smoking flax He will not quench, till He sends forth justice to victory.

COLLIER, Collyer

Language/Cultural Origin: Middle English
Inherent Meaning: Merchant or Miner
Spiritual Connotation: Guided of God
Scripture: 2 Samuel 22:33 NKJV
God is my strength and power, and He makes my way perfect.

COLSON, Coleson
Language/Cultural Origin: English
Inherent Meaning: Son of the Victor
Spiritual Connotation: Generously Gifted
Scripture: Ephesians 4:8 NRSV
Therefore it is said, "When he ascended on high he made captivity itself a captive; he gave gifts to his people."

COLTER, Colt
Language/Cultural Origin: English
Inherent Meaning: Lover of Animals
Spiritual Connotation: Gentle
Scripture: Romans 13:10 NASB
Love does no wrong to a neighbor; therefore love is the fulfillment of the law.

COLTON, Colten, Coltin, Kolten, Koltin, Kolton
Language/Cultural Origin: Anglo-Saxon
Inherent Meaning: From the Coal Town
Spiritual Connotation: Resourceful
Scripture: Romans 5:5 NKJV
Now hope does not disappoint, because the love of God has been poured out in our hearts by the Holy Spirit who was given to us.

CONAN, Connan
Language/Cultural Origin: Celtic
Inherent Meaning: Intelligent
Spiritual Connotation: Spiritual Discernment
Scripture: Exodus 31:3 NKJV
And I have filled him with the Spirit of God, in wisdom, in understanding, in knowledge, and in all manner of workmanship.

CONCETTA, Conchita, Conciana, Concianna, Concieta
Language/Cultural Origin: Italian
Inherent Meaning: Pure
Spiritual Connotation: Undefiled
Scripture: Titus 1:15 NKJV
To the pure all things are pure.

CONIAH, Coniyah
Language/Cultural Origin: Hebrew
Inherent Meaning: God-Appointed
Spiritual Connotation: Destined
Scripture: James 4:10 NASB
Humble yourselves in the presence of the Lord, and He will exalt you.

CONLAN, Conlen, Conley, Conlin
Language/Cultural Origin: Irish

Inherent Meaning: Hero
Spiritual Connotation: Gifted
Scripture: Proverbs 2:6 NKJV
For the LORD gives wisdom; from His mouth come knowledge and understanding.

CONNERY, Connary
Language/Cultural Origin: Irish
Inherent Meaning: Exalted
Spiritual Connotation: Humble
Scripture: Luke 14:11 NKJV
For whoever exalts himself will be humbled, and he who humbles himself will be exalted.

CONNIE, Connee, Conni, Conny, Konnie
Language/Cultural Origin: English
Inherent Meaning: Consistent
Spiritual Connotation: Unwavering
Scripture: 1 Peter 5:9 TLB
Stand firm when he attacks. Trust the Lord; and remember that other Christians all around the world are going through these sufferings too.

CONNOR, Conner, Konner, Konnor
Language/Cultural Origin: Irish
Inherent Meaning: Lofty Desire
Spiritual Connotation: Stronghold of God
Scripture: 2 Corinthians 10:5 NASB
We are taking every thought captive to the obedience of Christ.

CONRAD, Conrade, Konrad, Konrade
Language/Cultural Origin: German
Inherent Meaning: Bold Counselor
Spiritual Connotation: Discerner of Excellence
Scripture: Colossians 3:16 NKJV
Let the word of Christ dwell in you richly in all wisdom . . . singing with grace in your hearts to the Lord.

CONROY, Conroye
Language/Cultural Origin: Irish
Inherent Meaning: Wise
Spiritual Connotation: Strong Leader
Scripture: Ecclesiastes 2:26 NKJV
For God gives wisdom and knowledge and joy to a man who is good in His sight.

CONSTANCE, Constanze, Konstance, Konstanze (see also Connie)
Language/Cultural Origin: Latin

Inherent Meaning: Steadfast
Spiritual Connotation: Consecrated
Scripture: Romans 8:16 NKJV
The Spirit Himself bears witness with our spirit that we are children of God.

CONSUELA, Konsuela
Language/Cultural Origin: Spanish
Inherent Meaning: Consoling Friend
Spiritual Connotation: Compassionate
Scripture: Proverbs 27:9 NLT
The heartfelt counsel of a friend is as sweet as perfume and incense.

COOPER, Couper
Language/Cultural Origin: English
Inherent Meaning: Barrel Maker
Spiritual Connotation: Servant
Scripture: 1 Corinthians 16:16 TLB
Please follow their instructions and do everything you can to help them as well as all others like them who work hard at your side with such real devotion.

CORA, Corra, Kora, Korra
Language/Cultural Origin: Greek
Inherent Meaning: Maiden
Spiritual Connotation: Abiding in God
Scripture: 1 John 4:16 NKJV
And we have known and believed the love that God has for us. God is love, and he who abides in love abides in God, and God in him.

CORAL, Corral, Koral
Language/Cultural Origin: Latin
Inherent Meaning: Coral
Spiritual Connotation: Joyful Praise
Scripture: Psalm 69:34 NKJV
Let heaven and earth praise Him, the seas and everything that moves in them.

CORALEE, Coralea, Cora-Lee, Coralie, Coraline, Coralyn, Corilee, Koralee, Koralie, Koralyn
Language/Cultural Origin: English
Inherent Meaning: Maiden From the Sea
Spiritual Connotation: Beloved
Scripture: Psalm 139:9–10 NASB
If I take the wings of the dawn, if I dwell in the remotest part of the sea, even there Thy hand will lead me, and Thy right hand will lay hold of me.

CORBETT, Corbet, Corbitt
Language/Cultural Origin: Irish
Inherent Meaning: Raven
Spiritual Connotation: Attractive
Scripture: Song of Songs 5:11 NRSV
His head is the finest gold; his locks are wavy, black as a raven.

CORBIN, Corban, Corben, Korban, Korben, Korbin
Language/Cultural Origin: Latin
Inherent Meaning: Raven
Spiritual Connotation: For Whom the Lord Will Provide
Scripture: Job 38:41 NKJV
Who provides food for the raven, when its young ones cry to God, and wander about for lack of food?

CORDELL, Cordelle, Kordell
Language/Cultural Origin: French
Inherent Meaning: Rope Maker
Spiritual Connotation: Laborer
Scripture: Exodus 20:10 NKJV
The seventh day is the Sabbath of the LORD your God. In it you shall do no work.

CORDELIA, Cordey, Cordia, Cordie
Language/Cultural Origin: Welsh
Inherent Meaning: Jewel of the Sea
Spiritual Connotation: Precious
Scripture: Psalm 139:17 NKJV
How precious also are Your thoughts to me, O God! How great is the sum of them!

COREY, Coree, Correy, Corry, Cory (see also Korey)
Language/Cultural Origin: Irish
Inherent Meaning: From the Hollow
Spiritual Connotation: Prosperous
Scripture: Psalm 1:3 NKJV
He shall be like a tree planted by the rivers of water. . . . Whatever he does shall prosper.

CORI, Coriann, Corianne, Cori-Anne, Corie, Corri, Corrie, Corrienne (see also Cora, Korah)
Language/Cultural Origin: Irish
Inherent Meaning: From the Hollow
Spiritual Connotation: Empowered Spirit
Scripture: James 4:7 NKJV
Therefore submit to God. Resist the devil and he will flee from you.

CORIN, Coren, Corian, Corien, Corinn, Corrian, Corren, Corrin, Corryn, Coryn, Corynn
Language/Cultural Origin: English
Inherent Meaning: Little One
Spiritual Connotation: Trusting
Scripture: Hebrews 13:5 NRSV
Keep your lives free from the love of money, and be content with what you have; for he has said, I will never leave you or forsake you.

CORINA, Coreena, Corinna, Corrina (see also Carina, Cori, Korina)
Language/Cultural Origin: English
Inherent Meaning: Little Damsel
Spiritual Connotation: Innocent
Scripture: Titus 1:15 NKJV
To the pure all things are pure.

CORINNE, Coreen, Corine, Corinne, Correen, Corrinne
Language/Cultural Origin: Greek
Inherent Meaning: Fair Maiden
Spiritual Connotation: Illuminated
Scripture: Job 22:28 NKJV
You will also declare a thing, and it will be established for you; so light will shine on your ways.

CORISSA, Corisa, Korissa (see also Carissa)
Language/Cultural Origin: English
Inherent Meaning: Most Maidenly
Spiritual Connotation: Filled With Praise
Scripture: Psalm 145:3 RSV
Great is the LORD, and greatly to be praised, and his greatness is unsearchable.

CORLISS, Corlisa, Corlise, Corlissa, Korlisa, Korlise, Korliss
Language/Cultural Origin: English
Inherent Meaning: Good-Hearted
Spiritual Connotation: Sanctified
Scripture: 2 Corinthians 3:18 RSV
And we all, with unveiled face, beholding the glory of the Lord, are being changed into his likeness from one degree of glory to another.

CORNELIUS
☞ Language/Cultural Origin: Latin
Inherent Meaning: Sunbeam
Spiritual Connotation: Praise
Scripture: Psalm 113:3 RSV
From the rising of the sun to its setting the name of the LORD is to be praised!

CORRIGAN, Korrigan
Language/Cultural Origin: Irish
Inherent Meaning: Spearman
Spiritual Connotation: Proud Father
Scripture: Psalm 127:4 RSV
Like arrows in the hand of a warrior are the sons of one's youth.

CORT, see Courtney

CORTEZ, Courtez
Language/Cultural Origin: Spanish
Inherent Meaning: Conqueror
Spiritual Connotation: Valiant
Scripture: Revelation 6:2 NASB
And I looked, and behold, a white horse, and he who sat on it had a bow; and a crown was given to him; and he went out conquering, and to conquer.

CORWIN, Corwyn
Language/Cultural Origin: Latin
Inherent Meaning: Heart's Delight
Spiritual Connotation: Brilliant Countenance
Scripture: 2 Corinthians 4:6 NKJV
For it is the God who commanded light to shine out of darkness, who has shone in our hearts.

CORY, see Corey

COSETTE, Cosetta, Cossetta, Cossette
Language/Cultural Origin: French
Inherent Meaning: Victorious
Spiritual Connotation: Confident Spirit
Scripture: Isaiah 42:16 NKJV
I will bring the blind by a way they did not know; I will lead them in paths they have not known.

COSMO, Cozmo, Kosmo
Language/Cultural Origin: Greek
Inherent Meaning: Orderly
Spiritual Connotation: Peaceful
Scripture: 1 Thessalonians 4:11 TLB
This should be your ambition: to live a quiet life, minding your own business and doing your own work.

COURTLAND, Courtlin, Courtlyn
Language/Cultural Origin: English
Inherent Meaning: From the Farmstead
Spiritual Connotation: Truthful
Scripture: Psalm 19:14 NKJV
*Let the words of my mouth and the
meditation of my heart be acceptable in Your
sight, O LORD, my strength and my Redeemer.*

**COURTNEY, Cort, Cortnay, Cortne,
Cortnee, Cortney, Cortni, Cortnie,
Corttney, Court, Courtenay,
Courteney, Courtnae, Courtnay,
Courtnee, Courtnée, Courtni,
Courtnie, Courtny, Courtonie, Kort,
Kortnay, Kortnee, Kortney, Kortni,
Kortnie, Kortny, Kourtney, Kourtni,
Kourtny, Kourtinee**
Language/Cultural Origin: Old French
Inherent Meaning: From the Court
Spiritual Connotation: Amidst God's Love
Scripture: 1 John 4:16 NKJV
*And we have known and believed the love
that God has for us. God is love, and he who
abides in love abides in God, and God in
him.*

COWAN, Cowey
Language/Cultural Origin: Irish
Inherent Meaning: From the Hillside
Spiritual Connotation: Generous
Scripture: Luke 6:38 NKJV
*Give, and it will be given to you. . . . For with
the same measure that you use, it will be
measured back to you.*

COY, Coi, Koy
Language/Cultural Origin: English
Inherent Meaning: From the Woods
Spiritual Connotation: Focused
Scripture: 1 Corinthians 2:2 NLT
*For I decided to concentrate only on Jesus
Christ and his death on the cross.*

COYLE, Coyel
Language/Cultural Origin: Irish
Inherent Meaning: Courageous Leader
Spiritual Connotation: God's Warrior
Scripture: 1 Timothy 6:12 NKJV
*Fight the good fight of faith, lay hold on
eternal life, to which you were also called.*

**COZBI, Cosbey, Cosbie, Cosby, Coz,
⌖Cozbee, Cozbie, Cozby**
Language/Cultural Origin: Canaanite
Inherent Meaning: Deceiver
Spiritual Connotation: Loving
Scripture: 1 John 4:7 NKJV
*Beloved, let us love one another, for love is of
God; and everyone who loves is born of God
and knows God.*

CRAIG, Cregg, Crieg, Kraig
Language/Cultural Origin: Scottish
Inherent Meaning: From the Steep Rock
Spiritual Connotation: Enduring Spirit
Scripture: Matthew 7:24 NKJV
*Therefore whoever hears these sayings of
Mine, and does them, I will liken him to a
wise man who built his house on the rock:*

CRANDELL, Crandall
Language/Cultural Origin: English
Inherent Meaning: From the Valley
Spiritual Connotation: Freedom
Scripture: 2 Corinthians 3:17 NKJV
*Now the Lord is the Spirit; and where the
Spirit of the Lord is, there is liberty.*

CREED, Creedon
Language/Cultural Origin: Latin
Inherent Meaning: Belief
Spiritual Connotation: Power in Faith
Scripture: Matthew 8:10 NRSV
*Truly I tell you, in no one in Israel have I
found such faith.*

CREIGHTON, Cray, Crayton
Language/Cultural Origin: English
Inherent Meaning: From the Rocky Place
Spiritual Connotation: Humble Spirit
Scripture: 3 John 2 NKJV
*Beloved, I pray that you may prosper in all
things and be in health, just as your soul
prospers.*

CROSBY, Crosbie
Language/Cultural Origin: Scandinavian
Inherent Meaning: Shrine of the Cross
Spiritual Connotation: Reminder of Christ
Scripture: Luke 23:33 NASB
*And when they came to the place called The
Skull, there they crucified Him and the
criminals, one on the right and the other on
the left.*

CRUZ, Kruz
Language/Cultural Origin: Portuguese
Inherent Meaning: Cross
Spiritual Connotation: Symbol
Scripture: Philippians 2:8 NKJV
And being found in appearance as a man, He humbled Himself and became obedient to the point of death, even the death of the cross.

CRYSTAL, Christal, Christalin, Christall, Christalyn, Christel, Chrystal, Chrystel, Cristal, Cristel, Cristelle, Crystalee, Crystall, Crystallin, Crystallynn, Crystel, Crystilin, Crystol, Crystyl (see also Krystal)
Language/Cultural Origin: Latin
Inherent Meaning: Sparkling
Spiritual Connotation: Pure
Scripture: 1 Timothy 4:12 NCV
Do not let anyone treat you as if you are unimportant because you are young. Instead, be an example to the believers with . . . your pure life.

CULLEN, Cullan, Cullin, Cully
Language/Cultural Origin: Irish
Inherent Meaning: Pleasing to Look Upon
Spiritual Connotation: Loving
Scripture: Romans 13:10 NKJV
Love does no harm to a neighbor; therefore love is the fulfillment of the law.

CURRAN, Curan
Language/Cultural Origin: Irish
Inherent Meaning: Hero
Spiritual Connotation: Example
Scripture: 1 Corinthians 11:1 NKJV
Imitate me, just as I also imitate Christ.

CURTIS, Curt, Curtiss, Kurtis, Kurtiss (see also Kurt)
Language/Cultural Origin: Old French
Inherent Meaning: Courteous
Spiritual Connotation: Just and Honorable
Scripture: Zechariah 7:9 NKJV
Thus says the LORD of hosts: "Execute true justice, show mercy and compassion everyone to his brother."

CUSH, Kush
☞ Language/Cultural Origin: Hebrew
Inherent Meaning: Black
Spiritual Connotation: Forgiven
Scripture: 1 John 3:3 NCV
Christ is pure, and all who have this hope in Christ keep themselves pure like Christ.

CYBIL, see Sybil

CYNTHIA, Cindee, Cindi, Cindie, Cindy, Cydna, Cynda, Cyndee, Cyndi, Cyndie, Cyndy
Language/Cultural Origin: Greek
Inherent Meaning: Moon
Spiritual Connotation: Celestial Light
Scripture: Psalm 27:1 NKJV
The LORD is my light and my salvation; whom shall I fear? The LORD is the strength of my life; of whom shall I be afraid?

CYRIL, Cyrill, Cyrille
Language/Cultural Origin: Greek
Inherent Meaning: Lordly
Spiritual Connotation: Great Spiritual Potential
Scripture: Malachi 3:10 NKJV
I will . . . open for you the windows of heaven and pour out for you such blessing that there will not be room enough to receive it.

CYRUS, Cy, Cyris
☞ Language/Cultural Origin: Persian
Inherent Meaning: Sun
Spiritual Connotation: Spiritual Enlightenment
Scripture: Ephesians 1:18 NASB
I pray that the eyes of your heart may be enlightened, so that you may know . . . what are the riches of the glory of His inheritance in the saints.

CZARINA, Czareena, Czariana, Czarianna (see also Zorina)
Language/Cultural Origin: Russian
Inherent Meaning: Empress
Spiritual Connotation: Regal
Scripture: Psalm 45:9 NKJV
Kings' daughters are among Your honorable women; at Your right hand stands the queen in gold.

DACEY, Dacee, Daci, Dacie, Dacy, Daicee, Daycee, Daycie
Language/Cultural Origin: Gaelic
Inherent Meaning: Southerner
Spiritual Connotation: Friend of Christ
Scripture: Hebrews 2:7 NKJV
You have made him a little lower than the angels; you have crowned him with glory and honor, and set him over the works of Your hands.

DACIA, Dacya
Language/Cultural Origin: Latin
Inherent Meaning: Southerner
Spiritual Connotation: Divine Perspective
Scripture: Isaiah 65:17 NKJV
For behold, I create new heavens and a new earth; and the former shall not be remembered or come to mind.

DACIAN, Dacien
Language/Cultural Origin: Latin
Inherent Meaning: Southerner
Spiritual Connotation: Divine Perspective
Scripture: Isaiah 55:8 NKJV
"For My thoughts are not your thoughts, nor are your ways My ways," says the LORD.

DAGAN, Dagon
Language/Cultural Origin: Hebrew
Inherent Meaning: Grain
Spiritual Connotation: Wise
Scripture: Ecclesiastes 7:19 NKJV
Wisdom strengthens the wise more than ten rulers of the city.

DAGANA, Dagania, Daganna
Language/Cultural Origin: Hebrew
Inherent Meaning: Grain
Spiritual Connotation: Chosen
Scripture: Deuteronomy 33:28 NKJV
Then Israel shall dwell in safety, the fountain of Jacob alone, in a land of grain and new wine; His heavens shall also drop dew.

DAGMAR
Language/Cultural Origin: Old German
Inherent Meaning: Glorious Day
Spiritual Connotation: Redeemed
Scripture: Romans 8:2 NKJV
For the law of the Spirit of life in Christ Jesus has made me free from the law of sin and death.

DAHLIA, Dahliana, Dahlianna (see also Daliah)
Language/Cultural Origin: Scandinavian
Inherent Meaning: From the Valley
Spiritual Connotation: Example
Scripture: Job 21:33 NKJV
The clods of the valley shall be sweet to him; everyone shall follow him, as countless have gone before him.

DAISY, Daisee
Language/Cultural Origin: Old English
Inherent Meaning: Vision of the Day
Spiritual Connotation: Cleansed
Scripture: Ephesians 1:4 NKJV
He chose us in Him before the foundation of the world, that we should be holy and without blame before Him in love.

DAJUAN, Dawan, Dawon, Dejuan, Dewaun, Dijuan, D'Juan, Dujuan
Language/Cultural Origin: American
Inherent Meaning: God Is Gracious
Spiritual Connotation: Promise
Scripture: 2 Chronicles 30:9 NKJV
For if you return to the LORD, your brethren and your children will . . . come back to this land; for the LORD your God is gracious and merciful.

DAKOTA, Dakotah
Language/Cultural Origin: Sioux
Inherent Meaning: Friend
Spiritual Connotation: Sincere

Scripture: Proverbs 22:11 NCV
Whoever loves pure thoughts and kind words will have even the king as a friend.

DALE, Dayle
Language/Cultural Origin: Old English
Inherent Meaning: From the Valley
Spiritual Connotation: Peaceful
Scripture: Psalm 85:11 NKJV
Truth shall spring out of the earth, and righteousness shall look down from heaven.

DALIAH, Dalia, Daliyah (see also Dahlia)
Language/Cultural Origin: Hebrew
Inherent Meaning: Branch
Spiritual Connotation: Destined
Scripture: Isaiah 4:2 NKJV
In that day the Branch of the LORD shall be beautiful and glorious; and the fruit of the earth shall be excellent and appealing.

DALLAN, Daelan, Daelen, Daelin, Dalian, Daylan, Daylen, Daylin
Language/Cultural Origin: English
Inherent Meaning: From the Dale
Spiritual Connotation: Secure
Scripture: Joel 2:21 NASB
Do not fear, O land, rejoice and be glad, for the LORD has done great things.

DALLAS, Dallis, Dallys
Language/Cultural Origin: Scottish
Inherent Meaning: Gentle
Spiritual Connotation: Efficient
Scripture: Deuteronomy 15:10 NKJV
You shall surely give to him, and your heart should not be grieved . . . because for this thing the LORD your God will bless you.

DALTON, Dalten
Language/Cultural Origin: Old English
Inherent Meaning: From the Valley Town
Spiritual Connotation: Filled With Peace
Scripture: Luke 6:45 NKJV
A good man out of the good treasure of his heart brings forth good.

DALY, Daley
Language/Cultural Origin: Irish
Inherent Meaning: Assembly
Spiritual Connotation: Bringer of Light

Scripture: Isaiah 52:7 NKJV
How beautiful upon the mountains are the feet of him who brings good news . . . Who says to Zion, Your God reigns!

DAMARA, Damarrah
Language/Cultural Origin: Czech
Inherent Meaning: Glory of the Day
Spiritual Connotation: Promised Result
Scripture: Isaiah 29:18 NKJV
In that day the deaf shall hear the words of the book, and the eyes of the blind shall see out of obscurity and out of darkness.

DAMARIS, Damarius, Damarys, ☞Demaras, Demaris, Demarius
Language/Cultural Origin: Greek
Inherent Meaning: Gentle
Spiritual Connotation: Forgiving
Scripture: Hosea 11:4 NRSV
I led them with cords of human kindness, with bands of love. I was to them like those who lift infants to their cheeks. I bent down to them and fed them.

DAMIAN, Daemien, Daimyan, Dameion, Dameon, Damián, Damien, Damion, Daymian
Language/Cultural Origin: Russian
Inherent Meaning: Soother
Spiritual Connotation: One Who Restores
Scripture: Isaiah 40:1 NKJV
Comfort, yes, comfort My people! Says your God.

DAMIANA, Damianna
Language/Cultural Origin: Greek
Inherent Meaning: Soother
Spiritual Connotation: Healer
Scripture: Jeremiah 31:13 NRSV
Then shall the young women rejoice in the dance, and the young men and the old shall be merry. I will turn their mourning into joy.

DAMICA, Damika, Damikah, Demeeka, Demica, Demicah
Language/Cultural Origin: French
Inherent Meaning: Friendly
Spiritual Connotation: Seeker of Truth
Scripture: Psalm 25:14 RSV
The friendship of the LORD is for those who fear him, and he makes known to them his covenant.

DAMITA, Dametia, Dametra
Language/Cultural Origin: Spanish
Inherent Meaning: Noble Lady
Spiritual Connotation: Gracious Spirit
Scripture: Psalm 97:11 NKJV
Light is sown for the righteous, and gladness for the upright in heart.

DAMON, Daemon, Daman, Damen, Damonn, Daymon
Language/Cultural Origin: Greek
Inherent Meaning: Loyal
Spiritual Connotation: Walks With God
Scripture: Zechariah 8:16 NKJV
These are the things you shall do: speak each man the truth to his neighbor; give judgment in your gates for truth, justice, and peace.

DANA, Daina, Danah, Dayna, Daynah
Language/Cultural Origin: Scandinavian
Inherent Meaning: Bright as Day
Spiritual Connotation: Obedient
Scripture: Deuteronomy 16:20 NASB
Justice, and only justice, you shall pursue, that you may live and possess the land which the LORD your God is giving you.

DANAE, Danaë, Danay, Dannae (see also Denae)
Language/Cultural Origin: English
Inherent Meaning: God Is My Judge
Spiritual Connotation: Just
Scripture: 1 Kings 10:9 NKJV
Blessed be the LORD your God, who delighted in you, setting you on the throne of Israel!

DANE, Daine, Dayne, Dhane
Language/Cultural Origin: Old English
Inherent Meaning: Trickling Stream
Spiritual Connotation: Blessed
Scripture: Psalm 104:10 NKJV
He sends the springs into the valleys, they flow among the hills.

DANELLE, Danel, Danele, Danell, Dannell (see also Danielle)
Language/Cultural Origin: French
Inherent Meaning: God Is My Judge
Spiritual Connotation: Discerning
Scripture: Psalm 36:6 NCV
Your goodness is as high as the mountains. Your justice is as deep as the great ocean. LORD, you protect both people and animals.

DANETTE, Danett
Language/Cultural Origin: American
Inherent Meaning: God Is My Judge
Spiritual Connotation: Perceptive
Scripture: Psalm 45:6 TLB
Your throne, O God, endures forever. Justice is your royal scepter.

DANIA, Danee, Dani, Daniah, Danie, Danni, Danya
Language/Cultural Origin: Hebrew
Inherent Meaning: God Is My Judge
Spiritual Connotation: Intuitive
Scripture: Psalm 146:7 NCV
He does what is fair for those who have been wronged. He gives food to the hungry. The LORD sets the prisoners free.

DANICA, Daneeka, Danika, Dannika
Language/Cultural Origin: Slavic
Inherent Meaning: Morning Star
Spiritual Connotation: Attentive
Scripture: 2 Peter 1:19 NRSV
You will do well to be attentive to this as to a lamp shining in a dark place, until the day dawns and the morning star rises in your hearts.

DANIEL, Dan, Dániel, Daniël, ☞Daniyel, Danny, Donyel, Donyell
Language/Cultural Origin: Hebrew
Inherent Meaning: God Is My Judge
Spiritual Connotation: Discerning
Scripture: Psalm 119:142 NKJV
Your righteousness is an everlasting righteousness, and Your law is truth.

DANIELLE, Danialle, Daniela, Daniele, Daniell, Daniella, Dannielle, Danyel, Danyele, Danyelle (see also Danelle)
Language/Cultural Origin: French
Inherent Meaning: God Is My Judge
Spiritual Connotation: Perceptive
Scripture: Psalm 119:112 NKJV
I have inclined my heart to perform Your statutes forever, to the very end.

DANNON, Danaan, Danen, Danon
Language/Cultural Origin: American
Inherent Meaning: God Is My Judge
Spiritual Connotation: Preserved

Scripture: Numbers 6:24 NKJV

The LORD bless you and keep you; the LORD make His face shine upon you, and be gracious to you.

DANTE, Danté, Dauntay, Dauntaye, Daunte (see also Deon, Dontae)
Language/Cultural Origin: Latin
Inherent Meaning: Enduring
Spiritual Connotation: Loving
Scripture: 1 Corinthians 13:7 RSV

Love bears all things, believes all things, hopes all things, endures all things.

DANYA, Danyah, Donya (see also Dawn, Donna)
Language/Cultural Origin: Russian
Inherent Meaning: God Is My Judge
Spiritual Connotation: Vindicated
Scripture: Hebrews 13:10 TLB

We have an altar—the cross where Christ was sacrificed—where those who continue to seek salvation by obeying Jewish laws can never be helped.

DAPHNE, Daphaney, Daphanie, Daphany, Daphnee, Daphney
Language/Cultural Origin: Greek
Inherent Meaning: Laurel Tree
Spiritual Connotation: Victorious
Scripture: 1 Kings 3:12 NKJV

I have given you a wise and understanding heart, so that there has not been anyone like you before you, nor shall any like you arise after you.

DARA, Darah, Darra, Darrah
☞ Language/Cultural Origin: Hebrew
Inherent Meaning: Compassionate
Spiritual Connotation: Bearer of Mercy
Scripture: Matthew 25:40 NKJV

Assuredly, I say to you, inasmuch as you did it to one of the least of these My brethren, you did it to Me.

DARBY, Darbey, Darbi, Darbie
Language/Cultural Origin: Irish
Inherent Meaning: Freedom
Spiritual Connotation: Free Spirit
Scripture: Romans 8:21 NLT

All creation anticipates the day when it will join God's children in glorious freedom from death and decay.

DARCY, Darcee, Darcey, Darcie, Darcy, Darsey, Darsie
Language/Cultural Origin: French
Inherent Meaning: Fortress
Spiritual Connotation: Established in Strength
Scripture: Psalm 25:10 NKJV

All the paths of the LORD are mercy and truth, to such as keep His covenant and His testimonies.

DARIA, Darria, Darya
Language/Cultural Origin: Greek
Inherent Meaning: Wealthy
Spiritual Connotation: Gracious
Scripture: Psalm 9:1 NKJV

I will praise You, O LORD, with my whole heart; I will tell of all Your marvelous works.

DARIELLE, Dariel, Darriel, Darrielle
Language/Cultural Origin: French
Inherent Meaning: Little Darling
Spiritual Connotation: Cherished
Scripture: Psalm 108:6 TLB

Hear the cry of your beloved child—come with mighty power and rescue me.

DARIUS, Darian, Dariann, Darias, ☞Darien, Darion, Dárion
Language/Cultural Origin: Persian
Inherent Meaning: Prosperous
Spiritual Connotation: Preserved
Scripture: Isaiah 42:6 NKJV

I, the LORD, have called you in righteousness, and will hold your hand; I will keep you.

DARLENE, Darla, Darleen, Darling
Language/Cultural Origin: French
Inherent Meaning: Darling
Spiritual Connotation: Beloved
Scripture: Proverbs 4:23 NKJV

Keep your heart with all diligence, for out of it spring the issues of life.

DARNELLE, Darnall, Darnell
Language/Cultural Origin: Irish
Inherent Meaning: Magnificent
Spiritual Connotation: Loving
Scripture: 1 Peter 4:8 NRSV

Above all, maintain constant love for one another, for love covers a multitude of sins.

DARON, Darron, Daryn, Darynn, Darynne, Derrion, Derron, Diron (see also Darren, Darius, Deron)
Language/Cultural Origin: English
Inherent Meaning: Rocky Hill
Spiritual Connotation: Obedient
Scripture: 1 John 2:28 NKJV
And now, little children, abide in Him, that when He appears, we may have confidence and not be ashamed before Him at His coming.

DARRELL, Darelle, Daril, Darral, Darrel, Darril, Darryl, Darryll, Daryl, Derell, Derrel, Derril
Language/Cultural Origin: French
Inherent Meaning: Beloved
Spiritual Connotation: Blessed
Scripture: Psalm 18:32 NKJV
It is God who arms me with strength, and makes my way perfect.

DARWIN, Darwyn
Language/Cultural Origin: Old English
Inherent Meaning: Beloved
Spiritual Connotation: Treasured
Scripture: 2 Corinthians 4:7 NIV
But we have this treasure in jars of clay to show that this all-surpassing power is from God and not from us.

DARREN, Daran, Daren, Darin, Darran, Darrian, Darrien, Darrin, Deren, Derran, Derren, Derrin (see also Daron, Darius, Deron)
Language/Cultural Origin: Irish
Inherent Meaning: Great
Spiritual Connotation: Esteemed
Scripture: 2 Corinthians 9:8 NKJV
And God is able to make all grace abound toward you, that you . . . may have an abundance for every good work.

DASAN, Dassan
Language/Cultural Origin: Pomo
Inherent Meaning: Leader
Spiritual Connotation: Chosen
Scripture: Jeremiah 30:21 NASB
Their leader shall be one of them, and their ruler shall come forth from their midst.

DASHA, Dashah, Dasya
Language/Cultural Origin: Russian
Inherent Meaning: Divine Display
Spiritual Connotation: Miracle
Scripture: Joel 2:30 NLT
I will cause wonders in the heavens and on the earth—blood and fire and pillars of smoke.

DASHAWNA, Deshandra, Deshaundra, Deshawnda, Deshawna, Deshonda, Deshonna
Language/Cultural Origin: American
Inherent Meaning: God Is Gracious
Spiritual Connotation: Pardoned
Scripture: Isaiah 63:9 NLT
In all their suffering he also suffered, and he personally rescued them. In his love and mercy he redeemed them.

DATHAN, Dathon, Daythan, Daython
☞ Language/Cultural Origin: Hebrew
Inherent Meaning: Belonging to the Law
Spiritual Connotation: Redeemed
Scripture: Ephesians 2:5 NCV
Though we were spiritually dead because of the things we did against God, he gave us new life with Christ. You have been saved by God's grace.

DATIA, Datiah, Datiya, Datya
Language/Cultural Origin: Hebrew
Inherent Meaning: Faith in God
Spiritual Connotation: Strength
Scripture: Matthew 9:22 RSV
Take heart, daughter; your faith has made you well.

DAVID, Dave, Daved, Daveed, Davey, Davíde, Davy, Dayvid
☞ Language/Cultural Origin: Hebrew
Inherent Meaning: Beloved
Spiritual Connotation: Lover of All
Scripture: 1 John 4:16 NKJV
And we have known and believed the love that God has for us. God is love, and he who abides in love abides in God, and God in him.

DAVIN, Daevin, Daevon, Davohn, Davon, Davonn, Davontay, Davonte, Dayvin (see also Devin)
Language/Cultural Origin: Scandinavian
Inherent Meaning: Brilliant
Spiritual Connotation: Heavenly Light

Scripture: Psalm 148:3 NRSV
Praise him, sun and moon; praise him, all you shining stars!

DAVINA, Dava, Daveena, Davi, Daviana, Davine, Davinia, Davria, Devona, Devonda, Devonna, Devina
Language/Cultural Origin: Scottish
Inherent Meaning: Beloved
Spiritual Connotation: Enlightened
Scripture: Zechariah 4:6 NKJV
Not by might nor by power, but by My Spirit, says the LORD of hosts.

DAVIS, Davidson, Davies, Davison
Language/Cultural Origin: English
Inherent Meaning: Honorable
Spiritual Connotation: Loving
Scripture: 1 John 4:8 NKJV
He who does not love does not know God, for God is love.

DAWN, Dawana, Dawna, Dawne, Dawnn, Dawnna, Dawnya (see also Danya, Donna)
Language/Cultural Origin: Old English
Inherent Meaning: Beginning Anew
Spiritual Connotation: Joy and Praise
Scripture: Psalm 113:2–3 NKJV
Blessed be the name of the LORD from this time forth and forevermore! From the rising of the sun to its going down the Lord's name is to be praised.

DAWSON, Dawsen
Language/Cultural Origin: English
Inherent Meaning: Son of the Beloved
Spiritual Connotation: Victorious
Scripture: Psalm 60:5 RSV
That thy beloved may be delivered, give victory by thy right hand and answer us!

DAYA, Daeya, Daia
Language/Cultural Origin: Hebrew
Inherent Meaning: Bird
Spiritual Connotation: Secure
Scripture: Psalm 84:3 RSV
Even the sparrow finds a home, and the swallow a nest for herself, where she may lay her young, at thy altars, O LORD of hosts, my King and my God.

DAYANA, Dayahna
Language/Cultural Origin: Middle Eastern

Inherent Meaning: Divine
Spiritual Connotation: Warrior
Scripture: 2 Corinthians 10:4 NCV
We fight with weapons that are different from those the world uses. Our weapons have power from God that can destroy the enemy's strong places.

DEACON, Deke, Diakonos
Language/Cultural Origin: Greek
Inherent Meaning: One Who Serves
Spiritual Connotation: Honored
Scripture: 1 Timothy 3:8 NLT
In the same way, deacons must be people who are respected and have integrity. They must not be heavy drinkers and must not be greedy for money.

DEAN, Deane, Dene
Language/Cultural Origin: Old English
Inherent Meaning: Valley
Spiritual Connotation: Prosperous
Scripture: Matthew 12:35 NKJV
A good man out of the good treasure of his heart brings forth good things.

DEANDRA, Deandrá, Deandrea, Deandria, Deanndra, Diandre
Language/Cultural Origin: American
Inherent Meaning: Courageous
Spiritual Connotation: Heir
Scripture: Deuteronomy 31:7 NASB
Be strong and courageous, for you shall go with this people into the land which the LORD has sworn to their fathers to give them.

DEANDRE, D'Andre, Dandrae, Dandray, Dandré, Deandré, De Andre, Deaundre, Deondré
Language/Cultural Origin: French
Inherent Meaning: Courageous
Spiritual Connotation: Submissive
Scripture: 1 Chronicles 19:13 NRSV
Be strong, and let us be courageous for our people and for the cities of our God.

DEANNA, Deana, Deann, Déanne, Deeann, Deeanna
Language/Cultural Origin: Latin
Inherent Meaning: Divine
Spiritual Connotation: Brightness of the Dawn
Scripture: Psalm 143:8 NKJV
Cause me to hear Your lovingkindness in the morning, for in You do I trust.

DEBORAH, Deb, Debb, Debbi,
☞ **Debbie, Debbora, Debborah, Debby,**
Debi, Debora, Deborrah, Debra
Language/Cultural Origin: Hebrew
Inherent Meaning: Honey Bee
Spiritual Connotation: New Era of Leadership
Scripture: Isaiah 65:17 NKJV
For behold, I create new heavens and a new earth; and the former shall not be remembered or come to mind.

DEE, Dede, Deedee
Language/Cultural Origin: Welsh
Inherent Meaning: Dark
Spiritual Connotation: Loving
Scripture: 2 John 1:6 NRSV
And this is love, that we walk according to his commandments.

DEENA, see Dena

DEIRDRE, Dedra, Deedra, Deidra,
Deidre, Dierdra, Dierdre, Diérdre
Language/Cultural Origin: Irish
Inherent Meaning: Wanderer
Spiritual Connotation: Seeker of
   Righteousness and Truth
Scripture: Psalm 119:35 NKJV
Make me walk in the path of Your commandments, for I delight in it.

DEITRA, Deetra, Detria
Language/Cultural Origin: Greek
Inherent Meaning: Abundant
Spiritual Connotation: Refreshed
Scripture: Psalm 68:9 TLB
You sent abundant rain upon your land, O God, to refresh it in its weariness!

DEJA, Daija, Daja, Déja
Language/Cultural Origin: French
Inherent Meaning: Before
Spiritual Connotation: Compassionate
Scripture: Romans 12:15 NKJV
Rejoice with those who rejoice, and weep with those who weep.

DEJUAN, see Dajuan

DELAIAH, Dalaiah
☞ Language/Cultural Origin: Hebrew
Inherent Meaning: God Is the Deliverer

Spiritual Connotation: Redeemed
Scripture: Romans 11:26 NKJV
The Deliverer will come out of Zion.

DELANA, Dalanna, Dalayna, Dalena,
Dalina, Delaina, Delena, Delina
Language/Cultural Origin: German
Inherent Meaning: Noble Protector
Spiritual Connotation: Example
Scripture: Psalm 71:7 NLT
My life is an example to many, because you have been my strength and protection.

DELANO, Dellano
Language/Cultural Origin: French
Inherent Meaning: Nut Tree
Spiritual Connotation: Anchored
Scripture: Psalm 1:3 RSV
He is like a tree planted by streams of water, that yields its fruit in its season, and its leaf does not wither. In all that he does, he prospers.

DELANY, Dalaney, Delainey, Delanny,
Delaynie, Dellaney
Language/Cultural Origin: Irish
Inherent Meaning: Of the Champion
Spiritual Connotation: Victorious
Scripture: Psalm 98:2 NIV
The LORD has made his salvation known and revealed his righteousness to the nations.

DELIA, Dehlia, Deleah, Dellia, Delya
Language/Cultural Origin: Greek
Inherent Meaning: Visible
Spiritual Connotation: Divine Reflection
Scripture: 1 Corinthians 13:12 TLB
We can see and understand only a little about God now, as if we were peering at his reflection in a poor mirror; but someday we are going to see him . . . face to face.

DELICIA, Deleesha, Delisha, Delysia
Language/Cultural Origin: Latin
Inherent Meaning: Delightful
Spiritual Connotation: Joyous Spirit
Scripture: Psalm 16:11 NKJV
You will show me the path of life; in Your presence is fullness of joy; At Your right hand are pleasures forevermore.

DELLA, Dellie
Language/Cultural Origin: Old German

Inherent Meaning: Noble Maiden
Spiritual Connotation: Excellent Virtue
Scripture: 1 Corinthians 13:13 NKJV
And now abide faith, hope, love, these three; but the greatest of these is love.

DELMAR, Dalmar
Language/Cultural Origin: Latin
Inherent Meaning: By the Sea
Spiritual Connotation: Filled With Praise
Scripture: Psalm 69:34 NRSV
Let heaven and earth praise him, the seas and everything that moves in them.

DELORES, Deloria, Deloris, Dolores
Language/Cultural Origin: Spanish
Inherent Meaning: Sorrowful
Spiritual Connotation: Compassionate
Scripture: Psalm 121:1 NKJV
I will lift up my eyes to the hills; from whence comes my help?

DELSIE, Delcee, Delcie, Delsee
Language/Cultural Origin: English
Inherent Meaning: Oath of God
Spiritual Connotation: Promise
Scripture: Genesis 17:4 NRSV
As for me, this is my covenant with you: you shall be the ancestor of a multitude of nations.

DELTA, Deltra
Language/Cultural Origin: Greek
Inherent Meaning: Door
Spiritual Connotation: Seeker of Truth
Scripture: Revelation 3:20 NKJV
Behold, I stand at the door and knock. If anyone hears My voice and opens the door, I will come in to him and dine with him, and be with Me.

DEMAS, Deemas, Deimas
Language/Cultural Origin: Greek
Inherent Meaning: Ruler of People
Spiritual Connotation: Powerful
Scripture: Psalm 105:21 NKJV
He made him lord of his house, and ruler of all his possessions,

DEMETRIA, Demetra, Demitra
Language/Cultural Origin: Greek
Inherent Meaning: Plentiful
Spiritual Connotation: Fruitful

Scripture: John 10:10 NKJV
I have come that they may have life, and that they may have it more abundantly.

DEMETRIUS, Demetreus, Demetrias, Demetric, Demetrik, Demitrias, Dimitrios, Dimitrius, Dmetrius (see also Dimitri)
Language/Cultural Origin: Greek
Inherent Meaning: Lover of the Earth
Spiritual Connotation: Fruitful Increase
Scripture: Luke 11:10 NKJV
For everyone who asks receives, and he who seeks finds, and to him who knocks it will be opened.

DEMI, Demee, Demiah
Language/Cultural Origin: French
Inherent Meaning: Half
Spiritual Connotation: Dependent
Scripture: Zechariah 4:6 NASB
Not by might nor by power, but by My Spirit, says the LORD of hosts.

DEMPSEY, Dempsie
Language/Cultural Origin: Irish
Inherent Meaning: Proud
Spiritual Connotation: Honorable
Scripture: Galatians 5:1 NKJV
Stand fast therefore in the liberty by which Christ has made us free, and do not be entangled again with a yoke of bondage.

DENA, Deena
Language/Cultural Origin: Native American
Inherent Meaning: From the Valley
Spiritual Connotation: Peaceful
Scripture: John 16:33 NASB
These things I have spoken to you, so that in Me you may have peace. In the world you have tribulation, but take courage; I have overcome the world.

DENAE, Denaé, Denay, Deneé (see also Danae)
Language/Cultural Origin: Hebrew
Inherent Meaning: Vindicated
Spiritual Connotation: Example
Scripture: Ezekiel 39:27 RSV
Through them I have vindicated my holiness in the sight of many nations.

DENHAM, Denhem
Language/Cultural Origin: English

Inherent Meaning: From the Valley Village
Spiritual Connotation: One of Integrity
Scripture: Acts 24:16 NRSV
Therefore I do my best always to have a clear conscience toward God and all people.

DENISE, Danice, Deni, Dení, Denice, Deniece, Dennise
Language/Cultural Origin: French
Inherent Meaning: Favored
Spiritual Connotation: Reborn
Scripture: Isaiah 65:17 NKJV
For behold, I create new heavens and a new earth; and the former shall not be remembered or come to mind.

DENNIS, Dénes, Dennes, Denny
Language/Cultural Origin: Greek
Inherent Meaning: Happy
Spiritual Connotation: Effective
Scripture: Isaiah 55:11 NKJV
So shall My word be that goes forth from My mouth; it shall not return to Me void.

DENTON, Dentin
Language/Cultural Origin: English
Inherent Meaning: From a Happy Home
Spiritual Connotation: Trusting Spirit
Scripture: Romans 8:28 KJV
And we know that all things work together for good to them that love God, to them who are the called according to his purpose.

DENZEL, Danzel, Danzell, Dennzel, Denzell, Denzil
Language/Cultural Origin: English
Inherent Meaning: From Cornwall, England
Spiritual Connotation: Forgiven
Scripture: 1 John 3:20 NKJV
For if our heart condemns us, God is greater than our heart, and knows all things.

DEON, Deion, Deone, Deontée, Deontre, Dion, Diontae, Dionte (see also Dante, Dontae)
Language/Cultural Origin: English
Inherent Meaning: Joyful
Spiritual Connotation: Praise
Scripture: Habakkuk 3:18 NASB
Yet I will exult in the LORD, I will rejoice in the God of my salvation.

DEREK, Darek, Darik, Darrick, Darrik, Dereck, Derikk, Derreck, Derrek, Derric, Derrick, Derrik
Language/Cultural Origin: German
Inherent Meaning: Ruler
Spiritual Connotation: Gifted
Scripture: Ecclesiastes 2:26 NKJV
For God gives wisdom and knowledge and joy to a man who is good in His sight.

DERIKA, Dereka, Derica, Dericka, Derrica, Derrika
Language/Cultural Origin: German
Inherent Meaning: Ruler of the People
Spiritual Connotation: Generous
Scripture: Luke 11:13 TLB
Don't you realize that your heavenly Father will . . . give the Holy Spirit to those who ask for him?

DERON, De-Ron, Deronne, Derronn, Diron, Durron (see also Darius, Daron, Darren)
Language/Cultural Origin: Welsh
Inherent Meaning: Freedom
Spiritual Connotation: Spirit-Filled
Scripture: 2 Corinthians 3:17 NKJV
Now the Lord is the Spirit; and where the Spirit of the Lord is, there is liberty.

DESHAWNA, see Dashawna

DESHAY, Deshae, Deshea
Language/Cultural Origin: American
Inherent Meaning: Courteous
Spiritual Connotation: Kind
Scripture: Psalm 57:10 TLB
Your kindness and love are as vast as the heavens. Your faithfulness is higher than the skies.

DESI, Dési, Dezi
Language/Cultural Origin: French
Inherent Meaning: Longed-For
Spiritual Connotation: Faithful
Scripture: Philippians 4:1 NRSV
Therefore, my brothers and sisters, whom I love and long for, my joy and crown, stand firm in the Lord in this way, my beloved.

DESIREE, Desarae, Desaray, Desaré, Deserae, Deseray, Desirae, Desiray, Desirée, Désirée, Dezirae, Deziree
Language/Cultural Origin: French

Inherent Meaning: Desired
Spiritual Connotation: Likeness of God
Scripture: Isaiah 55:12 NKJV

The mountains and the hills shall break forth into singing before you, and all the trees of the field shall clap their hands.

DESMOND, Des, Desmon, Desmund, Dezmond

Language/Cultural Origin: Irish
Inherent Meaning: Youthful
Spiritual Connotation: Refreshing
Scripture: Ecclesiastes 3:17 NKJV

God shall judge the righteous and the wicked, for there is a time there for every purpose and for every work.

DESTIN, Deston, Destry

Language/Cultural Origin: French
Inherent Meaning: Fate
Spiritual Connotation: Confirmed
Scripture: Isaiah 11:10 NLT

The nations will rally to him, for the land where he lives will be a glorious place.

DESTINY, Destanee, Destanie, Destany, Destinee, Destinée, Destiney, Destinie

Language/Cultural Origin: Old French
Inherent Meaning: Fate
Spiritual Connotation: Fulfilled
Scripture: Psalm 132:14 NASB

This is My resting place forever; here I will dwell, for I have desired it.

DEVA, see Diva

DEVANY, Devaney, Devoney, Devony

Language/Cultural Origin: Gaelic
Inherent Meaning: Dark-Haired
Spiritual Connotation: Sacrifice
Scripture: Romans 12:1 NRSV

I appeal to you therefore, brothers and sisters . . . to present your bodies as a living sacrifice, holy and acceptable to God.

DEVIN, Devan, Deven, Devine, Devyn

Language/Cultural Origin: Irish
Inherent Meaning: Poet
Spiritual Connotation: Seeker of Wisdom
Scripture: Hebrews 13:16 NKJV

But do not forget to do good and to share, for with such sacrifices God is well pleased.

DEVON, Devonlee, Devonleigh, Devonn, Devonne (see also Davon)

Language/Cultural Origin: English
Inherent Meaning: From Devonshire
Spiritual Connotation: Obedient
Scripture: Exodus 19:5 NKJV

Now therefore, if you will indeed obey My voice and keep My covenant, then you shall be a special treasure to Me above all people.

DEWEY, Dewie

Language/Cultural Origin: Welsh
Inherent Meaning: Prized
Spiritual Connotation: Prosperous
Scripture: 3 John 1:2 NLT

Dear friend, I am praying that all is well with you and that your body is as healthy as I know your soul is.

DEXTER, Dextor

Language/Cultural Origin: Latin
Inherent Meaning: Skilled in Workmanship
Spiritual Connotation: Industrious
Scripture: Exodus 31:3 NLT

I have filled him with the Spirit of God, giving him great wisdom, intelligence, and skill in all kinds of crafts.

DIAMOND, Diamonique, Diamonté

Language/Cultural Origin: Latin
Inherent Meaning: Precious Gem
Spiritual Connotation: Carefully Guarded
Scripture: Isaiah 54:12 NCV

I will use rubies to build your walls and shining jewels for the gates and precious jewels for all your outer walls.

DIANA, Daiana, Daianna, Di, Diahann, Dianah, Diandra, Diane, Diann, Dianna, Dianne, Dyan, Dyana, Dyane, Dyann, Dyanna, Dyanne

Language/Cultural Origin: Latin
Inherent Meaning: Divine
Spiritual Connotation: Glorious
Scripture: Psalm 40:5 NKJV

Many, O LORD my God, are Your wonderful works which You have done. . . . They are more than can be numbered.

DIBRI, Díbri

Language/Cultural Origin: Hebrew
Inherent Meaning: God's Promise

Spiritual Connotation: Reverent
Scripture: Psalm 25:14 NASB

The secret of the LORD is for those who fear Him, and He will make them know His covenant.

DICK, Dic, Dickenson, Dickie, Dik, Dikk (see also Richard)
Language/Cultural Origin: English
Inherent Meaning: Powerful Ruler
Spiritual Connotation: Refuge
Scripture: Isaiah 32:2 NASB

And each will be like a refuge from the wind, and a shelter from the storm, like streams of water in a dry country, like the shade of a huge rock in a parched land.

DIEGO, Diaz
Language/Cultural Origin: Spanish
Inherent Meaning: Supplanter
Spiritual Connotation: Wise
Scripture: Proverbs 9:9 NRSV

Give instruction to the wise, and they will become wiser still; teach the righteous and they will gain in learning.

DIETER, Deiter
Language/Cultural Origin: German
Inherent Meaning: Army of the People
Spiritual Connotation: God's Warrior
Scripture: Isaiah 13:3 NASB

I have commanded My consecrated ones, I have even called My mighty warriors, My proudly exulting ones, to execute My anger.

DIETRICH, Dedric, Dedrick, Detrick, Didrik, Diedrick
Language/Cultural Origin: German
Inherent Meaning: Ruler of the People
Spiritual Connotation: Respected
Scripture: Hebrews 13:17 NKJV

Obey those who rule over you, and be submissive, for they watch out for your souls.... Let them do so with joy and not with grief.

DILBERT, Dalbert, Del, Delbert
Language/Cultural Origin: English
Inherent Meaning: Bright as Day
Spiritual Connotation: Obedient
Scripture: Deuteronomy 5:33 NKJV

You shall walk in all the ways which the LORD your God has commanded you ... that you may prolong your days in the land which you shall possess.

DILLON, Dillan, Dillen, Dillin (see also Dylan)
Language/Cultural Origin: Irish
Inherent Meaning: Faithful
Spiritual Connotation: Steadfast in Christ
Scripture: 1 John 3:18 NKJV

My little children, let us not love in word or in tongue, but in deed and in truth.

DIMITRI, Demitré, Demetri, Dimitrie, Dmitri, Dymitri (see also Demetrius)
Language/Cultural Origin: Russian
Inherent Meaning: Immeasurable
Spiritual Connotation: Gracious
Scripture: Jonah 4:2 NLT

I knew that you were a gracious and compassionate God, slow to get angry and filled with unfailing love.

DINAH, Dina, Dyna, Dynah
Language/Cultural Origin: Hebrew
Inherent Meaning: God Has Vindicated
Spiritual Connotation: Righteous
Scripture: 1 John 4:16 NKJV

God is love, and he who abides in love abides in God, and God in him.

DINO, Deeno
Language/Cultural Origin: German
Inherent Meaning: Little Sword
Spiritual Connotation: Covenant
Scripture: 1 Kings 3:14 RSV

And if you will walk in my ways, keeping my statutes and my commandments ... then I will lengthen your days.

DION, see Deon

DIONNE, Deondra, Deonna, Deonne, Dione, Dionna, Dionté, Diontée
Language/Cultural Origin: Greek
Inherent Meaning: Divine Queen
Spiritual Connotation: Promise
Scripture: 2 Peter 1:4 NRSV

Thus he has given us ... his precious and very great promises, so that through them you ... may become participants of the divine nature.

DIOR, Diora, Diore, Diorra
Language/Cultural Origin: French
Inherent Meaning: Golden
Spiritual Connotation: Seeker of Wisdom
Scripture: Colossians 2:3 NLT
In him lie hidden all the treasures of wisdom and knowledge.

DIRK, Derk
Language/Cultural Origin: German
Inherent Meaning: Ruler
Spiritual Connotation: Perceptive Leadership
Scripture: Psalm 91:2 NKJV
I will say of the LORD, He is my refuge and my fortress; my God, in Him I will trust.

DIVA, Deva
Language/Cultural Origin: Indo-Pakistani
Inherent Meaning: Blessed
Spiritual Connotation: Praise
Scripture: Psalm 8:1 NKJV
O LORD, our Lord, how excellent is Your name in all the earth, Who have set Your glory above the heavens!

DIVINA, Divinia
Language/Cultural Origin: English
Inherent Meaning: Beloved
Spiritual Connotation: Humble
Scripture: Galatians 6:14 NKJV
But God forbid that I should boast except in the cross of our Lord Jesus Christ, by whom the world has been crucified to me, and I to the world.

DIXIE, Dixee, Dixi, Dixy
Language/Cultural Origin: French
Inherent Meaning: Tenth
Spiritual Connotation: Blessing
Scripture: 2 Corinthians 4:15 NKJV
For all things are for your sakes, that grace, having spread through the many, may cause thanksgiving to abound to the glory of God.

DIXON, Dickson
Language/Cultural Origin: English
Inherent Meaning: Son of the Ruler
Spiritual Connotation: Youthful Courage
Scripture: Psalm 92:4 NKJV
For You, LORD, have made me glad through Your work; I will triumph in the works of Your hands.

DOLAN, Dolin, Dolyn
Language/Cultural Origin: Irish
Inherent Meaning: Dark-Haired
Spiritual Connotation: Full of Life
Scripture: Psalm 145:10 NKJV
All Your works shall praise You, O LORD, and Your saints shall bless You.

DOLPH, Dolf
Language/Cultural Origin: Slavic
Inherent Meaning: Famous
Spiritual Connotation: Great
Scripture: Ruth 4:14 NASB
Then the women said to Naomi, "Blessed is the LORD who has not left you without a redeemer today."

DOLLY, Dollee, Dolli, Dollie
Language/Cultural Origin: American
Inherent Meaning: Compassionate
Spiritual Connotation: Christlike
Scripture: Psalm 116:5 NASB
Gracious is the LORD, and righteous; yes, our God is compassionate.

DOMINIC, Dom, Domenico, Domenick, Domingo, Dominitric
Language/Cultural Origin: Latin
Inherent Meaning: Belonging to the Lord
Spiritual Connotation: Faithful Disciple
Scripture: John 6:39 NLT
And this is the will of God, that I should not lose even one of all those he has given me, but that I should raise them to eternal life at the last day.

DOMINIQUE, Dominica, Dominika
Language/Cultural Origin: Latin
Inherent Meaning: Belonging to the Lord
Spiritual Connotation: Consecrated
Scripture: Isaiah 58:11 NKJV
The LORD will guide you continually, and satisfy your soul in drought, and strengthen your bones; you shall be like a watered garden.

DONALD, Don, Donn, Donnie, Donny
Language/Cultural Origin: Gaelic
Inherent Meaning: World Leader
Spiritual Connotation: Faithful
Scripture: James 2:22 NKJV
Do you see that faith was working together with his works, and by works faith was made perfect?

DONATA, Donatta

Language/Cultural Origin: Latin
Inherent Meaning: Gift of God
Spiritual Connotation: Contemplative
Scripture: Psalm 25:5 NKJV

Lead me in Your truth and teach me, for You are the God of my salvation; on You I wait all the day.

DONATO, Donatello

Language/Cultural Origin: Italian
Inherent Meaning: Gift of God
Spiritual Connotation: Kind
Scripture: Proverbs 16:24 NKJV

Pleasant words are like a honeycomb, sweetness to the soul and health to the bones.

DONNA, Dona, Doña, Doni, Donia, Donica, Donie, Donika, Donni, Donya (see also Danya, Dawn)

Language/Cultural Origin: Italian
Inherent Meaning: Refined Lady
Spiritual Connotation: Dependent
Scripture: Matthew 4:4 NKJV

Man shall not live by bread alone, but by every word that proceeds from the mouth of God.

DONNELL, Donell, Donelle, Donnel, Donnelle

Language/Cultural Origin: Irish
Inherent Meaning: Brave
Spiritual Connotation: Vigilant
Scripture: 1 Corinthians 16:13 NKJV

Watch, stand fast in the faith, be brave, be strong.

DONOVAN, Donavan, Donavon, Donoven, Donovon

Language/Cultural Origin: Irish
Inherent Meaning: Dark Warrior
Spiritual Connotation: Refreshed
Scripture: Colossians 3:10 NKJV

Put on the new man who is renewed in knowledge according to the image of Him who created him.

DONTAE, Dontai, Dontay, Dontáy, Dontaye, Donté, Dontée

Language/Cultural Origin: American
Inherent Meaning: Presevering
Spiritual Connotation: Steadfast

Scripture: 1 Thessalonians 3:8 TLB

We can bear anything as long as we know that you remain strong in him.

DONYEL, see Daniel

DORA, Doralia, Doralie

Language/Cultural Origin: Greek
Inherent Meaning: Gift of God
Spiritual Connotation: Wise
Scripture: Isaiah 33:6 NKJV

Wisdom and knowledge will be the stability of your times, and the strength of salvation; the fear of the LORD is His treasure.

DORAN, Dorin, Doron, Dorran, Dorren

Language/Cultural Origin: Hebrew
Inherent Meaning: God's Gift
Spiritual Connotation: Sacrifice
Scripture: 1 Corinthians 9:23 NASB

And I do all things for the sake of the gospel, that I may become a fellow partaker of it.

DORCAS

Language/Cultural Origin: Greek
Inherent Meaning: Filled With Grace
Spiritual Connotation: Heir
Scripture: Psalm 37:18 NKJV

The LORD knows the days of the upright, and their inheritance shall be forever.

DOREEN, Dorene, Dorey, Dori, Dorie, Dorri, Dorrie, Dureen

Language/Cultural Origin: Gaelic
Inherent Meaning: Acrimonious
Spiritual Connotation: Peerless
Scripture: Psalm 100:5 NKJV

For the LORD is good; His mercy is everlasting, and His truth endures to all generations.

DORIAN, Doriana, Doriann, Dorianna, Dorien, Dorion, Dorrian, Dorrien

Language/Cultural Origin: Greek
Inherent Meaning: Gift
Spiritual Connotation: Gracious
Scripture: 1 John 3:2 NKJV

Beloved, now we are children of God . . . when He is revealed, we shall be like Him, for we shall see Him as He is.

DORIS, Dorice, Dorise, Dorris
Language/Cultural Origin: Greek
Inherent Meaning: From the Ocean
Spiritual Connotation: Strong
Scripture: Isaiah 33:6 NKJV
Wisdom and knowledge will be the stability of your times, and the strength of salvation; the fear of the LORD is His treasure.

DOROTHEA, Dorotheé, Dorothy, Dottie, Dotti, Dotty
Language/Cultural Origin: Greek
Inherent Meaning: Gift of God
Spiritual Connotation: Blessed
Scripture: Isaiah 52:7 NKJV
How beautiful upon the mountains are the feet of him who brings good news . . . who says to Zion, "your God reigns!"

DOUGLAS, Doug, Douglass
Language/Cultural Origin: Scottish
Inherent Meaning: From the Dark Stream
Spiritual Connotation: Adventurous
Scripture: 1 Corinthians 2:7 NKJV
But we speak the wisdom of God in a mystery, the hidden wisdom which God ordained before the ages for our glory.

DOYLE, Doyal
Language/Cultural Origin: Irish
Inherent Meaning: Dark Stranger
Spiritual Connotation: Guided by the Spirit
Scripture: 2 Corinthians 3:17 NKJV
Now the Lord is the Spirit; and where the Spirit of the Lord is, there is liberty.

DRAKE, Drago
Language/Cultural Origin: Latin
Inherent Meaning: Dragon
Spiritual Connotation: Symbol
Scripture: Psalm 104:25 NKJV
[In] this great and wide sea . . . the ships sail about; there is that Leviathan which You have made to play there.

DREW, Drewe, Dru, Drue
Language/Cultural Origin: Welsh
Inherent Meaning: Wise
Spiritual Connotation: Esteemed
Scripture: Romans 12:10 NKJV
Be kindly affectionate to one another with brotherly love, in honor giving preference to one another.

DRISANA, Drisanna
Language/Cultural Origin: Sanskrit
Inherent Meaning: Daughter of the Sun
Spiritual Connotation: Loyal
Scripture: Ruth 1:16 NLT
I will go wherever you go and live wherever you live. Your people will be my people, and your God will be my God.

DRUSILLA, Drucilla, Druscilla
Language/Cultural Origin: Latin
Inherent Meaning: Strong
Spiritual Connotation: Strong in Spirit
Scripture: John 15:7 NKJV
If you abide in Me, and My words abide in you, you will ask what you desire, and it shall be done for you.

DRYDEN, Drieden
Language/Cultural Origin: English
Inherent Meaning: From the Arid Valley
Spiritual Connotation: Trusting
Scripture: Proverbs 3:5–6 NKJV
Trust in the LORD with all your heart, and lean not on your own understanding; in all your ways acknowledge Him, and He shall direct your paths.

DUANA, Duanna
Language/Cultural Origin: Irish
Inherent Meaning: Cheerful Song
Spiritual Connotation: Harmonious
Scripture: Psalm 92:4 NKJV
For You, LORD, have made me glad through Your work; I will triumph in the works of Your hands.

DUANE, see Dwayne

DUDLEY, Dudly
Language/Cultural Origin: English
Inherent Meaning: From the Common Field
Spiritual Connotation: Free in Christ
Scripture: John 8:32 KJV
And ye shall know the truth, and the truth shall make you free.

DUGAN, Doogan, Duggan
Language/Cultural Origin: Scottish
Inherent Meaning: Dark
Spiritual Connotation: Gifted
Scripture: Psalm 150:4 NCV

Praise him with tambourines and dancing; praise him with stringed instruments and flutes.

DULCINEA, Dulcia, Dulciana, Dulcie

Language/Cultural Origin: Spanish
Inherent Meaning: Sweet
Spiritual Connotation: Delights in God's Grace
Scripture: Psalm 37:5 NKJV

Commit your way to the LORD, trust also in Him, and He shall bring it to pass.

DUNCAN, Duncon

Language/Cultural Origin: Scottish
Inherent Meaning: Steadfast Warrior
Spiritual Connotation: Strong in Faith
Scripture: Romans 10:8 NKJV

The word is near you, in your mouth and in your heart.

DUNSTAN, Dunsten

Language/Cultural Origin: English
Inherent Meaning: From the Stony Hill
Spiritual Connotation: Victorious
Scripture: John 5:26 NKJV

For as the Father has life in Himself, so He has granted the Son to have life in Himself.

DURANT, Durand, Durante, Durrant

Language/Cultural Origin: Latin
Inherent Meaning: Enduring
Spiritual Connotation: Protected
Scripture: Psalm 34:7 NKJV

The angel of the LORD encamps all around those who fear Him, and delivers them.

DUSTIN, Dustan, Dusten, Duston, Dusty, Dustyn

Language/Cultural Origin: German
Inherent Meaning: Valiant Warrior
Spiritual Connotation: Brave
Scripture: Acts 27:22 NLT

But take courage! None of you will lose your lives, even though the ship will go down.

DUSYA, Dusyanna

Language/Cultural Origin: Russian
Inherent Meaning: Hope
Spiritual Connotation: Steadfast
Scripture: Hebrews 3:6 NRSV

Christ, however, was faithful over God's house as a son, and we are his house if we hold firm the confidence and the pride that belong to hope.

DWAYNE, DeWayne, Duaine, Duane, Dwane

Language/Cultural Origin: Irish
Inherent Meaning: Dark
Spiritual Connotation: Transformed Heart
Scripture: Job 22:28 NKJV

You will also declare a thing, and it will be established for you; so light will shine on your ways.

DWIGHT, Dwieght

Language/Cultural Origin: English
Inherent Meaning: Fair
Spiritual Connotation: Diligent Leader
Scripture: Psalm 91:1 NKJV

He who dwells in the secret place of the Most High shall abide under the shadow of the Almighty.

DYLAN, Dyllan, Dyllon, Dylon (see also Dillon)

Language/Cultural Origin: Welsh
Inherent Meaning: From the Sea
Spiritual Connotation: Resolute Courage
Scripture: Deuteronomy 20:4 NKJV

The LORD your God is He who goes with you, to fight for you against your enemies, to save you.

DYLANA, Dylanna

Language/Cultural Origin: Welsh
Inherent Meaning: From the Sea
Spiritual Connotation: Devoted
Scripture: John 21:7 NASB

And so when Simon Peter heard that it was the Lord, he put his outer garment on . . . and threw himself into the sea.

I am the light of the world. Whoever follows me will never walk in darkness but will have the light of life.

EAGAN, see Egan

EAN, see Ian

EARL, Earle
Language/Cultural Origin: English
Inherent Meaning: Noble
Spiritual Connotation: Reflected Image
Scripture: Genesis 1:26 NKJV
Let Us make man in Our image, according to Our likeness.

EASTER, Eastre
Language/Cultural Origin: Old German
Inherent Meaning: Spring Festival
Spiritual Connotation: Celebration
Scripture: Matthew 28:6 NASB
He is not here, for He has risen, just as He said.

EASTON, Eason
Language/Cultural Origin: English
Inherent Meaning: From the Eastern Town
Spiritual Connotation: Christlike
Scripture: 2 Corinthians 4:6 NASB
Light shall shine out of darkness . . . to give the light of the knowledge of the glory of God in the face of Christ.

EBONY, Ebanee, Ebany, Ebonee, Eboney, Eboni, Ebonie
Language/Cultural Origin: American
Inherent Meaning: Hard, Dark Wood
Spiritual Connotation: Shining
Scripture: John 8:12 NRSV

ECHO, Ecko, Ekko
Language/Cultural Origin: Greek
Inherent Meaning: Repeated Sound
Spiritual Connotation: Constant Prayer
Scripture: 1 Thessalonians 5:17 NASB
Pray without ceasing; in everything give thanks; for this is God's will for you in Christ Jesus.

EDA, Edah
Language/Cultural Origin: Irish
Inherent Meaning: Loyal
Spiritual Connotation: Faithful
Scripture: Psalm 77:14 NKJV
You are the God who does wonders; You have declared Your strength among the peoples.

EDANA, Edanna, Edena
Language/Cultural Origin: Irish
Inherent Meaning: Ardent Flame
Spiritual Connotation: Unending Love
Scripture: Song of Songs 8:6 RSV
Set me as a seal upon your heart, as a seal upon your arm; for love is strong as death.

EDEN, Eaden, Eadin, Edin, Edyn
Language/Cultural Origin: Hebrew
Inherent Meaning: Delightful
Spiritual Connotation: Pleasing
Scripture: Zephaniah 3:17 NKJV
The LORD your God in your midst, the Mighty One, will save; He will rejoice over you with gladness, He will quiet you with His love.

EDGAR, Ed
Language/Cultural Origin: English
Inherent Meaning: Prosperous
Spiritual Connotation: Gifted
Scripture: 1 Corinthians 12:4 NKJV
There are diversities of gifts, but the same Spirit.

EDIE, Eadie, Edy, Eydie
Language/Cultural Origin: English
Inherent Meaning: Wealthy
Spiritual Connotation: Obedient
Scripture: 1 Kings 2:3 TLB
Obey the laws of God and follow all his ways;

keep each of his commands written in the law of Moses so that you will prosper in everything you do.

EDITH, Edythe

Language/Cultural Origin: Old English
Inherent Meaning: Valuable Gift
Spiritual Connotation: Wise
Scripture: Proverbs 3:15 RSV
She is more precious than jewels, and nothing you desire can compare with her.

EDMUND, Edmon, Edmond, Edmonde, Esmond

Language/Cultural Origin: Old English
Inherent Meaning: Blessed Peace
Spiritual Connotation: Prosperous Protector
Scripture: John 14:27 NKJV
Peace I leave with you, My peace I give to you; not as the world gives do I give to you. Let not your heart be troubled, neither let it be afraid.

EDNA, Ednah

Language/Cultural Origin: Hebrew
Inherent Meaning: Rejuvenated
Spiritual Connotation: Filled With Pleasure
Scripture: John 3:6 NASB
That which is born of the flesh is flesh, and that which is born of the Spirit is spirit.

EDOM

☞Language/Cultural Origin: Hebrew
Inherent Meaning: Red Earth
Spiritual Connotation: Strong
Scripture: Genesis 36:8 NCV
So Esau lived in the mountains of Edom. (Esau is also named Edom.)

EDRIC, Eddrick, Ederick, Edrick

Language/Cultural Origin: Old English
Inherent Meaning: Powerful With Property
Spiritual Connotation: Blessed
Scripture: Deuteronomy 30:9 RSV
The LORD your God will make you abundantly prosperous in all the work of your hand.

EDWARD, Ed, Eddie, Eddy, Eduardo, Edwardo, Edwards

Language/Cultural Origin: Old English
Inherent Meaning: Appointed to Protect
Spiritual Connotation: Guardian of Happiness
Scripture: John 14:13 NKJV

And whatever you ask in My name, that I will do, that the Father may be glorified in the Son.

EDWIN, Edwyn, Edwina

Language/Cultural Origin: Old English
Inherent Meaning: Prosperous Friend
Spiritual Connotation: Belonging to God
Scripture: John 17:10 NKJV
And all Mine are Yours, and Yours are Mine, and I am glorified in them.

EGAN, Eagan, Egann, Egen

Language/Cultural Origin: Irish
Inherent Meaning: Ardent
Spiritual Connotation: Filled With Zeal
Scripture: Psalm 69:9 NLT
Passion for your house burns within me, so those who insult you are also insulting me.

EILEEN, Eilean, Eilene, Eilleen (see also Aileen)

Language/Cultural Origin: English
Inherent Meaning: Bright Light
Spiritual Connotation: Glorious
Scripture: Psalm 23:6 KJV
Surely goodness and mercy shall follow me all the days of my life: and I will dwell in the house of the LORD for ever.

EINAR, Ejnar

Language/Cultural Origin: Old Norse
Inherent Meaning: Individualist
Spiritual Connotation: Free
Scripture: Galatians 5:1 NASB
It was for freedom that Christ set us free; therefore keep standing firm and do not be subject again to a yoke of slavery.

EIRA, Eirah

Language/Cultural Origin: Welsh
Inherent Meaning: Snow
Spiritual Connotation: Pure
Scripture: Psalm 51:7 NLT
Purify me from my sins, and I will be clean; wash me, and I will be whiter than snow.

ELADAH, Eilada, Eláda, Elahdah

☞Language/Cultural Origin: Hebrew
Inherent Meaning: Adorned of God
Spiritual Connotation: Lovely
Scripture: Psalm 45:11 NCV
The king loves your beauty. Because he is your master, you should obey him.

EIRENA, Eirana, Eiranna, Eirenna
Language/Cultural Origin: English
Inherent Meaning: Peace
Spiritual Connotation: Contentment
Scripture: Psalm 119:165 NASB
Those who love Your law have great peace, and nothing causes them to stumble.

ELAINE, Elain, Elane, Elayne, Eliane
Language/Cultural Origin: Old French
Inherent Meaning: Brilliant
Spiritual Connotation: Admirable
Scripture: Psalm 84:11 NKJV
For the LORD God is a sun and shield; the LORD will give grace and glory; no good thing will He withhold from those who walk uprightly.

ELAN, Elann
Language/Cultural Origin: Native American
Inherent Meaning: Friendly
Spiritual Connotation: Servant
Scripture: John 15:13 NKJV
Greater love has no one than this, than to lay down one's life for his friends.

ELANA, Elaina, Elainna, Elani, Elania, Elanna
Language/Cultural Origin: English
Inherent Meaning: Shining
Spiritual Connotation: Standard
Scripture: Isaiah 60:3 NCV
Nations will come to your light; kings will come to the brightness of your sunrise.

ELASAH, Elasa, Elása, Elasia, Elasya
☞ Language/Cultural Origin: Hebrew
Inherent Meaning: God Has Created
Spiritual Connotation: Image of God
Scripture: Genesis 5:2 NKJV
He created them male and female, and blessed them and called them Mankind in the day they were created.

ELDEN, Eldin
Language/Cultural Origin: Old English
Inherent Meaning: Wise Guardian
Spiritual Connotation: Good Judgment
Scripture: Hebrews 13:20 NKJV
Now may the God of peace who brought up our Lord Jesus from the dead . . . make you complete in every good work to do His will.

ELDON, Elldon
Language/Cultural Origin: English
Inherent Meaning: From the Holy Hill
Spiritual Connotation: Enlightened
Scripture: Isaiah 30:29 NKJV
You shall have a song as in the night when a holy festival is kept, and gladness of heart.

ELDRED, Eldrid
Language/Cultural Origin: Old English
Inherent Meaning: Elderly Counsel
Spiritual Connotation: Friend of God
Scripture: 1 John 2:13 NRSV
I am writing to you, fathers, because you know him who is from the beginning. I am writing to you, young people, because you have conquered the evil one.

ELDRIDGE, Eldredge
Language/Cultural Origin: German
Inherent Meaning: Mature Counselor
Spiritual Connotation: Godly
Scripture: Romans 12:2 NKJV
And do not be conformed to this world, but be transformed by the renewing of your mind.

ELEANOR, Eleanore, Elinor, Ellenora, Elynora
Language/Cultural Origin: Greek
Inherent Meaning: Bright as the Sun
Spiritual Connotation: Kindhearted
Scripture: Ephesians 4:32 NKJV
And be kind to one another, tenderhearted, forgiving one another, just as God in Christ forgave you.

ELEAZAR, Eléazar, Eliazar
☞ Language/Cultural Origin: Hebrew
Inherent Meaning: God Has Helped
Spiritual Connotation: Set Apart
Scripture: Numbers 4:16 NCV
Eleazar son of Aaron, the priest, will be responsible for the Holy Tent and for everything in it, for all the holy things.

ELECTRA, Elektra
Language/Cultural Origin: Greek
Inherent Meaning: Brilliant
Spiritual Connotation: Eternal Hope
Scripture: Isaiah 60:19 NRSV
The sun shall no longer be your light by day . . . but the LORD will be your everlasting light, and your God will be your glory.

ELENA, Eleena, Elina, Ellena
Language/Cultural Origin: Russian
Inherent Meaning: Radiant
Spiritual Connotation: Illuminated
Scripture: Psalm 16:11 NKJV
> You will show me the path of life; in Your presence is fullness of joy; at Your right hand are pleasures forevermore.

ELGIN, Elgen
Language/Cultural Origin: English
Inherent Meaning: Noble
Spiritual Connotation: Responsible
Scripture: Ezra 10:4 NASB
> Arise! For this matter is your responsibility, but we will be with you; be courageous and act.

ELI, Ely
☞ Language/Cultural Origin: Hebrew
Inherent Meaning: Uplifted
Spiritual Connotation: Delivered
Scripture: Psalm 50:15 NKJV
> Call upon Me in the day of trouble; I will deliver you, and you shall glorify Me.

ELIAB
☞ Language/Cultural Origin: Hebrew
Inherent Meaning: God Is My Father
Spiritual Connotation: God's Child
Scripture: Exodus 3:6 NCV
> I am the God of your ancestors—the God of Abraham, the God of Isaac, and the God of Jacob.

ELIADA, Eliadah, Elliada, Elyada
☞ Language/Cultural Origin: Hebrew
Inherent Meaning: God Knows
Spiritual Connotation: Revealed
Scripture: Luke 16:15 NKJV
> You are those who justify yourselves before men, but God knows your hearts.

ELIAH, Eliyah
☞ Language/Cultural Origin: Hebrew
Inherent Meaning: The Lord Is God
Spiritual Connotation: Believer
Scripture: Deuteronomy 4:39 NCV
> Know and believe today that the LORD is God. He is God in heaven above and on the earth below. There is no other god!

ELIANA, Elianna, Ellianna
(see also Iliana, Liana)
Language/Cultural Origin: Hebrew
Inherent Meaning: God Has Answered Me
Spiritual Connotation: Fulfilled Promise
Scripture: 1 Samuel 1:20 NKJV
> Hannah conceived and bore a son, and called his name Samuel, saying, "Because I have asked for him from the LORD."

ELIAS, Ellis
☞ Language/Cultural Origin: Greek
Inherent Meaning: God Is My Salvation
Spiritual Connotation: Mouthpeice of God
Scripture: Luke 12:11 NKJV
> Do not worry about how or what you should answer, or what you should say. For the Holy Spirit will teach you in that very hour what you ought to say.

ELIJAH, Elija, Eliyahu
☞ Language/Cultural Origin: Hebrew
Inherent Meaning: The Lord Is My God
Spiritual Connotation: Spiritual Champion
Scripture: Proverbs 3:6 KJV
> In all thy ways acknowledge him, and he shall direct thy paths.

ELIORA, Eliaura, Eliorra, Eliyora
Language/Cultural Origin: Hebrew
Inherent Meaning: My God Is Light
Spiritual Connotation: Beloved
Scripture: Isaiah 12:2 NRSV
> Surely God is my salvation; I will trust, and will not be afraid, for the LORD GOD is my strength and my might; he has become my salvation.

ELISE, Élise, Elisse, Ellice, Ellise, Ellyce, Ellyse, Elyce, Elyse
Language/Cultural Origin: French
Inherent Meaning: Oath of God
Spiritual Connotation: Dedicated
Scripture: Acts 11:23 NRSV
> When he came and saw the grace of God, he rejoiced, and he exhorted them all to remain faithful to the Lord with steadfast devotion.

ELISHA, Elishah, Elishia, Elishua
☞ Language/Cultural Origin: Hebrew
Inherent Meaning: God Will Save Me
Spiritual Connotation: Protected
Scripture: Psalm 62:7 TLB

My protection and success come from God alone. He is my refuge, a Rock where no enemy can reach me.

ELISSA, Elisia, Ellisa, Ellissa, Ellisia, Ellyssa, Elysa, Elyssa (see also Alisa, Elysia, Lissa)
Language/Cultural Origin: Italian
Inherent Meaning: Oath of God
Spiritual Connotation: Devoted
Scripture: Psalm 89:1 NRSV
I will sing of your steadfast love, O LORD, forever; with my mouth I will proclaim your faithfulness to all generations.

ELIZA, Aliza, Elizah
Language/Cultural Origin: Polish
Inherent Meaning: Oath of God
Spiritual Connotation: Pledged
Scripture: 2 Corinthians 11:2 NLT
I am jealous for you with the jealousy of God himself. For I promised you as a pure bride to one husband, Christ.

ELIZABETH, Elisabeth, Elisabethe
☞ Language/Cultural Origin: Hebrew
Inherent Meaning: Oath of God
Spiritual Connotation: Consecrated
Scripture: Romans 6:23 NKJV
But the gift of God is eternal life in Christ Jesus our Lord.

ELKANAH, Elkana
☞ Language/Cultural Origin: Hebrew
Inherent Meaning: God Is Jealous
Spiritual Connotation: Pure
Scripture: Deuteronomy 5:9 NLT
You must never worship or bow down to them, for I, the LORD your God, am a jealous God who will not share your affection with any other god!

ELKE, Elki
Language/Cultural Origin: German
Inherent Meaning: Nobility
Spiritual Connotation: Approved
Scripture: 1 Thessalonians 2:4 NLT
For we speak as messengers who have been approved by God to be entrusted with the Good News.

ELLA, Ellah
Language/Cultural Origin: Old German

Inherent Meaning: Beautiful
Spiritual Connotation: Sustained
Scripture: Psalm 91:11 KJV
For he shall give his angels charge over thee, to keep thee in all thy ways.

ELLEN, Elen, Ellan, Ellin
Language/Cultural Origin: English
Inherent Meaning: Bright
Spiritual Connotation: Heir
Scripture: Matthew 4:16 NKJV
The people who sat in darkness have seen a great light, and upon those who sat in the region and shadow of death Light has dawned.

ELLIE, Elie, Elli
Language/Cultural Origin: Estonian
Inherent Meaning: Illuminated
Spiritual Connotation: Shining Light
Scripture: Luke 11:36 TLB
If you are filled with light within, with no dark corners, then your face will be radiant too, as though a floodlight is beamed upon you.

ELLERY, Elleree, Ellerey
Language/Cultural Origin: English
Inherent Meaning: From Elder Tree Island
Spiritual Connotation: Creative Worker
Scripture: Psalm 31:23 NKJV
Oh, love the LORD, all you His saints! For the LORD preserves the faithful, and fully repays the proud person.

ELLIOT, Eliot, Eliott, Elliott
Language/Cultural Origin: Hebrew
Inherent Meaning: The Lord Is My God
Spiritual Connotation: Consecrated
Scripture: Isaiah 51:16 NASB
And I have put My words in your mouth, and have covered you with the shadow of My hand. . . . You are My people.

ELLIS, see Elias

ELLISON, Elison, Ellyson
Language/Cultural Origin: English
Inherent Meaning: Son of the Redeemed One
Spiritual Connotation: Near to God's Heart
Scripture: Psalm 32:7 NASB
You are my hiding place; You preserve me from trouble; You surround me with songs of deliverance.

ELMER, Ellmer
Language/Cultural Origin: Old English
Inherent Meaning: Famous
Spiritual Connotation: Trusting
Scripture: Psalm 36:7 NKJV
> How precious is Your lovingkindness, O God! Therefore the children of men put their trust under the shadow of Your wings.

ELMO, Almo
Language/Cultural Origin: Latin
Inherent Meaning: Vigilant
Spiritual Connotation: Secure
Scripture: John 14:1 NKJV
> Let not your heart be troubled; you believe in God, believe also in Me.

ELOISE
Language/Cultural Origin: Old German
Inherent Meaning: Wise
Spiritual Connotation: Sustained
Scripture: Psalms 121:5 NKJV
> The LORD is your keeper; the LORD is your shade at your right hand.

ELROY
Language/Cultural Origin: Latin
Inherent Meaning: Majestic
Spiritual Connotation: Noble
Scripture: Proverbs 17:24 NKJV
> Wisdom is in the sight of him who has understanding, but the eyes of a fool are on the ends of the earth.

ELSA, Ellsa
Language/Cultural Origin: Swedish
Inherent Meaning: Royal
Spiritual Connotation: Honorable
Scripture: Philippians 4:8 RSV
> Finally, brethren, whatever is true, . . . honorable, . . . just, whatever is pure, . . . lovely, . . . gracious, if there is any excellence, . . . [or] anything worthy of praise, think about these things.

ELSIE, Ellsey, Ellsie, Elsi, Elsy
Language/Cultural Origin: German
Inherent Meaning: Noble
Spiritual Connotation: Priceless Friend
Scripture: John 15:13 NKJV
> Greater love has no one than this, than to lay down one's life for his friends.

ELSTON, Ellston
Language/Cultural Origin: Old English
Inherent Meaning: From the Old Farm
Spiritual Connotation: Believer
Scripture: John 11:25 NKJV
> He who believes in Me, though he may die, he shall live.

ELTON, Alten, Alton, Ellton
Language/Cultural Origin: English
Inherent Meaning: From the Old Town
Spiritual Connotation: Steadfast
Scripture: Hebrews 4:14 NKJV
> Seeing then that we have a great High Priest who has passed through the heavens, Jesus the Son of God, let us hold fast our confession.

ELVA, Elvia (see also Alva)
Language/Cultural Origin: Old English
Inherent Meaning: Delicate
Spiritual Connotation: Enlightened
Scripture: Psalm 54:2 NKJV
> Hear my prayer, O God; Give ear to the words of my mouth.

ELVIN, Elvyn (see also Alvin)
Language/Cultural Origin: Old English
Inherent Meaning: Friend of All
Spiritual Connotation: Joyous
Scripture: Matthew 9:15 NKJV
> Can the friends of the bridegroom mourn as long as the bridegroom is with them?

ELVIRA, Elvera
Language/Cultural Origin: Spanish
Inherent Meaning: Fair
Spiritual Connotation: Wise
Scripture: James 3:17 NKJV
> But the wisdom that is from above is first pure, then peaceable, gentle, . . . [and] without partiality and without hypocrisy.

ELVIS, Elvys
Language/Cultural Origin: Old Norse
Inherent Meaning: All-Wise
Spiritual Connotation: Righteous
Scripture: Isaiah 58:8 NKJV
> Then your light shall break forth like the morning, your healing shall spring forth speedily, and your righteousness shall go before you.

ELYA, Elja, Elyah (see also Ilya)
Language/Cultural Origin: Hebrew
Inherent Meaning: The Lord Is My God
Spiritual Connotation: Filled With Praise
Scripture: Exodus 15:2 RSV
The LORD is my strength and my song, and he has become my salvation; this is my God, and I will praise him, my father's God, and I will exalt him.

ELYNN, Elinn, Elyne, Ellynn
Language/Cultural Origin: American
Inherent Meaning: Clear Pool
Spiritual Connotation: Cleansed
Scripture: Hebrews 10:22 NCV
We have been made free from a guilty conscience, and our bodies have been washed with pure water.

ELYSIA (see also Alisa, Elissa, Lissa)
Language/Cultural Origin: Latin
Inherent Meaning: Sweetly Blissful
Spiritual Connotation: Strong Faith
Scripture: Matthew 17:20 NKJV
If you have faith as a mustard seed, you will say to this mountain, Move from here to there, and it will move; and nothing will be impossible for you.

EMANUEL, Emanual, Emanuell, ☞Emmanuel, Immanuel
Language/Cultural Origin: Hebrew
Inherent Meaning: God With Us
Spiritual Connotation: Gift of God
Scripture: John 3:16 NKJV
For God so loved the world that He gave His only begotten Son, that whoever believes in Him should not perish but have everlasting life.

EMANUELA, Emmanuella, Emmanuelle, Imanuela
Language/Cultural Origin: Hebrew
Inherent Meaning: God With Us
Spiritual Connotation: Gift of God
Scripture: Isaiah 7:14 NKJV
Therefore the Lord Himself will give you a sign: Behold, the virgin shall conceive and bear a Son, and shall call His name Immanuel.

EMBER, Embur (see also Amber)
Language/Cultural Origin: Old English
Inherent Meaning: Ashes
Spiritual Connotation: Confirmed Faith
Scripture: Acts 10:40 NASB
God raised Him up on the third day, and granted that He should become visible.

EMELIA, Amilia, Emalia, Emilia (see also Amelia, Emily)
Language/Cultural Origin: Latin
Inherent Meaning: Industrious
Spiritual Connotation: Blessed
Scripture: Zephaniah 3:17 NKJV
The LORD your God in your midst, the Mighty One, will save; He will rejoice over you with gladness.

EMERALD, Emeralde
Language/Cultural Origin: French
Inherent Meaning: Green Gem
Spiritual Connotation: Breathtaking
Scripture: Revelation 4:3 NCV
The One who sat on the throne looked like precious stones.... All around the throne was a rainbow the color of an emerald.

EMERSON, Emmerson
Language/Cultural Origin: English
Inherent Meaning: Son of the Leader
Spiritual Connotation: Victorious
Scripture: Psalm 20:5 RSV
May we shout for joy over your victory, and in the name of our God set up our banners! May the LORD fulfil all your petitions!

EMERY, Emeri, Emmery, Emmory, Emory (see also Amery, Emre)
Language/Cultural Origin: German
Inherent Meaning: Industrious Leader
Spiritual Connotation: Authority Under God
Scripture: Proverbs 29:2 NKJV
When the righteous are in authority, the people rejoice.

EMIL, Emill
Language/Cultural Origin: German
Inherent Meaning: Industrious
Spiritual Connotation: Diligent Seeker
Scripture: Jeremiah 29:12 NKJV
Then you will call upon Me and go and pray to Me, and I will listen to you. And you will seek Me and find Me, when you search for Me with all your heart.

EMILIAN, Emille, Emillé, Emils
Language/Cultural Origin: Polish
Inherent Meaning: Eager
Spiritual Connotation: Purified
Scripture: 2 Corinthians 7:11 NRSV
For see what earnestness this godly grief has produced in you. . . . At every point you have proved yourselves guiltless in the matter.

EMILIO, Emillio
Language/Cultural Origin: Italian
Inherent Meaning: Glorifier
Spiritual Connotation: Obedient
Scripture: Isaiah 26:8 NLT
LORD, we love to obey your laws; our heart's desire is to glorify your name.

EMILY, Emalee, Emelie, Emile, Emilee, Emiley, Emilie, Emillie, Emilly, Emmélie, Emylee (see also Amelia, Emelia)
Language/Cultural Origin: German
Inherent Meaning: Industrious
Spiritual Connotation: Diligent Worker
Scripture: Matthew 5:16 NKJV
Let your light so shine before men, that they may see your good works and glorify your Father in heaven.

EMILIANNA, Emiliana, Emiliann, Emilianne, Emilyann, Emilyanne
Language/Cultural Origin: American
Inherent Meaning: Gracious
Spiritual Connotation: Thoughtful
Scripture: Ruth 3:10 NKJV
Blessed are you of the LORD, my daughter! For you have shown more kindness at the end than at the beginning.

EMMA, Ema
Language/Cultural Origin: Old German
Inherent Meaning: All-Embracing
Spiritual Connotation: Absolute Faith
Scripture: Mark 11:24 NKJV
Therefore I say to you, whatever things you ask when you pray, believe that you receive them, and you will have them.

EMMET, Emitt, Emmett, Emmit, Emmitt, Emmot, Emmott
Language/Cultural Origin: Old English
Inherent Meaning: Earnest

Spiritual Connotation: Genuine Devotion
Scripture: Philippians 4:4 NKJV
Rejoice in the Lord always. Again I will say, rejoice!

EMMY, Emee, Emi, Emmi, Emmie
Language/Cultural Origin: English
Inherent Meaning: Striving
Spiritual Connotation: Attentive
Scripture: Hebrews 2:1 NRSV
Therefore we must pay greater attention to what we have heard, so that we do not drift away from it.

EMRE, Emra, Emrah, Emree (see also Amery, Emery)
Language/Cultural Origin: Turkish
Inherent Meaning: Brother
Spiritual Connotation: God's Servant
Scripture: Mark 3:35 NKJV
For whoever does the will of God is My brother and My sister and mother.

ENID, Ennid
Language/Cultural Origin: Welsh
Inherent Meaning: Soul of Life
Spiritual Connotation: Obedient
Scripture: Hebrews 5:9 NASB
And having been made perfect, He became to all those who obey Him the source of eternal salvation.

ENNIS, Enis (see also Innes)
Language/Cultural Origin: Irish
Inherent Meaning: Chosen
Spiritual Connotation: Enduring
Scripture: Psalm 51:12 NRSV
Restore to me the joy of your salvation, and sustain in me a willing spirit.

ENOCH, Enoc, Enock
Language/Cultural Origin: Hebrew
Inherent Meaning: Consecrated
Spiritual Connotation: Dedicated to God
Scripture: Exodus 32:29 NKJV
Consecrate yourselves today to the LORD, that He may bestow on you a blessing this day, for every man has opposed his son and his brother.

ENOS, Enosh
Language/Cultural Origin: Hebrew
Inherent Meaning: Man

Spiritual Connotation: Expectant
Scripture: Jude 1:20 NCV
But dear friends, use your most holy faith to build yourselves up, praying in the Holy Spirit.

ENRICA, Enrikka
Language/Cultural Origin: French
Inherent Meaning: Home Ruler
Spiritual Connotation: Righteous
Scripture: Psalm 33:5 NKJV
He loves righteousness and justice; the earth is full of the goodness of the LORD.

ENRIQUE, Enrico, Enrikos, Enriqué
Language/Cultural Origin: Spanish
Inherent Meaning: Head of the Home
Spiritual Connotation: Servant
Scripture: Matthew 24:46 NKJV
Blessed is that servant whom his master, when he comes, will find so doing.

ENYA, Eina, Einya, Enyah
Language/Cultural Origin: Hebrew
Inherent Meaning: God's Eye
Spiritual Connotation: Beloved
Scripture: Psalm 17:8 NKJV
Keep me as the apple of Your eye; hide me under the shadow of Your wings.

EPHRAIM, Efraim, Efrayim, Ephrem
Language/Cultural Origin: Hebrew
Inherent Meaning: Fruitful
Spiritual Connotation: Prosperous
Scripture: John 6:35 NKJV
I am the bread of life. He who comes to Me shall never hunger, and he who believes in Me shall never thirst.

EPHRON
Language/Cultural Origin: Hebrew
Inherent Meaning: Strong
Spiritual Connotation: Thankful
Scripture: Psalm 21:13 RSV
Be exalted, O LORD, in thy strength! We will sing and praise thy power.

ERASMUS
Language/Cultural Origin: Greek
Inherent Meaning: Lovable
Spiritual Connotation: Endearing
Scripture: Psalm 116:15 NKJV
Precious in the sight of the LORD is the death of His saints.

ERHARD, Erhardt, Erhart
Language/Cultural Origin: German
Inherent Meaning: Resolute
Spiritual Connotation: Efficient
Scripture: Job 14:5 NCV
Our time is limited. You have given us only so many months to live and have set limits we cannot go beyond.

ERIC, Aric, Arik, Arick, Arrict, Erek, Erich, Erick, Erik, Ériq, Erric, Errick, Errict, Eryk
Language/Cultural Origin: Old Norse
Inherent Meaning: Powerful
Spiritual Connotation: Unifier
Scripture: John 13:34 NKJV
A new commandment I give to you, that you love one another; as I have loved you, that you also love one another.

ERICA, Arica, Aricka, Arika, Arikka, Ericca, Ericka, Erika, Erikka, Errica, Errika, Eryka, Erykka
Language/Cultural Origin: Old Norse
Inherent Meaning: Brave
Spiritual Connotation: Victorious
Scripture: Isaiah 60:1 NKJV
Arise, shine; for your light has come! And the glory of the LORD is risen upon you.

ERIN, Erine, Erinn, Erinne, Errin, Eryn, Erynn, Erynne (see also Arin)
Language/Cultural Origin: Irish
Inherent Meaning: Bringer of Peace
Spiritual Connotation: Benevolent
Scripture: Psalm 121:8 NKJV
The LORD shall preserve your going out and your coming in from this time forth, and even forevermore.

ERNEST, Ernesto, Ernie, Ernst
Language/Cultural Origin: English
Inherent Meaning: Sincere
Spiritual Connotation: Free in Spirit
Scripture: John 8:31 NKJV
If you abide in My word, you are My disciples indeed. And you shall know the truth, and the truth shall make you free.

ERROL, Erol, Erroll, Erryl
Language/Cultural Origin: Turkish
Inherent Meaning: Courageous

Spiritual Connotation: God's Messanger
Scripture: Acts 23:11 RSV
Take courage, for as you have testified about me at Jerusalem, so you must bear witness also at Rome.

ERVING, see Irving

ERWIN, see Irwin

ESAU, Esaw
🖙 Language/Cultural Origin: Hebrew
Inherent Meaning: Hairy
Spiritual Connotation: Strength
Scripture: Genesis 25:25 NASB
Now the first came forth red, all over like a hairy garment; and they named him Esau.

ESDRAS, Ezdras
Language/Cultural Origin: French
Inherent Meaning: Help
Spiritual Connotation: Supported
Scripture: Psalm 121:2 RSV
My help comes from the LORD, who made heaven and earth.

ESHBAN, Eshbán
🖙 Language/Cultural Origin: Hebrew
Inherent Meaning: Man of Understanding
Spiritual Connotation: Wise
Scripture: Proverbs 15:21 NCV
A person without wisdom enjoys being foolish, but someone with understanding does what is right.

ESHTON, Eshtonn
🖙 Language/Cultural Origin: Hebrew
Inherent Meaning: Rest
Spiritual Connotation: Humble
Scripture: Matthew 11:28 NLT
Come to me, all of you who are weary and carry heavy burdens, and I will give you rest.

ESMÉ, Esme, Esmée
Language/Cultural Origin: French
Inherent Meaning: Overcomer
Spiritual Connotation: Victor
Scripture: Romans 8:37 NRSV
No, in all these things we are more than conquerors through him who loved us.

ESMERALDA, Esmerelda, Esmiralda
Language/Cultural Origin: Spanish

Inherent Meaning: Victory
Spiritual Connotation: Triumphant Spirit
Scripture: Luke 12:32 NKJV
Do not fear, little flock, for it is your Father's good pleasure to give you the kingdom.

ESMOND, Esmonde, Esmunde
Language/Cultural Origin: Old English
Inherent Meaning: Rich Protector
Spiritual Connotation: Gracious
Scripture: 2 Corinthians 3:17 NKJV
Now the Lord is the Spirit; and where the Spirit of the Lord is, there is liberty.

ESTE, Estes
Language/Cultural Origin: Italian
Inherent Meaning: East
Spiritual Connotation: Armed
Scripture: Ephesians 6:13 NLT
Use every piece of God's armor to resist the enemy in the time of evil, so that after the battle you will still be standing firm.

ESTEBAN, Estéban
Language/Cultural Origin: Spanish
Inherent Meaning: Crowned
Spiritual Connotation: Wise
Scripture: Proverbs 14:18 TLB
The simpleton is crowned with folly; the wise man is crowned with knowledge.

ESTEE, Estée
Language/Cultural Origin: English
Inherent Meaning: Star
Spiritual Connotation: Fulfillment
Scripture: Numbers 24:17 NCV
I see someone who will come some day, someone who will come, but not soon. A star will come from Jacob; a ruler will rise from Israel.

ESTELLE, Estele
Language/Cultural Origin: French
Inherent Meaning: Star
Spiritual Connotation: Infinite Potential
Scripture: Matthew 9:29 NKJV
According to your faith let it be to you.

ESTHER, Ester, Esthur
🖙 **(see also Asther, Hester)**
Language/Cultural Origin: Persian
Inherent Meaning: Star

Spiritual Connotation: Victorious
Scripture: Esther 2:17 NKJV
The king loved Esther more than all the other women, and she obtained grace and favor in his sight.

ESTRELLA, Estelina, Estelita, Estella, Estrela, Estrellita, Estrietta
Language/Cultural Origin: Spanish
Inherent Meaning: Child of the Star
Spiritual Connotation: Witness
Scripture: Matthew 10:32 NASB
Everyone therefore who shall confess Me before men, I will also confess him before My Father who is in heaven.

ETHAN, Eathan, Ethen, Eythan
☞Language/Cultural Origin: Hebrew
Inherent Meaning: Firmness
Spiritual Connotation: Steadfast in Truth
Scripture: Romans 8:28 NKJV
And we know that all things work together for good to those who love God, to those who are the called according to His purpose.

ETHEL, Ethyl
Language/Cultural Origin: Old English
Inherent Meaning: One of High Regard
Spiritual Connotation: Noble
Scripture: Matthew 7:7 KJV
Ask, and it shall be given you; seek, and ye shall find; knock, and it shall be opened unto you.

ETHNI, Ethnee, Ethney
☞Language/Cultural Origin: Hebrew
Inherent Meaning: My Gift
Spiritual Connotation: Secure
Scripture: John 14:27 NASB
Peace I leave with you; My peace I give to you. . . . Do not let your heart be troubled, nor let it be fearful.

ETIENNE, Etiene
Language/Cultural Origin: French
Inherent Meaning: Enthroned
Spiritual Connotation: Humble
Scripture: Psalm 113:5 NLT
Who can be compared with the LORD our God, who is enthroned on high?

EUCLID
Language/Cultural Origin: Greek

Inherent Meaning: Brilliant
Spiritual Connotation: Creative
Scripture: Psalm 19:2 RSV
Day to day pours forth speech, and night to night declares knowledge.

EUDORA, Eldora, Eudorra
Language/Cultural Origin: Greek
Inherent Meaning: Honorable Gift
Spiritual Connotation: Invaluable
Scripture: John 4:10 NCV
If you only knew the free gift of God and who it is that is asking you for water, you would have asked him, and he would have given you living water.

EUGENE, Eugéne, Gene
Language/Cultural Origin: Greek
Inherent Meaning: Born to Nobility
Spiritual Connotation: Vivacious
Scripture: Isaiah 58:8 NKJV
Then your light shall break forth like the morning, your healing shall spring forth speedily, and your righteousness shall go before you.

EULALIA, Eulalie
Language/Cultural Origin: French
Inherent Meaning: Sweetly Speaking
Spiritual Connotation: Mouthpiece of God
Scripture: Matthew 10:20 NRSV
Do not worry about how you are to speak or what you are to say; for it is not you who speak, but the Spirit of your Father speaking through you.

EUNICE, Eunique, Eunise
☞Language/Cultural Origin: Greek
Inherent Meaning: Joyous
Spiritual Connotation: Victorious
Scripture: Psalm 40:5 NKJV
Many, O LORD my God, are Your wonderful works which You have done.

EUSTACE, Eustasius, Eustis
Language/Cultural Origin: Greek
Inherent Meaning: Productive
Spiritual Connotation: Diligent
Scripture: 2 Timothy 2:15 NASB
Be diligent to present yourself approved to God as a workman who does not need to be ashamed, handling accurately the word of truth.

EVE, Eva, Evah, Evie

Language/Cultural Origin: Hebrew
Inherent Meaning: Mother of Life
Spiritual Connotation: Full of Life
Scripture: Psalm 16:11 NKJV

You will show me the path of life; in Your presence is fullness of joy; at Your right hand are pleasures forevermore.

EVAN, Evann, Evans, Evin, Evyn

Language/Cultural Origin: Irish
Inherent Meaning: Young Warrior
Spiritual Connotation: Noble Protector
Scripture: Philippians 4:13 KJV

I can do all things through Christ which strengtheneth me.

EVANGELINE, Evangelina

Language/Cultural Origin: Greek
Inherent Meaning: Bringer of Good News
Spiritual Connotation: Happy Messenger
Scripture: Psalm 37:6 NKJV

He shall bring forth your righteousness as the light, And your justice as the noonday.

EVELYN, Evalina, Evaline, Evelynne

Language/Cultural Origin: English
Inherent Meaning: Hazelnut
Spiritual Connotation: Radiant
Scripture: 1 John 2:8 NASB

The darkness is passing away and the true Light is already shining.

EVERETT, Everet, Everette, Everitt

Language/Cultural Origin: German
Inherent Meaning: Courageous
Spiritual Connotation: Unending Praise
Scripture: Psalm 96:1 NKJV

Oh, sing to the LORD a new song! Sing to the LORD, all the earth.

EVERLEY, Everlea, Everlee, Everleigh

Language/Cultural Origin: English
Inherent Meaning: From the Boar Meadow
Spiritual Connotation: Faithful
Scripture: 1 Timothy 6:12 NCV

Fight the good fight of faith, grabbing hold of the life that continues forever.

EVETTE, see Yvette

EVITA, Evéeta

Language/Cultural Origin: Hispanic
Inherent Meaning: Youthful Life
Spiritual Connotation: Childlike
Scripture: Job 33:25 NLT

Then his body will become as healthy as a child's, firm and youthful again.

EVONNE, see Yvonne

EWING, Ewin, Ewynn

Language/Cultural Origin: English
Inherent Meaning: Friend of Justice
Spiritual Connotation: Benevolent Protector
Scripture: Psalm 28:7 NKJV

The LORD is my strength and my shield; my heart trusted in Him, and I am helped.

EYOTA, Eyotah

Language/Cultural Origin: Native American
Inherent Meaning: Greatest
Spiritual Connotation: Servant
Scripture: Matthew 23:11 NRSV

The greatest among you will be your servant.

EZEKIEL, Ezekial, Zeke

Language/Cultural Origin: Hebrew
Inherent Meaning: Whom God Makes Strong
Spiritual Connotation: God Is My Strength
Scripture: 1 Corinthians 2:12 NKJV

Now we have received, not the spirit of the world, but the Spirit who is from God.

EZRA, Esera, Esra, Ezera, Ezri (see also Izri)

Language/Cultural Origin: Hebrew
Inherent Meaning: Helper
Spiritual Connotation: Strong
Scripture: Luke 12:12 NKJV

For the Holy Spirit will teach you in that very hour what you ought to say.

EZRELA, Ezraela

Language/Cultural Origin: Hebrew
Inherent Meaning: God Is My Strength
Spiritual Connotation: Adoration
Scripture: Psalm 18:1 NLT

I love you, LORD; you are my strength.

FALINA, Falena, Faylina, Felina
Language/Cultural Origin: Latin
Inherent Meaning: Catlike
Spiritual Connotation: Upright
Scripture: Psalm 17:2 NASB
Let my judgment come forth from Your presence; let Your eyes look with equity.

FALKNER, Faulkner
Language/Cultural Origin: Old English
Inherent Meaning: Trainer of Falcons
Spiritual Connotation: One Who Disciples
Scripture: Philippians 1:21 KJV
For to me to live is Christ, and to die is gain.

FALLON, Falan, Falen, Falin, Fallan, Fallyn, Falyn
Language/Cultural Origin: Irish
Inherent Meaning: Grandchild of the Ruler
Spiritual Connotation: Heir
Scripture: Exodus 20:6 NRSV
But showing steadfast love to the thousandth generation of those who love me and keep my commandments.

FANNY, Fanney, Fanni, Fannie
Language/Cultural Origin: English
Inherent Meaning: French
Spiritual Connotation: Dedicated
Scripture: Psalm 62:1 NASB
My soul waits in silence for God only; from Him is my salvation.

FANYA, Fania, Fannia
Language/Cultural Origin: Russian
Inherent Meaning: Free
Spiritual Connotation: Vindicated
Scripture: Psalm 146:7 NCV
He does what is fair for those who have been wronged. He gives food to the hungry. The LORD sets the prisoners free.

FARLEY, Fairleigh, Farlay, Farrley
Language/Cultural Origin: English
Inherent Meaning: From the Sheep Meadow
Spiritual Connotation: Serene
Scripture: Exodus 14:14 NASB
The LORD will fight for you while you keep silent.

FARRAH, Fara, Farah, Farra
Language/Cultural Origin: English

FABIA, Fabiana, Fabianna, Fabianne, Fabria, Fabriana, Fabrianne
Language/Cultural Origin: English
Inherent Meaning: Bean Grower
Spiritual Connotation: Laborer
Scripture: Psalm 33:4 NKJV
For the word of the LORD is right, and all His work is done in truth.

FABIAN, Fabayan, Fabiano, Fabien, Fabio, Faybian
Language/Cultural Origin: Latin
Inherent Meaning: Bean Grower
Spiritual Connotation: Nourishing Spirit
Scripture: Jeremiah 31:16 NRSV
Thus says the LORD: "Keep your voice from weeping, and your eyes from tears; for there is a reward for your work."

FADEY, Faidee
Language/Cultural Origin: Ukrainian
Inherent Meaning: Father
Spiritual Connotation: Gentle
Scripture: Ephesians 6:4 NASB
And, fathers, do not provoke your children to anger; but bring them up in the discipline and instruction of the Lord.

FAITH, Fayth, Faythe
Language/Cultural Origin: English
Inherent Meaning: Firm Believer
Spiritual Connotation: Faith
Scripture: Mark 9:23 NCV
All things are possible for the one who believes.

Inherent Meaning: Beautiful
Spiritual Connotation: Favored
Scripture: Esther 2:9 NASB
Now the young lady pleased him and found favor with him.

FARREL, Farrel, Ferel, Ferell, Ferryl
Language/Cultural Origin: Irish
Inherent Meaning: Valiant
Spiritual Connotation: Servant
Scripture: 2 Samuel 17:10 NKJV
For all Israel knows that your father is a mighty man, and those who are with him are valiant men.

FARREN, Faran, Farin, Farrahn, Farran, Farrin, Farron, Farryn, Faryn (see also Ferran)
Language/Cultural Origin: English
Inherent Meaning: Wanderer
Spiritual Connotation: Foreigner
Scripture: Ruth 2:10 NKJV
Why have I found favor in your eyes, that you should take notice of me, since I am a foreigner?

FAUSTINA, Faustana
Language/Cultural Origin: Latin
Inherent Meaning: Fortunate
Spiritual Connotation: Blessed
Scripture: Genesis 1:28 NKJV
Then God blessed them, and God said to them, "Be fruitful and multiply."

FAWN, Faun, Fauna, Fawna, Fawne
Language/Cultural Origin: Old French
Inherent Meaning: Young Deer
Spiritual Connotation: Innocent
Scripture: Psalm 42:1 NRSV
As a deer longs for flowing streams, so my soul longs for you, O God.

FAXON, Faxan
Language/Cultural Origin: Old German
Inherent Meaning: Long-Haired
Spiritual Connotation: Devotion
Scripture: Judges 13:7 NKJV
Behold, you shall conceive and bear a son . . . for the child shall be a Nazirite to God from the womb to the day of his death.

FAYE, Fae, Fay, Fayanna, Fayla
Language/Cultural Origin: Latin

Inherent Meaning: Raven
Spiritual Connotation: Remembered
Scripture: Isaiah 65:24 NKJV
It shall come to pass that before they call, I will answer; and while they are still speaking, I will hear.

FELICIA, Falesha, Falisha, Felecia, Felicya, Felesha, Feleesha, Felisha
Language/Cultural Origin: Latin
Inherent Meaning: Fortunate
Spiritual Connotation: Joyful
Scripture: John 10:10 NKJV
The thief does not come except to steal, and to kill, and to destroy. I have come that they may have life, and that they may have it more abundantly.

FELICITY, Felicianna, Félicité, Felisianna, Felissa, Feliza, Felysse
Language/Cultural Origin: English
Inherent Meaning: Joyful
Spiritual Connotation: Content
Scripture: Philippians 4:4 NKJV
Rejoice in the Lord always. Again I will say, rejoice!

FELIPE, see Phillip

FELIX, Feliks, Félix
Language/Cultural Origin: Latin
Inherent Meaning: Fortunate
Spiritual Connotation: Blessed
Scripture: Isaiah 40:31 NKJV
But those who wait on the LORD shall renew their strength; they shall mount up with wings like eagles, they shall run and not be weary, they shall walk and not faint.

FELTON, Felten
Language/Cultural Origin: English
Inherent Meaning: From the Field Town
Spiritual Connotation: Hopeful
Scripture: Psalm 42:5 NKJV
Why are you cast down, O my soul? And why are you disquieted within me? Hope in God, for I shall yet praise Him for the help of His countenance.

FENTON, Fenny
Language/Cultural Origin: English
Inherent Meaning: From the Marshland Farm
Spiritual Connotation: Spirit of Life

Scripture: Galatians 6:8 NKJV
For he who sows to his flesh will of the flesh reap corruption, but he who sows to the Spirit will of the Spirit reap everlasting life.

FERDINAND, Ferdinánd, Fernand
Language/Cultural Origin: Gothic
Inherent Meaning: Adventurous
Spiritual Connotation: Seeker of Truth
Scripture: Psalm 33:3–4 NKJV
Sing to Him a new song; play skillfully with a shout of joy. For the word of the LORD is right, and all His work is done in truth.

FERGUS, Ferguson
Language/Cultural Origin: Irish
Inherent Meaning: Very Choice One
Spiritual Connotation: Esteemed
Scripture: Psalm 18:2 NKJV
The LORD is my rock and my fortress and my deliverer; my God, my strength, in whom I will trust; my shield and the horn of my salvation, my stronghold.

FERN, Ferne, Fernleigh
Language/Cultural Origin: Old English
Inherent Meaning: Sincere
Spiritual Connotation: Loving
Scripture: 1 John 4:11 KJV
Beloved, if God so loved us, we ought also to love one another.

FERNANDO, Fernandez
Language/Cultural Origin: Spanish
Inherent Meaning: Fearless
Spiritual Connotation: Redeemed
Scripture: Matthew 28:5–6 NKJV
Do not be afraid, for I know that you seek Jesus who was crucified. He is not here; for He is risen, as He said.

FERRAN, Feran, Ferren, Feron, Ferrin, Ferron, Ferryn (see also Farran)
Language/Cultural Origin: Middle Eastern
Inherent Meaning: Baker
Spiritual Connotation: Laborer for Souls
Scripture: Luke 10:2 NLT
The harvest is so great, but the workers are so few. Pray to the Lord . . . and ask him to send out more workers for his fields.

FERRAND, Farrand
Language/Cultural Origin: French

Inherent Meaning: Iron-Haired
Spiritual Connotation: Believer
Scripture: Ephesians 1:19 NCV
And you will know that God's power is very great for us who believe. That power is the same as the great strength.

FERRIS, Faris, Farris, Feris
Language/Cultural Origin: Middle Eastern
Inherent Meaning: Horseman
Spiritual Connotation: Fearsome
Scripture: Jeremiah 4:29 NASB
At the sound of the horseman and bowman every city flees.

FIDEL, Fidele, Fidéle, Fidelis
Language/Cultural Origin: Latin
Inherent Meaning: Faithful
Spiritual Connotation: Secure
Scripture: Romans 8:38–39 NKJV
For I am persuaded that neither death nor life . . . nor any other . . . thing, shall be able to separate us from the love of God which is in Christ Jesus our Lord.

FIDELITY, Fidelia
Language/Cultural Origin: Latin
Inherent Meaning: Faithful
Spiritual Connotation: Received
Scripture: Isaiah 26:2 NASB
Open the gates, that the righteous nation may enter, the one that remains faithful.

FIEVEL, Feivel, Fivel
Language/Cultural Origin: Yiddish
Inherent Meaning: Bright
Spiritual Connotation: Attentive
Scripture: 2 Peter 1:19 NRSV
You will do well to be attentive to this as to a lamp shining in a dark place, until the day dawns and the morning star rises in your hearts.

FINDLAY, Finlay, Finley
Language/Cultural Origin: Irish
Inherent Meaning: Valorous Soldier
Spiritual Connotation: Victorious Life
Scripture: Proverbs 12:28 NKJV
In the way of righteousness is life, and in its pathway there is no death.

FINIAN, Phinean
Language/Cultural Origin: Irish

Inherent Meaning: Fair Hero
Spiritual Connotation: Servant
Scripture: Proverbs 27:18 NASB
He who tends the fig tree will eat its fruit; and he who cares for his master will be honored.

FIONA, Fionna
Language/Cultural Origin: Irish
Inherent Meaning: Fair
Spiritual Connotation: Persevering
Scripture: Isaiah 66:22 RSV
For as the new heavens and the new earth which I will make shall remain before me, says the LORD; so shall your descendants and your name remain.

FISK, Fiske
Language/Cultural Origin: Middle English
Inherent Meaning: Fisherman
Spiritual Connotation: Witness
Scripture: Matthew 4:19 NKJV
Follow Me, and I will make you fishers of men.

FITZGERALD, Fitz
Language/Cultural Origin: Old English
Inherent Meaning: Son of the Mighty One
Spiritual Connotation: Hopeful
Scripture: Colossians 1:27 NKJV
To them God willed to make known what are the riches of the glory of this mystery among the Gentiles: which is Christ in you, the hope of glory.

FLAIR, Flaire, Flare
Language/Cultural Origin: English
Inherent Meaning: Vivacious
Spiritual Connotation: Glorified
Scripture: Psalm 64:10 RSV
Let the righteous rejoice in the LORD, and take refuge in him! Let all the upright in heart glory!

FLANA, Flanna
Language/Cultural Origin: Latin
Inherent Meaning: Blonde
Spiritual Connotation: Satisfied
Scripture: Psalm 90:14 NASB
O satisfy us in the morning with Thy lovingkindness, that we may sing for joy and be glad all our days.

FLANNERY, Flann
Language/Cultural Origin: Irish
Inherent Meaning: Redhead
Spiritual Connotation: Accountable
Scripture: Ecclesiastes 11:9 NCV
Young people, enjoy yourselves while you are young. . . . But remember that God will judge you for everything you do.

FLAVIA, Flavian, Flaviar, Flavio
Language/Cultural Origin: Latin
Inherent Meaning: Blond
Spiritual Connotation: Redeemed
Scripture: Isaiah 61:10 NASB
I will rejoice greatly in the LORD . . . For He has clothed me with garments of salvation, He has wrapped me with a robe of righteousness.

FLEMING, Flemming
Language/Cultural Origin: English
Inherent Meaning: From Denmark
Spiritual Connotation: Obedient
Scripture: Romans 16:19 NKJV
For your obedience has become known to all. Therefore I am glad on your behalf..

FLETCHER, Flecher, Fletch
Language/Cultural Origin: Anglo-Saxon
Inherent Meaning: Arrow Featherer
Spiritual Connotation: Ingenious
Scripture: John 14:12 NKJV
He who believes in Me, the works that I do he will do also; and greater works than these he will do, because I go to My Father.

FLEUR, Flure
Language/Cultural Origin: French
Inherent Meaning: Flower
Spiritual Connotation: Efficient
Scripture: Isaiah 40:6 NKJV
All flesh is grass, and all its loveliness is like the flower of the field.

FLINT, Flynt
Language/Cultural Origin: Old English
Inherent Meaning: Stream
Spiritual Connotation: Praise
Scripture: Psalm 78:16 RSV
He made streams come out of the rock, and caused waters to flow down like rivers.

FLIP, Flipp
Language/Cultural Origin: American

Inherent Meaning: Lover of Horses
Spiritual Connotation: Joyful
Scripture: Psalm 45:15 NRSV
With joy and gladness they are led along as they enter the palace of the king.

FLORA, Floria, Floriana, Florianna
Language/Cultural Origin: Latin
Inherent Meaning: Flower
Spiritual Connotation: Nurtured
Scripture: Isaiah 49:13 NASB
Shout for joy, O heavens! And rejoice, O earth! . . . For the LORD has comforted His people And will have compassion on His afflicted.

FLORENCE, Flo, Florance, Florann, Floren, Florida, Florrie, Flossie
Language/Cultural Origin: Latin
Inherent Meaning: Flourishing
Spiritual Connotation: Prosperous
Scripture: Psalm 91:1 NKJV
He who dwells in the secret place of the Most High shall abide under the shadow of the Almighty.

FLORIAN, Florien, Florrian
Language/Cultural Origin: English
Inherent Meaning: Blooming
Spiritual Connotation: Nourished
Scripture: Isaiah 35:1 NKJV
And the desert shall rejoice and blossom as the rose.

FLOYD, Floydd
Language/Cultural Origin: Welsh
Inherent Meaning: White- or Gray-Haired
Spiritual Connotation: Wise
Scripture: 1 Samuel 10:6 NKJV
Then the Spirit of the LORD will come upon you, and you will prophesy with them and be turned into another man.

FLYNN, Flinn, Flyn
Language/Cultural Origin: Gaelic
Inherent Meaning: Son of the Redhead
Spiritual Connotation: Blessed
Scripture: 1 Kings 8:56 NKJV
Blessed be the LORD, who has given rest to His people Israel. . . . There has not failed one word of all His good promise.

FONTANNA, Fontaine, Fontana
Language/Cultural Origin: French

Inherent Meaning: Fountain
Spiritual Connotation: Sustained
Scripture: Psalm 36:9 NKJV
For with You is the fountain of life; in Your light we see light.

FONZIE, Fonsie, Fonz
Language/Cultural Origin: German
Inherent Meaning: Zealous
Spiritual Connotation: Righteous
Scripture: Proverbs 23:17 NKJV
Do not let your heart envy sinners, but be zealous for the fear of the LORD all the day.

FORBES, Forbe
Language/Cultural Origin: Gaelic
Inherent Meaning: Prosperous
Spiritual Connotation: Blessed
Scripture: Proverbs 16:20 NLT
Those who listen to instruction will prosper; those who trust the LORD will be happy.

FORREST, Forest, Forster, Foster
Language/Cultural Origin: Latin
Inherent Meaning: Guardian of the Forest
Spiritual Connotation: Preserved
Scripture: Psalm 138:8 NKJV
The LORD will perfect that which concerns me; Your mercy, O LORD, endures forever; do not forsake the works of Your hands.

FRANCES, Fran, Francesca, Francess, Franchelle, Franchesca, Franchette, Francine, Frann, Frannie
Language/Cultural Origin: Latin
Inherent Meaning: Free
Spiritual Connotation: Triumphant
Scripture: Isaiah 65:24 NKJV
It shall come to pass that before they call, I will answer; and while they are still speaking, I will hear.

FRANCIS, Fran, Francesco, Franchot, Francisco, Franco, Francois, Franz
Language/Cultural Origin: Latin
Inherent Meaning: Free
Spiritual Connotation: Victorious
Scripture: John 5:24 NKJV
He who hears my word and believes in Him who sent Me has everlasting life, and shall not come into judgment, but has passed from death into life.

FRANK, Franc, Frankie, Franky
Language/Cultural Origin: English
Inherent Meaning: Free Man
Spiritual Connotation: Shining
Scripture: Matthew 5:14 NKJV
You are the light of the world. A city that is set on a hill cannot be hidden.

FRANKLIN, Francklin, Franklinn, Franklyn, Franklynn
Language/Cultural Origin: Old English
Inherent Meaning: Free Holder of Land
Spiritual Connotation: Joyful
Scripture: Nehemiah 8:10 NKJV
This day is holy to our LORD. Do not sorrow, for the joy of the LORD is your strength.

FRASER, Fraizer, Frasier, Frazer, Frazier
Language/Cultural Origin: French
Inherent Meaning: Strawberry
Spiritual Connotation: Filled With Life
Scripture: 2 Peter 1:4 NKJV
By which have been given to us exceedingly great and precious promises, that through these you may be partakers of the divine nature.

FRAYNE, Fraine, Freyne
Language/Cultural Origin: Old English
Inherent Meaning: Stranger
Spiritual Connotation: Accepting
Scripture: Deuteronomy 23:7 NRSV
You shall not abhor any of the Edomites, for they are your kin. You shall not abhor any of the Egyptians, because you were an alien residing in their land.

FREDERICA, Freddi, Fredericka, Frederina, Frederique, Fredrika
Language/Cultural Origin: Old German
Inherent Meaning: Peaceful Ruler
Spiritual Connotation: Compassionate
Scripture: Psalm 112:4 NKJV
Unto the upright there arises light in the darkness; He is gracious, and full of compassion, and righteous.

FREDERICK, Fred, Fredd, Freddi, Freddrick, Freddy, Frederic, Frederich, Frederico, Frederik, Frederric, Fredric, Fredrich, Fredrik, Freéderic, Fritz
Language/Cultural Origin: German
Inherent Meaning: Peaceful Ruler
Spiritual Connotation: Perceptive
Scripture: Proverbs 20:12 NKJV
The hearing ear and the seeing eye, the LORD has made them both.

FREEDOM
Language/Cultural Origin: Old German
Inherent Meaning: Freedom
Spiritual Connotation: Released
Scripture: James 2:12 NASB
So speak and so act, as those who are to be judged by the law of liberty.

FREEMAN, Freedman, Freemon
Language/Cultural Origin: English
Inherent Meaning: Free
Spiritual Connotation: Witness
Scripture: 1 Corinthians 10:31 NRSV
So, whether you eat or drink, or whatever you do, do everything for the glory of God.

FREIDA, Freda, Freeda, Freia, Frieda
Language/Cultural Origin: German
Inherent Meaning: Serene
Spiritual Connotation: Victorious
Scripture: Revelation 2:7 NKJV
To him who overcomes I will give to eat from the tree of life, which is in the midst of the Paradise of God.

FREJA, Fraya, Freya
Language/Cultural Origin: Swedish
Inherent Meaning: Virtuous Woman
Spiritual Connotation: Valuable
Scripture: Proverbs 31:10 NASB
An excellent wife, who can find? For her worth is far above jewels.

FREEMONT, Freemondt
Language/Cultural Origin: German
Inherent Meaning: Protector of Freedom
Spiritual Connotation: Righteous
Scripture: Psalm 146:7-8 NASB
The LORD sets the prisoners free. The LORD opens the eyes of the blind; the LORD raises up those who are bowed down; the LORD loves the righteous.

FRITZI, Fritzie, Fritzy
Language/Cultural Origin: German
Inherent Meaning: Restful
Spiritual Connotation: Righteous

Scripture: Hebrews 12:11 RSV

For the moment all discipline seems painful rather than pleasant; later it yields the peaceful fruit of righteousness.

FULLER, Fullar

Language/Cultural Origin: English
Inherent Meaning: Cloth Worker
Spiritual Connotation: Diligent

Scripture: Psalm 103:1–4 NKJV

Bless the LORD, O my soul; and all that is within me, bless His holy name!

FULTON, Fultan

Language/Cultural Origin: English
Inherent Meaning: From Near the Town
Spiritual Connotation: Spirit-Filled Life
Scripture: Galatians 5:22–23 NKJV

But the fruit of the Spirit is love, joy, peace, longsuffering, kindness, goodness, faithfulness, gentleness, self-control.

Inherent Meaning: From Southern Italy
Spiritual Connotation: Redeemed
Scripture: Romans 5:2 RSV
Through him we have obtained access to this grace in which we stand, and we rejoice in our hope of sharing the glory of God.

GAGE, Gaege
Language/Cultural Origin: French
Inherent Meaning: Promise
Spiritual Connotation: Vision
Scripture: Zechariah 9:9 NRSV
Rejoice greatly, O daughter Zion! . . . Lo, your king comes to you; triumphant and victorious is he, humble and riding on a donkey.

GAIL, Gael, Gaila, Gale, Gayle
Language/Cultural Origin: Old English
Inherent Meaning: My Father Rejoices
Spiritual Connotation: Lively
Scripture: Zephaniah 3:17 NKJV
The LORD your God in your midst, the Mighty One, will save; He will rejoice over you with gladness.

GAIUS, Caius
Language/Cultural Origin: Latin
Inherent Meaning: One Who Rejoices
Spiritual Connotation: Bold
Scripture: Joel 2:21 TLB
Fear not, my people; be glad now and rejoice, for he has done amazing things for you.

GALA, Galla
Language/Cultural Origin: Old Norse
Inherent Meaning: Singer
Spiritual Connotation: Filled With Praise
Scripture: Psalm 84:4 RSV
Blessed are those who dwell in thy house, ever singing thy praise!

GALATIA
Language/Cultural Origin: Greek
Inherent Meaning: Pure
Spiritual Connotation: Courageous
Scripture: Psalm 27:1 NKJV
The LORD is my light and my salvation; whom shall I fear? The LORD is the strength of my life; of whom shall I be afraid?

GALEN, Gaelen, Gaylen
Language/Cultural Origin: Greek

GABOR, Gábor
Language/Cultural Origin: Hungarian
Inherent Meaning: God Is My Strength
Spiritual Connotation: Grounded in Faith
Scripture: Isaiah 12:2 NASB
Behold, God is my salvation, I will trust and not be afraid; for the LORD GOD is my strength and song, and He has become my salvation.

GABRIEL, Gab, Gabe, Gabriël, Gabriell, Gabrielli, Gabriello, Gibbee, Gibbie
Language/Cultural Origin: Hebrew
Inherent Meaning: Devoted to God
Spiritual Connotation: Brave
Scripture: Joshua 1:9 NKJV
Have I not commanded you? Be strong and of good courage; do not be afraid, nor be dismayed, for the LORD your God is with you wherever you go.

GABRIELLE, Gabbey, Gabbi, Gabbie, Gabrial, Gabriala, Gabrialla, Gabriana, Gabrianna, Gabriela, Gabriele, Gabriella
Language/Cultural Origin: Hebrew
Inherent Meaning: Devoted to God
Spiritual Connotation: Confident
Scripture: 2 Corinthians 7:16 RSV
I rejoice, because I have perfect confidence in you.

GAETAN, Gaetano
Language/Cultural Origin: Italian

Inherent Meaning: Healer
Spiritual Connotation: Established in Truth
Scripture: Psalm 37:5 NKJV
Commit your way to the LORD, trust also in Him, and He shall bring it to pass.

GALENA, Galeena
Language/Cultural Origin: Greek
Inherent Meaning: Calm
Spiritual Connotation: Amiable
Scripture: Proverbs 15:18 NRSV
Those who are hot-tempered stir up strife, but those who are slow to anger calm contention.

GALIANA, Galianna, Galiena, Galienna
Language/Cultural Origin: Old German
Inherent Meaning: Supreme
Spiritual Connotation: Respectful
Scripture: 1 Timothy 5:2 NLT
Treat the older women as you would your mother, and treat the younger women with all purity as your own sisters.

GALINA, Gailina
Language/Cultural Origin: Russian
Inherent Meaning: Shining
Spiritual Connotation: Glorified
Scripture: Isaiah 60:1 NKJV
Arise, shine; for your light has come! And the glory of the LORD is risen upon you.

GALLIO, Galio
Language/Cultural Origin: Hebrew
Inherent Meaning: He That Sucks
Spiritual Connotation: Mighty
Scripture: Isaiah 54:17 NKJV
No weapon formed against you shall prosper.

GALVIN, Galvan, Galven
Language/Cultural Origin: Gaelic
Inherent Meaning: Glowing
Spiritual Connotation: Blessed
Scripture: Isaiah 49:4 NKJV
I have labored in vain, I have spent my strength for nothing and in vain; yet surely my just reward is with the LORD, and my work with my God.

GALYA, Galia, Gallia
Language/Cultural Origin: Russian
Inherent Meaning: Illuminated

Spiritual Connotation: Untainted
Scripture: Luke 11:36 NRSV
If then your whole body is full of light, with no part of it in darkness, it will be as full of light as when a lamp gives you light with its rays.

GAMALIEL, Gaméliel
Language/Cultural Origin: Hebrew
Inherent Meaning: God Is My Reward
Spiritual Connotation: Blessed
Scripture: Ruth 2:12 NASB
May the LORD reward your work, and your wages be full from the LORD, the God of Israel, under whose wings you have come to seek refuge.

GAMARYA, Gamara, Gamária, Gamariya
Language/Cultural Origin: Hebrew
Inherent Meaning: Act of God
Spiritual Connotation: Pledged
Scripture: Micah 7:15 NASB
As in the days when you came out from the land of Egypt, I will show you miracles.

GANNON, Gannan, Gannen
Language/Cultural Origin: Irish
Inherent Meaning: White
Spiritual Connotation: Devout
Scripture: Matthew 4:10 NKJV
Away with you, Satan! For it is written, "You shall worship the LORD your God, and Him only you shall serve."

GANYA, Gania, Ganyah
Language/Cultural Origin: Hebrew
Inherent Meaning: Garden of God
Spiritual Connotation: Refreshed
Scripture: Isaiah 51:3 NLT
The LORD will comfort Israel again and make her deserts blossom. Her barren wilderness will become as beautiful as Eden—the garden of the LORD.

GARETH, Garith, Garreth
Language/Cultural Origin: Welsh
Inherent Meaning: Gentle
Spiritual Connotation: Peaceful
Scripture: Proverbs 15:1 RSV
A soft answer turns away wrath, but a harsh word stirs up anger.

GARNER, Garnier
Language/Cultural Origin: French
Inherent Meaning: Guard
Spiritual Connotation: One of Integrity
Scripture: 1 Timothy 6:20 NCV
*Timothy, guard what God has trusted to you.
Stay away from foolish, useless talk and
from the arguments of what is falsely
called knowledge.*

GARNET, Garnette
Language/Cultural Origin: Latin
Inherent Meaning: Precious Stone
Spiritual Connotation: Invaluable
Scripture: Isaiah 49:8 NKJV
*In an acceptable time I have heard You, and
in the day of salvation I have helped You; I
will preserve You.*

GARNETT, Garnatt
Language/Cultural Origin: Anglo-Saxon
Inherent Meaning: Protection
Spiritual Connotation: Obedient
Scripture: Deuteronomy 11:1 NKJV
*Therefore you shall love the LORD your God,
and keep His charge, His statutes, His
judgments, and His commandments always.*

**GARRETT, Garett, Garret,
Gerrett (see also Jarrett)**
Language/Cultural Origin: Irish
Inherent Meaning: Warrior
Spiritual Connotation: Free
Scripture: Galatians 5:1 NKJV
*Stand fast therefore in the liberty by which
Christ has made us free, and do not be
entangled again with a yoke of bondage.*

**GARRICK, Garick, Garreck,
Garrik (see also Carrick)**
Language/Cultural Origin: English
Inherent Meaning: Ruler
Spiritual Connotation: Champion
Scripture: Psalm 24:3 NKJV
*Who may ascend into the hill of the LORD?
Or who may stand in His holy place? He
who has clean hands and a pure heart.*

GARRIN, Garran, Garren, Garron
Language/Cultural Origin: Old English
Inherent Meaning: Spearman
Spiritual Connotation: Preserved
Scripture: Philippians 4:7 RSV

*And the peace of God, which passes all
understanding, will keep your hearts and
your minds in Christ Jesus.*

GARRISON, Garris
Language/Cultural Origin: Old French
Inherent Meaning: Fortress
Spiritual Connotation: Guided of God
Scripture: Psalm 31:3 NRSV
*You are indeed my rock and my fortress; for
your name's sake lead me and guide me.*

GARTH, Gar
Language/Cultural Origin: Old Norse
Inherent Meaning: From the Garden
Spiritual Connotation: Wise
Scripture: Job 28:28 NKJV
*Behold, the fear of the Lord, that is wisdom,
and to depart from evil is understanding.*

GARVEY, Garrvey
Language/Cultural Origin: Irish
Inherent Meaning: Rugged Place
Spiritual Connotation: Increasing Faithfulness
Scripture: Ephesians 5:8 NKJV
*For you were once darkness, but now you are
light in the Lord. Walk as children of light.*

GARVIN, Garvan, Garvyn
Language/Cultural Origin: English
Inherent Meaning: Friend in Battle
Spiritual Connotation: Peaceful
Scripture: Colossians 3:15 NKJV
*And let the peace of God rule in your hearts,
to which also you were called in one body;
and be thankful.*

GARY, Garry
Language/Cultural Origin: German
Inherent Meaning: Mighty
Spiritual Connotation: Regenerated
Scripture: 2 Corinthians 5:17 NKJV
*Therefore, if anyone is in Christ, he is a new
creation; old things have passed away;
behold, all things have become new.*

GASTON, Gascon, Gastón
Language/Cultural Origin: French
Inherent Meaning: From Gascony
Spiritual Connotation: Protected
Scripture: 2 Samuel 22:2 NCV
*The LORD is my rock, my protection, my
Savior.*

GAVIN, Gavan, Gaven, Gavyn

Language/Cultural Origin: Welsh
Inherent Meaning: White Hawk
Spiritual Connotation: Content
Scripture: Psalm 119:34 NKJV

Give me understanding, and I shall keep Your law; Indeed, I shall observe it with my whole heart.

GAYLORD, Gayler, Gaylor

Language/Cultural Origin: Old French
Inherent Meaning: Lively
Spiritual Connotation: Gifted
Scripture: Psalm 84:11 NKJV

For the LORD God is a sun and shield; the LORD will give grace and glory; no good thing will He withhold From those who walk uprightly.

GEARY, Gearey

Language/Cultural Origin: English
Inherent Meaning: Changeable
Spiritual Connotation: Courageous
Scripture: Psalm 16:8 NKJV

I have set the LORD always before me; because He is at my right hand I shall not be moved.

GEMINI, Gemelle, Gemina, Gemmina

Language/Cultural Origin: Greek
Inherent Meaning: Twin
Spiritual Connotation: Righteous
Scripture: Isaiah 61:1 RSV

The Spirit of the Lord GOD is upon me, because the LORD has anointed me to bring good tidings to the afflicted.

GENA, see Gina

GENE, see Eugene

GENEEN, see Jeanine

GENEVA, Jeneva

Language/Cultural Origin: French
Inherent Meaning: Juniper Tree
Spiritual Connotation: Wise
Scripture: Psalm 111:10 NKJV

The fear of the LORD is the beginning of wisdom; a good understanding have all those who do His commandments. His praise endures forever.

GENEVIEVE, Genavieve, Geneviéve, Jenavieve

Language/Cultural Origin: French
Inherent Meaning: Fair
Spiritual Connotation: Inner Beauty
Scripture: Proverbs 31:10 RSV

A good wife who can find? She is far more precious than jewels.

GENNA, see Jenna

GENNIFER, see Jennifer

GEOFFREY, Geffery, Geffrey, Geoff, Geoffery, Giotto, Gottfried (see also Godfrey, Jeffrey)

Language/Cultural Origin: Old German
Inherent Meaning: Perfectly Tranquil
Spiritual Connotation: Restful
Scripture: Isaiah 32:18 NRSV

My people will abide in a peaceful habitation, in secure dwellings, and in quiet resting places.

GEORGE, Georges, Georgio, Gheorghe, Giorgio, Giorgios

Language/Cultural Origin: Greek
Inherent Meaning: Land Worker
Spiritual Connotation: Walks With God
Scripture: Genesis 5:24 NRSV

Enoch walked with God; then he was no more, because God took him.

GEORGIA, Georgeann, Georgeanna, Georgene, Georgette, Georgie

Language/Cultural Origin: Greek
Inherent Meaning: Farmer
Spiritual Connotation: Promise of God
Scripture: Hebrews 8:10 NKJV

I will put My laws in their mind and write them on their hearts; and I will be their God, and they shall be My people.

GERALD, Geraldo, Gerrald, Gerrold, Gerry, Jerald, Jeraldo, Jeri, Jerrald, Jerri, Jerrold, Jerry

Language/Cultural Origin: Old German
Inherent Meaning: Mighty
Spiritual Connotation: Loyal
Scripture: Psalm 25:5 NKJV

Lead me in Your truth and teach me, for You are the God of my salvation; on You I wait all the day.

GERALDINE, Geraldina, Geralyn, Geri, Gerianna, Gerry, Jeraldine
Language/Cultural Origin: Old German
Inherent Meaning: Powerful
Spiritual Connotation: Victorious
Scripture: Psalm 118:14 NKJV
The LORD is my strength and song, and He has become my salvation.

GERARD, Gérard, Gerardo, Gerrard, Gerry, Girard
Language/Cultural Origin: Old German
Inherent Meaning: Strong, Powerful
Spiritual Connotation: Trusting Heart
Scripture: Psalm 138:8 NKJV
The LORD will perfect that which concerns me; Your mercy, O LORD, endures forever; do not forsake the works of Your hands.

GERMAIN, Germaine, Germana, Germane, Germaya, Germayne (see also Jermaine)
Language/Cultural Origin: French
Inherent Meaning: From Germany
Spiritual Connotation: Bringer of Unity
Scripture: 2 Timothy 2:22 NKJV
Flee also youthful lusts; but pursue righteousness, faith, love, peace with those who call on the Lord out of a pure heart.

GERSHOM, Gershon
Language/Cultural Origin: Hebrew
Inherent Meaning: Stranger
Spiritual Connotation: Visitor
Scripture: John 8:23 NKJV
You are from beneath; I am from above. You are of this world; I am not of this world.

GIANNA, Giana, Gianella, Giannella, Gianni, Jiana, Jianna, Jianella
Language/Cultural Origin: Italian
Inherent Meaning: God Is Gracious
Spiritual Connotation: Sanctified
Scripture: 1 Corinthians 1:4 RSV
I give thanks to God always for you because of the grace of God which was given you in Christ Jesus.

GIBBAR, Gibbár
Language/Cultural Origin: Hebrew
Inherent Meaning: Mighty Man

Spiritual Connotation: Empowered
Scripture: Judges 6:12 NRSV
The LORD is with you, you mighty warrior.

GIBSON, Gilson
Language/Cultural Origin: English
Inherent Meaning: Son of the Honest Man
Spiritual Connotation: Fruitful
Scripture: Luke 8:15 NASB
And the seed in the good soil, these are the ones who have heard the word in an honest and good heart . . . and bear fruit with perseverance.

GIDEON, Gedeon, Gideón
Language/Cultural Origin: Hebrew
Inherent Meaning: Tree Cutter
Spiritual Connotation: Victorious
Scripture: Judges 8:28 NRSV
So Midian was subdued before the Israelites, and they lifted up their heads no more. So the land had rest forty years in the days of Gideon.

GIGI, G.G., Geegee
Language/Cultural Origin: French
Inherent Meaning: Trustworthy
Spiritual Connotation: True Friend
Scripture: Proverbs 11:13 NLT
A gossip goes around revealing secrets, but those who are trustworthy can keep a confidence.

GILANA, Gilanna
Language/Cultural Origin: Hebrew
Inherent Meaning: Hill of the Monument
Spiritual Connotation: Testimony
Scripture: Matthew 10:8 NKJV
Heal the sick, cleanse the lepers, raise the dead, cast out demons. Freely you have received, freely give.

GILBERT, Gibb, Gibbs, Gil, Guilbert
Language/Cultural Origin: Old German
Inherent Meaning: Bright Pledge
Spiritual Connotation: Devoted
Scripture: Psalm 119:38 NLT
Reassure me of your promise, which is for those who honor you.

GILDA, Gildé
Language/Cultural Origin: Anglo-Saxon
Inherent Meaning: Covered With Gold

Spiritual Connotation: Blessed
Scripture: Psalm 68:13 NLT
Though they lived among the sheepfolds, now they are covered with silver and gold, as a dove is covered by its wings.

GILEAD, Giliad
Language/Cultural Origin: Hebrew
Inherent Meaning: Mass of Testimony
Spiritual Connotation: Witness
Scripture: Matthew 10:18 NKJV
You will be brought before governors and kings for my sake, as a testimony to them and to the Gentiles.

GILEN, Gilan
Language/Cultural Origin: Basque
Inherent Meaning: Notable Promise
Spiritual Connotation: Protected
Scripture: Psalm 18:30 RSV
This God—his way is perfect; the promise of the LORD proves true; he is a shield for all those who take refuge in him.

GILES, Gilles, Gyles
Language/Cultural Origin: French
Inherent Meaning: Shield
Spiritual Connotation: Strength
Scripture: Psalm 66:1–2 NKJV
Make a joyful shout to God, all the earth! Sing out the honor of His name; make His praise glorious.

GILLIAN, see Jillian

GILMORE, Gilmour
Language/Cultural Origin: Irish
Inherent Meaning: Devout
Spiritual Connotation: Dependent
Scripture: Job 10:12 NKJV
You have granted me life and favor, and Your care has preserved my spirit.

GILSEY, Gilsea, Gilsee
Language/Cultural Origin: English
Inherent Meaning: Flower
Spiritual Connotation: Flourishing
Scripture: Psalm 92:12 TLB
But the godly shall flourish like palm trees and grow tall as the cedars of Lebanon.

**GINA, Geena, Gena, Ginah, Ginia
(see also Jean)**
Language/Cultural Origin: Italian

Inherent Meaning: Queen
Spiritual Connotation: Full of Love
Scripture: Colossians 3:12 NRSV
Above all, clothe yourselves with love, which binds everything together in perfect harmony.

GINGER, Gingata
Language/Cultural Origin: English
Inherent Meaning: Pure
Spiritual Connotation: Respectful
Scripture: 1 Timothy 5:2 NLT
Treat the older women as you would your mother, and treat the younger women with all purity as your own sisters.

**GINNY, Gini, Ginni, Ginnie, Jinnee,
Jinney, Jinni, Jinnie, Jinny
(see also Jina)**
Language/Cultural Origin: English
Inherent Meaning: Unblemished
Spiritual Connotation: Spotless
Scripture: Matthew 5:48 NKJV
Therefore you shall be perfect, just as your Father in heaven is perfect.

GINO, Geno
Language/Cultural Origin: Greek
Inherent Meaning: Of Noteworthy Birth
Spiritual Connotation: Delivered
Scripture: Ezekiel 34:29 NRSV
I will provide for them a splendid vegetation so that they shall no more be consumed with hunger in the land.

**GIOVANNA, Giovana
(see also Jovanna)**
Language/Cultural Origin: Italian
Inherent Meaning: God Is Gracious
Spiritual Connotation: Blessed
Scripture: Titus 2:11 NRSV
For the grace of God has appeared, bringing salvation to all.

**GIOVANNI, Geovani, Geovanni, Gian,
Giani, Gianni, Giavani, Giovanno
(see also Jovan)**
Language/Cultural Origin: Italian
Inherent Meaning: God Is Gracious
Spiritual Connotation: Servant
Scripture: 1 Peter 4:10 NCV
Each of you has received a gift to use to serve others. Be good servants of God's various gifts of grace.

GIUSEPPE, Giusepe
Language/Cultural Origin: Italian
Inherent Meaning: God Will Increase
Spiritual Connotation: Joyful
Scripture: Isaiah 29:19 NKJV
The humble also shall increase their joy in the LORD, And the poor among men shall rejoice In the Holy One of Israel.

GIZELLE, Gissell, Giselle, Jizella, Jiselle, Jizelle
Language/Cultural Origin: Old German
Inherent Meaning: Pledge
Spiritual Connotation: Approved
Scripture: 2 Corinthians 1:22 NCV
He put his mark on us to show that we are his, and he put his Spirit in our hearts to be a guarantee for all he has promised.

GLADYS, Gladis
Language/Cultural Origin: Irish
Inherent Meaning: Princess
Spiritual Connotation: Spiritual Understanding
Scripture: 1 Peter 2:5 NKJV
You also, as living stones, are being built up a spiritual house, a holy priesthood, to offer up spiritual sacrifices.

GLENDON, Glenden
Language/Cultural Origin: Scottish
Inherent Meaning: From the Valley Fortress
Spiritual Connotation: Secure
Scripture: 2 Samuel 22:33 TLB
God is my strong fortress; He has made me safe.

GLENN, Glen
Language/Cultural Origin: Irish
Inherent Meaning: From the Valley
Spiritual Connotation: Excellent Worth
Scripture: Psalm 84:4 NKJV
Blessed are those who dwell in Your house; they will still be praising You.

GLENNA, Glenda
Language/Cultural Origin: Irish
Inherent Meaning: From the Valley
Spiritual Connotation: Blooming
Scripture: Psalm 52:8 NKJV
But I am like a green olive tree in the house of God; I trust in the mercy of God forever and ever.

GLORIA, Gloriela, Gloriella, Glorielle, Glory, Glorya
Language/Cultural Origin: Latin
Inherent Meaning: Glory
Spiritual Connotation: Glorious
Scripture: 2 Corinthians 3:18 NRSV
And all of us ... are being transformed into the same image from one degree of glory to another; for this comes from the Lord, the Spirit.

GLYN, Glynn
Language/Cultural Origin: Scottish
Inherent Meaning: From the Ravine
Spiritual Connotation: Protected
Scripture: Psalm 3:3 NASB
But Thou, O LORD, art a shield about me, my glory, and the One who lifts my head.

GODFREY, Godfry
(see also Geoffrey)
Language/Cultural Origin: Irish
Inherent Meaning: Man of God's Peace
Spiritual Connotation: Divinely Peaceful
Scripture: John 7:38 NKJV
He who believes in Me, as the Scripture has said, out of his heart will flow rivers of living water.

GOLDA, Golden, Goldi, Goldie
Language/Cultural Origin: English
Inherent Meaning: Golden
Spiritual Connotation: Divine Perspective
Scripture: Psalms 119:127 NLT
Truly, I love your commands more than gold, even the finest gold.

GOMER
Language/Cultural Origin: Hebrew
Inherent Meaning: Completion
Spiritual Connotation: Preserved
Scripture: Philippians 1:6 NCV
God began doing a good work in you, and I am sure he will continue it until it is finished when Jesus Christ comes again.

GORDON, Gordan, Gordie, Gordy
Language/Cultural Origin: Anglo-Saxon
Inherent Meaning: From the Round Hill
Spiritual Connotation: Shining
Scripture: Matthew 5:14 NKJV
You are the light of the world. A city that is set on a hill cannot be hidden.

GORMAN, Gormon

Language/Cultural Origin: Gaelic
Inherent Meaning: Blue-eyed
Spiritual Connotation: Walks With God
Scripture: Psalm 84:11 NKJV

For the LORD God is a sun and shield; the LORD will give grace and glory; no good thing will He withhold From those who walk uprightly.

GOWON, Gowan

Language/Cultural Origin: Tiv
Inherent Meaning: Born During a Storm
Spiritual Connotation: Rainmaker
Scripture: Joel 2:23 TLB

Rejoice, O people of Jerusalem, rejoice in the Lord your God! For the rains he sends are tokens of forgiveness.

GRACE, Gracey, Graci, Gracia, Graciana, Gracianna, Gracie

Language/Cultural Origin: Latin
Inherent Meaning: Patient
Spiritual Connotation: Full of Grace
Scripture: 1 Corinthians 16:14 TLB

And whatever you do, do it with kindness and love.

GRADY, Gradey

Language/Cultural Origin: Gaelic
Inherent Meaning: Noble
Spiritual Connotation: Strong
Scripture: Joshua 1:9 NKJV

Be strong and of good courage; do not be afraid, nor be dismayed, for the LORD your God is with you wherever you go.

GRAHAM, Graeham, Graeme

Language/Cultural Origin: English
Inherent Meaning: From a Grand Home
Spiritual Connotation: Generous
Scripture: 1 Corinthians 13:13 NKJV

And now abide faith, hope, love, these three; but the greatest of these is love.

GRANGER, Grainger, Grange

Language/Cultural Origin: French
Inherent Meaning: Farmer
Spiritual Connotation: God's Follower
Scripture: Isaiah 48:17 NKJV

I am the LORD your God, who teaches you to profit, who leads you by the way you should go.

GRANT, Grantham, Grantley

Language/Cultural Origin: French
Inherent Meaning: Tall
Spiritual Connotation: Assurance
Scripture: Psalm 18:2 NKJV

The LORD is my rock and my fortress and my deliverer; my God, my strength, in whom I will trust; my shield and the horn of my salvation, my stronghold.

GRANTLAND, Grantlund

Language/Cultural Origin: Old English
Inherent Meaning: From the Great Plains
Spiritual Connotation: Strength in God
Scripture: Proverbs 3:5–6 NKJV

Trust in the LORD with all your heart, and lean not on your own understanding; in all your ways acknowledge Him, and He shall direct your paths.

GRANVILLE, Grenville

Language/Cultural Origin: French
Inherent Meaning: From the Large Village
Spiritual Connotation: Righteous
Scripture: Psalm 37:6 NKJV

He shall bring forth your righteousness as the light, and your justice as the noonday.

GRAYSON, Greyson

Language/Cultural Origin: Middle English
Inherent Meaning: Son of the Bailiff
Spiritual Connotation: One of Knowledge
Scripture: Proverbs 13:14 NKJV

The law of the wise is a fountain of life, to turn one away from the snares of death.

GREER, Grier

Language/Cultural Origin: English
Inherent Meaning: Watchful
Spiritual Connotation: Vigilant
Scripture: 1 Peter 5:8–9 NKJV

Be sober, be vigilant; because your adversary the devil walks about like a roaring lion, seeking whom he may devour. Resist him, steadfast in the faith.

GREGORY, Greg, Gregg, Greggory, Gregori, Greig, Grigori

Language/Cultural Origin: Greek
Inherent Meaning: Guardian
Spiritual Connotation: God's Trustee
Scripture: 1 Corinthians 16:13 NKJV

Watch, stand fast in the faith, be brave, be strong. Let all that you do be done with love.

GRESHAM, Grisham

Language/Cultural Origin: English
Inherent Meaning: From the Village
by the Pasture
Spiritual Connotation: Peaceful
Scripture: Psalm 23:2 NKJV
*He makes me to lie down in green pastures;
He leads me beside the still waters.*

GRETA, Gretal, Grethal, Gretta

Language/Cultural Origin: English
Inherent Meaning: Pearl
Spiritual Connotation: Eternal Hope
Scripture: Revelation 21:21 NKJV
*The twelve gates were twelve pearls: each
individual gate was of one pearl. And the
street of the city was pure gold, like
transparent glass.*

GRETCHEN, Gretchin

Language/Cultural Origin: German
Inherent Meaning: Pearl
Spiritual Connotation: Invaluable
Scripture: Psalm 36:7 NIV
*How priceless is your unfailing love! Both
high and low among men find refuge in the
shadow of your wings.*

GRIFFITH, Griffey

Language/Cultural Origin: Welsh
Inherent Meaning: Great Strength
Spiritual Connotation: Blessed of God
Scripture: Psalm 8:5–6 NKJV
*You have crowned him with glory and honor.
You have made him to have dominion over
the works of Your hands; You have put all
things under his feet.*

GROVER, Grove

Language/Cultural Origin: German
Inherent Meaning: Gardener
Spiritual Connotation: Consecrated
Scripture: Psalm 37:37 NKJV
*Mark the blameless man, and observe the
upright; for the future of that man is peace.*

GUADALUPE, Guadulupe

Language/Cultural Origin: Spanish
Inherent Meaning: From the Valley of Wolves
Spiritual Connotation: Wondrous
Scripture: Psalm 29:4 NASB
*The voice of the LORD is powerful, the voice
of the LORD is majestic.*

GUILLAUME, Guillermo

Language/Cultural Origin: French
Inherent Meaning: Strong Guardian
Spiritual Connotation: Shielded
Scripture: Psalm 5:11 NASB
*But let all who take refuge in You be glad, let
them ever sing for joy; and may You shelter
them, that those who love Your name may
exult in You.*

GUINEVERE, Guenevere

Language/Cultural Origin: Welsh
Inherent Meaning: Unstained
Spiritual Connotation: Ransomed
Scripture: 1 Peter 1:19 TLB
*But he paid for you with the precious
lifeblood of Christ, the sinless, spotless Lamb
of God.*

GUNNAR, Gunner, Gunthar, Gunther, Günther

Language/Cultural Origin: Old Norse
Inherent Meaning: Warrior-King
Spiritual Connotation: Obedient
Scripture: Psalm 119:34 NKJV
*Give me understanding, and I shall keep Your
law; Indeed, I shall observe it with my whole
heart.*

GURION, Guri, Guriel

Language/Cultural Origin: Hebrew
Inherent Meaning: Young Lion
Spiritual Connotation: Righteous
Scripture: Proverbs 28:1 NKJV
*The wicked flee when no one pursues, but the
righteous are bold as a lion.*

GUSTAVE, Gus, Guss, Gustaf, Gustáv, Gustavus

Language/Cultural Origin: Scandinavian
Inherent Meaning: God's Staff
Spiritual Connotation: Blessed
Scripture: Psalm 24:5 NKJV
*He shall receive blessing from the LORD, and
righteousness from the God of his salvation.*

GUTHRIE, Gutherie, Guthrey

Language/Cultural Origin: German
Inherent Meaning: War Hero
Spiritual Connotation: Great
Scripture: Colossians 3:16 NKJV
*Let the word of Christ dwell in you richly in
all wisdom.*

GUY, Guido, Gui
Language/Cultural Origin: French
Inherent Meaning: Director
Spiritual Connotation: Peaceful
Scripture: James 3:18 NKJV
Now the fruit of righteousness is sown in peace by those who make peace.

GWENDOLYN, Gwen, Gwendalyn, Gwendolin, Gwendolynn, Gwenn
Language/Cultural Origin: Welsh
Inherent Meaning: Fair
Spiritual Connotation: Full of Honor

Scripture: Psalm 18:35 NKJV
You have also given me the shield of Your salvation; Your right hand has held me up, Your gentleness has made me great.

GWYNN, Gwinn, Gwyn, Gwynne
Language/Cultural Origin: Welsh
Inherent Meaning: Spotless
Spiritual Connotation: Seeker of Wisdom
Scripture: Isaiah 58:14 NKJV
Then you shall delight yourself in the LORD; and I will cause you to ride on the high hills of the earth.

H

HABAIAH, Habiyah (see also Abia)
Language/Cultural Origin: Hebrew
Inherent Meaning: God Has Hidden
Spiritual Connotation: Preserved
Scripture: Isaiah 49:2 NKJV
And He has made My mouth like a sharp sword; in the shadow of His hand He has hidden Me.

HADAD, Haddad
Language/Cultural Origin: Hebrew
Inherent Meaning: Mighty
Spiritual Connotation: Strength of God
Scripture: Psalm 66:3 NRSV
How awesome are your deeds! Because of your great power, your enemies cringe before you.

HADASSAH, Hadása, Hadassa
Language/Cultural Origin: Hebrew
Inherent Meaning: Star
Spiritual Connotation: Precious
Scripture: Genesis 1:16 NASB
God made the two great lights, the greater light to govern the day, and the lesser light to govern the night; He made the stars also.

HADDEN, Haddan, Haddon (see also Hayden)
Language/Cultural Origin: English
Inherent Meaning: From the Hill of Heather
Spiritual Connotation: Great Confidence
Scripture: Jeremiah 32:17 NKJV
Ah, Lord GOD! Behold, You have made the

heavens and the earth by Your great power and outstretched arm. There is nothing too hard for You.

HADLAI, Haddlai (see also Adlai)
Language/Cultural Origin: Hebrew
Inherent Meaning: Frail
Spiritual Connotation: Child of God
Scripture: 2 Corinthians 12:9 NCV
My grace is enough for you. When you are weak, my power is made perfect in you.

HADLEY, Hadlee, Hadleigh
Language/Cultural Origin: Anglo-Saxon
Inherent Meaning: From the Field of Heather
Spiritual Connotation: Peaceful Spirit
Scripture: Psalm 25:21 NKJV
Let integrity and uprightness preserve me, for I wait for You.

HADRIAN, Hadrien
Language/Cultural Origin: Swedish
Inherent Meaning: Dark
Spiritual Connotation: Just
Scripture: Colossians 4:1 NKJV
Masters, give your bondservants what is just and fair, knowing that you also have a Master in heaven.

HAGAN, Haggan
Language/Cultural Origin: German
Inherent Meaning: Strong Defense
Spiritual Connotation: Immovable
Scripture: Psalm 62:6 NRSV
He alone is my rock and my salvation, my fortress; I shall not be shaken.

HAGAR, Haggar
Language/Cultural Origin: Hebrew
Inherent Meaning: Fugitive
Spiritual Connotation: Assurance
Scripture: Genesis 21:18 NASB
Arise, lift up the lad, and hold him by the hand, for I will make a great nation of him.

HAGEN, Haggen
Language/Cultural Origin: Irish
Inherent Meaning: Youthful
Spiritual Connotation: Accountable
Scripture: Ecclesiastes 12:1 KJV
Remember now thy Creator in the days of thy youth, while the evil days come not.

HAI, Haian
Language/Cultural Origin: Vietnamese
Inherent Meaning: Sea
Spiritual Connotation: Filled With Praise
Scripture: Psalm 69:34 NKJV
Let heaven and earth praise Him, the seas and everything that moves in them.

HAIDAR, Haidor
Language/Cultural Origin: Middle Eastern
Inherent Meaning: Lion
Spiritual Connotation: Warrior of God
Scripture: Isaiah 31:4 KJV
Like as the lion and the young lion roaring on its prey . . . so shall the LORD of hosts come down to fight for Mount Zion.

HAIDEE, Haiday, Haydee
(see also Heidi)
Language/Cultural Origin: English
Inherent Meaning: Modest
Spiritual Connotation: Humble
Scripture: Ezra 8:21 NKJV
Then I proclaimed a fast . . . that we might humble ourselves before our God, to seek from Him the right way for us and our little ones and all our possessions.

HAKIM, Hakeem, Hákeem
(see also Akim, Joachim)
Language/Cultural Origin: Ethiopian
Inherent Meaning: Doctor
Spiritual Connotation: Healer
Scripture: Psalm 147:3 NKJV
He heals the brokenhearted and binds up their wounds.

HAL, see Harold

HALE, Haile
Language/Cultural Origin: Hawaiian
Inherent Meaning: Military Power
Spiritual Connotation: Act of God
Scripture: Psalm 106:8 RSV
Yet he saved them for his name's sake, that he might make known his mighty power.

HALEN, Haylan
Language/Cultural Origin: Swedish
Inherent Meaning: Hall
Spiritual Connotation: Gracious
Scripture: Romans 12:14 NKJV
Bless those who persecute you; bless and do not curse.

HALEY, Haeley, Hailee, Hailey, Hailie,
Halee, Haleigh, Halie, Haylee,
Hayleigh, Hayley, Haylie
Language/Cultural Origin: Scandinavian
Inherent Meaning: Heroine
Spiritual Connotation: Creative
Scripture: Colossians 3:23–24 NKJV
And whatever you do, do it heartily, as to the Lord and not to men . . . for you serve the Lord Christ.

HALIA, Halianna, Hallia, Halliana
Language/Cultural Origin: Hawaiian
Inherent Meaning: In Remembrance of a Loved One
Spiritual Connotation: Reflective
Scripture: Luke 22:19 NKJV
And He took bread, gave thanks and broke it, and gave it to them, saying, "This is My body which is given for you; do this in remembrance of Me."

HALIAN, Halien
Language/Cultural Origin: Zuni
Inherent Meaning: Young
Spiritual Connotation: Righteous
Scripture: 2 Timothy 2:2 NKJV
And the things that you have heard from me among many witnesses, commit these to faithful men who will be able to teach others also.

HALIM, Haleem
Language/Cultural Origin: Middle Eastern
Inherent Meaning: Patient
Spiritual Connotation: Persistent
Scripture: 2 Timothy 4:2 NLT
Preach the word of God. Be persistent, whether the time is favorable or not. Patiently correct, rebuke, and encourage your people with good teaching.

HALINA, Halinah (see also Helena)
Language/Cultural Origin: Russian
Inherent Meaning: Glowing
Spiritual Connotation: Godly Example
Scripture: Matthew 5:14 NLT
You are the light of the world—like a city on a mountain, glowing in the night for all to see.

HALLAN, Hallin
Language/Cultural Origin: English

Inherent Meaning: **From the Manor**
Spiritual Connotation: **Generous**
Scripture: **2 Corinthians 9:9** TLB
The godly man gives generously to the poor. His good deeds will be an honor to him forever.

HALLE, Halla, Halley, Halli, Hally
Language/Cultural Origin: **Nigerian**
Inherent Meaning: **Unexpected Gift**
Spiritual Connotation: **Blessing**
Scripture: **2 Corinthians 9:13** TLB
Those you help . . . will praise God for this proof that your deeds are as good as your doctrine.

HALONA, Halonah
Language/Cultural Origin: **Native American**
Inherent Meaning: **Fortunate**
Spiritual Connotation: **Blessed**
Scripture: **Proverbs 3:18** NKJV
She is a tree of life to those who take hold of her, and happy are all who retain her.

HALSEY, Halsee, Halseigh, Halzee
Language/Cultural Origin: **English**
Inherent Meaning: **From the Ruler's Island**
Spiritual Connotation: **Righteous**
Scripture: **3 John 11** NKJV
Beloved, do not imitate what is evil, but what is good. He who does good is of God, but he who does evil has not seen God.

HAMAL, Hamaal
Language/Cultural Origin: **Middle Eastern**
Inherent Meaning: **Lamb**
Spiritual Connotation: **Hopeful**
Scripture: **Isaiah 11:6** NKJV
The wolf also shall dwell with the lamb, the leopard shall lie down with the young goat. . . . And a little child shall lead them.

HAMAN, Hayman
☞Language/Cultural Origin: **Hebrew**
Inherent Meaning: **Well Disposed**
Spiritual Connotation: **Blessed**
Scripture: **Deuteronomy 30:5** NLT
He will make you even more prosperous and numerous than your ancestors!

HAMILTON, Hamelton
Language/Cultural Origin: **Old English**
Inherent Meaning: **From the Fortified Castle**

Spiritual Connotation: **Faithful**
Scripture: **Proverbs 20:6** RSV
Many a man proclaims his own loyalty, but a faithful man who can find?

HAMLET, Hamlett
Language/Cultural Origin: **Old Norse**
Inherent Meaning: **From the Village**
Spiritual Connotation: **Compassionate**
Scripture: **Luke 6:36** NKJV
Therefore be merciful, just as your Father also is merciful.

HAMLIN, Hamelin, Hamlyn
Language/Cultural Origin: **Old German**
Inherent Meaning: **Loves His Home**
Spiritual Connotation: **Godly Example**
Scripture: **Ephesians 5:25** NKJV
Husbands, love your wives, just as Christ also loved the church and gave Himself for her.

HAMMOND, Hamond
Language/Cultural Origin: **English**
Inherent Meaning: **From the Village**
Spiritual Connotation: **Witness**
Scripture: **1 Peter 2:21** NASB
For you have been called for this purpose, since Christ also suffered for you, leaving you an example for you to follow in His steps.

HAMUEL, Hammuel
☞Language/Cultural Origin: **Hebrew**
Inherent Meaning: **Warmth of God**
Spiritual Connotation: **Loving**
Scripture: **Isaiah 60:3** NLT
All nations will come to your light. Mighty kings will come to see your radiance.

HANA, Hanita
Language/Cultural Origin: **Japanese**
Inherent Meaning: **Flower**
Spiritual Connotation: **Joyful**
Scripture: **Psalm 96:12–13** NCV
Let the fields and everything in them rejoice. Then all the trees of the forest will sing for joy before the LORD, because he is coming.

HANAN, Hannan, Hannen, Hannon
☞Language/Cultural Origin: **Hebrew**
Inherent Meaning: **Merciful**
Spiritual Connotation: **Compassionate**

Scripture: Matthew 9:13 NRSV
I desire mercy, not sacrifice. For I have come to call not the righteous but sinners.

HANANI, Hannani, Hananni
Language/Cultural Origin: Hebrew
Inherent Meaning: God Has Shown Mercy
Spiritual Connotation: Promised
Scripture: Deuteronomy 4:31 TLB
For the Lord your God is merciful—he will not abandon you.

HANANIAH, Hananiyah
Language/Cultural Origin: Hebrew
Inherent Meaning: God Is Gracious
Spiritual Connotation: Blessed
Scripture: Numbers 6:24 NKJV
The LORD bless you and keep you; the LORD make His face shine upon you, and be gracious to you.

HANIA, Hanja, Hanya
Language/Cultural Origin: Hebrew
Inherent Meaning: Resting Place
Spiritual Connotation: Peaceful
Scripture: Psalm 132:14 NLT
This is my home where I will live forever, he said. I will live here, for this is the place I desired.

HANIEL, Hanniel
Language/Cultural Origin: Hebrew
Inherent Meaning: Grace of God
Spiritual Connotation: Restored
Scripture: Joel 2:13 NLT
Return to the LORD your God, for he is gracious and merciful.

HANLEY, Hanlee, Hanleigh, Henlee, Henleigh, Henley, Hensley
Language/Cultural Origin: English
Inherent Meaning: From the High Pasture
Spiritual Connotation: Protector, Shepherd
Scripture: Isaiah 49:10 NKJV
They shall neither hunger nor thirst, neither heat nor sun shall strike them; for He who has mercy on them will lead them.

HANNAH, Hanna
Language/Cultural Origin: Hebrew
Inherent Meaning: Gracious
Spiritual Connotation: Compassionate

Scripture: Psalm 145:8 NKJV
The LORD is gracious and full of compassion, Slow to anger and great in mercy.

HANNIBAL, Hanibal
Language/Cultural Origin: Phoenician
Inherent Meaning: Grace
Spiritual Connotation: Merciful
Scripture: Psalm 18:25 NKJV
With the merciful You will show Yourself merciful; with a blameless man You will show Yourself blameless.

HANS, Hansel, Hansen, Hanz
Language/Cultural Origin: Swedish
Inherent Meaning: God Is Gracious
Spiritual Connotation: Discerning Spirit
Scripture: 1 Corinthians 15:10 NKJV
But by the grace of God I am what I am, and His grace toward me was not in vain.

HARAN, Harran
Language/Cultural Origin: Hebrew
Inherent Meaning: Enlightened
Spiritual Connotation: Sanctified
Scripture: Ephesians 1:18 NASB
I pray that the eyes of your heart may be enlightened.

HARBIN, Harbyn
Language/Cultural Origin: German
Inherent Meaning: Little Warrior
Spiritual Connotation: Obedient
Scripture: Matthew 8:9 NKJV
For I also am a man under authority, having soldiers under me. And I say to this one, "Go," and he goes; and to another, "Come," and he comes.

HARDIN, Hardan
Language/Cultural Origin: English
Inherent Meaning: From the Hares' Valley
Spiritual Connotation: Righteous
Scripture: Philippians 3:17 NCV
Brothers and sisters, all of you should try to follow my example and to copy those who live the way we showed you.

HARDY, Hardey
Language/Cultural Origin: English
Inherent Meaning: Bold
Spiritual Connotation: Confident
Scripture: Hebrews 4:16 NKJV

Let us therefore come boldly to the throne of grace, that we may obtain mercy and find grace to help in time of need.

HAREL, Hariel, Harrel
Language/Cultural Origin: Hebrew
Inherent Meaning: Mountain of God
Spiritual Connotation: Holy
Scripture: Exodus 3:1 NKJV
Now Moses . . . led the flock to the back of the desert, and came to Horeb, the mountain of God.

HARLAN, Harland, Harlon
Language/Cultural Origin: Old English
Inherent Meaning: From the Land
Spiritual Connotation: Resolute
Scripture: Deuteronomy 31:6 NKJV
Be strong and of good courage, do not fear nor be afraid of them; for the LORD your God, He is the One who goes with you. He will not leave you nor forsake you.

HARLEY, Harlee, Harleigh
Language/Cultural Origin: Old English
Inherent Meaning: From the Rabbit Pasture
Spiritual Connotation: Chosen of God
Scripture: John 15:19 NCV
If you belonged to the world, it would love you as it loves its own. But I have chosen you out of the world, so you don't belong to it. That is why the world hates you.

HARMONY, Harmoni, Harmonie
Language/Cultural Origin: Latin
Inherent Meaning: Oneness
Spiritual Connotation: Unifier
Scripture: Colossians 3:14 NCV
Do all these things; but most important, love each other. Love is what holds you all together in perfect unity.

HAROLD, Hal, Herald, Herold
Language/Cultural Origin: Old English
Inherent Meaning: Army Leader
Spiritual Connotation: Born of God
Scripture: Acts 17:28 NKJV
For in Him we live and move and have our being, as also some of your own poets have said, for we are also His offspring.

HARPER, Harpo
Language/Cultural Origin: English

Inherent Meaning: Harp Player
Spiritual Connotation: Instrument of Praise
Scripture: Psalm 33:2 NKJV
Praise the LORD with the harp; make melody to Him with an instrument of ten strings.

HARRIET, Harriett, Hattie
Language/Cultural Origin: Old German
Inherent Meaning: Ruler of the Household
Spiritual Connotation: Discerner of Excellence
Scripture: Philippians 4:8 NASB
Finally, brethren, whatever is true, . . . honorable, . . . right, . . . pure, . . . lovely, . . . [or] of good repute, if there is any excellence and if anything worthy of praise, let your mind dwell on these things.

HARRIS, Harrison
Language/Cultural Origin: Old English
Inherent Meaning: Son of the Strong Man
Spiritual Connotation: Courageous
Scripture: Proverbs 24:5 NKJV
A wise man is strong, yes, a man of knowledge increases strength.

HARRY, Harray, Harrey
Language/Cultural Origin: Old German
Inherent Meaning: Home Ruler
Spiritual Connotation: Integrity
Scripture: Ephesians 6:8 NKJV
Whatever good anyone does, he will receive the same from the Lord, whether he is a slave or free.

HARTLEY, Hartlee, Hartleigh
Language/Cultural Origin: Anglo-Saxon
Inherent Meaning: From the Deer Meadow
Spiritual Connotation: Victorious
Scripture: Psalm 50:15 NKJV
Call upon Me in the day of trouble; I will deliver you, and you shall glorify Me.

HARVEY, Harv (see also Hervé)
Language/Cultural Origin: Celtic
Inherent Meaning: Noble
Spiritual Connotation: Brave
Scripture: Psalm 100:3 NKJV
Know that the LORD, He is God; it is He who has made us, and not we ourselves; we are His people and the sheep of His pasture.

HASAD, Hasád, Hasaad (see also Asad)
Language/Cultural Origin: Turkish

Inherent Meaning: Harvester
Spiritual Connotation: Evangelist
Scripture: John 4:35 NCV
You have a saying, "Four more months till harvest." But I tell you, open your eyes and look at the fields ready for harvest now.

HASANA, Haseina
Language/Cultural Origin: Swahili
Inherent Meaning: Firstborn
Spiritual Connotation: Follower of Christ
Scripture: Colossians 1:15 NKJV
He is the image of the invisible God, the firstborn over all creation.

HASANI, Hasaan, Hasán, Hashaan (see also Ahsan, Ihsan)
Language/Cultural Origin: Swahili
Inherent Meaning: Handsome
Spiritual Connotation: Chosen
Scripture: 1 Samuel 16:12 NKJV
He was ruddy, with bright eyes, and good-looking. And the LORD said, "Arise, anoint him; for this is the one!"

HASRAH, Hazrah
Language/Cultural Origin: Hebrew
Inherent Meaning: Splendor
Spiritual Connotation: Praise
Scripture: Exodus 15:11 RSV
Who is like thee, majestic in holiness, terrible in glorious deeds, doing wonders?

HATIPHA, Hateefa, Hatifa, Hateepha
Language/Cultural Origin: Hebrew
Inherent Meaning: Captive
Spiritual Connotation: Obedient
Scripture: 2 Corinthians 10:5 NRSV
We take every thought captive to obey Christ.

HAVEN, Havan, Havin
Language/Cultural Origin: Dutch
Inherent Meaning: Harbor
Spiritual Connotation: Preserved
Scripture: Leviticus 25:18 NKJV
So you shall observe My statutes and keep My judgments, and perform them; and you will dwell in the land in safety.

HAYDEN, Haden, Haydn, Haydon (see also Hadden)
Language/Cultural Origin: English

Inherent Meaning: From the Hedged Valley
Spiritual Connotation: Victorious
Scripture: 2 Corinthians 6:2 NKJV
In the day of salvation I have helped you. Behold, now is the accepted time; behold, now is the day of salvation.

HAYES, Hays
Language/Cultural Origin: English
Inherent Meaning: From the Hedged Valley
Spiritual Connotation: Moderate
Scripture: 1 Corinthians 6:12 NCV
I am allowed to do all things, but all things are not good for me to do. I am allowed to do all things, but I will not let anything make me its slave.

HAYLEY, see Haley

HAYWARD, Heyward
Language/Cultural Origin: English
Inherent Meaning: Guardian/Protector of the Hedged Area
Spiritual Connotation: Secure
Scripture: Isaiah 26:3 NLT
You will keep in perfect peace all who trust in you, whose thoughts are fixed on you!

HAYWOOD, Heywood
Language/Cultural Origin: English
Inherent Meaning: From the Hedged Forest
Spiritual Connotation: Chosen
Scripture: Acts 13:48 NKJV
And as many as had been appointed to eternal life believed.

HAZEL, Hazyl
Language/Cultural Origin: English
Inherent Meaning: Commander of Authority
Spiritual Connotation: Cleansed
Scripture: 1 John 1:7 NKJV
But if we walk in the light as He is in the light, we have fellowship with one another, and the blood of Jesus Christ His Son cleanses us from all sin.

HAZIEL, Hazael
Language/Cultural Origin: Hebrew
Inherent Meaning: God Sees
Spiritual Connotation: Witness
Scripture: John 8:38 NRSV
I declare what I have seen in the Father's presence.

HEATH, Heathe

Language/Cultural Origin: English
Inherent Meaning: Shrub
Spiritual Connotation: Protector
Scripture: Ephesians 6:16 NKJV

Above all, taking the shield of faith with which you will be able to quench all the fiery darts of the wicked one.

HEATHER, Heatherlee

Language/Cultural Origin: Middle English
Inherent Meaning: Flowering, Blooming
Spiritual Connotation: Cover of Beauty
Scripture: Matthew 6:28–29 NKJV

So why do you worry about clothing? Consider the lilies of the field. . . . I say to you that even Solomon in all his glory was not arrayed like one of these.

HEBRON

☞Language/Cultural Origin: Hebrew
Inherent Meaning: Company
Spiritual Connotation: Inheritance
Scripture: Joshua 14:14 RSV

So Hebron became the inheritance of Caleb.

HECTOR, Hectar

Language/Cultural Origin: Greek
Inherent Meaning: Steadfast
Spiritual Connotation: One of Integrity
Scripture: Luke 6:38 NKJV

Give, and it will be given to you. . . . For with the same measure that you use, it will be measured back to you.

HEIDI, Heide, Heidee, Hidee, Hiedi (see also Haidee)

Language/Cultural Origin: Old German
Inherent Meaning: Honored
Spiritual Connotation: Blessed
Scripture: Psalm 29:11 KJV

The LORD will give strength unto his people; the LORD will bless his people with peace.

HEINRICH, Heinrick, Heinrik

Language/Cultural Origin: German
Inherent Meaning: Household Ruler
Spiritual Connotation: Just
Scripture: 1 Chronicles 18:14 NRSV

So David reigned over all Israel; and he administered justice and equity to all his people.

HELEN, Hellen

Language/Cultural Origin: Greek
Inherent Meaning: Light
Spiritual Connotation: Righteous
Scripture: Psalm 37:6 NKJV

He shall bring forth your righteousness as the light, and your justice as the noonday.

HELENA, Haleena, Halena, Helana, Heleana, Heleena (see also Halina)

Language/Cultural Origin: English
Inherent Meaning: Brightness
Spiritual Connotation: Testimony
Scripture: Isaiah 60:3 NRSV

Nations shall come to your light, and kings to the brightness of your dawn.

HENLEY, see Hanley

HENRIETTA, Henrieta

Language/Cultural Origin: English
Inherent Meaning: Household Ruler
Spiritual Connotation: Strong
Scripture: Psalm 18:32 NKJV

It is God who arms me with strength, and makes my way perfect.

HENRY, Hank, Henri, Henrí

Language/Cultural Origin: Old German
Inherent Meaning: Ruler of the Household
Spiritual Connotation: Trusted
Scripture: Psalm 37:23 NKJV

The steps of a good man are ordered by the LORD, and He delights in his way.

HERBERT, Herb, Herbie

Language/Cultural Origin: Old German
Inherent Meaning: Shining Soldier
Spiritual Connotation: Powerful Protector
Scripture: Psalm 37:31 NKJV

The law of his God is in his heart; none of his steps shall slide.

HERCULES

Language/Cultural Origin: Greek
Inherent Meaning: Glorious Gift
Spiritual Connotation: Enduring
Scripture: Jude 1:24,25 NRSV

Now to him who is able to keep you from falling, be glory, majesty, power, and authority, before all time and now and forever. Amen.

HERMAN, Hermann, Hermon

Language/Cultural Origin: Old German
Inherent Meaning: Noble Soldier
Spiritual Connotation: Righteous
Scripture: Psalm 37:37 NKJV
Mark the blameless man, and observe the upright; for the future of that man is peace.

HERICK, Herrik

Language/Cultural Origin: German
Inherent Meaning: War Ruler
Spiritual Connotation: Chosen
Scripture: 2 Thessalonians 2:13 RSV
But we are bound to give thanks to God always for you, brethren beloved by the Lord, because God chose you from the beginning to be saved.

HERSHEL, Herschel, Hershell

Language/Cultural Origin: Hebrew
Inherent Meaning: Deer
Spiritual Connotation: Promise
Scripture: Isaiah 35:6 NKJV
Then the lame shall leap like a deer, and the tongue of the dumb sing. For waters shall burst forth in the wilderness, and streams in the desert.

HERVÉ, Hervay (see also Harvey)

Language/Cultural Origin: French
Inherent Meaning: Warrior
Spiritual Connotation: Steadfast
Scripture: 1 Timothy 6:12 NASB
Fight the good fight of faith; take hold of the eternal life to which you were called.

HESED, Heséd

Language/Cultural Origin: Hebrew
Inherent Meaning: Kindness
Spiritual Connotation: Gentle
Scripture: Proverbs 3:3 NASB
Do not let kindness and truth leave you.

HESTER, Hestar (see also Esther)

Language/Cultural Origin: English
Inherent Meaning: Star
Spiritual Connotation: Gift of God
Scripture: Psalm 139:9–10 NKJV
If I take the wings of the morning, and dwell in the uttermost parts of the sea, even there Your hand shall lead me, and Your right hand shall hold me.

HEZEKIAH

Language/Cultural Origin: Hebrew
Inherent Meaning: God Has Strengthened
Spiritual Connotation: Hopeful
Scripture: 2 Thessalonians 3:3 NRSV
But the Lord is faithful; he will strengthen you and guard you from the evil one.

HEZRAI, Hezrael

Language/Cultural Origin: Hebrew
Inherent Meaning: Beautiful
Spiritual Connotation: Testimony
Scripture: Romans 10:15 RSV
How beautiful are the feet of those who preach good news!

HILDA, Hilde

Language/Cultural Origin: Old German
Inherent Meaning: Battle Maid
Spiritual Connotation: Courageous
Scripture: Psalm 73:26 NKJV
My flesh and my heart fail; but God is the strength of my heart and my portion forever.

HILLARY, Hilaree, Hilari, Hilary, Hillaree, Hillarie, Hilleree, Hillory

Language/Cultural Origin: English
Inherent Meaning: Cheerful
Spiritual Connotation: Blessed
Scripture: James 1:17 NKJV
Every good gift and every perfect gift is from above, and comes down from the Father of lights, with whom there is no variation or shadow of turning.

HILLEL, Hillal

Language/Cultural Origin: Hebrew
Inherent Meaning: Greatly Praised
Spiritual Connotation: Humble
Scripture: Psalm 109:30 NKJV
I will greatly praise the LORD with my mouth; yes, I will praise Him among the multitude.

HILTON, Hillton

Language/Cultural Origin: English
Inherent Meaning: From the Hill Town
Spiritual Connotation: Obedient
Scripture: Revelation 22:7 NASB
And behold, I am coming quickly. Blessed is he who heeds the words of the prophecy of this book.

HIRAH, Hierah

Language/Cultural Origin: Hebrew

Inherent Meaning: Noble
Spiritual Connotation: Holy
Scripture: Romans 6:18 NLT
Now you are free from sin, your old master, and you have become slaves to your new master, righteousness.

HIRAM, Hi, Hirom
Language/Cultural Origin: Hebrew
Inherent Meaning: Most Noble
Spiritual Connotation: Righteous
Scripture: Psalm 84:11 NKJV
For the LORD God is a sun and shield; the LORD will give grace and glory; no good thing will He withhold from those who walk uprightly.

HIROKO, Hirokoh
Language/Cultural Origin: Japanese
Inherent Meaning: Self-Sacrificing
Spiritual Connotation: Glorified
Scripture: Hebrews 9:26 NASB
Otherwise, He would have needed to suffer often since the foundation of the world; but now once at the consummation of the ages He has been manifested to put away sin by the sacrifice of Himself.

HIROSHI, Hirashi
Language/Cultural Origin: Japanese
Inherent Meaning: Generous
Spiritual Connotation: Cheerful
Scripture: 2 Corinthians 9:7 NCV
Each one should give as you have decided in your heart to give. You should not be sad when you give, and you should not give because you feel forced to give.

HISA, Hisae, Hisayo
Language/Cultural Origin: Japanese
Inherent Meaning: Long-Lasting
Spiritual Connotation: Wise
Scripture: John 6:27 NKJV
Do not labor for the food which perishes, but for the food which endures to everlasting life.

HODIAH, Hodiyah
Language/Cultural Origin: Hebrew
Inherent Meaning: Splendor of God
Spiritual Connotation: Majestic
Scripture: Psalm 29:2 NRSV
Ascribe to the LORD the glory of his name; worship the LORD in holy splendor.

HOGAN, Hogen
Language/Cultural Origin: Gaelic
Inherent Meaning: Youthful
Spiritual Connotation: Generous Soul
Scripture: 2 Corinthians 9:12 NCV
This service you do not only helps the needs of God's people, it also brings many more thanks to God.

HOLBROOK, Holbrooke
Language/Cultural Origin: Old English
Inherent Meaning: From the Brook
Spiritual Connotation: Peaceful
Scripture: Psalm 122:7 NKJV
Peace be within your walls, prosperity within your palaces.

HOLDEN, Holdin
Language/Cultural Origin: English
Inherent Meaning: From the Valley Hollow
Spiritual Connotation: Fearless
Scripture: Joel 2:21 NKJV
Fear not, O land; be glad and rejoice, for the LORD has done marvelous things!

HOLLIS, Hollyss
Language/Cultural Origin: Old English
Inherent Meaning: From the Holly Trees
Spiritual Connotation: Righteous
Scripture: Isaiah 58:8 NKJV
Then your light shall break forth like the morning, your healing shall spring forth speedily, and your righteousness shall go before you.

HOLLY, Hollee, Holley, Holli, Hollie
Language/Cultural Origin: Old English
Inherent Meaning: Holly Tree
Spiritual Connotation: Peaceful
Scripture: Philippians 4:7 NKJV
And the peace of God, which surpasses all understanding, will guard your hearts and minds through Christ Jesus.

HOLLYANN, Hollianna, Hollyanne
Language/Cultural Origin: English
Inherent Meaning: Gracious
Spiritual Connotation: Kind
Scripture: Ephesians 4:32 NKJV
And be kind to one another, tenderhearted, forgiving one another, just as God in Christ forgave you.

HOMER
Language/Cultural Origin: Greek
Inherent Meaning: Covenant
Spiritual Connotation: Doer of God's Word
Scripture: Jeremiah 32:40 NKJV
> And I will make an everlasting covenant with them, that I will not turn away from doing them good.

HONORIA, Honor, Honora, Honoré
Language/Cultural Origin: Latin
Inherent Meaning: Honorable Woman
Spiritual Connotation: Thankful
Scripture: Psalm 100:4 NKJV
> Enter into His gates with thanksgiving, and into His courts with praise. Be thankful to Him, and bless His name.

HOPE, Hopie
Language/Cultural Origin: Old English
Inherent Meaning: Trust in the Future
Spiritual Connotation: Understanding Heart
Scripture: Psalm 37:4 NKJV
> Delight yourself also in the LORD, and He shall give you the desires of your heart.

HOPHNI, Hophnee, Hophney
☞ Language/Cultural Origin: Hebrew
Inherent Meaning: Strong
Spiritual Connotation: Arm of God
Scripture: 2 Corinthians 12:9 RSV
> My grace is sufficient for you, for my power is made perfect in weakness.

HORACE, Horacio, Horatio, Horatius
Language/Cultural Origin: Latin
Inherent Meaning: Keeper of Time
Spiritual Connotation: Efficient
Scripture: Ephesians 5:15–16 NKJV
> See then that you walk circumspectly, not as fools but as wise, redeeming the time, because the days are evil.

HORTON, Horten
Language/Cultural Origin: Old English
Inherent Meaning: From the Garden Estate
Spiritual Connotation: Faithful Steward
Scripture: 1 Peter 4:10 NRSV
> Like good stewards of the manifold grace of God, serve one another with whatever gift each of you has received.

HOSANNA, Hosana
☞ (see also Osanna)
Language/Cultural Origin: Hebrew
Inherent Meaning: God Has Heard
Spiritual Connotation: Praise the Lord
Scripture: John 12:13 NRSV
> Hosanna! Blessed is the one who comes in the name of the Lord—the King of Israel!

HOSEA, Hoshea
☞ Language/Cultural Origin: Hebrew
Inherent Meaning: Deliverance
Spiritual Connotation: Strength
Scripture: 2 Corinthians 12:9 NKJV
> My grace is sufficient for you, for My strength is made perfect in weakness.

HOSHAMA, Hoshamma
☞ Language/Cultural Origin: Hebrew
Inherent Meaning: God Has Heard
Spiritual Connotation: Godly
Scripture: 1 John 5:14 NRSV
> If we ask anything according to his will, he hears us.

HOWARD, Howie
Language/Cultural Origin: English
Inherent Meaning: Chief Guardian
Spiritual Connotation: Discerning
Scripture: Psalm 37:23 NKJV
> The steps of a good man are ordered by the LORD, and He delights in his way.

HOWE, Howey
Language/Cultural Origin: German
Inherent Meaning: Eminent
Spiritual Connotation: Protected
Scripture: Job 36:4 NKJV
> For truly my words are not false; One who is perfect in knowledge is with you.

HOWELL, Howel
Language/Cultural Origin: Welsh
Inherent Meaning: Remarkable
Spiritual Connotation: Reconciled
Scripture: 2 Corinthians 5:18 NKJV
> Now all things are of God, who has reconciled us to Himself through Jesus Christ, and has given us the ministry of reconciliation.

HOYT, Hoyte
Language/Cultural Origin: Irish

Inherent Meaning: Spirited
Spiritual Connotation: Zealous
Scripture: Titus 2:14 NCV
He gave himself for us so he might pay the price to free us from all evil and to make us pure people who belong only to him.

HUBERT, Hubbard, Hubie
Language/Cultural Origin: Old German
Inherent Meaning: Clear-Minded
Spiritual Connotation: Obedient
Scripture: Deuteronomy 6:5 NKJV
You shall love the LORD your God with all your heart, with all your soul, and with all your strength.

HUGH, Huey, Hughes, Hugo
Language/Cultural Origin: Old German
Inherent Meaning: Thoughtful
Spiritual Connotation: Wise
Scripture: James 3:17 NKJV
But the wisdom that is from above is first pure, then peaceable, gentle, willing to yield, full of mercy and good fruits, without partiality and without hypocrisy.

HUMPHREY, Humfrey
Language/Cultural Origin: Old German
Inherent Meaning: Protector
Spiritual Connotation: Peaceful Strength
Scripture: Ecclesiastes 7:12 NKJV
For wisdom is a defense as money is a defense, but the excellence of knowledge is that wisdom gives life to those who have it.

HUNTER, Huntar
Language/Cultural Origin: Old English
Inherent Meaning: Hunter
Spiritual Connotation: Pursuer of Truth

Scripture: Lamentations 4:19 NRSV
Our pursuers were swifter than the eagles in the heavens; they chased us on the mountains, they lay in wait for us in the wilderness.

HUR, Hurr
Language/Cultural Origin: Hebrew
Inherent Meaning: Noble
Spiritual Connotation: Purified
Scripture: Ephesians 4:24 NLT
You must display a new nature because you are a new person, created in God's likeness—righteous, holy, and true.

HURLEY, Hurlee, Hurleigh
Language/Cultural Origin: Gaelic
Inherent Meaning: Lover of the Sea
Spiritual Connotation: Blessed
Scripture: James 1:17 NKJV
Every good gift and every perfect gift is from above, and comes down from the Father of lights, with whom there is no variation or shadow of turning.

HUXLEY, Huxlee
Language/Cultural Origin: Old English
Inherent Meaning: From the Wise Man's Meadow
Spiritual Connotation: Tranquil Spirit
Scripture: Romans 8:14 NKJV
For as many as are led by the Spirit of God, these are sons of God.

HYATT, Hyett
Language/Cultural Origin: English
Inherent Meaning: From the High Gate
Spiritual Connotation: Righteous
Scripture: Psalm 55:22 NASB
Cast your burden upon the LORD, and He will sustain you; He will never allow the righteous to be shaken.

Yes, there will be an abundance of flowers and singing and joy! The deserts will become as green as the Lebanon mountains.

IBRI, Ibree
☞ Language/Cultural Origin: Hebrew
Inherent Meaning: Passes Over
Spiritual Connotation: Symbol
Scripture: Exodus 12:13 NRSV
When I see the blood, I will pass over you, and no plague shall destroy you when I strike the land of Egypt.

ICHABOD
☞ Language/Cultural Origin: Hebrew
Inherent Meaning: The Glory Has Departed
Spiritual Connotation: Grief
Scripture: 1 Samuel 4:22 RSV
The glory has departed from Israel, for the ark of God has been captured.

IAGO, Jago, Yago
Language/Cultural Origin: Welsh
Inherent Meaning: Supplanter
Spiritual Connotation: Replacement
Scripture: Isaiah 9:10 NKJV
The bricks have fallen down, but we will rebuild with hewn stones; the sycamores are cut down, but we will replace them with cedars.

IDA, Idaleena, Idarina
Language/Cultural Origin: German
Inherent Meaning: Youthful
Spiritual Connotation: Industrious
Scripture: Psalm 16:11 NKJV
You will show me the path of life; In Your presence is fullness of joy; at Your right hand are pleasures forevermore.

IAN, Ean, Iain
Language/Cultural Origin: Scottish
Inherent Meaning: God Is Gracious
Spiritual Connotation: Discreet
Scripture: Matthew 6:6 NKJV
When you pray, go into your room, and . . . pray to your Father who is in the secret place; and your Father who sees in secret will reward you openly.

IDALIA, Idalis, Idalys
Language/Cultural Origin: American
Inherent Meaning: Creative
Spiritual Connotation: Gifted
Scripture: Psalm 19:1 NCV
The heavens tell the glory of God, and the skies announce what his hands have made.

IANOS, Iano, Iános
Language/Cultural Origin: Czech
Inherent Meaning: God Is Gracious
Spiritual Connotation: Divine Vision
Scripture: Acts 14:20 NLT
But as the believers stood around him, he got up and went back into the city. The next day he left with Barnabas for Derbe.

IESHA, Ieasha, Ieesha, Ieisha, Ieshia (see also Aiesha)
Language/Cultural Origin: American
Inherent Meaning: Woman
Spiritual Connotation: Blessed
Scripture: Exodus 3:22 TLB
Every woman will ask for jewels, silver, gold, and the finest of clothes from her Egyptian master's wife and neighbors. You will clothe your sons and daughters with the best of Egypt!

IANTHE, Iantha, Yantha
Language/Cultural Origin: Greek
Inherent Meaning: Violet Flower
Spiritual Connotation: Restored
Scripture: Isaiah 35:2 TLB

IGNATIA, Ignacia, Ignashia
Language/Cultural Origin: Latin
Inherent Meaning: Ardent

Spiritual Connotation: **Full of Honor**
Scripture: **Psalm 51:10** KJV
*Create in me a clean heart, O God; and
renew a right spirit within me.*

IGNATIUS, Ignacius, Ignashus
Language/Cultural Origin: **Latin**
Inherent Meaning: **Ardent**
Spiritual Connotation: **Diligent**
Scripture: **Romans 12:11** NRSV
*Do not lag in zeal, be ardent in spirit,
serve the Lord.*

IGOR, Igorr
Language/Cultural Origin: **Russian**
Inherent Meaning: **Protected**
Spiritual Connotation: **Preserved**
Scripture: **Psalm 20:1** NKJV
*May the LORD answer you in the day of
trouble; may the name of the God of
Jacob defend you.*

IHSAN, Ihsaan, Ihsán
(see also Ahsan, Hasani)
Language/Cultural Origin: **Turkish**
Inherent Meaning: **Compassionate**
Spiritual Connotation: **Loving**
Scripture: **Psalm 63:3** RSV
*Because thy steadfast love is better than
life, my lips will praise thee.*

ILAN, Illan
Language/Cultural Origin: **Hebrew**
Inherent Meaning: **Youth**
Spiritual Connotation: **Pride of the Father**
Scripture: **Psalm 127:4** NCV
*Children who are born to a young man are
like arrows in the hand of a warrior.*

ILANA, Ilani, Illana, Illanda, Illani
Language/Cultural Origin: **Hebrew**
Inherent Meaning: **Tree**
Spiritual Connotation: **Firmly Rooted**
Scripture: **Psalm 1:3** NLT
*They are like trees planted along the
riverbank ... and in all they do, they
prosper.*

ILIANA, Ileana, Illiana
(see also Eliana, Liana)
Language/Cultural Origin: **Greek**
Inherent Meaning: **From Troy**

Spiritual Connotation: **Believer**
Scripture: **Romans 1:16** NKJV
*For I am not ashamed of the gospel of Christ,
for it is the power of God to salvation for
everyone who believes, for the Jew first and
also for the Greek.*

ILONA, Ileena, Ilina
Language/Cultural Origin: **Hungarian**
Inherent Meaning: **Light**
Spiritual Connotation: **Disciple of Christ**
Scripture: **John 15:8** NRSV
*My Father is glorified by this, that you bear
much fruit and become my disciples.*

ILYA, Ilias, Iljah (see also Elya)
Language/Cultural Origin: **Russian**
Inherent Meaning: **The Lord Is My God**
Spiritual Connotation: **Confessor**
Scripture: **Matthew 27:54** NKJV
*So when the centurion ... saw the
earthquake and the things that had
happened, [he] feared greatly, saying, "Truly
this was the Son of God!"*

IMAN, Imani
Language/Cultural Origin: **Middle Eastern**
Inherent Meaning: **Believer**
Spiritual Connotation: **Illuminated**
Scripture: **John 12:46** NASB
*I have come as light into the world, that
everyone who believes in Me may not remain
in darkness.*

IMELDA, Imalda
Language/Cultural Origin: **Swiss**
Inherent Meaning: **All-Encompassing Battle**
Spiritual Connotation: **Victorious**
Scripture: **Nehemiah 1:10** NASB
*They are Your servants and Your people
whom You redeemed by Your great power
and by Your strong hand.*

IMLA, Imlah
Language/Cultural Origin: **Hebrew**
Inherent Meaning: **Fulfilling**
Spiritual Connotation: **Prosperous**
Scripture: **John 10:10** NKJV
*I have come that they may have life, and that
they may have it more abundantly.*

IMMANUEL, IMMANUELA,
see Emanuel, Emanuela

IMOGENE, Imogenia
Language/Cultural Origin: Latin
Inherent Meaning: Image
Spiritual Connotation: Likeness of God
Scripture: Hebrews 8:10 NKJV
I will put My laws in their mind and write them on their hearts; and I will be their God, and they shall be My people.

IMRA, Imrah
☞Language/Cultural Origin: Hebrew
Inherent Meaning: Stubborn
Spiritual Connotation: Learner of Obedience
Scripture: Hosea 4:16 TLB
Don't be like Israel, stubborn as a heifer, resisting the Lord's attempts to lead her in green pastures.

IMRAN, Imrand
Language/Cultural Origin: Hebrew
Inherent Meaning: Host
Spiritual Connotation: Gracious
Scripture: Romans 16:23 NCV
Gaius is letting me and the whole church here use his home. He also sends greetings to you.

IMRI, Imree, Imrée
☞Language/Cultural Origin: Hebrew
Inherent Meaning: Speech
Spiritual Connotation: Empowered
Scripture: Acts 11:15 RSV
As I began to speak, the Holy Spirit fell on them just as on us at the beginning.

INA, Inah
Language/Cultural Origin: Irish
Inherent Meaning: Pure
Spiritual Connotation: Divine Inspiration
Scripture: Job 22:28 NKJV
You will also declare a thing, and it will be established for you; so light will shine on your ways.

INDIA, Indya
Language/Cultural Origin: English
Inherent Meaning: From India
Spiritual Connotation: Gift of Faith
Scripture: Job 19:25 NRSV
For I know that my Redeemer lives, and that at the last he will stand upon the earth.

INDIGO
Language/Cultural Origin: Latin
Inherent Meaning: Dark Blue
Spiritual Connotation: Strengthened
Scripture: Psalm 42:5 RSV
Why are you cast down, O my soul, and why are you disquieted within me? Hope in God.

INDIRA, Indra
Language/Cultural Origin: Indo-Pakistani
Inherent Meaning: Splendid
Spiritual Connotation: Miraculous
Scripture: 1 Chronicles 16:24 NKJV
Declare His glory among the nations, His wonders among all peoples.

INESSA, Innessa
Language/Cultural Origin: Russian
Inherent Meaning: Innocent
Spiritual Connotation: Cleansed
Scripture: Psalm 36:6 NKJV
Your righteousness is like the great mountains; Your judgments are a great deep; O LORD

INGEMAR, Ingeborg
Language/Cultural Origin: Old Norse
Inherent Meaning: Famous Son
Spiritual Connotation: Adventurous
Scripture: Job 23:14 NKJV
For He performs what is appointed for me, And many such things are with Him.

INGER, Ing, Inga, Inge
Language/Cultural Origin: Old Norse
Inherent Meaning: Army of the Son
Spiritual Connotation: Kind
Scripture: Matthew 25:40 NKJV
Assuredly, I say to you, inasmuch as you did it to one of the least of these My brethren, you did it to Me.

INGERLISA, Ingerlise
Language/Cultural Origin: Norwegian
Inherent Meaning: Praised Daughter
Spiritual Connotation: Consecrated to God
Scripture: Romans 12:1 NCV
So brothers and sisters, since God has shown us great mercy, I beg you to offer your lives as a living sacrifice to Him.

INGRAM, Ingraham, Ingrim
Language/Cultural Origin: Old Norse

Inherent Meaning: King's Raven
Spiritual Connotation: Wise
Scripture: Psalm 121:1 NKJV
I will lift up my eyes to the hills; from whence comes my help?

INGRID, Ingela
Language/Cultural Origin: Old Norse
Inherent Meaning: Hero's Daughter
Spiritual Connotation: Cherished
Scripture: 1 Corinthians 2:9 NKJV
Eye has not seen, nor ear heard, nor have entered into the heart of man the things which God has prepared for those who love Him.

INIKO, Ineeko
Language/Cultural Origin: Ibo
Inherent Meaning: Born During Hard Times
Spiritual Connotation: Forever Preserved
Scripture: Psalm 27:5 NRSV
For he will hide me in his shelter in the day of trouble; he will conceal me under the cover of his tent; he will set me high on a rock.

INKA, Inkah
Language/Cultural Origin: Russian
Inherent Meaning: Heavenly
Spiritual Connotation: Image of God
Scripture: Matthew 5:48 NKJV
Therefore you shall be perfect, just as your Father in heaven is perfect.

INNIS, Innes, Inness
(see also Ennis)
Language/Cultural Origin: Gaelic
Inherent Meaning: From the Island
Spiritual Connotation: Obedient
Scripture: Psalm 119:30 NKJV
I have chosen the way of truth; Your judgments I have laid before me.

IOAN, Ioann
Language/Cultural Origin: Romanian
Inherent Meaning: God Is Gracious
Spiritual Connotation: Cherished
Scripture: Titus 2:11 NRSV
For the grace of God has appeared, bringing salvation to all.

IOANNA, Ioana
Language/Cultural Origin: Russian

Inherent Meaning: God Is Gracious
Spiritual Connotation: Set Apart
Scripture: Ephesians 3:2 NCV
Surely you have heard that God gave me this work through his grace to help you.

IOLA, Iolia
Language/Cultural Origin: Greek
Inherent Meaning: Dawn of Day
Spiritual Connotation: One Made Worthy
Scripture: Revelation 2:7 NKJV
To him who overcomes I will give to eat from the tree of life, which is in the midst of the Paradise of God.

IOLANA, Iolanna
Language/Cultural Origin: Hawaiian
Inherent Meaning: Soaring Like a Hawk
Spiritual Connotation: Steadfast
Scripture: Isaiah 40:31 RSV
But they who wait for the LORD shall renew their strength, they shall mount up with wings like eagles, they shall run and not be weary, they shall walk and not faint.

IONA, Ione, Ionia
Language/Cultural Origin: Greek
Inherent Meaning: Violet Flower
Spiritual Connotation: Inner Beauty
Scripture: Psalm 119:34 NKJV
Give me understanding, and I shall keep Your law; indeed, I shall observe it with my whole heart.

IRA, Irah
Language/Cultural Origin: Hebrew
Inherent Meaning: Watchful
Spiritual Connotation: Led by the Spirit
Scripture: Galatians 5:22–23 NKJV
But the fruit of the Spirit is love, joy, peace, longsuffering, kindness, goodness, faithfulness, gentleness, self-control.

IRAM, Irram
Language/Cultural Origin: Hebrew
Inherent Meaning: Brightness
Spiritual Connotation: Profound
Scripture: Psalm 18:12 NLT
The brilliance of his presence broke through the clouds, raining down hail and burning coals.

IRENE, Irena, Iryna
Language/Cultural Origin: Greek

Inherent Meaning: Messenger of Peace
Spiritual Connotation: Victorious Spirit
Scripture: Job 22:28 NKJV
> You will also declare a thing, and it will be established for you; so light will shine on your ways.

IRI, Iree, Ireigh
Language/Cultural Origin: Hebrew
Inherent Meaning: God Watches
Spiritual Connotation: In the Light
Scripture: John 2:25 NIV
> He did not need man's testimony about man, for he knew what was in a man.

IRIJAH, Irija, Iriya, Iriyah
Language/Cultural Origin: Hebrew
Inherent Meaning: God Sees
Spiritual Connotation: One of Integrity
Scripture: Job 31:4 NASB
> Does He not see my ways, and number all my steps?

IRINA, Irana, Iriana, Irianna (see also Ariana)
Language/Cultural Origin: Russian
Inherent Meaning: Serenity
Spiritual Connotation: Absolute Peace
Scripture: Exodus 11:7 NASB
> But against any of the sons of Israel a dog shall not even bark . . . that you may understand how the LORD makes a distinction between Egypt and Israel.

IRIS, Irisa, Irisha, Irissa, Irusya
Language/Cultural Origin: Greek
Inherent Meaning: Rainbow
Spiritual Connotation: God's Promise
Scripture: Psalm 104:24 NKJV
> O LORD, how manifold are Your works! In wisdom You have made them all. The earth is full of Your possessions.

IRMA, Erma, Irmina
Language/Cultural Origin: Latin
Inherent Meaning: Exalted
Spiritual Connotation: Excellent Virtue
Scripture: Acts 2:28 NKJV
> You have made known to me the ways of life; You will make me full of joy in Your presence.

IRVING, Earvin, Erv, Ervin, Ervine, Erving, Irv, Irvin, Irvine
Language/Cultural Origin: Irish
Inherent Meaning: Handsome
Spiritual Connotation: Trusting Spirit
Scripture: Isaiah 26:3 NKJV
> You will keep him in perfect peace, Whose mind is stayed on You, Because he trusts in You.

IRWIN, Erwin, Erwyn, Irwyn
Language/Cultural Origin: Old English
Inherent Meaning: Friend
Spiritual Connotation: Triumphant Spirit
Scripture: Zechariah 4:6 NKJV
> This is the word of the LORD to Zerubbabel: "Not by might nor by power, but by My Spirit," says the LORD of hosts.

ISAAC, Ike, Isaak, Isac, Isak, Ishaq, Itzak, Izaac, Izaak, Izac, Izak, Izák, Izakk, Izzy, Yitzak, Yitzhak
Language/Cultural Origin: Hebrew
Inherent Meaning: Laughter
Spiritual Connotation: Child of Promise
Scripture: Genesis 21:6 NASB
> God has made laughter for me; everyone who hears will laugh with me.

ISSACHAR
Language/Cultural Origin: Hebrew
Inherent Meaning: Reward
Spiritual Connotation: Righteous
Scripture: 1 Samuel 24:19 NKJV
> Therefore may the LORD reward you with good for what you have done to me this day.

ISABEL, Isabela, Isabella, Isabelle, Izabel, Izabele, Izabella
Language/Cultural Origin: Spanish
Inherent Meaning: Consecrated to God
Spiritual Connotation: Discerning Spirit
Scripture: Isaiah 60:1 NKJV
> Arise, shine; for your light has come! And the glory of the LORD is risen upon you.

ISADORA, Isidora
Language/Cultural Origin: Greek
Inherent Meaning: Gift of the Goddess
Spiritual Connotation: Inspired
Scripture: John 5:30 NKJV

I can of Myself do nothing. . . . I do not seek My own will but the will of the Father who sent Me.

ISAIAH, Isaia, Isiah, Izaiah
☞ Language/Cultural Origin: Hebrew
Inherent Meaning: God Is My Salvation
Spiritual Connotation: Steadfast
Scripture: Matthew 17:20 NKJV
If you have faith as a mustard seed, you will say to this mountain, Move from here to there, and it will move; and nothing will be impossible for you.

ISHMAEL, Ishmeil, Ismael,
☞ Ishmaiah, Ismail
Language/Cultural Origin: Hebrew
Inherent Meaning: God Will Hear
Spiritual Connotation: Blessed
Scripture: Genesis 17:20 NCV
As for Ishmael, I have heard you. I will bless him and give him many descendants. . . . I will make him into a great nation.

ISHMAELA, Ismaela
Language/Cultural Origin: Hebrew
Inherent Meaning: God Will Hear
Spiritual Connotation: Trusting
Scripture: Philemon 1:22 NCV
One more thing—prepare a room for me in which to stay, because I hope God will answer your prayers and I will be able to come to you.

ISRAEL, Izrael, Yisrael
☞ Language/Cultural Origin: Hebrew
Inherent Meaning: Wrestled With God
Spiritual Connotation: Reminder
Scripture: Genesis 32:25 NKJV
Now when He saw that He did not prevail against him, He touched the socket of his hip; and the socket of Jacob's hip was out of joint as He wrestled with him.

ITALIA, Italie, Italya
Language/Cultural Origin: Italian
Inherent Meaning: From Italy
Spiritual Connotation: Flexible
Scripture: Isaiah 64:8 NKJV
But now, O LORD, You are our Father; we are the clay, and You our potter; and all we are the work of Your hand.

IVAN, Iven
Language/Cultural Origin: Russian

Inherent Meaning: God Is Gracious
Spiritual Connotation: Triumphant
Scripture: Luke 6:38 NKJV
Give, and it will be given to you. . . . For with the same measure that you use, it will be measured back to you.

IVANA, Ivania, Ivanna
Language/Cultural Origin: Slavic
Inherent Meaning: God Is Gracious
Spiritual Connotation: Thankful
Scripture: Galatians 2:21 NKJV
I do not set aside the grace of God; for if righteousness comes through the law, then Christ died in vain.

IVAR, Iver, Ivor
Language/Cultural Origin: Old Norse
Inherent Meaning: Noble
Spiritual Connotation: Peaceful
Scripture: John 14:27 NKJV
Peace I leave with you, My peace I give to you; not as the world gives do I give to you. Let not your heart be troubled, neither let it be afraid.

IVES, see Yves

IVONNE, Ivette, Ivete, Ivonn
(see also Yvonne)
Language/Cultural Origin: Scandinavian
Inherent Meaning: Yew Wood
Spiritual Connotation: Devout
Scripture: Luke 7:50 TLB
Your faith has saved you; go in peace.

IVORY, Ivori
Language/Cultural Origin: American
Inherent Meaning: Made of Ivory
Spiritual Connotation: Fearless
Scripture: Matthew 14:27 NASB
Take courage, it is I; do not be afraid.

IVRIA, Ivriah
Language/Cultural Origin: Hebrew
Inherent Meaning: From the Far Side of the Euphrates River
Spiritual Connotation: Fruitful
Scripture: John 7:38 NRSV
Out of the believer's heart shall flow rivers of living water.

IVY, Ivey, Ivie
Language/Cultural Origin: English

Inherent Meaning: Ivy Plant
Spiritual Connotation: Trusting
Scripture: Isaiah 26:3 NKJV
You will keep him in perfect peace, whose mind is stayed on You, because he trusts in You.

IWAN, Iwann
Language/Cultural Origin: Polish
Inherent Meaning: God Is Gracious
Spiritual Connotation: Grateful
Scripture: 1 Corinthians 15:10 NCV
But God's grace has made me what I am, and his grace to me was not wasted.

IZRI, Izree (see also Ezra)
☞ Language/Cultural Origin: Hebrew

Inherent Meaning: Creative
Spiritual Connotation: Skilled
Scripture: Exodus 31:3 NKJV
And I have filled him with the Spirit of God . . . in all manner of workmanship.

IZUSA, Izussa
Language/Cultural Origin: Native American
Inherent Meaning: White Stone
Spiritual Connotation: Overcomer
Scripture: Revelation 2:17 NRSV
To everyone who conquers I will give . . . a white stone, and on the white stone is written a new name that no one knows except the one who receives it.

Inherent Meaning: God Is My Maker
Spiritual Connotation: Thankful
Scripture: Psalm 139:14 NASB
I will give thanks to Thee, for I am fearfully and wonderfully made.

JAAZIEL, Jaziel
Language/Cultural Origin: Hebrew
Inherent Meaning: God Is My Comfort
Spiritual Connotation: Nurtured
Scripture: Isaiah 66:13 NRSV
As a mother comforts her child, so I will comfort you; you shall be comforted in Jerusalem.

JABARI, Jabaar, Jabar, Jabbar, Jabier
Language/Cultural Origin: Swahili
Inherent Meaning: Fearless
Spiritual Connotation: Leader
Scripture: Matthew 28:5–6 NKJV
Do not be afraid, for I know that you seek Jesus who was crucified. He is not here; for He is risen, as He said.

JABEZ, Jabe, Jabesh
Language/Cultural Origin: Hebrew
Inherent Meaning: Born in Pain
Spiritual Connotation: Blessed
Scripture: Joel 2:25 NKJV
So I will restore to you the years that the swarming locust has eaten.

JABIN, Jaban
Language/Cultural Origin: Hebrew
Inherent Meaning: God Has Formed
Spiritual Connotation: Chosen
Scripture: Psalm 139:13 NCV
You made my whole being; you formed me in my mother's body.

JACHAN, Jacan, Jachon, Jacon
☞ (see also Jaakan)
Language/Cultural Origin: Hebrew
Inherent Meaning: Trouble
Spiritual Connotation: Victorious
Scripture: John 16:33 NASB
These things I have spoken to you, that in Me you may have peace. In the world you have tribulation, but take courage; I have overcome the world.

JAAKAN, Jaekan, Jakan, Jaikan
☞ (see also Jachan)
Language/Cultural Origin: Hebrew
Inherent Meaning: Intelligent
Spiritual Connotation: Discerning
Scripture: Proverbs 4:5 NASB
Acquire wisdom! Acquire understanding! Do not forget, nor turn away from the words of my mouth.

JAALA, Jala
☞ Language/Cultural Origin: Hebrew
Inherent Meaning: Doe
Spiritual Connotation: Loving
Scripture: Psalm 42:1 NRSV
As a deer longs for flowing streams, so my soul longs for you, O God.

JAALAM, Jalam
☞ Language/Cultural Origin: Hebrew
Inherent Meaning: Hidden
Spiritual Connotation: Guardian of Wisdom
Scripture: 1 Corinthians 1:27 NKJV
But God has chosen the foolish things of the world to put to shame the wise.

JAAN, Jaann, Jaano, Yaan, JayAnn
Language/Cultural Origin: Estonian
Inherent Meaning: Disciple of Christ
Spiritual Connotation: Anointed
Scripture: John 8:31 NRSV
If you continue in my word, you are truly my disciples.

JAASIEL, Jasiel
☞ Language/Cultural Origin: Hebrew

JACEY, J.C., Jace, Jacee, Jacie,
Jaciel, Jayce, Jaycee, Jaycey, Jaycie
(see also Jacy)
Language/Cultural Origin: American
Inherent Meaning: Prestigous
Spiritual Connotation: Blessed
Scripture: Ezekiel 34:29 RSV
*And I will provide for them prosperous
plantations so that they shall no more be
consumed with hunger in the land.*

JACINDA, Jacenda, Jacinta
Language/Cultural Origin: Hispanic
Inherent Meaning: Beautiful
Spiritual Connotation: Cherished
Scripture: Song of Songs 1:15 NASB
*How beautiful you are, my darling, How
beautiful you are! Your eyes are like doves.*

JACK, Jackie, Jacky, Jax
Language/Cultural Origin: English
Inherent Meaning: God Is Gracious
Spiritual Connotation: Redeemed
Scripture: Colossians 1:6 TLB
*The same Good News that came to you is
going out all over the world and changing
lives everywhere.*

JACKSON, Jakson, Jaxon
Language/Cultural Origin: English
Inherent Meaning: Son of Jack
Spiritual Connotation: Gracious
Scripture: Psalm 111:4 NKJV
*He has made His wonderful works to be
remembered; the LORD is gracious and full
of compassion.*

JACOB, Jacobb, Jacobs, Jakab, Jakiv,
☞Jakov, Jakub (see also Yakov)
Language/Cultural Origin: Hebrew
Inherent Meaning: Supplanter
Spiritual Connotation: Benevolent
Scripture: 1 John 2:17 NKJV
*And the world is passing away, and the lust
of it; but he who does the will of God abides
forever.*

JACOBI, Jackobi
Language/Cultural Origin: Scottish
Inherent Meaning: Replacement
Spiritual Connotation: Joyous
Scripture: Isaiah 9:10 NASB

*The bricks have fallen down, but we will
rebuild with smooth stones; the sycamores
have been cut down, but we will replace
them with cedars.*

JACQUELINE, Jacalyn, Jackalyn,
Jackee, Jacki, Jackie, Jacklyn,
Jacquelyn, Jacquelynn, Jacqué,
Jacqui, Jakki, Jaquelynn, Jaqui
Language/Cultural Origin: French
Inherent Meaning: Substitute
Spiritual Connotation: Renewal
Scripture: Job 33:4 NKJV
*The Spirit of God has made me, and the
breath of the Almighty gives me life.*

JACQUES, Jacquan, Jacque,
Jacquees, Jacquez, Jaques
Language/Cultural Origin: French
Inherent Meaning: Supplanter
Spiritual Connotation: Redeemed
Scripture: Titus 3:5 NASB
*He saved us . . . according to His mercy, by
the washing of regeneration and renewing by
the Holy Spirit.*

JACY, Jaicy (see also Jacey)
Language/Cultural Origin: Guarani
Inherent Meaning: Moon
Spiritual Connotation: Reverent
Scripture: Psalm 72:5 NIV
*He will endure as long as the sun, as long as
the moon, through all generations.*

JADA, Jaeda, Jaida, Jayda
☞Language/Cultural Origin: Hebrew
Inherent Meaning: Wise
Spiritual Connotation: Blessed
Scripture: Proverbs 4:7 NIV
*Wisdom is supreme; therefore get
wisdom. Though it cost all you have,
get understanding.*

JADE, Jadah, Jadi, Jadie,
Jady, Jaide, Jayde
Language/Cultural Origin: Spanish
Inherent Meaning: Precious Gem
Spiritual Connotation: Priceless
Scripture: James 1:17 NKJV
*Every good gift and every perfect gift is from
above, and comes down from the Father of
lights, with whom there is no variation or
shadow of turning.*

JADON, Jaden, Jadin, Jaeden, Jaedon
Language/Cultural Origin: Hebrew
Inherent Meaning: God Has Heard
Spiritual Connotation: Seeker of the Truth
Scripture: Psalm 5:3 NIV

*In the morning, O LORD, you hear my voice;
in the morning I lay my requests before you
and wait in expectation.*

JAE, see Jaye

JAEGAR, Jaager
Language/Cultural Origin: German
Inherent Meaning: Hunter
Spiritual Connotation: Increase
Scripture: Genesis 1:22 NKJV

*Be fruitful and multiply, and fill the waters
in the seas, and let birds multiply on the
earth.*

JAE-HWA, Jaewah
Language/Cultural Origin: Korean
Inherent Meaning: Prosperous
Spiritual Connotation: Blessed
Scripture: Jeremiah 29:11 NLT

*For I know the plans I have for you, says the
LORD. They are plans for good and not for
disaster, to give you a future and a hope.*

JAEL, Jaela, Jaelle (see also Yael)
Language/Cultural Origin: Hebrew
Inherent Meaning: Mountain Climber
Spiritual Connotation: God's Servant
Scripture: Psalm 90:2 NRSV

*Before the mountains were brought forth, or
ever you had formed the earth and the world,
from everlasting to everlasting you are God.*

JA'FAR, Jafar, Jaffar
Language/Cultural Origin: Sanskrit
Inherent Meaning: Little Stream
Spiritual Connotation: Refreshing
Scripture: Psalm 46:4 NASB

*There is a river whose streams make glad the
city of God, the holy dwelling places of the
Most High.*

JAFFA, see Yaffa

JAGA, Yaga
Language/Cultural Origin: Polish
Inherent Meaning: Innocent

Spiritual Connotation: Cleansed
Scripture: 2 Chronicles 29:18 RSV

We have cleansed all the house of the LORD.

JAGO, see Iago

JAHDIEL, Jadiel, Yadiel
Language/Cultural Origin: Hebrew
Inherent Meaning: God Gladdens
Spiritual Connotation: Cheerful
Scripture: Nehemiah 8:10 NKJV

*Do not sorrow, for the joy of the LORD is your
strength.*

JAHZEEL, Jahziel, Jazeel, Jaziel
Language/Cultural Origin: Hebrew
Inherent Meaning: God Distributes
Spiritual Connotation: Righteousness of Christ
Scripture: Zechariah 3:4 NKJV

*See, I have removed your iniquity from you,
and I will clothe you with rich robes.*

**JAIME, Jaimey, Jaimee, Jaimmie,
Jaimy, Jayme (see also Jamie)**
Language/Cultural Origin: French
Inherent Meaning: I Love
Spiritual Connotation: Devoted
Scripture: Psalm 18:1 NKJV

I will love You, O LORD, my strength.

JAIRUS, Jairo, Jarius
Language/Cultural Origin: Hebrew
Inherent Meaning: God Enlightens
Spiritual Connotation: Wise
Scripture: Isaiah 5:16 NKJV

*But the LORD of hosts shall be exalted in
judgment, and God who is holy shall be
hallowed in righteousness.*

**JAJUAN, Jauan, Jawaan, Jawan,
Jawann, Jawaun, Jawon, Jawuan,
Jujuan, Juwaan, Juwan, Juwann,
Juwaun, Juwon, Juwuan**
Language/Cultural Origin: American
Inherent Meaning: God Is Gracious
Spiritual Connotation: Blessed
Scripture: Jonah 4:2 NKJV

*For I know that You are a gracious and
merciful God, slow to anger and abundant in
lovingkindness, One who relents from doing
harm.*

JAKE, Jayke
Language/Cultural Origin: English

Inherent Meaning: Substitute
Spiritual Connotation: New Covenant
Scripture: Colossians 3:11 TLB
In this new life one's nationality or race or education or social position is unimportant. . . . Whether a person has Christ is what matters.

JAKIM, Jakeem
Language/Cultural Origin: Hebrew
Inherent Meaning: Uplifted
Spiritual Connotation: Chosen
Scripture: John 12:32 NRSV
And I, when I am lifted up from the earth, will draw all people to myself.

JALILA, Jalile
Language/Cultural Origin: Middle Eastern
Inherent Meaning: Great
Spiritual Connotation: Humble
Scripture: Matthew 20:16 NKJV
So the last will be first, and the first last. For many are called, but few chosen.

JAMAAL, Jamar, see Jhamil

JAMARCUS, Jamarco, Jemarcus
Language/Cultural Origin: American
Inherent Meaning: Aggressive
Spiritual Connotation: Zealous
Scripture: 1 Corinthians 14:12 NKJV
Even so you, since you are zealous for spiritual gifts, let it be for the edification of the church that you seek to excel.

JAMARIO, Jamari, Jamariel, Jamarius, Jemarus
Language/Cultural Origin: American
Inherent Meaning: Of the Sea
Spiritual Connotation: Filled With Praise
Scripture: Psalm 69:34 NKJV
Let heaven and earth praise Him, the seas and everything that moves in them.

JAMES, Jaimes, Jaymes, Jim, Jimi, Jimmee, Jimmie, Jimmy, Jimy
Language/Cultural Origin: Hebrew
Inherent Meaning: Supplanter
Spiritual Connotation: Nurtured
Scripture: Psalm 23:4 KJV
Yea, though I walk through the valley of the shadow of death, I will fear no evil: for thou art with me; thy rod and thy staff they comfort me.

JAMESON, Jamerson, Jamison, Jemisian
Language/Cultural Origin: English
Inherent Meaning: Son of James
Spiritual Connotation: Persevering
Scripture: Jude 1:21 NKJV
Keep yourselves in the love of God, looking for the mercy of our Lord Jesus Christ unto eternal life.

JAMIE, Jamee, Jamey, Jami, Jamia, Jamian, Jamii, Jammie, Jamya, Jaymee, Jaymie (see also Jaime)
Language/Cultural Origin: English
Inherent Meaning: Replacement
Spiritual Connotation: Wise
Scripture: Matthew 13:28-29 NASB
Do you want us, then, to go and gather them up? No, lest while you are gathering up the tares, you may root up the wheat with them.

JAMILA, Jahmela, Jahmelia, Jameela, Jamelia, Jamelle, Jamelya, Jamilia, Jamillia, Yamila, Yamilla
Language/Cultural Origin: Middle Eastern
Inherent Meaning: Beautiful
Spiritual Connotation: Loving
Scripture: Philippians 4:8 NKJV
Finally, brethren, whatever things are true, . . . noble, . . . just, . . . pure, . . . lovely, . . . of good report, if there is any virtue and if there is anything praiseworthy; meditate on these things.

JAMIN, Jaman, Jamial, Jamian, Jamiel, Jamien, Jaymin
Language/Cultural Origin: Hebrew
Inherent Meaning: Favored
Spiritual Connotation: Triumphant
Scripture: Psalm 44:3 NASB
Their own arm did not save them, but Your right hand and Your arm and the light of Your presence, for You favored them.

JAMOND, Jamand, Jamon, Jamón (see also Jemond)
Language/Cultural Origin: American
Inherent Meaning: Mighty Protector
Spiritual Connotation: Exalted
Scripture: Psalm 25:20 NRSV
O guard my life, and deliver me; do not let me be put to shame, for I take refuge in you.

JAN, Jani, Jania, Jann

Language/Cultural Origin: German
Inherent Meaning: God's Gift
Spiritual Connotation: Cherished
Scripture: Psalm 70:4 NKJV

Let all those who seek You rejoice and be glad in You; and let those who love Your salvation say continually, let God be magnified!

JANA, Janna (See also Yana)

Language/Cultural Origin: Slavic
Inherent Meaning: Gift of God
Spiritual Connotation: Cherished
Scripture: Deuteronomy 6:11 NKJV

Houses full of all good things, which you did not fill, hewn-out wells which you did not dig, vineyards and olive trees which you did not plant.

JANAE, Janaé, Janaya, Janea, Janée, Janay, Jannay, Jenay, Jenaya, Jennae, Jennay, Jennaya

Language/Cultural Origin: American
Inherent Meaning: God Is Gracious
Spiritual Connotation: Treasured
Scripture: Numbers 6:24–25 NKJV

The LORD bless you and keep you; the LORD make His face shine upon you, and be gracious to you.

JANAN, Janani, Janann

Language/Cultural Origin: Middle Eastern
Inherent Meaning: Tenderhearted
Spiritual Connotation: Gentle
Scripture: Ephesians 4:32 NASB

And be kind to one another, tender-hearted, forgiving each other, just as God in Christ also has forgiven you.

JANE, Jaine, Janet, Janett, Janey, Janie, Janice, Janis, Jannie, Jayna, Jayne, Jaynee

Language/Cultural Origin: English
Inherent Meaning: God Is Gracious
Spiritual Connotation: Beloved
Scripture: Romans 12:2 NKJV

And do not be conformed to this world, but be transformed by the renewing of your mind.

JANELLE, Janel, Janele, Janell, Janella, Janiel, Janielle, Jannel, Jannell, Jannelle, Jenell, Jenelle, Jennell, Jennelle, Jonell, Jonelle

Language/Cultural Origin: English
Inherent Meaning: God Is Gracious
Spiritual Connotation: Blessed
Scripture: Psalm 138:8 NKJV

The LORD will perfect that which concerns me; your mercy, O LORD, endures forever; do not forsake the works of Your hands.

JANESSA, Janiesha, Janissa, Jannisha, Jannissa, Jenisa, Jenisha, Jenissa, Jennisha, Jennisse

Language/Cultural Origin: American
Inherent Meaning: God Is Gracious
Spiritual Connotation: Delivered
Scripture: Nehemiah 9:31 RSV

Nevertheless in thy great mercies thou didst not make an end of them or forsake them; for thou art a gracious and merciful God.

JANSON, Jansen, Janssen, Jantzen, Janzen, Jensen

Language/Cultural Origin: Scandinavian
Inherent Meaning: Son of Jan
Spiritual Connotation: Joyful
Scripture: 1 Peter 1:8 NRSV

Although you have not seen him, you love him; and even though you do not see him now, you believe in him and rejoice with an indescribable and glorious joy.

JAPHETH, Japeth, Yaphet, Yapheth

Language/Cultural Origin: Hebrew
Inherent Meaning: May He Expand
Spiritual Connotation: Ancestor
Scripture: Genesis 9:27 NASB

May God enlarge Japheth, and let him dwell in the tents of Shem; and let Canaan be his servant.

JARAH, Jarrah (see also Jerah)

Language/Cultural Origin: Hebrew
Inherent Meaning: Sweet as Honey
Spiritual Connotation: Discerner
Scripture: Revelation 10:10 NKJV

Then I took the little book out of the angel's hand and ate it, and it was as sweet as honey in my mouth.

JARDAN, Jarden, Jardena, Jardina (see also Jordan)
Language/Cultural Origin: Hebrew
Inherent Meaning: Descender
Spiritual Connotation: Aide
Scripture: Psalm 10:14 NKJV
The helpless commits himself to You; You are the helper of the fatherless.

JARED, Jarad, Ja'red, Jarod, Jarrad, Jarred, Jarrod, Jarryd, Jerad, Jerod, Jerrad, Jerrod, Jerryd, Yarod, Yarrod
Language/Cultural Origin: Hebrew
Inherent Meaning: Descendent
Spiritual Connotation: Favored
Scripture: Matthew 21:22 NKJV
And whatever things you ask in prayer, believing, you will receive.

JAREK, Jarrek
Language/Cultural Origin: Slavic
Inherent Meaning: Born in January
Spiritual Connotation: Promised Assurance
Scripture: 1 Timothy 1:14 NKJV
And the grace of our Lord was exceedingly abundant, with faith and love which are in Christ Jesus.

JARELL, Jarel, Jarelle, Jarrell, Jerall, Jerel, Jerral, Jerell, Jerrel, Jerrell
Language/Cultural Origin: Scandinavian
Inherent Meaning: Mighty
Spiritual Connotation: Power of God
Scripture: Exodus 9:16 NKJV
But indeed for this purpose I have raised you up, that I may show My power in you, and that My name may be declared in all the earth.

JAROAH, Jaroha, Jaroyah
Language/Cultural Origin: Hebrew
Inherent Meaning: New Moon
Spiritual Connotation: Festive
Scripture: Psalm 81:3 RSV
Blow the trumpet at the new moon, at the full moon, on our feast day.

JARON, Jaaron, Jairon, Jaren, Jarón, Jarone (see also Jeron, Yaron)
Language/Cultural Origin: Hebrew
Inherent Meaning: He Will Sing; He Will Cry Out
Spiritual Connotation: Joyful
Scripture: Job 8:21 NKJV
He will yet fill your mouth with laughing, and your lips with rejoicing.

JARRETT, Jaret, Jareth, Jarratt, Jarret, Jarrot, Jarrott, Jerrat, Jerrett, Jerott (see also Garrett)
Language/Cultural Origin: English
Inherent Meaning: Warrior
Spiritual Connotation: Brave
Scripture: 1 Corinthians 16:13 NRSV
Keep alert, stand firm in your faith, be courageous, be strong.

JARVIS, Jarvas, Javares, Javaris, Javarius, Javaron, Javarus
Language/Cultural Origin: German
Inherent Meaning: Skilled
Spiritual Connotation: Inspired
Scripture: 2 Corinthians 6:2 NKJV
And in the day of salvation I have helped you. Behold, now is the accepted time; behold, now is the day of salvation.

JASIA, Jasha, Jasio, Jasya, Jazya
Language/Cultural Origin: Polish
Inherent Meaning: God Is Gracious
Spiritual Connotation: Forgiven
Scripture: Joel 2:13 TLB
Return to the Lord your God, for he is gracious and merciful. He is not easily angered; he is full of kindness and anxious not to punish you.

JASMINE, Jas, Jasmain, Jasmaine, Jasman, Jasmin, Jasmon, Jasmyn, Jass, Jassmin, Jassmine, Jassmyn, Jaz, Jazmin, Jazmine, Jazminn, Jazmon, Jazmyne, Jazz, Jazze, Jazzman, Jazzmin, Jazzmon, Jazzmyn (see also Yasmine)
Language/Cultural Origin: Persian
Inherent Meaning: Jasmine Flower
Spiritual Connotation: Messenger of Love
Scripture: Isaiah 55:11 NKJV
So shall My word be that goes forth from My mouth; it shall not return to Me void.

JASON, Jacen, Jaeson, Jaison, Jasan, Jasen, Jasun, Jaysen, Jayson
Language/Cultural Origin: Greek

Inherent Meaning: Healer
Spiritual Connotation: Benevolent
Scripture: Luke 6:45 NKJV
A good man out of the good treasure of his heart brings forth good. . . . For out of the abundance of the heart his mouth speaks.

JASPER, Jaspar
Language/Cultural Origin: English
Inherent Meaning: Treasure-Holder
Spiritual Connotation: Richly Blessed
Scripture: Matthew 25:29 NKJV
For to everyone who has, more will be given, and he will have abundance; but from him who does not have, even what he has will be taken away.

JAVAN, Jaavon, Jahvon, Javaughn, ☞Javon, Javoni, Javonn (see also Jevan, Jovan)
Language/Cultural Origin: Hebrew
Inherent Meaning: Clay
Spiritual Connotation: Example
Scripture: Deuteronomy 4:10 NASB
Assemble the people to Me, that I may let them hear My words so they . . . may teach their children.

JAVANA, Javanna, Javonna, Javonne, Javonya
Language/Cultural Origin: Malayan
Inherent Meaning: From Java
Spiritual Connotation: Honest
Scripture: Joshua 24:14 NKJV
Now therefore, fear the LORD, serve Him in sincerity and in truth.

JAVIER, Javiare
Language/Cultural Origin: Spanish
Inherent Meaning: Owner of a New House
Spiritual Connotation: Prosperous
Scripture: Zechariah 8:12 NLT
For I am planting seeds of peace and prosperity among you.

JAWAUN, see Jajuan

JAY, Jai, Jey
Language/Cultural Origin: Old French
Inherent Meaning: Vivacious
Spiritual Connotation: Adventurous
Scripture: Psalm 139:3 NKJV
You comprehend my path and my lying down, and are acquainted with all my ways.

JAYA, Jaea, Jaia, Jayla, Jaylah
Language/Cultural Origin: Indo-Pakistani
Inherent Meaning: Victory
Spiritual Connotation: Overcomer
Scripture: Romans 8:37 NRSV
No, in all these things we are more than conquerors through him who loved us.

JAYE, Jae, Jaela, Jaelin, Jaelynn, Jalen, Jalin, Jaylan, Jaylee, Jayleen, Jaylene, Jaylin, Jaylyn
Language/Cultural Origin: Latin
Inherent Meaning: Jaybird
Spiritual Connotation: Source of Joy
Scripture: Acts 8:39 NCV
When they came up out of the water, the Spirit of the Lord took Philip away. . . . And the officer continued on his way home, full of joy.

JEAN, Jéan, Jeana, Jeane, Jeanee, Jeanie, Jeanna, Jeanne, Jene (see also Gina)
Language/Cultural Origin: Scottish
Inherent Meaning: God Is Gracious
Spiritual Connotation: Gifted
Scripture: 2 Chronicles 1:12 NKJV
Wisdom and knowledge are granted to you; and I will give you riches and wealth and honor.

JEANETTE, Janeen, Janette, Jannine, Jeaneen, Jeanett, Jeanine, Jeannette, Jeannine, Jenine
Language/Cultural Origin: French
Inherent Meaning: God Is Gracious
Spiritual Connotation: Preserved
Scripture: Isaiah 33:2 NRSV
O LORD, be gracious to us; we wait for you. Be our arm every morning, our salvation in the time of trouble.

JEDAIAH, Jedaia, Jediah
☞Language/Cultural Origin: Hebrew
Inherent Meaning: Hand of God
Spiritual Connotation: Guided
Scripture: 2 Chronicles 30:12 NASB
The hand of God was also on Judah to give them one heart to do what the king and the princes commanded by the word of the LORD.

JEDIDIAH, Jeb, Jebadiah, ☞Jebediah, Jed, Jedediah
Language/Cultural Origin: Hebrew

Inherent Meaning: Beloved of God
Spiritual Connotation: Perceptive
Scripture: Psalm 145:10 NKJV
*All Your works shall praise You, O LORD,
and Your saints shall bless You.*

JEFFERSON, Jeferson
Language/Cultural Origin: English
Inherent Meaning: Son of the Peaceful Man
Spiritual Connotation: Contemplative
Scripture: Genesis 25:27 NKJV
*So the boys grew. And Esau was a skillful
hunter, a man of the field; but Jacob was
a mild man, dwelling in tents.*

JEFFREY, Jefery, Jeff, Jefferay, Jefferey, Jefferie, Jefferies, Jeffery, Jeffrie, Jeffries, Jeffry (see also Geoffrey)
Language/Cultural Origin: English
Inherent Meaning: Divine Peace
Spiritual Connotation: Wise
Scripture: Proverbs 3:13 NKJV
*Happy is the man who finds wisdom,
and the man who gains understanding.*

JEHAN, Jehahn, Jehann
Language/Cultural Origin: French
Inherent Meaning: God Is Gracious
Spiritual Connotation: Godly Example
Scripture: Isaiah 30:18 NRSV
*Therefore the LORD waits to be gracious
to you; therefore he will rise up to
show mercy to you.*

JEHOHANAN
Language/Cultural Origin: Hebrew
Inherent Meaning: God Is Gracious
Spiritual Connotation: Contrite
Scripture: Joel 2:13 NASB
*Now return to the LORD your God, for
He is gracious and compassionate.*

JEHONATHAN
Language/Cultural Origin: Hebrew
Inherent Meaning: God Has Given
Spiritual Connotation: Blessed
Scripture: 2 Timothy 1:7 NCV
*God did not give us a spirit that makes us
afraid but a spirit of power and love and
self-control.*

JEHORAM
Language/Cultural Origin: Hebrew

Inherent Meaning: God Is Exalted
Spiritual Connotation: Majestic
Scripture: Psalm 118:16 NLT
*The strong right arm of the LORD is raised in
triumph.*

JEHU, Jaehu, Jayhue, Yayhu, Yayhue
Language/Cultural Origin: Hebrew
Inherent Meaning: God Is
Spiritual Connotation: Divine Perspective
Scripture: Exodus 3:6 NKJV
*I am the God of your father; the God of
Abraham, the God of Isaac, and the God of
Jacob.*

JEKAMIAH, Jekamiyah
Language/Cultural Origin: Hebrew
Inherent Meaning: God Will Gather
Spiritual Connotation: Blessed Promise
Scripture: Nehemiah 1:9 NCV
*I will gather your people from the far ends of
the earth.*

JELANI, Jelanee, Jeláni, Jelanni, Jellani
Language/Cultural Origin: Swahili
Inherent Meaning: Mighty
Spiritual Connotation: Strength of God
Scripture: Psalm 21:13 NKJV
*Be exalted, O LORD, in Your own strength! We
will sing and praise Your power.*

JELENA, Jelina (see also Yelina)
Language/Cultural Origin: Russian
Inherent Meaning: Shining
Spiritual Connotation: Filled With Praise
Scripture: Psalm 148:3 RSV
*Praise him, sun and moon, praise him, all
you shining stars!*

JEMAL, see Jhamil

JEMIMA, Jamima, Jemimah, Jemma, Jemmia, Jemmiah
Language/Cultural Origin: Hebrew
Inherent Meaning: Dove
Spiritual Connotation: Serene
Scripture: Isaiah 32:18 NASB
*Then my people will live in a peaceful
habitation, and in secure dwellings and in
undisturbed resting places.*

JEMOND, Jemon, Jémond, Jemonde, Jemone (see also Jamond)
Language/Cultural Origin: French
Inherent Meaning: Temporal
Spiritual Connotation: Mind of Christ
Scripture: Colossians 3:2 NRSV
Set your minds on things that are above, not on things that are on earth.

JEMUEL, Jemuél
☞Language/Cultural Origin: Hebrew
Inherent Meaning: God Is Light
Spiritual Connotation: Set Apart
Scripture: John 8:12 NRSV
I am the light of the world. Whoever follows me will never walk in darkness.

JENDAYA, Jenndaya
Language/Cultural Origin: Shona
Inherent Meaning: Give Thanks
Spiritual Connotation: Adoration
Scripture: Revelation 7:12 NKJV
Amen! Blessing and glory and wisdom, thanksgiving and honor and power and might, be to our God forever and ever. Amen.

JENEVIEVE, see Genevieve

JENKIN, Jenkins, Jenkyn, Jenkyns
Language/Cultural Origin: Flemish
Inherent Meaning: Little John
Spiritual Connotation: Reverent
Scripture: Psalm 2:11 NKJV
Serve the LORD with fear, and rejoice with trembling.

JENNA, Jena, Jenah, Jennah, Jennay
Language/Cultural Origin: Middle Eastern
Inherent Meaning: Small Bird
Spiritual Connotation: Nurtured
Scripture: Matthew 10:29 RSV
Are not two sparrows sold for a penny? And not one of them will fall to the ground without your Father's will.

JENNIFER, Jen, Jenefer, Jeni, Jenifer, Jeniffer, Jenn, Jennafer, Jennee, Jenney, Jennie, Jenniffer, Jenny
Language/Cultural Origin: Welsh
Inherent Meaning: Fair
Spiritual Connotation: Trusting
Scripture: Psalm 28:7 NKJV

The LORD is my strength and my shield; my heart trusted in Him, and I am helped. . . . With my song I will praise Him.

JERAH, Jerrah (see also Jarah)
☞Language/Cultural Origin: Hebrew
Inherent Meaning: Moon
Spiritual Connotation: Glorious Hope
Scripture: Isaiah 30:26 NASB
And the light of the moon will be as the light of the sun.

JEREMIAH, Jeramiah, Jeramaya, ☞Jeremai, Jeremia, Jeremias, Yermiya, Yirmaya
Language/Cultural Origin: Hebrew
Inherent Meaning: God Is Exalted
Spiritual Connotation: Seeker of Truth
Scripture: Luke 12:31 NKJV
But seek the kingdom of God, and all these things shall be added to you.

JEREMY, Jeramee, Jerami, Jeramy, ☞Jéreme, Jeremee, Jeremey, Jeremii
Language/Cultural Origin: English
Inherent Meaning: God Is Exalted
Spiritual Connotation: Humble
Scripture: James 4:10 NKJV
Humble yourselves in the sight of the Lord, and He will lift you up.

JERENI, Jerani, Jeraney, Jerenee
Language/Cultural Origin: Russian
Inherent Meaning: Peace
Spiritual Connotation: Filled With the Spirit
Scripture: Luke 1:79 NCV
It will shine on those who live in darkness, in the shadow of death. It will guide us into the path of peace.

JERIAH, Jariah, Jariya, Jeriya
☞Language/Cultural Origin: Hebrew
Inherent Meaning: God Has Seen
Spiritual Connotation: Proven
Scripture: Psalm 33:14–15 NRSV
From where he sits enthroned he watches all the inhabitants of the earth—he who fashions the hearts of them all, and observes all their deeds.

JERIEL, Jerriel (see also Yeriel)
☞Language/Cultural Origin: Hebrew
Inherent Meaning: God's Foundation

Spiritual Connotation: Reflection of Christ
Scripture: Ephesians 2:20 NLT
We are his house.... And the cornerstone is Christ Jesus himself.

JERMAINE, Jermain, Jermane, Jermayne, Jhirmaine (see also Germain)
Language/Cultural Origin: English
Inherent Meaning: Sprout
Spiritual Connotation: Constant Growth
Scripture: Isaiah 45:8 NKJV
Rain down, you heavens, from above ... let them bring forth salvation, and let righteousness spring up together. I, the LORD, have created it.

JEROHAM, Jeroam
☞ Language/Cultural Origin: Hebrew
Inherent Meaning: Loved
Spiritual Connotation: Treasured
Scripture: 1 John 4:7 NASB
Beloved, let us love one another, for love is from God.

JEROME, Jérome, Jerôme, Jerrome
Language/Cultural Origin: Latin
Inherent Meaning: Sacred
Spiritual Connotation: Holy
Scripture: Leviticus 11:45 NASB
For I am the LORD, who brought you up from the land of Egypt, to be your God; thus you shall be holy for I am holy.

JERON, Jéron, Jerone, Jerron (see also Jaron)
Language/Cultural Origin: English
Inherent Meaning: Set Apart
Spiritual Connotation: Chosen
Scripture: Psalm 4:3 RSV
But know that the LORD has set apart the godly for himself; the LORD hears when I call to him.

JESAIAH, Jeshaiah
☞ Language/Cultural Origin: Hebrew
Inherent Meaning: God Is Wealthy
Spiritual Connotation: Eternal Perspective
Scripture: Luke 12:34 TLB
Wherever your treasure is, there your heart and thoughts will also be.

JESSE, Jesee, Jess, Jessé, ☞Jessee, Jessey, Jessie
Language/Cultural Origin: Hebrew
Inherent Meaning: God Exists
Spiritual Connotation: Upright
Scripture: Job 19:25 NIV
I know that my Redeemer lives, and that in the end he will stand upon the earth.

JESSENIA, Jeseenya
Language/Cultural Origin: Middle Eastern
Inherent Meaning: Flower
Spiritual Connotation: Spiritual Maturity
Scripture: Mark 4:27 NCV
Night and day, whether the person is asleep or awake, the seed still grows, but the person does not know how it grows.

JESSICA, Jesi, Jesica, Jesika, Jess, Jessa, Jessaca, Jesseca, Jessi, Jessie, Jessika, Jessy, Jessyca, Yessica, Yessika
Language/Cultural Origin: Hebrew
Inherent Meaning: Wealthy
Spiritual Connotation: Blessed
Scripture: 1 Corinthians 13:13 NKJV
And now abide faith, hope, love, these three; but the greatest of these is love.

JETHRO, Jethroe
☞ Language/Cultural Origin: Hebrew
Inherent Meaning: Excellence
Spiritual Connotation: Abundant Praise
Scripture: Psalm 98:4 NKJV
Shout joyfully to the LORD, all the earth; break forth in song, rejoice, and sing praises.

JEVAN, Jevaughn, Jevaun, Jevohn, Jevon, Jevoni, Jevonn, Jevonne (see also Javan, Jovan)
Language/Cultural Origin: English
Inherent Meaning: Abundance
Spiritual Connotation: Heir
Scripture: Psalm 37:11 NKJV
But the meek shall inherit the earth, and shall delight themselves in the abundance of peace.

JEWEL, Jewell, Jewelle
Language/Cultural Origin: French
Inherent Meaning: Gem
Spiritual Connotation: Precious

Scripture: **Psalm 16:11** NKJV
You will show me the path of life; in Your presence is fullness of joy; at Your right hand are pleasures forevermore.

JEZANIAH, Jezánia, Jezzania
Language/Cultural Origin: Hebrew
Inherent Meaning: God Determines
Spiritual Connotation: In God's Hands
Scripture: **Job 14:5** NLT
You have decided the length of our lives. You know how many months we will live, and we are not given a minute longer.

JEZIEL, Jezziel
Language/Cultural Origin: Hebrew
Inherent Meaning: Assembly of God
Spiritual Connotation: Restored
Scripture: **Ezra 5:15** NCV
Put them back in the Temple in Jerusalem and rebuild the Temple of God where it was.

JEZREEL, Jezriel
Language/Cultural Origin: Hebrew
Inherent Meaning: God Sows
Spiritual Connotation: Proclaimer of the Word
Scripture: **Matthew 13:3** NKJV
Behold, a sower went out to sow.

JHAMIL, Jahmal, Jahmel, Jamaal, Jamaar, Jamaari, Jamahl, Jamail, Jamal, Jamall, Jamar, Jamara, Jamarr, Jameel, Jamel, Jamell, Jamelle, Jamiel, Jamil, Jamill, Jamille, Jammal, Jammel, Jemaal, Jemal, Jemar, Jemel, Jhamaal, Jhamal, Jhamar, Jhameel, Jhamel, Jhamell, Jhamelle, Jhamiel, Jhamielle, Jimaal, Jimell, Jimelle
Language/Cultural Origin: Hebrew
Inherent Meaning: Handsome
Spiritual Connotation: Image of Christ
Scripture: **Titus 2:10** NCV
They ... should show their masters they can be fully trusted so that in everything they do they will make the teaching of God our Savior attractive.

JIANNA, see Gianna

JILLIAN, Gillian, Jil, Jilaine, Jilayne, Jileesa, Jilian, Jiliana, Jiliann, Jilianna, Jill, Jillana, Jillene, Jilliana, Jillianne, Jillisa
Language/Cultural Origin: Latin

Inherent Meaning: Youthful
Spiritual Connotation: Regenerated
Scripture: **Psalm 103:5** TLB
He fills my life with good things! My youth is renewed like the eagle's!

JIN, Jinn
Language/Cultural Origin: Chinese
Inherent Meaning: Gold
Spiritual Connotation: True Worth
Scripture: **Proverbs 3:14** NLT
For the profit of wisdom is better than silver, and her wages are better than gold.

JINA, Jinna (see also Ginny)
Language/Cultural Origin: Swahili
Inherent Meaning: Name
Spiritual Connotation: Destined
Scripture: **Revelation 2:17** NRSV
To everyone who conquers I will ... give a white stone, and on the white stone is written a new name that no one knows except the one who receives it.

JINDRICH, Jindrick
Language/Cultural Origin: Czech
Inherent Meaning: Head of the Household
Spiritual Connotation: Trusted
Scripture: **Psalm 105:21** NKJV
He made him lord of his house, and ruler of all his possessions.

JINNY, see Ginny

JIRI, Jirian
Language/Cultural Origin: Czech
Inherent Meaning: Farmer
Spiritual Connotation: Skilled
Scripture: **2 Samuel 9:10** NASB
And you and your sons and your servants shall cultivate the land for him. ...

JIRINA, Jirana, Jiranna, Jireena
Language/Cultural Origin: Czech
Inherent Meaning: Farmer
Spiritual Connotation: Expectant
Scripture: **James 5:7** NLT
Dear brothers and sisters, you must be patient as you wait for the Lord's return.

JIZELLE, see Gizelle

JOAB, Joäb, Yoab, Yoav
Language/Cultural Origin: Hebrew

Inherent Meaning: Praise the Lord
Spiritual Connotation: Adoration
Scripture: Psalm 34:1 NKJV
I will bless the LORD at all times; His praise shall continually be in my mouth.

JOACHIM, Joakim, Joaquim
☞ **(see also Akim, Hakim, Joaquin)**
Language/Cultural Origin: Hebrew
Inherent Meaning: God Will Establish
Spiritual Connotation: Enthroned
Scripture: 1 Chronicles 17:12 NKJV
He shall build Me a house, and I will establish his throne forever.

JOAH, Yoah
☞ Language/Cultural Origin: Hebrew
Inherent Meaning: God Is Father
Spiritual Connotation: Secure
Scripture: Psalm 89:26 NKJV
You are my Father, My God, and the rock of my salvation.

JOAN, Joane, Joanelle, Joanie, Joann, Jo-Anne, Joanne, Joanie, Joni
Language/Cultural Origin: English
Inherent Meaning: God Is Gracious
Spiritual Connotation: Wise
Scripture: Proverbs 4:7 NKJV
Wisdom is the principal thing; therefore get wisdom. And in all your getting, get understanding.

JOANNA, Jo, Joana, Jo-Anna,
☞ **Joannah, Joey, Johana, Johannah, Yoana, Yoanna, Yohana, Yohanna**
Language/Cultural Origin: German
Inherent Meaning: God Is Gracious
Spiritual Connotation: Delivered
Scripture: 1 Corinthians 15:10 RSV
But by the grace of God I am what I am, and his grace toward me was not in vain.

JOAQUIN, Joaquín, Jocquin, Juquin
Language/Cultural Origin: Portuguese
Inherent Meaning: God Is My Salvation
Spiritual Connotation: Filled With Praise
Scripture: Isaiah 12:2 NASB
Behold, God is my salvation, I will trust and not be afraid; for the LORD GOD is my strength and song, and He has become my salvation.

JOASH
☞ Language/Cultural Origin: Hebrew
Inherent Meaning: God Hastens to Help
Spiritual Connotation: Delivered
Scripture: 2 Kings 17:39 NLT
You must worship only the LORD your God. He is the one who will rescue you from all your enemies.

JOB, Jobe
☞ Language/Cultural Origin: Hebrew
Inherent Meaning: Afflicted
Spiritual Connotation: Delivered
Scripture: Job 36:15 NLT
But by means of their suffering, he rescues those who suffer. For he gets their attention through adversity.

JOBEN, Joban
Language/Cultural Origin: Japanese
Inherent Meaning: Cleanliness
Spiritual Connotation: White as Snow
Scripture: Acts 15:9 TLB
He made no distinction between them and us, for he cleansed their lives through faith, just as he did ours.

JOCELYN, Jocelin, Jocelynn, Joscelyn, Joscelynn, Josalene, Joselyn
Language/Cultural Origin: Old German
Inherent Meaning: Joyous
Spiritual Connotation: Righteous
Scripture: Ezekiel 36:26 NKJV
I will give you a new heart and put a new spirit within you; I will take the heart of stone out of your flesh and give you a heart of flesh.

JODY, Jodee, Jodene, Jodey, Jodi, Jodie, Jodine
Language/Cultural Origin: American
Inherent Meaning: Praised
Spiritual Connotation: Humble
Scripture: 1 Chronicles 16:25 NKJV
For the LORD is great and greatly to be praised; He is also to be feared above all gods.

JOEL, Jôel, Joël, Jole
☞ Language/Cultural Origin: Hebrew
Inherent Meaning: The Lord Is God
Spiritual Connotation: God's Messenger
Scripture: Romans 12:2 NKJV

And do not be conformed to this world, but be transformed by the renewing of your mind.

JOELLE, Joella, Joëlle
Language/Cultural Origin: French
Inherent Meaning: The Lord Is God
Spiritual Connotation: Beloved
Scripture: Psalm 100:3 NKJV
Know that the LORD, He is God; it is He who has made us, and not we ourselves; we are His people and the sheep of His pasture.

JOERGEN, Jergen, Jöergen, Jörgen, Jürgen
Language/Cultural Origin: Danish
Inherent Meaning: Farmer
Spiritual Connotation: Persevering
Scripture: 2 Timothy 2:6 NASB
The hard-working farmer ought to be the first to receive his share of the crops.

JOHANN, Joannes, Johan, Johanan, Johannas, Johannes, Yohan, Yohann, Yohannes
Language/Cultural Origin: German
Inherent Meaning: God Is Gracious
Spiritual Connotation: Generosity of Spirit
Scripture: Galatians 5:22–23 NKJV
But the fruit of the Spirit is love, joy, peace, longsuffering, kindness, goodness, faithfulness, gentleness, self-control.

JOHANNA, see Joanna

JOHN, Jahn, Jhan, Jhon, Johnnie, Johnny, Jon, Jonn, Jonnie, Jonny (see also Jonathan)
Language/Cultural Origin: Greek
Inherent Meaning: God Is Gracious
Spiritual Connotation: Strength of God
Scripture: Psalm 118:14 NKJV
The LORD is my strength and song, and He has become my salvation.

JOLAN, Jolán, Jolánda, Jolánta
Language/Cultural Origin: Hungarian
Inherent Meaning: Violet Flower
Spiritual Connotation: Steady Growth
Scripture: Hosea 14:5 NKJV
I will be like the dew to Israel; he shall grow like the lily, and lengthen his roots like Lebanon.

JOLENE, Jolayne, Jolean, Joleane, Joleen, Joline, Jolinn, Jolynn
Language/Cultural Origin: English
Inherent Meaning: God Will Increase
Spiritual Connotation: Reborn
Scripture: Isaiah 38:5 NASB
I have heard your prayer, I have seen your tears; behold, I will add fifteen years to your life.

JONAH, Jona, Jonas, Yona, Yonah
Language/Cultural Origin: Hebrew
Inherent Meaning: Dove
Spiritual Connotation: Declarer of Joy and Salvation
Scripture: Acts 4:20 NLT
We cannot stop telling about the wonderful things we have seen and heard.

JONATHAN, Johnathan, Johnathon, Jonathon, Jonnathan (see also John)
Language/Cultural Origin: Hebrew
Inherent Meaning: Gift of the Lord
Spiritual Connotation: God's Precious Gift
Scripture: Psalm 92:4 NKJV
For You, LORD, have made me glad through Your work; I will triumph in the works of Your hands.

JONINA, Jeneena, Joneena, Jonika, Joniqua, Jonita, Jonnina, Jontaya
Language/Cultural Origin: Hebrew
Inherent Meaning: Dove
Spiritual Connotation: Reflection of God
Scripture: Luke 3:22 NKJV
And the Holy Spirit descended in bodily form like a dove upon Him, and a voice came from heaven which said, "You are My beloved Son; in You I am well pleased."

JONTAE, see Shantae

JORAH, Jora, Yora, Yorah
Language/Cultural Origin: Hebrew
Inherent Meaning: Autumn Rain
Spiritual Connotation: Blessing
Scripture: Joel 2:23 NIV
Rejoice in the LORD your God, for he has given you the autumn rains in righteousness. He sends you abundant showers, both autumn and spring rains, as before.

JORAM, Jorim
Language/Cultural Origin: Hebrew
Inherent Meaning: God Is Exalted
Spiritual Connotation: Reverent
Scripture: Isaiah 25:1 NKJV
O LORD, You are my God. I will exalt You, I will praise Your name.

JORDAN, Jordaan, Jordain, Jordane, Jorden, Jordenn, Jordenne, Jordin, Jordon, Jordyn, Joree, Jorée, Jori, Jorie, Jorii, Jorin, Jorrdan, Jorrie, Jorrín, Jorry, Jory, Jourdan
Language/Cultural Origin: Hebrew
Inherent Meaning: Descender
Spiritual Connotation: Wise in Judgment
Scripture: Proverbs 21:30 NCV
There is no wisdom, understanding, or advice that can succeed against the LORD.

JORDANA, see Yordana

JORELL, Jorel, Jorrel, Jorrell
Language/Cultural Origin: American
Inherent Meaning: He Preserves
Spiritual Connotation: Witness
Scripture: Isaiah 42:6 RSV
I am the LORD, I have called you in righteousness, I have taken you by the hand and kept you.

JORGEN, see Joergen

JORIANNA, Joriann, Jori-Anna, Jorianne, Jorrianna, Yoriann, Yorianna, Yorianne
Language/Cultural Origin: American
Inherent Meaning: Increasing in Grace
Spiritual Connotation: Blessed
Scripture: Joel 2:13 NASB
Now return to the LORD your God, for He is gracious and compassionate, slow to anger, abounding in lovingkindness, and relenting of evil.

JOSEPH, Joe, Joey, Joeseph, José, Josée, Josef, Joseff, Josephe, Josephus, Jozef, Yosef, Yoseff, Yosif, Yousef, Yusif
Language/Cultural Origin: Hebrew
Inherent Meaning: God Will Add
Spiritual Connotation: Wise and Understanding

Scripture: Proverbs 28:5 NKJV
Evil men do not understand justice, but those who seek the LORD understand all.

JOSEPHINE, Jo, Joey, Josée, Joselle, Josetta, Josette, Josephina, Josey, Josie
Language/Cultural Origin: French
Inherent Meaning: She Shall Increase in Wisdom
Spiritual Connotation: Spiritual Understanding
Scripture: Romans 12:2 NKJV
And do not be conformed to this world, but be transformed by the renewing of your mind.

JOSHUA, Jeshua, Jeshuah, Josh, Joshe, Joshuah, Joshuwa, Jozua
Language/Cultural Origin: Hebrew
Inherent Meaning: God Is My Salvation
Spiritual Connotation: Bringer of Truth
Scripture: James 1:25 NKJV
But he who looks into the perfect law of liberty and continues in it . . . this one will be blessed in what he does.

JOSIAH, Josia, Josias
Language/Cultural Origin: Hebrew
Inherent Meaning: Fire of the Lord
Spiritual Connotation: Intuitive Perception
Scripture: 1 Corinthians 2:7 NKJV
But we speak the wisdom of God in a mystery, the hidden wisdom which God ordained before the ages for our glory.

JOVAN, Jeovani, Jeovanni, Jiovani, Jiovanni, Jovaan, Jovani, Jovann, Jovanni, Jovonn, Yovaan, Yovan, Yovani, Yovann, Yovanni (see also Giovanni, Javan, Jevan)
Language/Cultural Origin: Latin
Inherent Meaning: Majestic
Spiritual Connotation: Delightful
Scripture: Psalm 16:3 NASB
As for the saints who are in the earth, they are the majestic ones in whom is all my delight.

JOVANNA, Jeovana, Jeovanna, Jovana, Jovena, Jovonna (see also Giovanna)
Language/Cultural Origin: Latin
Inherent Meaning: Majestic

Spiritual Connotation: Lovely
Scripture: Psalm 76:4 NASB
You are resplendent, more majestic than the mountains of prey.

JOY, Joya, Joyanna, Joye
Language/Cultural Origin: Latin
Inherent Meaning: Joyful
Spiritual Connotation: Follower of Truth
Scripture: Psalm 119:105 NKJV
Your word is a lamp to my feet and a light to my path.

JOYCE, Joice, Joyous
Language/Cultural Origin: Latin
Inherent Meaning: Vivacious
Spiritual Connotation: God's Gracious Gift
Scripture: Psalm 16:11 NKJV
You will show me the path of life; in Your presence is fullness of joy; at Your right hand are pleasures forevermore.

JUAN, Juanito, Juaun
Language/Cultural Origin: Spanish
Inherent Meaning: God Is Gracious
Spiritual Connotation: Righteous
Scripture: Psalm 97:11 NKJV
Light is sown for the righteous, and gladness for the upright in heart.

JUANITA, Juana, Juanequa, Juanesha, Juanna
Language/Cultural Origin: Spanish
Inherent Meaning: God Is Gracious
Spiritual Connotation: Famous
Scripture: Ezekiel 16:14 NRSV
Your fame spread among the nations on account of your beauty, for it was perfect because of my splendor that I had bestowed on you.

JUBAL, Jubel
Language/Cultural Origin: Hebrew
Inherent Meaning: Ram's Horn
Spiritual Connotation: Victorious
Scripture: Joshua 6:5 NRSV
When they make a long blast with the ram's horn . . . then all the people shall shout with a great shout; and the wall of the city will fall down flat.

JUDAH, Jud, Juda, Judas, Judd, Jude
Language/Cultural Origin: Hebrew

Inherent Meaning: Praised
Spiritual Connotation: Full of Love
Scripture: John 13:34 NKJV
A new commandment I give to you, that you love one another; as I have loved you, that you also love one another.

JUDSON, Judsen
Language/Cultural Origin: English
Inherent Meaning: Son of the Praised One
Spiritual Connotation: Glory to God
Scripture: Daniel 4:34 NKJV
I blessed the Most High and praised and honored Him who lives forever: for His dominion is an everlasting dominion, and His kingdom is from generation to generation.

JUDITH, Judi, Judie, Judy
Language/Cultural Origin: Hebrew
Inherent Meaning: She Who Praises
Spiritual Connotation: Righteous
Scripture: Isaiah 58:8 NKJV
Then your light shall break forth like the morning, your healing shall spring forth speedily, and your righteousness shall go before you.

JULIA, Julee, Juleen, Juli, Juliana, Juliane, Juliann, Julianna, Julie, Julieann, Juliene, Julienne, Julila, Julilla, Julina, Juline, Julisa, Julissa, Julliana, Jullianna
Language/Cultural Origin: Latin
Inherent Meaning: Youthful
Spiritual Connotation: Guided by Faith
Scripture: Matthew 9:29 NKJV
According to your faith let it be to you.

JULIET, Julieta, Juliete, Julietta, Juliette, Julliet, Jullietta
Language/Cultural Origin: French
Inherent Meaning: Youthful
Spiritual Connotation: Immovable
Scripture: Psalm 16:8 NKJV
I have set the LORD always before me; because He is at my right hand I shall not be moved.

JULIUS, Jule, Jules, Julian, Juliano, Julias, Julien, Julio, Jullian
Language/Cultural Origin: Latin
Inherent Meaning: Youthful

Spiritual Connotation: Regenerated
Scripture: Ephesians 4:23–24 NKJV

And be renewed in the spirit of your mind, and that you put on the new man . . . in true righteousness and holiness.

JUNE, Junelle, Junia
Language/Cultural Origin: Latin
Inherent Meaning: Born in the Fourth Month
Spiritual Connotation: Loving
Scripture: Romans 13:10 NKJV

Love does no harm to a neighbor; therefore love is the fulfillment of the law.

JURI, see Yuri

JURRIEN, Jurian, Jurien, Jurrian
Language/Cultural Origin: Dutch
Inherent Meaning: God Will Uplift
Spiritual Connotation: Humble
Scripture: James 4:10 NKJV

Humble yourselves in the sight of the Lord, and He will lift you up.

JUSTIN, Justan, Justen, Justinn, Justinus, Juston, Justun, Justyn
Language/Cultural Origin: Latin
Inherent Meaning: Upright
Spiritual Connotation: Righteous
Scripture: Psalm 138:8 NKJV

The LORD will perfect that which concerns me; your mercy, O LORD, endures forever; do not forsake the works of Your hands.

JUSTINA, Justeen, Justine, Justinna
Language/Cultural Origin: French
Inherent Meaning: Upright
Spiritual Connotation: Righteous
Scripture: Psalm 139:17 NKJV

How precious also are Your thoughts to me, O God! How great is the sum of them!

JUSTUS, Justas, Justice, Justis
Language/Cultural Origin: Hebrew
Inherent Meaning: Just
Spiritual Connotation: Righteous
Scripture: Isaiah 26:7 NIV

O upright One, you make the way of the righteous smooth.

JUWAN, see Jajuan

**KAARINA, Kaariana, Kaarianna
(see also Carina, Karina, Karena)**
Language/Cultural Origin: Finnish
Inherent Meaning: Pure
Spiritual Connotation: Spotless
Scripture: 2 Peter 3:14 RSV
Therefore, beloved, since you wait for these, be zealous to he found by him without spot or blemish, and at peace.

KACEY, see Casey

KACHINA, Kachéna
Language/Cultural Origin: Native American
Inherent Meaning: Sacred Dancer
Spiritual Connotation: Pleasant Offering
Scripture: Exodus 15:20 NASB
And Miriam the prophetess, Aaron's sister, took the timbrel in her hand, and all the women went out after her with timbrels and with dancing.

KACIA, Cacia, Casia, Kaycia, Kaysia
Language/Cultural Origin: Greek
Inherent Meaning: Thorny
Spiritual Connotation: Holy
Scripture: 2 Corinthians 7:1 NASB
Therefore, having these promises, beloved, let us cleanse ourselves from all defilement of flesh and spirit, perfecting holiness in the fear of God.

**KADEE, K.D., Kadey, Kadie, Kady, Kaydee, Kaydi, Kaydie, Kaydy
(see also Cady, Katy)**
Language/Cultural Origin: English

Inherent Meaning: Stainless
Spiritual Connotation: Sanctified
Scripture: Ephesians 5:27 NCV
He died so that he could give the church to himself like a bride in all her beauty. He died so that the church could be pure and without fault.

**KADIM, Kadeem, Kadím, Khadeem
(see also Qadim)**
Language/Cultural Origin: Middle Eastern
Inherent Meaning: Servant
Spiritual Connotation: Messenger
Scripture: Matthew 12:18 NRSV
Here is my servant, whom I have chosen, my beloved, with whom my soul is well pleased. . . . He will proclaim justice to the Gentiles.

KADIN, Kaden, Kadeen, Kaiden, Kadon
Language/Cultural Origin: Middle Eastern
Inherent Meaning: Confidant
Spiritual Connotation: Peacemaker
Scripture: Proverbs 21:14 NKJV
A gift in secret pacifies anger.

KADMIEL, Kadmielle
Language/Cultural Origin: Hebrew
Inherent Meaning: God Is of Old
Spiritual Connotation: Eternal
Scripture: Matthew 22:32 NKJV
God is not the God of the dead, but of the living.

**KAELA, Kaelah, Kahla, Kahlah, Keila, Keilah, Keyla, Keylah
(see also Cayla, Kaila, Kayla, Kyla)**
Language/Cultural Origin: Middle Eastern
Inherent Meaning: Cherished
Spiritual Connotation: Adored
Scripture: Song of Songs 6:3 NKJV
I am my beloved's, and my beloved is mine.

KAELYN, see Kaylyn

**KAHLIL, Kahleil, Kahlíl
(see also Kalil)**
Language/Cultural Origin: Turkish
Inherent Meaning: Young
Spiritual Connotation: Accountable
Scripture: Ecclesiastes 11:9 NRSV

*Rejoice, young man, while you are young
... but know that for all these things God
will bring you into judgment.*

KAI

Language/Cultural Origin: Navaho
Inherent Meaning: Willow Tree
Spiritual Connotation: Firmly Rooted
Scripture: Psalm 1:3 NKJV
*He shall be like a tree planted by the rivers of
water, that brings forth its fruit in its season.*

KAIJA, Kaijah, Kaiya, Kaiyah

Language/Cultural Origin: Russian
Inherent Meaning: Life
Spiritual Connotation: Eternal
Scripture: Psalm 23:6 RSV
*Surely goodness and mercy shall follow me
all the days of my life; and I shall dwell in
the house of the LORD for ever.*

KAILA, Kailah, Kailla, Kaillah
(see also Cayla, Kaela, Kayla, Kyla)

Language/Cultural Origin: Hebrew
Inherent Meaning: Crowned
Spiritual Connotation: Wise
Scripture: Proverbs 14:18 NASB
*The naive inherit foolishness, but the sensible
are crowned with knowledge.*

KAILEE, KAILEY, see Kaylee

KAITLIN, Kaatlan, Kaetlin, Kaetlynn, Kaitlan, Kaitland, Kaitlen, Kaitlinn, Kaitlyn, Kaitlynn, Kateland, Katelin, Katelyn, Katlyn, Kaytlin, Kaytlynn (see also Caitlin)

Language/Cultural Origin: Irish
Inherent Meaning: Virtuous
Spiritual Connotation: Favored
Scripture: Ruth 3:11 NKJV
*And now, my daughter, do not fear. I will do
for you all that you request, for all the people
of my town know that you are a virtuous
woman.*

KALA, Kalah, Kalla, Kallah
(see also Cala)

Language/Cultural Origin: American
Inherent Meaning: Refuge
Spiritual Connotation: Guarded of God
Scripture: Psalm 91:2 NKJV
*He is my refuge and my fortress; My God, in
Him I will trust.*

KALAMA, Kalam, Kallam, Kallama

Language/Cultural Origin: Hawaiian
Inherent Meaning: Flaming Torch
Spiritual Connotation: Testimony
Scripture: 2 Kings 1:12 NKJV
*If I am a man of God, let fire come down
from heaven and consume you and your fifty
men. And the fire of God came down from
heaven and consumed him and his fifty.*

KALANI, Kalan, Kalana, Kalanna, Kailana, Kailani, Kalanee, Kalanie (see also Keilani)

Language/Cultural Origin: Hawaiian
Inherent Meaning: Chieftain
Spiritual Connotation: Guardian
Scripture: Psalm 61:2 NASB
*From the end of the earth I call to Thee,
when my heart is faint; lead me to the rock
that is higher than I.*

KALE, Kayle

Language/Cultural Origin: Hawaiian
Inherent Meaning: Farmer
Spiritual Connotation: Sower of Truth
Scripture: Mark 4:14 NCV
*The farmer is like a person who plants God's
message in people.*

KALEA, Kahlea, Kahleah, Kallea, Khalea, Khaleah

Language/Cultural Origin: Hawaiian
Inherent Meaning: Clear
Spiritual Connotation: Righteous
Scripture: John 3:21 NRSV
*But those who do what is true come to the
light, so that it may be clearly seen that their
deeds have been done in God.*

KALEENA, Kalena (see also Kalina)

Language/Cultural Origin: Hawaiian
Inherent Meaning: Spotless
Spiritual Connotation: Respectful
Scripture: 1 Timothy 5:2 NLT
*Treat the older women as you would your
mother, and treat the younger women with
all purity as your own sisters.*

KALEI, Kahléi, Kallei, Khalei
(see also Callie, Kali, Kalli)

Language/Cultural Origin: Hawaiian
Inherent Meaning: Wreath of Flowers
Spiritual Connotation: Adorned

Scripture: Revelation 12:1 NASB
And a great sign appeared in heaven: a woman clothed with the sun, and the moon under her feet, and on her head a crown of twelve stars.

KALEY, see Kaylee

KALI (see also Callie, Kalli)
Language/Cultural Origin: Hawaiian
Inherent Meaning: Hesitating
Spiritual Connotation: Examiner of Truth
Scripture: Acts 17:11 NASB
For they received the word with great eagerness, examining the Scriptures daily, to see whether these things were so.

KALIANA, See Kaulana

KALIL, Kahleel, Kaleel, Kaléel (see also Kahlil)
Language/Cultural Origin: Hebrew
Inherent Meaning: Complete
Spiritual Connotation: Righteous
Scripture: Philippians 1:6 NRSV
I am confident of this, that the one who began a good work among you will bring it to completion by the day of Jesus Christ.

KALILA, Kahlila, Kaleela, Kalilla, Kaylila, Khalilah, Kylila, Kylilah
Language/Cultural Origin: Middle Eastern
Inherent Meaning: Sweetheart
Spiritual Connotation: Beloved
Scripture: Genesis 24:67 TLB
And Isaac brought Rebekah into his mother's tent, and she became his wife. He loved her very much.

KALIN, KALYN, see Kaylyn

KALINA, Kalinna (see also Kaleena)
Language/Cultural Origin: Slavic
Inherent Meaning: Flower
Spiritual Connotation: Nurtured
Scripture: Isaiah 35:2 NKJV
It shall blossom abundantly and rejoice, even with joy and singing.

KALISA, Kalissa, Kalysa, Kalyssa
Language/Cultural Origin: American
Inherent Meaning: Pure Offering
Spiritual Connotation: Sweet Sacrifice

Scripture: Exodus 29:18 NKJV
And you shall burn the whole ram on the altar. It is a burnt offering to the LORD; it is a sweet aroma, an offering made by fire to the LORD.

KALLAN, Kallen, Kallin, Kallon, Kallun, Kallyn (see also Kellen)
Language/Cultural Origin: Slavic
Inherent Meaning: River
Spiritual Connotation: Joyful
Scripture: Psalm 98:8 NASB
Let the rivers clap their hands; let the mountains sing together for joy.

KALLI, Kaleigh, Kallee, Kalley, Kallie, Kally
Language/Cultural Origin: English
Inherent Meaning: Lark
Spiritual Connotation: Cheerful
Scripture: Psalm 100:2 NKJV
Serve the LORD with gladness; come before His presence with singing.

KALYCA, Kaleecia, Kalica, Kalicia, Kalicya
Language/Cultural Origin: Greek
Inherent Meaning: Rosebud
Spiritual Connotation: Promise
Scripture: Isaiah 35:1 NKJV
The wilderness and the wasteland shall be glad for them, and the desert shall rejoice and blossom as the rose.

KAMA, Kamah, Khama
Language/Cultural Origin: Hebrew
Inherent Meaning: Ripe Harvest
Spiritual Connotation: Reaper
Scripture: Revelation 14:15 NKJV
Thrust in Your sickle and reap, for the time has come for You to reap, for the harvest of the earth is ripe.

KAMAL, Kamaal, Kamâl, Kamîl
Language/Cultural Origin: Middle Eastern
Inherent Meaning: Perfect
Spiritual Connotation: Power of God
Scripture: 2 Samuel 22:33 NKJV
God is my strength and power, and He makes my way perfect.

KAMALI, Kamalaya, Kamalee, Kamaleah, Kamaleigh
Language/Cultural Origin: Mahona

Inherent Meaning: Protector
Spiritual Connotation: Chosen
Scripture: Nehemiah 13:22 NKJV
Remember me, O my God, concerning this also, and spare me according to the greatness of Your mercy!

KAMARIA, Kamara, Kamari
Language/Cultural Origin: Swahili
Inherent Meaning: Moonlight
Spiritual Connotation: Deliverance
Scripture: Isaiah 30:26 NKJV
Moreover the light of the moon will be as the light of the sun. . . . In the day that the LORD binds up the bruise of His people and heals the stroke of their wound.

KAMEA, Kameah
Language/Cultural Origin: Hawaiian
Inherent Meaning: Precious
Spiritual Connotation: Honored
Scripture: Isaiah 43:4 NKJV
Since you were precious in My sight, You have been honored, and I have loved you; therefore I will give men for you, and people for your life.

KAMEKO, Kameka, Kamika, Kamiko
Language/Cultural Origin: Japanese
Inherent Meaning: Turtle Child
Spiritual Connotation: Humble
Scripture: Proverbs 15:33 NRSV
The fear of the LORD is instruction in wisdom, and humility goes before honor.

**KAMI, Kamee, Kámi, Kahmi
(see also Cami)**
Language/Cultural Origin: Japanese
Inherent Meaning: Divine Aura
Spiritual Connotation: Gifted
Scripture: 2 Peter 1:4 NASB
For by these He has granted to us His precious and magnificent promises, in order that by them you might become partakers of the divine nature.

**KAMILAH, Kameela, Kameelah,
Kamila, Kamilla, Kamillah**
Language/Cultural Origin: Middle Eastern
Inherent Meaning: Perfect
Spiritual Connotation: Holy
Scripture: Hebrews 10:14 NCV
With one sacrifice he made perfect forever those who are being made holy.

KANA, Kána, Kaena, Kaina, Kayna
Language/Cultural Origin: Japanese
Inherent Meaning: Powerful
Spiritual Connotation: Strength of God
Scripture: Psalm 106:8 NKJV
Nevertheless He saved them for His name's sake, that He might make His mighty power known.

KANANI, Kananee, Kananie
Language/Cultural Origin: Hawaiian
Inherent Meaning: Beautiful
Spiritual Connotation: Obedient
Scripture: Psalm 45:11 NCV
The king loves your beauty. Because he is your master, you should obey him.

KANE, Kané (see also Cain)
Language/Cultural Origin: Celtic
Inherent Meaning: Beautiful
Spiritual Connotation: Hopeful
Scripture: Psalm 31:24 NKJV
Be of good courage, and He shall strengthen your heart, all you who hope in the LORD.

KANGE, Kainge, Kangé
Language/Cultural Origin: Lakota
Inherent Meaning: Raven
Spiritual Connotation: Genuine
Scripture: Song of Songs 5:11 NCV
His head is like the finest gold; his hair is wavy and black like a raven.

KANIEL, Kahniel, Kahnyell, Kanyel
Language/Cultural Origin: Hebrew
Inherent Meaning: God Is My Reed
Spiritual Connotation: God Has Bought Me
Scripture: 1 Corinthians 6:20 NASB
For you have been bought with a price: therefore glorify God in your body.

KANIKA, Kanicka, Kaneeka, Kanikah
Language/Cultural Origin: Kenyan
Inherent Meaning: Black Cloth
Spiritual Connotation: Reverent
Scripture: Hebrews 12:29 NKJV
For our God is a consuming fire.

**KANNON, Kanen, Kannen, Kanon
(see also Cannon)**
Language/Cultural Origin: Polynesian
Inherent Meaning: Unchained

Spiritual Connotation: Free
Scripture: Psalm 107:14 NKJV

He brought them out of darkness and the shadow of death, And broke their chains in pieces.

KANYA, Kania, Kanyah
Language/Cultural Origin: Thai
Inherent Meaning: Young Lady
Spiritual Connotation: Prosperous
Scripture: Zechariah 9:17 NKJV

For how great is its goodness and how great its beauty! Grain shall make the young men thrive, and new wine the young women.

KAORI, Kaory
Language/Cultural Origin: Japanese
Inherent Meaning: Strong
Spiritual Connotation: Majestic
Scripture: 1 Chronicles 16:27 NKJV

Honor and majesty are before Him; strength and gladness are in His place.

KARA, Kaira, Kairah, Karah, Karrah (see also Cara, Kerani)
Language/Cultural Origin: Danish
Inherent Meaning: Pure
Spiritual Connotation: Cherished
Scripture: Psalm 36:9 NKJV

For with You is the fountain of life; in Your light we see light.

KARAL, KAREL, see Carl

KARALEE, Karalea, Karaleah, Karaleigh, Karalie
Language/Cultural Origin: English
Inherent Meaning: Innocent
Spiritual Connotation: Righteous
Scripture: Job 33:9 NKJV

I am pure, without transgression; I am innocent, and there is no iniquity in me.

KARE, Kåre, Kareé
Language/Cultural Origin: Norwegian
Inherent Meaning: Enormous
Spiritual Connotation: Saved by Faith
Scripture: Psalm 33:16 TLB

The best-equipped army cannot save a king—for great strength is not enough to save anyone.

KAREEM, see Karim

KAREN, Kaaren, Karan, Karon, Karren, Karron, Karryn, Karyn, Karynn (see also Caryn, Karin)
Language/Cultural Origin: German
Inherent Meaning: Pure
Spiritual Connotation: Beloved
Scripture: Nehemiah 8:10 NKJV

Do not sorrow, for the joy of the LORD is your strength.

KAREAH, Kareeah
Language/Cultural Origin: Hebrew
Inherent Meaning: Bald
Spiritual Connotation: Forgiven
Scripture: Romans 5:8 NRSV

But God proves his love for us in that while we still were sinners Christ died for us.

KARENA, Kareena, Karyna, Karynna (see also Corina, Kaarina, Karina)
Language/Cultural Origin: Norwegian
Inherent Meaning: Spotless
Spiritual Connotation: Purchased
Scripture: 1 Peter 1:19 NLT

He paid for you with the precious lifeblood of Christ, the sinless, spotless Lamb of God.

KARI, Karee, Karie, Karri (see also Cari, Carrie)
Language/Cultural Origin: Greek
Inherent Meaning: Pure
Spiritual Connotation: Righteous
Scripture: 2 Timothy 2:22 NKJV

Flee also youthful lusts; but pursue righteousness, faith, love, peace with those who call on the Lord out of a pure heart.

KARIANNE, Cariana, Cariann, Carrianna, Carianne, Kariana, Kariann, Karianna, Karriana (see also Kerianne)
Language/Cultural Origin: English
Inherent Meaning: Virtuous
Spiritual Connotation: Godly
Scripture: 2 Peter 1:3 NRSV

His divine power has given us everything needed for life and godliness, through the knowledge of him who called us by his own glory and goodness.

KARIF, Kareef
Language/Cultural Origin: Middle Eastern

Inherent Meaning: Born in the Fall
Spiritual Connotation: Prosperous
Scripture: Jeremiah 33:9 NKJV
They shall fear and tremble for all the goodness and all the prosperity that I provide for it.

KARILYNN, Karilin, Karilyne, Karilynne, Karylin, Karylynn (see also Caroline, Karolyn)
Language/Cultural Origin: American
Inherent Meaning: Clear, Pure Water
Spiritual Connotation: Cleansed
Scripture: Hebrews 10:22 NKJV
Let us draw near with a true heart in full assurance of faith, having our hearts sprinkled from an evil conscience and our bodies washed with pure water.

KARIM, Kareem, Karém, Karriem
Language/Cultural Origin: Middle Eastern
Inherent Meaning: Distinguished
Spiritual Connotation: Chosen
Scripture: Psalm 4:3 NKJV
But know that the LORD has set apart for Himself him who is godly; the LORD will hear when I call to Him.

KARIN, Kaarin, Kárin, Karrin (see also Caryn, Karen)
Language/Cultural Origin: Scandinavian
Inherent Meaning: Unblemished
Spiritual Connotation: Righteous
Scripture: Psalm 18:2 NCV
The LORD is my rock, my protection, my Savior. My God is my rock. I can run to him for safety. He is my shield and my saving strength, my defender.

KARINA, Karine, Karinna, Karrina, Karrine, Karyna (see also Carina, Kaarina, Karena)
Language/Cultural Origin: Russian
Inherent Meaning: Innocent
Spiritual Connotation: Pure
Scripture: Psalm 26:6 NKJV
I will wash my hands in innocence; so I will go about Your altar, O LORD.

KARIS, Kariss, Karris, Karys, Karyss (see also Carys)
Language/Cultural Origin: Greek
Inherent Meaning: Graceful

Spiritual Connotation: Discreet
Scripture: Proverbs 3:21–22 NKJV
Keep sound wisdom and discretion; So they will be life to your soul and grace to your neck.

KARISSA, see Carissa

KARL, see Carl

KARLA, see Carla

KARLANA, see Carlana

KARLENE, see Carlene

KARLIN, KARLEE, see Carlin

KARLINA, see Carlina

KARLISSA, see Carlissa

KARLYNN, Karlyn
Language/Cultural Origin: Slavic
Inherent Meaning: Womanly
Spiritual Connotation: Valuable
Scripture: Proverbs 31:10 NKJV
Who can find a virtuous wife? For her worth is far above rubies.

KARMEN, see Carmen

KAROLYN, Kåralyn, Karalynn, Karilyn, Karilynn, Karrolyn (see also Caroline, Karilynn)
Language/Cultural Origin: American
Inherent Meaning: Womanly
Spiritual Connotation: Cherished
Scripture: Ephesians 5:25 NKJV
Husbands, love your wives, just as Christ also loved the church and gave Himself for her.

KARSTEN, Karstan, Kärsten, Karstin, Karstine
Language/Cultural Origin: Swedish
Inherent Meaning: Anointed
Spiritual Connotation: Chosen
Scripture: 1 Samuel 16:13 NKJV
Then Samuel took the horn of oil and anointed him ... and the Spirit of the LORD came upon David from that day forward.

KASEM, Casem
Language/Cultural Origin: Thai
Inherent Meaning: Joy
Spiritual Connotation: Fulfilled
Scripture: John 15:11 NRSV
I have said these things to you so that my joy may be in you, and that your joy may be complete.

KASEY, see Casey

KASHA, Kahasha, Kahsha, Kasa
Language/Cultural Origin: Native American
Inherent Meaning: Fur Robe
Spiritual Connotation: Righteous
Scripture: Isaiah 61:10 NKJV
He has clothed me with the garments of salvation, He has covered me with the robe of righteousness.

KASHAWNA, Kashana, Kashaun, Kashauna, Kashawn, Kashonda
Language/Cultural Origin: American
Inherent Meaning: Pure Promise
Spiritual Connotation: Eternal Gift
Scripture: Joshua 23:14 NKJV
Not one thing has failed of all the good things which the LORD your God spoke concerning you. All have come to pass for you; not one word of them has failed.

KASIM, Kaseem, Kazeem
Language/Cultural Origin: Middle Eastern
Inherent Meaning: Divided
Spiritual Connotation: Holy
Scripture: Philippians 1:23–24 NRSV
I am hard pressed between the two: my desire is to depart and be with Christ, for that is far better; but to remain in the flesh is more necessary for you.

KASIMIR, see Casimir

KASSANDRA, see Cassandra

KASSIDY, see Cassidy

KATARINA, Catarina, Caterina, Ecatarina, Ecaterina, Ekatarina, Ekaterina, Katareena, Katerina (see also Katrina)
Language/Cultural Origin: Czech/Russian
Inherent Meaning: Unblemished
Spiritual Connotation: Purified
Scripture: Hebrews 9:14 NRSV
How much more will the blood of Christ . . . purify our conscience from dead works to worship the living God!

KATE, Cait, Cate, Kait
Language/Cultural Origin: English
Inherent Meaning: Innocent
Spiritual Connotation: Godly Example
Scripture: Philippians 2:15 NASB
So that you will prove yourselves to be blameless and innocent, children of God above reproach.

KATHERINE, Katharin, Katharine, Katheren, Kathereen, Katherin, Katheryn, Kathren, Kathryn (see also Catherine)
Language/Cultural Origin: Greek
Inherent Meaning: Pure
Spiritual Connotation: Perceptive
Scripture: Jeremiah 33:3 NKJV
Call to Me, and I will answer you, and show you great and mighty things, which you do not know.

KATHLEEN, Katheleen, Kathlynn, Katleen (see also Cathleen)
Language/Cultural Origin: Irish
Inherent Meaning: Pure
Spiritual Connotation: Treasured
Scripture: Psalm 115:15 NKJV
May you be blessed by the LORD, who made heaven and earth.

KATO, Katón (see also Cato)
Language/Cultural Origin: English
Inherent Meaning: Wise
Spiritual Connotation: Humble
Scripture: Proverbs 13:10 RSV
By insolence the heedless make strife, but with those who take advice is wisdom.

KATONE, Katóne
Language/Cultural Origin: Hungarian
Inherent Meaning: The Lord Exalts
Spiritual Connotation: Obedient
Scripture: Isaiah 42:21 NKJV
The LORD is well pleased for His righteousness' sake; He will exalt the law and make it honorable.

KATRIEL, Catriel, Catrielle, Cattriel, Katrielle, Kattriel
Language/Cultural Origin: Hebrew
Inherent Meaning: God Is My Crown
Spiritual Connotation: Redeemed
Scripture: Hebrews 2:9 NKJV
But we see Jesus, who was . . . for the suffering of death crowned with glory and honor, that He, by the grace of God, might taste death for everyone.

KATRINA, Cateena, Catina, Catreen, Catreena, Catrien, Catrién, Catrin, Catrina, Catrine, Catrinia, Catriona, Catryn, Catryna, Cattrina, Cattrinna, Cattryna, Ecatrinna, Ekatrinna, Kateena, Katina, Katreen, Katreena, Katrene, Katrien, Katrién, Katrin, Katrine, Katrinia, Katriona, Katryn, Katryna, Kattrina, Kattryna
Language/Cultural Origin: Russian/German
Inherent Meaning: Spotless
Spiritual Connotation: Cleansed
Scripture: 1 Peter 1:19 NKJV
But with the precious blood of Christ, as of a lamb without blemish and without spot.

KATURAH, Katura (see also Keturah)
Language/Cultural Origin: Rhodesian
Inherent Meaning: Relieved
Spiritual Connotation: Righteous
Scripture: Psalm 119:142 NKJV
Your righteousness is an everlasting righteousness, and Your law is truth.

KATY, Catey, Caytee, Caytie, Katey, Kati, Katie, Kaytee, Kaytie (see also Cady, Kadee)
Language/Cultural Origin: Estonian
Inherent Meaning: Spotless
Spiritual Connotation: Unblemished
Scripture: Ephesians 5:27 NLT
He did this to present her to himself as a glorious church without a spot or wrinkle or any other blemish.

KATYA, Cata, Catia, Catja, Catka, Cattiah, Catya, Kata, Katia, Katica, Katja, Katka, Kattiah
Language/Cultural Origin: Russian
Inherent Meaning: Pure

Spiritual Connotation: Righteous
Scripture: Psalm 119:1 NRSV
Happy are those whose way is blameless, who walk in the law of the LORD.

KAULANA, Kaliana, Kalianna
Language/Cultural Origin: Hawaiian
Inherent Meaning: Famous
Spiritual Connotation: Strength of God
Scripture: Psalm 89:13 NKJV
You have a mighty arm; strong is Your hand, and high is Your right hand.

KAY, Kae, Kaye
Language/Cultural Origin: Latin
Inherent Meaning: Rejoicer
Spiritual Connotation: Joyful
Scripture: Proverbs 15:23 NRSV
To make an apt answer is a joy to anyone, and a word in season, how good it is!

KAYA, Kayah
Language/Cultural Origin: Hopi
Inherent Meaning: Child of Wisdom
Spiritual Connotation: Youthful Example
Scripture: Luke 2:49 NKJV
Why did you seek Me? Did you not know that I must be about My Father's business?

KAYLA, Kaylia, Kayliah (see also Cayla, Kaela, Kaila, Kyla)
Language/Cultural Origin: Middle Eastern
Inherent Meaning: Crowned
Spiritual Connotation: Exalted
Scripture: Psalm 8:5 NKJV
For You have made him a little lower than the angels, and You have crowned him with glory and honor.

KAYLEE, Kaeleah, Kaelee, Kaeleigh, Kaelie, Kailee, Kaileigh, Kailey, Kalee, Kaleigh, Kaley, Kayleah, Kayleigh, Kayley, Kaylie (see also Caeley)
Language/Cultural Origin: American
Inherent Meaning: Crowned
Spiritual Connotation: Wise
Scripture: Proverbs 14:18 NASB
The naive inherit foolishness, but the sensible are crowned with knowledge.

KAYLEEN, Caeleen, Caileen, Cayleen, Caylene, Kaeleen, Kaileen, Kaylene
Language/Cultural Origin: Middle Eastern
Inherent Meaning: Sweetheart
Spiritual Connotation: Beloved
Scripture: Song of Songs 2:14 NKJV
Let me see your face, let me hear your voice; for your voice is sweet, and your face is lovely.

KAYLYN, Kaelan, Kaelen, Kaelin, Kaelyn, Kaelynn, Kailyn, Kalan, Kalen, Kalin, Kalyn, Kaylan, Kaylin, Kaylon, Kaylynn (see also Caelan, Cailin)
Language/Cultural Origin: American
Inherent Meaning: Crowned
Spiritual Connotation: Delivered
Scripture: Hebrews 2:9 NKJV
But we see Jesus who was . . . for the suffering of death crowned with glory and honor, that He, by the grace of God, might taste death for everyone.

KAYSA, Kajsa
Language/Cultural Origin: Swedish
Inherent Meaning: Clean
Spiritual Connotation: Innocent
Scripture: 2 Samuel 22:21 NLT
The LORD rewarded me for doing right; he compensated me because of my innocence.

KEANDRE, Kendre, Keondre (see also Kendre)
Language/Cultural Origin: American
Inherent Meaning: Manly
Spiritual Connotation: Gentle
Scripture: Philippians 4:5 NRSV
Let your gentleness be known to everyone. The Lord is near.

KEANE, Kean, Keano, Keanu
Language/Cultural Origin: Irish
Inherent Meaning: Commander
Spiritual Connotation: Steadfast
Scripture: Psalm 16:8 NKJV
I have set the LORD always before me; because He is at my right hand I shall not be moved.

KEARA, Kearra, Keera, Keira, Keirra, Kera (see also Kiera, Kira, Kyrie)
Language/Cultural Origin: Irish
Inherent Meaning: Dark
Spiritual Connotation: Obedient
Scripture: Isaiah 50:10 NKJV
Who among you fears the LORD? . . . Who walks in darkness and has no light? Let him trust in the name of the LORD and rely upon his God.

KEARNEY, Kearn, Kearny
Language/Cultural Origin: Irish
Inherent Meaning: Victorious
Spiritual Connotation: Thankful
Scripture: Psalm 20:5 NASB
We will sing for joy over your victory, and in the name of our God we will set up our banners. May the LORD fulfill all your petitions.

KEATON, Keaten, Keeton
Language/Cultural Origin: English
Inherent Meaning: From Where Hawks Fly
Spiritual Connotation: Reverent
Scripture: Exodus 3:5 NRSV
Come no closer! Remove the sandals from your feet, for the place on which you are standing is holy ground.

KEEGAN, Kaegan, Keagan, Kegan, Keghan
Language/Cultural Origin: Gaelic
Inherent Meaning: Fiery
Spiritual Connotation: Righteous
Scripture: Psalm 37:37 NKJV
Mark the blameless man, and observe the upright; for the future of that man is peace.

KEELAN, Kealyn, Keelen, Keelin, Keelyn, Kielan, Kielyn
Language/Cultural Origin: Irish
Inherent Meaning: Slender
Spiritual Connotation: Holy
Scripture: Leviticus 26:12 NKJV
I will walk among you and be your God, and you shall be My people.

KEELY, Kealey, Kealy, Keelee, Keeleigh, Keelie, Keely, Keilee, Kieley
Language/Cultural Origin: Gaelic

Inherent Meaning: Beautiful
Spiritual Connotation: Trusting
Scripture: Proverbs 30:5 NKJV
Every word of God is pure; He is a shield to those who put their trust in Him.

KEENA, Kina
Language/Cultural Origin: Irish
Inherent Meaning: Brave
Spiritual Connotation: Given Strength
Scripture: Acts 28:15 NKJV
When Paul saw them, he thanked God and took courage.

KEENAN, Keanan, Keenen, Keenon, Kienan, Kienon
Language/Cultural Origin: Irish
Inherent Meaning: Little Commander
Spiritual Connotation: Honored
Scripture: Isaiah 12:2 NKJV
Behold, God is my salvation, I will trust and not be afraid; for YAH, the LORD, is my strength and song; He also has become my salvation.

KEIANNA, Kayana, Kayanna, Keiana (see also Kiana, Kiona, Quiana)
Language/Cultural Origin: Japanese
Inherent Meaning: Reverent
Spiritual Connotation: Heir
Scripture: Hebrews 12:28 NKJV
Therefore, since we are receiving a kingdom which cannot be shaken, let us have grace, by which we may serve God acceptably with reverence and godly fear.

KEIFFER, Keefer, Kieffer
Language/Cultural Origin: German
Inherent Meaning: Barrel Maker
Spiritual Connotation: Beloved
Scripture: John 14:23 NKJV
If anyone loves Me, he will keep My word; and My Father will love him, and We will come to him and make Our home with him.

KEIKO, Keiki
Language/Cultural Origin: Japanese
Inherent Meaning: Happy Child
Spiritual Connotation: Chosen
Scripture: Psalm 65:4 NRSV
Happy are those whom you choose and bring near to live in your courts. We shall be satisfied with the goodness of your house, your holy temple.

KEILA, see Kaela

KEILANI, Keilana, Keilanna (see also Kalani)
Language/Cultural Origin: Hawaiian
Inherent Meaning: Glorious
Spiritual Connotation: Likeness of God
Scripture: 2 Corinthians 3:18 NLT
As the Spirit of the Lord works within us, we become more and more like him and reflect his glory even more.

KEISHA, Keesha, Keeshawna, Keisha, Kesha, Keshia, Keshonda, Keysha, Kiesha, Kisha (see also Queisha)
Language/Cultural Origin: American
Inherent Meaning: Beautiful Woman
Spiritual Connotation: Gentle
Scripture: 1 Peter 3:4 TLB
Be beautiful inside, in your hearts, with the lasting charm of a gentle and quiet spirit that is so precious to God.

KEITA, Keeta
Language/Cultural Origin: Scottish
Inherent Meaning: Enclosed Place
Spiritual Connotation: Joyful
Scripture: Zechariah 2:10 RSV
Sing and rejoice, O daughter of Zion; for lo, I come and I will dwell in the midst of you, says the LORD.

KEITH, Keath
Language/Cultural Origin: Scottish
Inherent Meaning: From the Place of Battle
Spiritual Connotation: Brave
Scripture: Galatians 5:25 NKJV
If we live in the Spirit, let us also walk in the Spirit.

KELBY, Kelbee, Kelbey, Kellby
Language/Cultural Origin: Old German
Inherent Meaning: From the Spring Farm
Spiritual Connotation: Petition
Scripture: Matthew 18:20 NKJV
For where two or three are gathered together in My name, I am there in the midst of them.

KELISSA, Kalisa, Kalissa, Kelisa
Language/Cultural Origin: English
Inherent Meaning: Fighter

Spiritual Connotation: Witness
Scripture: 1 Timothy 6:12 NKJV

Fight the good fight of faith, lay hold on eternal life, to which you were also called.

KELITA, Kellita, Kelitta
Language/Cultural Origin: Hebrew
Inherent Meaning: Poverty
Spiritual Connotation: Unselfish
Scripture: John 12:8 NCV

You will always have the poor with you, but you will not always have me.

KELLEN, Kellan, Kellin, Kellon, Kellyn (see also Kallen)
Language/Cultural Origin: English
Inherent Meaning: Mighty Warrior
Spiritual Connotation: Triumphant
Scripture: Jeremiah 50:9 NKJV

Their arrows shall be like those of an expert warrior; none shall return in vain.

KELLER, Keler
Language/Cultural Origin: Irish
Inherent Meaning: Little Friend
Spiritual Connotation: Selfless
Scripture: John 15:13 NASB

Greater love has no one than this, that one lay down his life for his friends.

KELLY, Kelia, Keli, Keliana, Kelianna, Kellee, Kelley, Kelli, Kellia, Kelliana, Kellie
Language/Cultural Origin: Irish
Inherent Meaning: Warrior
Spiritual Connotation: Loyal and Brave
Scripture: Proverbs 2:7 NKJV

He stores up sound wisdom for the upright; He is a shield to those who walk uprightly.

KELSEY, Kelcea, Kelcee, Kelcey, Kelcie, Kelcy, Kellsea, Kellsee, Kellsie, Kelsee, Kelsi, Kelsie, Kelsy
Language/Cultural Origin: Old Norse
Inherent Meaning: From Ship Island
Spiritual Connotation: Malleable
Scripture: Jeremiah 18:6 NKJV

Look, as the clay is in the potter's hand, so are you in My hand, O house of Israel!

KELVIN, Kelvan, Kelvyn
Language/Cultural Origin: Celtic

Inherent Meaning: From the Narrow River
Spiritual Connotation: Reasonable
Scripture: Psalm 119:130 NKJV

The entrance of Your words gives light; it gives understanding to the simple.

KEMP, Khemp
Language/Cultural Origin: English
Inherent Meaning: Champion
Spiritual Connotation: Zealous
Scripture: Psalm 19:5 NCV

The sun comes out like a bridegroom from his bedroom. It rejoices like an athlete eager to run a race.

KENDA, Kendi, Kendie, Kennda, Kindi, Kinnda, Kynda
Language/Cultural Origin: English
Inherent Meaning: Water Baby
Spiritual Connotation: Pure
Scripture: 2 Corinthians 11:2 NLT

I am jealous for you with the jealousy of God himself. For I promised you as a pure bride to one husband, Christ.

KENDALL, Kendahl, Kendal, Kendel, Kendell, Kindal, Kindall, Kyndal, Kyndall
Language/Cultural Origin: English
Inherent Meaning: From the Clear Valley
Spiritual Connotation: Thankful
Scripture: Psalm 126:3 NKJV

The LORD has done great things for us, and we are glad.

KENDRA, Kenndra, Kindra, Kyndra
Language/Cultural Origin: English
Inherent Meaning: Understanding
Spiritual Connotation: Filled With Wisdom
Scripture: Proverbs 24:3 NKJV

Through wisdom a house is built, and by understanding it is established.

KENDRE, Kendrae, Kendré, Kendrei (see also Keandre)
Language/Cultural Origin: American
Inherent Meaning: Strong
Spiritual Connotation: Victorious
Scripture: Joshua 10:25 NKJV

Do not be afraid, nor be dismayed; be strong and of good courage, for thus the LORD will do to all your enemies against whom you fight.

**KENDRICK, Kendric, Kendrik
(see also Kenrick)**
Language/Cultural Origin: Celtic
Inherent Meaning: Royal Chief
Spiritual Connotation: Subject of God
Scripture: Deuteronomy 11:1 NKJV
Therefore you shall love the LORD your God, and keep His charge, His statutes, His judgments, and His commandments always.

**KENEISHA, Kaneisha, Kaneshia,
Keneesha, Keneshia, Kenishia,
Kennesha, Kennisha, Kineesha,
Kineisha, Kinesha, Kineshia
(see also Quaneisha)**
Language/Cultural Origin: American
Inherent Meaning: Beautiful Woman
Spiritual Connotation: Promise
Scripture: Isaiah 4:2 NKJV
In that day the Branch of the LORD shall be beautiful and glorious; and the fruit of the earth shall be excellent and appealing.

**KENNEDY, Kenadee,
Kenedy, Kennady**
Language/Cultural Origin: Irish
Inherent Meaning: Ugly-Headed
Spiritual Connotation: Obedient
Scripture: 2 John 1:9 NCV
But whoever continues to follow the teaching of Christ has both the Father and the Son.

**KENNETH, Ken, Keneth,
Kenney, Kennith, Kenny**
Language/Cultural Origin: Old English
Inherent Meaning: Royal Oath
Spiritual Connotation: Trustworthy
Scripture: Luke 19:17 NRSV
Well done, good slave! Because you have been trustworthy in a very small thing, take charge of ten cities.

**KENEESE, Kenese, Keniece,
Keniese, Kennise**
Language/Cultural Origin: English
Inherent Meaning: Fair
Spiritual Connotation: Companion
Scripture: Psalm 55:14 NASB
We who had sweet fellowship together, walked in the house of God in the throng.

KENNAN, Kenan, Kennen, Kennon
Language/Cultural Origin: Scottish

Inherent Meaning: Little Ken
Spiritual Connotation: Encourager
Scripture: 1 Thessalonians 3:2 NKJV
To establish you and encourage you concerning your faith.

**KENRICK, Kenric, Kenrik
(see also Kendrick)**
Language/Cultural Origin: Old English
Inherent Meaning: Bold Ruler
Spiritual Connotation: Loyal
Scripture: Psalms 119:112 NKJV
I have inclined my heart to perform Your statutes forever, to the very end.

KENT, Khent
Language/Cultural Origin: Welsh
Inherent Meaning: Radiant
Spiritual Connotation: Wise
Scripture: Colossians 3:16 NKJV
Let the word of Christ dwell in you richly in all wisdom.

KENYA, Kenia, Kenja
Language/Cultural Origin: Hebrew
Inherent Meaning: Animal Horn
Spiritual Connotation: Accountable
Scripture: Hebrews 10:24 NKJV
And let us consider one another in order to stir up love and good works, but exhorting one another.

KENYON, Kenyan
Language/Cultural Origin: Irish
Inherent Meaning: Blond/White-Haired
Spiritual Connotation: Righteous
Scripture: Philippians 1:27 NRSV
Only, live your life in a manner worthy of the gospel of Christ.

**KENZIE, Kensie, Kenzy, Kinzie
(see also Mackenzie)**
Language/Cultural Origin: English
Inherent Meaning: Child of the Wise Leader
Spiritual Connotation: Destined
Scripture: Isaiah 11:2 NASB
The Spirit of the LORD will rest on Him, the spirit of wisdom and understanding, the spirit of counsel and strength, the spirit of knowledge and the fear of the LORD.

KEON, Keion, Keionne, Keón, Keyon
Language/Cultural Origin: Irish

Inherent Meaning: God Is Gracious
Spiritual Connotation: Blessed
Scripture: 1 Corinthians 1:4 RSV
I give thanks to God always for you because of the grace of God which was given you in Christ Jesus.

KERANI, Kera, Kurani, Kura
Language/Cultural Origin: Indo-Pakistani
Inherent Meaning: Sacred Bells
Spiritual Connotation: Protected
Scripture: Psalm 23:5 NKJV
You prepare a table before me in the presence of my enemies; You anoint my head with oil; my cup runs over.

KERENSA, Karenza, Kerenza
Language/Cultural Origin: Cornish
Inherent Meaning: Loving
Spiritual Connotation: Beloved
Scripture: Isaiah 43:4 NCV
Because you are precious to me, because I give you honor and love you . . . I will give other nations to save your life.

KERMIT, Kermet, Kermic
Language/Cultural Origin: Irish
Inherent Meaning: Free of Envy
Spiritual Connotation: Steadfast
Scripture: Isaiah 33:5–6 NKJV
The LORD is exalted, for He dwells on high; He has filled Zion with justice and righteousness. Wisdom and knowledge will be the stability of your times.

KERN, Kerne
Language/Cultural Origin: Irish
Inherent Meaning: Dark
Spiritual Connotation: Righteous
Scripture: Romans 12:21 NKJV
Do not be overcome by evil, but overcome evil with good.

KEROS, Karos
☞Language/Cultural Origin: Hebrew
Inherent Meaning: Reed of a Weaver's Beam
Spiritual Connotation: Gifted
Scripture: Exodus 35:35 NRSV
He has filled them with skill to do every kind of work done . . . by any sort of artisan or skilled designer.

KERRIANNE, Karriann, Karrianne, Keriann, Kerianne, Kerriann, Kerryann, Kerryanne (see also Karianne)
Language/Cultural Origin: English
Inherent Meaning: Grace of the People
Spiritual Connotation: Child of Grace
Scripture: Romans 9:8 NCV
Abraham's true children are those who become God's children because of the promise God made to Abraham.

KERRY, Kearie, Keary, Keree, Kerey, Keri, Kerrey, Kerri, Kerrie (see also Carey, Cary)
Language/Cultural Origin: Irish
Inherent Meaning: Dark-Haired
Spiritual Connotation: Diligent
Scripture: Colossians 3:23 NKJV
And whatever you do, do it heartily, as to the Lord and not to men.

KERSTEN, see Kirsten

KERSEN, Kersan, Kersun
Language/Cultural Origin: Indonesian
Inherent Meaning: Cherry
Spiritual Connotation: Destined
Scripture: Isaiah 27:6 NASB
In the days to come Jacob will take root, Israel will blossom and sprout; and they will fill the whole world with fruit.

KESHIA, see Keisha

KESHAWN, Keshaun, Keshon, Keyshaun, Keyshawn
Language/Cultural Origin: American
Inherent Meaning: God Is Gracious
Spiritual Connotation: Forgiven
Scripture: Psalm 116:5 RSV
Gracious is the LORD, and righteous; our God is merciful.

KESSIE, Kessa, Kessey, Kessi, Kessia, Kessiah
Language/Cultural Origin: Ashanti
Inherent Meaning: Chubby Baby
Spiritual Connotation: Nourished
Scripture: 1 Peter 2:2 NRSV
Like newborn infants, long for the pure, spiritual milk, so that by it you may grow into salvation.

KESTER, Kesster
Language/Cultural Origin: English
Inherent Meaning: Bearer of Christ
Spiritual Connotation: Servant
Scripture: Mark 8:34 NRSV
If any want to become my followers, let them deny themselves and take up their cross and follow me.

KETURAH, Keturia, Keturyah
☞(see also Katurah)
Language/Cultural Origin: Hebrew
Inherent Meaning: Incense
Spiritual Connotation: Holy
Scripture: Psalm 141:2 NCV
Let my prayer be like incense placed before you, and my praise like the evening sacrifice.

KEVIN, Kev, Keven, Kévin, Kevinn, Kevon (see also Cavan)
Language/Cultural Origin: Irish
Inherent Meaning: Handsome
Spiritual Connotation: Honored
Scripture: Psalm 91:15 NKJV
He shall call upon Me, and I will answer him; I will be with him in trouble; I will deliver him and honor him.

KEVYN, Kevan, Kevynn
Language/Cultural Origin: Irish
Inherent Meaning: Beautiful
Spiritual Connotation: Attractive
Scripture: Song of Songs 2:14 NASB
Let me see your form, let me hear your voice; for your voice is sweet, and your form is lovely.

KEZIA, Kazia, Kaziah, Ketzia,
☞Ketziah, Keziah, Kizzie, Kizzy
Language/Cultural Origin: Hebrew
Inherent Meaning: Cinnamonlike Bark
Spiritual Connotation: Valuable
Scripture: Luke 12:24 NKJV
Consider the ravens. . . . God feeds them. Of how much more value are you than the birds?

KHALID, Khaled, Khälid
Language/Cultural Origin: Middle Eastern
Inherent Meaning: Eternal
Spiritual Connotation: Divine
Scripture: John 6:51 NRSV
I am the living bread that came down from heaven.

KHAN, Khanh (see also Quanah)
Language/Cultural Origin: Turkish
Inherent Meaning: Prince
Spiritual Connotation: Promise
Scripture: Psalm 45:16 NASB
In place of your fathers will be your sons; You shall make them princes in all the earth.

KHRISTIAN, KHRISTOPHER,
see Christian, Christopher

KIA, Kiah
Language/Cultural Origin: Nigerian
Inherent Meaning: Beginning of the Season
Spiritual Connotation: Sign
Scripture: Psalm 104:19 NRSV
You have made the moon to mark the seasons; the sun knows its time for setting.

KIANA, Keanna, Keiana, Kianna, Kiauna, Kiaunna (see also Keianna, Kiona, Quiana)
Language/Cultural Origin: American
Inherent Meaning: Grace of God
Spiritual Connotation: Restored
Scripture: Isaiah 30:18 NKJV
Therefore the LORD will wait, that He may be gracious to you; and therefore He will be exalted, that He may have mercy on you.

KIARIA, Kiariah, Kiariana, Kiarianna
Language/Cultural Origin: Japanese
Inherent Meaning: Fortunate
Spiritual Connotation: Blessed
Scripture: Ruth 3:10 NKJV
Blessed are you of the LORD, my daughter!

KIELE, Kiela, Kieli
Language/Cultural Origin: Hawaiian
Inherent Meaning: Fragrant Blossom
Spiritual Connotation: Sacrifice
Scripture: 2 Corinthians 2:15 NKJV
For we are to God the fragrance of Christ among those who are being saved and among those who are perishing.

KIERA, Kiara, Kiarra, Kierlyn, Kierlynn, Kierra (see also Keara, Kira, Kyrie)
Language/Cultural Origin: Irish
Inherent Meaning: Little and Dark
Spiritual Connotation: Contemplative

Scripture: Psalm 46:10 NKJV

Be still, and know that I am God; I will be exalted among the nations, I will be exalted in the earth!

KIERAN, Keiran, Kernan, Kiernan, Kieron

Language/Cultural Origin: Irish
Inherent Meaning: Little
Spiritual Connotation: Blessed
Scripture: Proverbs 3:13 NKJV

Happy is the man who finds wisdom, and the man who gains understanding.

KILEY, Kilee, Kileigh (see also Kylie)

Language/Cultural Origin: Irish
Inherent Meaning: Attractive
Spiritual Connotation: Desirable
Scripture: Zechariah 9:17 NLT

How wonderful and beautiful they will be! The young men and women will thrive on the abundance of grain and new wine.

KILLIAN, Kilian

Language/Cultural Origin: Irish
Inherent Meaning: Little Warrior
Spiritual Connotation: Attentive
Scripture: 1 Corinthians 14:8 NLT

And if the bugler doesn't sound a clear call, how will the soldiers know they are being called to battle?

KIMANA, Kimanna

Language/Cultural Origin: Shushone
Inherent Meaning: Butterfly
Spiritual Connotation: Unchained
Scripture: Galatians 5:1 NASB

It was for freedom that Christ set us free; therefore keep standing firm and do not be subject again to a yoke of slavery.

KIMBALL, Kim, Kimbal, Kimble

Language/Cultural Origin: Celtic
Inherent Meaning: Ruler
Spiritual Connotation: Subject of God
Scripture: Psalm 29:2 NKJV

Give unto the LORD the glory due to His name; worship the LORD in the beauty of holiness.

KIMBERLY, Kim, Kimba, Kimber, Kimberlea, Kimberlee, Kimberleigh, Kimberley, Kimberli, Kimberlyn, Kimberlynn, Kimbria, Kym, Kymberlee, Kymberly

Language/Cultural Origin: Old English
Inherent Meaning: From the Royal Meadow
Spiritual Connotation: Seeker of Truth
Scripture: Psalm 119:2 NKJV

Blessed are those who keep His testimonies, who seek Him with the whole heart!

KIMI, Kimie, Kimia, Kimika, Kimiko

Language/Cultural Origin: Japanese
Inherent Meaning: Peerless
Spiritual Connotation: Honored
Scripture: Hebrews 8:11 NRSV

And they shall not teach one another or say to each other, know the Lord, for they shall all know me, from the least of them to the greatest.

KINEISHA, see Keneisha

KINSEY, Kingsley, Kingsly, Kinsea, Kinsee, Kinslea, Kinsleigh, Kinslee

Language/Cultural Origin: Old English
Inherent Meaning: Relative
Spiritual Connotation: Protected
Scripture: Ruth 3:13 NASB

Remain this night, and when morning comes, if he will redeem you, good; let him redeem you.

KIOKO, Kiyoko (see also Kyoko)

Language/Cultural Origin: Japanese
Inherent Meaning: Happy Child
Spiritual Connotation: Respectful
Scripture: Proverbs 29:18 NASB

Where there is no vision, the people are unrestrained, but happy is he who keeps the law.

KIONA, Kionia, Kionna, Kionya (see also Keianna, Kiana, Quiana)

Language/Cultural Origin: Native American
Inherent Meaning: Dark Hills
Spiritual Connotation: Preserved
Scripture: Psalm 121:1–2 NASB

I will lift up my eyes to the mountains; from whence shall my help come? My help comes from the LORD, who made heaven and earth.

KIPP, Kip, Kippar, Kipper, Kippie, Kippy
Language/Cultural Origin: English
Inherent Meaning: From the Pointed Hill
Spiritual Connotation: Near the Heart of God
Scripture: Exodus 24:13 RSV
So Moses rose with his servant Joshua, and Moses went up into the mountain of God.

KIRA, Kiri, Kiria, Kiriana (see also Keara, Kiera, Kyrie)
Language/Cultural Origin: Bulgarian
Inherent Meaning: Throne
Spiritual Connotation: Temple of God
Scripture: Isaiah 37:16 NRSV
O LORD of hosts, God of Israel, who are enthroned above the cherubim, you are God, you alone.

KIRAL, Kieral
Language/Cultural Origin: Turkish
Inherent Meaning: King
Spiritual Connotation: Obedient
Scripture: 1 Samuel 13:4 TLB
Saul sounded the call to arms throughout Israel. He announced that he had destroyed the Philistine garrison.

KIRBY, Kerbey, Kerbie, Kerby, Kirbey, Kirbie
Language/Cultural Origin: Anglo-Saxon
Inherent Meaning: From the Church Village
Spiritual Connotation: Follower of God
Scripture: Psalm 1:3 NKJV
He shall be like a tree planted by the rivers of water, that brings forth its fruit in its season.

KIRIMA, Kireema
Language/Cultural Origin: Eskimo
Inherent Meaning: Hill
Spiritual Connotation: Joyful Praise
Scripture: Psalm 98:8 NASB
Let the rivers clap their hands, let the mountains sing together for joy,

KIRI, Kiree, Kirie, Kirey (see also Kuri)
Language/Cultural Origin: Cambodian
Inherent Meaning: Mountain
Spiritual Connotation: Abundance
Scripture: Amos 9:13 NCV

The time is coming when there will be all kinds of food. People will still be harvesting crops when it's time to plow again.

KIRK, Kerk
Language/Cultural Origin: Old Norse
Inherent Meaning: From the Church
Spiritual Connotation: Glad in Heart
Scripture: Psalm 4:7 TLB
Yes, the gladness you have given me is far greater than their joys at harvest time as they gaze at their bountiful crops.

KIRSI, Kirsea, Kirsee
Language/Cultural Origin: Indo-Pakistani
Inherent Meaning: Blossoming Flower
Spiritual Connotation: Blessed
Scripture: Hosea 14:5 NCV
I will be like the dew to Israel, and they will blossom like a lily.

KIRSTEN, Keirstan, Kersten, Kerstin, Kerstine, Kerston, Kerstyn, Kiersten, Kirstan, Kirstien, Kirstin, Kirstine, Kirston, Kirstyn, Kjersten, Kurstan, Kursten, Kurstyn (see also Karsten)
Language/Cultural Origin: Greek
Inherent Meaning: Follower of Christ
Spiritual Connotation: Anointed
Scripture: 2 Chronicles 6:42 NLT
O LORD God, do not reject your anointed one. Remember your unfailing love for your servant David.

KIRSTY, Kersta, Kerstee, Kersti, Kerstie, Kersty, Kirsta, Kirstee, Kirsti, Kirstie, Kjersti
Language/Cultural Origin: Scandinavian
Inherent Meaning: Follower of Christ
Spiritual Connotation: Anointed
Scripture: Psalm 28:8 RSV
The LORD is the strength of his people, he is the saving refuge of his anointed.

KISA, Keesa, Keeson, Kissa, Kison
Language/Cultural Origin: Russian
Inherent Meaning: Kitten
Spiritual Connotation: Formed of God
Scripture: Genesis 2:20 NCV
The man gave names to all the tame animals, to the birds in the sky, and to all the wild animals.

KISH

☞ Language/Cultural Origin: Hebrew
Inherent Meaning: Straw
Spiritual Connotation: Faithful
Scripture: 1 Corinthians 3:14 NRSV
If what has been built on the foundation survives, the builder will receive a reward.

KJELL, Kjele

Language/Cultural Origin: Swedish
Inherent Meaning: Landworker
Spiritual Connotation: Blessed
Scripture: Psalm 80:9 TLB
You cleared the ground and tilled the soil, and we took root and filled the land.

KLARISSA, Klaresa, Klaressa, Klarisa, Klarisse, Klarrisa, Klarrissa, Klerissa (see also Clarissa)

Language/Cultural Origin: German
Inherent Meaning: Bright
Spiritual Connotation: Glorious Reflection
Scripture: Psalm 148:3 NRSV
Praise him, sun and moon; praise him, all you shining stars!

KLAUS, Claas, Claus, Clas, Klaas, Klas, Klause

Language/Cultural Origin: German
Inherent Meaning: Victory of the People
Spiritual Connotation: Triumphant
Scripture: Deuteronomy 20:4 NLT
For the LORD your God is going with you! He will fight for you against your enemies, and he will give you victory!

KNOX, Knoxx

Language/Cultural Origin: Old English
Inherent Meaning: From the Hills
Spiritual Connotation: Peaceful
Scripture: Psalm 72:3 NASB
Let the mountains bring peace to the people, and the hills in righteousness.

KNUTE, Canute, Knut

Language/Cultural Origin: Old Norse
Inherent Meaning: Knot
Spiritual Connotation: Victorious
Scripture: Psalm 18:32 NKJV
It is God who arms me with strength, and makes my way perfect.

KOBI, see Coby

KODY, see Cody

KOHANA, Kohanna

Language/Cultural Origin: Lakota
Inherent Meaning: Speedy
Spiritual Connotation: Efficient
Scripture: Psalm 147:15 NRSV
He sends out his command to the earth; his word runs swiftly.

KOKO, Kokko (see also Coco)

Language/Cultural Origin: Japanese
Inherent Meaning: Stork
Spiritual Connotation: Created
Scripture: Genesis 1:20 NASB
Let the waters teem with swarms of living creatures, and let birds fly above the earth in the open expanse of the heavens.

KOLEY, see Coley

KOLYA, Kollya

Language/Cultural Origin: Russian
Inherent Meaning: Victory of the People
Spiritual Connotation: Exalted
Scripture: Psalm 44:7 NLT
It is you who gives us victory over our enemies; it is you who humbles those who hate us.

KONA, Konia, Konya

Language/Cultural Origin: Hawaiian
Inherent Meaning: Lady
Spiritual Connotation: Loving
Scripture: 2 John 1:5 NASB
And now I ask you, lady, not as writing to you a new commandment, but the one which we have had from the beginning, that we love one another.

KONSTANCE, see Constance

KORAH, Korrah

☞ Language/Cultural Origin: Hebrew
Inherent Meaning: Baldness
Spiritual Connotation: Covenant
Scripture: Genesis 9:15 NIV
Never again will the waters become a flood to destroy all life.

KORDELL, see Cordell

KOREN, Coren, Corren, Korren
Language/Cultural Origin: Hebrew
Inherent Meaning: Shining
Spiritual Connotation: Image of Christ
Scripture: 1 John 2:8 NKJV
The darkness is passing away, and the true light is already shining.

KOREY, Koree, Korrey, Korry, Kory (see also Corey)
Language/Cultural Origin: English
Inherent Meaning: From the Hollow
Spiritual Connotation: Heir
Scripture: Psalm 2:8 NKJV
Ask of Me, and I will give you the nations for your inheritance, and the ends of the earth for your possession.

KORINA, Koren, Koreen, Koreena, Korey, Kori, Korie, Korianna, Korine, Korri, Korrie, Korrin, Korrina, Korrine, Koryn (see also Cora, Cori, Corina, Corinne, Kaarina, Karina, Korah)
Language/Cultural Origin: Greek
Inherent Meaning: Maiden
Spiritual Connotation: Pure
Scripture: 1 Peter 1:22 NASB
Since you have in obedience to the truth purified your souls for a sincere love of the brethren, fervently love one another from the heart.

KORISSA, see Corissa

KORTNEY, see Courtney

KRISSY, Khris, Kris, Krissey, Krissi, Krissi
Language/Cultural Origin: American
Inherent Meaning: Follower of Christ
Spiritual Connotation: Disciple
Scripture: Matthew 28:19 NKJV
Go therefore and make disciples of all the nations, baptizing them in the name of the Father and of the Son and of the Holy Spirit.

KRISTA, Khrissa, Khrista, Khryssa, Khrysta, Krisa, Kriska, Krissa, Kristia, Kryssa, Krysta (see also Christa, Kirsty)
Language/Cultural Origin: Latvian
Inherent Meaning: Follower of Christ
Spiritual Connotation: Disciple
Scripture: Luke 6:20 RSV
And he lifted up his eyes on his disciples, and said: "Blessed are you poor, for yours is the kingdom of God."

KRISTEN, Kristan, Kristi, Kristie, Kristii, Kristin, Kristy, Kristyn, Krysten, Krysti, Krystin (see also Christen, Karsten, Kirsten)
Language/Cultural Origin: Scandinavian
Inherent Meaning: Follower of Christ
Spiritual Connotation: Anointed
Scripture: Psalm 84:9 NRSV
Behold our shield, O God; look on the face of your anointed.

KRISTIAN, see Christian

KRISTIANA, Kristi-Ann, Kristianna, Kristi-Anna, Kristianne, Kristyana, Kristyanna, Krystiana, Krystianna
Language/Cultural Origin: Greek
Inherent Meaning: Follower of Christ
Spiritual Connotation: Joyful
Scripture: Luke 11:37 NASB
Now when He had spoken, a Pharisee asked Him to have lunch with him; and He went in, and reclined at the table.

KRISTINA, Khristina, Kristeena, Krysteena, Krystina, Krystyna (see also Christina)
Language/Cultural Origin: Swedish
Inherent Meaning: Follower of Christ
Spiritual Connotation: Near to God
Scripture: John 6:3 NKJV
And Jesus went up on the mountain, and there He sat with His disciples.

KRISTINE, Kristeen, Kristene, Krystine (see also Christine)
Language/Cultural Origin: Norwegian
Inherent Meaning: Follower of Christ
Spiritual Connotation: Chosen
Scripture: John 8:31–32 NRSV
If you continue in my word, you are truly my disciples; and you will know the truth, and the truth will make you free.

KRISTOPHER, see Christopher

KRUIN, Kruan
Language/Cultural Origin: Afrikaans
Inherent Meaning: Mountain Top
Spiritual Connotation: Sacred
Scripture: Ezekiel 43:12 RSV
This is the law of the temple: the whole territory round about upon the top of the mountain shall be most holy.

KRUZ, see Cruz

KRYSTAL, Kristal, Kristalin, Kristall, Kristalyn, Krisstal, Kristal, Kristalee, Kristel, Kristelle, Krystall, Krystallin, Krystel, Krystell Krystilin, Krystol, Krystylyn (see also Crystal)
Language/Cultural Origin: American
Inherent Meaning: Clear, Sparkling
Spiritual Connotation: Blessed
Scripture: Isaiah 54:12 NASB
Moreover, I will make your battlements of rubies, and your gates of crystal, and your entire wall of precious stones.

KRYSTALYNN, Krystaleen, Krystalina, Kristalyn, Kristilynn, Krystalin, Krystalin
Language/Cultural Origin: English
Inherent Meaning: Perfectly Clear Water
Spiritual Connotation: Symbol
Scripture: Revelation 21:21 NASB
And the twelve gates were twelve pearls; each one of the gates was a single pearl. And the street of the city was pure gold, like transparent glass.

KUMI, Kumie, Kumika, Kumiko
Language/Cultural Origin: Japanese
Inherent Meaning: Braided Hair
Spiritual Connotation: Lovely Sacrifice
Scripture: Luke 7:38 TLB
Going in, she knelt behind him at his feet, weeping, with her tears falling down upon his feet; and she wiped them off with her hair and kissed them and poured the perfume on them.

KURI, Kuree, Kurie, Kurii, Kurri (see also Kiri)
Language/Cultural Origin: Japanese
Inherent Meaning: Chestnut
Spiritual Connotation: Expectant
Scripture: Song of Songs 6:11 NCV
I went down into the orchard of nut trees to see the blossoms of the valley, to look for buds on the vines, to see if the pomegranate trees had bloomed.

KURT, Kort (see also Curtis)
Language/Cultural Origin: German
Inherent Meaning: Bold Counselor
Spiritual Connotation: Wise and Just
Scripture: Colossians 2:3 NLT
In him lie hidden all the treasures of wisdom and knowledge.

KWAN, Kwanan
Language/Cultural Origin: Korean
Inherent Meaning: Strong
Spiritual Connotation: Upright
Scripture: 1 Corinthians 10:13 NLT
But remember that the temptations that come into your life are no different from what others experience. And God is faithful.

KYLA, Kylah, Kylla, Kyllah (see also Cayla, Kaela, Kaila, Keila)
Language/Cultural Origin: Yiddish
Inherent Meaning: Crowned
Spiritual Connotation: Purchased
Scripture: Hebrews 2:9 NASB
But we do see ... Jesus, because of the suffering of death crowned with glory and honor, that by the grace of God He might taste death for everyone.

KYLE, Kile, Kylan, Kylen, Kyler
Language/Cultural Origin: Gaelic
Inherent Meaning: From the Strait
Spiritual Connotation: Perceptive Insight
Scripture: Proverbs 15:33 NKJV
The fear of the LORD is the instruction of wisdom, and before honor is humility.

KYLIE, Kylee, Kyleigh, Kylen, Kylyn (see also Kiley)
Language/Cultural Origin: Aboriginal
Inherent Meaning: Boomerang
Spiritual Connotation: Generous
Scripture: Ecclesiastes 11:1 NASB
Cast your bread on the surface of the waters, for you will find it after many days.

KYRIE, Kyra, Kyrah, Kyria, Kyriah (see also Keara, Kiera, Kira)
Language/Cultural Origin: Greek
Inherent Meaning: Feminine, Ladylike
Spiritual Connotation: Tenderhearted
Scripture: 2 John 1:5 NRSV
But now, dear lady, I ask you, not as though I were writing you a new commandment, but one we have had from the beginning, let us love one another.

KYOKO, Kyokoh (see also Kioko)
Language/Cultural Origin: Japanese
Inherent Meaning: Mirror
Spiritual Connotation: Reflection
Scripture: 1 Corinthians 13:12 NRSV
For now we see in a mirror, dimly, but then we will see face to face.

LABAN, Laben, Labon
Language/Cultural Origin: Hebrew
Inherent Meaning: White
Spiritual Connotation: Glorious
Scripture: Matthew 28:3 NASB
And his appearance was like lightning, and his garment as white as snow.

LACEY, Lacee, Laci, Lacie, Lacy
Language/Cultural Origin: Latin
Inherent Meaning: Joyful
Spiritual Connotation: Filled With Praise
Scripture: Psalm 98:4 RSV
Make a joyful noise to the LORD, all the earth; break forth into joyous song and sing praises!

LACHELLE, Lachele, Lachell
Language/Cultural Origin: American/French
Inherent Meaning: Lock
Spiritual Connotation: Steadfast
Scripture: Revelation 2:17 NRSV
To everyone who conquers I will give . . . a white stone, and on the white stone is written a new name that no one knows except the one who receives it.

LACHLAN, Lachlann, Lochlan, Lochlann
Language/Cultural Origin: Scottish
Inherent Meaning: From the Land of Lakes
Spiritual Connotation: Reverent
Scripture: Mark 4:41 NCV
The followers were very afraid and asked each other, "Who is this? Even the wind and the waves obey him!"

LACHLANA, Lachlanna, Lochlanna, Lochlanne
Language/Cultural Origin: Scottish
Inherent Meaning: From the Land of Lakes
Spiritual Connotation: Strength Through Faith
Scripture: Mark 11:23 NASB
Whoever says to this mountain, Be taken up and cast into the sea, and does not doubt in his heart, but believes that what he says is going to happen, it shall be granted him.

LADA, Ladah
Language/Cultural Origin: Russian
Inherent Meaning: Beauty
Spiritual Connotation: Useful
Scripture: Romans 10:15 NKJV
How beautiful are the feet of those who preach the gospel of peace, who bring glad tidings of good things!

LADONNA, Ladona, La Donna, Ladonia, Ladonya
Language/Cultural Origin: American
Inherent Meaning: Refined Lady
Spiritual Connotation: Loving
Scripture: 2 John 1:5 NRSV
But now, dear lady, I ask you, not as though I were writing you a new commandment, but one we have had from the beginning, let us love one another.

LAELA, see Layla

LAHELA, Lahaela, Lahaila
Language/Cultural Origin: Hawaiian
Inherent Meaning: Lamb
Spiritual Connotation: Redeemed
Scripture: 1 Peter 1:19 NLT
He paid for you with the precious lifeblood of Christ, the sinless, spotless Lamb of God.

LAINE, Laina, Lainee, Lainey (see also Lane)
Language/Cultural Origin: French
Inherent Meaning: Brilliant
Spiritual Connotation: Righteous
Scripture: Proverbs 4:18 RSV
But the path of the righteous is like the light of dawn, which shines brighter and brighter until full day.

LAIRD, Layrd
Language/Cultural Origin: Scottish

176 ~ THE NAME BOOK

Inherent Meaning: Wealthy Landowner
Spiritual Connotation: Prosperous
Scripture: Proverbs 4:7 NKJV
Wisdom is the principal thing; therefore get wisdom. And in all your getting, get understanding.

LAKEISHA, Lakaisha, Lakasha, Lakecia, Lakeesha, Lakesha, Lakeshia, Lakesia, Lakeysha, Lakicia, Lakisha, Laqueisha, Laquesha, Laquiesha, Laquisha, Lekasha, Lekeesha, Lekeisha, Lekesha, Lekeshia, Lekicia, Lekisha
Language/Cultural Origin: American
Inherent Meaning: Lovely
Spiritual Connotation: Thankful
Scripture: Psalm 27:4 NASB
One thing . . . I shall seek: That I may dwell in the house of the LORD all the days of my life, to behold the beauty of the LORD, and to meditate in His temple.

LAKENYA, Lakeena, Lakeenya, Lakena, Lakenia, Lakinya, Lekenya
Language/Cultural Origin: American
Inherent Meaning: Horn
Spiritual Connotation: Symbol of Strength
Scripture: Psalm 89:17 NKJV
For You are the glory of their strength, and in Your favor our horn is exalted.

LAKIA, Lakita, Lakiya, Lakya
Language/Cultural Origin: Middle Eastern
Inherent Meaning: Treasure Discovered
Spiritual Connotation: Wise
Scripture: Isaiah 33:6 NASB
And He will be the stability of your times, a wealth of salvation, wisdom and knowledge; the fear of the LORD is his treasure.

LAKRESHA, see Lucretia

LALA, Lalla
Language/Cultural Origin: Slavic
Inherent Meaning: Tulip
Spiritual Connotation: Enduring
Scripture: Isaiah 40:8 NKJV
The grass withers, the flower fades, but the word of our God stands forever.

LAMAR, Lamarr, Lemar, Lemarr
Language/Cultural Origin: Latin

Inherent Meaning: From the Sea
Spiritual Connotation: Preserved
Scripture: Psalm 139:9–10 NKJV
If I take the wings of the morning, and dwell in the uttermost parts of the sea, even there Your hand shall lead me, and Your right hand shall hold me.

LAMBERT, Lambard
Language/Cultural Origin: Old German
Inherent Meaning: From the Bright Land
Spiritual Connotation: Protected
Scripture: Psalm 121:8 NKJV
The LORD shall preserve your going out and your coming in from this time forth, and even forevermore.

LAMOND, Lammond, Lemond
Language/Cultural Origin: French
Inherent Meaning: From the Earth
Spiritual Connotation: Blessed
Scripture: Acts 3:25 NRSV
You are the descendants of the prophets and of the covenant that God gave to your ancestors,

LAMONT, Lamonte, Lemont
Language/Cultural Origin: Old Norse
Inherent Meaning: Lawman
Spiritual Connotation: Fearless
Scripture: Haggai 2:5 NKJV
According to the word that I covenanted with you when you came out of Egypt, so My Spirit remains among you; do not fear!

LANA, Lanna, Lannah
Language/Cultural Origin: Irish
Inherent Meaning: Attractive
Spiritual Connotation: Peaceful
Scripture: Psalm 37:3 NKJV
Trust in the LORD, and do good; dwell in the land, and feed on His faithfulness.

LANAE, Lanai, Lanay, Lannay
Language/Cultural Origin: Hawaiian
Inherent Meaning: Buoyant
Spiritual Connotation: Full of Faith
Scripture: Matthew 14:31 RSV
Jesus immediately reached out his hand and caught him.

LANCE, Lantz, Launce
Language/Cultural Origin: German

Inherent Meaning: From the Land
Spiritual Connotation: Witness
Scripture: Acts 13:47 NLT
For this is as the Lord commanded us when he said, I have made you a light to the Gentiles, to bring salvation to the farthest corners of the earth.

LANCELOT, Launcelot
Language/Cultural Origin: Old French
Inherent Meaning: Attendant
Spiritual Connotation: God's Helper
Scripture: Ezekiel 18:31 NKJV
Get yourselves a new heart and a new spirit. For why should you die, O house of Israel?

LANDER, Landers
Language/Cultural Origin: Basque
Inherent Meaning: Like a Lion
Spiritual Connotation: Powerful
Scripture: Genesis 49:9 NCV
Judah is like a young lion. . . . Like a lion, he stretches out and lies down to rest, and no one is brave enough to wake him.

LANDO, Landro
Language/Cultural Origin: Portuguese
Inherent Meaning: From the Famous Land
Spiritual Connotation: Destined
Scripture: Acts 17:26 NLT
From one man he created all the nations throughout the whole earth.

LANDON, Landan, Landin
Language/Cultural Origin: Old English
Inherent Meaning: From the Grassy Meadow
Spiritual Connotation: Comforted
Scripture: John 10:9 NRSV
I am the gate. Whoever enters by me will be saved, and will come in and go out and find pasture.

LANDRY, Landré
Language/Cultural Origin: French
Inherent Meaning: Ruler
Spiritual Connotation: Subject of God
Scripture: Luke 1:33 NKJV
And He will reign over the house of Jacob forever, and of His kingdom there will be no end.

LANE, Laney, Lanie, Layne (see also Laine)
Language/Cultural Origin: English

Inherent Meaning: Road
Spiritual Connotation: Eternal
Scripture: Matthew 7:14 NLT
But the gateway to life is small, and the road is narrow, and only a few ever find it.

LANG, Lange
Language/Cultural Origin: Old Norse
Inherent Meaning: Tall
Spiritual Connotation: Lifted Up
Scripture: Psalm 18:33 NRSV
He made my feet like the feet of a deer, and set me secure on the heights.

LANGLEY, Langlee
Language/Cultural Origin: Old English
Inherent Meaning: From the Long Meadow
Spiritual Connotation: Peaceful
Scripture: Psalm 147:8 RSV
He covers the heavens with clouds, he prepares rain for the earth, he makes grass grow upon the hills.

LANGSTON, Langsdon
Language/Cultural Origin: Old English
Inherent Meaning: From the Tall Man's Town
Spiritual Connotation: Rescued
Scripture: Isaiah 49:9 NCV
You will tell the prisoners, "Come out of your prison." You will tell those in darkness, "Come into the light."

LANI, Lanata, Lanita
Language/Cultural Origin: Hawaiian
Inherent Meaning: Heavenly
Spiritual Connotation: Thankful
Scripture: Psalm 111:3 NCV
What he does is glorious and splendid, and his goodness continues forever.

LANNY, see Lawrence

LAQUISHA, see Lakeisha

LARA, Larah (see also Laura)
Language/Cultural Origin: Latin
Inherent Meaning: Famous
Spiritual Connotation: God's Gracious Gift
Scripture: Romans 8:28 NKJV
And we know that all things work together for good to those who love God, to those who are the called according to His purpose.

LARAMIE, Laramee

Language/Cultural Origin: French
Inherent Meaning: Tears of Love
Spiritual Connotation: Vital
Scripture: Ecclesiastes 3:4 NKJV

A time to weep, and a time to laugh; a time to mourn, and a time to dance.

LARAINE, Larain, Larayne, Larine, Lauraine (see also Lorraine)

Language/Cultural Origin: Latin
Inherent Meaning: Freedom
Spiritual Connotation: Free Spirit
Scripture: Malachi 3:1 NKJV

Behold, I send My messenger, and he will prepare the way before Me.

LARI, Laree, Larey, Larii

Language/Cultural Origin: English
Inherent Meaning: Bay
Spiritual Connotation: Protected
Scripture: Isaiah 4:6 NLT

It will be a shelter from daytime heat and a hiding place from storms and rain.

LARINA, Larena

Language/Cultural Origin: Greek
Inherent Meaning: Sea Bird
Spiritual Connotation: Free
Scripture: Matthew 6:26 NRSV

Look at the birds of the air; they neither sow nor reap . . . and yet your heavenly Father feeds them. Are you not of more value than they?

LARISSA, Larisa, Laryssa

Language/Cultural Origin: Greek
Inherent Meaning: Cheerful
Spiritual Connotation: Grateful
Scripture: James 5:13 NRSV

Are any among you suffering? They should pray. Are any cheerful? They should sing songs of praise.

LARK, Larke

Language/Cultural Origin: English
Inherent Meaning: Skylark
Spiritual Connotation: Spiritual Freedom
Scripture: Galatians 5:1 NASB

It was for freedom that Christ set us free; therefore keep standing firm and do not be subject again to a yoke of slavery.

LARKIN, Larkan

Language/Cultural Origin: Irish
Inherent Meaning: Fierce
Spiritual Connotation: Strength of God
Scripture: Psalm 29:4 NASB

The voice of the LORD is powerful, the voice of the LORD is majestic.

LARRY, see Lawrence

LARS, Larsen, Larson, Larss, Larsson

Language/Cultural Origin: Scandinavian
Inherent Meaning: Crowned With Honor
Spiritual Connotation: Redeemed
Scripture: Hebrews 2:9 NRSV

But we do see Jesus, who . . . was . . . now crowned with glory and honor because of the suffering of death, so that by the grace of God he might taste death for everyone.

LASHONDA, Lashana, Lashandra, Lashanna, Lashannon, Lashauna, Lashaunda, Lashaundra, Lashawnda, Lashawndra, Lashawnia, Lashona, Lashondia, Lashondra, Lashonna, Lashunda, Lashundra, Leshandra, Leshondra, Leshundra, Leshawna

Language/Cultural Origin: American
Inherent Meaning: God Is Gracious
Spiritual Connotation: Victorious
Scripture: Romans 16:20 NLT

The God of peace will soon crush Satan under your feet. May the grace of our Lord Jesus Christ be with you.

LATANYA, Latana, Latania, Latanja, Latanna, Latona, Latonia, Latonna, Latonya (see also Litonya)

Language/Cultural Origin: American
Inherent Meaning: Queen
Spiritual Connotation: Righteous
Scripture: Psalm 45:6 NKJV

Your throne, O God, is forever and ever; a scepter of righteousness is the scepter of Your kingdom.

LATASHA, Latacia, Latashia, Lataysha, Letasha, Letashia

Language/Cultural Origin: American
Inherent Meaning: Christmas Child
Spiritual Connotation: Witness of Christ
Scripture: Revelation 1:18 NCV

I am the One who lives; I was dead, but look, I am alive forever and ever! And I hold the keys to death and to the place of the dead.

LATAVIA, Latavya
Language/Cultural Origin: Middle Eastern
Inherent Meaning: Pleasant
Spiritual Connotation: Wise
Scripture: Proverbs 2:10 NCV
Wisdom will come into your mind, and knowledge will be pleasing to you.

LATEEFAH, Latifa, Latifah
Language/Cultural Origin: Hebrew
Inherent Meaning: Caress
Spiritual Connotation: Tender
Scripture: Matthew 5:5 NASB
Blessed are the gentle, for they shall inherit the earth.

LATHAM, Laith, Lathe
Language/Cultural Origin: Old Norse
Inherent Meaning: From the Farmstead
Spiritual Connotation: Strong
Scripture: Micah 3:8 NKJV
But truly I am full of power by the Spirit of the LORD, and of justice and might, to declare to Jacob his transgression and to Israel his sin.

LATISHA, Latecia, Lateesha, Lateisha, Latishia, Latissa
Language/Cultural Origin: Latin
Inherent Meaning: Gladness
Spiritual Connotation: Joyful
Scripture: Psalm 4:7 NLT
You have given me greater joy than those who have abundant harvests of grain and wine.

LATORIA, Latora, Latorya
Language/Cultural Origin: American
Inherent Meaning: Victorious
Spiritual Connotation: Faithful
Scripture: 1 John 5:4 NKJV
For whatever is born of God overcomes the world. And this is the victory that has overcome the world; our faith.

LATOYA, Latoiya, LaToya
Language/Cultural Origin: American
Inherent Meaning: Victorious
Spiritual Connotation: Exalted

Scripture: Matthew 12:20 NLT
He will not crush those who are weak, or quench the smallest hope, until he brings full justice with his final victory.

LAURA, Lauralee, Laureana, Lauret, Laurette, Lauriana, Lauriane, Laurianna, Laurina, Lora, Lorah, Loretta, Lorra, Lorrah, Lorreta (see also Lara, Lori)
Language/Cultural Origin: Latin
Inherent Meaning: Crowned With Honor
Spiritual Connotation: Victorious
Scripture: 1 Thessalonians 4:4 NLT
Then each of you will control your body and live in holiness and honor.

LAUREL, Laural, Laurell, Laurelle
Language/Cultural Origin: Latin
Inherent Meaning: Laurel
Spiritual Connotation: Faithful
Scripture: John 15:5 NRSV
I am the vine, you are the branches. Those who abide in me and I in them bear much fruit, because apart from me you can do nothing.

LAUREN, Lauran, Laurene, Laurin, Lauryn, Laurynn (see also Loren)
Language/Cultural Origin: English
Inherent Meaning: Bay
Spiritual Connotation: Guarded of God
Scripture: Isaiah 25:4 TLB
But to the poor, O Lord, you are a refuge from the storm, a shadow from the heat.

LAURIE, see Lori

LAVEDA, Lavedia
Language/Cultural Origin: Latin
Inherent Meaning: Purified
Spiritual Connotation: Blessed
Scripture: Psalm 84:11 NKJV
For the LORD God is a sun and shield; the LORD will give grace and glory; no good thing will He withhold from those who walk uprightly.

LAVERNE, LaVerne, Laverna
Language/Cultural Origin: Latin
Inherent Meaning: Springtime
Spiritual Connotation: Peaceful

Scripture: Isaiah 9:7 NKJV
Of the increase of His government and peace there will be no end.

LAVINIA, Lavenia, Lavina
Language/Cultural Origin: Latin
Inherent Meaning: Pure
Spiritual Connotation: Priceless
Scripture: Job 22:26 NKJV
For then you will have your delight in the Almighty, and lift up your face to God.

LAVONNE, Lavanna, Lavonda, Lavondria, LaVonne, Lavonya
Language/Cultural Origin: Latin
Inherent Meaning: Warm, Cheerful
Spiritual Connotation: Fruitful
Scripture: Psalm 8:6 NKJV
You have made him to have dominion over the works of Your hands; You have put all things under his feet.

LAWRENCE, Lanny, Larrance, Larrence, Larry, Laurence, Laurens, Laurant, Laurent, Lauris, Lauritz, Lawrance, Lorence, Lorentz, Lorenzo, Lorinzo, Lorrenzo (see also Loren)
Language/Cultural Origin: Latin
Inherent Meaning: Crowned With Laurel
Spiritual Connotation: Joyful
Scripture: Psalm 118:24 NKJV
This is the day the LORD has made; We will rejoice and be glad in it.

LAWTON, Laughton
Language/Cultural Origin: English
Inherent Meaning: From the Hill Town
Spiritual Connotation: Seeker of Truth
Scripture: Matthew 6:33 NKJV
But seek first the kingdom of God and His righteousness, and all these things shall be added to you.

LAYLA, Laela, Laylah, Laylee, Laylie (see also Leala, Leila, Lila)
Language/Cultural Origin: Middle Eastern
Inherent Meaning: Born at Night
Spiritual Connotation: Cause for Joy
Scripture: Luke 2:11 TLB
The Savior—yes, the Messiah, the Lord—has been born tonight in Bethlehem!

LAZARUS, Lazaros
☞ Language/Cultural Origin: Greek
Inherent Meaning: He Whom God Helps
Spiritual Connotation: Friend of God
Scripture: John 16:13 NKJV
When He, the Spirit of truth, has come, He will guide you into all truth.

LEAH, Lea, Léa, Leeah, Leia
☞ **(see also Leigh, Lia, Liya)**
Language/Cultural Origin: Hebrew
Inherent Meaning: Gazelle
Spiritual Connotation: Beauty and Grace
Scripture: Psalm 18:32–33 NKJV
It is God who arms me with strength, and makes my way perfect. He makes my feet like the feet of deer, and sets me on my high places.

LEALA, Lealia, Leial, Leiala (see also Layla, Leila, Lila)
Language/Cultural Origin: French
Inherent Meaning: Loyal
Spiritual Connotation: Faithful
Scripture: Proverbs 3:3 RSV
Let not loyalty and faithfulness forsake you; bind them about your neck, write them on the tablet of your heart.

LEANDER, Léandre
Language/Cultural Origin: Greek
Inherent Meaning: Brave as a Lion
Spiritual Connotation: Strong in Spirit
Scripture: John 15:4 NCV
Remain in me, and I will remain in you. . . . You cannot produce fruit alone but must remain in me.

LEANDRA, Leandrea, Leandria, Leeandra
Language/Cultural Origin: English
Inherent Meaning: Brave as a Lion
Spiritual Connotation: Steadfast
Scripture: Psalm 86:15 NASB
But You, O Lord, are a God merciful and gracious, slow to anger and abundant in lovingkindness and truth.

LEANN, Leann, Leanne, Leean, Leeanne, Leiann, Leianne (see also Lian)
Language/Cultural Origin: English
Inherent Meaning: Youthful

Spiritual Connotation: Righteous
Scripture: 2 Timothy 2:22 NIV
Flee the evil desires of youth, and pursue righteousness, faith, love and peace, along with those who call on the Lord out of a pure heart.

LEANNA, see Liana

LEANORE, Lanore, Leanora, Lenora, Lenore, Leonora, Leonorah
Language/Cultural Origin: English
Inherent Meaning: Bright Like the Sun
Spiritual Connotation: Reflection of Christ
Scripture: Revelation 1:16 NASB
His face was like the sun shining in its strength.

LEE
Language/Cultural Origin: German
Inherent Meaning: From the Sheltered Place
Spiritual Connotation: Gracious
Scripture: Romans 8:16 NKJV
The Spirit Himself bears witness with our spirit that we are children of God.

LEEANN, see Leann

LEEDON, Leydon, Lidon, Liedon
Language/Cultural Origin: Hebrew
Inherent Meaning: Justice Is Mine
Spiritual Connotation: Defended
Scripture: Deuteronomy 32:35 NLT
I will take vengeance; I will repay those who deserve it.

LEESHA, Lecia, Leecia, Leesia, Lesha, Leshia
Language/Cultural Origin: English
Inherent Meaning: Happy
Spiritual Connotation: Obedient
Scripture: Psalm 119:35 NLT
Make me walk along the path of your commands, for that is where my happiness is found.

LEEZA, Leza (see also Lisa, Liza)
Language/Cultural Origin: American
Inherent Meaning: Surrendered to God
Spiritual Connotation: Sacrifice
Scripture: Luke 23:46 RSV
Then Jesus, crying with a loud voice, said, "Father, into thy hands I commit my spirit!"

LEIF, Léif, Lief
Language/Cultural Origin: Old Norse
Inherent Meaning: Beloved
Spiritual Connotation: Chosen
Scripture: Matthew 3:17 RSV
And lo, a voice from heaven, saying, "This is my beloved Son, with whom I am well pleased."

LEIGH, Leigha, Leighann, Leighanna (see also Leah, Lia, Liya)
Language/Cultural Origin: American
Inherent Meaning: Meadow
Spiritual Connotation: Guided of God
Scripture: Psalm 95:7 RSV
For he is our God, and we are the people of his pasture, and the sheep of his hand. O that today you would hearken to his voice!

LEIGHTON, Layton, Leyton
Language/Cultural Origin: Old English
Inherent Meaning: From the Meadow Farm
Spiritual Connotation: Rescued
Scripture: Isaiah 49:9 TLB
Come out! I am giving you your freedom! They will be my sheep, grazing in green pastures and on the grassy hills.

LEILA, Laila, Leala, Lela (see also Layla, Leala, Lila)
Language/Cultural Origin: Hebrew
Inherent Meaning: Dark Beauty
Spiritual Connotation: Bringer of Light
Scripture: Ecclesiastes 3:11 NKJV
He has made everything beautiful in its time. Also He has put eternity in their hearts.

LEILANI, Lelani, Lelania
Language/Cultural Origin: Hawaiian
Inherent Meaning: Heavenly Flower
Spiritual Connotation: Priceless
Scripture: Luke 12:32 NKJV
Do not fear, little flock, for it is your Father's good pleasure to give you the kingdom.

LEITH, Léith
Language/Cultural Origin: Scottish
Inherent Meaning: From the Broad River
Spiritual Connotation: Blessed
Scripture: Acts 3:19–20 NRSV
Repent therefore, and turn to God so that your sins may be wiped out, so that times of refreshing may come from the presence of the Lord.

LEKEISHA, see Lakeisha

LELAND, Leeland, Leyland
Language/Cultural Origin: English
Inherent Meaning: From the Meadowland
Spiritual Connotation: Prosperous
Scripture: Deuteronomy 30:9 NASB
Then the LORD your God will prosper you abundantly in all the work of your hand.

LEMUEL, Lem
☞ Language/Cultural Origin: Hebrew
Inherent Meaning: Consecrated to God
Spiritual Connotation: Holy
Scripture: 2 Timothy 1:7 NKJV
For God has not given us a spirit of fear, but of power and of love and of a sound mind.

LENA, Leena, Lenah, Lina
Language/Cultural Origin: Greek
Inherent Meaning: Gentle
Spiritual Connotation: Blessed Peacemaker
Scripture: Matthew 7:12 NKJV
Therefore, whatever you want men to do to you, do also to them, for this is the Law and the Prophets.

**LENITA, Leneisha, Lenice,
Lenis, Lenise, Lenisha**
Language/Cultural Origin: Latin
Inherent Meaning: White Lily
Spiritual Connotation: Discerning Spirit
Scripture: Proverbs 16:20 NLT
Those who listen to instruction will prosper; those who trust the LORD will be happy.

LENNON, Lennan, Lennen
Language/Cultural Origin: Irish
Inherent Meaning: Small Cloak
Spiritual Connotation: Selfless
Scripture: Luke 6:29 NKJV
To him who strikes you on the one cheek, offer the other also. And from him who takes away your cloak, do not withhold your tunic either.

LENNOX, Lenox
Language/Cultural Origin: Scottish
Inherent Meaning: Placid Stream
Spiritual Connotation: God Is All-Sufficient
Scripture: Jeremiah 32:27 TLB
I am the Lord, the God of all mankind; is there anything too hard for me?

LENORE, see Leanore

LEO, Léo
Language/Cultural Origin: Latin
Inherent Meaning: Lionhearted
Spiritual Connotation: Courageous
Scripture: Deuteronomy 31:6 NASB
Be strong and courageous, do not be afraid or tremble at them, for the LORD your God is the one who goes with you. He will not fail you or forsake you.

LEON, Léon, Leone
Language/Cultural Origin: English
Inherent Meaning: Brave as a Lion
Spiritual Connotation: Brave
Scripture: Joshua 1:7 NASB
Only be strong and very courageous; be careful to do according to all the law which Moses My servant commanded you . . . so that you may have success wherever you go.

LEONA, Leone, Leonia, Liona
Language/Cultural Origin: Latin
Inherent Meaning: Lioness
Spiritual Connotation: Courageous Spirit
Scripture: Psalm 25:5 RSV
Lead me in thy truth, and teach me, for thou art the God of my salvation; for thee I wait all the day long.

**LEONARD, Len, Lenard, Lennard,
Lennie, Lenno, Lenny, Leno,
Léonard, Leonardo**
Language/Cultural Origin: Old German
Inherent Meaning: Strong as a Lion
Spiritual Connotation: Fearless Spirit
Scripture: Proverbs 8:14 NKJV
Counsel is mine, and sound wisdom; I am understanding, I have strength.

LEORA, see Liora

LEROY, Leeroy, LeeRoy, LeRoy
Language/Cultural Origin: Old French
Inherent Meaning: Royal
Spiritual Connotation: Esteemed
Scripture: 1 Corinthians 2:10 NKJV
But God has revealed them to us through His Spirit. For the Spirit searches all things, yes, the deep things of God.

LESLIE, Leslea, Leslee, Lesley, Lesli, Lesslie, Lezlee, Lezley, Lezlie

Language/Cultural Origin: Scottish
Inherent Meaning: From the Low Meadow
Spiritual Connotation: Remembered
Scripture: Isaiah 42:16 NKJV

I will bring the blind by a way they did not know; I will lead them in paths they have not known. I will make darkness light before them.

LESTER, Les

Language/Cultural Origin: English
Inherent Meaning: From the Chosen Camp
Spiritual Connotation: Shining Spirit
Scripture: 2 Corinthians 5:17 NKJV

Therefore, if anyone is in Christ, he is a new creation; old things have passed away; behold, all things have become new.

LEVANA, Lévana, Levanna, Livana, Livanna

Language/Cultural Origin: Hebrew
Inherent Meaning: Moon
Spiritual Connotation: Symbol
Scripture: Psalm 89:37 NRSV

It shall be established forever like the moon, an enduring witness in the skies.

LEVANON, Levanan, Levanen, Levannon

Language/Cultural Origin: Hebrew
Inherent Meaning: Moon
Spiritual Connotation: Blessed
Scripture: Psalm 136:9 NCV

He made the moon and stars to rule the night. His love continues forever.

LEVI, Leevi, Levey, Levy

☞ Language/Cultural Origin: Hebrew
Inherent Meaning: Harmonious
Spiritual Connotation: Enlightened
Scripture: Psalm 18:28 NKJV

For You will light my lamp; the LORD my God will enlighten my darkness.

LEVIA, Levya

Language/Cultural Origin: Hebrew
Inherent Meaning: Attached
Spiritual Connotation: One With God
Scripture: Zechariah 2:11 NKJV

Many nations shall be joined to the LORD in that day, and they shall become My people. And I will dwell in your midst.

LEVINA, Leveena

Language/Cultural Origin: Latin
Inherent Meaning: Flash of Lightning
Spiritual Connotation: Ardent Praise
Scripture: Psalm 36:7 NLT

How precious is your unfailing love, O God! All humanity finds shelter in the shadow of your wings.

LEVONA, Livona

Language/Cultural Origin: Hebrew
Inherent Meaning: Incense
Spiritual Connotation: Sacrifice
Scripture: Psalm 141:2 NRSV

Let my prayer be counted as incense before you, and the lifting up of my hands as an evening sacrifice.

LEWIS, Lew, Lewie

Language/Cultural Origin: Old English
Inherent Meaning: Safeguard of the People
Spiritual Connotation: Righteous
Scripture: Matthew 12:35 NLT

A good person produces good words from a good heart, and an evil person produces evil words from an evil heart.

LEX, Lexx

Language/Cultural Origin: English
Inherent Meaning: Defender of Mankind
Spiritual Connotation: Protector
Scripture: Psalm 9:9 TLB

All who are oppressed may come to him. He is a refuge for them in their times of trouble.

LEXI, Leksa, Lexa, Lexey, Lexee, Lexia, Lexie, Lexxa, Lexxia, Lexxie, Lexy

Language/Cultural Origin: Czech
Inherent Meaning: Defender of Mankind
Spiritual Connotation: Stronghold
Scripture: Isaiah 4:6 NASB

There will be a shelter to give shade from the heat by day, and refuge and protection from the storm and the rain.

LIA, Liah (see also Leah, Leigh, Liya)

Language/Cultural Origin: Greek
Inherent Meaning: Bringer of Good News
Spiritual Connotation: Messenger
Scripture: Luke 2:10 NASB

And the angel said to them, "Do not be afraid; for behold, I bring you good news of a great joy which shall be for all the people."

**LIAN, Liane, Lianne
(see also Leann)**
Language/Cultural Origin: Chinese
Inherent Meaning: Willow
Spiritual Connotation: Eternal
Scripture: Jeremiah 17:8 NRSV
*They shall be like a tree planted by water,
sending out its roots by the stream. It shall
not . . . cease to bear fruit.*

**LIANA, Leana, Leanna, Leeanna,
Leiana, Leianna, Lianna
(see also Iliana, Eliana)**
Language/Cultural Origin: Hebrew
Inherent Meaning: My God Has Answered Me
Spiritual Connotation: Important
Scripture: Genesis 21:17 NRSV
*Do not be afraid; for God has heard the voice
of the boy where he is.*

LIBBY, Libbee, Libbey, Libbie
Language/Cultural Origin: English
Inherent Meaning: Promise of God
Spiritual Connotation: Preserved
Scripture: Isaiah 59:21 NASB
*My Spirit which is upon you, and My words
which I have put in your mouth shall not
depart from your mouth.*

LIBERTY, Libertee
Language/Cultural Origin: Latin
Inherent Meaning: Freedom
Spiritual Connotation: Unchained
Scripture: Galatians 5:1 NASB
*It was for freedom that Christ set us free;
therefore keep standing firm and do not be
subject again to a yoke of slavery.*

LIDA, Leeda, Lita
Language/Cultural Origin: Slavic
Inherent Meaning: Love
Spiritual Connotation: Beloved
Scripture: Ephesians 4:32 NASB
*Be kind to one another, tender-hearted,
forgiving each other, just as God in Christ
also has forgiven you.*

**LIESEL, Leisel, Liesl,
Liezel, Liezl, Lisel**
Language/Cultural Origin: German
Inherent Meaning: Oath of God
Spiritual Connotation: Promise

Scripture: Zechariah 9:11 NASB
*As for you also, because of the blood of My
covenant with you, I have set your prisoners
free from the waterless pit.*

**LILA, Lilah, Lyla, Lylah
(see also Layla, Leala, Leila)**
Language/Cultural Origin: Persian
Inherent Meaning: Lilac
Spiritual Connotation: Lovely Aroma
Scripture: 2 Corinthians 2:15 NKJV
*For we are to God the fragrance of Christ
among those who are being saved and among
those who are perishing.*

LILITH, Lillith
Language/Cultural Origin: Hebrew
Inherent Meaning: Night Owl
Spiritual Connotation: Wise
Scripture: Proverbs 8:9 NKJV
*They are all plain to him who understands,
and right to those who find knowledge.*

**LILLIAN, Lili, Lilia, Lilian,
Liliana, Liliane, Liljana, Lilliana,
Lillianna, Lillyan, Lily**
Language/Cultural Origin: Latin
Inherent Meaning: Purity
Spiritual Connotation: Shining Light
Scripture: Zechariah 2:10 NKJV
*Sing and rejoice, O daughter of Zion! For
behold, I am coming and I will dwell in your
midst.*

LIN, Linh, Linn (see also Lynn)
Language/Cultural Origin: Chinese
Inherent Meaning: Jade
Spiritual Connotation: Beautiful
Scripture: Revelation 4:3 NKJV
*And He who sat there was like a jasper and a
sardius stone in appearance; and there was a
rainbow around the throne, in appearance
like an emerald.*

LINCOLN, Lincon
Language/Cultural Origin: Old English
Inherent Meaning: From the Pool Town
Spiritual Connotation: Victorious
Scripture: 1 John 5:4 RSV
*For whatever is born of God overcomes the
world; and this is the victory that overcomes
the world, our faith.*

LINDA, Linnea, Linnie, Lynda
Language/Cultural Origin: Spanish
Inherent Meaning: Beautiful
Spiritual Connotation: Excellent Virtue
Scripture: James 5:16 NRSV
*Therefore confess your sins to one another,
and pray for one another, so that you may
be healed. The prayer of the righteous is
powerful and effective.*

LINDEE, Lindey, Lindi, Lindie, Lindy
Language/Cultural Origin: American
Inherent Meaning: Lovely
Spiritual Connotation: Witness
Scripture: Romans 10:15 NLT
*How beautiful are the feet of those who
bring good news!*

**LINDELL, Lendell, Lindall,
Lindel, Lyndel, Lyndell**
Language/Cultural Origin: Anglo-Saxon
Inherent Meaning: From the Linden Trees
Spiritual Connotation: Inheritor
Scripture: Luke 12:32 NASB
*Do not be afraid, little flock, for your Father
has chosen gladly to give you the kingdom.*

**LINDSEY, Lindsay, Lindsee, Lindsi,
Lindsie, Lindsy, Lindzee, Linsay,
Linsey, Linsi, Linsie, Linzee, Linzey,
Lyndsay, Lyndsee, Lyndsey, Lynnsey,
Lynnzey, Lynsay, Lynsee, Lynsey,
Lynzey, Lynzi, Lynzie**
Language/Cultural Origin: English
Inherent Meaning: From the Pool Island
Spiritual Connotation: Peaceful
Scripture: Hebrews 12:11 RSV
*For the moment all discipline seems painful
rather than pleasant; later it yields the
peaceful fruit of righteousness.*

LINFORD, Lynford
Language/Cultural Origin: Middle English
Inherent Meaning: From the Lime-Tree Ford
Spiritual Connotation: Gentle
Scripture: Matthew 11:29 NRSV
*Take my yoke upon you, and learn from me;
for I am gentle and humble in heart, and you
will find rest for your souls.*

LINLEY, Lindlee, Linlea, Linlee
Language/Cultural Origin: Old English

Inherent Meaning: From the Flax Meadow
Spiritual Connotation: Abiding in God
Scripture: Acts 17:28 NRSV
*For in him we live and move and have our
being; as even some of your own poets have
said . . . we too are his offspring.*

LINUS, Linas
☞ Language/Cultural Origin: Greek
Inherent Meaning: Fair-Haired
Spiritual Connotation: Treasurer of
Wisdom and Knowledge
Scripture: Colossians 2:2 NRSV
*I want their hearts to . . . have the knowledge
of God's mystery, that is, Christ himself, in
whom are hidden all the treasures of wisdom
and knowledge.*

LIONEL, Lional, Lionell, Lyonel
Language/Cultural Origin: Latin
Inherent Meaning: Little Lion
Spiritual Connotation: Strong in Faith
Scripture: Psalm 26:3 RSV
*For thy steadfast love is before my eyes, and I
walk in faithfulness to thee.*

LIORA, Leora
Language/Cultural Origin: Hebrew
Inherent Meaning: Glowing Light
Spiritual Connotation: Brilliance
Scripture: Revelation 21:11 NCV
*It was shining with the glory of God and was
bright like a very expensive jewel, like a
jasper, clear as crystal.*

**LISA, Leesa, Liesa, Liisa, Lisana,
Lisann, Lisanna, Lisanne, Lise
(see also Leeza, Liza)**
Language/Cultural Origin: English
Inherent Meaning: Consecrated to God
Spiritual Connotation: Redeemed
Scripture: Romans 11:27 NKJV
*For this is My covenant with them, when I
take away their sins.*

**LISSA, Lissee, Lissey, Lissi,
Lissie, Lissy, Lyssa
(see also Alisa, Elissa, Elysia)**
Language/Cultural Origin: English
Inherent Meaning: Honeybee
Spiritual Connotation: Servant
Scripture: 1 Corinthians 16:16 NRSV

I urge you to put yourselves at the service of such people, and of everyone who works and toils with them.

LISETTE, Lissette
Language/Cultural Origin: French
Inherent Meaning: Promise of God
Spiritual Connotation: One With Christ
Scripture: Romans 8:38–39 NKJV
For I am persuaded that neither death nor life . . . nor anything else in all creation, will be able to separate us from the love of God in Christ Jesus our Lord.

LITA, see Lida

LITONYA, Litania, Litanya, Litonia (see also Latanya)
Language/Cultural Origin: Moquelumnan
Inherent Meaning: Darting Hummingbird
Spiritual Connotation: Child of God
Scripture: Matthew 6:26 RSV
Look at the birds of the air: they neither sow nor reap . . . and yet your heavenly Father feeds them. Are you not of more value than they?

LIVIA, Levia, Leviya, Levya, Livie, Liviya, Livy, Livya (see also Olivia)
Language/Cultural Origin: Hebrew
Inherent Meaning: Royal Crown
Spiritual Connotation: Exalted
Scripture: Psalm 89:19 NRSV
Then you spoke in a vision to your faithful one, and said: I have set the crown on one who is mighty, I have exalted one chosen from the people.

LIVINGSTON, Livingstone
Language/Cultural Origin: Old English
Inherent Meaning: From Leif's Town
Spiritual Connotation: Chosen
Scripture: Isaiah 55:5 NKJV
Surely you shall call a nation you do not know, and nations who do not know you shall run to you, because of the LORD your God . . . for He has glorified you.

LIYA, Leeya (see also Leah, Leigh, Lia)
Language/Cultural Origin: Hebrew
Inherent Meaning: Belonging to God
Spiritual Connotation: Trusting
Scripture: John 1:12 TLB
But to all who received him, he gave the right to become children of God. All they needed to do was to trust him to save them.

LIZA, Liz, Lizann, Lizanne, Lizbeth, Lizina, Lizzey, Lizzie, Lizzy, Lyza (see also Leeza, Lisa)
Language/Cultural Origin: American
Inherent Meaning: Covenant of God
Spiritual Connotation: Established
Scripture: Psalm 132:12 NCV
If your sons keep my agreement and the rules that I teach them, then their sons after them will rule on your throne forever and ever.

LLEWELLYN, Lewellyn
Language/Cultural Origin: Celtic
Inherent Meaning: Ruler
Spiritual Connotation: Peaceful
Scripture: 1 John 4:18 NASB
There is no fear in love; but perfect love casts out fear, because fear involves punishment, and the one who fears is not perfected in love.

LLOYD, Loyd
Language/Cultural Origin: Welsh
Inherent Meaning: Wise
Spiritual Connotation: Seeker of Holiness
Scripture: Proverbs 12:28 NKJV
In the way of righteousness is life, and in its pathway there is no death.

LOCKE, Lock
Language/Cultural Origin: Old English
Inherent Meaning: From the Forest
Spiritual Connotation: Wise
Scripture: Proverbs 23:24 NKJV
The father of the righteous will greatly rejoice, and he who begets a wise child will delight in him.

LOGAN, Logen
Language/Cultural Origin: Celtic
Inherent Meaning: From the Little Hollow
Spiritual Connotation: Devoted to God
Scripture: Philippians 4:6 NCV
Do not worry about anything, but pray and ask God for everything you need, always giving thanks.

LOIS
☞Language/Cultural Origin: Greek
Inherent Meaning: Desired
Spiritual Connotation: Established in Truth
Scripture: 2 Samuel 22:29 NKJV
For You are my lamp, O LORD; the LORD shall enlighten my darkness.

LOLA, Lolita
Language/Cultural Origin: Latin
Inherent Meaning: Crowned With Compassion and Grace
Spiritual Connotation: Perceptive Insight
Scripture: Psalm 16:11 NKJV
You will show me the path of life; in Your presence is fullness of joy; at Your right hand are pleasures forevermore.

LOMAN, Lomán
Language/Cultural Origin: Serbian
Inherent Meaning: Delicate
Spiritual Connotation: Loving
Scripture: Ephesians 4:32 NKJV
And be kind to one another, tenderhearted, forgiving one another, just as God in Christ forgave you.

LOMAS, Lomás
Language/Cultural Origin: English
Inherent Meaning: From Lomas
Spiritual Connotation: Reverent
Scripture: Psalm 33:8 NKJV
Let all the earth fear the LORD; let all the inhabitants of the world stand in awe of Him.

LONDON, Londan, Londen, Londyn
Language/Cultural Origin: English
Inherent Meaning: Castle of the Moon
Spiritual Connotation: Unique
Scripture: 1 Corinthians 15:41 NCV
The sun has one kind of beauty, the moon has another beauty, and the stars have another. And each star is different in its beauty.

LONNA, Lona, Loni, Lonie
Language/Cultural Origin: German
Inherent Meaning: Lioness
Spiritual Connotation: Courageous
Scripture: Joshua 1:9 RSV
Be strong and of good courage; be not frightened, neither be dismayed; for the LORD your God is with you wherever you go.

LONNIE, Lon, Lonn, Lonny
Language/Cultural Origin: English
Inherent Meaning: Ready for Battle
Spiritual Connotation: God's Soldier
Scripture: Exodus 13:18 RSV
But God led the people . . . and the people of Israel went up out of the land of Egypt equipped for battle.

LORA, see Laura

LORELEI, Loralee, Loralie, Lorilee
Language/Cultural Origin: Old German
Inherent Meaning: Alluring
Spiritual Connotation: Witness
Scripture: Titus 2:10 NCV
They . . . should show their masters they can be fully trusted so that in everything they do they will make the teaching of God our Savior attractive.

LOREN, Larian, Larien, Laurin, Lawren, Loring, Lorin, Lorne, Lorren, Lorrin, Loryn (see also Lauren, Lawrence)
Language/Cultural Origin: Basque
Inherent Meaning: Son of the Famous Warrior
Spiritual Connotation: God's Warrior
Scripture: Ephesians 6:17 NKJV
And take the helmet of salvation, and the sword of the Spirit, which is the word of God.

LORI, Lari, Laure, Lauré, Lauri, Laurie, Loree, Lorey, Lorianna, Lorie, Lorrie (see also Laura)
Language/Cultural Origin: English
Inherent Meaning: Crowned With Honor
Spiritual Connotation: Hopeful
Scripture: Isaiah 28:5 NASB
In that day the LORD of hosts will become a beautiful crown and a glorious diadem to the remnant of His people.

LORITZ, Lauritz
Language/Cultural Origin: Danish
Inherent Meaning: Evergreen
Spiritual Connotation: Promise
Scripture: Isaiah 55:13 NIV
Instead of the thornbush will grow the pine tree, and instead of briers the myrtle will grow. This will be for . . . an everlasting sign.

LORRETA, see Laura

LORRAINE, Loraine, Lorayne, Lorrayne (see also Laraine)
Language/Cultural Origin: German
Inherent Meaning: Warrior
Spiritual Connotation: Strength of God
Scripture: Isaiah 45:2 NKJV
> I will go before you and make the crooked places straight; I will break in pieces the gates of bronze and cut the bars of iron.

LOT, Lott
☞ Language/Cultural Origin: Hebrew
Inherent Meaning: Covered
Spiritual Connotation: Protected
Scripture: Isaiah 32:2 NASB
> And each will be like a refuge from the wind, and a shelter from the storm, . . . like the shade of a huge rock in a parched land.

LOUIS, Lou, Louie, Luigi, Luis
Language/Cultural Origin: Old German
Inherent Meaning: Famous Warrior
Spiritual Connotation: Declarer of God
Scripture: Isaiah 43:19 NASB
> Behold, I will do something new, now it will spring forth. . . . I will even make a roadway in the wilderness, rivers in the desert.

LOUISE, Louisa, Luisa, Luiza
Language/Cultural Origin: Old German
Inherent Meaning: Protectress
Spiritual Connotation: Watchful
Scripture: 1 Peter 2:25 NRSV
> For you were going astray like sheep, but now you have returned to the shepherd and guardian of your souls.

LOURDES, Lordes
Language/Cultural Origin: French
Inherent Meaning: From Lourdes
Spiritual Connotation: Redeemed
Scripture: Romans 5:8 RSV
> But God shows his love for us in that while we were yet sinners Christ died for us.

LOWELL, Lovell, Lowel
Language/Cultural Origin: Latin
Inherent Meaning: Little Wolf
Spiritual Connotation: Peaceful
Scripture: Colossians 3:15 NKJV
> And let the peace of God rule in your hearts, to which also you were called in one body; and be thankful.

LUANN, Luana, Luanna, Luanne
Language/Cultural Origin: Hebrew
Inherent Meaning: Graceful Warrior
Spiritual Connotation: Righteous
Scripture: Psalm 55:22 NASB
> Cast your burden upon the LORD, and He will sustain you; He will never allow the righteous to be shaken.

LUCILE, Luci, Lucia, Luciann, Lucie, Lucienne, Lucile, Lucille, Lucina, Lucinda, Lucy
Language/Cultural Origin: English
Inherent Meaning: Light Bringer
Spiritual Connotation: Chosen of God
Scripture: Romans 8:28 NKJV
> And we know that all things work together for good to those who love God, to those who are the called according to His purpose.

LUCIUS, Lucas, Lucian, Luciano, ☞ Lucien (see also Luke)
Language/Cultural Origin: Latin
Inherent Meaning: Bringer of Light
Spiritual Connotation: Enlightened
Scripture: Psalm 139:9–10 NRSV
> If I take the wings of the morning and settle at the farthest limits of the sea, even there your hand shall lead me, and your right hand shall hold me fast.

LUCRETIA, Lacresha, Lacreshia, Lacretia, Lakresha, Lakreshia, Lucresha, Lucreshia
Language/Cultural Origin: Latin
Inherent Meaning: Riches, Rewards
Spiritual Connotation: Prosperous
Scripture: 2 Chronicles 20:20 KJV
> Believe in the LORD your God, so shall ye be established; believe his prophets, so shall ye prosper.

LUDWIG, Ludvig
Language/Cultural Origin: German
Inherent Meaning: Famous Warrior
Spiritual Connotation: Gifted
Scripture: Psalm 89:18 NKJV
> For our shield belongs to the LORD, and our king to the Holy One of Israel.

LUKE, Luc, Luk (see also Lucius)
Language/Cultural Origin: Greek
Inherent Meaning: Luminous
Spiritual Connotation: Talented
Scripture: Exodus 31:3 NKJV
And I have filled him with the Spirit of God, in wisdom, in understanding, in knowledge, and in all manner of workmanship.

LUPE, Lupé
Language/Cultural Origin: Spanish
Inherent Meaning: Wolf
Spiritual Connotation: Courageous
Scripture: Psalm 91:11 NKJV
For He shall give His angels charge over you, to keep you in all your ways.

LUTHER, Lothar, Luthor
Language/Cultural Origin: Old German
Inherent Meaning: Famous Warrior
Spiritual Connotation: Honored
Scripture: Isaiah 41:13 RSV
For I, the LORD your God, hold your right hand.... Fear not, I will help you.

LYDIA, Lidi, Lidia, Lidiya
Language/Cultural Origin: Greek
Inherent Meaning: Womanly
Spiritual Connotation: Beautiful Light
Scripture: 2 Corinthians 4:6 NASB
For God ... is the One who has shone in our hearts to give the Light of the knowledge of the glory of God in the face of Christ.

LYLE, Lisle, Lysle
Language/Cultural Origin: Old French
Inherent Meaning: From the Island
Spiritual Connotation: Joyous Spirit
Scripture: Psalm 32:11 NASB
Be glad in the LORD and rejoice, you righteous ones; and shout for joy, all you who are upright in heart.

LYNDON, Lindan, Linden, Lindon, Lynden
Language/Cultural Origin: English
Inherent Meaning: From the Lime Tree Hill
Spiritual Connotation: Excellent Worth
Scripture: Luke 12:7 NASB
Indeed, the very hairs of your head are all numbered. Do not fear; you are of more value than many sparrows.

LYNELLE, Linell, Linnell, Lynell, Lynnell, Lynnelle
Language/Cultural Origin: English
Inherent Meaning: Pretty
Spiritual Connotation: Virtuous
Scripture: Proverbs 31:30 RSV
Charm is deceitful, and beauty is vain, but a woman who fears the LORD is to be praised.

LYNN, Linette, Lyn, Lynetta, Lynette, Lynne (see also Lin)
Language/Cultural Origin: English
Inherent Meaning: Clear Pool
Spiritual Connotation: Holy
Scripture: Proverbs 9:10 NKJV
The fear of the LORD is the beginning of wisdom, and the knowledge of the Holy One is understanding.

LYSANDER, Lisander
Language/Cultural Origin: Greek
Inherent Meaning: Liberator
Spiritual Connotation: Freedom
Scripture: John 8:32 NASB
And you shall know the truth, and the truth shall make you free.

LYSANDRA, Lisandra
Language/Cultural Origin: Greek
Inherent Meaning: Liberator
Spiritual Connotation: Freedom
Scripture: Galatians 5:1 NKJV
Stand fast therefore in the liberty by which Christ has made us free, and do not be entangled again with a yoke of bondage.

MAAYAN, Maayana, Maeanna, Maion, Mayon, Mayani (see also Mahon, Maon)
Language/Cultural Origin: Hebrew
Inherent Meaning: Water Source
Spiritual Connotation: Fountain of Life
Scripture: John 4:14 NRSV
But those who drink of the water that I will give them will never be thirsty. The water that I will give will become in them a spring of water gushing up to eternal life.

MABEL, Mable
Language/Cultural Origin: Latin
Inherent Meaning: Lovable
Spiritual Connotation: Beautiful in Spirit
Scripture: John 15:5 NKJV
I am the vine, you are the branches. He who abides in Me, and I in him, bears much fruit; for without Me you can do nothing.

MACABEE, Maccabee, Mákabi
Language/Cultural Origin: Hebrew
Inherent Meaning: Who Is Like God?
Spiritual Connotation: Reverent
Scripture: Exodus 15:11 NASB
Who is like Thee among the gods, O LORD? Who is like Thee, majestic in holiness, awesome in praises, working wonders?

MACARTHUR, MacArthur, McArthur
Language/Cultural Origin: Scottish
Inherent Meaning: Child of the Brave Man
Spiritual Connotation: Forgiven
Scripture: Matthew 9:2 NASB
Take courage, My son, your sins are forgiven.

MACAULAY, Macauley, McCauley
Language/Cultural Origin: Scottish
Inherent Meaning: Child of Righteousness
Spiritual Connotation: Mature
Scripture: Proverbs 22:6 NKJV
Train up a child in the way he should go, and when he is old he will not depart from it.

MACDONALD, McDonald, McDonnell
Language/Cultural Origin: Scottish
Inherent Meaning: Child of the Great Ruler
Spiritual Connotation: Honest
Scripture: Proverbs 20:11 TLB
The character of even a child can be known by the way he acts—whether what he does is pure and right.

MACIA, Macya
Language/Cultural Origin: Polish
Inherent Meaning: Wished-for
Spiritual Connotation: Blameless
Scripture: Psalm 37:4 NASB
Delight yourself in the LORD; and He will give you the desires of your heart.

MACKAY, MacKay, McKay
Language/Cultural Origin: Scottish
Inherent Meaning: Son of the Rejoicer
Spiritual Connotation: Received With Glory
Scripture: Zephaniah 3:17 RSV
The LORD, your God, is in your midst, a warrior who gives victory; he will rejoice over you with gladness.

MACKENZIE, Mackensie, Mackenzee, McKensi, McKenzee, McKenzie
Language/Cultural Origin: Gaelic
Inherent Meaning: Child of the Wise Leader
Spiritual Connotation: Witness
Scripture: Proverbs 23:24 NKJV
The father of the righteous will greatly rejoice, and he who begets a wise child will delight in him.

MACKINNLEY, MacKinnley, Mckinnlee, McKinnley
Language/Cultural Origin: Irish
Inherent Meaning: Child of the Scholarly Ruler

Spiritual Connotation: **Peaceful**
Scripture: **Isaiah 11:6 RSV**
The wolf shall dwell with the lamb . . . and a little child shall lead them.

MACNAIR, McNair
Language/Cultural Origin: **Scottish**
Inherent Meaning: **Child of the Heir**
Spiritual Connotation: **Favored**
Scripture: **Galatians 3:29 NLT**
And now that you belong to Christ, you are the true children of Abraham. . . . All the promises God gave to him belong to you.

MACY, Macee, Macey, Maci, Macie
Language/Cultural Origin: **French**
Inherent Meaning: **From Matthew's Estate**
Spiritual Connotation: **Enlightened**
Scripture: **John 1:29 NKJV**
The next day John saw Jesus coming toward him, and said, Behold! The Lamb of God who takes away the sin of the world!

MADDOX, Madox
Language/Cultural Origin: **Welsh**
Inherent Meaning: **Son of the Benefactor**
Spiritual Connotation: **Promise**
Scripture: **Hebrews 11:11 RSV**
By faith Sarah herself received power to conceive, even when she was past the age, since she considered him faithful who had promised.

MADELINE, Mada, Madalaina, Madaline, Madalyn, Madalynn, Maddi, Maddie, Maddy, Madelaine, Madeleine, Madelene, Madelynn, Madelynne, Madlen, Madlin, Madoline
Language/Cultural Origin: **Greek**
Inherent Meaning: **Magnificent**
Spiritual Connotation: **Prayerful**
Scripture: **1 Corinthians 14:15 NKJV**
I will pray with the spirit, and I will also pray with the understanding. I will sing with the spirit, and I will also sing with the understanding.

MADISON, Maddison, Madisen, Madissen, Madisson
Language/Cultural Origin: **Old English**
Inherent Meaning: **Child of the Valiant Warrior**

Spiritual Connotation: **Brave**
Scripture: **Luke 18:27 NKJV**
The things which are impossible with men are possible with God.

MADONNA, Madona
Language/Cultural Origin: **Latin**
Inherent Meaning: **My Lady**
Spiritual Connotation: **Pure**
Scripture: **1 Timothy 5:2 NLT**
Treat the older women as you would your mother, and treat the younger women with all purity as your own sisters.

MAE, see May

MAGDALENE, Magdalen, Magdalina, ☞Magdaline, Magdalyn, Magdelana, Magdelena, Magdelene, Magdelina, Magdeline, Magdelyn, Magdelynn
Language/Cultural Origin: **Greek**
Inherent Meaning: **High Fortress**
Spiritual Connotation: **Protected**
Scripture: **Psalm 144:2 NLT**
He is my loving ally and my fortress, my tower of safety, my deliverer. He stands before me as a shield, and I take refuge in him.

MAGGIE, Maggee, Maggi
Language/Cultural Origin: **Greek**
Inherent Meaning: **Pearl**
Spiritual Connotation: **Of Great Value**
Scripture: **Revelation 21:21 NKJV**
The twelve gates were twelve pearls: each individual gate was of one pearl. And the street of the city was pure gold, like transparent glass.

MAGNUS, Magnes
Language/Cultural Origin: **Latin**
Inherent Meaning: **Great**
Spiritual Connotation: **Privileged**
Scripture: **Jeremiah 33:3 NKJV**
Call to Me, and I will answer you, and show you great and mighty things, which you do not know.

MAGUIRE, MacGuire, McGwire
Language/Cultural Origin: **Irish**
Inherent Meaning: **Child of the Fair One**
Spiritual Connotation: **Trustworthy**
Scripture: **James 2:5 NRSV**

Has not God chosen the poor in the world to be rich in faith and to be heirs of the kingdom that he has promised to those who love him?

MAHALAH, Mahala, Mahalah,
☞Mahalia, Mahaliah, Mahalla,
Mahlah, Mehalia, Mehalla
Language/Cultural Origin: Hebrew
Inherent Meaning: Tenderness
Spiritual Connotation: Gentle
Scripture: Ephesians 4:32 RSV
And be kind to one another, tenderhearted, forgiving one another, as God in Christ forgave you.

MAHINA, Maheina
Language/Cultural Origin: Hawaiian
Inherent Meaning: Moon
Spiritual Connotation: Testimony
Scripture: Psalm 89:37 NRSV
It shall be established forever like the moon, an enduring witness in the skies.

MAHIRA, Maheira
Language/Cultural Origin: Hebrew
Inherent Meaning: Industrious
Spiritual Connotation: Diligent
Scripture: Matthew 9:37 RSV
Then he said to his disciples, the harvest is plentiful, but the laborers are few.

MAHON, Mahan
(see also Maayan, Maon)
Language/Cultural Origin: Irish
Inherent Meaning: Bear
Spiritual Connotation: Favored
Scripture: Ephesians 1:5 NRSV
He destined us for adoption as his children through Jesus Christ, according to the good pleasure of his will.

MAIA, Maiah
(see also Maija, Maya, Mia, Miya)
Language/Cultural Origin: Greek
Inherent Meaning: Nurse ?
Spiritual Connotation: Healer
Scripture: Psalm 147:3 RSV
He heals the brokenhearted, and binds up their wounds.

MAIJA, Maja, Majalyn
(see also Maia, Maya, Mia, Miya)
Language/Cultural Origin: Middle Eastern

Inherent Meaning: Splendid
Spiritual Connotation: Wondrous
Scripture: Micah 7:15 RSV
As in the days when you came out of the land of Egypt I will show them marvelous things.

MAITLAND, Maitlan, Maitlen
Language/Cultural Origin: English
Inherent Meaning: From the Meadowland
Spiritual Connotation: Blessed
Scripture: Isaiah 30:23 NASB
Then He will give you rain . . . and bread from the yield of the ground, and it will be rich and plenteous; on that day your livestock will graze in a roomy pasture.

MAJOR, Majar, Majer
Language/Cultural Origin: Latin
Inherent Meaning: Greater
Spiritual Connotation: Selfless
Scripture: John 15:13 NKJV
Greater love has no one than this, than to lay down one's life for his friends.

MAKANA, Makanna
Language/Cultural Origin: Hawaiian
Inherent Meaning: Present
Spiritual Connotation: Priceless Gift
Scripture: Romans 6:23 NKJV
For the wages of sin is death, but the gift of God is eternal life in Christ Jesus our Lord.

MAKANI, Makánee
Language/Cultural Origin: Hawaiian
Inherent Meaning: Wind
Spiritual Connotation: Mysterious
Scripture: John 3:8 TLB
Just as you can hear the wind but can't tell where it comes from or where it will go next, so it is with the Spirit.

MALA, Malea
(see also Malaya, Malia)
Language/Cultural Origin: English
Inherent Meaning: High Fortress
Spiritual Connotation: Child of God
Scripture: Joel 3:16 NKJV
The heavens and earth will shake; but the LORD will be a shelter for His people, and the strength of the children of Israel.

MALACHI, Malakai
☞Language/Cultural Origin: Hebrew

Inherent Meaning: Messenger of the Lord
Spiritual Connotation: Trustworthy
Scripture: Proverbs 25:13 RSV
Like the cold of snow in the time of harvest is a faithful messenger to those who send him, he refreshes the spirit of his masters.

MALANA, Malanna
Language/Cultural Origin: Hawaiian
Inherent Meaning: Buoyant
Spiritual Connotation: Preserved
Scripture: John 10:9 NRSV
I am the gate. Whoever enters by me will be saved, and will come in and go out and find pasture.

MALAYA, Malaea
(see also Mala, Malia)
Language/Cultural Origin: Filipino
Inherent Meaning: Free
Spiritual Connotation: Liberated
Scripture: John 8:32 NKJV
And you shall know the truth, and the truth shall make you free.

MALCOLM, Malcom
Language/Cultural Origin: Scottish
Inherent Meaning: Diligent Servant
Spiritual Connotation: Teachable Spirit
Scripture: Isaiah 42:16 NRSV
I will lead the blind by a road they do not know, by paths they have not known I will guide them. I will turn the darkness before them into light.

MALI, Malee, Maley, Malí
(see also Malley)
Language/Cultural Origin: Thai
Inherent Meaning: Flower
Spiritual Connotation: Joyful
Scripture: Isaiah 35:2 NKJV
It shall blossom abundantly and rejoice, even with joy and singing.

MALIA, Maleah, Maleia, Maliea
(see also Mala, Malaya)
Language/Cultural Origin: Zuni
Inherent Meaning: Bitterness
Spiritual Connotation: Forgiven
Scripture: 1 John 2:12 NRSV
I am writing to you, little children, because your sins are forgiven on account of his name.

MALIK, Maalik, Málik, Maliq, Malique
Language/Cultural Origin: Middle Eastern
Inherent Meaning: The Lord's Messenger
Spiritual Connotation: Forerunner
Scripture: Mark 1:2 RSV
As it is written in Isaiah the prophet, "Behold, I send my messenger before thy face, who shall prepare thy way."

MALIKA, Maleeka, Maleka
Language/Cultural Origin: Hungarian
Inherent Meaning: Industrious
Spiritual Connotation: Committed
Scripture: Colossians 3:23 TLB
Work hard and cheerfully at all you do, just as though you were working for the Lord and not merely for your masters.

MALIN, Mallin, Mallon, Maylin
Language/Cultural Origin: Old English
Inherent Meaning: Little Warrior
Spiritual Connotation: Champion
Scripture: Matthew 5:6 NKJV
Blessed are those who hunger and thirst for righteousness, for they shall be filled.

MALINA, Malena
(see also Milana, Milena)
Language/Cultural Origin: Hebrew
Inherent Meaning: Tower
Spiritual Connotation: Secure
Scripture: Proverbs 18:10 NKJV
The name of the LORD is a strong tower; the righteous run to it and are safe.

MALINDA, Malinde, Malynda
(see also Melinda)
Language/Cultural Origin: Greek
Inherent Meaning: Gentle
Spiritual Connotation: Tenderhearted
Scripture: 1 Corinthians 3:16 NKJV
Do you not know that you are the temple of God and that the Spirit of God dwells in you?

MALLEY, Malli, Mallie
(see also Mali)
Language/Cultural Origin: English
Inherent Meaning: Bitterness
Spiritual Connotation: Peaceful
Scripture: Isaiah 38:17 NKJV
Indeed it was for my own peace that I had

great bitterness; but You have lovingly
delivered my soul . . . for You have cast all
my sins behind Your back.

MALLORY, Mallari, Mallary, Malerie, Mallerie, Mallery, Malloree, Mallorey, Mallori, Mallorie, Malori, Malorie, Malory
Language/Cultural Origin: German
Inherent Meaning: Counselor
Spiritual Connotation: Joyful
Scripture: John 15:11 NKJV
These things I have spoken to you, that My joy may remain in you, and that your joy may be full.

MAMIE, Maymee
Language/Cultural Origin: English
Inherent Meaning: Desired
Spiritual Connotation: Righteous
Scripture: Psalm 27:4 NCV
I ask only one thing from the LORD. . . . Let me live in the LORD's house all my life. Let me see the LORD's beauty and look with my own eyes at his temple.

MANASSEH, Manassah
Language/Cultural Origin: Hebrew
Inherent Meaning: Cause to Forget
Spiritual Connotation: Restored
Scripture: Psalm 103:12 NASB
As far as the east is from the west, so far has He removed our transgressions from us.

MANDEL, Mandell
Language/Cultural Origin: German
Inherent Meaning: Almond
Spiritual Connotation: Sign
Scripture: Numbers 17:8 NCV
[Moses] saw that Aaron's stick (which stood for the family of Levi) had grown leaves. It had even budded, blossomed, and produced almonds.

MANDIE, Manda, Mandaline, Mandalyn, Mandee, Mandi, Mandy (see also Amanda)
Language/Cultural Origin: Latin
Inherent Meaning: Lovable
Spiritual Connotation: Eternal
Scripture: John 3:16 NKJV
For God so loved the world that He gave His

only begotten Son, that whoever believes in
Him should not perish but have everlasting
life.

MANLEY, Manlea, Manleigh
Language/Cultural Origin: English
Inherent Meaning: Heroic
Spiritual Connotation: Victorious Spirit
Scripture: Isaiah 58:8 NKJV
Then your light shall break forth like the morning, your healing shall spring forth speedily, and your righteousness shall go before you.

MANNING, Maning
Language/Cultural Origin: English
Inherent Meaning: Child of the Hero
Spiritual Connotation: Obedient
Scripture: Proverbs 1:8 RSV
Hear, my son, your father's instruction, and reject not your mother's teaching.

MANON, Mannon
Language/Cultural Origin: French
Inherent Meaning: Wished-for
Spiritual Connotation: Fulfilled
Scripture: Psalm 132:14 NLT
This is my home where I will live forever, he said. I will live here, for this is the place I desired.

MANOR, Mannor
Language/Cultural Origin: Hebrew
Inherent Meaning: Weaver's Beam
Spiritual Connotation: Creative
Scripture: Exodus 39:29 NIV
The sash was of finely twisted linen and blue, purple and scarlet yarn—the work of an embroiderer—as the LORD commanded Moses.

MANSEL, Mansell
Language/Cultural Origin: Old English
Inherent Meaning: From the Pastor's House
Spiritual Connotation: Discerning
Scripture: 1 John 2:14 RSV
I write to you, fathers, because you know him who is from the beginning.

MANSIE, Mancey, Manci, Mancie, Mansey, Mansy
Language/Cultural Origin: Hopi
Inherent Meaning: Pruned Blossom

Spiritual Connotation: Fruitful
Scripture: Hebrews 12:6 NLT
For the Lord disciplines those he loves, and he punishes those he accepts as his children.

MANTON, Manten
Language/Cultural Origin: Old English
Inherent Meaning: From the Hero's Town
Spiritual Connotation: Wise
Scripture: Titus 2:6 TLB
In the same way, urge the young men to behave carefully, taking life seriously.

MANUEL, Manni, Mannuel, Manny (see also Emanuel)
Language/Cultural Origin: Spanish
Inherent Meaning: God With Us
Spiritual Connotation: Consecrated to God
Scripture: Isaiah 9:6 NKJV
For unto us a Child is born, unto us a Son is given; and the government will be upon His shoulder.

MANUELA, Manuelle (see also Emanuela)
Language/Cultural Origin: Spanish
Inherent Meaning: God With Us
Spiritual Connotation: Consecrated to God
Scripture: Isaiah 7:14 NKJV
Therefore the Lord Himself will give you a sign: Behold, the virgin shall conceive and bear a Son, and shall call His name Immanuel.

MANYA, Manyah
Language/Cultural Origin: Russian
Inherent Meaning: Wished-for
Spiritual Connotation: Faithful
Scripture: Proverbs 19:22 NRSV
What is desirable in a person is loyalty, and it is better to be poor than a liar.

MAON, Maeon, Mayon, Meion, Meyon (see also Maayan, Mahon)
Language/Cultural Origin: Hebrew
Inherent Meaning: Habitation
Spiritual Connotation: Beautiful
Scripture: Psalm 84:1 RSV
How lovely is thy dwelling place, O LORD of hosts!

MARA, Marah, Marra ☞ (see also Maria)
Language/Cultural Origin: Hebrew

Inherent Meaning: Bitterness
Spiritual Connotation: Blessed
Scripture: Matthew 5:4 NKJV
Blessed are those who mourn, for they shall be comforted.

MARCEL, Marcele, Marcelis, Marcelius, Marcell, Marcello, Marcellus, Marsel, Marsello
Language/Cultural Origin: Latin
Inherent Meaning: Industrious Worker
Spiritual Connotation: Strong in Spirit
Scripture: Proverbs 4:23 NKJV
Keep your heart with all diligence, for out of it spring the issues of life.

MARCELLA, Marceil, Marcele, Marcelia, Marcelle, Marcilla, Marcille, Marselle
Language/Cultural Origin: Latin
Inherent Meaning: Warlike
Spiritual Connotation: Steadfast in Spirit
Scripture: Psalm 27:1 NKJV
The LORD is my light and my salvation; whom shall I fear? The LORD is the strength of my life; of whom shall I be afraid?

MARCIA, Marcee, Marci, Marciana, Marcianna, Marcie, Marcy, Marsey, Marsha, Marsi, Marsie, Marsy
Language/Cultural Origin: Latin
Inherent Meaning: Fearless
Spiritual Connotation: Excellent Worth
Scripture: 1 John 3:2 NKJV
Beloved, now we are children of God. . . . We shall be like Him, for we shall see Him as He is.

MARCUS, MARCO, see Mark

MAREN, Marin, Miren
Language/Cultural Origin: Aramaic
Inherent Meaning: Longed-for
Spiritual Connotation: Holy
Scripture: Isaiah 26:9 RSV
My soul yearns for thee in the night, my spirit within me earnestly seeks thee.

MARGARET, Margara, Margarett, Margarita, Margaux, Marge, Margeret, Margerite, Margi, Margie, Margo, Margot, Margret, Marguerite (see also Maggie, Marjorie)
Language/Cultural Origin: Greek

Inherent Meaning: Pearl
Spiritual Connotation: Gift of God
Scripture: Psalm 18:32 NKJV
> *It is God who arms me with strength, and makes my way perfect.*

MARIA, Marea, Mareah, Marija, Mariya, Mariyah, Marja, Marya (see also Mara, Marie)
Language/Cultural Origin: Italian
Inherent Meaning: Bitterness
Spiritual Connotation: Delivered
Scripture: Isaiah 38:17 NKJV
> *Indeed it was for my own peace that I had great bitterness; but You have lovingly delivered my soul . . . For You have cast all my sins behind Your back.*

MARIAH, Maraia, Maraya, Mariyah, Marriah (see also Moriah)
Language/Cultural Origin: English
Inherent Meaning: Bitterness
Spiritual Connotation: Comforted
Scripture: 1 Samuel 1:27 NKJV
> *For this child I prayed, and the LORD has granted me my petition which I asked of Him.*

MARIAN, Mariana, Mariane, Mariann, Marianna, Marianne, Mariene, Marion, Marrian, Marrianne, Maryana, Maryanna
Language/Cultural Origin: English
Inherent Meaning: Bitterness
Spiritual Connotation: Grace
Scripture: Isaiah 60:19 NRSV
> *The sun shall no longer be your light by day . . . but the LORD will be your everlasting light, and your God will be your glory.*

MARIE, Maree (see also Maria, Mary)
Language/Cultural Origin: French
Inherent Meaning: Bitterness
Spiritual Connotation: Consoled
Scripture: Isaiah 2:11 NCV
> *Proud people will be made humble, and they will bow low with shame. At that time only the LORD will still be praised.*

MARIEL, Marial, Mariela, Mariele, Mariella, Marielle (see also Maurelle, Merial, Muriel)
Language/Cultural Origin: English
Inherent Meaning: Bitterness
Spiritual Connotation: Exonerated
Scripture: Romans 8:30 NRSV
> *And those whom he predestined he also called; and those whom he called he also justified; and those whom he justified he also glorified.*

MARIKA, Marica, Marrika, Maryka, Merika
Language/Cultural Origin: Greek
Inherent Meaning: Bitterness
Spiritual Connotation: Vindicated
Scripture: Micah 5:9 NCV
> *So you will raise your fist in victory over your enemies, and all your enemies will be destroyed.*

MARIKO, Meriko
Language/Cultural Origin: Japanese
Inherent Meaning: Circle
Spiritual Connotation: Believer
Scripture: Isaiah 40:22 NCV
> *God sits on his throne above the circle of the earth, and compared to him, people are like grasshoppers.*

MARILEE, Marrilee, Merrilee, Merrily
Language/Cultural Origin: English
Inherent Meaning: Bitterness
Spiritual Connotation: Vindicated
Scripture: Job 13:18 NLT
> *I have prepared my case; I will be proved innocent.*

MARILU, Marilow, Marylou
Language/Cultural Origin: American
Inherent Meaning: Bitter Grace
Spiritual Connotation: Blessed
Scripture: Ephesians 1:6 TLB
> *Now all praise to God for his wonderful kindness to us and his favor that he has poured out upon us, because we belong to his dearly loved Son.*

MARILYN, Maralin, Maralyn, Maralyne, Maralynn, Marillyn, Marilynn, Marralin, Marrilyn, Marrilynn, Marylin
Language/Cultural Origin: English
Inherent Meaning: Bitterness
Spiritual Connotation: Sacrifice of Praise
Scripture: Psalm 69:30 NASB
I will praise the name of God with song, and shall magnify Him with thanksgiving.

MARINA, Marena, Marrina, Merina
Language/Cultural Origin: Russian
Inherent Meaning: From the Sea
Spiritual Connotation: Wonder of God
Scripture: Psalm 93:4 NRSV
More majestic than the thunders of mighty waters, more majestic than the waves of the sea, majestic on high is the LORD!

MARIO, Marios, Marrio
Language/Cultural Origin: Italian
Inherent Meaning: Sailor
Spiritual Connotation: Regenerated
Scripture: John 6:63 NRSV
It is the spirit that gives life; the flesh is useless. The words that I have spoken to you are spirit and life.

MARION, see Marian

MARISSA, Maressa, Maris, Marisa, Marise, Marisha, Marishka, Mariska, Marisse, Marris, Marrisa, Marrissa, Marrissia, Marysa, Maryssa, Meris, Merisa, Merissa
Language/Cultural Origin: English
Inherent Meaning: Bitterness
Spiritual Connotation: Eternally Steadfast
Scripture: Job 13:15 NKJV
Though He slay me, yet will I trust Him. Even so, I will defend my own ways before Him.

MARIT, Marita, Merit
Language/Cultural Origin: Aramaic
Inherent Meaning: Lady
Spiritual Connotation: Righteous
Scripture: Proverbs 31:10 TLB
If you can find a truly good wife, she is worth more than precious gems!

MARIUS, Mariano, Marino
Language/Cultural Origin: Latin

Inherent Meaning: Warlike
Spiritual Connotation: Powerful
Scripture: Joel 2:7 NRSV
Like warriors they charge, like soldiers they scale the wall. Each keeps to its own course, they do not swerve from their paths.

MARJORIE, Margerie, Marjarie, Marjerie, Marji, Marjie, Marjorey, Marjori, Marjory
Language/Cultural Origin: Latin
Inherent Meaning: Pearl
Spiritual Connotation: Gift of Praise
Scripture: Psalm 104:24 NASB
O LORD, how many are Your works! In wisdom You have made them all; the earth is full of Your possessions.

MARK, Marc, Marciano, Marcio, Marco, Marcos, Marcus, Marek, Marke, Markeese, Markei, Markey, Markice, Marko, Markos, Markques, Markus, Márkus, Marqes, Marques, Marquez, Marqui, Marquis, Marx
Language/Cultural Origin: Latin
Inherent Meaning: Martial
Spiritual Connotation: Servant of God
Scripture: John 4:24 RSV
God is spirit, and those who worship him must worship in spirit and truth.

MARKITA, Markeeta
Language/Cultural Origin: Bulgarian
Inherent Meaning: Pearl
Spiritual Connotation: Wise
Scripture: Job 28:18 NKJV
No mention shall be made of coral or quartz, for the price of wisdom is above rubies.

MARLAND, Marlan
Language/Cultural Origin: Old Englilsh
Inherent Meaning: From the Lake Land
Spiritual Connotation: Destined
Scripture: Ephesians 2:10 NKJV
For we are His workmanship, created in Christ Jesus for good works, which God prepared beforehand that we should walk in them.

MARLENE, Marla, Marlah, Marlaina, Marlaine, Marlana, Marlanna, Marlayne, Marlea, Marleah, Marlee, Marleen, Marleena, Marleigh, Marlena, Marli, Marlie, Marlina, Marline, Marlis, Marlo, Marlow, Marly, Marlys, Marlysa, Marlyssa
Language/Cultural Origin: Slavic
Inherent Meaning: High Fortress
Spiritual Connotation: Shielded
Scripture: Psalm 61:3 TLB
For you are my refuge, a high tower where my enemies can never reach me.

MARLON, Marlin
Language/Cultural Origin: Welsh
Inherent Meaning: From the Hill by the Sea
Spiritual Connotation: Victorious Spirit
Scripture: Psalm 8:6 NKJV
You have made him to have dominion over the works of Your hands; You have put all things under his feet.

MARNINA, Marna, Marne, Marnee, Marney, Marni, Marnie, Marnia, Marnja, Marnya
Language/Cultural Origin: Hebrew
Inherent Meaning: Rejoice
Spiritual Connotation: Content
Scripture: Philippians 4:4 NKJV
Rejoice in the Lord always. Again I will say, rejoice!

MARSDEN, Marsdon
Language/Cultural Origin: English
Inherent Meaning: From the Boundary Valley
Spiritual Connotation: Preserved
Scripture: Psalm 46:1 NKJV
God is our refuge and strength, a very present help in trouble.

MARSHA, see Marcia

MARSHALL, Marschal, Marshal, Marshel, Marshell
Language/Cultural Origin: Old French
Inherent Meaning: Caretaker
Spiritual Connotation: Faithful
Scripture: Psalm 40:4 NKJV
Blessed is that man who makes the LORD his trust, and does not respect the proud, nor such as turn aside to lies.

MARTHA, Marta, Marti, Martie, Martika, Marty, Mattie
Language/Cultural Origin: Aramaic
Inherent Meaning: Mistress of the House
Spiritual Connotation: Helpful Spirit
Scripture: Proverbs 31:27 NKJV
She watches over the ways of her household, and does not eat the bread of idleness.

MARTIN, Martan, Marten, Martinez, Marton, Marty, Martyn
Language/Cultural Origin: Latin
Inherent Meaning: Warlike
Spiritual Connotation: Seeker of Truth
Scripture: John 15:7 NKJV
If you abide in Me, and My words abide in you, you will ask what you desire, and it shall be done for you.

MARTINA, Martel, Martelle, Marthina, Martinia, Martiza, Martoya, Martrina, Martyna
Language/Cultural Origin: Hispanic
Inherent Meaning: Lady of the House
Spiritual Connotation: Virtuous
Scripture: 1 Timothy 2:10 NLT
For women who claim to be devoted to God should make themselves attractive by the good things they do.

MARVEL, Marvelle
Language/Cultural Origin: Latin
Inherent Meaning: Miracle
Spiritual Connotation: Sustained
Scripture: 2 Corinthians 12:9 NKJV
My grace is sufficient for you, for My strength is made perfect in weakness.

MARVIN, Marv, Marven, Merv, Mervin
Language/Cultural Origin: Welsh
Inherent Meaning: Lover of the Sea
Spiritual Connotation: Trusting Spirit
Scripture: Psalm 91:2 NLT
This I declare of the LORD: He alone is my refuge, my place of safety; he is my God, and I am trusting him.

MARY, Mari, Marietta, Meri (see also Mara, Maria, Marie)
Language/Cultural Origin: Hebrew
Inherent Meaning: Sea of Bitterness
Spiritual Connotation: Blessed

Scripture: Luke 1:28 NKJV
And having come in, the angel said to her,
"Rejoice, highly favored one, the Lord is with
you; blessed are you among women!"

MARYLOU, see Marilu

MASADA, Massada
Language/Cultural Origin: Hebrew
Inherent Meaning: Foundation
Spiritual Connotation: Enlightened
Scripture: Matthew 21:42 NKJV
The stone which the builders rejected has
become the chief cornerstone. This was the
Lord's doing, and it is marvelous in our eyes.

MASLIN, Maslen
Language/Cultural Origin: French
Inherent Meaning: Little Twin
Spiritual Connotation: Bold
Scripture: John 11:16 NRSV
Thomas, who was called the Twin, said to his
fellow disciples, "Let us also go, that we may
die with him."

MASON, Maison
Language/Cultural Origin: Old French
Inherent Meaning: Stoneworker
Spiritual Connotation: Overcomer
Scripture: Revelation 2:17 NRSV
To everyone who conquers . . . I will give a
white stone, and on the white stone is
written a new name that no one knows
except the one who receives it.

MATANA, Matanna
Language/Cultural Origin: Hebrew
Inherent Meaning: Gift
Spiritual Connotation: Blessed
Scripture: Ephesians 4:7 NKJV
But to each one of us grace was given
according to the measure of Christ's gift.

MATHER, Mathre
Language/Cultural Origin: English
Inherent Meaning: Conqueror
Spiritual Connotation: Intuitive
Scripture: Luke 6:45 TLB
A good man produces good deeds from a
good heart. . . . Whatever is in the heart
overflows into speech.

MATHILDA, Tilda, Tillie
Language/Cultural Origin: German

Inherent Meaning: Noble Lady
Spiritual Connotation: Beloved
Scripture: Luke 12:32 NKJV
Do not fear, little flock, for it is your Father's
good pleasure to give you the kingdom.

MATRIKA, Matreika
Language/Cultural Origin: Indo-Pakastani
Inherent Meaning: Mother
Spiritual Connotation: Nurturing
Scripture: 1 Timothy 5:2 NLT
Treat the older women as you would your
mother, and treat the younger women with
all purity as your own sisters.

MATSUKO, Metsuko
Language/Cultural Origin: Japanese
Inherent Meaning: Evergreen
Spiritual Connotation: Perpetual
Scripture: Isaiah 55:13 NIV
Instead of the thornbush will grow the pine
tree, and instead of briers the myrtle will
grow. This will be . . . an everlasting sign.

MATTEA, Matea, Mathea
Language/Cultural Origin: Hebrew
Inherent Meaning: Gift of God
Spiritual Connotation: Blessed
Scripture: Ephesians 2:8–9 RSV
For by grace you have been saved through
faith; . . . it is the gift of God—not because
of works, lest any man should boast.

MATTHEW, Mateo, Mathew, Mathias,
☞Mathieux, Matt, Matthias
Language/Cultural Origin: Hebrew
Inherent Meaning: Gift of God
Spiritual Connotation: Honor to God
Scripture: Psalm 104:1 KJV
Bless the LORD, O my soul. O LORD my God,
thou art very great; thou art clothed with
honour and majesty.

MAUDE, Maud
Language/Cultural Origin: English
Inherent Meaning: Noble Lady
Spiritual Connotation: Victorious
Scripture: Isaiah 25:8 NKJV
He will swallow up death forever, and the
Lord GOD will wipe away tears from all faces.

MAUREEN, Maura, Maurene,
Maurine
Language/Cultural Origin: Irish

Inherent Meaning: Wished-for Child
Spiritual Connotation: Beloved
Scripture: Psalm 139:17 NASB

How precious also are Your thoughts to me,
O God! How vast is the sum of them!

MAURELLE, Maurial, Mauriall, Mauriel, Mauriell, Maurielle (see also Mariel, Merial, Muriel)
Language/Cultural Origin: French
Inherent Meaning: Dark
Spiritual Connotation: Peaceful
Scripture: James 3:17 NKJV

But the wisdom that is from above is first pure, then peaceable, gentle, willing to yield, full of mercy and good fruits, without partiality and without hypocrisy.

MAURICE, Maury, Morrice, Morrie, Morris, Morry
Language/Cultural Origin: Latin
Inherent Meaning: From the Marshland
Spiritual Connotation: Conciliatory
Scripture: Proverbs 16:7 NKJV

When a man's ways please the LORD, he makes even his enemies to be at peace with him.

MAVIS, Mayvis
Language/Cultural Origin: French
Inherent Meaning: Songbird
Spiritual Connotation: Praise
Scripture: Psalm 138:2 NCV

I will bow down facing your holy Temple, and I will thank you for your love and loyalty. You have made your name and your word greater than anything.

MAXIMILLIAN, Max, Maxx
Language/Cultural Origin: Latin
Inherent Meaning: Greatest in Excellence
Spiritual Connotation: Teachable Spirit
Scripture: Isaiah 64:8 NRSV

Yet, O LORD, you are our Father; we are the clay, and you are our potter; we are all the work of your hand.

MAXINE, Maxeen, Maxene
Language/Cultural Origin: Latin
Inherent Meaning: Greatest in Excellence
Spiritual Connotation: Secure in Truth
Scripture: Philippians 3:15 NKJV

Therefore let us, as many as are mature, have this mind; and if in anything you think otherwise, God will reveal even this to you.

MAXWELL, Max, Maxx
Language/Cultural Origin: Scottish
Inherent Meaning: From the Great Spring
Spiritual Connotation: Righteous
Scripture: Matthew 6:22 NASB

The eye is the lamp of the body; so then if your eye is clear, your whole body will be full of light.

MAY, Mae, Maye
Language/Cultural Origin: Hebrew
Inherent Meaning: Gift of God
Spiritual Connotation: Blessed
Scripture: Psalm 92:4 KJV

For thou, Lord, hast made me glad through thy work: I will triumph in the works of thy hands.

MAYA, Mayah (see also Maia, Maija, Mia, Miya)
Language/Cultural Origin: Latin
Inherent Meaning: Esteemed
Spiritual Connotation: Honored
Scripture: Psalm 143:8 TLB

Let me see your kindness to me in the morning, for I am trusting you. Show me where to walk, for my prayer is sincere.

MAYER, Mayor (see also Meyer)
Language/Cultural Origin: Latin
Inherent Meaning: Renowned
Spiritual Connotation: Enlightened
Scripture: Romans 12:2 NRSV

Do not be conformed to this world, but be transformed by the renewing of your minds.

MAYHEW, Maihew
Language/Cultural Origin: Latin
Inherent Meaning: Gift of God
Spiritual Connotation: United in Spirit
Scripture: 2 Corinthians 13:11 NKJV

Be of good comfort, be of one mind, live in peace; and the God of love and peace will be with you.

MAYNARD, Ménard
Language/Cultural Origin: Old English
Inherent Meaning: Powerful
Spiritual Connotation: Spirit of Praise

Scripture: 1 Corinthians 14:15 NLT
Well then, what shall I do? I will do both. I will pray [and sing] in the spirit, and I will pray [and sing] in words I understand.

MAYO, Maiyo
Language/Cultural Origin: Irish
Inherent Meaning: From the Yew-Tree Plain
Spiritual Connotation: Heart of Praise
Scripture: Psalm 96:1 KJV
O sing unto the LORD a new song: sing unto the LORD, all the earth.

MEARA, Mearah
(see also Meira, Mira, Mura)
Language/Cultural Origin: Irish
Inherent Meaning: Mirthful
Spiritual Connotation: Gift of Discernment
Scripture: Psalm 119:18 NKJV
Open my eyes, that I may see wondrous things from Your law.

MEDINA, Medaena,
Medaina, Medinah
Language/Cultural Origin: Hebrew
Inherent Meaning: State/country
Spiritual Connotation: Intercessor
Scripture: Exodus 33:13 NCV
If I have truly pleased you, show me your plans so that I may know you and continue to please you. Remember that this nation is your people.

MEDORA, Medorra
Language/Cultural Origin: English
Inherent Meaning: Mother's Gift
Spiritual Connotation: Blessing
Scripture: Luke 2:7 NRSV
And she gave birth to her firstborn son and wrapped him in bands of cloth, and laid him in a manger, because there was no place for them in the inn.

MEGAN, Maegan, Maeghan, Magan,
Magen, Meagan, Meagann, Meagen,
Meaghan, Meaghann, Meg, Megan,
Megen, Meggan, Meggen, Meggie,
Meghan, Meghann
Language/Cultural Origin: Welsh
Inherent Meaning: Mighty
Spiritual Connotation: Victorious Spirit
Scripture: Isaiah 2:5 NRSV
O house of Jacob, come, let us walk in the light of the LORD!

MEIRA, Meera
(see also Meara, Mira, Mura)
Language/Cultural Origin: Hebrew
Inherent Meaning: Light
Spiritual Connotation: Exalted
Scripture: Isaiah 60:1 RSV
Arise, shine; for your light has come, and the glory of the LORD has risen upon you.

MELANIE, Melainie, Melanee,
Melaney, Melani, Mélanie,
Melaniya, Melanney, Melannie,
Melanya, Mellanie
Language/Cultural Origin: Greek
Inherent Meaning: Dark
Spiritual Connotation: Child of God
Scripture: Ezekiel 37:13 NASB
Then you will know that I am the LORD, when I have opened your graves and caused you to come up out of your graves, My people.

MELINDA, Mellinda, Melynda
(see also Malinda)
Language/Cultural Origin: Greek
Inherent Meaning: Honey
Spiritual Connotation: Cherished
Scripture: Isaiah 58:11 NKJV
The LORD will guide you continually, and satisfy your soul in drought, and strengthen your bones; you shall be like a watered garden.

MELISSA, Malissa, Mallissa, Melisa,
Mélisa, Mélissa, Mellisa, Mellissa,
Milissa, Millisa, Millissa, Missi,
Missie, Missy, Mylis, Mylissa
Language/Cultural Origin: Greek
Inherent Meaning: Honey Bee
Spiritual Connotation: Industrious, Creative
Scripture: James 2:22 NASB
You see that faith was working with his works, and as a result of the works, faith was perfected.

MELITA, Malita
Language/Cultural Origin: Greek
Inherent Meaning: Sweetened With Honey
Spiritual Connotation: Content
Scripture: Psalm 145:16 NASB
Thou dost open Thy hand, and dost satisfy the desire of every living thing.

MELODY, Melodee, Melodey, Melodi, Melodie

Language/Cultural Origin: English
Inherent Meaning: Song
Spiritual Connotation: Joyful
Scripture: Psalm 63:5 NRSV

My soul is satisfied as with a rich feast, and my mouth praises you with joyful lips.

MELORA, Melorra

Language/Cultural Origin: Latin
Inherent Meaning: Improved
Spiritual Connotation: Sanctified
Scripture: Philippians 1:6 NRSV

I am confident of this, that the one who began a good work among you will bring it to completion by the day of Jesus Christ.

MELVIN, Malvin, Mel

Language/Cultural Origin: Middle English
Inherent Meaning: Reliable Friend
Spiritual Connotation: Excellent Virtue
Scripture: Ephesians 3:19 TLB

And so at last you will be filled up with God himself.

MENDEL, Mendell

Language/Cultural Origin: Hebrew
Inherent Meaning: Wisdom
Spiritual Connotation: Studious
Scripture: Proverbs 19:8 NLT

To acquire wisdom is to love oneself; people who cherish understanding will prosper.

MENORA, Manora

Language/Cultural Origin: Hebrew
Inherent Meaning: Candelabrum
Spiritual Connotation: Witness
Scripture: Matthew 5:14 NASB

You are the light of the world. A city set on a hill cannot be hidden.

MERCEDES, Mersade

Language/Cultural Origin: Latin
Inherent Meaning: Gift
Spiritual Connotation: Esteemed
Scripture: Isaiah 52:7 NRSV

How beautiful upon the mountains are the feet of the messenger who announces peace, who brings good news.

MEREDITH, Meredithe, Meredyth, Merideth, Meridith, Merridith, Merry

Language/Cultural Origin: Welsh
Inherent Meaning: Guardian of the Sea
Spiritual Connotation: Faithful Friend
Scripture: Proverbs 2:10–11 NKJV

When wisdom enters your heart, and knowledge is pleasant to your soul, discretion will preserve you; understanding will keep you.

MERIAL, Meriel, Meriol (see also Mariel, Maurelle, Muriel)

Language/Cultural Origin: Irish
Inherent Meaning: Shining Sea
Spiritual Connotation: Cherished
Scripture: Psalm 139:9–10 RSV

If I take the wings of the morning and dwell in the uttermost parts of the sea, even there thy hand shall lead me, and thy right hand shall hold me.

MERLIN, Merle, Merlen

Language/Cultural Origin: Old English
Inherent Meaning: Falcon
Spiritual Connotation: Courageous
Scripture: Deuteronomy 31:6 RSV

Be strong and of good courage, do not fear or be in dread of them: for it is the LORD your God who goes with you; he will not fail you or forsake you.

MERRILL, Meril, Merill, Merril (see also Meryl)

Language/Cultural Origin: French
Inherent Meaning: Famous
Spiritual Connotation: Honored
Scripture: Ecclesiastes 2:26 NASB

For to a person who is good in His sight He has given wisdom and knowledge and joy.

MERRILY, see Marilee

MERTON, Murton

Language/Cultural Origin: Middle English
Inherent Meaning: From the Town by the Sea
Spiritual Connotation: Child of God
Scripture: Romans 8:16 NKJV

The Spirit Himself bears witness with our spirit that we are children of God.

MERVIN, see Marvin

MERYL, Meral, Merel, Merrall,
Merryl, Meryll (see also Merrill)
Language/Cultural Origin: German
Inherent Meaning: Famous
Spiritual Connotation: Chosen
Scripture: Isaiah 52:13 NASB
Behold, My servant will prosper, he will be
high and lifted up and greatly exalted.

MEYER, Meier, Myer
(see also Mayer)
Language/Cultural Origin: German
Inherent Meaning: Farmer
Spiritual Connotation: Blessed
Scripture: Isaiah 28:26 NLT
The farmer knows just what to do, for God
has given him understanding.

MIA, Meah, Miah
(see also Maia, Maija, Maya, Miya)
Language/Cultural Origin: English
Inherent Meaning: Wished-for
Spiritual Connotation: Devout
Scripture: Psalm 27:4 RSV
One thing have I asked of the LORD: . . . that
I may dwell in the house of the LORD all the
days of my life, to behold the beauty of the
LORD, and to inquire in his temple.

MICAH, Mica, Micaiah,
☞**Michah, Mycah**
Language/Cultural Origin: Hebrew
Inherent Meaning: Who Is Like God?
Spiritual Connotation: Reverent
Scripture: Psalm 113:5 NKJV
Who is like the LORD our God, who dwells
on high?

MICHAEL, Mekhail, Micael, Mical,
☞**Michale, Micheal, Michel, Mick,**
Mickey, Mickie, Micky, Mikael,
Mikáele, Mikal, Mike, Mikhael,
Mikhail, Miki, Mikki, Mychal,
Mychael, Mycheal, Mykael, Mykal
Language/Cultural Origin: Hebrew
Inherent Meaning: Who Is Like God?
Spiritual Connotation: Esteemed
Scripture: Exodus 15:11 NKJV
Who is like You, O LORD, among the gods?
Who is like You, glorious in holiness,
fearful in praises, doing wonders?

MICHAL, Machelle, Makayla,
☞**Mekaela, Mekala, Mekayla,**
Meshelle, Micaela, Michaele,
Michaelle, Michala, Michayla,
Michayle, Michele, Michèle,
Michelle, Mikaela, Mikalya, Mikyla,
Mischel, Mishayle, Mychaela,
Mykala, Mykaela
Language/Cultural Origin: Hebrew
Inherent Meaning: Who Is Like God?
Spiritual Connotation: Godliness
Scripture: Psalm 71:19 NASB
For Your righteousness, O God, reaches to the
heavens, You who have done great things; O
God, who is like You?

MIDORI, Midoree
Language/Cultural Origin: Japanese
Inherent Meaning: Green
Spiritual Connotation: Restful
Scripture: Psalm 23:2 RSV
He makes me lie down in green pastures. He
leads me beside still waters.

MIGUEL, Migel
Language/Cultural Origin: Portuguese
Inherent Meaning: Who Is Like God?
Spiritual Connotation: Victorious Spirit
Scripture: Philippians 2:13 RSV
For God is at work in you, both to will and
to work for his good pleasure.

MILADA, Miladah, Milady
Language/Cultural Origin: Czech
Inherent Meaning: My Love
Spiritual Connotation: Beloved
Scripture: 1 Corinthians 16:24 NKJV
My love be with you all in Christ Jesus. Amen.

MILAN, Milen, Mylan, Mylen, Mylon
Language/Cultural Origin: Italian
Inherent Meaning: From Milan
Spiritual Connotation: Witness
Scripture: Romans 1:16 NKJV
For I am not ashamed of the gospel of Christ,
for it is the power of God to salvation for
everyone who believes, for the Jew first and
also for the Greek.

MILANA, Milani, Milanna, Milania
(see also Malina)
Language/Cultural Origin: Italian

Inherent Meaning: From Milan
Spiritual Connotation: Blessed
Scripture: Romans 2:10 NLT
But there will be glory and honor and peace from God for all who do good—for the Jew first and also for the Gentile.

MILDRED, Midge, Mildrid
Language/Cultural Origin: Old English
Inherent Meaning: Gentle Spirit
Spiritual Connotation: Loving
Scripture: 1 John 4:7 NLT
Dear friends, let us continue to love one another, for love comes from God. Anyone who loves is born of God and knows God.

MILENA, Milèna, Milenia, Milenya (see also Malina)
Language/Cultural Origin: Slavic
Inherent Meaning: Dark
Spiritual Connotation: Prepared
Scripture: 1 Thessalonians 5:2 NRSV
For you yourselves know very well that the day of the Lord will come like a thief in the night.

MILES, Myles
Language/Cultural Origin: German
Inherent Meaning: Merciful
Spiritual Connotation: Heart of Compassion
Scripture: Proverbs 18:16 NRSV
A gift opens doors; it gives access to the great.

MILIANI, Milianni
Language/Cultural Origin: Hawaiian
Inherent Meaning: Caress
Spiritual Connotation: Treasured
Scripture: Song of Songs 4:7 NCV
My darling, everything about you is beautiful, and there is nothing at all wrong with you.

MILLARD, Miller, Myller
Language/Cultural Origin: Latin
Inherent Meaning: Caretaker
Spiritual Connotation: Excellent Worth
Scripture: 1 Chronicles 29:12 NCV
Riches and honor come from you. You rule everything. You have the power and strength to make anyone great and strong.

MILLICENT, Melisenda, Mellicent, Millee, Millie, Milly
Language/Cultural Origin: Old German

Inherent Meaning: Industrious
Spiritual Connotation: Strong Spirit
Scripture: 1 Corinthians 1:25 NKJV
Because the foolishness of God is wiser than men, and the weakness of God is stronger than men.

MILO, Mylo
Language/Cultural Origin: Old German
Inherent Meaning: Generous
Spiritual Connotation: Helpful Spirit
Scripture: Isaiah 30:29 NKJV
You shall have a song as in the night when a holy festival is kept, and gladness of heart.

MILTON, Milt, Mytlon
Language/Cultural Origin: English
Inherent Meaning: From the Mill Town
Spiritual Connotation: Blessed of God
Scripture: Romans 12:6 NKJV
Having then gifts differing according to the grace that is given to us, let us use them.

MIMI, Mimee, Mimie, Mimii
Language/Cultural Origin: English
Inherent Meaning: Wished-for
Spiritual Connotation: Spiritual Passion
Scripture: Psalm 27:4 NKJV
One thing I have desired of the LORD . . . that I may dwell in the house of the LORD all the days of my life, to behold the beauty of the LORD, and to inquire in His temple.

MINDY, Mindee, Mindi, Mindie, Myndee, Myndie
Language/Cultural Origin: English
Inherent Meaning: Sweet as Honey
Spiritual Connotation: Genuine
Scripture: Revelation 10:10 NRSV
So I took the little scroll from the hand of the angel and ate it; it was sweet as honey in my mouth.

MINGAN, Mingen
Language/Cultural Origin: Native American
Inherent Meaning: Gray Wolf
Spiritual Connotation: Vigilant
Scripture: 1 Peter 5:8 NRSV
Discipline yourselves, keep alert. Like a roaring lion your adversary the devil prowls around, looking for someone to devour.

MINH, Min
Language/Cultural Origin: Vietnamese

Inherent Meaning: Light
Spiritual Connotation: Enlightened
Scripture: John 8:12 NRSV

Again Jesus spoke to them, saying, I am the light of the world. Whoever follows me will never walk in darkness but will have the light of life.

MINNA, Meena, Mena, Mina, Mini, Minni, Minnie, Minny
Language/Cultural Origin: Old German
Inherent Meaning: Love
Spiritual Connotation: Cherished
Scripture: Isaiah 35:1 NASB

The wilderness and the desert will be glad, and the Arabah will rejoice.

MIRA, Mirra, Mirah
(see also Meara, Meira, Mura)
Language/Cultural Origin: English
Inherent Meaning: Wonderful
Spiritual Connotation: Worshipful
Scripture: 1 Chronicles 16:9 TLB

Sing to him; yes, sing his praises and tell of his marvelous works.

MIRANDA, Maranda, Meranda, Mirranda, Myranda
Language/Cultural Origin: Latin
Inherent Meaning: Admirable
Spiritual Connotation: Beloved
Scripture: Proverbs 3:6 TLB

In everything you do, put God first, and he will direct you and crown your efforts with success.

MIRIAM, Mariam, Mariame, ☞Mariamne, Miriame, Mirriam, Myriam, Myriame
Language/Cultural Origin: Hebrew
Inherent Meaning: Bitterness
Spiritual Connotation: Discerning
Scripture: Jeremiah 30:3 NRSV

For the days are surely coming, says the LORD, when I will restore the fortunes of my people.

MIRON, Miran (see also Myron)
Language/Cultural Origin: Polish
Inherent Meaning: Peace
Spiritual Connotation: Commissioned
Scripture: John 20:21 NASB

Jesus therefore said to them again, "Peace be with you; as the Father has sent Me, I also send you."

MISHA, Mischa, Mishka
Language/Cultural Origin: Russian
Inherent Meaning: Who Is Like God?
Spiritual Connotation: Disciple
Scripture: Psalm 71:19 NASB

For Thy righteousness, O God, reaches to the heavens, Thou who hast done great things; O God, who is like Thee?

MISHAN, Mishán, Mishaun, Mishawn, Mishon
Language/Cultural Origin: Hebrew
Inherent Meaning: Support
Spiritual Connotation: Helpful
Scripture: Galatians 6:2 TLB

Share each other's troubles and problems, and so obey our Lord's command.

MITCHELL, Mitch, Mitchall, Mytch, Mytchell
Language/Cultural Origin: English
Inherent Meaning: Who Is Like God?
Spiritual Connotation: Consecrated to God
Scripture: Numbers 6:8 NKJV

All the days of his separation he shall be holy to the LORD.

MITZI, Mitzee, Mitzie
Language/Cultural Origin: German
Inherent Meaning: Bitterness
Spiritual Connotation: Vindicated
Scripture: Acts 3:21 NCV

But Jesus must stay in heaven until the time comes when all things will be made right again.

MIYA, Miyana, Miyanna
(see also Maia, Maija, Maya, Mia)
Language/Cultural Origin: Japanese
Inherent Meaning: Temple
Spiritual Connotation: Pure
Scripture: 1 Corinthians 6:19 TLB

Haven't you yet learned that your body is the home of the Holy Spirit God gave you? . . . Your own body does not belong to you.

MIYO, Miyoko, Miyuko
Language/Cultural Origin: Japanese
Inherent Meaning: Beautiful Generation

Spiritual Connotation: Spirit of Praise
Scripture: Psalm 79:13 NRSV

Then we your people, the flock of your pasture, will give thanks to you forever; from generation to generation we will recount your praise.

MOHALA, Moala
Language/Cultural Origin: Hawaiian
Inherent Meaning: Blooming
Spiritual Connotation: Destined
Scripture: Hosea 14:7 NCV

The people of Israel will again live under my protection. They will grow like the grain, they will bloom like a vine.

MOIRA, Moirah, Moyra, Moyrah (see also Mora)
Language/Cultural Origin: Irish
Inherent Meaning: Wished-for
Spiritual Connotation: Zealous
Scripture: Psalm 119:20 NRSV

My soul is consumed with longing for your ordinances at all times.

MOISES, see Moses

MOLLY, Mollee, Molley, Molli, Mollie
Language/Cultural Origin: English
Inherent Meaning: Desired
Spiritual Connotation: Righteous
Scripture: Isaiah 26:9 NRSV

My soul yearns for you in the night. . . . For when your judgments are in the earth, the inhabitants of the world learn righteousness.

MONA, Monna, Moyna
Language/Cultural Origin: Irish
Inherent Meaning: Noble
Spiritual Connotation: Reflection of Wisdom
Scripture: Proverbs 2:6 NKJV

For the LORD gives wisdom; from His mouth come knowledge and understanding.

MONICA, Moneka, Moni, Monicka, Monika, Monique, Monnica, Monnika
Language/Cultural Origin: Latin
Inherent Meaning: Advisor
Spiritual Connotation: Consecrated
Scripture: 2 Corinthians 1:21 NRSV

But it is God who establishes us with you in Christ and has anointed us.

MONROE, Munroe
Language/Cultural Origin: Irish
Inherent Meaning: From the Hill
Spiritual Connotation: Trusting
Scripture: Mark 9:23 NRSV

All things can be done for the one who believes.

MONTANA, Montanna
Language/Cultural Origin: Spanish
Inherent Meaning: Mountain
Spiritual Connotation: Joyful
Scripture: Psalm 48:1 NASB

Great is the LORD, and greatly to be praised, in the city of our God, His holy mountain.

MONTGOMERY, Montaé, Monte, Montee, Monty
Language/Cultural Origin: Old English
Inherent Meaning: From the Mountain of the Wealthy One
Spiritual Connotation: Prosperous
Scripture: Psalm 37:5 NKJV

Commit your way to the LORD, trust also in Him, and He shall bring it to pass.

MORA, Morra (see also Moira)
Language/Cultural Origin: Spanish
Inherent Meaning: Blueberry
Spiritual Connotation: Lovely
Scripture: Genesis 1:11 NASB

Then God said, "Let the earth sprout vegetation, plants yielding seed, and fruit trees bearing fruit after their kind; . . ." and it was so.

MORASHA, Morascha, Morrasha
Language/Cultural Origin: Hebrew
Inherent Meaning: Legacy
Spiritual Connotation: Heritage
Scripture: Isaiah 54:17 RSV

No weapon that is fashioned against you shall prosper. . . . This is the heritage of the servants of the LORD and their vindication from me, says the LORD.

MORDECAI, Mordechai
Language/Cultural Origin: Persian
Inherent Meaning: Warlike
Spiritual Connotation: Reknowned
Scripture: Esther 9:4 NKJV

For Mordecai was great in the king's palace,

and his fame spread throughout all the provinces; for this man Mordecai became increasingly prominent.

MORGAN, Morgana, Morgann, Morganna, Morganne, Morgen, Morgun, Morrgan, Morrgana
Language/Cultural Origin: Welsh
Inherent Meaning: White Sea
Spiritual Connotation: Bright
Scripture: Isaiah 12:2 NLT
See, God has come to save me. I will trust in him and not be afraid. The LORD GOD is my strength and my song; he has become my salvation.

MORRELL, Morell
Language/Cultural Origin: French
Inherent Meaning: Dark
Spiritual Connotation: Redeemed
Scripture: Isaiah 9:2 RSV
The people who walked in darkness have seen a great light; those who dwelt in a land of deep darkness, on them has light shined.

MORIAH, Moria, Moriya, Moriel, ☞ Morriah (see also Mariah)
Language/Cultural Origin: Hebrew
Inherent Meaning: God Is My Teacher
Spiritual Connotation: Privileged
Scripture: John 1:49 RSV
Nathanael answered him, Rabbi, you are the Son of God! You are the King of Israel!

MORRIS, see Maurice

MORTON, Mort, Mortey
Language/Cultural Origin: English
Inherent Meaning: From the Town Near the Moor Estate
Spiritual Connotation: Empowered
Scripture: Matthew 28:18 NASB
And Jesus came up and spoke to them, saying, "All authority has been given to Me in heaven and on earth."

MOSELLE, Mozelle
Language/Cultural Origin: Hebrew
Inherent Meaning: Drawn From the Water
Spiritual Connotation: Rescued
Scripture: Acts 20:28 NRSV
Keep watch over yourselves and over all the flock . . . to shepherd the church of God that he obtained with the blood of his own Son.

MOSES, Moe, Moïse, Moisei, Moises, ☞ Moisés, Moishe, Moisis, Mose, Moshe, Moyses, Mozes
Language/Cultural Origin: Hebrew
Inherent Meaning: Drawn From the Water
Spiritual Connotation: Delivered
Scripture: Ecclesiastes 3:11 NRSV
He has made everything suitable for its time; moreover he has put a sense of past and future into their minds.

MOYA, Moia
Language/Cultural Origin: English
Inherent Meaning: Wished-for
Spiritual Connotation: Hopeful
Scripture: Psalm 119:81 NLT
I faint with longing for your salvation; but I have put my hope in your word.

MURA, Murah (see also Meara, Meira, Mira)
Language/Cultural Origin: Japanese
Inherent Meaning: Village
Spiritual Connotation: High Praise
Scripture: Daniel 4:3 NASB
How great are His signs, and how mighty are His wonders! His kingdom is an everlasting kingdom, and His dominion is from generation to generation.

MURIEL, Murial, Muriell, Murielle (see also Mariel, Maurelle, Merial)
Language/Cultural Origin: Middle Eastern
Inherent Meaning: Myrrh
Spiritual Connotation: Fragrant
Scripture: Ephesians 5:2 NKJV
And walk in love, as Christ also has loved us and given Himself for us, an offering and a sacrifice to God for a sweet-smelling aroma.

MURPHY, Murfey
Language/Cultural Origin: Irish
Inherent Meaning: Sea Warrior
Spiritual Connotation: Full of Praise
Scripture: Psalm 100:4 RSV
Enter his gates with thanksgiving, and his courts with praise! Give thanks to him, bless his name!

MURRAY, Murrey
Language/Cultural Origin: Gaelic
Inherent Meaning: Sailor
Spiritual Connotation: Discerning

Scripture: 1 Kings 3:9 NRSV
Give your servant therefore an understanding mind to govern your people, able to discern between good and evil.

MUSTAFA, Mostafa, Mustafah, Mustapha
Language/Cultural Origin: Middle Eastern
Inherent Meaning: Chosen
Spiritual Connotation: Destined
Scripture: Luke 18:7 NRSV
And will not God grant justice to his chosen ones who cry to him day and night? Will he delay long in helping them?

MYISHA, Miyesha, Myesha, Myeshia, Myeisha, Myeishia
Language/Cultural Origin: Middle Eastern
Inherent Meaning: Woman
Spiritual Connotation: Invaluable
Scripture: Proverbs 31:10 NRSV
A capable wife who can find? She is far more precious than jewels.

MYLA, Mylah, Mylea, Mylie
Language/Cultural Origin: English
Inherent Meaning: Merciful
Spiritual Connotation: Compassionate
Scripture: Hosea 6:6 NIV
For I desire mercy, not sacrifice, and acknowledgment of God rather than burnt offerings.

MYLES, see Miles

MYLON, see Milan

MYRA, Myrah, Myria
Language/Cultural Origin: Latin

Inherent Meaning: Fragrant
Spiritual Connotation: Abundant Praise
Scripture: Psalm 32:11 NKJV
Be glad in the LORD and rejoice, you righteous; and shout for joy, all you upright in heart!

MYRNA, Mirna
Language/Cultural Origin: Scottish
Inherent Meaning: Gentle
Spiritual Connotation: Beloved
Scripture: Isaiah 55:12 NKJV
The mountains and the hills shall break forth into singing before you, and all the trees of the field shall clap their hands.

MYRON, Myran (see also Miron)
Language/Cultural Origin: Greek
Inherent Meaning: Fragrant Ointment
Spiritual Connotation: Peaceful Praise
Scripture: Philippians 4:7 RSV
And the peace of God, which passes all understanding, will keep your hearts and your minds in Christ Jesus.

MYSIE, Mysie
Language/Cultural Origin: Scottish
Inherent Meaning: Pearl
Spiritual Connotation: Treasured
Scripture: Matthew 13:45 NKJV
Again, the kingdom of heaven is like a merchant seeking beautiful pearls.

MYSTIQUE, Mistique
Language/Cultural Origin: French
Inherent Meaning: Intriguing
Spiritual Connotation: Reverent
Scripture: Psalm 33:8 NRSV
Let all the earth fear the LORD; let all the inhabitants of the world stand in awe of him.

NAARAN, Naaren, Naran, Naren
Language/Cultural Origin: Hebrew
Inherent Meaning: Young Man
Spiritual Connotation: Temperate
Scripture: Titus 2:6 NRSV
Likewise, urge the younger men to be self-controlled.

NAARIA, Naarya, Naria (see also Nara, Narah)
Language/Cultural Origin: Hebrew
Inherent Meaning: Child of God
Spiritual Connotation: Heir
Scripture: John 1:12 TLB
But to all who received him, he gave the right to become children of God. All they needed to do was to trust him to save them.

NADIA, Nadea, Nadiya, Nadja, Nadya (see also Nydia)
Language/Cultural Origin: Slavic
Inherent Meaning: Hopeful
Spiritual Connotation: Blessed
Scripture: Deuteronomy 16:15 NKJV
The LORD your God will bless you in all your produce and in all the work of your hands, so that you surely rejoice.

NADIM, Nadeem, Nadím
Language/Cultural Origin: Middle Eastern
Inherent Meaning: Friend
Spiritual Connotation: Friend of God
Scripture: Luke 12:8 TLB
I, the Messiah, will publicly honor you in the presence of God's angels if you publicly acknowledge me here on earth as your Friend.

NADINE, Nadean, Nadeen
Language/Cultural Origin: French
Inherent Meaning: Hope
Spiritual Connotation: Spiritual Potential
Scripture: Psalm 18:28 TLB
You have turned on my light! The Lord my God has made my darkness turn to light.

NAIDA, Nayda
Language/Cultural Origin: Greek
Inherent Meaning: Water Nymph
Spiritual Connotation: Gifted
Scripture: Psalm 90:17 NRSV
Let the favor of the Lord our God be upon us, and prosper for us the work of our hands— O prosper the work of our hands!

NAJILA, Naiyila, Najah
Language/Cultural Origin: Middle Eastern
Inherent Meaning: Has Beautiful Eyes
Spiritual Connotation: Anointed
Scripture: 1 Samuel 16:12 NASB
Now he was ruddy, with beautiful eyes and a handsome appearance. And the LORD said, "Arise, anoint him; for this is he."

NAKITA, see Nikita

NALANI, Nalanee
Language/Cultural Origin: Hawaiian
Inherent Meaning: Calm as the Heavens
Spiritual Connotation: Discerning
Scripture: Isaiah 55:9 RSV
For as the heavens are higher than the earth, so are my ways higher than your ways and my thoughts than your thoughts.

NANCY, Nan, Nana, Nancee, Nanci, Nancie, Nanette, Nanna
Language/Cultural Origin: English
Inherent Meaning: Grace
Spiritual Connotation: Gracious
Scripture: Psalm 145:9 NRSV
The LORD is good to all, and his compassion is over all that he has made.

NANI, Nanie
Language/Cultural Origin: Hawaiian
Inherent Meaning: Beautiful

Spiritual Connotation: Lovely
Scripture: Romans 10:15 NRSV
*How beautiful are the feet of those who
bring good news!*

NAOMI, Naomie, Neomi
Language/Cultural Origin: Hebrew
Inherent Meaning: Delightful Renewal
Spiritual Connotation: Trusting
Scripture: Psalm 52:8 NKJV
*But I am like a green olive tree in the
house of God; I trust in the mercy of
God forever and ever.*

NAPHTALI, Naftali,
Naftalie, Naphtalie
Language/Cultural Origin: Hebrew
Inherent Meaning: Struggle
Spiritual Connotation: Seeker of Truth
Scripture: Genesis 32:24 NASB
*Then Jacob was left alone, and a man
wrestled with him until daybreak.*

NAPOLEON, Nap, Napoléon
Language/Cultural Origin: Greek
Inherent Meaning: Lion of the Woodland
Spiritual Connotation: Bold
Scripture: Proverbs 28:1 NKJV
*The wicked flee when no one pursues,
but the righteous are bold as a lion.*

NARA, Narra (see also Naaria, Narah)
Language/Cultural Origin: Japanese
Inherent Meaning: Oak
Spiritual Connotation: Holy
Scripture: Joshua 24:26 NKJV
*Then Joshua wrote these words in the Book
of the Law of God. And he took a large
stone, and set it up there under the oak
that was by the sanctuary of the LORD.*

NARAH, Naara, Naari
(see also Naaria, Nara)
Language/Cultural Origin: Hebrew
Inherent Meaning: Young Woman
Spiritual Connotation: Respectful
Scripture: 1 Timothy 5:2 NLT
*Treat the older women as you would your
mother, and treat the younger women with
all purity as your own sisters.*

NARI, Naree
Language/Cultural Origin: Japanese

Inherent Meaning: Thunder
Spiritual Connotation: Attentive
Scripture: Job 37:2 NCV
*Listen! Listen to the thunder of God's voice
and to the rumbling that comes from his
mouth.*

NARIKO, Nareeko
Language/Cultural Origin: Japanese
Inherent Meaning: Humble Child
Spiritual Connotation: Righteous
Scripture: Proverbs 23:24 NRSV
*The father of the righteous will greatly
rejoice; he who begets a wise son will be glad
in him.*

NASSER, Nassar, Nassor
Language/Cultural Origin: Middle Eastern
Inherent Meaning: Victorious
Spiritual Connotation: Delivered
Scripture: Psalm 60:5 NRSV
*Give victory with your right hand, and
answer us, so that those whom you love may
be rescued.*

NATALIE, Natalea, Natalee, Natali,
Natalia, Nataliana, Natalina,
Natallia, Natalya, Nattalie
Language/Cultural Origin: Latin
Inherent Meaning: Christmas Child
Spiritual Connotation: God's Gift of Joy
Scripture: Psalm 9:2 NKJV
*I will be glad and rejoice in You; I will sing
praise to Your name, O Most High.*

NATANIA, Nathania
Language/Cultural Origin: Hebrew
Inherent Meaning: Gift of God
Spiritual Connotation: Righteous
Scripture: Psalm 119:11 NASB
*Thy word I have treasured in my heart, that I
may not sin against Thee.*

NATARA, Natarra (see also Nitara)
Language/Cultural Origin: Middle Eastern
Inherent Meaning: Sacrifice
Spiritual Connotation: Generous
Scripture: Philippians 4:18 NKJV
*I am full, having received . . . the things sent
from you, a sweet-smelling aroma, an
acceptable sacrifice, well pleasing to God.*

NATASHA, Natachia, Natacia, Natascha, Natashah, Natashia, Natasia, Nathasha, Nitasha (see also Tasha)
Language/Cultural Origin: Russian
Inherent Meaning: Christmas Child
Spiritual Connotation: Innocent
Scripture: Matthew 18:3 NRSV
Truly I tell you, unless you change and become like children, you will never enter the kingdom of heaven.

NATHANIEL, Nat, Natan, Nataniel,
☞**Nate, Nathan, Nathanael, Nathaneal, Nathanial, Nathann, Nathanyal, Nathanyel, Nathen, Nathon, Natt, Naython, Nethanial, Nethanyal**
Language/Cultural Origin: Hebrew
Inherent Meaning: Gift of God
Spiritual Connotation: Victorious
Scripture: 1 Corinthians 15:57 NRSV
But thanks be to God, who gives us the victory through our Lord Jesus Christ.

NATIFA, Nateefah, Natifah
Language/Cultural Origin: Middle Eastern
Inherent Meaning: Untainted
Spiritual Connotation: Pure
Scripture: Ephesians 5:27 NCV
He died so that he could give the church to himself like a bride in all her beauty. He died so that the church could be pure and without fault.

NAVIN, Navan, Naven (see also Nevan)
Language/Cultural Origin: Indo-Pakistani
Inherent Meaning: New
Spiritual Connotation: Regenerated
Scripture: 2 Corinthians 5:17 NRSV
So if anyone is in Christ, there is a new creation: everything old has passed away; see, everything has become new!

NED, Nedd, Nedra
Language/Cultural Origin: English
Inherent Meaning: Guardian
Spiritual Connotation: Preserved
Scripture: Philippians 4:7 RSV
And the peace of God, which passes all understanding, will keep your hearts and your minds in Christ Jesus.

NEHEMIAH, Nehmiah
☞Language/Cultural Origin: Hebrew
Inherent Meaning: God Comforts
Spiritual Connotation: Righteous
Scripture: 2 Corinthians 1:4 NCV
He comforts us every time we have trouble, so when others have trouble, we can comfort them with the same comfort God gives us.

NEIL, Neal, Neale, Nealon, Neile, Neill, Neilon
Language/Cultural Origin: Irish
Inherent Meaning: Champion
Spiritual Connotation: Beloved
Scripture: 1 John 4:7 NKJV
Beloved, let us love one another, for love is of God; and everyone who loves is born of God and knows God.

NELLIE, Nel, Nell, Nelle, Nellee, Nelley, Nelli
Language/Cultural Origin: English
Inherent Meaning: Shining
Spiritual Connotation: Witness
Scripture: Isaiah 60:3 NKJV
The Gentiles shall come to your light, and kings to the brightness of your rising.

NELSON, Neilson, Nelsen, Nilsson
Language/Cultural Origin: English
Inherent Meaning: Son of the Champion
Spiritual Connotation: Honored
Scripture: Isaiah 33:15–16 NASB
He who walks righteously, and speaks with sincerity, He who rejects unjust gain . . . His bread will be given him; His water will be sure.

NERIAH, Neri, Neria, Neriya, Nerriah (see also Nuria)
Language/Cultural Origin: Hebrew
Inherent Meaning: Light of the Lord
Spiritual Connotation: Witness
Scripture: Matthew 5:14 NKJV
You are the light of the world. A city that is set on a hill cannot be hidden.

NERISSA, Narissa
Language/Cultural Origin: English
Inherent Meaning: Sea Nymph
Spiritual Connotation: Expectant
Scripture: Luke 21:31 NKJV

So you also, when you see these things happening, know that the kingdom of God is near.

NESS, Nes
Language/Cultural Origin: Hebrew
Inherent Meaning: Miracle
Spiritual Connotation: Act of God
Scripture: Acts 14:3 NKJV
Therefore they stayed there a long time, speaking boldly in the Lord, who was . . . granting signs and wonders to be done by their hands.

NEVA, Neyva
Language/Cultural Origin: English
Inherent Meaning: New
Spiritual Connotation: Obedient Spirit
Scripture: Psalm 119:2 NKJV
Blessed are those who keep His testimonies, who seek Him with the whole heart!

**NEVAN, Neven, Nevin, Nevon
(see also Navin)**
Language/Cultural Origin: Irish
Inherent Meaning: Holy
Spiritual Connotation: Righteous
Scripture: 2 Corinthians 7:1 NRSV
Let us cleanse ourselves from every defilement of body and of spirit, making holiness perfect in the fear of God.

NEVILLE, Nevil, Nevile, Nevill
Language/Cultural Origin: Old French
Inherent Meaning: From the New Town
Spiritual Connotation: Compassionate Spirit
Scripture: Zechariah 7:9 TLB
Tell them to be honest and fair—and not to take bribes—and to be merciful and kind to everyone.

NEWELL, Newall
Language/Cultural Origin: Middle English
Inherent Meaning: From the New Hall
Spiritual Connotation: Sincere
Scripture: Isaiah 58:14 NRSV
Then you shall take delight in the LORD, and I will make you ride upon the heights of the earth.

NEWTON, Newtyn
Language/Cultural Origin: Middle English
Inherent Meaning: From the New Town

Spiritual Connotation: Helpful Counselor
Scripture: Proverbs 20:5 NKJV
Counsel in the heart of man is like deep water, but a man of understanding will draw it out.

NEYLAN, Neyla, Neylen
Language/Cultural Origin: Turkish
Inherent Meaning: Granted Wish
Spiritual Connotation: Made Whole
Scripture: Luke 9:11 NCV
But the people learned where Jesus went and followed him. He welcomed them and talked with them about God's kingdom and healed those who needed to be healed.

NICHOLAS, see Nicolas

**NICOLE, Nichola, Nichole, Nicholette, Nicholle, Nicki, Nickie, Nickola, Nickole, Nicky, Nicolette, Nicolle, Nicolyn, Niki, Nikkey, Nikki, Nikkie, Nikkola, Nikkole, Nikkolette, Nikky, Nikola, Nikole, Nikolette, Nikolle, Nikolyn, Niquole, Nykola
(see also Colette, Nikita)**
Language/Cultural Origin: French
Inherent Meaning: Victory of the People
Spiritual Connotation: Overcomer
Scripture: Revelation 2:7 NRSV
To everyone who conquers, I will give permission to eat from the tree of life that is in the paradise of God.

**NICOLAS, Nic, Niccolas, Nichalas,
☞Nicholas, Nicholsen, Nicholson, Nick, Nickey, Nickolas, Nickolaus, Nickolus, Nicky, Nicolaas, Nicolai, Nicolás, Nicolo, Nik, Niki, Nikk, Nikki, Niklas, Niklaus, Niklos, Nikolaas, Nikolai, Nikolas, Nikolaus, Nikoli, Nikolos, Nycholas, Nykolas (see also Nikita)**
Language/Cultural Origin: Greek
Inherent Meaning: Victory of the People
Spiritual Connotation: Triumphant Spirit
Scripture: 1 Corinthians 15:57 RSV
But thanks be to God, who gives us the victory through our Lord Jesus Christ.

NIESHA, Neisha, Neishia, Nesha, Neshia, Nisha
Language/Cultural Origin: Hebrew

Inherent Meaning: Sign
Spiritual Connotation: Glorious Manifestation
Scripture: Luke 2:12 NRSV
This will be a sign for you: you will find a child wrapped in bands of cloth and lying in a manger.

NIGEL, Niegel, Nigell, Nijel, Nygel
Language/Cultural Origin: Latin
Inherent Meaning: Champion
Spiritual Connotation: Adventurous Spirit
Scripture: 2 Corinthians 2:14 NASB
But thanks be to God, who always leads us in His triumph in Christ.

NIKA, Neika
Language/Cultural Origin: Russian
Inherent Meaning: Belonging to God
Spiritual Connotation: Purchased
Scripture: 1 Corinthians 6:19 NRSV
Or do you not know that your body is a temple of the Holy Spirit within you, which you have from God, and that you are not your own?

NIKITA, Nakeeta, Nakita, Nakkita, Nakyta, Nikkita, Naquita, Niquita
Language/Cultural Origin: Russian
Inherent Meaning: Victory of the People
Spiritual Connotation: Eternal Hope
Scripture: 1 Thessalonians 4:17 NKJV
Then we . . . shall be caught up together with them in the clouds to meet the Lord in the air. And thus we shall always be with the Lord.

NILS, Niels, Niles
Language/Cultural Origin: Scandinavian
Inherent Meaning: Champion
Spiritual Connotation: Triumphant
Scripture: Zechariah 9:9 TLB
Rejoice greatly, O my people! Shout with joy! For look—your King is coming! He is the Righteous One, the Victor!

NIMROD
Language/Cultural Origin: Hebrew
Inherent Meaning: Rebel
Spiritual Connotation: Mighty
Scripture: Genesis 10:9 NRSV
He was a mighty hunter before the LORD.

NINA, Neena, Neenah, Ninah
Language/Cultural Origin: English

Inherent Meaning: Grace of God
Spiritual Connotation: Delivered
Scripture: 2 Corinthians 2:14 RSV
But thanks be to God, who in Christ always leads us in triumph, and through us spreads the fragrance of the knowledge of him everywhere.

NIRAN, Nieran
Language/Cultural Origin: Thai
Inherent Meaning: Eternal
Spiritual Connotation: Gift of Faith
Scripture: 2 Corinthians 4:18 NCV
We set our eyes not on what we see but on what we cannot see. . . . What we cannot see will last forever.

NISHAN, Nishana, Nissim
Language/Cultural Origin: Armenian
Inherent Meaning: Miracle
Spiritual Connotation: Spirit-Filled
Scripture: Galatians 3:5 NASB
Does He then, who provides you with the Spirit and works miracles among you, do it by the works of the Law, or by hearing with faith?

NITA, Nitika (see also Anita)
Language/Cultural Origin: Hebrew
Inherent Meaning: Planter
Spiritual Connotation: Sower of Truth
Scripture: Luke 8:15 NCV
And the seed that fell on the good ground is like those who hear God's teaching with good, honest hearts and obey it and patiently produce good fruit.

NITARA, Nitarah (see also Natara)
Language/Cultural Origin: Indo-Pakistani
Inherent Meaning: Deeply Rooted
Spiritual Connotation: Steadfast
Scripture: Psalm 1:3 NRSV
They are like trees planted by streams of water, which yield their fruit in its season, and their leaves do not wither.

NIXON, Nickson, Nikson, Nixson
Language/Cultural Origin: English
Inherent Meaning: Son of the Victor
Spiritual Connotation: Overcomer
Scripture: Romans 8:37 RSV
No, in all these things we are more than conquerors through him who loved us.

NIZANA, Nizanna
Language/Cultural Origin: Hebrew
Inherent Meaning: Flower Bud
Spiritual Connotation: Joyful
Scripture: Isaiah 35:1 NKJV
The wilderness and the wasteland shall be glad for them, and the desert shall rejoice and blossom as the rose.

NOAH, Noé
☞ Language/Cultural Origin: Hebrew
Inherent Meaning: Peaceful
Spiritual Connotation: Provider of Comfort
Scripture: Nahum 1:7 NASB
The LORD is good, a stronghold in the day of trouble, and He knows those who take refuge in Him.

NOAM, Noame
Language/Cultural Origin: Hebrew
Inherent Meaning: Friend
Spiritual Connotation: Chosen
Scripture: Isaiah 41:8 TLB
But as for you, O Israel, you are mine, my chosen ones; for you are Abraham's family, and he was my friend.

NOEL, Noél, Noël, Noela, Noele, Noelia, Noell, Noella, Noelle
Language/Cultural Origin: Latin
Inherent Meaning: Christmas Child
Spiritual Connotation: Precious Gift
Scripture: Isaiah 9:6 NKJV
For unto us a Child is born, unto us a Son is given. . . . And His name will be called Wonderful, Counselor, Mighty God, Everlasting Father, Prince of Peace.

NOKOMIS, Nokomas
Language/Cultural Origin: Dakota
Inherent Meaning: Moon Child
Spiritual Connotation: Great Promise
Scripture: Isaiah 30:26 NRSV
Moreover the light of the moon will be like the light of the sun . . . on the day when the LORD binds up the injuries of his people.

NOLA, Nuala
Language/Cultural Origin: Latin
Inherent Meaning: Small Bell
Spiritual Connotation: Harmonious
Scripture: Proverbs 25:11 TLB
Timely advice is as lovely as gold apples in a silver basket.

NOLAN, Noland, Nolyn
Language/Cultural Origin: Gaelic
Inherent Meaning: Noble
Spiritual Connotation: Honorable
Scripture: Micah 6:8 NKJV
He has shown you, O man, what is good; and what does the LORD require of you but to do justly, to love mercy, and to walk humbly with your God?

NONA, Nonah, Noni, Nonie, Nonna, Nony, Nonya
Language/Cultural Origin: Latin
Inherent Meaning: Ninth
Spiritual Connotation: Full of Wisdom
Scripture: Proverbs 2:6 NRSV
For the LORD gives wisdom; from his mouth come knowledge and understanding.

NORA, Norah, Nordia
Language/Cultural Origin: Greek
Inherent Meaning: Light
Spiritual Connotation: Esteemed
Scripture: Isaiah 30:21 NASB
Your ears will hear a word behind you [which says] this is the way, walk in it.

NORI, Noria
Language/Cultural Origin: Japanese
Inherent Meaning: Tradition
Spiritual Connotation: Honored
Scripture: Exodus 31:16 TLB
Work six days only, for the seventh day is a special day to remind you of my covenant— a weekly reminder forever of my promises to the people of Israel.

NORMA, Noma
Language/Cultural Origin: Latin
Inherent Meaning: Perfection
Spiritual Connotation: Model of Excellence
Scripture: 1 Timothy 4:14 NRSV
Do not neglect the gift that is in you, which was given to you through prophecy with the laying on of hands by the council of elders.

NORMAN, Norm, Normand, Normen, Normie
Language/Cultural Origin: Old English
Inherent Meaning: Man From the North
Spiritual Connotation: Courageous Spirit
Scripture: Psalm 17:7 NLT

Show me your unfailing love in wonderful ways. You save with your strength those who seek refuge from their enemies.

NORRIS, Noris

Language/Cultural Origin: Old English
Inherent Meaning: Northerner
Spiritual Connotation: Wise
Scripture: Psalm 111:10 RSV

The fear of the LORD is the beginning of wisdom; a good understanding have all those who practice it. His praise endures for ever!

NORTON, Nortan

Language/Cultural Origin: Middle English
Inherent Meaning: From the North Town
Spiritual Connotation: Integrity
Scripture: Psalm 42:8 KJV

Yet the LORD will command his lovingkindness in the daytime, and in the night his song shall be with me, and my prayer unto the God of my life.

NORWOOD, Norrwood

Language/Cultural Origin: Middle English
Inherent Meaning: From the North Forest
Spiritual Connotation: Noble
Scripture: Philippians 3:14 TLB

I strain to reach the end of the race and receive the prize for which God is calling us up to heaven because of what Christ Jesus did for us.

NOVIA, Nuvia

Language/Cultural Origin: Spanish
Inherent Meaning: Sweetheart
Spiritual Connotation: Beloved
Scripture: 1 John 3:1 NKJV

Behold what manner of love the Father has bestowed on us, that we should be called children of God!

NURI, Nurie, Nury

Language/Cultural Origin: Hebrew
Inherent Meaning: Fire of God
Spiritual Connotation: Guided of God
Scripture: Exodus 13:21 NASB

The LORD was going before them in a pillar of cloud by day to lead them on the way, and in a pillar of fire by night to give them light.

NURIA, Noura, Nura, Nuriah, Nuriel, Nuriya (see also Neriah)

Language/Cultural Origin: Aramaic
Inherent Meaning: Fire of God
Spiritual Connotation: Dependent Upon God
Scripture: Numbers 14:14 NCV

The Egyptians will tell this to those who live in this land.... They know that ... you lead your people ... with fire at night.

NYDIA, Nydya (see also Nadia)

Language/Cultural Origin: Latin
Inherent Meaning: Nest
Spiritual Connotation: Spiritual Potential
Scripture: Colossians 3:12 NASB

And so, as those who have been chosen of God, holy and beloved, put on a heart of compassion, kindness, humility, gentleness and patience.

NYUSHA, Nyasha

Language/Cultural Origin: Russian
Inherent Meaning: Pure
Spiritual Connotation: Patient
Scripture: 1 Peter 1:7 NLT

These trials are only to test your faith, to show that it is strong and pure.

OCTAVIUS, Octavian, Octavio, Octavien, Octavious
Language/Cultural Origin: Latin
Inherent Meaning: Eighth
Spiritual Connotation: Abiding Place of God
Scripture: Psalm 18:28 NKJV
For You will light my lamp; the LORD my God will enlighten my darkness.

ODELIA, Odeleya
Language/Cultural Origin: Hebrew
Inherent Meaning: I Will Praise God
Spiritual Connotation: Thankful Spirit
Scripture: Luke 19:40 RSV
I tell you, if these were silent, the very stones would cry out.

OAKLEY, Oaklee, Oakleigh
Language/Cultural Origin: Old English
Inherent Meaning: From the Oak Trees
Spiritual Connotation: Immovable
Scripture: Psalm 1:3 NASB
And he will be like a tree firmly planted by streams of water. . . . And in whatever he does, he prospers.

ODELL, Odie
Language/Cultural Origin: Middle English
Inherent Meaning: From the Wooded Hill
Spiritual Connotation: Hopeful
Scripture: Psalm 119:114 NRSV
You are my hiding place and my shield; I hope in your word.

OBADIAH, Obediah
☞ Language/Cultural Origin: Hebrew
Inherent Meaning: Servant of God
Spiritual Connotation: Discerning
Scripture: Romans 12:2 NRSV
Do not be conformed to this world, but be transformed by the renewing of your minds.

ODESSA, Odyssa
Language/Cultural Origin: Greek
Inherent Meaning: Long Voyage
Spiritual Connotation: Preserved
Scripture: 2 Corinthians 11:26 TLB
I have traveled many weary miles. . . . I have faced grave dangers from mobs in the cities and from death in the deserts and in the stormy seas and from men who claim to be brothers in Christ but are not.

OCEANA, Ocean
Language/Cultural Origin: Greek
Inherent Meaning: Sea
Spiritual Connotation: Praise
Scripture: Psalm 65:5 NASB
By awesome deeds You answer us in righteousness, O God of our salvation, You who are the trust of all the ends of the earth and of the farthest sea.

ODYSSEUS, Odesseus
Language/Cultural Origin: Greek
Inherent Meaning: Wrathful
Spiritual Connotation: Righteous
Scripture: Isaiah 26:20 NLT
Go home, my people, and lock your doors! Hide until the Lord's anger against your enemies has passed.

OCTAVIA, Octivia
Language/Cultural Origin: Latin
Inherent Meaning: Eighth
Spiritual Connotation: Abiding Place of God
Scripture: Psalm 23:6 KJV
Surely goodness and mercy shall follow me all the days of my life: and I will dwell in the house of the LORD for ever.

OGDEN, Ogdan
Language/Cultural Origin: Old English
Inherent Meaning: From the Oak Valley
Spiritual Connotation: One of Dignity
Scripture: Psalm 92:12 KJV
The righteous shall flourish like the palm tree: he shall grow like a cedar in Lebanon.

OKALANI, Okilani

Language/Cultural Origin: Hawaiian
Inherent Meaning: Heavenly
Spiritual Connotation: Eternal
Scripture: Colossians 3:2 NKJV
Set your mind on things above, not on things on the earth.

OLAF, Ole, Olav, Olie, Olle

Language/Cultural Origin: Old Norse
Inherent Meaning: Ancestor
Spiritual Connotation: Protector
Scripture: Psalm 18:2 RSV
The LORD is my rock, and my fortress, and my deliverer, my God, my rock, in whom I take refuge, my shield, and the horn of my salvation, my stronghold.

OLAJUWON, Olajuwan

Language/Cultural Origin: Nigerian
Inherent Meaning: Honor of God
Spiritual Connotation: Reverent
Scripture: Daniel 2:20 NLT
Praise the name of God forever and ever, for he alone has all wisdom and power.

OLEG, Olleg

Language/Cultural Origin: Latvian
Inherent Meaning: Holy
Spiritual Connotation: Unending Praise
Scripture: Revelation 4:8 NRSV
Day and night without ceasing they sing, Holy, holy, holy, the Lord God the Almighty, who was and is and is to come.

OLESIA, Olesha, Olésya

Language/Cultural Origin: Polish
Inherent Meaning: Defender
Spiritual Connotation: Protector of Truth
Scripture: 1 Timothy 6:20 NRSV
Guard what has been entrusted to you. Avoid the profane chatter and contradictions of what is falsely called knowledge.

OLGA, Olya

Language/Cultural Origin: Scandinavian
Inherent Meaning: Holy
Spiritual Connotation: Wise
Scripture: Proverbs 15:33 NKJV
The fear of the LORD is the instruction of wisdom, and before honor is humility.

OLIANA, Olianna

Language/Cultural Origin: Hawaiian
Inherent Meaning: Flowering Evergreen
Spiritual Connotation: Preserved
Scripture: Hosea 14:8 TLB
I look after you and care for you. I am like an evergreen tree, yielding my fruit to you throughout the year. My mercies never fail.

OLIVER, Olley, Ollie, Olliver

Language/Cultural Origin: Old Norse
Inherent Meaning: Kind and Affectionate
Spiritual Connotation: Bringer of Peace
Scripture: Psalm 23:1 KJV
The LORD is my shepherd; I shall not want. He maketh me to lie down in green pastures: he leadeth me beside the still waters.

OLIVIA, Olive, Olivea, Olyvia (see also Livia)

Language/Cultural Origin: Latin
Inherent Meaning: Peace
Spiritual Connotation: Walks With God
Scripture: Matthew 13:44 NCV
The kingdom of heaven is like a treasure hidden in a field. One day a man found the treasure. . . . He was so happy that he went and sold everything he owned to buy that field.

OLUJIMI, Oluyimi

Language/Cultural Origin: Nigerian
Inherent Meaning: Given by God
Spiritual Connotation: Righteous
Scripture: Isaiah 42:6 NRSV
I am the LORD, I have called you in righteousness, I have taken you by the hand and kept you; I have given you as a covenant to the people, a light to the nations.

OLYA, Ollya

Language/Cultural Origin: Russian
Inherent Meaning: Holy
Spiritual Connotation: High Praise
Scripture: Isaiah 6:3 NLT
In a great chorus they sang, Holy, holy, holy is the LORD Almighty! The whole earth is filled with his glory!

OLYMPIA, Olympa

Language/Cultural Origin: Greek
Inherent Meaning: Heavenly
Spiritual Connotation: Beloved
Scripture: Psalm 103:11 NKJV

*For as the heavens are high above the earth,
so great is His mercy toward those who fear
Him.*

OMA, Omah

Language/Cultural Origin: Hebrew
Inherent Meaning: Eloquent
Spiritual Connotation: Voice of God
Scripture: 1 Corinthians 1:17 NIV

*For Christ did not send me to baptize, but
to preach the gospel—not with words
of human wisdom.*

OMAR, Omarr

☞ Language/Cultural Origin: Hebrew
Inherent Meaning: Eloquent
Spiritual Connotation: Successful
Scripture: Romans 8:37 NKJV

*Yet in all these things we are more than
conquerors through Him who loved us.*

ONA

Language/Cultural Origin: Lithuanian
Inherent Meaning: Grace of God
Spiritual Connotation: Viewed With Favor
Scripture: Matthew 13:43 NRSV

*Then the righteous will shine like the
sun in the kingdom of their Father. Let
anyone with ears listen!*

ONI, Onii

Language/Cultural Origin: Nigerian
Inherent Meaning: Born on Holy Ground
Spiritual Connotation: Sacred
Scripture: Exodus 3:5 NRSV

*Then he said, "Come no closer! Remove the
sandals from your feet, for the place on
which you are standing is holy ground."*

OONA, see Una

OPAL, Opall

Language/Cultural Origin: Sanskrit
Inherent Meaning: Jewel
Spiritual Connotation: Treasure
Scripture: Malachi 3:17 NKJV

*"They shall be Mine," says the LORD of hosts,
"On the day that I make them My jewels."*

OPHELIA, Ophilia

Language/Cultural Origin: Greek
Inherent Meaning: Helper
Spiritual Connotation: Consecrated

Scripture: 2 Corinthians 3:18 NKJV

*But we all, with unveiled face, beholding as
in a mirror the glory of the Lord, are being
transformed into the same image from glory
to glory.*

OPRAH, see Orpah

ORA, Orah

Language/Cultural Origin: Latin
Inherent Meaning: Prayerful
Spiritual Connotation: Precious
Scripture: 1 John 4:7 NKJV

*Beloved, let us love one another, for love is of
God; and everyone who loves is born of God
and knows God.*

ORAN, Orane (see also Orin)

Language/Cultural Origin: Irish
Inherent Meaning: Green
Spiritual Connotation: Fruitful
Scripture: Jeremiah 17:8 NKJV

*For he shall be like a tree planted by the
waters, which spreads out its roots by the
river. . . . Its leaf will be green.*

OREN, Oreen (see also Orin)

☞ Language/Cultural Origin: Hebrew
Inherent Meaning: Ash Tree
Spiritual Connotation: Blessed
Scripture: Psalm 1:3 NASB

*And he will be like a tree firmly planted by
streams of water, which yields its fruit in its
season, and its leaf does not wither; and in
whatever he does, he prospers.*

ORESTES, Orastes

Language/Cultural Origin: Greek
Inherent Meaning: From the Mountain
Spiritual Connotation: Peaceful
Scripture: Isaiah 56:7 NLT

*I will bring them also to my holy mountain
of Jerusalem and will fill them with joy in my
house of prayer.*

ORIANA, Orania, Oriane, Oriann, Orianna

Language/Cultural Origin: Latin
Inherent Meaning: Dawning Sun
Spiritual Connotation: Enlightened for Service
Scripture: Ephesians 6:7 NKJV

*Whatever good anyone does, he will receive
the same from the Lord, whether he is a
slave or free.*

ORIN, Orinn, Orrie, Orrin (see also Oran, Oren)
Language/Cultural Origin: Greek
Inherent Meaning: Mountain
Spiritual Connotation: God-Revealed Insight
Scripture: 2 Peter 1:18 NKJV
And we heard this voice which came from heaven when we were with Him on the holy mountain.

ORION, Orien
Language/Cultural Origin: Greek
Inherent Meaning: Son of Fire
Spiritual Connotation: Zealous
Scripture: Psalm 104:4 NCV
You make the winds your messengers, and flames of fire are your servants.

ORLANDO, Orlanda, Orlondo
Language/Cultural Origin: Italian
Inherent Meaning: Famous Throughout the Land
Spiritual Connotation: Reknowned
Scripture: James 4:10 NASB
Humble yourselves in the presence of the Lord, and He will exalt you.

ORLI, Ori, Orlie
Language/Cultural Origin: Hebrew
Inherent Meaning: My Light
Spiritual Connotation: Fearless
Scripture: Psalm 27:1 NKJV
The LORD is my light and my salvation; whom shall I fear? The LORD is the strength of my life; of whom shall I be afraid?

ORPAH, Ophra, Opra, Oprah
Language/Cultural Origin: Hebrew
Inherent Meaning: Runaway
Spiritual Connotation: Chaste
Scripture: 1 Corinthians 6:18 NKJV
Flee sexual immorality. Every sin that a man does is outside the body, but he who commits sexual immorality sins against his own body.

ORRICK, Orric, Orrik
Language/Cultural Origin: English
Inherent Meaning: Aged Oak Tree
Spiritual Connotation: Great Joy
Scripture: Isaiah 55:12 NRSV
For you shall go out in joy, and be led back in peace . . . and all the trees of the field shall clap their hands.

ORSON, Orsen
Language/Cultural Origin: Latin
Inherent Meaning: Little Bear
Spiritual Connotation: Loyal, Steadfast
Scripture: 1 Corinthians 15:58 RSV
Be steadfast, immovable, always abounding in the work of the Lord, knowing that in the Lord your labor is not in vain.

ORVILLE, Orv, Orval
Language/Cultural Origin: French
Inherent Meaning: From the Golden Town
Spiritual Connotation: Benevolent
Scripture: 2 Corinthians 9:6 NKJV
But this I say: He who sows sparingly will also reap sparingly, and he who sows bountifully will also reap bountifully.

OSANNA, Osana (see also Hosanna)
Language/Cultural Origin: Hebrew
Inherent Meaning: Save Us
Spiritual Connotation: Remnant
Scripture: Psalm 102:18 NRSV
Let this be recorded for a generation to come, so that a people yet unborn may praise the LORD.

OSBORN, Osborne
Language/Cultural Origin: English
Inherent Meaning: Divine Warrior
Spiritual Connotation: Victorious in Truth
Scripture: Isaiah 61:2-3 NRSV
To proclaim the year of the Lord's favor . . . to comfort all who mourn . . . to give them the oil of gladness instead of mourning. . . . They will . . . display his glory.

OSCAR, Oskar
Language/Cultural Origin: Old English
Inherent Meaning: Divine Spearman
Spiritual Connotation: Appointed of God
Scripture: Colossians 3:23 RSV
Whatever your task, work heartily, as serving the Lord and not men.

OSMOND, Osmund
Language/Cultural Origin: Old English
Inherent Meaning: Divine Protector
Spiritual Connotation: God's Warrior
Scripture: Psalm 5:11 NRSV
But let all who take refuge in you rejoice; let them ever sing for joy. Spread your protection over them, so that those who love your name may exult in you.

OSWALD, Osvaldo, Oswaldo

Language/Cultural Origin: English
Inherent Meaning: God's Power
Spiritual Connotation: Honored
Scripture: Psalm 77:11 NRSV

I will call to mind the deeds of the LORD; I will remember your wonders of old.

OTHELLO, Othella

Language/Cultural Origin: Spanish
Inherent Meaning: Wealthy
Spiritual Connotation: Obedient
Scripture: Joshua 1:8 NKJV

This Book of the Law shall not depart from your mouth, but you shall meditate in it day and night. . . . For then you will make your way prosperous. . . .

OTIS, Ottis

Language/Cultural Origin: Greek
Inherent Meaning: Keen of Hearing
Spiritual Connotation: Open to Divine Inspiration
Scripture: Psalm 46:10 NKJV

Be still, and know that I am God; I will be exalted among the nations, I will be exalted in the earth!

OTTO, Oto

Language/Cultural Origin: German
Inherent Meaning: Prosperous
Spiritual Connotation: Esteemed
Scripture: Jeremiah 29:11 NLT

For I know the plans I have for you, says the LORD. They are plans for good and not for disaster, to give you a future and a hope.

OURAY, Orray

Language/Cultural Origin: Cherokee
Inherent Meaning: Arrow
Spiritual Connotation: Guardian of Truth
Scripture: Isaiah 54:17 NKJV

No weapon formed against you shall prosper, and every tongue which rises against you in judgment You shall condemn.

OWEN, Owens

Language/Cultural Origin: Greek
Inherent Meaning: Distinguished
Spiritual Connotation: Pleasant to Look Upon
Scripture: 2 Samuel 23:4 NKJV

And he shall be like the light of the morning when the sun rises, a morning without clouds, like the tender grass springing out of the earth, by clear shining after rain.

OXFORD, Oxforde

Language/Cultural Origin: Old English
Inherent Meaning: From the Place Where the Oxen Cross the River
Spiritual Connotation: Restful
Scripture: Matthew 11:28, 30 NRSV

Come to me, all you that are weary and are carrying heavy burdens, and I will give you rest. For my yoke is easy, and my burden is light.

OYA, Oiya

Language/Cultural Origin: Miwok
Inherent Meaning: Called Forth
Spiritual Connotation: Witness
Scripture: Acts 10:42 NLT

And he ordered us to preach everywhere and to testify that Jesus is ordained of God to be the judge of all—the living and the dead.

OZ, Ozz, Ozzey, Ozzi, Ozzie

Language/Cultural Origin: Hebrew
Inherent Meaning: Courage
Spiritual Connotation: Overcomer
Scripture: John 16:33 NRSV

I have said this to you, so that in me you may have peace. In the world you face persecution. But take courage; I have conquered the world!

OZARA, Ozarra

Language/Cultural Origin: Hebrew
Inherent Meaning: Treasure
Spiritual Connotation: Divine Perspective
Scripture: Matthew 6:21 KJV

For where your treasure is, there will your heart be also.

PABLO, Paublo

Language/Cultural Origin: Spanish
Inherent Meaning: Small
Spiritual Connotation: Great Faith
Scripture: Mark 4:31–32 NCV

The kingdom of God is like a mustard seed, the smallest seed you plant in the ground. But when planted, this seed grows and becomes the largest of all garden plants.

PAIGE, Page, Payge

Language/Cultural Origin: French
Inherent Meaning: Young Assistant
Spiritual Connotation: Blessed Helper
Scripture: Philippians 2:13 RSV

For God is at work in you, both to will and to work for his good pleasure.

PALANI, Pallani

Language/Cultural Origin: Hawaiian
Inherent Meaning: Free
Spiritual Connotation: Unchained
Scripture: John 8:36 NKJV

Therefore if the Son makes you free, you shall be free indeed.

PALASHA, Pasha, Pelasha

Language/Cultural Origin: Russian
Inherent Meaning: From the Sea
Spiritual Connotation: Protected
Scripture: Psalm 139:9–10 RSV

If I take the wings of the morning and dwell in the uttermost parts of the sea, even there thy hand shall lead me, and thy right hand shall hold me.

PALMER, Palmar

Language/Cultural Origin: Old English
Inherent Meaning: Peaceful Pilgrim
Spiritual Connotation: Bringer of Peace
Scripture: Zechariah 4:6 NASB

Not by might nor by power, but by My Spirit, says the LORD of hosts.

PALOMA, Palloma

Language/Cultural Origin: Spanish
Inherent Meaning: Dove
Spiritual Connotation: Symbol
Scripture: Luke 3:22 NKJV

And the Holy Spirit descended in bodily form like a dove upon Him, and a voice came from heaven which said, "You are My beloved Son; in You I am well pleased."

PAMELA, Pam, Pamala, Pamella, Pammela

Language/Cultural Origin: Greek
Inherent Meaning: Honey
Spiritual Connotation: Righteous
Scripture: Matthew 13:43 NRSV

Then the righteous will shine like the sun in the kingdom of their Father. Let anyone with ears listen!

PANCHO, Poncho

Language/Cultural Origin: Spanish
Inherent Meaning: Frenchman
Spiritual Connotation: God's Witness
Scripture: Daniel 7:27 NKJV

His kingdom is an everlasting kingdom, and all dominions shall serve and obey Him.

PANDORA, Pandorra, Panndora

Language/Cultural Origin: Greek
Inherent Meaning: Skilled
Spiritual Connotation: Gifted
Scripture: 1 Corinthians 12:4–5 NRSV

Now there are varieties of gifts, but the same Spirit; and there are varieties of services, but the same Lord.

PANYA, Pania

Language/Cultural Origin: Russian
Inherent Meaning: Crowned
Spiritual Connotation: Wise
Scripture: Proverbs 14:18 NASB

The naive inherit folly, but the prudent are crowned with knowledge.

PARI, Pári, Parri
Language/Cultural Origin: Persian
Inherent Meaning: Eagle
Spiritual Connotation: Renewed
Scripture: Isaiah 40:31 RSV
But they who wait for the LORD shall renew their strength, they shall mount up with wings like eagles, they shall run and not be weary, they shall walk and not faint.

PARIS, Parras, Parris
Language/Cultural Origin: Greek
Inherent Meaning: Attractive
Spiritual Connotation: Godly
Scripture: Psalm 27:4 NKJV
One thing I have desired of the LORD . . . that I may dwell in the house of the LORD all the days of my life, to behold the beauty of the LORD, and to inquire in His temple.

PARK, Parke
Language/Cultural Origin: Chinese
Inherent Meaning: Cyprus Tree
Spiritual Connotation: Blessed
Scripture: Isaiah 41:19–20 NKJV
I will set in the desert the cypress tree and the pine and the box tree together, that they may see and know . . . that the hand of the LORD has done this.

PARKER, Parkker
Language/Cultural Origin: Middle English
Inherent Meaning: Guardian of the Park
Spiritual Connotation: Spiritual Light
Scripture: Matthew 5:14 NASB
You are the light of the world. A city set on a hill cannot be hidden.

PARNELL, Parnel, Pernell
Language/Cultural Origin: French
Inherent Meaning: Little Peter
Spiritual Connotation: Faithfulness
Scripture: Lamentations 3:23 NLT
Great is his faithfulness; his mercies begin afresh each day.

PARRISH, Parish
Language/Cultural Origin: English
Inherent Meaning: From the Church District
Spiritual Connotation: Devout
Scripture: Hebrews 10:25 NCV
You should not stay away from the church meetings, as some are doing, but you should meet together and encourage each other.

PARRY, Parrey, Perry
Language/Cultural Origin: Welsh
Inherent Meaning: Son of the Leader
Spiritual Connotation: Humble
Scripture: Psalm 37:11 RSV
But the meek shall possess the land, and delight themselves in abundant prosperity.

PASCAL, Pascale, Paschale, Pascual, Pascuale
Language/Cultural Origin: French
Inherent Meaning: Easter Child
Spiritual Connotation: Resurrected
Scripture: Mark 16:6 NKJV
But he said to them, "Do not be alarmed. You seek Jesus of Nazareth, who was crucified. He is risen! He is not here. See the place where they laid Him."

PATIENCE, Paishence
Language/Cultural Origin: English
Inherent Meaning: Endurance, Fortitude
Spiritual Connotation: Firmness of Spirit
Scripture: Psalm 77:12 NASB
I will meditate on all Thy work, and muse on Thy deeds.

PATRICIA, Pat, Patreice, Patrice, Patriece, Patrisha, Patsey, Patsi, Patsy, Patti, Pattrice, Patty
Language/Cultural Origin: Latin
Inherent Meaning: Noble
Spiritual Connotation: Victorious
Scripture: Romans 8:37 NKJV
Yet in all these things we are more than conquerors through Him who loved us.

PATRICK, Pat, Patric, Patrique, Patrik, Patryck, Patryk
Language/Cultural Origin: Latin
Inherent Meaning: Nobleman
Spiritual Connotation: Obedient
Scripture: Romans 12:2 RSV
Do not be conformed to this world but be transformed by the renewal of your mind.

PATTON, Patten
Language/Cultural Origin: Old English
Inherent Meaning: From the Warrior's Town
Spiritual Connotation: Immovable
Scripture: Psalm 147:5 NRSV
Great is our Lord, and abundant in power; his understanding is beyond measure.

PAUL, Pasha, Pauley, Pauli, Paulis,
☞Paolo, Paulo, Paulus, Pavel
Language/Cultural Origin: Latin
Inherent Meaning: Small
Spiritual Connotation: Dynamo of
 Energy and Faith
Scripture: 2 Timothy 1:11 NRSV
 For this gospel I was appointed a herald
 and an apostle and a teacher, and for
 this reason I suffer as I do.

PAULA, Paola, Paolina, Paulette,
Paulina, Pauline, Paulla
Language/Cultural Origin: Latin
Inherent Meaning: Small
Spiritual Connotation: Loving
Scripture: John 15:12 NKJV
 This is My commandment, that you love
 one another as I have loved you.

PAXTON, Paxon, Paxten
Language/Cultural Origin: Old English
Inherent Meaning: From the Peaceful Town
Spiritual Connotation: Prepared
Scripture: Ephesians 6:15 NLT
 For shoes, put on the peace that comes
 from the Good News, so that you will
 be fully prepared.

PAYNE, Paine
Language/Cultural Origin: Latin
Inherent Meaning: From the Country
Spiritual Connotation: Sacred
Scripture: Psalm 99:9 NKJV
 Exalt the LORD our God, and worship at His
 holy hill; for the LORD our God is holy.

PAYTON, see Peyton

PEARL, Pearle
Language/Cultural Origin: Latin
Inherent Meaning: Priceless Jewel
Spiritual Connotation: Health and Long Life
Scripture: Jeremiah 29:11 NKJV
 For I know the thoughts that I think toward
 you, says the LORD, thoughts of peace and not
 of evil, to give you a future and a hope.

PEARSON, Pierson
Language/Cultural Origin: English
Inherent Meaning: Son of the Rock
Spiritual Connotation: Joyful Praise

Scripture: Deuteronomy 32:4 NKJV
 He is the Rock, His work is perfect; for all His
 ways are justice, a God of truth and without
 injustice; righteous and upright is He.

PEDRO, Pédro
Language/Cultural Origin: Spanish
Inherent Meaning: Rock
Spiritual Connotation: Steadfast in Christ
Scripture: 1 Corinthians 15:58 NRSV
 Be steadfast, immovable, always excelling in
 the work of the Lord, because you know that
 in the Lord your labor is not in vain.

PEGGY, Peg, Pegg, Peggi
Language/Cultural Origin: English
Inherent Meaning: Pearl
Spiritual Connotation: Promise
Scripture: Revelation 21:21 NASB
 And the twelve gates were twelve pearls; each
 one of the gates was a single pearl. And the
 street of the city was pure gold, like
 transparent glass.

PELE, Pelé, Peleh
Language/Cultural Origin: Hebrew
Inherent Meaning: Miracle
Spiritual Connotation: Strong Faith
Scripture: Micah 7:15 NASB
 As in the days when you came out from the
 land of Egypt, I will show you miracles.

PELI, Pelí
Language/Cultural Origin: Basque
Inherent Meaning: Happy
Spiritual Connotation: Filled With Joy
Scripture: Psalm 84:4 NRSV
 Happy are those who live in your house, ever
 singing your praise.

PENELOPE, Pennelope, Penney,
Penni, Pennie, Penny
Language/Cultural Origin: Greek
Inherent Meaning: Industrious Weaver
Spiritual Connotation: Creative Spirit
Scripture: Deuteronomy 28:12 RSV
 The LORD will open to you his good treasury
 the heavens ... to bless all the work of your
 hands.

PERCIVAL, Percivall, Percie,
Percy, Purcell
Language/Cultural Origin: Old French

Inherent Meaning: Pierce the Veil
Spiritual Connotation: Miracle
Scripture: Matthew 27:51 NLT
At that moment the curtain in the temple was torn in two, from top to bottom. The earth shook, rocks split apart.

PERKIN, Perkins, Perkyn, Perkyns
Language/Cultural Origin: English
Inherent Meaning: Little Rock
Spiritual Connotation: Joyful
Scripture: Psalm 95:1 NASB
O come, let us sing for joy to the LORD, let us shout joyfully to the rock of our salvation.

PERRY, see Parry

PERVIS, Purvis
Language/Cultural Origin: Latin
Inherent Meaning: Passage
Spiritual Connotation: Messenger
Scripture: Isaiah 40:3 NRSV
A voice cries out: In the wilderness prepare the way of the LORD, make straight in the desert a highway for our God.

PETER, Peder, Petar, Pete, Péter, ☞Petey, Petr, Petras, Petros, Pietro
Language/Cultural Origin: Greek
Inherent Meaning: Rock
Spiritual Connotation: Powerful Faith
Scripture: Matthew 16:18 RSV
And I tell you, you are Peter, and on this rock I will build my church, and the powers of death shall not prevail against it.

PETRA, Petrina, Pietra
Language/Cultural Origin: Greek
Inherent Meaning: Small Rock
Spiritual Connotation: Strong and Everlasting
Scripture: John 14:27 NRSV
Peace I leave with you. . . . Do not let your hearts be troubled, and do not let them be afraid.

PEYTON, Paiton, Payden, Payton
Language/Cultural Origin: Middle English
Inherent Meaning: From the Leader's Town
Spiritual Connotation: Christlike
Scripture: Isaiah 11:6 NLT
In that day the wolf and the lamb will live together; the leopard and the goat will be at peace . . . and a little child will lead them all.

PHEBE, Phoebe
☞Language/Cultural Origin: Greek
Inherent Meaning: Bright
Spiritual Connotation: Cherished
Scripture: Matthew 5:14 KJV
Ye are the light of the world. A city that is set on an hill cannot be hid.

PHELAN, Phaelan
Language/Cultural Origin: Irish
Inherent Meaning: Little Wolf
Spiritual Connotation: Exalted
Scripture: James 4:10 RSV
Humble yourselves before the Lord and he will exalt you.

PHELPS, Phellps
Language/Cultural Origin: Middle English
Inherent Meaning: Son of Phillip
Spiritual Connotation: Loving Spirit
Scripture: 2 Peter 1:3 NASB
His divine power has granted to us everything pertaining to life and godliness, through the true knowledge of Him who called us by His own glory and excellence.

PHILANA, Philina
Language/Cultural Origin: Greek
Inherent Meaning: Lover of Humankind
Spiritual Connotation: Gracious
Scripture: Matthew 22:39 NKJV
You shall love your neighbor as yourself.

PHILANTHA, Phillantha
Language/Cultural Origin: Greek
Inherent Meaning: Lover of Flowers
Spiritual Connotation: Seeker of Truth
Scripture: Proverbs 4:9 NCV
[Wisdom] will be like flowers in your hair and like a beautiful crown on your head.

PHILEMON, Philémon
☞Language/Cultural Origin: Greek
Inherent Meaning: Kiss
Spiritual Connotation: Affectionate
Scripture: Romans 16:16 NASB
Greet one another with a holy kiss. All the churches of Christ greet you.

PHILLIP, Felipe, Felípe, Filip, ☞Fillip, Phil, Philip, Philipp, Philippe, Phill, Phillipp
Language/Cultural Origin: Greek

Inherent Meaning: Lover of Horses
Spiritual Connotation: Transformed
Scripture: 2 Corinthians 3:18 NKJV
But we all, with unveiled face, beholding as in a mirror the glory of the Lord, are being transformed into the same image from glory to glory.

PHINEAS, Phinehas

Language/Cultural Origin: Hebrew
Inherent Meaning: Face of Compassion
Spiritual Connotation: Merciful
Scripture: Nehemiah 9:31 NASB
Nevertheless, in Your great compassion You did not make an end of them or forsake them, for You are a gracious and compassionate God.

PHOEBE, see Phebe

PHYLICIA, see Felicia

PHYLLIS, Philyss, Phylis, Phyllis, Phylliss

Language/Cultural Origin: Greek
Inherent Meaning: Green Branch
Spiritual Connotation: Youthful Trust
Scripture: Psalm 86:11 NKJV
Teach me Your way, O LORD; I will walk in Your truth; unite my heart to fear Your name.

PIA, Piya

Language/Cultural Origin: Italian
Inherent Meaning: Devoted
Spiritual Connotation: Focused
Scripture: 1 Corinthians 7:35 NKJV
And this I say for your own profit, not that I may put a leash on you, but for what is proper, and that you may serve the Lord without distraction.

PIERCE, Pearce, Peerce, Peirce

Language/Cultural Origin: English
Inherent Meaning: Stone
Spiritual Connotation: Strong in Spirit
Scripture: Psalm 18:32 NRSV
The God who girded me with strength, and made my way safe. He made my feet like the feet of a deer, and set me secure on the heights.

PIERRE, Peirre, Piere, Piero, Pierro

Language/Cultural Origin: French

Inherent Meaning: Rock
Spiritual Connotation: Dependent Upon God
Scripture: Psalm 62:7 NKJV
In God is my salvation and my glory; the rock of my strength, and my refuge, is in God.

PILAR, Pillar

Language/Cultural Origin: Latin
Inherent Meaning: Pillar
Spiritual Connotation: Strong in Faith
Scripture: Matthew 17:20 NKJV
If you have faith as a mustard seed, you will say to this mountain, move from here to there, and it will move; and nothing will be impossible for you.

PIPER

Language/Cultural Origin: English
Inherent Meaning: Pipe Player
Spiritual Connotation: Joyous Spirit
Scripture: Isaiah 61:11 NCV
The Lord GOD will make goodness and praise come from all the nations.

PIPPI, Pippen, Pippie, Pippin

Language/Cultural Origin: English
Inherent Meaning: Lover of Horses
Spiritual Connotation: Eternal
Scripture: 1 Corinthians 15:52 NKJV
For the trumpet will sound, and the dead will be raised incorruptible, and we shall be changed.

PIRAN, Pieran

Language/Cultural Origin: Irish
Inherent Meaning: Prayer
Spiritual Connotation: Supplicant
Scripture: Philippians 4:6 NRSV
Do not worry about anything, but in everything by prayer and supplication with thanksgiving let your requests be made known to God.

PITNEY, Pittnee, Pittney

Language/Cultural Origin: English
Inherent Meaning: Strong-Willed
Spiritual Connotation: Act of God
Scripture: John 1:12 NKJV
But as many as received Him, to them He gave the right to become children of God, to those who believe in His name.

PLACIDO, Placydo
Language/Cultural Origin: Spanish
Inherent Meaning: Tranquil
Spiritual Connotation: Serene
Scripture: Philippians 4:7 NRSV
And the peace of God, which surpasses all understanding, will guard your hearts and your minds in Christ Jesus.

PLATO, Plaeto, Platón
Language/Cultural Origin: Greek
Inherent Meaning: Broad-Shouldered
Spiritual Connotation: Wise
Scripture: Proverbs 19:8 NLT
To acquire wisdom is to love oneself; people who cherish understanding will prosper.

POLLY, Pollee, Polli, Pollyana, Pollyanna
Language/Cultural Origin: English
Inherent Meaning: Gentle
Spiritual Connotation: Loving Spirit
Scripture: Psalm 149:1 NCV
Praise the LORD! Sing a new song to the LORD; sing his praise in the meeting of his people.

PONCE, Poncé
Language/Cultural Origin: Spanish
Inherent Meaning: Fifth
Spiritual Connotation: Increase
Scripture: Acts 6:7 NASB
And the word of God kept on spreading; and the number of the disciples continued to increase greatly in Jerusalem.

POPPY, Poppey, Poppi, Poppie
Language/Cultural Origin: Latin
Inherent Meaning: Poppy Flower
Spiritual Connotation: Nourished
Scripture: Isaiah 35:2 NKJV
It shall blossom abundantly and rejoice, even with joy and singing. . . . They shall see the glory of the LORD, the excellency of our God.

PORTER, Port
Language/Cultural Origin: Latin
Inherent Meaning: Gatekeeper
Spiritual Connotation: Watchful Spirit
Scripture: Isaiah 12:2 RSV
Behold, God is my salvation; I will trust, and will not be afraid; for the LORD GOD is my strength and my song, and he has become my salvation.

PORTIA, Porsché, Porschia, Porsha
Language/Cultural Origin: Latin
Inherent Meaning: Offering
Spiritual Connotation: Gift of God
Scripture: Psalm 37:5 NKJV
Commit your way to the LORD, trust also in Him, and He shall bring it to pass.

POWELL, Powel
Language/Cultural Origin: English
Inherent Meaning: Prepared
Spiritual Connotation: Purified
Scripture: James 1:2 NKJV
My brethren, count it all joy when you fall into various trials, knowing that the testing of your faith produces patience.

PRENTICE, Prentis, Prentiss
Language/Cultural Origin: Middle English
Inherent Meaning: Learner
Spiritual Connotation: Seeker of Truth
Scripture: Isaiah 30:21 NRSV
And when you turn to the right or when you turn to the left, your ears shall hear a word behind you, saying, "This is the way; walk in it."

PRESCOTT, Prescot
Language/Cultural Origin: Old English
Inherent Meaning: From the Priest's Dwelling
Spiritual Connotation: Blessed
Scripture: 1 John 5:11 NASB
And the witness is this, that God has given us eternal life, and this life is in His Son.

PRESLEY, Presleigh
Language/Cultural Origin: Old English
Inherent Meaning: From the Priest's Meadow
Spiritual Connotation: Peaceful Spirit
Scripture: Psalm 146:5 NASB
How blessed is he whose help is the God of Jacob, whose hope is in the LORD his God.

PRESTON, Prestan
Language/Cultural Origin: Old English
Inherent Meaning: From the Priest's Home
Spiritual Connotation: Consecrated to God
Scripture: Psalm 50:14 NRSV
Offer to God a sacrifice of thanksgiving, and pay your vows to the Most High.

PRICE, Pryce
Language/Cultural Origin: Welsh

Inherent Meaning: Son of the Ardent One
Spiritual Connotation: Eager
Scripture: Psalm 69:9 NRSV
It is zeal for your house that has consumed me; the insults of those who insult you have fallen on me.

PRIEL, Poriel, Priela, Priella
Language/Cultural Origin: Hebrew
Inherent Meaning: Fruit of God
Spiritual Connotation: Righteous
Scripture: Galatians 5:22–23 NRSV
By contrast, the fruit of the Spirit is love, joy, peace, patience, kindness, generosity, faithfulness, gentleness, and self-control.

PRISCILLA, Prescilla, Pricilla, Priscila, Prisilla, Prissilla, Prysilla
Language/Cultural Origin: Latin
Inherent Meaning: Primitive, Ancient
Spiritual Connotation: Eternal Value
Scripture: Philippians 4:8 NCV

Think about the things that are good and worthy of praise. Think about the things that are true and honorable and right and pure and beautiful and respected.

PRUDENCE, Prudy
Language/Cultural Origin: Latin
Inherent Meaning: Discretion
Spiritual Connotation: Awareness of God
Scripture: Psalm 19:8 NKJV
The statutes of the LORD are right, rejoicing the heart; the commandment of the LORD is pure, enlightening the eyes.

PRYOR, Prior
Language/Cultural Origin: Latin
Inherent Meaning: Head of the Monastery
Spiritual Connotation: Respected
Scripture: 1 Timothy 5:17 NASB
Let the elders who rule well be considered worthy of double honor, especially those who work hard at preaching and teaching.

I pray that you will begin to understand how incredibly great his power is to help those who believe him.

QAMAR, Quamar

Language/Cultural Origin: Middle Eastern
Inherent Meaning: Moon
Spiritual Connotation: Glorious Joy
Scripture: Isaiah 60:20 TLB

Your sun shall never set; the moon shall not go down—for the Lord will be your everlasting light; your days of mourning all will end.

QITARAH, Qitara

Language/Cultural Origin: Middle Eastern
Inherent Meaning: Fragrance
Spiritual Connotation: Pleasing
Scripture: 2 Corinthians 2:15 RSV

For we are the aroma of Christ to God among those who are being saved and among those who are perishing.

QABIL, Qabial, Qabiel, Qabiele, Qabielle

Language/Cultural Origin: Middle Eastern
Inherent Meaning: Able
Spiritual Connotation: Strength of God
Scripture: Hebrews 2:18 RSV

For because he himself has suffered and been tempted, he is able to help those who are tempted.

QUANAH, Quan, Quanh (see also Khan)

Language/Cultural Origin: Comanche
Inherent Meaning: Fragrance
Spiritual Connotation: Beloved
Scripture: Song of Songs 1:12 NASB

While the king was at his table, my perfume gave forth its fragrance.

QADIM, Qadeem, Qadím (see also Kadim)

Language/Cultural Origin: Middle Eastern
Inherent Meaning: Ancient
Spiritual Connotation: Eternal
Scripture: Revelation 21:6 NKJV

It is done! I am the Alpha and the Omega, the Beginning and the End. I will give of the fountain of the water of life freely to him who thirsts.

QUANEISHA, Quanesha, Quanisha, Quanishia, Quenisha, Quenishia (see also Keneisha)

Language/Cultural Origin: American
Inherent Meaning: Beautiful
Spiritual Connotation: Righteous
Scripture: Proverbs 31:30 NLT

Charm is deceptive, and beauty does not last; but a woman who fears the LORD will be greatly praised.

QADIR, Qadeer

Language/Cultural Origin: Middle Eastern
Inherent Meaning: Powerful
Spiritual Connotation: Witness
Scripture: Psalm 106:8 RSV

Yet he saved them for his name's sake, that he might make known his mighty power.

QUBILAH, Quabilah

Language/Cultural Origin: Middle Eastern
Inherent Meaning: Conciliatory
Spiritual Connotation: Peacemaker
Scripture: Hebrews 12:14 NIV

Make every effort to live in peace with all men and to be holy; without holiness no one will see the Lord.

QADIRA, Qadeera

Language/Cultural Origin: Middle Eastern
Inherent Meaning: Powerful
Spiritual Connotation: Power of God
Scripture: Ephesians 1:19 TLB

QUEISHA, Queshia, Quisha
(see also Keisha)
Language/Cultural Origin: American
Inherent Meaning: Beautiful
Spiritual Connotation: Unblemished
Scripture: Ecclesiastes 11:9 NCV
Young people, enjoy yourselves while you are young. . . . But remember that God will judge you for everything you do.

QUENBY, Quenbie
Language/Cultural Origin: Swedish
Inherent Meaning: Feminine
Spiritual Connotation: Holy
Scripture: 1 Timothy 5:2 NLT
Treat the older women as you would your mother, and treat the younger women with all purity as your own sisters.

QUENNELL, Quenell, Quennel
Language/Cultural Origin: Old French
Inherent Meaning: From by the Oak Tree
Spiritual Connotation: Steadfast
Scripture: Psalm 1:3 NLT
They are like trees planted along the riverbank, bearing fruit each season without fail. Their leaves never wither.

QUENTIN, Quenton, Qwentin
Language/Cultural Origin: Middle English
Inherent Meaning: From the Queen's Town
Spiritual Connotation: Forgiven
Scripture: Romans 8:1 NRSV
There is therefore now no condemnation for those who are in Christ Jesus.

QUERIDA, Queridah
Language/Cultural Origin: Spanish
Inherent Meaning: Beloved
Spiritual Connotation: Loving
Scripture: 1 John 4:7 NRSV
Beloved, let us love one another, because love is from God; everyone who loves is born of God and knows God.

QUIANA, Quianna
(see also Keianna, Kiana, Kiona)
Language/Cultural Origin: American
Inherent Meaning: Gracious
Spiritual Connotation: Blessed
Scripture: Numbers 6:24–25 KJV
The LORD bless thee, and keep thee: The LORD make his face shine upon thee, and be gracious unto thee.

QUILLAN, Quillen, Quillon
Language/Cultural Origin: Gaelic
Inherent Meaning: Little Cub
Spiritual Connotation: Beloved
Scripture: Psalm 91:15 RSV
When he calls to me, I will answer him; I will be with him in trouble, I will rescue him and honor him.

QUIMBY, Quinby
Language/Cultural Origin: Scandinavian
Inherent Meaning: From the Queen's Estate
Spiritual Connotation: Vigilant Spirit
Scripture: Matthew 24:42 NASB
Therefore be on the alert, for you do not know which day your Lord is coming.

QUINCY, Quincey, Quinci, Quincie
Language/Cultural Origin: Old French
Inherent Meaning: From the Fifth Son's Estate
Spiritual Connotation: Freedom in Christ
Scripture: Romans 8:2 NRSV
For the law of the Spirit of life in Christ Jesus has set you free from the law of sin and of death.

QUINN, Quin
Language/Cultural Origin: Gaelic
Inherent Meaning: Intelligent
Spiritual Connotation: Godly Insight
Scripture: 1 John 3:2 NKJV
Beloved, now we are children of God; and . . . we shall be like Him, for we shall see Him as He is.

QUINTANA, Quinta, Quintanna, Quintara, Quintarah, Quintina
Language/Cultural Origin: English
Inherent Meaning: Fifth
Spiritual Connotation: Compassionate
Scripture: Galatians 6:1 KJV
If a man be overtaken in a fault, ye which are spiritual, restore such an one in the spirit of meekness; considering thyself, lest thou also be tempted.

QUINTESSA, Quintesa
Language/Cultural Origin: English
Inherent Meaning: Efficiency
Spiritual Connotation: Steward
Scripture: Ephesians 5:15 NRSV
Be careful then how you live, not as unwise people but as wise, making the most of the time, because the days are evil.

QUINTIN, Quint, Quintan, Quinten, Quinton, Quintus, Qwinton

Language/Cultural Origin: Latin

Inherent Meaning: Fifth

Spiritual Connotation: Brave

Scripture: 1 Corinthians 16:13 NRSV

Keep alert, stand firm in your faith, be courageous, be strong.

QUON, Quonn

Language/Cultural Origin: Chinese

Inherent Meaning: Bright

Spiritual Connotation: Righteous

Scripture: Daniel 12:3 NRSV

Those who are wise shall shine like the brightness of the sky, and those who lead many to righteousness, like the stars forever and ever.

RAANAN, Ranaan, Ranan
(see also Rhiannon, Ranon)
Language/Cultural Origin: Hebrew
Inherent Meaning: Luxuriant
Spiritual Connotation: Sacrifice
Scripture: John 12:3 NASB

> Mary therefore took a pound of very costly
> perfume . . . and anointed the feet of Jesus,
> and wiped His feet with her hair; and the
> house was filled with the fragrance.

RABIAH, Rabiya
Language/Cultural Origin: Middle Eastern
Inherent Meaning: Breeze
Spiritual Connotation: Miracle
Scripture: John 3:8 NLT

> Just as you can hear the wind but can't tell
> where it comes from or where it is going, so
> you can't explain how people are born of the
> Spirit.

RACHEL, Rachael, Rachaele,
Rachal, Rachele, Racquel,
Raechel, Raechele, Raquel,
Raquela, Riquelle, Rashel
Language/Cultural Origin: Hebrew
Inherent Meaning: Lamb
Spiritual Connotation: Innocence
Scripture: Hosea 14:9 NRSV

> Those who are wise understand these things;
> those who are discerning know them. For the
> ways of the LORD are right, and the upright
> walk in them.

RACHELLE, see Rochelle

RADLEY, Radlee, Radleigh
Language/Cultural Origin: English
Inherent Meaning: From the Reed Meadow
Spiritual Connotation: Spirit-Filled
Scripture: John 14:16 NLT

> And I will ask the Father, and he will give you
> another Counselor, who will never leave you.

RAE, Ralina (see also Ray)
Language/Cultural Origin: English
Inherent Meaning: Doe
Spiritual Connotation: Full of Grace
Scripture: Psalm 50:23 NKJV

> Whoever offers praise glorifies Me; and to
> him who orders his conduct aright I will
> show the salvation of God.

RAEANN, Raeanna, Raeanne, Rayana,
Rayann, Rayanna, Reana, Reane,
Reann, Reanna, Reanne, Reyanna,
Reyanne (see also Rhian)
Language/Cultural Origin: English
Inherent Meaning: Gracious
Spiritual Connotation: Gentle
Scripture: Matthew 12:20 NRSV

> He will not break a bruised reed or quench a
> smoldering wick until he brings justice to
> victory.

RAELENE, Raeleen, Raelina, Raelle,
Raelyn, Raelynn, Rayele, Rayelle,
Rayleen, Raylene, Raylynn
Language/Cultural Origin: English
Inherent Meaning: Lovely
Spiritual Connotation: Compassionate
Scripture: Jeremiah 12:15 NASB

> I will again have compassion on them; and I
> will bring them back, each one to his
> inheritance and each one to his land.

RAFAEL, RAFAELA,
see Raphael, Raphaela

RAFER, Rafar
Language/Cultural Origin: Gaelic
Inherent Meaning: Prosperous
Spiritual Connotation: Gifted
Scripture: Jeremiah 29:11 NRSV

> For surely I know the plans I have for you,
> says the LORD, plans for your welfare and not
> for harm, to give you a future with hope.

RAGHIB, Raquib

Language/Cultural Origin: Middle Eastern
Inherent Meaning: Desirous
Spiritual Connotation: Ardent
Scripture: Psalm 69:9 NKJV

Because zeal for Your house has eaten me up, and the reproaches of those who reproach You have fallen on me.

RAHIM, Raheem, Rahím, Rahiim

Language/Cultural Origin: Middle Eastern
Inherent Meaning: Compassionate
Spiritual Connotation: Merciful
Scripture: James 5:11 NKJV

Indeed we count them blessed who endure. . . . The Lord is very compassionate and merciful.

RAINA, Raenah, Rainna (see also Rana, Rayna)

Language/Cultural Origin: Russian
Inherent Meaning: Queenly
Spiritual Connotation: Gracious
Scripture: Psalm 143:8 RSV

Let me hear in the morning of thy steadfast love, for in thee I put my trust. Teach me the way I should go, for to thee I lift up my soul.

RAINOR, Rainar, Rainer, Rainos, Ranos (see also Rainier)

Language/Cultural Origin: Greek
Inherent Meaning: Counselor
Spiritual Connotation: Promise
Scripture: Isaiah 9:6 NKJV

For unto us a Child is born, unto us a Son is given. . . . And His name will be called Wonderful, Counselor, Mighty God, Everlasting Father, Prince of Peace.

RAINEY, Rainée, Raini, Rainie

Language/Cultural Origin: English
Inherent Meaning: Regal
Spiritual Connotation: Praised
Scripture: Esther 6:9 NCV

Let the robe and the horse be given to [him]. Let . . . the servants . . . lead him on the horse through the city streets. . . . Let them announce: "This is what is done for the man whom the king wants to honor!"

RAINIER, Ráinier, Rainios, Ranios (see also Rainor)

Language/Cultural Origin: Old German

Inherent Meaning: Mighty Army
Spiritual Connotation: Strength of God
Scripture: Psalm 66:7 NASB

He rules by His might forever; His eyes keep watch on the nations; let not the rebellious exalt themselves.

RAIZA, Raissa, Raisza

Language/Cultural Origin: Russian
Inherent Meaning: Rose
Spiritual Connotation: Lovely
Scripture: Isaiah 35:1 NKJV

The wilderness and the wasteland shall be glad for them, and the desert shall rejoice and blossom as the rose.

RAIZEL, Raisel (see also Rasia)

Language/Cultural Origin: Yiddish
Inherent Meaning: Rose
Spiritual Connotation: Adorned
Scripture: Isaiah 35:2 NKJV

It shall blossom abundantly and rejoice, even with joy and singing.

RAJA, Raija, Raiya

Language/Cultural Origin: Middle Eastern
Inherent Meaning: Hopeful
Spiritual Connotation: Gift of Faith
Scripture: Romans 4:18 NRSV

Hoping against hope, he believed that he would become the father of many nations.

RALEIGH, Rawley

Language/Cultural Origin: Old English
Inherent Meaning: From the Deer Meadow
Spiritual Connotation: Excellent Worth
Scripture: 2 Corinthians 9:8 TLB

There will not only be enough for your own needs but plenty left over to give joyfully to others.

RALPH, Ralf (see also Rolf)

Language/Cultural Origin: Anglo-Saxon
Inherent Meaning: Counselor
Spiritual Connotation: Discerning
Scripture: Psalm 13:5 KJV

But I have trusted in thy mercy; my heart shall rejoice in thy salvation.

RAMA, Ramah

Language/Cultural Origin: Hebrew
Inherent Meaning: Praised
Spiritual Connotation: Glory to God

Scripture: Psalm 86:12 RSV
I give thanks to thee, O Lord my God, with my whole heart, and I will glorify thy name for ever.

RAMIRO, Rami, Ramierez, Ramieros, Ramos
Language/Cultural Origin: Spanish
Inherent Meaning: Judge
Spiritual Connotation: Accountable
Scripture: Deuteronomy 16:20 NASB
Justice, and only justice, you shall pursue, that you may live and possess the land which the LORD your God is giving you.

RAMON, Raimon, Ramón, Ramone (see also Raymond)
Language/Cultural Origin: Spanish
Inherent Meaning: Mighty Protector
Spiritual Connotation: Vigilant
Scripture: Habakkuk 2:1 NCV
I will stand like a guard to watch and place myself at the tower. I will wait to see what he will say to me.

RAMONA, Ramonda, Rimona, Romona
Language/Cultural Origin: Old German
Inherent Meaning: Protector
Spiritual Connotation: Virtuous
Scripture: Proverbs 31:10 NKJV
Who can find a virtuous wife? For her worth is far above rubies.

RAMSEY, Ramsay, Ramzee
Language/Cultural Origin: Old English
Inherent Meaning: From the Wooded Island
Spiritual Connotation: Believer
Scripture: Matthew 16:16 NKJV
Simon Peter answered and said, "You are the Christ, the Son of the living God."

RANA, Rahna, Rahni, Ranee, Rania (see also Raina, Rayna)
Language/Cultural Origin: Sanskrit
Inherent Meaning: Regal
Spiritual Connotation: Noble
Scripture: James 4:10 NKJV
Humble yourselves in the sight of the Lord, and He will lift you up.

RANDALL, Rand, Randal, Randel, Randell, Randle, Randy, Ranndy
Language/Cultural Origin: English

Inherent Meaning: Shield
Spiritual Connotation: Protected
Scripture: Psalm 3:3 NASB
But Thou, O LORD, art a shield about me, my glory, and the One who lifts my head.

RANDI, Randalin, Randalyn, Randee, Randie, Randii
Language/Cultural Origin: English
Inherent Meaning: Shield
Spiritual Connotation: Guarded
Scripture: Proverbs 30:5 RSV
Every word of God proves true; he is a shield to those who take refuge in him.

RANDOLPH, Randolf
Language/Cultural Origin: Old English
Inherent Meaning: Shield
Spiritual Connotation: Established in Peace
Scripture: Matthew 6:33 KJV
But seek ye first the kingdom of God, and his righteousness; and all these things shall be added unto you.

RANGER, Rainger, Range
Language/Cultural Origin: French
Inherent Meaning: Keeper of the Forest
Spiritual Connotation: Covenant
Scripture: Isaiah 32:15 NCV
This will continue until God pours his Spirit from above upon us. Then the desert will be like a fertile field and the fertile field like a forest.

RANITA, Ranata, Ranitta (see also Renata)
Language/Cultural Origin: Hebrew
Inherent Meaning: Song
Spiritual Connotation: Filled With Joy
Scripture: Isaiah 55:12 RSV
The mountains and the hills before you shall break forth into singing, and all the trees of the field shall clap their hands.

RANON, Ranen, Rani, Ranie
Language/Cultural Origin: Hebrew
Inherent Meaning: My Song
Spiritual Connotation: Praise
Scripture: Psalm 9:2 NKJV
I will be glad and rejoice in You; I will sing praise to Your name, O Most High.

RANKIN, Randkin
Language/Cultural Origin: Old English

Inherent Meaning: Small Shield
Spiritual Connotation: Valiant Spirit
Scripture: Psalm 27:14 RSV
Wait for the LORD; be strong, and let your heart take courage; yea, wait for the LORD!

RANSOM, Randsom, Ransome
Language/Cultural Origin: Latin
Inherent Meaning: Redeemer
Spiritual Connotation: Hopeful
Scripture: Job 19:25 NRSV
For I know that my Redeemer lives, and that at the last he will stand upon the earth.

RAOUL, Raul, Raúl
Language/Cultural Origin: French
Inherent Meaning: Counselor
Spiritual Connotation: Divine Wisdom
Scripture: Romans 11:34 TLB
For who among us can know the mind of the Lord? Who knows enough to be his counselor and guide?

RAPHAEL, see Rephael

RAPHAELA, Rafaela, Rafaell, Rafaelle, Raphaéla
Language/Cultural Origin: Hebrew
Inherent Meaning: Healed by God
Spiritual Connotation: God's Anointed
Scripture: 2 Chronicles 1:12 NKJV
Wisdom and knowledge are granted to you; and I will give you riches and wealth and honor.

RAQUEL, see Rachel

RASHA, Rahsha, Rashia
Language/Cultural Origin: Middle Eastern
Inherent Meaning: Little Gazelle
Spiritual Connotation: Freedom
Scripture: Proverbs 6:5 NKJV
Deliver yourself like a gazelle from the hand of the hunter, and like a bird from the hand of the fowler.

RASHAD, Raashad, Rashaad, Reshaad, Rhashad, Rishaad
Language/Cultural Origin: Middle Eastern
Inherent Meaning: Wise Leader
Spiritual Connotation: Discerning
Scripture: Proverbs 4:7 NRSV
The beginning of wisdom is this: Get wisdom, and whatever else you get, get insight.

RASHAWNA, Rashana, Rashanda, Rashaunda, Rashona, Rashonda, Reshana, Reshanna, Reshaunda, Reshawnda, Reshonda
Language/Cultural Origin: American
Inherent Meaning: God Is Gracious
Spiritual Connotation: Preserved
Scripture: 2 Chronicles 30:9 NLT
For if you return to the LORD, your relatives and your children . . . will be able to return to this land. For the LORD your God is gracious and merciful.

RASHID, Rasheed, Rasheid, Rashied, Rausheed
Language/Cultural Origin: Turkish
Inherent Meaning: Well-Directed
Spiritual Connotation: Humble
Scripture: Proverbs 3:5–6 NKJV
Trust in the LORD with all your heart, and lean not on your own understanding; in all your ways acknowledge Him, and He shall direct your paths.

RASHIDA, Rahsheda, Rasheda, Rasheeda, Rasheida
Language/Cultural Origin: Swahili
Inherent Meaning: Well-Directed
Spiritual Connotation: Discerning
Scripture: John 16:13 NRSV
When the Spirit of truth comes, he will guide you into all the truth.

RASIA, Rasha, Rasya (see also Raizel)
Language/Cultural Origin: Greek
Inherent Meaning: Rose
Spiritual Connotation: Joyful
Scripture: Isaiah 35:1 NKJV
The wilderness and the wasteland shall be glad for them, and the desert shall rejoice and blossom as the rose.

RATANA, Ratania, Ratanya
Language/Cultural Origin: Thai
Inherent Meaning: Made of Crystal
Spiritual Connotation: Priceless
Scripture: Revelation 21:11 NCV
It was shining with the glory of God and was bright like a very expensive jewel, like a jasper, clear as crystal.

RAUL, see Raoul

RAVEN, Ravan, Ravin, Ravon, Ravyn
Language/Cultural Origin: Old German
Inherent Meaning: Blackbird
Spiritual Connotation: Cherished
Scripture: Matthew 6:26 TLB

Look at the birds! They don't worry about what to eat . . . for your heavenly Father feeds them. And you are far more valuable to him than they are.

RAY, Raye (see also Rae)
Language/Cultural Origin: French
Inherent Meaning: Royal
Spiritual Connotation: Wise
Scripture: Proverbs 9:10 NASB

The fear of the LORD is the beginning of wisdom, and the knowledge of the Holy One is understanding.

RAYAH, Raia, Raya (see also Rhea)
Language/Cultural Origin: Hebrew
Inherent Meaning: Companion
Spiritual Connotation: Friend of God
Scripture: Hebrews 13:6 TLB

That is why we can say without any doubt or fear, the Lord is my Helper, and I am not afraid of anything that mere man can do to me.

RAYANNE, see Raeann

RAYLEEN, see Raelene

RAYMOND, Raimond, Ramond, Raymon, Raymont (see also Ramon)
Language/Cultural Origin: Old German
Inherent Meaning: Mighty Protector
Spiritual Connotation: Sanctified
Scripture: Philippians 1:6 NRSV

I am confident of this, that the one who began a good work among you will bring it to completion by the day of Jesus Christ.

RAYNA, Reyna (see also Raina, Rana)
Language/Cultural Origin: Yiddish
Inherent Meaning: Pure
Spiritual Connotation: Virtuous
Scripture: Philippians 4:8 NKJV

Finally, brethren, whatever things are true, . . . noble, . . . just, . . . pure, . . . lovely, . . .

[and] of good report, if there is any virtue and if there is anything praiseworthy; meditate on these things.

**REA, Reah, Reha
(see also Rayah, Rhea, Ria)**
Language/Cultural Origin: Greek
Inherent Meaning: Poppy Flower
Spiritual Connotation: Firmly Grounded
Scripture: Hosea 14:5 NLT

I will be to Israel like a refreshing dew from heaven. It will blossom like the lily; it will send roots deep into the soil like the cedars in Lebanon.

REAGAN, see Regan

REANNE, see Raeann

REBA, Reva, Rheba
☞Language/Cultural Origin: English
Inherent Meaning: Bound
Spiritual Connotation: Witness
Scripture: Acts 4:20 NCV

We cannot keep quiet. We must speak about what we have seen and heard.

**REBECCA, Rabecca, Rebeca,
☞Rébecca, Rebeccah, Rebecka,
Rebeckah, Rebeka, Rebekah,
Rebekka (see also Becky)**
Language/Cultural Origin: Hebrew
Inherent Meaning: Bound
Spiritual Connotation: Refreshed
Scripture: Psalm 23:1–2 KJV

The LORD is my shepherd; I shall not want. He maketh me to lie down in green pastures: he leadeth me beside the still waters.

REED, see Reid

REENA, Rena (see also Rina)
Language/Cultural Origin: Greek
Inherent Meaning: Peaceful
Spiritual Connotation: Abiding in God
Scripture: Philippians 4:7 RSV

And the peace of God, which passes all understanding, will keep your hearts and your minds in Christ Jesus.

**REESA, Resa, Reesha, Risa,
Risha, Ryssa, Rysha**
Language/Cultural Origin: Latin

Inherent Meaning: Laughter
Spiritual Connotation: Blessed
Scripture: Psalm 126:2 NLT

We were filled with laughter, and we sang for joy. And the other nations said, "What amazing things the LORD has done for them."

REESE, Reece, Rhys
Language/Cultural Origin: Welsh
Inherent Meaning: Enthusiastic
Spiritual Connotation: Dedicated
Scripture: Numbers 25:13 NLT

In this covenant, he and his descendants will be priests for all time, because he was zealous for his God and made atonement for the people of Israel.

REEVE, Reaves, Reeves
Language/Cultural Origin: Middle English
Inherent Meaning: Steward
Spiritual Connotation: Servant
Scripture: 1 Peter 4:10 NRSV

Like good stewards of the manifold grace of God, serve one another with whatever gift each of you has received.

REGAN, Raegan, Reagan, Reaganne, Reganne, Reegan, Reegen
Language/Cultural Origin: Irish
Inherent Meaning: Ruler
Spiritual Connotation: Spiritual Strength
Scripture: Proverbs 24:5 NCV

Wise people have great power, and those with knowledge have great strength.

REGINA, Regeena, Reggi, Reggie, Regi, Regie, Reginia, Reginna
Language/Cultural Origin: Latin
Inherent Meaning: Queen
Spiritual Connotation: Gracious
Scripture: Psalm 19:14 NKJV

Let the words of my mouth and the meditation of my heart be acceptable in Your sight, O LORD, my strength and my Redeemer.

REGINALD, Reg, Reggie, Reginauld, Reginault
Language/Cultural Origin: Middle English
Inherent Meaning: Powerful Counselor
Spiritual Connotation: Humble
Scripture: Micah 6:8 RSV

He has showed you, O man, what is good;

and what does the LORD require of you but to do justice, and to love kindness, and to walk humbly with your God?

REGIS, Reggis
Language/Cultural Origin: Latin
Inherent Meaning: Regal
Spiritual Connotation: Honored
Scripture: Esther 6:9 NCV

Let the robe and the horse be given to one of the king's most important men. . . . Let them announce: This is what is done for the man whom the king wants to honor!

REID, Raed, Reade, Reed, Reide, Ried
Language/Cultural Origin: Old English
Inherent Meaning: Fair Countenance
Spiritual Connotation: Blessed
Scripture: Psalm 118:14 NKJV

The LORD is my strength and song, and He has become my salvation.

REIKO, Reyko
Language/Cultural Origin: Japanese
Inherent Meaning: Pleasant Child
Spiritual Connotation: Blessing
Scripture: Proverbs 23:24 NLT

The father of godly children has cause for joy. What a pleasure it is to have wise children.

REMEZ, Rémez
Language/Cultural Origin: Hebrew
Inherent Meaning: Sign
Spiritual Connotation: Miraculous
Scripture: Luke 2:12 NRSV

This will be a sign for you: you will find a child wrapped in bands of cloth and lying in a manger.

REMI, Remee, Rémi, Remie, Remy, Remmie, Remmy
Language/Cultural Origin: French
Inherent Meaning: From Rheims
Spiritual Connotation: Obedient
Scripture: Psalm 119:105 KJV

Thy word is a lamp unto my feet, and a light unto my path.

REMINGTON, Remingten
Language/Cultural Origin: Old English
Inherent Meaning: From the Home of the Raven

Spiritual Connotation: Devoted
Scripture: 2 Timothy 3:16 NRSV
All scripture is inspired by God and is useful for teaching, for reproof, for correction, and for training in righteousness.

REMUS, Reemus
Language/Cultural Origin: Latin
Inherent Meaning: Speedy
Spiritual Connotation: Joyful
Scripture: Matthew 28:7 NASB
Go quickly and tell His disciples that He has risen from the dead.

RENATA, Ranata, Renada, Reneeta, Renita, Rinata (see also Ranita)
Language/Cultural Origin: Latin
Inherent Meaning: Reborn
Spiritual Connotation: Quickened Spirit
Scripture: Romans 12:2 NASB
And do not be conformed to this world, but be transformed by the renewing of your mind.

RENDOR, Renndor
Language/Cultural Origin: Hungarian
Inherent Meaning: Police Officer
Spiritual Connotation: Trusted
Scripture: 1 Peter 2:13 NIV
Submit yourselves for the Lord's sake to every authority instituted among men.

RENÉ, Raenée, Rainato, Ranato, Renato, Rene, Renne, Rennie
Language/Cultural Origin: Latin
Inherent Meaning: Reborn
Spiritual Connotation: Forgiven
Scripture: John 3:3 NLT
Jesus replied, "I assure you, unless you are born again, you can never see the Kingdom of God."

RENEE, Renae, Renay, Renée, Reonne
Language/Cultural Origin: French
Inherent Meaning: Born Again
Spiritual Connotation: Joyful
Scripture: Galatians 2:20 RSV
I have been crucified with Christ; it is no longer I who live, but Christ who lives in me.

REPHAEL, Rafael, Rafeal, ☞Raffael, Raffeal, Raphaél
Language/Cultural Origin: Hebrew

Inherent Meaning: Healed by God
Spiritual Connotation: God's Anointed
Scripture: 1 Samuel 2:10 NASB
Those who contend with the LORD will be shattered. . . . He will give strength to His king, and will exalt the horn of His anointed.

RESEDA, Resada
Language/Cultural Origin: Spanish
Inherent Meaning: Fragrant Blossom
Spiritual Connotation: Pleasing Aroma
Scripture: 2 Corinthians 2:15 NASB
For we are a fragrance of Christ to God among those who are being saved and among those who are perishing.

RESEL, Rcisel
Language/Cultural Origin: German
Inherent Meaning: Summer
Spiritual Connotation: Blessing
Scripture: Psalm 74:17 NASB
You have established all the boundaries of the earth; You have made summer and winter.

RESHAWNA, see Rashawna

REUBEN, Reuban, Reubin, ☞Rheuben, Rube, Rubin
Language/Cultural Origin: Hebrew
Inherent Meaning: Behold, a Son
Spiritual Connotation: Wondrous Recognition
Scripture: Psalm 119:16 NKJV
I will delight myself in Your statutes; I will not forget Your word.

REX, Rexx
Language/Cultural Origin: Latin
Inherent Meaning: King
Spiritual Connotation: Leadership
Scripture: 1 Peter 5:3 NLT
Don't lord it over the people assigned to your care, but lead them by your good example.

REYNARD, Reinhart, Renárd, Rennard, Rey, Reynardo
Language/Cultural Origin: German
Inherent Meaning: Courageous
Spiritual Connotation: Brave
Scripture: Joshua 1:9 NKJV
Have I not commanded you? Be strong and of good courage; do not be afraid, nor be dismayed, for the LORD your God is with you wherever you go.

REYNOLD, Reinhold, Renaldo, Renault, Rey, Reynald, Reynaldo, Reynolds

Language/Cultural Origin: German

Inherent Meaning: Counselor

Spiritual Connotation: Wise

Scripture: Proverbs 13:10 NASB

Through insolence comes nothing but strife, but wisdom is with those who receive counsel.

RHEA, Rhaya, Rhéa, Rhia (see also Rayah, Rea, Ria)

Language/Cultural Origin: Greek

Inherent Meaning: Flowing Stream

Spiritual Connotation: Refreshing

Scripture: Isaiah 35:6 NRSV

For waters shall break forth in the wilderness, and streams in the desert.

RHETT, Rhet

Language/Cultural Origin: Welsh

Inherent Meaning: Ardent

Spiritual Connotation: Shepherd

Scripture: 1 Peter 5:2 TLB

Feed the flock of God; care for it willingly, not grudgingly; not for what you will get out of it but because you are eager to serve the Lord.

RHIAN, Rhiana, Rhianna, Rhiauna, Rhyan, Rhyanna, Rian, Riana, Riann, Rianna, Rihana, Rihanna (see also Raeann, Ryan)

Language/Cultural Origin: Welsh

Inherent Meaning: Maiden

Spiritual Connotation: Joyful

Scripture: Isaiah 62:5 NCV

As a young man marries a woman, so your children will marry your land. As a man rejoices over his new wife, so your God will rejoice over you.

RHIANNON, Rhianen, Rhiannan, Rhiannen, Rhianon, Riannon (see also Raana, Ranon)

Language/Cultural Origin: Welsh

Inherent Meaning: Goddess

Spiritual Connotation: Mortal

Scripture: John 6:40 NRSV

This is indeed the will of my Father, that all

who see the Son and believe in him may have eternal life; and I will raise them up on the last day.

RHODA, Rhodi, Rhody

Language/Cultural Origin: Greek

Inherent Meaning: From the Island of Roses

Spiritual Connotation: God's Unfolded Love

Scripture: Isaiah 35:1 NKJV

The wilderness and the wasteland shall be glad for them, and the desert shall rejoice and blossom as the rose.

RHODES, Rhoads

Language/Cultural Origin: Greek

Inherent Meaning: From the Island of Roses

Spiritual Connotation: Formed of God

Scripture: Isaiah 24:15 NCV

People in the east, praise the LORD. People in the islands of the sea, praise the name of the LORD, the God of Israel.

RHONDA, Ronda

Language/Cultural Origin: Welsh

Inherent Meaning: Grand

Spiritual Connotation: Beloved

Scripture: Jeremiah 15:16 NRSV

Your words became to me a joy and the delight of my heart; for I am called by your name, O LORD, God of hosts.

RIA, Ría, Riah (see also Rayah, Rea, Rhea)

Language/Cultural Origin: Spanish

Inherent Meaning: River

Spiritual Connotation: Sacred

Scripture: Psalm 46:4 NCV

There is a river that brings joy to the city of God, the holy place where God Most High lives.

RICHARD, Ric, Ricardo, Ricardos, Ricci, Rich, Richards, Richie, Rick, Rickey, Ricki, Rickie, Ricky, Rico, Ricqui, Ricquie, Rik, Riki, Rikk, Rikki, Rikky, Riks, Riq, Riqee, Riqui, Riquie, Ritch, Ritchard, Ritchie, Rykk (see also Dick)

Language/Cultural Origin: Old German

Inherent Meaning: Powerful Ruler

Spiritual Connotation: Benevolent

Scripture: Psalm 111:10 NKJV

The fear of the LORD is the beginning of

wisdom; a good understanding have all those who do His commandments. His praise endures forever.

RICHELLE, Richela, Richele, Richella (see also Rochelle)
Language/Cultural Origin: German
Inherent Meaning: Strong Ruler
Spiritual Connotation: Hand of God
Scripture: Psalm 68:28 NRSV
Summon your might, O God; show your strength, O God, as you have done for us before.

RICHMOND, Richmon
Language/Cultural Origin: French
Inherent Meaning: From the Hill of Wealthy Vegetation
Spiritual Connotation: Nourished
Scripture: Isaiah 27:6 NCV
Israel will grow like a plant beginning to bloom. Then the world will be filled with their children.

RIDER, Ryder
Language/Cultural Origin: English
Inherent Meaning: Travels by Horse
Spiritual Connotation: Great Faith
Scripture: Psalm 20:7 NKJV
Some trust in chariots, and some in horses; but we will remember the name of the LORD our God.

RIGEL, Reigel, Reigell, Rigell
Language/Cultural Origin: Middle Eastern
Inherent Meaning: Foot
Spiritual Connotation: Secure
Scripture: John 11:9 NRSV
Those who walk during the day do not stumble, because they see the light of this world.

RILEY, Reilly, Rileigh, Rylee, Rylie
Language/Cultural Origin: Irish
Inherent Meaning: Valiant
Spiritual Connotation: Protected
Scripture: Psalm 36:7 NASB
How precious is Your lovingkindness, O God! And the children of men take refuge in the shadow of Your wings.

RINA, Rinnah (see also Reena)
Language/Cultural Origin: Hebrew
Inherent Meaning: Song of Joy
Spiritual Connotation: Filled With Gladness
Scripture: Psalm 47:1 KJV
O clap your hands, all ye people; shout unto God with the voice of triumph.

RINGO, Rengo
Language/Cultural Origin: Japanese
Inherent Meaning: Apple
Spiritual Connotation: Beloved
Scripture: Psalm 17:8 NKJV
Keep me as the apple of Your eye; hide me under the shadow of Your wings.

RIORDAN, Reardon
Language/Cultural Origin: Irish
Inherent Meaning: Poet/Singer
Spiritual Connotation: Full of Wisdom
Scripture: Isaiah 50:4 RSV
The Lord GOD has given me the tongue of those who are taught, that I may know how to sustain with a word him that is weary.

RIPLEY, Rip, Ripleigh
Language/Cultural Origin: English
Inherent Meaning: From the Meadow of the One Who Shouts
Spiritual Connotation: Thankful
Scripture: Psalm 32:11 NASB
Be glad in the LORD and rejoice, you righteous ones, and shout for joy, all you who are upright in heart.

RISHON, Rishán, Rishaun, Rishawn
Language/Cultural Origin: Hebrew
Inherent Meaning: First
Spiritual Connotation: Servant
Scripture: Mark 10:45 NKJV
For even the Son of Man did not come to be served, but to serve, and to give His life a ransom for many.

RITA, Reeta, Rheta
Language/Cultural Origin: Spanish
Inherent Meaning: Pearl
Spiritual Connotation: Priceless
Scripture: Matthew 13:45 NRSV
Again, the kingdom of heaven is like a merchant in search of fine pearls.

RIVER, Rivers
Language/Cultural Origin: English
Inherent Meaning: Large Stream

Spiritual Connotation: Vessel of God
Scripture: Psalm 74:15 NASB
You broke open springs and torrents; You dried up ever-flowing streams.

ROANNA, Rohana, Rohanna, Roana, Roann, Roanne (see also Ruana)
Language/Cultural Origin: Hebrew
Inherent Meaning: Reminder of Sweet Incense
Spiritual Connotation: Spiritual Understanding
Scripture: Psalm 51:6 NKJV
Behold, You desire truth in the inward parts, and in the hidden part You will make me to know wisdom.

ROARKE, Rourke
Language/Cultural Origin: Irish
Inherent Meaning: Famous Ruler
Spiritual Connotation: Courageous Spirit
Scripture: Psalm 31:24 NKJV
Be of good courage, and He shall strengthen your heart, all you who hope in the LORD.

ROBERT, Bob, Bobb, Bobby, Rob, Robb, Robbert, Robbie, Robby, Roberto, Roberts, Robertson, Robinson, Rupert
Language/Cultural Origin: Old English
Inherent Meaning: Bright in Counsel
Spiritual Connotation: Abiding in God
Scripture: 1 John 4:13 TLB
And he has put his own Holy Spirit into our hearts as a proof to us that we are living with him and he with us.

ROBERTA, Birdee, Birdie, Bobbi, Robbi
Language/Cultural Origin: English
Inherent Meaning: Famous Brilliance
Spiritual Connotation: Excellent Worth
Scripture: Ephesians 2:10 NASB
For we are His workmanship, created in Christ Jesus for good works, which God prepared beforehand, that we should walk in them.

ROBIN, Robbin, Robbyn, Robyn, Robynn
Language/Cultural Origin: English
Inherent Meaning: Shining Fame
Spiritual Connotation: Victorious Spirit

Scripture: Psalm 18:32 NKJV
It is God who arms me with strength, and makes my way perfect.

ROCCO, Rock, Rocko, Rocky, Rokko, Roque
Language/Cultural Origin: Italian
Inherent Meaning: Rest
Spiritual Connotation: Restored
Scripture: Psalm 23:2–23 KJV
He maketh me to lie down in green pastures: he leadeth me beside the still waters. He restoreth my soul.

ROCHELLE, Rachalle, Raechell, Raeshelle, Rochell, Rochella, Rochette, Roshele, Roshell, Roshelle (see also Richelle)
Language/Cultural Origin: French
Inherent Meaning: Little Rock
Spiritual Connotation: Established
Scripture: Psalm 62:2 NIV
He alone is my rock and my salvation; he is my fortress, I will never be shaken.

RODERICK, Rodderick, Roderic, Roderigo, Roderique, Rodric, Rodrigo, Rodriguez, Rodrik, Rodrique, Rodriquez (see also Broderick)
Language/Cultural Origin: Old German
Inherent Meaning: Famous Ruler
Spiritual Connotation: Arm of God
Scripture: Psalm 33:16 NASB
The king is not saved by a mighty army; a warrior is not delivered by great strength.

RODMAN, Rodmond, Rodmund
Language/Cultural Origin: Old English
Inherent Meaning: Heroic
Spiritual Connotation: Famous
Scripture: Isaiah 19:20 NLT
It will be a sign and a witness to the LORD Almighty in the land of Egypt. . . . He will send them a savior who will rescue them.

RODNEY, Rod, Rhodney, Rodnee
Language/Cultural Origin: Anglo-Saxon
Inherent Meaning: From the Clearing on the Island
Spiritual Connotation: Joyful
Scripture: Psalm 40:3 NKJV

He has put a new song in my mouth; praise to our God; many will see it and fear, and will trust in the LORD.

ROGAN, Rogann
Language/Cultural Origin: Irish
Inherent Meaning: Redhead
Spiritual Connotation: Persevering
Scripture: Hebrews 12:1 NKJV
Let us lay aside every weight, and the sin which so easily ensnares us, and let us run with endurance the race that is set before us.

ROGER, Rodger, Rog, Rogers, Rutger
Language/Cultural Origin: Old German
Inherent Meaning: Famous Warrior
Spiritual Connotation: Strong in Counsel
Scripture: Isaiah 48:17 NKJV
I am the LORD your God, who teaches you to profit, who leads you by the way you should go.

ROLAND, Rolando, Rolland, Rollando, Rolle, Rollie, Rowland
Language/Cultural Origin: Old German
Inherent Meaning: Famous Throughout the Land
Spiritual Connotation: Full of Wisdom
Scripture: Psalm 106:3 NKJV
Blessed are those who keep justice, and he who does righteousness at all times!

ROLANDA, Rollanda
Language/Cultural Origin: German
Inherent Meaning: Famous Throughout the Land
Spiritual Connotation: Peaceful
Scripture: Numbers 6:26 NKJV
The LORD lift up His countenance upon you, and give you peace.

ROLF, Rolfe, Rolph (see also Ralph)
Language/Cultural Origin: Scandinavian
Inherent Meaning: Counselor
Spiritual Connotation: Wise
Scripture: Psalm 90:12 NASB
So teach us to number our days, that we may present to Thee a heart of wisdom.

ROMAINE, Romana, Romanda, Romayne, Romi, Romy
Language/Cultural Origin: French
Inherent Meaning: From Rome

Spiritual Connotation: Blessed
Scripture: Romans 1:7 RSV
To all God's beloved in Rome, who are called to be saints: Grace to you and peace from God our Father and the Lord Jesus Christ.

ROMAN, Román
Language/Cultural Origin: Latin
Inherent Meaning: From Rome
Spiritual Connotation: Protector of Truth
Scripture: Ephesians 6:10 NKJV
Finally, my brethren, be strong in the Lord and in the power of His might.

ROMEO, Roméo
Language/Cultural Origin: Italian
Inherent Meaning: Pilgrim to Rome
Spiritual Connotation: Steadfast
Scripture: Hebrews 11:13 NKJV
These all died in faith, not having received the promises, but having seen them afar off were assured of them, embraced them and confessed that they were strangers and pilgrims on the earth.

RONALD, Ron, Ronny
Language/Cultural Origin: Old English
Inherent Meaning: Mighty Power
Spiritual Connotation: Authority
Scripture: Micah 6:8 NKJV
He has shown you, O man, what is good; and what does the LORD require of you but to do justly, to love mercy, and to walk humbly with your God?

RONAN, Ronán, Rónán (see also Raanan, Rhiannon)
Language/Cultural Origin: Irish
Inherent Meaning: Little Seal
Spiritual Connotation: Playful
Scripture: Zechariah 8:5 NLT
And the streets of the city will be filled with boys and girls at play.

RONDEL, Rondell, Rondrell
Language/Cultural Origin: French
Inherent Meaning: Poem
Spiritual Connotation: Gifted
Scripture: Psalm 40:3 RSV
He put a new song in my mouth, a song of praise to our God. Many will see and fear, and put their trust in the LORD.

RONNI, Ronee, Roni, Ronia, Ronnee, Ronney, Ronnie, Ronny, Ronya
Language/Cultural Origin: English
Inherent Meaning: Power
Spiritual Connotation: Strength
Scripture: Zechariah 4:6 NKJV
Not by might nor by power, but by My Spirit, Says the LORD of hosts.

ROOSEVELT, Rosevelt
Language/Cultural Origin: Dutch
Inherent Meaning: From the Field of Roses
Spiritual Connotation: Blessed
Scripture: Isaiah 35:1 NKJV
The wilderness and the wasteland shall be glad for them, and the desert shall rejoice and blossom as the rose.

RORY, Roari, Rorey, Rori
Language/Cultural Origin: Gaelic
Inherent Meaning: King
Spiritual Connotation: Worthy of Honor
Scripture: Psalm 97:11 TLB
Light is sown for the godly and joy for the good.

ROSALIND, Rosalea, Rosalee, Rosalia, Rosalin, Rosalina, Rosalinda, Rosalyn, Rosalynn, Roselynn, Rosetta, Rosette, Rosilyn, Roslyn, Rozália, Rozalee, Rozalie, Rozalin, Rozalyn, Rozlyn
Language/Cultural Origin: Spanish
Inherent Meaning: Beautiful Rose
Spiritual Connotation: Wise
Scripture: Psalm 49:3 NKJV
My mouth shall speak wisdom, and the meditation of my heart shall give understanding.

ROSAMOND, Rosamund
Language/Cultural Origin: Old German
Inherent Meaning: Guardian
Spiritual Connotation: Protector of Truth
Scripture: 1 Timothy 6:20 NASB
Guard what has been entrusted to you, avoiding worldly and empty chatter and the opposing arguments of what is falsely called knowledge.

ROSCOE, Rosco
Language/Cultural Origin: Old Norse

Inherent Meaning: From the Deer Forest
Spiritual Connotation: Discerning
Scripture: Proverbs 2:11 NLT
Wise planning will watch over you. Understanding will keep you safe.

ROSEANNA, Rosana, Rosannah, Rosangela, Roseann, Rose Ann, Rose Anne, Roseannah, Rossana, Rossanna, Rozana, Rozangela, Rozanna, Rozeanne
Language/Cultural Origin: English
Inherent Meaning: Rose
Spiritual Connotation: Gracious
Scripture: Psalm 111:4 NASB
He has made His wonders to be remembered; the LORD is gracious and compassionate.

ROSE, Rosa, Rosey, Rosi, Rosie, Rosy, Roza, Rozee, Rozy
Language/Cultural Origin: Latin
Inherent Meaning: Rose
Spiritual Connotation: God's Gracious Gift
Scripture: Isaiah 35:1 NKJV
The wilderness and the wasteland shall be glad for them, and the desert shall rejoice and blossom as the rose.

ROSEMARY, Rosemaria, Rosemarie
Language/Cultural Origin: Latin
Inherent Meaning: Dew of the Sea
Spiritual Connotation: Crowned
Scripture: Psalm 121:1–2 NASB
I will lift up my eyes to the mountains; from whence shall my help come? My help comes from the LORD, who made heaven and earth.

ROSINE, Rosina
Language/Cultural Origin: Italian
Inherent Meaning: Cherished
Spiritual Connotation: Bold
Scripture: Isaiah 41:13 NRSV
For I, the LORD your God, hold your right hand; it is I who say to you, "Do not fear, I will help you."

ROSS, Roess
Language/Cultural Origin: Gaelic
Inherent Meaning: Knight
Spiritual Connotation: Victorious Spirit
Scripture: 1 Corinthians 15:57 NKJV
But thanks be to God, who gives us the victory through our Lord Jesus Christ.

ROWEN, Rowan
Language/Cultural Origin: Irish
Inherent Meaning: Red
Spiritual Connotation: Purchased
Scripture: 1 Peter 1:18–19 NKJV
You were not redeemed with corruptible things, . . . but with the precious blood of Christ, as of a lamb without blemish and without spot.

ROWENA, Rowina
Language/Cultural Origin: Welsh
Inherent Meaning: Peaceful
Spiritual Connotation: Wise
Scripture: Proverbs 24:3 NKJV
Through wisdom a house is built, and by understanding it is established.

ROXANNE, Roxana, Roxane, Roxann, Roxanna, Roxi, Roxie, Roxy
Language/Cultural Origin: Persian
Inherent Meaning: Sunrise
Spiritual Connotation: Heavenly Light
Scripture: Psalm 113:3 NRSV
From the rising of the sun to its setting the name of the LORD is to be praised.

ROY, Roi
Language/Cultural Origin: French
Inherent Meaning: King
Spiritual Connotation: Seeker of Wisdom
Scripture: Psalm 119:34 NRSV
Give me understanding, that I may keep your law and observe it with my whole heart.

ROYCE, Roice
Language/Cultural Origin: Old English
Inherent Meaning: Son of the King
Spiritual Connotation: Tranquil Spirit
Scripture: Matthew 5:9 NKJV
Blessed are the peacemakers, for they shall be called sons of God.

ROZEN, Roszen
Language/Cultural Origin: Hebrew
Inherent Meaning: Ruler
Spiritual Connotation: Gifted
Scripture: Proverbs 28:2 NRSV
When a land rebels it has many rulers; but with an intelligent ruler there is lasting order.

RUANA, Ruanna (see also Roanna)
Language/Cultural Origin: Indo-Pakistani

Inherent Meaning: Stringed Instrument
Spiritual Connotation: Joyful Praise
Scripture: Psalm 108:2 NASB
Awake, harp and lyre; I will awaken the dawn!

RUBY, Rubia, Rubey, Rubi, Rubie
Language/Cultural Origin: French
Inherent Meaning: Beautiful Jewel
Spiritual Connotation: Full of Grace
Scripture: Psalm 26:3 NKJV
For Your lovingkindness is before my eyes, and I have walked in Your truth.

RUDOLPH, Rudi, Rudy
Language/Cultural Origin: Old German
Inherent Meaning: Great and Famous
Spiritual Connotation: Resourceful
Scripture: Exodus 31:3 NKJV
And I have filled him with the Spirit of God, in wisdom, in understanding, in knowledge, and in all manner of workmanship.

RUFUS, Ruffus
Language/Cultural Origin: Latin
Inherent Meaning: Red-Haired
Spiritual Connotation: Excellent Virtue
Scripture: Zechariah 7:9 NLT
This is what the LORD Almighty says: Judge fairly and honestly, and show mercy and kindness to one another.

RUNE, Roone
Language/Cultural Origin: Swedish
Inherent Meaning: Secret
Spiritual Connotation: Guarded of God
Scripture: Psalm 91:4 TLB
He will shield you with his wings! They will shelter you. His faithful promises are your armor.

RUPERT, see Robert

RURI, Rurika, Ruriko
Language/Cultural Origin: Japanese
Inherent Meaning: Emerald
Spiritual Connotation: Future Hope
Scripture: Revelation 21:19 NASB
The foundation stones of the city wall were adorned with every kind of precious stone.

RUSH, Rusch
Language/Cultural Origin: English

Inherent Meaning: Redhead
Spiritual Connotation: Strength
Scripture: Genesis 25:25 NASB

Now the first came forth red, all over like a hairy garment; and they named him Esau.

RUSSELL, Russ, Russel, Rusty

Language/Cultural Origin: French
Inherent Meaning: Redhead
Spiritual Connotation: Trusting
Scripture: Psalm 143:8 RSV

Let me hear in the morning of thy steadfast love, for in thee I put my trust. Teach me the way I should go, for to thee I lift up my soul.

RUTH, Ruthann, Ruthanne, ☞Ruthe, Ruthey, Ruthie

Language/Cultural Origin: Hebrew
Inherent Meaning: Companion
Spiritual Connotation: Faithful
Scripture: Psalm 119:73 NKJV

Your hands have made me and fashioned me; give me understanding, that I may learn Your commandments.

RUTHERFORD, Rutherforde

Language/Cultural Origin: Scottish
Inherent Meaning: From the Cattle Ford
Spiritual Connotation: Vigilant

Scripture: Proverbs 22:12 NKJV

The eyes of the LORD preserve knowledge, but He overthrows the words of the faithless.

RUTLEDGE, Rutlege

Language/Cultural Origin: Scandinavian
Inherent Meaning: From the Red Land
Spiritual Connotation: Loyal
Scripture: Isaiah 38:3 NKJV

Remember now, O LORD, I pray, how I have walked before You in truth and with a loyal heart, and have done what is good in Your sight.

RUZA, Runzena, Ruzenka, Ruzina, Ruzsa

Language/Cultural Origin: Czech
Inherent Meaning: Rose
Spiritual Connotation: Lovely
Scripture: Isaiah 35:1 NKJV

The wilderness and the wasteland shall be glad for them, and the desert shall rejoice and blossom as the rose.

RYAN, Rhyan, Rhyne, Rian, Riann, Ryann, Ryanne, Ryen, Ryne, Ryon (see also Rhian)

Language/Cultural Origin: Irish
Inherent Meaning: Little Ruler
Spiritual Connotation: Youthful Heart
Scripture: Zechariah 8:5 NLT

And the streets of the city will be filled with boys and girls at play.

SABA, Sabah, Sabbah (see also Shaba)

Language/Cultural Origin: English
Inherent Meaning: Oath of God
Spiritual Connotation: Promise
Scripture: Romans 11:27 NLT
And then I will keep my covenant with them and take away their sins.

SABER, Sabre

Language/Cultural Origin: French
Inherent Meaning: Sword
Spiritual Connotation: Spiritual Warrior
Scripture: Ephesians 6:17 NKJV
And take the helmet of salvation, and the sword of the Spirit, which is the word of God.

SABINA, Sabinna, Sebina, Sebinah

Language/Cultural Origin: Latin
Inherent Meaning: Planter of Vines
Spiritual Connotation: Spiritual Discernment
Scripture: Philippians 1:9 NRSV
And this is my prayer, that your love may overflow more and more with knowledge and full insight.

SABIYA, Sabaya

Language/Cultural Origin: Middle Eastern
Inherent Meaning: Morning
Spiritual Connotation: Lovely
Scripture: Psalm 50:1 NRSV
The mighty one, God the LORD, speaks and summons the earth from the rising of the sun to its setting.

SABLE, Sabel

Language/Cultural Origin: English
Inherent Meaning: Sleek
Spiritual Connotation: Prudent
Scripture: Ephesians 5:16 NCV
Use every chance you have for doing good, because these are evil times.

SABRA, Sabrah, Sabriya

Language/Cultural Origin: Hebrew
Inherent Meaning: Cactus
Spiritual Connotation: Joyful
Scripture: Isaiah 35:1 NKJV
The wilderness and the wasteland shall be glad for them, and the desert shall rejoice and blossom as the rose.

SABRINA, Sabreena, Sabrinna, Sebrina, Zabreena, Zabrina

Language/Cultural Origin: Latin
Inherent Meaning: Boundary
Spiritual Connotation: Protected, Guarded
Scripture: Psalm 104:9 NCV
You set borders for the seas that they cannot cross, so water will never cover the earth again.

SADANNA, Sadana, Sadhana

Language/Cultural Origin: Indo-Pakistani
Inherent Meaning: Devotion
Spiritual Connotation: Persistent
Scripture: Psalm 119:97 NRSV
Oh, how I love your law! It is my meditation all day long.

SADIE, Sáde, Sadé, Sadee, Saydee

Language/Cultural Origin: English
Inherent Meaning: Princess
Spiritual Connotation: Beautiful
Scripture: Psalm 45:13 NIV
All glorious is the princess within her chamber; her gown is interwoven with gold.

SADIYA, Sadeea, Sadia, Sadya

Language/Cultural Origin: Middle Eastern
Inherent Meaning: Fortunate
Spiritual Connotation: Blessed
Scripture: Isaiah 3:10 RSV
Tell the righteous that it shall be well with them, for they shall eat the fruit of their deeds.

SAFARI, Safáree, Safaria, Safarya

Language/Cultural Origin: Swahili

Inherent Meaning: Born While Traveling
Spiritual Connotation: Promise
Scripture: Jeremiah 31:8 NASB
> And I will gather them from the remote parts of the earth . . . The woman with child and she who is in labor with child, together; a great company, they will return here.

SAFFORD, Saford
Language/Cultural Origin: Middle English
Inherent Meaning: From the Place of the Willow-River Crossing
Spiritual Connotation: Beloved
Scripture: 1 John 4:9 NCV
> This is how God showed his love to us: He sent his one and only Son into the world so that we could have life through him.

SAFFRON, Saffrón
Language/Cultural Origin: English
Inherent Meaning: Flower
Spiritual Connotation: Valuable Spice
Scripture: Proverbs 4:9 NCV
> [Wisdom] will be like flowers in your hair and like a beautiful crown on your head.

SAGE, Saige
Language/Cultural Origin: English
Inherent Meaning: Wise
Spiritual Connotation: Discerning
Scripture: Proverbs 14:8 NRSV
> It is the wisdom of the clever to understand where they go, but the folly of fools misleads.

SAHARA, Saharah
Language/Cultural Origin: Middle Eastern
Inherent Meaning: Wilderness
Spiritual Connotation: Strengthened
Scripture: Isaiah 32:16 NLT
> Justice will rule in the wilderness and righteousness in the fertile field.

SAKARI, Sakaree
Language/Cultural Origin: Indo-Pakistani
Inherent Meaning: Heart of Sweetness
Spiritual Connotation: Forgiving
Scripture: Job 42:10 NASB
> And the LORD restored the fortunes of Job when he prayed for his friends, and the LORD increased all that Job had twofold.

SAKURA, Sakhura
Language/Cultural Origin: Japanese

Inherent Meaning: Cherry Blossom
Spiritual Connotation: Promise
Scripture: Deuteronomy 1:25 NLT
> They picked some of its fruit and brought it back to us. And they reported that the land the LORD our God had given us was indeed a good land.

SALAAM, see Selam

SALIM, Saleem, Salím
Language/Cultural Origin: Middle Eastern
Inherent Meaning: Safe
Spiritual Connotation: Shielded
Scripture: Psalm 28:9 TLB
> Defend your people, Lord; defend and bless your chosen ones. Lead them like a shepherd and carry them forever in your arms.

**SALINA, Salena, Saleena
(see also Selena)**
Language/Cultural Origin: French
Inherent Meaning: Dignified
Spiritual Connotation: Delivered
Scripture: Leviticus 26:13 TLB
> For I am the Lord your God. . . . I have broken your chains so that you can walk with dignity.

SALLY, Sallee, Salley, Salli, Sallie
Language/Cultural Origin: Old English
Inherent Meaning: Princess
Spiritual Connotation: Beloved
Scripture: 1 Peter 2:9 NRSV
> But you are a chosen race, a royal priesthood, a holy nation, God's own people, in order that you may proclaim the mighty acts of him who called you out of darkness into his marvelous light.

**SALMAN, Salamen, Salmun
(see also Solomon)**
Language/Cultural Origin: Czech
Inherent Meaning: Serenity
Spiritual Connotation: Strong in Character
Scripture: Hebrews 12:11 RSV
> For the moment all discipline seems painful rather than pleasant; later it yields the peaceful fruit of righteousness to those who have been trained by it.

SALOME, Saloma, Salomé
Language/Cultural Origin: Hebrew

Inherent Meaning: Peaceful
Spiritual Connotation: Restful
Scripture: Mark 4:39 NIV
He got up, rebuked the wind and said to the waves, "Quiet! Be still!" Then the wind died down and it was completely calm.

SALVADOR, Sal, Salvadore, Salvatore
Language/Cultural Origin: Italian
Inherent Meaning: Savior
Spiritual Connotation: Faithful
Scripture: Hosea 13:4 NIV
You shall acknowledge no God but me, no Savior except me.

SAMANTHA, Sam, Samanthia, Sami, Sammantha, Semantha, Simantha, Symantha
Language/Cultural Origin: Aramaic
Inherent Meaning: Listener
Spiritual Connotation: Attentive to God's Voice
Scripture: Job 22:28 NLT
Whatever you decide to do will be accomplished, and light will shine on the road ahead of you.

SAMARA, Samarra, Samira, Sammara, Samora
Language/Cultural Origin: Hebrew
Inherent Meaning: Guarded by God
Spiritual Connotation: Proven Faithful
Scripture: Revelation 3:10 TLB
Because you have patiently obeyed me despite the persecution, therefore I will protect you from the time of Great Tribulation.

SAMINA, Sameena, Samayna
Language/Cultural Origin: Middle Eastern
Inherent Meaning: Praised
Spiritual Connotation: Honorable
Scripture: 1 Peter 2:17 TLB
Show respect for everyone. Love Christians everywhere. Fear God and honor the government.

SAMONA, see Simona

SAMSON, Sam, Sampson
☞ Language/Cultural Origin: Hebrew
Inherent Meaning: Like the Sun
Spiritual Connotation: Strength of Spirit

Scripture: Psalm 33:16 NASB
The king is not saved by a mighty army; a warrior is not delivered by great strength.

SAMUEL, Sam, Samm, Sammie, ☞Sammuel, Sammy, Samuele
Language/Cultural Origin: Hebrew
Inherent Meaning: God Has Heard
Spiritual Connotation: Instructed of God
Scripture: 1 Samuel 1:20 NASB
Hannah ... gave birth to a son; and she named him "Samuel," saying, "Because I have asked him of the LORD."

SANBORN, Sanborne, Sandbourne
Language/Cultural Origin: English
Inherent Meaning: From the Sandy Brook
Spiritual Connotation: Defender of the Faith
Scripture: 1 Corinthians 8:6 NLT
But we know that there is only one God, the Father. ... And there is only one Lord, Jesus Christ.

SANCHO, Sanchez
Language/Cultural Origin: Latin
Inherent Meaning: Sanctified
Spiritual Connotation: Appointed of God
Scripture: Nehemiah 9:6 NKJV
You alone are the LORD; You have made heaven ... with all their host, the earth and everything on it.

SANCIA, Sancha, Sanchia, Sancie, Sanzia
Language/Cultural Origin: Spanish
Inherent Meaning: Holy
Spiritual Connotation: Chosen
Scripture: Leviticus 20:26 NRSV
You shall be holy to me; for I the LORD am holy, and I have separated you from the other peoples to be mine.

SANDERS, Sander, Sándor, Sandey, Sandy, Saunder, Saunders
Language/Cultural Origin: English
Inherent Meaning: Defender
Spiritual Connotation: Beloved
Scripture: Psalm 119:18 NRSV
Open my eyes, so that I may behold wondrous things out of your law.

SANDRA, Sahndra, Sandee, Sandi,
Sandie, Sandrea, Sandreea,
Sandreia, Sandria, Sandy,
Saundra, Sondra, Sonndra
(see also Xandra, Zandra)
Language/Cultural Origin: English
Inherent Meaning: Defender
Spiritual Connotation: Guardian of Truth
Scripture: 1 Timothy 6:20 NLT

*Guard what God has entrusted to you. Avoid
godless, foolish discussions with those who
oppose you with their so-called knowledge.*

SANFORD, Sandford
Language/Cultural Origin: Old English
Inherent Meaning: From the Place of the
Sandy River Crossing
Spiritual Connotation: Gentle
Scripture: Matthew 11:29 NKJV

*Take My yoke upon you and learn from Me,
for I am gentle and lowly in heart, and you
will find rest for your souls.*

SANTIAGO, Sántiago
Language/Cultural Origin: Spanish
Inherent Meaning: Saint
Spiritual Connotation: Gifted
Scripture: Ephesians 4:12 NCV

*Christ gave those gifts to prepare God's holy
people for the work of serving, to make the
body of Christ stronger.*

SANYA, Sania, Saniya
Language/Cultural Origin: Indo-Pakistani
Inherent Meaning: Born on Saturday
Spiritual Connotation: Believer
Scripture: John 14:6 NKJV

*Jesus said to him, "I am the way, the truth,
and the life. No one comes to the Father
except through Me."*

SAPPHIRA, Safire, Saffire, Sapphire
Language/Cultural Origin: Greek
Inherent Meaning: Gem
Spiritual Connotation: Precious
Scripture: Proverbs 8:11 NKJV

*For wisdom is better than rubies, and all the
things one may desire cannot be compared
with her.*

SARAH, Saara, Saarah, Sahra, Sara,
Sarai, Sarra, Sarrah, Sharai,
Sharaiah, Sharaya, Sharayah
(see also Soraya, Zara)
Language/Cultural Origin: Hebrew
Inherent Meaning: Princess
Spiritual Connotation: Beloved
Scripture: Psalm 45:13 NIV

*All glorious is the princess within her
chamber; her gown is interwoven with gold.*

SARIYA, Sareeya
Language/Cultural Origin: Middle Eastern
Inherent Meaning: Night Clouds
Spiritual Connotation: Guided of God
Scripture: Exodus 13:22 NLT

*And the LORD did not remove the pillar of
cloud or pillar of fire from their sight.*

SASHA, Sacha, Sascha, Sashah,
Sashana, Sashia, Sashka, Sausha,
Shasha, Shashia, Zasha
Language/Cultural Origin: Russian
Inherent Meaning: Defender of Mankind
Spiritual Connotation: Heart of God
Scripture: Deuteronomy 10:18 TLB

*He gives justice to the fatherless and widows.
He loves foreigners and gives them food and
clothing.*

SASON, Sasóne, Sassón
Language/Cultural Origin: Hebrew
Inherent Meaning: Delight
Spiritual Connotation: Godly
Scripture: Psalm 37:4 NKJV

*Delight yourself also in the LORD, and He
shall give you the desires of your heart.*

SATIN, Sattin
Language/Cultural Origin: French
Inherent Meaning: Smooth
Spiritual Connotation: Freedom
Scripture: John 8:32 KJV

*And ye shall know the truth, and the truth
shall make you free.*

SAUL, Saül, Sol
Language/Cultural Origin: Hebrew
Inherent Meaning: Asked-for
Spiritual Connotation: God's Blessing
Scripture: Isaiah 44:3 NCV

I will pour out water for the thirsty land and

make streams flow on dry land. I will pour out my Spirit into your children and my blessing on your descendants.

SAVANNAH, Sahvannah, Savana, Savanah, Savanna, Savauna, Sevana, Sevanah, Sevanna
Language/Cultural Origin: Spanish
Inherent Meaning: From the Treeless Plain
Spiritual Connotation: Cherished
Scripture: James 4:8 NKJV
Draw near to God and He will draw near to you.

SAVILLE, Savill, Seville, Sevilla
Language/Cultural Origin: French
Inherent Meaning: From the Willow Village
Spiritual Connotation: Trusting
Scripture: Psalm 143:8 NLT
Let me hear of your unfailing love to me in the morning, for I am trusting you. Show me where to walk, for I have come to you in prayer.

SAWYER, Soiyer
Language/Cultural Origin: English
Inherent Meaning: Wood Worker
Spiritual Connotation: Gifted
Scripture: Exodus 31:3 NKJV
And I have filled him with the Spirit of God, in wisdom, in understanding, in knowledge, and in all manner of workmanship.

SAXON, Sax, Saxen
Language/Cultural Origin: Middle English
Inherent Meaning: Swordsman
Spiritual Connotation: Valorous
Scripture: Ephesians 6:17 NCV
Accept God's salvation as your helmet, and take the sword of the Spirit, which is the word of God.

SCHAFER, Schaefer, Shäffer, Shayfer
Language/Cultural Origin: German
Inherent Meaning: Shepherd
Spiritual Connotation: Leader
Scripture: John 10:14 NKJV
I am the good shepherd; and I know My sheep, and am known by My own.

SCHUYLER, see Skyler

SCOTT, Scot, Scottie, Scotty
Language/Cultural Origin: Old English

Inherent Meaning: From Scotland
Spiritual Connotation: Temple of God
Scripture: 1 Corinthians 3:16 NRSV
Do you not know that you are God's temple and that God's Spirit dwells in you?

SEAN, Séan, Seán, Seane, Shaan (see also Shane, Shawn)
Language/Cultural Origin: Irish
Inherent Meaning: God Is Gracious
Spiritual Connotation: Servant
Scripture: 1 Peter 4:10 NRSV
Like good stewards of the manifold grace of God, serve one another with whatever gift each of you has received.

SEANA, see Shauna

SEBASTIAN, Sabastien, Sébastien
Language/Cultural Origin: Greek
Inherent Meaning: Venerable
Spiritual Connotation: Esteemed
Scripture: Philippians 2:13 NLT
For God is working in you, giving you the desire to obey him and the power to do what pleases him.

SEELEY, see Ceeley

SELAM, Saalam, Salaam, Selaam
Language/Cultural Origin: Ethiopian
Inherent Meaning: Peaceful
Spiritual Connotation: Content
Scripture: Philippians 4:7 RSV
And the peace of God, which passes all understanding, will keep your hearts and your minds in Christ Jesus.

SELBY, Selbey
Language/Cultural Origin: English
Inherent Meaning: From the Mansion
Spiritual Connotation: Child of God
Scripture: Acts 17:28 NRSV
For in him we live and move and have our being; as even some of your own poets have said, for we too are his offspring.

SELENA, Selenia, Selina, Selyna, Sylena, Sylina (see also Salina)
Language/Cultural Origin: Greek
Inherent Meaning: Fair as the Moon
Spiritual Connotation: Full of Wisdom
Scripture: Matthew 10:20 NLT

For it won't be you doing the talking—it will be the Spirit of your Father speaking through you.

SELMA, Selmah, Zelma
Language/Cultural Origin: Celtic
Inherent Meaning: Divinely Protected
Spiritual Connotation: Enlightened Spirit
Scripture: Luke 12:31 NKJV
But seek the kingdom of God, and all these things shall be added to you.

SEQUOIA, Seqora, Sequora, Sequoya
Language/Cultural Origin: Cherokee
Inherent Meaning: Redwood Tree
Spiritual Connotation: Filled With Praise
Scripture: Psalm 96:12 NCV
Let the fields and everything in them rejoice. Then all the trees of the forest will sing for joy.

SERAPHINA, Sarafina, Saraphina, Serafina, Syrafina
Language/Cultural Origin: Hebrew
Inherent Meaning: Ardent
Spiritual Connotation: Zealous
Scripture: Psalm 42:8 NRSV
By day the LORD commands his steadfast love, and at night his song is with me, a prayer to the God of my life.

SERENA, Sarina, Sereena, Serenah, Serenna, Serenity
Language/Cultural Origin: Latin
Inherent Meaning: Secure
Spiritual Connotation: Content
Scripture: 1 Corinthians 2:12 NCV
Now we did not receive the spirit of the world, but we received the Spirit that is from God so that we can know all that God has given us.

SERGEI, Serg, Serge, Sergey, Sergio, Sergios, Sirgio, Sirgios
Language/Cultural Origin: Russian
Inherent Meaning: Servant
Spiritual Connotation: Humble
Scripture: Mark 10:43 NKJV
Whoever desires to become great among you shall be your servant.

SETH, Sethe
Language/Cultural Origin: Hebrew

Inherent Meaning: Appointed of God
Spiritual Connotation: Chosen
Scripture: James 2:5 NLT
Hasn't God chosen the poor in this world to be rich in faith? Aren't they the ones who will inherit the kingdom God promised to those who love him?

SHABA, Shahba (see also Saba)
Language/Cultural Origin: Hispanic
Inherent Meaning: Rose
Spiritual Connotation: Virtuous
Scripture: Isaiah 35:1 NKJV
The wilderness and the wasteland shall be glad for them, and the desert shall rejoice and blossom as the rose.

SHAE, see Shea

SHAELA, Shaila, Shalah, Shaylah, Shaylan, Shaylea, Shaylee, Shaylie, Shaylin, Shaylyn, Shaylynn
Language/Cultural Origin: Afghani
Inherent Meaning: Lovely Eyes
Spiritual Connotation: Beautiful
Scripture: Song of Songs 4:1A RSV
Behold, you are beautiful, my love, behold, you are beautiful! Your eyes are doves behind your veil.

SHAINA, Shaena, Shainah, Shainna, Shayna
Language/Cultural Origin: Yiddish
Inherent Meaning: Beautiful
Spiritual Connotation: Witness
Scripture: Romans 10:15B NRSV
How beautiful are the feet of those who bring good news!

SHAKARA, Shacara, Shaccara, Shakkara
Language/Cultural Origin: American
Inherent Meaning: Pure
Spiritual Connotation: Innocent
Scripture: Titus 1:15 NKJV
To the pure all things are pure.

SHAKIA, Shakeeya, Shakeya, Shakiya, Shaqiya, Shaquiya, Shekia, Shekeeya
Language/Cultural Origin: American
Inherent Meaning: Season's Beginning
Spiritual Connotation: Miraculous

Scripture: Genesis 1:14 NCV

Let there be lights in the sky to separate day from night. These lights will be used for signs, seasons, days, and years.

SHAKILA, Shakaela, Shakeela, Shaquilla, Shekaela, Shequilla, Shikeela, Shiquilla
Language/Cultural Origin: Middle Eastern
Inherent Meaning: Pretty
Spiritual Connotation: Beautiful
Scripture: Proverbs 31:30 NRSV

Charm is deceitful, and beauty is vain, but a woman who fears the LORD is to be praised.

SHAKIRA, Shaakira, Shakeira, Shakira, Shakiria
Language/Cultural Origin: Middle Eastern
Inherent Meaning: Grateful
Spiritual Connotation: Unifier
Scripture: Colossians 3:15 NASB

And let the peace of Christ rule in your hearts, to which indeed you were called in one body; and be thankful.

SHALANA, Shalaina, Shalauna, Shelanna, Shilauna
Language/Cultural Origin: American
Inherent Meaning: Attractive
Spiritual Connotation: Peaceful
Scripture: Isaiah 26:3 NLT

You will keep in perfect peace all who trust in you, whose thoughts are fixed on you!

SHALMAN, Shalmon
☞ Language/Cultural Origin: Hebrew
Inherent Meaning: Peacemaker
Spiritual Connotation: Pure
Scripture: 2 Peter 3:14 NCV

Dear friends, since you are waiting for this to happen, do your best to be without sin and without fault. Try to be at peace with God.

SHALOM, Salóm, Shalum, Sholome
☞ Language/Cultural Origin: Hebrew
Inherent Meaning: Peace
Spiritual Connotation: Hopeful
Scripture: Romans 12:18 NKJV

If it is possible, as much as depends on you, live peaceably with all men.

SHAMARA, Shamarah, Shamarra, Shammara
Language/Cultural Origin: Middle Eastern
Inherent Meaning: Prepared for Battle
Spiritual Connotation: Vigilant
Scripture: 1 Corinthians 14:8 NLT

And if the bugler doesn't sound a clear call, how will the soldiers know they are being called to battle?

SHAMIR, Shahmir, Shameer
Language/Cultural Origin: Hebrew
Inherent Meaning: Precious Stone
Spiritual Connotation: Invaluable
Scripture: 2 Chronicles 32:27 NCV

He made treasuries for his silver, gold, gems, spices, shields, and other valuable things.

SHAMIRA, Shamiria
Language/Cultural Origin: Hebrew
Inherent Meaning: Precious Stone
Spiritual Connotation: Destined
Scripture: Zechariah 9:16 RSV

On that day the LORD their God will save them for they are the flock of his people; for like the jewels of a crown they shall shine on his land.

SHAMMAI, Shamai, Shammae, ☞ Shammay, Shammei
Language/Cultural Origin: Hebrew
Inherent Meaning: Appraiser
Spiritual Connotation: Discerning
Scripture: Revelation 4:11 NASB

Worthy are You, our Lord and our God, to receive glory and honor and power; for You created all things.

SHANA, SHANAE, see Shauna

SHANAHAN, Shannahan
Language/Cultural Origin: Irish
Inherent Meaning: Wise
Spiritual Connotation: Gifted
Scripture: 1 Kings 3:28 NRSV

All Israel heard of the judgment that the king had rendered; and they stood in awe of the king, because they perceived that the wisdom of God was in him.

SHANDRA, see Chandra

SHANE, Shaine, Shayne
(see also Sean, Shawn)
Language/Cultural Origin: Irish
Inherent Meaning: God Is Gracious
Spiritual Connotation: Redeemed
Scripture: Hebrews 2:9 NCV
But we see Jesus . . . wearing a crown of glory and honor because he suffered and died. And by God's grace, he died for everyone.

SHANEISHA, Shaneesha, Shanesha,
Shaneshia, Shanisha, Shannisa
Language/Cultural Origin: American
Inherent Meaning: Beautiful
Spiritual Connotation: Witness
Scripture: Romans 10:15 NLT
How beautiful are the feet of those who bring good news!

SHANEL, see Chanel

SHANEQUA, Shaneequa, Shaniqua
Language/Cultural Origin: American
Inherent Meaning: God Is Gracious
Spiritual Connotation: Anointed
Scripture: Colossians 1:6 TLB
The same Good News that came to you is going out all over the world and changing lives everywhere.

SHANLEY, Shanlea, Shanlee,
Shanleigh, Shanly
Language/Cultural Origin: Irish
Inherent Meaning: Child of the Hero
Spiritual Connotation: Mature
Scripture: Proverbs 23:24 NRSV
The father of the righteous will greatly rejoice; he who begets a wise son will be glad in him.

SHANNA, see Shauna

SHANNON, Shanan, Shannan,
Shannen, Shannin, Shannyn, Shanon
Language/Cultural Origin: Irish
Inherent Meaning: Wise
Spiritual Connotation: Inspired of God
Scripture: Matthew 10:20 TLB
For it won't be you doing the talking—it will be the Spirit of your heavenly Father speaking through you!

SHANTAE, Jhontae, Jhontay, Jontae,
Jontáe, Jonté, Jontée, Shanta,
Shantai, Shantay, Shantaya, Shanté,
Shantée (see also Chante)
Language/Cultural Origin: American
Inherent Meaning: Singer
Spiritual Connotation: Joyful
Scripture: Psalm 101:1 NLT
I will sing of your love and justice. I will praise you, LORD, with songs.

SHANTEL, Shantell, Shanntell,
Shantal, Shantrell, Shauntel,
Shauntell, Shauntelle
(see also Chantal)
Language/Cultural Origin: American
Inherent Meaning: Song
Spiritual Connotation: Spirit of Worship
Scripture: Psalm 13:6 NLT
I will sing to the LORD because he has been so good to me.

SHAQUANDA, Shaquana,
Shaquandra, Shaquani, Shaquanna
Language/Cultural Origin: American
Inherent Meaning: Wanderer
Spiritual Connotation: Seeker of Truth
Scripture: Matthew 6:33 KJV
But seek ye first the kingdom of God, and his righteousness; and all these things shall be added unto you.

SHAQUILLE, Shaquile
Language/Cultural Origin: Middle Eastern
Inherent Meaning: Handsome
Spiritual Connotation: Attractive
Scripture: Song of Songs 1:16 NKJV
Behold, you are handsome, my beloved!

SHAREEF, Sharéf, Sharíf, Shariff
Language/Cultural Origin: Middle Eastern
Inherent Meaning: Honest
Spiritual Connotation: Eternal
Scripture: Proverbs 12:19 RSV
Truthful lips endure for ever, but a lying tongue is but for a moment.

SHARI, Sharaé, Sharee, Shareen,
Sharene, Sharie, Sharree, Sharrie,
Sheree, Sheeree, Sheri, Sherie,
Sherri, Sherrie (see also Cherie)
Language/Cultural Origin: American

Inherent Meaning: Dearest
Spiritual Connotation: Cherished
Scripture: 1 Thessalonians 2:8 TLB
We loved you dearly—so dearly that we gave you not only God's message, but our own lives too.

SHARICE, see Cherise

SHARISSA, see Charissa

SHARLEEN, see Charleen

SHARMAIN, see Charmain

SHARON, Shaara, Shaaron, Sharen, ☞ Sharona, Sharone, Sharonna, Sharra, Sharran, Sharren, Sharron, Sharyn, Sheronna, Sherryn (see also Cheran)
Language/Cultural Origin: Hebrew
Inherent Meaning: Floral Plain
Spiritual Connotation: Vision of Beauty
Scripture: Song of Songs 2:1 NASB
I am the rose of Sharon, the lily of the valleys.

SHAULA, Shala, Shaola
Language/Cultural Origin: Hebrew
Inherent Meaning: Borrowed
Spiritual Connotation: Dedicated
Scripture: 1 Samuel 1:28 NLT
Now I am giving him to the LORD, and he will belong to the LORD his whole life.

SHAUNA, Seana, Seandra, Seanna, Shaana, Shana, Shanea, Shanna, Shannah, Shannay, Shannea, Shaunah, Shaundel, Shaundell, Shaundelle, Shaunelle, Shaunia, Shaunna, Shauntrel, Shauntrell, Shaunya, Shawna, Shawndel, Shawndelle, Shawndrelle, Shawnelle, Shawnna, Shawntel, Shawntelle, Shawntreice, Shona, Shonah, Shonda, Shondel, Shondelle, Shonelle, Shonna, Shonnika, Shonta, Shontá, Shontara, Shontasya, Shonte, Shonté, Shontel, Shontelle, Shontrail, Shontreece, Shunna, Shunnel, Shunnelle, Shunta, Shuntel, Shuntelle, Shuntia
Language/Cultural Origin: English

Inherent Meaning: God Is Gracious
Spiritual Connotation: Accountable
Scripture: 1 Peter 4:10 NRSV
Like good stewards of the manifold grace of God, serve one another with whatever gift each of you has received.

SHAVON, see Chavon

SHAWN, Shaughn, Shaune, Shaunn, Shawne, Shawnn, Shawon (see also Sean, Shane)
Language/Cultural Origin: American
Inherent Meaning: God Is Gracious
Spiritual Connotation: Forgiven
Scripture: 2 Chronicles 30:9 NKJV
For the LORD your God is gracious and merciful, and will not turn His face from you if you return to Him.

SHAY, see Shea

SHAYLA, see Shaela

SHAYNA, see Shaina

SHEA, Shae, Shaelea, Shaelee, Shaeleigh, Shaena, Shaeya, Shaia, Shay, Shaya, Shaye, Shayia, Shaelyn, Shealy, Shéana, Sheanna, Shey
Language/Cultural Origin: Irish
Inherent Meaning: From the Fairy Palace
Spiritual Connotation: Blessed
Scripture: Ephesians 3:20 NCV
With God's power working in us, God can do much, much more than anything we can ask or imagine.

SHEENA, Sheenah, Sheenna, Sheina, Shena
Language/Cultural Origin: Scottish
Inherent Meaning: God Is Gracious
Spiritual Connotation: Instrument of Grace
Scripture: Joel 2:13 TLB
Let your remorse tear at your hearts and not your garments. Return to the Lord your God, for he is gracious and merciful.

SHEILA, Sheela, Sheelah, Sheilah, Shiela, Shyla
Language/Cultural Origin: English
Inherent Meaning: Blind

Spiritual Connotation: Wise
Scripture: Psalm 111:10 RSV
The fear of the LORD is the beginning of wisdom.

SHELBY, Shelbee, Shelbey, Shelbie, Shellby
Language/Cultural Origin: Old English
Inherent Meaning: From the Estate on the Slope
Spiritual Connotation: Faithful Steward
Scripture: 1 Corinthians 4:2 NCV
Now in this way those who are trusted with something valuable must show they are worthy of that trust.

SHELDON, Shelden, Sheldin
Language/Cultural Origin: Middle English
Inherent Meaning: From the Steep Valley
Spiritual Connotation: Man of Virtue
Scripture: Ezekiel 36:27 NRSV
I will put my spirit within you, and make you follow my statutes and be careful to observe my ordinances.

SHELLEY, Shelee, Sheley, Shellee, Shelli, Shellie, Shelly
Language/Cultural Origin: Old English
Inherent Meaning: From the Meadow on the Slope
Spiritual Connotation: Walks With God
Scripture: John 15:5 NRSV
I am the vine, you are the branches. Those who abide in me and I in them bear much fruit, because apart from me you can do nothing.

SHELTON, Shelten
Language/Cultural Origin: Middle English
Inherent Meaning: From the Edge of Town
Spiritual Connotation: Divinely Bestowed
Scripture: 1 Corinthians 2:12 RSV
Now we have received not the spirit of the world, but the Spirit which is from God.

SHEM, Shemm
Language/Cultural Origin: Hebrew
Inherent Meaning: Reputation
Spiritual Connotation: Honest
Scripture: 2 Corinthians 8:21 NRSV
We intend to do what is right not only in the Lord's sight but also in the sight of others.

SHERIDAN, Sherridan
Language/Cultural Origin: Irish
Inherent Meaning: Ambitious
Spiritual Connotation: Free in Spirit
Scripture: Job 33:4 NKJV
The Spirit of God has made me, and the breath of the Almighty gives me life.

SHERIKA, Shereka, Sherica, Shericka, Sherrika
Language/Cultural Origin: Middle Eastern
Inherent Meaning: Easterner
Spiritual Connotation: Stranger
Scripture: Isaiah 43:5 NKJV
Fear not, for I am with you; I will bring your descendants from the east.

SHERMAN, Scherman, Shermann
Language/Cultural Origin: Anglo-Saxon
Inherent Meaning: Sheepshearer
Spiritual Connotation: Gifted of God
Scripture: James 1:17 NASB
Every good thing given and every perfect gift is from above.

SHERROD, Sherod, Sherrard, Sherrodd
Language/Cultural Origin: Anglo-Saxon
Inherent Meaning: Clearer of Land
Spiritual Connotation: Messenger
Scripture: John 4:35 TLB
Look around you! Vast fields of human souls are ripening all around us, and are ready now for reaping.

SHERWIN, Sherwyn
Language/Cultural Origin: Anglo-Saxon
Inherent Meaning: Swift Runner
Spiritual Connotation: Steady Judgment
Scripture: Psalm 103:6 NLT
The LORD gives righteousness and justice to all who are treated unfairly.

SHERYL, Sharilyn, Sharyl, Sherey, Sheri, Sheril, Sherill, Sherleen, Sherrey, Sherri, Sherrie, Sherril, Sherrilynn, Sherryl (see also Cheryl, Shari)
Language/Cultural Origin: English
Inherent Meaning: Dearest
Spiritual Connotation: Treasured

Scripture: 1 Peter 5:7 NRSV
Cast all your anxiety on him, because he cares for you.

SHIANTE, Shianda, Shianta, Shianté, Shianna, Shianne, Shyanna, Shyanne, Shyenna, Shyenne (see also Cheyenne, Shantae)
Language/Cultural Origin: Native American
Inherent Meaning: Tribe
Spiritual Connotation: Regenerated
Scripture: Ezekiel 11:19 NLT
And I will give them singleness of heart and put a new spirit within them. I will take away their hearts of stone and give them tender hearts instead.

SHILO, Shiloh
☞Language/Cultural Origin: Hebrew
Inherent Meaning: God's Gift
Spiritual Connotation: Precious Sacrifice
Scripture: Genesis 49:10 NASB
The scepter shall not depart from Judah, nor the ruler's staff from between his feet, until Shiloh comes.

SHIONA, Shéona, Sheyona
Language/Cultural Origin: Scottish
Inherent Meaning: God Is Gracious
Spiritual Connotation: Redeemed
Scripture: Titus 2:11 NLT
For the grace of God has been revealed, bringing salvation to all people.

SHIRLEY, Sherlee, Shirlee
Language/Cultural Origin: Old English
Inherent Meaning: From the Bright Meadow
Spiritual Connotation: Happiness of Heart
Scripture: 1 John 4:12 NRSV
No one has ever seen God; if we love one another, God lives in us, and his love is perfected in us.

SHONA, Shonda, see Shauna

SIBLEY, Siblee, Sibleigh, Syblie
Language/Cultural Origin: Middle English
Inherent Meaning: Friendly
Spiritual Connotation: Reverent
Scripture: Psalm 25:14 NRSV
The friendship of the LORD is for those who fear him, and he makes his covenant known to them.

SIDNEY, Cyd, Cydna, Cydnee, Cydney, Sidanni, Sidona, Sidonia, Sidonio, Sidony, Sydna, Sydnee, Sydney, Sydnie, Sydonia (see also Cid)
Language/Cultural Origin: Old French
Inherent Meaning: From St. Denis, France
Spiritual Connotation: Righteous
Scripture: Psalm 32:11 RSV
Be glad in the LORD, and rejoice, O righteous, and shout for joy, all you upright in heart!

SIEGFRIED, Seifert, Siegfred, Sig (see also Zigfrid)
Language/Cultural Origin: German
Inherent Meaning: Victorious Peace
Spiritual Connotation: Grateful
Scripture: Colossians 3:15 NASB
And let the peace of Christ rule in your hearts, to which indeed you were called in one body; and be thankful.

SIERRA, Ciaara, Ciara, Ciera, Siaara, Siara, Siarra, Sieara, Siera
Language/Cultural Origin: Irish
Inherent Meaning: Black
Spiritual Connotation: Pure
Scripture: 1 John 1:9 RSV
If we confess our sins, he is faithful and just, and will forgive our sins and cleanse us from all unrighteousness.

SIGMUND
Language/Cultural Origin: Old German
Inherent Meaning: Victorious Protector
Spiritual Connotation: Guardian
Scripture: Psalm 3:3 RSV
But thou, O LORD, art a shield about me, my glory, and the lifter of my head.

SIGOURNEY, Sigourny
Language/Cultural Origin: Old English
Inherent Meaning: Conqueror
Spiritual Connotation: Victor
Scripture: Romans 8:37 NKJV
Yet in all these things we are more than conquerors through Him who loved us.

SILAS, Sylas
☞Language/Cultural Origin: Latin
Inherent Meaning: From the Forest
Spiritual Connotation: Steadfast in Trust

Scripture: Proverbs 29:25 TLB
Fear of man is a dangerous trap, but to trust in God means safety.

SILVIA, see Sylvia

SIMBA, Symba
Language/Cultural Origin: Swahili
Inherent Meaning: Lion
Spiritual Connotation: Blessed
Scripture: Numbers 24:9 NIV
Like a lion they crouch and lie down, like a lioness—who dares to rouse them? May those who bless you be blessed and those who curse you be cursed!

SIMON, Shimon, Shimóne, Simeon, ☞Simmons, Simion, Symon
Language/Cultural Origin: Hebrew
Inherent Meaning: God Heard
Spiritual Connotation: Diligent
Scripture: Psalm 61:5 NASB
For You have heard my vows, O God; You have given me the inheritance of those who fear Your name.

SIMONE, Samona, Simmona, Simmone, Simoane, Simona, Simonne, Symone
Language/Cultural Origin: French
Inherent Meaning: God Hears
Spiritual Connotation: Steadfast
Scripture: John 8:26 NKJV
He who sent Me is true; and I speak to the world those things which I heard from Him.

SINCLAIR, Sinclaire
Language/Cultural Origin: French
Inherent Meaning: Prayer
Spiritual Connotation: Heavenly Minded
Scripture: 1 Thessalonians 5:16–17 NCV
Always be joyful. Pray continually.

SINEAD, Sineád
Language/Cultural Origin: Irish
Inherent Meaning: God Is Gracious
Spiritual Connotation: Blessed
Scripture: Psalm 67:1 NRSV
May God be gracious to us and bless us and make his face to shine upon us.

SIONA, Siauna, Siaunna, Sionna
Language/Cultural Origin: Hebrew

Inherent Meaning: Apex
Spiritual Connotation: Productive
Scripture: Colossians 3:23 NLT
Work hard and cheerfully at whatever you do, as though you were working for the Lord rather than for people.

SKEETER, Skeet
Language/Cultural Origin: English
Inherent Meaning: Fast
Spiritual Connotation: Efficient
Scripture: 2 Kings 1:11 NKJV
Man of God, thus has the king said, "Come down quickly!"

SKELLY, Skelley
Language/Cultural Origin: Gaelic
Inherent Meaning: Storyteller
Spiritual Connotation: Treasurer of Knowledge
Scripture: Exodus 10:2 NLT
You will be able to tell wonderful stories to your children and grandchildren about the marvelous things I am doing . . . to prove that I am the LORD.

SKIPPER, Skip, Skipp
Language/Cultural Origin: Old Norse
Inherent Meaning: Master of a Ship
Spiritual Connotation: Leader
Scripture: Psalm 104:26 NLT
See the ships sailing along, and Leviathan, which you made to play in the sea.

SKYE, Sky
Language/Cultural Origin: Middle Eastern
Inherent Meaning: Supplier of Water
Spiritual Connotation: Miraculous Creation
Scripture: Psalm 19:1 NCV
The heavens tell the glory of God, and the skies announce what his hands have made.

SKYLER, Schylar, Schyler, Skyelar, Skyla, Skylah, Skylar, Skylee, Skylie, Skyllar, Skyller, Skylor
Language/Cultural Origin: Dutch
Inherent Meaning: Scholar
Spiritual Connotation: Wise
Scripture: Romans 15:4 RSV
For whatever was written in former days was written for our instruction, that by steadfastness and by the encouragement of the scriptures we might have hope.

SLADE, Slayde

Language/Cultural Origin: Old English
Inherent Meaning: Child of the Valley
Spiritual Connotation: Fearless
Scripture: Psalm 23:4 NASB

Even though I walk through the valley of the shadow of death, I fear no evil; for Thou art with me; Thy rod and Thy staff, they comfort me.

SLATER, Slaeter

Language/Cultural Origin: English
Inherent Meaning: Roof Slater
Spiritual Connotation: Skilled
Scripture: Exodus 31:3 NKJV

And I have filled him with the Spirit of God, in wisdom, in understanding, in knowledge, and in all manner of workmanship.

SLOAN, Sloane

Language/Cultural Origin: Irish
Inherent Meaning: Warrior
Spiritual Connotation: Victorious Spirit
Scripture: 1 John 5:4 RSV

For whatever is born of God overcomes the world; and this is the victory that overcomes the world, our faith.

SOCRATES, Socratis

Language/Cultural Origin: Greek
Inherent Meaning: Learned
Spiritual Connotation: Brilliant
Scripture: 1 Corinthians 1:21 NCV

In the wisdom of God the world did not know God through its own wisdom. So God chose to use the message that sounds foolish to save those who believe.

SOLANA, Solanna, Soliana, Solianna

Language/Cultural Origin: Spanish
Inherent Meaning: Sunshine
Spiritual Connotation: Righteous
Scripture: Proverbs 4:18 NKJV

But the path of the just is like the shining sun, that shines ever brighter unto the perfect day.

SOLOMON, Salamun, Sol, Solaman, ☞ Sulaiman (see also Salman)

Language/Cultural Origin: Hebrew
Inherent Meaning: Peaceful
Spiritual Connotation: Where God Dwells

Scripture: Job 22:26 NKJV

For then you will have your delight in the Almighty, and lift up your face to God.

SOMMER, Summar, Summer

Language/Cultural Origin: English
Inherent Meaning: Summer
Spiritual Connotation: Ordained
Scripture: Psalm 74:17 NIV

It was you who set all the boundaries of the earth; you made both summer and winter.

SONYA, Sonia, Sonja, Sonjia, Sunya

Language/Cultural Origin: Russian
Inherent Meaning: Wisdom
Spiritual Connotation: Spiritual Discernment
Scripture: Hebrews 5:14 NLT

Solid food is for those who are mature, who have trained themselves to recognize the difference between right and wrong and then do what is right.

SOPHIA, Sofi, Soffi, Sofia, Sofie, Sofiya, Sofya, Sophey, Sophi, Sophie, Zofia, Zophia

Language/Cultural Origin: Greek
Inherent Meaning: Wisdom
Spiritual Connotation: Excellent Virtue
Scripture: James 1:5 NASB

But if any of you lacks wisdom, let him ask of God, who gives to all men generously and without reproach, and it will be given to him.

SORAYA, Sorayah, Suraya, Surayah

Language/Cultural Origin: Persian
Inherent Meaning: Princess
Spiritual Connotation: Beautiful
Scripture: Psalm 45:13 NIV

All glorious is the princess within her chamber; her gown is interwoven with gold.

SOREN, Sören

Language/Cultural Origin: Danish
Inherent Meaning: Thunder
Spiritual Connotation: Power of God
Scripture: Revelation 14:2 RSV

And I heard a voice from heaven like the sound of many waters and like the sound of loud thunder.

SORREL, Sorel, Sorell

Language/Cultural Origin: French

Inherent Meaning: Reddish Brown
Spiritual Connotation: Witness
Scripture: Acts 4:12 TLB
There is salvation in no one else! Under all heaven there is no other name for men to call upon to save them.

SPENCER, Spence, Spenser
Language/Cultural Origin: English
Inherent Meaning: Dispenser of Provisions
Spiritual Connotation: Faithful Steward
Scripture: 1 Corinthians 4:1 NRSV
Think of us in this way, as servants of Christ and stewards of God's mysteries.

SPIKE, Spyke
Language/Cultural Origin: English
Inherent Meaning: Ear of Grain
Spiritual Connotation: Content
Scripture: Psalm 4:7 NLT
You have given me greater joy than those who have abundant harvests of grain and wine.

SPIRO, Spiros, Spyros
Language/Cultural Origin: Greek
Inherent Meaning: Breath
Spiritual Connotation: One of Integrity
Scripture: Job 27:3--4 NLT
As long as I live, while I have breath from God, my lips will speak no evil, and my tongue will speak no lies.

SPRING
Language/Cultural Origin: English
Inherent Meaning: Springtime
Spiritual Connotation: Renewed
Scripture: Psalm 72:6 NLT
May his reign be as refreshing as the springtime rains—like the showers that water the earth.

STACEY, Stacia, Stacee, Stacie, Stacy, Stasia, Stasha, Stashia, Stasia, Stasya
Language/Cultural Origin: English
Inherent Meaning: Resurrection
Spiritual Connotation: Strengthened
Scripture: Isaiah 40:31 NKJV
But those who wait on the LORD shall renew their strength; they shall mount up with wings like eagles, they shall run and not be weary, they shall walk and not faint.

STAFFORD, Stafforde
Language/Cultural Origin: English
Inherent Meaning: From the Riverbank Landing
Spiritual Connotation: High Praise
Scripture: Psalm 98:8 NASB
Let the rivers clap their hands, let the mountains sing together for joy.

STAMOS, Staemos, Stémos
Language/Cultural Origin: Greek
Inherent Meaning: Crowned
Spiritual Connotation: Exalted
Scripture: Hebrews 2:9 NCV
But we see Jesus . . . wearing a crown of glory and honor because he suffered and died. And by God's grace, he died for everyone.

STANA, Stano, Stas, Stasik, Stasio
Language/Cultural Origin: Czech
Inherent Meaning: Stand of Glory
Spiritual Connotation: Rewarded
Scripture: 1 Peter 5:4 NRSV
And when the chief shepherd appears, you will win the crown of glory that never fades away.

STANFORD, Stamford
Language/Cultural Origin: English
Inherent Meaning: From the Rocky Riverbank
Spiritual Connotation: Voice of God
Scripture: Proverbs 21:1 RSV
The king's heart is a stream of water in the hand of the LORD; he turns it wherever he will.

STANLEY, Stan, Stanlee
Language/Cultural Origin: English
Inherent Meaning: From the Rocky Meadow
Spiritual Connotation: Sincere Devotion
Scripture: Colossians 1:23 NCV
You must not be moved away from the hope brought to you by the Good News that you heard.

STANTON, Stanten
Language/Cultural Origin: English
Inherent Meaning: From the Stony Farm
Spiritual Connotation: Excellent Worth
Scripture: 1 John 2:10 NRSV

Whoever loves a brother or sister lives in the light, and in such a person there is no cause for stumbling.

STARLING, Starrling
Language/Cultural Origin: English
Inherent Meaning: Bird
Spiritual Connotation: Treasured
Scripture: Matthew 6:26 NLT
Look at the birds. . . . Your heavenly Father feeds them. And you are far more valuable to him than they are.

STASHA, see Stacey

STEADMAN, Stedman
Language/Cultural Origin: English
Inherent Meaning: Landowner
Spiritual Connotation: Generous
Scripture: Acts 2:45 NLT
They sold their possessions and shared the proceeds with those in need.

STEFAN, Stefane, Stéfane, Stefano, Stefanos, Stefon, Stefón, Stefone, Stefóne, Steffan, Steffon (see also Stephen)
Language/Cultural Origin: Polish/Swedish
Inherent Meaning: Crowned
Spiritual Connotation: Wise
Scripture: Proverbs 14:18 RSV
The prudent are crowned with knowledge.

STELLA, Stellar
Language/Cultural Origin: Latin
Inherent Meaning: Star
Spiritual Connotation: Esteemed
Scripture: Psalm 91:11 NRSV
For he will command his angels concerning you to guard you in all your ways.

STEPHEN, Steeve, Steeven, Stephan, ☞Stephán, Stephon, Stephón, Stephone, Stevan, Steve, Steven, Stevens, Stevie (see also Stefan)
Language/Cultural Origin: Greek
Inherent Meaning: Crowned
Spiritual Connotation: Blessed
Scripture: 2 Timothy 2:5 NASB
Also if anyone competes as an athlete, he does not win the prize unless he competes according to the rules.

STEPHANIE, Stafani, Stafanie, Staffany, Stefaney, Stefani, Stefany, Stefenie, Steffani, Steffanie, Steffi, Steffie, Stephana, Stephaney, Stephani, Stephania, Stephany, Stephanya, Stephenie, Stephi, Stephie, Stephney, Stephnie
Language/Cultural Origin: Greek
Inherent Meaning: Crowned
Spiritual Connotation: Illuminated
Scripture: 1 Corinthians 2:9 NRSV
What no eye has seen, nor ear heard, nor the human heart conceived, what God has prepared for those who love him.

STERLING, Stirling
Language/Cultural Origin: Middle English
Inherent Meaning: Of Genuine Value
Spiritual Connotation: Excellent Worth
Scripture: 1 Corinthians 2:12 RSV
Now we have received not the spirit of the world, but the Spirit which is from God, that we might understand the gifts bestowed on us by God.

STEVEN, see Stephen

STING
Language/Cultural Origin: English
Inherent Meaning: Spike of Grain
Spiritual Connotation: Blessed
Scripture: Psalm 4:7 NLT
You have given me greater joy than those who have abundant harvests of grain and wine.

STOCKTON, Stokkton
Language/Cultural Origin: English
Inherent Meaning: From the Town Full of Tree-Stumps
Spiritual Connotation: Thankful
Scripture: Psalm 96:12 TLB
Praise him for the growing fields, for they display his greatness. Let the trees of the forest rustle with praise.

STORM, Stormy
Language/Cultural Origin: Middle English
Inherent Meaning: Turbulent
Spiritual Connotation: Courageous
Scripture: Psalm 145:18 RSV
The LORD is near to all who call upon him, to all who call upon him in truth.

STRATFORD, Strattford
Language/Cultural Origin: Old English
Inherent Meaning: Bridge Over the River
Spiritual Connotation: Comforted
Scripture: Job 11:16 NLT
You will forget your misery. It will all be gone like water under the bridge.

STROM, Stromm
Language/Cultural Origin: German
Inherent Meaning: Stream
Spiritual Connotation: Seeker of Truth
Scripture: Psalm 42:1 NCV
As a deer thirsts for streams of water, so I thirst for you, God.

STUART, Stu, Steward, Stewart
Language/Cultural Origin: Old English
Inherent Meaning: Caretaker
Spiritual Connotation: Helpful Spirit
Scripture: Galatians 6:2 NCV
By helping each other with your troubles, you truly obey the law of Christ.

SUKE, Sukee, Sukée
Language/Cultural Origin: Hawaiian
Inherent Meaning: Lily
Spiritual Connotation: Adorned
Scripture: Luke 12:27 NLT
Look at the lilies and how they grow. They don't work or make their clothing, yet Solomon in all his glory was not dressed as beautifully as they are.

SUKI, Sukie, Suky
Language/Cultural Origin: Japanese
Inherent Meaning: Beloved
Spiritual Connotation: Image of Christ
Scripture: 1 John 4:7 NCV
Dear friends, we should love each other, because love comes from God. Everyone who loves has become God's child and knows God.

SULLIVAN, Sulley, Sullie, Sully
Language/Cultural Origin: Irish
Inherent Meaning: Black-Eyed or Hawk-Eyed
Spiritual Connotation: Deep Wisdom
Scripture: Proverbs 13:14 NASB
The teaching of the wise is a fountain of life, to turn aside from the snares of death.

SULTAN, Sultaan
Language/Cultural Origin: Swahili

Inherent Meaning: Ruler
Spiritual Connotation: Kind
Scripture: Proverbs 22:9 NRSV
Those who are generous are blessed, for they share their bread with the poor.

SUMMER, see Sommer

SUMMIT, Summet
Language/Cultural Origin: English
Inherent Meaning: Peak
Spiritual Connotation: Righteous
Scripture: Luke 12:3 NLT
Whatever you have said in the dark will be heard in the light, and what you have whispered behind closed doors will be shouted from the housetops for all to hear!

SUMIKO, Sumyko
Language/Cultural Origin: Japanese
Inherent Meaning: Lovely Child
Spiritual Connotation: Pleasing
Scripture: Proverbs 10:1 NRSV
A wise child makes a glad father.

SUNI, Sunni
Language/Cultural Origin: Zuni
Inherent Meaning: Native
Spiritual Connotation: Restored
Scripture: Zephaniah 3:20 TLB
At that time, I will gather you together and bring you home again, and give you a good name.

SUNNY, Sunney, Sunnie
Language/Cultural Origin: English
Inherent Meaning: Cheerful
Spiritual Connotation: Peaceful
Scripture: Psalm 98:6 NLT
Make a joyful symphony before the LORD, the King!

SUSANNA, Suanne, Sue, Sueanne,
☞ **Susan, Susana, Susanah, Susann, Susannah, Susanne, Susette, Susi, Susie, Suzan, Suzana, Suzann, Suzanna, Suzanne, Suzette, Suzi, Suzie, Suzy**
Language/Cultural Origin: Hebrew
Inherent Meaning: Graceful Lily
Spiritual Connotation: Purity
Scripture: Proverbs 4:18 NRSV

But the path of the righteous is like the light of dawn, which shines brighter and brighter until full day.

SUTHERLAND, Sutherlend
Language/Cultural Origin: Scandinavian
Inherent Meaning: Southern Land
Spiritual Connotation: Blessed
Scripture: Psalm 85:1 NLT
LORD, you have poured out amazing blessings on your land! You have restored the fortunes of Israel.

SVEN, Svein, Swen
Language/Cultural Origin: Scandinavian
Inherent Meaning: Youth
Spiritual Connotation: Loving
Scripture: Proverbs 5:18 NKJV
Let your fountain be blessed, and rejoice with the wife of your youth.

SVETLANA, Sveta, Svetlania, Svetlanna, Svetlanya
Language/Cultural Origin: Russian
Inherent Meaning: Bright Light
Spiritual Connotation: Image of Christ
Scripture: Matthew 4:16 NCV
These people who live in darkness will see a great light. They live in a place covered with the shadows of death, but a light will shine on them.

SWALEY, Swailee, Swailey
Language/Cultural Origin: Old English
Inherent Meaning: Winding Stream
Spiritual Connotation: Expectant
Scripture: Psalm 126:4 NLT
Restore our fortunes, LORD, as streams renew the desert.

SWINDEL, Swindell
Language/Cultural Origin: Old English

Inherent Meaning: From the Valley of the Pigs
Spiritual Connotation: Beloved
Scripture: 1 John 3:1 NKJV
Behold what manner of love the Father has bestowed on us, that we should be called children of God!

SYBIL, Cybel, Cybele, Cybil, Cybill, Sibbel, Sibbill, Sibel, Sibyl, Sybille
Language/Cultural Origin: Latin
Inherent Meaning: Prophet
Spiritual Connotation: Chosen
Scripture: Joel 2:28 NRSV
Your sons and your daughters shall prophesy, your old men shall dream dreams, and your young men shall see visions.

SYDNEY, see Sidney

SYLVESTER, Silvester, Sylvain, Sylvestre
Language/Cultural Origin: Latin
Inherent Meaning: From the Forest
Spiritual Connotation: Strong in Spirit
Scripture: 1 Kings 8:61 NRSV
Therefore devote yourselves completely to the LORD our God, walking in his statutes and keeping his commandments.

SYLVIA, Silva, Silvana, Silvanna, Silvia, Sylvana, Sylvania, Sylvanna, Sylvanya, Sylvya
Language/Cultural Origin: Latin
Inherent Meaning: From the Forest
Spiritual Connotation: Dwelling in Spirit
Scripture: Psalm 138:8 NRSV
The LORD will fulfill his purpose for me; your steadfast love, O LORD, endures forever. Do not forsake the work of your hands.

TABER, Tabor, Taibor, Tayber
Language/Cultural Origin: Persian
Inherent Meaning: Drummer
Spiritual Connotation: Merry of Heart
Scripture: Proverbs 15:13 NASB
A joyful heart makes a cheerful face.

TABITHA, Tabatha, Tabathia, Tabby, Tabytha
Language/Cultural Origin: Aramaic
Inherent Meaning: Gazelle
Spiritual Connotation: Graceful
Scripture: Psalm 90:16 NCV
Show your servants the wonderful things you do; show your greatness to their children.

TACI, Tace, Tacee, Tacey, Tacia, Taciana, Tacianna, Tacie, Taceya
Language/Cultural Origin: Zuni
Inherent Meaning: Washtub
Spiritual Connotation: Forgiven
Scripture: Psalm 51:2 NKJV
Wash me thoroughly from my iniquity, and cleanse me from my sin.

TADAN, Taedan, Taidan
Language/Cultural Origin: Native American
Inherent Meaning: Plenty
Spiritual Connotation: Nourished
Scripture: Psalm 72:16 NLT
May there be abundant crops throughout the land, flourishing even on the mountaintops.

TAESHA, Taheisha, Tahisha, Taiesha, Taisha, Teisha, Tyeisha, Tyeshia, Tyishia (see also Tisha)
Language/Cultural Origin: American
Inherent Meaning: Beautiful
Spiritual Connotation: Testimony
Scripture: Romans 10:15 NRSV
How beautiful are the feet of those who bring good news!

TAGGERT, Taggart
Language/Cultural Origin: Gaelic
Inherent Meaning: Son of the Priest
Spiritual Connotation: Full of Life
Scripture: John 6:63 NLT
It is the Spirit who gives eternal life. Human effort accomplishes nothing. And the very words I have spoken to you are spirit and life.

TAJA, Taeja, Taija, Teijah, Tiájara
Language/Cultural Origin: Indo-Pakistani
Inherent Meaning: Crown
Spiritual Connotation: Child of God
Scripture: Zechariah 9:16 TLB
The Lord their God will save his people in that day, as a Shepherd caring for his sheep. They shall shine in his land as glittering jewels in a crown.

TAKENYA, Takenia
Language/Cultural Origin: Moquelumnan
Inherent Meaning: Swooping Hawk
Spiritual Connotation: Humble
Scripture: Job 39:26 NRSV
Is it by your wisdom that the hawk soars, and spreads its wings toward the south?

TAKIA, Takéya, Takía, Takiya, Taquiia
Language/Cultural Origin: Middle Eastern
Inherent Meaning: Worshiper
Spiritual Connotation: True Believer
Scripture: John 4:24 RSV
God is spirit, and those who worship him must worship in spirit and truth.

TAKARA, Takaria, Takarya, Taqara, Taqaria
Language/Cultural Origin: Japanese
Inherent Meaning: Beloved Jewel
Spiritual Connotation: Discerning
Scripture: Proverbs 20:15 NASB

There is gold, and an abundance of jewels; but the lips of knowledge are a more precious thing.

TAL, Talley, Tally
Language/Cultural Origin: Hebrew
Inherent Meaning: Rain
Spiritual Connotation: Blessing
Scripture: Acts 14:17 NCV
Yet he proved he is real by showing kindness, by giving you rain from heaven and . . . by giving you food and filling your hearts with joy.

TALA, Tallah
Language/Cultural Origin: Native American
Inherent Meaning: Stalking Wolf
Spiritual Connotation: Tamed
Scripture: Isaiah 11:6 NKJV
The wolf also shall dwell with the lamb . . . And a little child shall lead them.

TALBOT, Talbott
Language/Cultural Origin: Old German
Inherent Meaning: Bright Valley
Spiritual Connotation: Promise
Scripture: Isaiah 40:4 NKJV
Every valley shall be exalted and every mountain and hill brought low; the crooked places shall be made straight and the rough places smooth.

TALIA, Talaya, Talea, Tahila, Taliah, Taliya, Tallia, Tallie, Tally, Talya, Thalia, Tylia
Language/Cultural Origin: Hebrew
Inherent Meaning: Heaven's Dew
Spiritual Connotation: Richly Blessed
Scripture: Genesis 27:28 NIV
May God give you of heaven's dew and of earth's richness—an abundance of grain and new wine.

TALITHA, Talétha
Language/Cultural Origin: Aramaic
Inherent Meaning: Little/Young Girl
Spiritual Connotation: Heavenly Vision
Scripture: Zechariah 8:5 NLT
And the streets of the city will be filled with boys and girls at play.

TALLIS, Tallys
Language/Cultural Origin: French

Inherent Meaning: From the Forest
Spiritual Connotation: Thankful
Scripture: Psalm 96:12 NASB
Let the field exult, and all that is in it. Then all the trees of the forest will sing for joy.

TALMAN, Talmon
Language/Cultural Origin: Aramaic
Inherent Meaning: Oppressed
Spiritual Connotation: Vindicated
Scripture: Psalm 146:7 NCV
He does what is fair for those who have been wronged. He gives food to the hungry. The LORD sets the prisoners free.

TALON, Talan, Talin, Tallin, Tallon, Tallyn, Talyn
Language/Cultural Origin: French
Inherent Meaning: Claw
Spiritual Connotation: Eternal
Scripture: Isaiah 40:31 NCV
But the people who trust the LORD will become strong again. They will rise up as an eagle in the sky; they will run and not need rest; they will walk and not become tired.

TAMAR, Tamara, Tamarah, Tamaria, Tamarra, Tamarria, Tamary, Tamera, Tamerai, Tamerey, Tameriás, Tamia, Tamie, Tamiya, Tammara, Tammee, Tammera, Tammey, Tammi, Tammie, Tammra, Tammy, Tamra, Tamy, Tamya
Language/Cultural Origin: Hebrew
Inherent Meaning: Palm Tree
Spiritual Connotation: Victorious Spirit
Scripture: Micah 5:9 RSV
Your hand shall be lifted up over your adversaries, and all your enemies shall be cut off.

TANI, Tahnee, Tahni, Tahnie, Tanee, Taney, Tanie, Tany (see also Tawny)
Language/Cultural Origin: Japanese
Inherent Meaning: Valley
Spiritual Connotation: Secure
Scripture: Psalm 23:4 NKJV
Yea, though I walk through the valley of the shadow of death, I will fear no evil; for You are with me; Your rod and Your staff, they comfort me.

TANIA, Tahnia, Tahniya, Tahnya, Taina, Tana, Tanae, Tanalia, Tanasha, Tanaya, Tanea, Taneia, Taneya, Tanija, Taniya, Tanna, Tannia, Tannis, Tanniya, Tannya, Tanya, Taunia, Tauniya, Taunya, Tawnia, Tawnya, Tonasha, Tonaya, Tonia, Tonja, Tonnia, Tonniya, Tonnya, Tonya (see also Tatiana)
Language/Cultural Origin: Russian
Inherent Meaning: Queen
Spiritual Connotation: Honorable
Scripture: 1 Corinthians 3:16 NRSV
Do you not know that you are God's temple and that God's Spirit dwells in you?

TANNER, Tannar, Tannor
Language/Cultural Origin: Old English
Inherent Meaning: Leather Worker
Spiritual Connotation: Diligent
Scripture: Colossians 3:23 NLT
Work hard and cheerfully at whatever you do, as though you were working for the Lord rather than for people.

TAPANI, Tapánee, Tapáney
Language/Cultural Origin: Finnish
Inherent Meaning: Crowned
Spiritual Connotation: Partaker in Grace
Scripture: Hebrews 2:9 NCV
But we see Jesus, who . . . is wearing a crown of glory and honor because he suffered and died. And by God's grace, he died for everyone.

TARIQ, Tareek, Tarék, Tarick, Tarik, Táriq, Tarreq
Language/Cultural Origin: Middle Eastern
Inherent Meaning: Conqueror
Spiritual Connotation: Victorious
Scripture: Romans 8:37 NKJV
Yet in all these things we are more than conquerors through Him who loved us.

TARAH, Taira, Tairra, Tara, Tarai, Taran, Tarasha, Taraya, Tari, Taria, Tarin, Taris, Tarisa, Tarise, Tarissa, Tarra, Tarren, Tarrin, Tarron, Tarryn, Taryn, Tayra (see also Tera)
Language/Cultural Origin: Hebrew
Inherent Meaning: Wild Goat
Spiritual Connotation: Excellent Worth

Scripture: 1 Corinthians 2:12 NRSV
Now we have received not the spirit of the world, but the Spirit that is from God, so that we may understand the gifts bestowed on us by God.

TARRANT, Terrant (see also Terrence)
Language/Cultural Origin: Welsh
Inherent Meaning: Thunder
Spiritual Connotation: Mighty Power
Scripture: 1 Samuel 12:18 TLB
So Samuel called to the Lord, and the Lord sent thunder and rain.

TARVER, Tarvar
Language/Cultural Origin: English
Inherent Meaning: Leader
Spiritual Connotation: Dependent Upon God
Scripture: Isaiah 11:6 NKJV
The wolf also shall dwell with the lamb. . . . And a little child shall lead them.

TASHA, Tacha, Tachia, Tachiana, Tachianna, Tahsha, Tashana, Tashanna, Tashi, Tashia, Tashiana, Tashianna, Tashina, Tashira, Tashiya, Thasha (see also Natasha)
Language/Cultural Origin: Russian
Inherent Meaning: Christmas Child
Spiritual Connotation: Glorious Gift
Scripture: Matthew 1:21 NCV
She will give birth to a son, and you will name him Jesus, because he will save his people from their sins.

TASHANA, Tashanda, Tashanna, Tashauna, Tashaunna, Tashawna, Tashonda, Tashondra, Tiashauna, Tyshanna, Tyshauna, Tyshawna
Language/Cultural Origin: American
Inherent Meaning: Christmas Child
Spiritual Connotation: Miraculous
Scripture: Matthew 1:23 NRSV
Look, the virgin shall conceive and bear a son, and they shall name him Emmanuel, which means, God is with us.

TASIA, Tasja, Tasiya, Tasiana, Tasianna, Tasiyana, Tassiana, Tassianna, Tassie, Tasya (see also Anastasia)
Language/Cultural Origin: Slavic

Inherent Meaning: Resurrection
Spiritual Connotation: Eternal Hope
Scripture: Luke 24:5–6 NKJV
Why do you seek the living among the dead? He is not here, but is risen!

TASMINE, Tasmin
Language/Cultural Origin: English
Inherent Meaning: Twin
Spiritual Connotation: Worthy
Scripture: Galatians 3:28 NASB
There is neither Jew nor Greek, there is neither slave nor free man, there is neither male nor female; for you are all one in Christ Jesus.

TATIANA, Taitiana, Taitianna, Tatanya, Tatia, Tatiania, Tatianya, Tatjana, Tatyana, Tatyanna (see also Tania)
Language/Cultural Origin: Slavic
Inherent Meaning: Queen
Spiritual Connotation: Lovely
Scripture: Psalm 45:11 NKJV
So the King will greatly desire your beauty; because He is your Lord, worship Him.

TATUM, Taetum, Taitum, Tate, Tayte, Taytum
Language/Cultural Origin: Middle English
Inherent Meaning: Cheerful
Spiritual Connotation: Happy
Scripture: Proverbs 15:13 NASB
A joyful heart makes a cheerful face.

TAWNY, Tahnee, Tauna, Tauni, Tawnee, Tawney, Tawni, Tawnie (see also Tani)
Language/Cultural Origin: Gypsy
Inherent Meaning: Little One
Spiritual Connotation: Trusting
Scripture: Matthew 10:42 NCV
Those who give one of these little ones a cup of cold water because they are my followers will truly get their reward.

TAYLOR, Tailor, Talor, Taya, Tayana, Tayanna, Tayla, Taylar, Tayler, Taylore, Taylour, Tayna, Taynie, Tayny, Teylar, Teyler, Teylor
Language/Cultural Origin: English
Inherent Meaning: Tailor

Spiritual Connotation: Gifted
Scripture: Exodus 31:3 RSV
I have filled him with the Spirit of God, with ability and intelligence, with knowledge and all craftsmanship.

TEAGAN, Taegan, Teaghen, Teegan, Teégan, Tegan, Teigen, Tiegan
Language/Cultural Origin: Welsh
Inherent Meaning: Attractive
Spiritual Connotation: Faithful
Scripture: Titus 2:10 NCV
They . . . should show their masters they can be fully trusted so that in everything they do they will make the teaching of God our Savior attractive.

TEMPEST, Tempestt
Language/Cultural Origin: Latin
Inherent Meaning: Stormy
Spiritual Connotation: Serene
Scripture: Psalm 89:9 NKJV
You rule the raging of the sea; when its waves rise, You still them.

TERA, Terra (see also Tarah)
Language/Cultural Origin: Latin
Inherent Meaning: Earth
Spiritual Connotation: Miraculous
Scripture: Daniel 6:27 NASB
He delivers and rescues and performs signs and wonders in heaven and on earth.

TERESA, see Theresa

TERRELL, Tarell, Terel, Terell, Terral, Terrell, Terrelle, Terriel, Terryl, Tyrel, Tyrell, Tyrelle, Tyrell
Language/Cultural Origin: English
Inherent Meaning: Thunder Ruler
Spiritual Connotation: Mighty Protector
Scripture: Psalm 5:11 NRSV
Spread your protection over them, so that those who love your name may exult in you.

TERRENCE, Tarrence, Tarry, Teran, Teren, Terence, Terin, Terran, Terrance, Terren, Terri, Terry (see also Tarrant)
Language/Cultural Origin: Latin
Inherent Meaning: Tender
Spiritual Connotation: Gently Formed

Scripture: Job 33:4 NRSV
The spirit of God has made me, and the breath of the Almighty gives me life.

TESSA, Tesia, Tessey, Tessi, Tessia, Tessie, Tessy
Language/Cultural Origin: English
Inherent Meaning: Reaper
Spiritual Connotation: Servant
Scripture: Luke 10:2 TLB
Plead with the Lord of the harvest to send out more laborers to help you, for the harvest is so plentiful and the workers so few.

THADDEUS, Tad, Tadd, Thad, ☞Thadd, Thaddaeus
Language/Cultural Origin: Aramaic
Inherent Meaning: Loving
Spiritual Connotation: Joyful
Scripture: Psalm 28:7 NKJV
The LORD is my strength and my shield; my heart trusted in Him, and I am helped; therefore my heart greatly rejoices, and with my song I will praise Him.

THALIA, see Talia

THANE, Thain, Thaine, Thayne
Language/Cultural Origin: Old English
Inherent Meaning: Follower
Spiritual Connotation: Loyal
Scripture: Psalm 40:8 RSV
I delight to do thy will, O my God; thy law is within my heart.

THATCHER, Thaxter
Language/Cultural Origin: Old English
Inherent Meaning: Repairer of Roofs
Spiritual Connotation: Diligent
Scripture: Deuteronomy 33:11 NIV
Bless all his skills, O LORD, and be pleased with the work of his hands.

THAYER, Thayor
Language/Cultural Origin: French
Inherent Meaning: National Army
Spiritual Connotation: Brave Defender
Scripture: Isaiah 19:20 NRSV
When they cry to the LORD because of oppressors, he will send them a savior, and will defend and deliver them.

THELMA, Thellma
Language/Cultural Origin: Greek

Inherent Meaning: Willful
Spiritual Connotation: Strong in Spirit
Scripture: 2 Timothy 1:7 NKJV
For God has not given us a spirit of fear, but of power and of love and of a sound mind.

THEODORE, Ted, Teddie, Teddy, Theo, Theódore
Language/Cultural Origin: Greek
Inherent Meaning: Divine Gift
Spiritual Connotation: Gift of God
Scripture: Ecclesiastes 2:26 TLB
For God gives those who please him wisdom, knowledge, and joy.

THERESA, Taresa, Tarisa, Tarise, Tarissa, Teree, Tereese, Terese, Teresa, Teresea, Terezia, Teri, Terie, Terisa, Terise, Terisha, Teriza, Terree, Terresa, Terri, Terrie, Terry, Therese, Thérèse, Theressa, Thereza, Trescha, Tresha, Treshana, Tresa, Tressa, Treysa, Treyssa
Language/Cultural Origin: Greek
Inherent Meaning: Harvester
Spiritual Connotation: Bountiful Spirit
Scripture: John 4:35 NLT
Look around you! Vast fields are ripening all around us and are ready now for the harvest.

THERON, Theran, Therron
Language/Cultural Origin: Greek
Inherent Meaning: Hunter
Spiritual Connotation: Efficient
Scripture: 2 Thessalonians 3:10 NRSV
For even when we were with you, we gave you this command: Anyone unwilling to work should not eat.

THOMAS, Thom, Thompson, Tom, ☞Tomás, Tomm, Tommie, Tommy
Language/Cultural Origin: Aramaic
Inherent Meaning: Twin
Spiritual Connotation: Divinely Preserved
Scripture: Proverbs 2:11 NASB
Discretion will guard you, understanding will watch over you.

THOR, Thorin
Language/Cultural Origin: Old Norse
Inherent Meaning: Thunder

Spiritual Connotation: God's Warrior
Scripture: Exodus 15:3 NASB
The LORD is a warrior; the LORD is His name.

THORNTON, Thorntin
Language/Cultural Origin: Old English
Inherent Meaning: From the Town
Near the Thorns
Spiritual Connotation: Wise
Scripture: Proverbs 22:5 TLB
The rebel walks a thorny, treacherous road; the man who values his soul will stay away.

TIA, Téa, Teeya, Teia, Tialeigh, Tiamarie, Tiandria, Tianika, Tiia
Language/Cultural Origin: Spanish
Inherent Meaning: Aunt
Spiritual Connotation: Pure
Scripture: 1 Timothy 5:2 NLT
Treat the older women as you would your mother, and treat the younger women with all purity as your own sisters.

TIANA, Teana, Teanna, Tianna
Language/Cultural Origin: Greek
Inherent Meaning: Princess
Spiritual Connotation: Praised
Scripture: Psalm 45:13 NIV
All glorious is the princess within her chamber; her gown is interwoven with gold.

TIARA, Tearra, Teira, Teirra, Tiára, Tiaria, Tiarra, Tiárra, Tiera, Tiéra, Tierra, Tyara, Tyarra
Language/Cultural Origin: Latin
Inherent Meaning: Crowned
Spiritual Connotation: Thankful
Scripture: Hebrews 2:9 RSV
But we see Jesus . . . crowned with glory and honor because of the suffering of death, so that by the grace of God he might taste death for every one.

TIERNEY, Tiernan
Language/Cultural Origin: Irish
Inherent Meaning: Lordly
Spiritual Connotation: Gracious Spirit
Scripture: Ephesians 4:7 NKJV
But to each one of us grace was given according to the measure of Christ's gift.

TIFARA, Tifára, Tifarra, Tifaria, Tifarra, Tiffarya
Language/Cultural Origin: Hebrew

Inherent Meaning: Splendor
Spiritual Connotation: Reverent
Scripture: Isaiah 2:10 NASB
Enter the rock and hide in the dust from the terror of the LORD and from the splendor of His majesty.

TIFFANY, Tifanee, Tifaney, Tifani, Tifanie, Tifany, Tiff, Tiffanee, Tiffaney, Tiffani, Tiffanie, Tiffanny, Tiffeney, Tiffenie, Tiffeni, Tiffennie, Tiffinee, Tiffiney, Tiffini, Tiffinie, Tiffiny, Tiffney, Tifnee, Tifnie, Tifny, Tiphanee, Tiphaney, Tiphani, Tiphanie, Tiphany, Tyfanny, Tyffani, Tyffini, Typhanee, Typhany
Language/Cultural Origin: English
Inherent Meaning: Divine Showing
Spiritual Connotation: Beloved
Scripture: 1 John 4:7 NKJV
Beloved, let us love one another, for love is of God; and everyone who loves is born of God and knows God.

TIGER, Tig, Tige, Tyger
Language/Cultural Origin: English
Inherent Meaning: Powerful
Spiritual Connotation: Strength of God
Scripture: Psalm 106:8 NRSV
Yet he saved them for his name's sake, so that he might make known his mighty power.

TILDA, TILLIE, see Matilda

TILDEN, Tildan
Language/Cultural Origin: Old English
Inherent Meaning: From the Blessed Valley
Spiritual Connotation: Peaceful Spirit
Scripture: Psalm 23:6 KJV
Surely goodness and mercy shall follow me all the days of my life: and I will dwell in the house of the LORD for ever.

TILTAN, Tilton
Language/Cultural Origin: Hebrew
Inherent Meaning: Clover
Spiritual Connotation: Blossom
Scripture: Isaiah 27:6 NLT
The time is coming when my people will take root. Israel will bud and blossom and fill the whole earth with her fruit!

TIMOTHY, Tim, Timmie, Timmothy,
☞**Timmy, Timothé, Timothée,**
Timothi, Tymothee, Tymothy
Language/Cultural Origin: Greek
Inherent Meaning: Honor to God
Spiritual Connotation: Blessed of God
Scripture: 1 Timothy 1:2 RSV
To Timothy, my true child in the faith: Grace,
mercy, and peace from God the Father and
Christ Jesus our Lord.

TINA, Teena, Téna, Tyna
Language/Cultural Origin: English
Inherent Meaning: Anointed
Spiritual Connotation: Protected
Scripture: Psalm 20:6 NKJV
Now I know that the LORD saves His anointed;
He will answer him from His holy heaven
with the saving strength of His right hand.

TINO, Tíno
Language/Cultural Origin: Hispanic
Inherent Meaning: Venerable
Spiritual Connotation: Promised Hope
Scripture: 2 Thessalonians 1:10 NCV
This will happen on the day when the Lord
Jesus comes to receive glory because
of his holy people.

TIPPER, Typper
Language/Cultural Origin: Gaelic
Inherent Meaning: Water Pourer
Spiritual Connotation: Generous
Scripture: Matthew 10:42 NASB
And whoever in the name of a disciple gives
to one of these little ones even a cup of cold
water to drink, truly I say to you, he shall
not lose his reward.

TIRA, Teara, Teera
(see also Tyra)
Language/Cultural Origin: Hebrew
Inherent Meaning: Small Village
Spiritual Connotation: Treasured
Scripture: Romans 5:8 NRSV
But God proves his love for us in that while
we still were sinners Christ died for us.

TIRZA, Thira, Tirsa, Tirzah,
☞**Tirzha, Tyrza, Tyrzah**
Language/Cultural Origin: Hebrew
Inherent Meaning: Pleasant
Spiritual Connotation: Gentle

Scripture: Psalm 133:1 NCV
It is good and pleasant when God's people
live together in peace!

TISHA, Tiesha, Tieshia, Tish, Tishia,
Tysha, Tyshia (see also Taesha)
Language/Cultural Origin: English
Inherent Meaning: Joy
Spiritual Connotation: Thankful
Scripture: Psalm 66:1 NKJV
Make a joyful shout to God, all the earth!

TISHREY, Tishrae, Tishray, Tishreigh
Language/Cultural Origin: Akkadian
Inherent Meaning: Beginning
Spiritual Connotation: Wise
Scripture: Proverbs 8:23 NKJV
I have been established from everlasting,
from the beginning, before there was ever an
earth.

TITUS, Tito, Titos, Tytus
☞ Language/Cultural Origin: Greek
Inherent Meaning: Of the Giants
Spiritual Connotation: Honorable
Scripture: Matthew 12:35 NKJV
A good man out of the good treasure of his
heart brings forth good things.

TOBIAS, Tobee, Tobey, Tobiah,
Tobie, Tobi, Toby
Language/Cultural Origin: Hebrew
Inherent Meaning: The Lord Is Good
Spiritual Connotation: God's Workmanship
Scripture: Matthew 5:16 NKJV
Let your light so shine before men, that they
may see your good works and glorify your
Father in heaven.

TODD, Tod
Language/Cultural Origin: Scottish
Inherent Meaning: Fox Hunter
Spiritual Connotation: Divine Ingenuity
Scripture: Genesis 25:27 NCV
When the boys grew up, Esau became a
skilled hunter. He loved to be out in the
fields.

TONI, Tonee, Tonie
Language/Cultural Origin: English
Inherent Meaning: Priceless
Spiritual Connotation: Lovely

Scripture: Psalm 36:7 NRSV
How precious is your steadfast love, O God!
All people may take refuge in the shadow
of your wings.

TONY, Toney
Language/Cultural Origin: English
Inherent Meaning: Praiseworthy
Spiritual Connotation: Pure
Scripture: Philippians 4:8 NKJV
Whatever things are true . . . noble . . . just
. . . pure . . . lovely . . . [and] of good report,
if there is any virtue and if there is anything
praiseworthy; meditate on these things.

TONYA, see Tania

TOPAZ
Language/Cultural Origin: Latin
Inherent Meaning: Gem
Spiritual Connotation: Fidelity
Scripture: Revelation 2:10 NKJV
Do not fear any of those things which you
are about to suffer. . . . Be faithful until
death, and I will give you the crown of life.

TOPHER, Tofer
Language/Cultural Origin: Greek
Inherent Meaning: Bearer
Spiritual Connotation: Helper
Scripture: Galatians 6:2 NRSV
Bear one another's burdens, and in this way
you will fulfill the law of Christ.

TORI, Toria, Torian, Toriana, Torianna, Torie, Torii, Torri, Torria, Torriana, Torrianna, Torrie (see also Tory)
Language/Cultural Origin: Japanese
Inherent Meaning: Bird
Spiritual Connotation: Great Worth
Scripture: Matthew 6:26 NKJV
Look at the birds of the air. . . your heavenly
Father feeds them. Are you not of more value
than they?

TORRANCE, Torance
Language/Cultural Origin: Irish
Inherent Meaning: From the Knolls
Spiritual Connotation: Man of Peace
Scripture: Psalm 91:15 NKJV
He shall call upon Me, and I will answer him;
I will be with him in trouble; I will deliver
him and honor him.

TORY, Torey, Torre, Torrey, Torry (see also Tori)
Language/Cultural Origin: English
Inherent Meaning: Tower
Spiritual Connotation: Preserved
Scripture: Proverbs 18:10 NKJV
The name of the LORD is a strong tower; the
righteous run to it and are safe.

TOWNSEND, Townshend
Language/Cultural Origin: English
Inherent Meaning: From the Edge of Town
Spiritual Connotation: Industrious
Scripture: 1 Corinthians 12:4 RSV
Now there are varieties of gifts, but the same
Spirit.

TRACEY, Trace, Tracee, Traci, Tracia, Tracie, Traciya, Tracy, Tracya, Traecee, Traeecey, Traicey, Trasee, Trasey (see also Taci)
Language/Cultural Origin: Latin
Inherent Meaning: Warrior
Spiritual Connotation: Noble Spirit
Scripture: 2 Corinthians 8:21 NLT
We are careful to be honorable before the
Lord, but we also want everyone else to know
we are honorable.

TRAVERS, Travis
Language/Cultural Origin: Old French
Inherent Meaning: From the Crossroads
Spiritual Connotation: Courageous
Scripture: Psalm 29:11 NKJV
The LORD will give strength to His people; the
LORD will bless His people with peace.

TRAYTON, Traeton, Traiton
Language/Cultural Origin: Old French
Inherent Meaning: From the Settlement
Near the Forest
Spiritual Connotation: Treasured
Scripture: Psalm 121:8 NASB
The LORD will guard your going out and your
coming in from this time forth and forever.

TREMAINE, Tremain, Tremayne
Language/Cultural Origin: Celtic
Inherent Meaning: From the House
by the Rock
Spiritual Connotation: High Praise

Scripture: 2 Samuel 22:47 NKJV

The LORD lives! Blessed be my Rock! Let God be exalted, the Rock of my salvation!

TRENT, Trente
Language/Cultural Origin: English
Inherent Meaning: Rapid Stream
Spiritual Connotation: Renewed
Scripture: Isaiah 65:17 NKJV

For behold, I create new heavens and a new earth; and the former shall not be remembered or come to mind.

TRENTON, Trendon, Trenten, Trentin
Language/Cultural Origin: Old English
Inherent Meaning: From the Town by the Rapid Stream
Spiritual Connotation: Rooted in Faith
Scripture: Psalm 1:3 NRSV

They are like trees planted by streams of water, which yield their fruit in its season, and their leaves do not wither. In all that they do, they prosper.

TREVOR, Trev, Trevar, Trever
Language/Cultural Origin: Irish
Inherent Meaning: Prudent and Discreet
Spiritual Connotation: Righteous
Scripture: Psalm 84:11 NKJV

For the LORD God is a sun and shield; the LORD will give grace and glory; no good thing will He withhold from those who walk uprightly.

TREY, Trae, Trai
Language/Cultural Origin: Middle English
Inherent Meaning: Third
Spiritual Connotation: Sacrifice
Scripture: 1 Chronicles 16:29 RSV

Ascribe to the LORD the glory due his name; bring an offering, and come before him!

TRILBY, Trilbee, Trilbey, Trilbie
Language/Cultural Origin: English
Inherent Meaning: Hat
Spiritual Connotation: Covered
Scripture: Psalm 36:7 RSV

How precious is thy steadfast love, O God! The children of men take refuge in the shadow of thy wings.

TRINA, Treena, Treina, Tria, Triana, Trianna, Trinette, Trinice, Triniece, Trinique, Triya
Language/Cultural Origin: English
Inherent Meaning: Pure
Spiritual Connotation: Gentle
Scripture: Proverbs 22:11 NRSV

Those who love a pure heart and are gracious in speech will have the king as a friend.

TRISHA, Tricha, Tricia, Trisa, Trish, Trishana, Trishanna, Trishara, Trissa, Tryssa
Language/Cultural Origin: English
Inherent Meaning: Noble
Spiritual Connotation: Honest
Scripture: Proverbs 3:3 NRSV

Do not let loyalty and faithfulness forsake you; bind them around your neck, write them on the tablet of your heart.

TRISTEN, Trista, Tristan, Tristia, Tristian, Tristiana, Tristianna, Tristin, Tristina, Triston, Tristya, Trystan, Trysten, Trystia, Trystian, Trystin (see also Trusten)
Language/Cultural Origin: Welsh
Inherent Meaning: Bold
Spiritual Connotation: Valiant
Scripture: Deuteronomy 31:6 NRSV

Be strong and bold; have no fear or dread of them, because it is the LORD your God who goes with you; he will not fail you or forsake you.

TRIXIE, Trix, Trixi
Language/Cultural Origin: American
Inherent Meaning: Bringer of Joy
Spiritual Connotation: Peaceful
Scripture: Psalm 46:4 NASB

There is a river whose streams make glad the city of God, the holy dwelling places of the Most High.

TROY, Troi, Troye
Language/Cultural Origin: Gaelic
Inherent Meaning: Foot Soldier
Spiritual Connotation: Steadfast
Scripture: 2 Corinthians 9:8 NASB

And God is able to make all grace abound to you, that always having all sufficiency in everything, you may have an abundance for every good deed.

TRUMAN, Trumann
Language/Cultural Origin: English
Inherent Meaning: Honest
Spiritual Connotation: Faithful
Scripture: Proverbs 19:22 NLT
Loyalty makes a person attractive. And it is better to be poor than dishonest.

TRUSTEN, Trustan, Trustin (see also Tristen)
Language/Cultural Origin: English
Inherent Meaning: Trustworthy
Spiritual Connotation: Reliable
Scripture: Psalm 101:1 NRSV
I will sing of loyalty and of justice; to you, O LORD, I will sing.

TRYGVE, Trigve, Trygvee
Language/Cultural Origin: Norwegian
Inherent Meaning: Victor
Spiritual Connotation: Triumphant
Scripture: 1 John 5:4 NCV
Everyone who is a child of God conquers the world. And this is the victory that conquers the world—our faith.

TUCKER
Language/Cultural Origin: Old English
Inherent Meaning: Folder of Cloth
Spiritual Connotation: Efficient
Scripture: Colossians 3:23 NLT
Work hard and cheerfully at whatever you do, as though you were working for the Lord rather than for people.

TULLIS, Tullias, Tullius
Language/Cultural Origin: Latin
Inherent Meaning: Rank
Spiritual Connotation: Admirable
Scripture: 1 Peter 2:17 NCV
Show respect for all people: Love the brothers and sisters of God's family, respect God, honor the king.

TURNER, Turnar
Language/Cultural Origin: English
Inherent Meaning: Woodworker
Spiritual Connotation: Infinite Creativity
Scripture: Exodus 35:35 TLB
God has filled them both with unusual skills as jewelers, carpenters . . . and as weavers— they excel in all the crafts we will be needing in the work.

TUSHIYA, Tuschiya
Language/Cultural Origin: Hebrew
Inherent Meaning: Wisdom
Spiritual Connotation: Righteous
Scripture: Proverbs 4:11 RSV
I have taught you the way of wisdom; I have led you in the paths of uprightness.

TWAIN, Twaine, Twayne
Language/Cultural Origin: English
Inherent Meaning: Divided in Two
Spiritual Connotation: Renewed
Scripture: 2 Corinthians 7:1 RSV
Since we have these promises, beloved, let us cleanse ourselves from every defilement of body and spirit, and make holiness perfect in the fear of God.

TWYLA, Twila, Twilla, Twylla
Language/Cultural Origin: English
Inherent Meaning: Doubly Woven
Spiritual Connotation: Strong
Scripture: Proverbs 31:25 NLT
She is clothed with strength and dignity, and she laughs with no fear of the future.

TYLER, Ty, Tylar, Tyller, Tylor
Language/Cultural Origin: Middle English
Inherent Meaning: Tile Maker
Spiritual Connotation: Resourceful
Scripture: Mark 11:24 NRSV
So I tell you, whatever you ask for in prayer, believe that you have received it, and it will be yours.

TYRA, Tyraa, Tyrah, Tyresa, Tyrisa, Tyrina, Tyrinia (see also Tira)
Language/Cultural Origin: Scandinavian
Inherent Meaning: Warrior
Spiritual Connotation: Blessed
Scripture: Psalm 127:4 NRSV
Like arrows in the hand of a warrior are the sons of one's youth.

TYREL, see Terrell

TYRONE, Ty, Tyronne
Language/Cultural Origin: Greek
Inherent Meaning: Sovereign
Spiritual Connotation: Steadfast
Scripture: Psalm 1:3 NKJV
He shall be like a tree planted by the rivers of

water, that brings forth its fruit in its season,
whose leaf also shall not wither; and
whatever he does shall prosper.

TYSON, Tison, Tyce, Tysen

Language/Cultural Origin: French
Inherent Meaning: Son of the Ruler
Spiritual Connotation: Gifted
Scripture: 1 Timothy 4:14 NASB

Do not neglect the spiritual gift within you.

Inherent Meaning: Mother
Spiritual Connotation: Blessed
Scripture: Genesis 17:16 RSV
I will bless her, and she shall be a mother of nations; kings of peoples shall come from her.

UMI, Umee
Language/Cultural Origin: Yao
Inherent Meaning: Life
Spiritual Connotation: Energetic
Scripture: Isaiah 43:19 TLB
For I'm going to do a brand new thing. See, I have already begun!

UNA, Oona
Language/Cultural Origin: Hopi
Inherent Meaning: Strong Memory
Spiritual Connotation: Humble
Scripture: Isaiah 41:13 NRSV
Do not fear, I will help you.

ULANI, Ulana, Ulanna, Ulanni
Language/Cultural Origin: Hawaiian
Inherent Meaning: Cheerful
Spiritual Connotation: Filled With Joy
Scripture: Isaiah 12:5 NIV
Sing to the LORD, for he has done glorious things; let this be known to all the world.

UNIQUE
Language/Cultural Origin: Latin
Inherent Meaning: One
Spiritual Connotation: Incomparable
Scripture: Psalm 139:14 NRSV
I praise you, for I am fearfully and wonderfully made.

ULRIC, Ulrik
Language/Cultural Origin: Old German
Inherent Meaning: Ruler of All
Spiritual Connotation: Regenerated
Scripture: Colossians 3:10 NRSV
[Clothe] yourselves with the new self, which is being renewed in knowledge according to the image of its creator.

UNITY
Language/Cultural Origin: Latin
Inherent Meaning: Togetherness
Spiritual Connotation: Harmonious
Scripture: Psalm 133:1 NRSV
How very good and pleasant it is when kindred live together in unity!

ULRICA, Ulrika
Language/Cultural Origin: Old German
Inherent Meaning: Ruler
Spiritual Connotation: Strong in Virtue
Scripture: Proverbs 31:10 NKJV
Who can find a virtuous wife? For her worth is far above rubies.

UPTON, Uptonn
Language/Cultural Origin: Old English
Inherent Meaning: From the Hill Town
Spiritual Connotation: Honorable
Scripture: Deuteronomy 8:3 NIV
Man does not live on bread alone but on every word that comes from the mouth of the LORD.

ULYSSES, Ulisses
Language/Cultural Origin: Latin
Inherent Meaning: One Who Detests Deceit or Injustice
Spiritual Connotation: Seeker of truth
Scripture: Jeremiah 29:12 NASB
Then you will call upon Me and come and pray to Me, and I will listen to you.

URBAN, Urbain
Language/Cultural Origin: Latin
Inherent Meaning: From the City
Spiritual Connotation: Peaceful
Scripture: Psalm 46:4 RSV

UMA, Ooma, Umah
Language/Cultural Origin: Indo-Pakistani

There is a river whose streams make glad the city of God, the holy habitation of the Most High.

URBANA, Urbanna
Language/Cultural Origin: Latin
Inherent Meaning: From the City
Spiritual Connotation: Majestic
Scripture: Psalm 87:3 NLT
O city of God, what glorious things are said of you!

URI, Uree, Urii (see also Yuri)
Language/Cultural Origin: Hebrew
Inherent Meaning: My Light
Spiritual Connotation: Righteous
Scripture: 2 Samuel 22:29 NLT
O LORD, you are my light; yes, LORD, you light up my darkness.

URIAH, Urias, Uriyah
☞ Language/Cultural Origin: Hebrew
Inherent Meaning: God Is My Light
Spiritual Connotation: Excellent Virtue
Scripture: Proverbs 12:28 NRSV
In the path of righteousness there is life, in walking its path there is no death.

URIEL, Uriela, Uriell, Uriella, ☞ Urielle (see also Ariel)
Language/Cultural Origin: Hebrew
Inherent Meaning: Flame of God
Spiritual Connotation: Transformed
Scripture: Deuteronomy 4:24 NASB
For the LORD your God is a consuming fire.

URIKA, Uraeka, Uriqua
Language/Cultural Origin: Omaha
Inherent Meaning: Universally Useful
Spiritual Connotation: Student of the Word
Scripture: 2 Timothy 3:16 NRSV
All scripture is inspired by God and is useful for teaching, for reproof, for correction, and for training in righteousness.

URSULA, Ursa
Language/Cultural Origin: Latin
Inherent Meaning: Little Bear
Spiritual Connotation: Courageous
Scripture: Deuteronomy 31:6 NKJV
Be strong and of good courage, do not fear nor be afraid of them; for the LORD your God, He is the One who goes with you.

UZIEL, Uzziah, Uzziel
☞ Language/Cultural Origin: Hebrew
Inherent Meaning: God Is My Strength
Spiritual Connotation: God's Servant
Scripture: Psalm 18:1 NRSV
I love you, O LORD, my strength.

VAIL, Vael, Vaile, Vale, Vayle
Language/Cultural Origin: English
Inherent Meaning: Valley
Spiritual Connotation: Praise
Scripture: Isaiah 40:4 NKJV
Every valley shall be exalted and every mountain and hill brought low.

VALERIE, Val, Valarae, Valaree, Valarie, Valeree, Valeri, Valery, Vallerie, Vallery, Vallory
Language/Cultural Origin: Latin
Inherent Meaning: Strength
Spiritual Connotation: Spiritual Purpose
Scripture: Ecclesiastes 3:1 NKJV
To everything there is a season, a time for every purpose under heaven:

VALESKA, Valisha, Valishia
Language/Cultural Origin: Slavic
Inherent Meaning: Glorious Ruler
Spiritual Connotation: Esteemed
Scripture: Psalm 92:4 NKJV
For You, LORD, have made me glad through Your work; I will triumph in the works of Your hands.

VALIN, Vaylin (see also Balin)
Language/Cultural Origin: Indo-Pakistani
Inherent Meaning: Mighty Warrior
Spiritual Connotation: Arm of God
Scripture: Deuteronomy 9:29 RSV
For they are thy people and thy heritage, whom thou didst bring out by thy great power and by thy outstretched arm.

VALLI, Vallee, Valley, Vallie, Vally
Language/Cultural Origin: Latin
Inherent Meaning: Strong
Spiritual Connotation: God's Leader
Scripture: Micah 5:4 NASB
And He will arise and shepherd His flock in the strength of the LORD.

VAN, Vann
Language/Cultural Origin: Dutch
Inherent Meaning: Water Dam
Spiritual Connotation: Forgiving
Scripture: Ecclesiastes 1:15 TLB
What is wrong cannot be righted; it is water over the dam; and there is no use thinking of what might have been.

VANCE, Vanse
Language/Cultural Origin: English
Inherent Meaning: Thresher
Spiritual Connotation: Hard Worker
Scripture: Deuteronomy 16:15 NASB
The LORD your God will bless you in all your produce and in all the work of your hands, so that you shall be altogether joyful.

VANDA, Vandelia, Vandi, Vandie, Vannda (see also Wanda)
Language/Cultural Origin: Slavic
Inherent Meaning: Wanderer
Spiritual Connotation: Redeemed
Scripture: Ephesians 2:19 TLB
Now you are no longer strangers to God and foreigners to heaven, but you are members of God's very own family, citizens of God's country.

VANESSA, Vanesa, Vanissa, Venessa
Language/Cultural Origin: Greek
Inherent Meaning: Butterfly
Spiritual Connotation: Free Spirit
Scripture: John 8:36 NKJV
Therefore if the Son makes you free, you shall be free indeed.

VANNA, Vana, Vania, Vannah, Vanya
Language/Cultural Origin: English
Inherent Meaning: Butterfly
Spiritual Connotation: Liberated
Scripture: Galatians 5:1 NASB
It was for freedom that Christ set us free; therefore keep standing firm and do not be subject again to a yoke of slavery.

VARINA, Vareena, Vareyna, Varia, Varya (see also Verena)
Language/Cultural Origin: Slavic
Inherent Meaning: Foreigner
Spiritual Connotation: Sanctified
Scripture: Ephesians 2:13 NCV
But now in Christ Jesus, you who were far away from God are brought near through the blood of Christ's death.

VASHAWN, Vashaun, Vashon, Vishaun, Vishawn, Voshan, Voshon, Voshaun, Voshawn
Language/Cultural Origin: American
Inherent Meaning: God Is Gracious
Spiritual Connotation: Blessed
Scripture: Numbers 6:25 NKJV
The LORD make His face shine upon you, and be gracious to you.

VASHTI, Vashtee, Vashtie
☞ Language/Cultural Origin: Persian
Inherent Meaning: Lovely
Spiritual Connotation: Beautiful
Scripture: Esther 1:11 NCV
He commanded them to bring him Queen Vashti . . . because she was very beautiful.

VAUGHN, Von
Language/Cultural Origin: Welsh
Inherent Meaning: Small
Spiritual Connotation: Compassionate
Scripture: Matthew 9:13 NKJV
I desire mercy and not sacrifice. For I did not come to call the righteous, but sinners, to repentance.

VEGA, Veyga
Language/Cultural Origin: Middle Eastern
Inherent Meaning: Falling Star
Spiritual Connotation: Prophetic
Scripture: Matthew 24:29 NLT
The sun will be darkened, the moon will not give light, the stars will fall from the sky, and the powers of heaven will be shaken.

VELMA, Valma, Vellma
Language/Cultural Origin: Old German
Inherent Meaning: Determined Protector
Spiritual Connotation: Watchful
Scripture: Matthew 25:13 NCV
So always be ready, because you don't know the day or the hour the Son of Man will come.

VENUS, Veenus
Language/Cultural Origin: Latin
Inherent Meaning: Love
Spiritual Connotation: Greatest Power
Scripture: Titus 3:4 NLT
But then God our Savior showed us his kindness and love.

VERA, Vara, Vira
Language/Cultural Origin: Latin
Inherent Meaning: Truth
Spiritual Connotation: Strong in Virtue
Scripture: Psalm 32:11 NLT
So rejoice in the LORD and be glad, all you who obey him! Shout for joy, all you whose hearts are pure!

VERENA, Verasha, Verasia, Vereena, Verina, Verity (see also Varina)
Language/Cultural Origin: Latin
Inherent Meaning: Truthful
Spiritual Connotation: Forthright
Scripture: Proverbs 12:19 NLT
Truth stands the test of time; lies are soon exposed.

VERNON, Vern, Verne
Language/Cultural Origin: Latin
Inherent Meaning: Youthful
Spiritual Connotation: Vigorous
Scripture: Colossians 3:23 NLT
Work hard and cheerfully at whatever you do, as though you were working for the Lord rather than for people.

VERONICA, Varonica, Veronika, Véronique, Vonnie, Vonny, Vronica
Language/Cultural Origin: Latin
Inherent Meaning: True Image
Spiritual Connotation: In God's Reflection
Scripture: 1 Corinthians 13:12 NCV
Now we see a dim reflection, as if we were looking into a mirror, but then we shall see clearly.

VIANNA, Viana (see also Vienna)
Language/Cultural Origin: American
Inherent Meaning: Gracious
Spiritual Connotation: Blessed
Scripture: 2 Chronicles 30:9 NKJV
For the LORD your God is gracious and merciful, and will not turn His face from you if you return to Him.

VICTOR, Vic, Victer, Vik, Viktor
Language/Cultural Origin: Latin
Inherent Meaning: Conqueror
Spiritual Connotation: Triumphant Spirit
Scripture: Mark 11:24 RSV
Therefore I tell you, whatever you ask in prayer, believe that you have received it, and it will be yours.

VICTORIA, Vicci, Vickee, Vicki, Vickie, Vicky, Victori, Victoriana, Victorianna, Victorina, Victorya, Viki, Vikki, Vikkie, Vikky, Viktori, Viktoria, Viktoriana, Viktorianna, Viktorina, Viktory, Viktorya
Language/Cultural Origin: Latin
Inherent Meaning: Conqueror
Spiritual Connotation: Triumphant Spirit
Scripture: Philippians 4:13 NKJV
I can do all things through Christ who strengthens me.

VIENNA, Viena (see also Vianna)
Language/Cultural Origin: Latin
Inherent Meaning: Capital of Austria
Spiritual Connotation: Chosen
Scripture: Psalm 106:5 NCV
Let me be happy along with your happy nation; let me join your own people in praising you.

VINCENT, Vicente, Vince, Vincente, Vinnie, Vinny
Language/Cultural Origin: Latin
Inherent Meaning: Conquering
Spiritual Connotation: Strength Through Faith
Scripture: Matthew 9:29 NASB
It shall be done to you according to your faith.

VINSON, Vinnson
Language/Cultural Origin: English
Inherent Meaning: Son of the Victor
Spiritual Connotation: Redeemed
Scripture: Romans 5:8 NKJV
But God demonstrates His own love toward us, in that while we were still sinners, Christ died for us.

VIOLET, Vi, Viola, Violette, Vyolet
Language/Cultural Origin: Latin
Inherent Meaning: Modest Flower
Spiritual Connotation: Humble
Scripture: James 4:10 NASB
Humble yourselves in the presence of the Lord, and He will exalt you.

VIRGIL, Vergil
Language/Cultural Origin: Latin
Inherent Meaning: Staff Bearer
Spiritual Connotation: Loyal Spirit
Scripture: Isaiah 41:13 NKJV
For I, the LORD your God, will hold your right hand.... Fear not, I will help you.

VIRGILIA, Virgillia
Language/Cultural Origin: Latin
Inherent Meaning: Staff Bearer
Spiritual Connotation: Protector
Scripture: Psalm 23:4 NLT
Your rod and your staff protect and comfort me.

VIRGINIA, Virg, Virgenia
Language/Cultural Origin: Latin
Inherent Meaning: Pure
Spiritual Connotation: Unblemished
Scripture: 2 Corinthians 5:17 NRSV
So if anyone is in Christ, there is a new creation: everything old has passed away; see, everything has become new!

VIVIAN, Viv, Vivia, Viviana, Vivianna, Viviane, Vivianne, Vivien, Vivienne
Language/Cultural Origin: Latin
Inherent Meaning: Lively
Spiritual Connotation: Joyous Spirit
Scripture: Psalm 37:4 NRSV
Take delight in the LORD, and he will give you the desires of your heart.

VLADIMIR, Vladamir, Vlade, Vladé
Language/Cultural Origin: Russian
Inherent Meaning: Famous Prince
Spiritual Connotation: Upright
Scripture: Jeremiah 29:13 NCV
When you search for me with all your heart, you will find me!

VONDRA, Vonda, Vondraea, Vondrea, Vondraya
Language/Cultural Origin: Czech
Inherent Meaning: Loving
Spiritual Connotation: Reborn
Scripture: 1 John 4:7 RSV

Beloved, let us love one another; for love is of God, and he who loves is born of God and knows God.

VOSHAWN, see Vashawn

Inherent Meaning: **Strong**
Spiritual Connotation: **Thankful**
Scripture: **Philippians 4:6** NASB
Be anxious for nothing, but in everything by prayer and supplication with thanksgiving let your requests be made known to God.

WALKER, Wallker
Language/Cultural Origin: **English**
Inherent Meaning: **Cloth Cleaner**
Spiritual Connotation: **Diligent**
Scripture: **Colossians 3:23** NCV
In all the work you are doing, work the best you can. Work as if you were doing it for the Lord, not for people.

WADE, Wayde
Language/Cultural Origin: **Old English**
Inherent Meaning: **One Who Advances**
Spiritual Connotation: **Generous Spirit**
Scripture: **Matthew 10:8** TLB
Give as freely as you have received!

WAGNER, Waggner
Language/Cultural Origin: **Old German**
Inherent Meaning: **Wagon Maker**
Spiritual Connotation: **Trusting Spirit**
Scripture: **Isaiah 26:3** NKJV
You will keep him in perfect peace, whose mind is stayed on You, because he trusts in You.

WAKANDA, Wakandra
Language/Cultural Origin: **Dakota**
Inherent Meaning: **Power**
Spiritual Connotation: **Faithful**
Scripture: **2 Corinthians 6:7** NLT
God's power has been working in us. We have righteousness as our weapon, both to attack and to defend ourselves.

WALDEN, Waldon
Language/Cultural Origin: **Old English**
Inherent Meaning: **From the Forest Valley**
Spiritual Connotation: **Calm Spirit**
Scripture: **Psalm 73:26** NCV
My body and my mind may become weak, but God is my strength. He is mine forever.

WALDO, Wald
Language/Cultural Origin: **German**

WALLACE, Wallach, Wallis, Wally, Walsh, Welsh
Language/Cultural Origin: **English**
Inherent Meaning: **From Wales**
Spiritual Connotation: **Man of Peace**
Scripture: **Isaiah 26:3** NCV
You, LORD, give true peace to those who depend on you, because they trust you.

WALTER, Walt
Language/Cultural Origin: **Old German**
Inherent Meaning: **Powerful Ruler**
Spiritual Connotation: **Strong Protector**
Scripture: **Psalm 121:8** RSV
The LORD will keep your going out and your coming in from this time forth and for evermore.

WALTON, Walten
Language/Cultural Origin: **English**
Inherent Meaning: **From the Fortified Town**
Spiritual Connotation: **Freedom of Spirit**
Scripture: **John 8:32** NKJV
And you shall know the truth, and the truth shall make you free.

WANDA, Wahnda, Wannda (see also Vanda, Wendy)
Language/Cultural Origin: **Old German**
Inherent Meaning: **Wanderer**
Spiritual Connotation: **Seeker of Truth**
Scripture: **Psalm 139:17** NASB
How precious also are Thy thoughts to me, O God! How vast is the sum of them!

WARD, Warde
Language/Cultural Origin: Old English
Inherent Meaning: Guardian
Spiritual Connotation: Watchful Spirit
Scripture: Luke 21:36 NCV
So be ready all the time. Pray that you will be strong enough to escape all these things that will happen.

WARDELL, Wardel
Language/Cultural Origin: Old English
Inherent Meaning: From the Watchman's Hill
Spiritual Connotation: Protector
Scripture: Isaiah 40:29 NASB
He gives strength to the weary, and to him who lacks might He increases power.

WARNER (see also Werner)
Language/Cultural Origin: Old French
Inherent Meaning: Defender
Spiritual Connotation: Courageous Spirit
Scripture: Luke 12:32 NKJV
Do not fear, little flock, for it is your Father's good pleasure to give you the kingdom.

WARREN, Warrin
Language/Cultural Origin: German
Inherent Meaning: Protecting Friend
Spiritual Connotation: Righteous
Scripture: Psalm 112:4 NIV
Even in darkness light dawns for the upright, for the gracious and compassionate and righteous man.

WARWICK, Warick, Warrick
Language/Cultural Origin: Old English
Inherent Meaning: From Near the Dam
Spiritual Connotation: Led by the Spirit
Scripture: Psalm 23:3 NKJV
He restores my soul; He leads me in the paths of righteousness for His name's sake.

WASHINGTON
Language/Cultural Origin: English
Inherent Meaning: From the Town Near the Water
Spiritual Connotation: Witness
Scripture: Psalm 71:18 NRSV
So even to old age and gray hairs, O God, do not forsake me, until I proclaim your might to all the generations to come.

WAVA, Waiva
Language/Cultural Origin: Slavic

Inherent Meaning: Foreigner
Spiritual Connotation: Child of God
Scripture: Ephesians 2:19 NRSV
So then you are no longer strangers and aliens, but you are citizens with the saints and also members of the household of God.

WAYMAN, Waymon
Language/Cultural Origin: Middle English
Inherent Meaning: Traveler
Spiritual Connotation: Shielded
Scripture: Deuteronomy 23:14 NKJV
For the LORD your God walks in the midst of your camp, to deliver you and give your enemies over to you.

WAYNE, Waiyne
Language/Cultural Origin: English
Inherent Meaning: Wagon Maker
Spiritual Connotation: Industrious
Scripture: Philippians 2:16 NRSV
It is by your holding fast to the word of life that I can boast on the day of Christ that I did not run in vain or labor in vain.

WEBSTER, Web
Language/Cultural Origin: Old English
Inherent Meaning: Weaver
Spiritual Connotation: Example
Scripture: Titus 2:7 NIV
In everything set them an example by doing what is good. In your teaching show integrity.

WELBY, Wellby
Language/Cultural Origin: Old English
Inherent Meaning: From Near the Well
Spiritual Connotation: Trusting Spirit
Scripture: Psalm 36:7 NKJV
How precious is Your lovingkindness, O God! Therefore the children of men put their trust under the shadow of Your wings.

WELDON, Welden
Language/Cultural Origin: Old English
Inherent Meaning: From the Hill Near the Well
Spiritual Connotation: Preserved
Scripture: Isaiah 42:6 NASB
I am the LORD, I have called you in righteousness, I will also hold you by the hand and watch over you.

WELLINGTON, Wellingtun

Language/Cultural Origin: Old English
Inherent Meaning: Prosperous
Spiritual Connotation: Conquering Spirit
Scripture: Acts 2:25 NKJV

I foresaw the LORD always before my face, for He is at my right hand, that I may not be shaken.

WENDELL, Wendal, Wendall, Wendel

Language/Cultural Origin: Old German
Inherent Meaning: Wanderer
Spiritual Connotation: Messenger of Truth
Scripture: 1 Corinthians 2:9 NRSV

No eye has seen, nor ear heard, nor the human heart conceived, what God has prepared for those who love him.

WENDY, Wenda, Wendee, Wendey, Wendi, Wendie (see also Wanda)

Language/Cultural Origin: Welsh
Inherent Meaning: Wanderer
Spiritual Connotation: Redeemed
Scripture: Ephesians 2:13 NCV

But now in Christ Jesus, you who were far away from God are brought near through the blood of Christ's death.

WERNER (see also Warner)

Language/Cultural Origin: Old German
Inherent Meaning: Protector
Spiritual Connotation: Peaceful
Scripture: John 14:27 NRSV

Peace I leave with you; my peace I give to you. Do not let your hearts be troubled, and do not let them be afraid.

WESLEY, Wes, Weslee, Westlee, Westley

Language/Cultural Origin: English
Inherent Meaning: From the Western Meadow
Spiritual Connotation: Steadfast
Scripture: Proverbs 3:23 RSV

Then you will walk on your way securely and your foot will not stumble.

WHEATLEY, Wheatleigh

Language/Cultural Origin: English
Inherent Meaning: From the Wheat Field
Spiritual Connotation: Witness
Scripture: John 4:35 NLT

Look around you! Vast fields are ripening all around us and are ready now for the harvest.

WHITLEY, Whitlee, Whitleigh

Language/Cultural Origin: English
Inherent Meaning: From the White Field
Spiritual Connotation: Joyful
Scripture: Psalm 96:12 NASB

Let the field exult, and all that is in it. Then all the trees of the forest will sing for joy.

WHITNEY, Whitnee, Whitnée, Whitneigh, Whitnie, Whittany, Whittney, Witney, Wittney

Language/Cultural Origin: Old English
Inherent Meaning: From the White Island
Spiritual Connotation: Protected
Scripture: Psalm 91:11 NKJV

For He shall give His angels charge over you, To keep you in all your ways.

WILBUR, Wilber

Language/Cultural Origin: Old German
Inherent Meaning: Resolute
Spiritual Connotation: Obedient
Scripture: James 1:25 NRSV

But those who look into the perfect law, the law of liberty, and persevere . . . they will be blessed in their doing.

WILDER, Willder

Language/Cultural Origin: Old English
Inherent Meaning: From the Wilderness
Spiritual Connotation: Sower
Scripture: Isaiah 40:3 NRSV

In the wilderness prepare the way of the LORD, make straight in the desert a highway for our God.

WILHELM, Willhelm

Language/Cultural Origin: Old German
Inherent Meaning: Determined Guardian
Spiritual Connotation: Wise
Scripture: Proverbs 2:11 NASB

Discretion will guard you, understanding will watch over you.

WILLARD, Wilard

Language/Cultural Origin: Old English
Inherent Meaning: Resolute and Brave
Spiritual Connotation: Champion
Scripture: Romans 8:28 KJV

And we know that all things work together for good to them that love God, to them who are the called according to his purpose.

WILLIAM, Bill, Billy, Wil, Wiley, Will, Willey, Willie, Willy, Wilson
Language/Cultural Origin: Old German
Inherent Meaning: Resolute Protector
Spiritual Connotation: Noble Spirit
Scripture: Deuteronomy 5:33 NKJV
You shall walk in all the ways which the LORD your God has commanded you . . . that you may prolong your days in the land which you shall possess.

WILLIS, Willus
Language/Cultural Origin: English
Inherent Meaning: Son of the Guardian
Spiritual Connotation: Cautious
Scripture: Psalm 141:3 RSV
Set a guard over my mouth, O LORD, keep watch over the door of my lips!

WILLOW, Wilow
Language/Cultural Origin: English
Inherent Meaning: Willow Tree
Spiritual Connotation: Great Hope
Scripture: Ezekiel 17:5 TLB
There he planted it in fertile ground beside a broad river, where it would grow as quickly as a willow tree.

WILONA, Willona
Language/Cultural Origin: English
Inherent Meaning: Desired
Spiritual Connotation: Seeker of Truth
Scripture: Psalm 42:1 NCV
As a deer thirsts for streams of water, so I thirst for you, God.

WINIFRED, Winn, Winnie, Winny, Wyn, Wynnie
Language/Cultural Origin: German
Inherent Meaning: Peaceful Friend
Spiritual Connotation: Cheerful Heart
Scripture: Psalm 4:7 NKJV
You have put gladness in my heart.

WINONA, Wenonah, Wenonah, Winonah, Wynnona, Wynona
Language/Cultural Origin: Sioux
Inherent Meaning: First-Born Daughter
Spiritual Connotation: Peaceful
Scripture: Philippians 4:7 NRSV
And the peace of God, which surpasses all understanding, will guard your hearts and your minds in Christ Jesus.

WINSTON, Winsten, Wynston
Language/Cultural Origin: Old English
Inherent Meaning: From the Friendly Town
Spiritual Connotation: Trusting
Scripture: Proverbs 3:5–6 NKJV
Trust in the LORD with all your heart, and lean not on your own understanding; in all your ways acknowledge Him, and He shall direct your paths.

WINTHROP, Wynthrop
Language/Cultural Origin: Old English
Inherent Meaning: From the Friend's Home
Spiritual Connotation: Benevolent
Scripture: Proverbs 18:24 NASB
A man of too many friends comes to ruin, but there is a friend who sticks closer than a brother.

WOLFGANG, Wolfgong
Language/Cultural Origin: Old German
Inherent Meaning: Quarrel of the Wolves
Spiritual Connotation: Faithful
Scripture: 1 Timothy 6:12 NKJV
Fight the good fight of faith, lay hold on eternal life, to which you were also called.

WOODROW, Woody, Woodson
Language/Cultural Origin: Old English
Inherent Meaning: From the Woods
Spiritual Connotation: Excellent Worth
Scripture: John 3:33 NKJV
He who has received His testimony has certified that God is true.

WOODWARD, Woodard
Language/Cultural Origin: Old English
Inherent Meaning: Forest Warden
Spiritual Connotation: Guardian
Scripture: Isaiah 26:3 NKJV
You will keep him in perfect peace, whose mind is stayed on You, because he trusts in You.

WORRELL, Worrel
Language/Cultural Origin: Old English
Inherent Meaning: From the Honest Home
Spiritual Connotation: Faith
Scripture: Mark 9:23 NCV
All things are possible for the one who believes.

WORTH, Worthington

Language/Cultural Origin: Old English
Inherent Meaning: Farmstead
Spiritual Connotation: Steadfast
Scripture: Psalm 1:3 NKJV

He shall be like a tree planted by the rivers of water, that brings forth its fruit in its season.

WYATT, Wyat, Wyatte

Language/Cultural Origin: Old French
Inherent Meaning: Little Warrior
Spiritual Connotation: Immoveable
Scripture: 2 Timothy 4:7 NKJV

I have fought the good fight, I have finished the race, I have kept the faith.

WYMAN, Wymon

Language/Cultural Origin: Old English
Inherent Meaning: Warrior
Spiritual Connotation: Determined
Scripture: 1 Corinthians 9:26 TLB

So I run straight to the goal with purpose in every step. I fight to win.

WYNN, Wyn, Wynette, Wynne

Language/Cultural Origin: Welsh
Inherent Meaning: Fair
Spiritual Connotation: Righteous
Scripture: Proverbs 4:18 RSV

But the path of the righteous is like the light of dawn, which shines brighter and brighter until full day.

WYNONNA, see Winona

XANDRA, Xandraea, Xandraya, Xandrea, Xandria, Xandriana (see also Sandra, Zandra)
Language/Cultural Origin: English
Inherent Meaning: Defender
Spiritual Connotation: Protector
Scripture: Isaiah 19:20 NRSV
He will send them a savior, and will defend and deliver them.

XANTHE, Xantha, Xanthia, Zantha, Zanthe, Zanthia
Language/Cultural Origin: Greek
Inherent Meaning: Blond
Spiritual Connotation: Lovely
Scripture: Song of Songs 1:15 NKJV
Behold, you are fair, my love! Behold, you are fair!

XAVIER, Xavian, Xavion, Xaven, Xavon, Zavier, Zavon
Language/Cultural Origin: Arabic
Inherent Meaning: Bright
Spiritual Connotation: Wise
Scripture: Proverbs 2:10–11 NKJV
When wisdom enters your heart, and knowledge is pleasant to your soul, discretion will preserve you; understanding will keep you.

XENIA, Xena (see also Zena, Zina)
Language/Cultural Origin: Greek
Inherent Meaning: Hospitable
Spiritual Connotation: Blessed

Scripture: 1 Peter 4:9 NLT
Cheerfully share your home with those who need a meal or a place to stay.

XERXES, Xerxus
Language/Cultural Origin: Persian
Inherent Meaning: Ruler
Spiritual Connotation: Benevolent
Scripture: 2 Peter 1:7 NCV
To your service for God, add kindness for your brothers and sisters in Christ; and to this kindness, add love.

XIMINES, Ximenes
Language/Cultural Origin: Spanish
Inherent Meaning: God Heard
Spiritual Connotation: Vindicated
Scripture: Psalm 66:19 NKJV
But certainly God has heard me; He has attended to the voice of my prayer.

XUAN, Xuann
Language/Cultural Origin: Vietnamese
Inherent Meaning: Spring
Spiritual Connotation: Refreshed
Scripture: Isaiah 58:11 NCV
The LORD will always lead you. . . . You will be like a garden that has much water, like a spring that never runs dry.

XUXA, Xúxa
Language/Cultural Origin: Brazilian
Inherent Meaning: Lily
Spiritual Connotation: Beautiful
Scripture: Song of Songs 2:2 NIV
Like a lily among thorns is my darling among the maidens.

XYLIA, Xyleah, Xyliana, Xylina
Language/Cultural Origin: Greek
Inherent Meaning: Wood
Spiritual Connotation: One of Integrity
Scripture: Proverbs 26:20 TLB
Fire goes out for lack of fuel, and tensions disappear when gossip stops.

XYLON, Xylen
Language/Cultural Origin: Greek
Inherent Meaning: From the Forest
Spiritual Connotation: Joyful
Scripture: Psalm 96:12 NCV
Let the fields and everything in them rejoice. Then all the trees of the forest will sing for joy.

YADIN, Yadeen, Yadín
Language/Cultural Origin: Hebrew
Inherent Meaning: God Will Judge
Spiritual Connotation: Righteous
Scripture: Psalm 98:9 NCV
Let them sing before the LORD, because he is coming to judge the world. He will judge the world fairly; he will judge the peoples with fairness.

YAEL, Yaella, Yaelle (see also Jael)
Language/Cultural Origin: Hebrew
Inherent Meaning: Strength of God
Spiritual Connotation: Arm of God
Scripture: Psalm 68:28 NRSV
Summon your might, O God; show your strength, O God, as you have done for us before.

YAGO, see Iago

YALE, Yail, Yayle
Language/Cultural Origin: Old English
Inherent Meaning: From the Hill
Spiritual Connotation: Prosperous
Scripture: Psalm 72:3 NIV
The mountains will bring prosperity to the people, the hills the fruit of righteousness.

YAMILA, see Jamila

YAMINAH, Yamina
Language/Cultural Origin: Middle Eastern
Inherent Meaning: Proper
Spiritual Connotation: Respectful
Scripture: 1 Timothy 5:2 NLT
Treat the older women as you would your mother, and treat the younger women with all purity as your own sisters.

YANA, Yanah, Yanna, Yannam, Yannah, Yannica, Yannick, Yannika (see also Jana)
Language/Cultural Origin: Polish
Inherent Meaning: Gift of God
Spiritual Connotation: Purchased
Scripture: Romans 6:23 NKJV
For the wages of sin is death, but the gift of God is eternal life in Christ Jesus our Lord.

YARDAN, Yarden
Language/Cultural Origin: Middle Eastern
Inherent Meaning: King
Spiritual Connotation: Victorious
Scripture: 2 Chronicles 20:15 NKJV
Do not be afraid nor dismayed because of this great multitude, for the battle is not yours, but God's.

YARINA, Yariana, Yarianna, Yaryna
Language/Cultural Origin: Russian
Inherent Meaning: Peace
Spiritual Connotation: Secure
Scripture: Philippians 4:7 NRSV
And the peace of God, which surpasses all understanding, will guard your hearts and your minds in Christ Jesus.

YARON, Yairon, Yaróne (see also Jaron)
Language/Cultural Origin: Hebrew
Inherent Meaning: He Will Sing; He Will Cry Out
Spiritual Connotation: High Praise
Scripture: Romans 15:9 TLB
I will praise you among the Gentiles and sing to your name.

YASMINE, Yasmen, Yasmon, Yazmen, Yazmin, Yazmine (see also Jasmine)
Language/Cultural Origin: Persian
Inherent Meaning: Jasmine Flower
Spiritual Connotation: Blossom
Scripture: Isaiah 35:2 TLB
Yes, there will be an abundance of flowers and singing and joy!

YEIRA, Yeirah
Language/Cultural Origin: Hebrew

Inherent Meaning: Light
Spiritual Connotation: Witness
Scripture: Matthew 5:14 KJV
Ye are the light of the world. A city that is set on an hill cannot be hid.

YELINA, Yelana, Yelanna (see also Jelena)
Language/Cultural Origin: Russian
Inherent Meaning: Shining
Spiritual Connotation: Glory of God
Scripture: Exodus 34:30 NASB
So when Aaron and all the sons of Israel saw Moses, behold, the skin of his face shone, and they were afraid to come near him.

YEMENA, Yemina
Language/Cultural Origin: Hebrew
Inherent Meaning: Capable
Spiritual Connotation: Exalted
Scripture: Proverbs 22:29 NKJV
Do you see a man who excels in his work? He will stand before kings; he will not stand before unknown men.

YERIEL, Yeriell, Yerielle (see also Jeriel)
Language/Cultural Origin: Hebrew
Inherent Meaning: Taught by God
Spiritual Connotation: Wise
Scripture: John 7:16 NCV
The things I teach are not my own, but they come from him who sent me.

YOHANN, see Johann

YOHANNA, see Johanna

YOKO, Yoki
Language/Cultural Origin: Japanese
Inherent Meaning: Good Girl
Spiritual Connotation: Justified
Scripture: Romans 3:10 NKJV
There is none righteous, no, not one.

YOLANDA, Yalonda, Yolana, Yolanna, Yolonda, Yulonda
Language/Cultural Origin: Greek
Inherent Meaning: Violet Flower
Spiritual Connotation: Sign of Life
Scripture: Psalm 36:9 NKJV
For with You is the fountain of life; in Your light we see light.

YONINA, Yonita
Language/Cultural Origin: Hebrew
Inherent Meaning: Dove
Spiritual Connotation: Graceful
Scripture: Song of Songs 4:1 NRSV
How beautiful you are, my love, how very beautiful! Your eyes are doves behind your veil.

YORDANA, Jordana, Jordanna, Yordanna
Language/Cultural Origin: Hebrew
Inherent Meaning: Descender
Spiritual Connotation: Praise
Scripture: Psalm 25:1 NKJV
To You, O LORD, I lift up my soul.

YORI, Yoriko
Language/Cultural Origin: Japanese
Inherent Meaning: Trustworthy
Spiritual Connotation: Honest
Scripture: Psalm 25:21 NLT
May integrity and honesty protect me, for I put my hope in you.

YORIANNA, see Jorianna

YORK, Yorick, Yorke, Yorrick
Language/Cultural Origin: Celtic
Inherent Meaning: From the Yew-Tree Estate
Spiritual Connotation: Vigilant
Scripture: Proverbs 3:23 NKJV
Then you will walk safely in your way, and your foot will not stumble.

YOSHI, Yóshi, Yoshie
Language/Cultural Origin: Japanese
Inherent Meaning: Respectful
Spiritual Connotation: Obedient
Scripture: Ephesians 6:5 NCV
Slaves, obey your masters here on earth with fear and respect and from a sincere heart, just as you obey Christ.

YUKI, Yukie
Language/Cultural Origin: Japanese
Inherent Meaning: Snow
Spiritual Connotation: Cleansed
Scripture: Isaiah 1:18 NKJV
Though your sins are like scarlet, they shall be as white as snow.

YUL, Yule, Yuul
Language/Cultural Origin: Mongolian

Inherent Meaning: Beyond the Horizon
Spiritual Connotation: Worshiper
Scripture: Psalm 113:3 NASB
From the rising of the sun to its setting the name of the LORD is to be praised.

YUMA, Yumia
Language/Cultural Origin: Native American
Inherent Meaning: Son of the Chief
Spiritual Connotation: Beloved
Scripture: Proverbs 17:6 NRSV
Grandchildren are the crown of the aged, and the glory of children is their parents.

YURI, Juri, Jurii, Jurri, Yurii, Yurri, Yury (see also Uri)
Language/Cultural Origin: Russian
Inherent Meaning: Farmer
Spiritual Connotation: Gifted
Scripture: Isaiah 28:26 NLT
The farmer knows just what to do, for God has given him understanding.

YURIKO, Yuríko
Language/Cultural Origin: Japanese

Inherent Meaning: Lily Child
Spiritual Connotation: Blessed
Scripture: Hosea 14:5 TLB
She will blossom as the lily and root deeply in the soil.

YVANNA, see Ivana

YVES, Ives
Language/Cultural Origin: French
Inherent Meaning: Little Archer
Spiritual Connotation: Trusting Spirit
Scripture: Psalm 37:5 RSV
Commit your way to the LORD; trust in him, and he will act.

YVONNE, Ivette, Ivonne, Yavonne, Yevette, Yvette
Language/Cultural Origin: French
Inherent Meaning: Young Archer
Spiritual Connotation: Shielded
Scripture: Leviticus 25:18 NRSV
You shall observe my statutes and faithfully keep my ordinances, so that you may live on the land securely.

Come, you blessed of My Father, inherit the
kingdom prepared for you from the
foundation of the world.

ZAFINA, Zafeena
Language/Cultural Origin: Middle Eastern
Inherent Meaning: Victorious
Spiritual Connotation: Strength of God
Scripture: 1 Corinthians 15:57 NKJV
*But thanks be to God, who gives us the
victory through our Lord Jesus Christ.*

ZAIM, Zaime, Zaimee, Zayme, Zaymee
Language/Cultural Origin: Middle Eastern
Inherent Meaning: Brigadier General
Spiritual Connotation: Leader
Scripture: Psalm 127:4 NKJV
*Like arrows in the hand of a warrior, so are
the children of one's youth.*

ZABRINA, see Sabrina

ZACHARIAH, Zac, Zacariah,
☞**Zacarias, Zacary, Zacc, Zaccari,**
Zaccary, Zach, Zacharee, Zacharey,
Zacharia, Zacharias, Zacharie,
Zachary, Zacherey, Zacherie,
Zachery, Zachrey, Zachry, Zack,
Zackari, Zackarie, Zackary, Zackery,
Zackory, Zacory, Zak, Zakarey,
Zakari, Zakarie, Zakary, Zakery,
Zakree, Zakry, Zaqary
Language/Cultural Origin: Hebrew
Inherent Meaning: God Has Remembered
Spiritual Connotation: Humble Before God
Scripture: Psalm 25:14 RSV
*The friendship of the LORD is for those who
fear him, and he makes known to them his
covenant.*

ZADA, Zaida, Zayda
Language/Cultural Origin: Middle Eastern
Inherent Meaning: Fortunate
Spiritual Connotation: Faithful
Scripture: Matthew 10:22 TLB
*Everyone shall hate you because you belong
to me. But all of you who endure to the end
shall be saved.*

ZADOK, Zaydok
☞ Language/Cultural Origin: Hebrew
Inherent Meaning: Righteous
Spiritual Connotation: Rewarded
Scripture: Matthew 25:34 NKJV

ZAMIR, Zameer, Zameir
Language/Cultural Origin: Hebrew
Inherent Meaning: Song
Spiritual Connotation: Joyful
Scripture: Psalm 40:3 RSV
*He put a new song in my mouth, a song of
praise to our God.*

ZANDRA, Zahndra, Zandraea,
Zandrea, Zandria, Zanndra, Zondra
(see also Sandra, Xandra)
Language/Cultural Origin: English
Inherent Meaning: Defender
Spiritual Connotation: Protector
Scripture: Jeremiah 51:36 NASB
*Behold, I am going to plead your case and
exact full vengeance for you.*

ZANE, Zain, Zayne
Language/Cultural Origin: English
Inherent Meaning: God Is Gracious
Spiritual Connotation: Blessed
Scripture: Numbers 6:25 NASB
*The LORD make His face shine on you, and be
gracious to you.*

ZANNA, Zana (see also Zaynah)
Language/Cultural Origin: English
Inherent Meaning: Lily
Spiritual Connotation: Beautiful
Scripture: Song of Songs 2:2 NKJV
*Like a lily among thorns, so is my love
among the daughters.*

ZANTHA, see Xanthe

ZARA, Zaira, Zarah, Zaria, Zariana, Zarya
Language/Cultural Origin: Middle Eastern
Inherent Meaning: Princess
Spiritual Connotation: Beloved
Scripture: Psalm 45:13 NIV
All glorious is the princess within her chamber; her gown is interwoven with gold.

ZAVIER, see Xavier

ZAYNAH, Zayna (see also Zanna)
Language/Cultural Origin: Middle Eastern
Inherent Meaning: Lovely
Spiritual Connotation: Beautiful
Scripture: Song of Songs 2:14 NKJV
Let me see your face, let me hear your voice; for your voice is sweet, and your face is lovely.

ZEBEDIAH, Zebedee
Language/Cultural Origin: Hebrew
Inherent Meaning: God's Gift
Spiritual Connotation: Redeemed
Scripture: Romans 1:16 NIV
I am not ashamed of the gospel, because it is the power of God for the salvation of everyone who believes: first for the Jew, then for the Gentile.

ZEBULON, Zebulun
Language/Cultural Origin: Hebrew
Inherent Meaning: Exalted
Spiritual Connotation: Wise
Scripture: James 4:10 NKJV
Humble yourselves in the sight of the Lord, and He will lift you up.

ZEDEKIAH, Zedekias
Language/Cultural Origin: Hebrew
Inherent Meaning: God Is Mighty and Just
Spiritual Connotation: Glory to God
Scripture: Proverbs 3:6 NKJV
In all your ways acknowledge Him, and He shall direct your paths.

ZEKE, see Ezekiel

ZELDA, Zellda
Language/Cultural Origin: German
Inherent Meaning: Warrior

Spiritual Connotation: Gifted
Scripture: Ecclesiastes 2:26 NRSV
For to the one who pleases him God gives wisdom and knowledge and joy.

ZELENKA, Zelenkia
Language/Cultural Origin: Czech
Inherent Meaning: Budding Blossom
Spiritual Connotation: Nurtured
Scripture: Isaiah 35:2 NKJV
It shall blossom abundantly and rejoice, even with joy and singing.

ZENA, Zeena, Zeenia, Zeenya, Zeina, Zenah, Zenia (see also Xenia, Zina)
Language/Cultural Origin: Persian
Inherent Meaning: Woman
Spiritual Connotation: Cherished
Scripture: Genesis 2:22 NKJV
Then the rib which the LORD God had taken from man He made into a woman, and He brought her to the man.

ZEPHANIAH, Zephan, Zephania
Language/Cultural Origin: Hebrew
Inherent Meaning: Protected by God
Spiritual Connotation: Precious
Scripture: Proverbs 4:6 NLT
Don't turn your back on wisdom, for she will protect you. Love her, and she will guard you.

ZEPHYR, Zephria, Zephriana
Language/Cultural Origin: Greek
Inherent Meaning: West Wind
Spiritual Connotation: Reborn
Scripture: John 3:8 NRSV
The wind blows where it chooses, and you hear the sound of it, but you do not know where it comes from or where it goes.

ZERLINA, Zerleyna
Language/Cultural Origin: Spanish
Inherent Meaning: Dawn
Spiritual Connotation: Blessed
Scripture: Psalms 139:9–10 NASB
If I take the wings of the dawn, if I dwell in the remotest part of the sea, even there Thy hand will lead me, and Thy right hand will lay hold of me.

ZIA, Zea, Zeah, Zeya
Language/Cultural Origin: Middle Eastern
Inherent Meaning: Light

Spiritual Connotation: Fearless
Scripture: Psalm 27:1 NKJV
The LORD is my light and my salvation;
whom shall I fear?

ZIGFRID, Ziggy (see also Siegfried)
Language/Cultural Origin: Latvian
Inherent Meaning: Victorious Peace
Spiritual Connotation: Secure in Christ
Scripture: Philippians 4:7 NRSV
And the peace of God, which surpasses all
understanding, will guard your hearts and
your minds in Christ Jesus.

ZIMRA, Zamora, Zemora
Language/Cultural Origin: Hebrew
Inherent Meaning: Song of Praise
Spiritual Connotation: Thankful
Scripture: Psalm 147:1 NRSV
Praise the LORD! How good it is to sing
praises to our God; for he is gracious, and a
song of praise is fitting.

ZIMRAAN, Zimran
Language/Cultural Origin: Middle Eastern
Inherent Meaning: Praise
Spiritual Connotation: Reverent
Scripture: Psalm 145:21 NIV
My mouth will speak in praise of the LORD.
Let every creature praise his holy name for
ever and ever.

ZINA, Zinah (see also Xenia, Zena)
Language/Cultural Origin: English
Inherent Meaning: Hospitable
Spiritual Connotation: Radiant Love
Scripture: 1 Peter 4:9 NLT
Cheerfully share your home with those who
need a meal or a place to stay.

ZOE, Zoa, Zöe, Zoé, Zoë, Zoee,
Zoey, Zoia, Zoie, Zoya
Language/Cultural Origin: Greek
Inherent Meaning: Life
Spiritual Connotation: Delivered
Scripture: Psalm 91:14 NRSV
Those who love me, I will deliver; I will
protect those who know my name.

ZORA, Zorah, Zorana, Zoranna,
Zoriana, Zorianna, Zorya
Language/Cultural Origin: Slavic
Inherent Meaning: Dawn
Spiritual Connotation: Bringer of Light
Scripture: Isaiah 60:1 RSV
Arise, shine; for your light has come, and the
glory of the LORD has risen upon you.

ZORG, Zörg
Language/Cultural Origin: Intergalactic Space
Inherent Meaning: Descendant of Blurgon
Spiritual Connotation: Intelligent Life
Scripture: Hebrews 11:3 NLT
By faith we understand that the entire
universe was formed at God's command, that
what we now see did not come from
anything that can be seen.

ZORINA, Zori, Zoriana, Zorianna,
Zorie, Zory (see also Czarina)
Language/Cultural Origin: Slavic
Inherent Meaning: Golden
Spiritual Connotation: Attractive
Scripture: Song of Songs 6:10 NKJV
Who is she who looks forth as the morning,
fair as the moon, clear as the sun.

ZSA ZSA, Zha Zha
Language/Cultural Origin: Hungarian
Inherent Meaning: Lily
Spiritual Connotation: Lovely
Scripture: Song of Songs 2:2 NASB
Like a lily among the thorns, so is my darling
among the maidens.

ZULEMA, Zulima
Language/Cultural Origin: Middle Eastern
Inherent Meaning: Peace
Spiritual Connotation: Secure
Scripture: Philippians 4:7 NASB
And the peace of God, which surpasses all
comprehension, will guard your hearts and
your minds in Christ Jesus.

ZURI, Zuria, Zuriya
Language/Cultural Origin: Swahili
Inherent Meaning: Beautiful
Spiritual Connotation: Messanger
Scripture: Romans 10:15 NRSV
How beautiful are the feet of those who bring
good news!

LIST OF

BIBLE

NAMES

Women's Names

Abi
Abia
Abiah
Abigail
Abihail
Abijah
Abishag
Achsa
Achsah
Agar
Ahinoam
Ahlai
Aholibamah
Anah
Anna
Apphia
Asenath
Atarah
Athaliah
Azubah

Baara
Bashemath
Basmath
Bathsheba
Bernice
Bilhah
Bithiah

Candace
Chloe
Claudia
Cozbi

Damaris
Deborah
Delilah
Dinah
Dorcas
Drusilla

Eglah
Elisabeth
Elisheba

Elizabeth
Ephah
Ephrath
Esther
Eunice
Euodias
Eve

Gomer

Hadassah
Hagar
Haggith
Hammoleketh
Hamutal
Hannah
Hazelelponi
Helah
Hephzibah
Herodias
Hodesh
Hodiah
Hoglah
Huldah
Hushim

Iscah

Jael
Jecholiah
Jecoliah
Jedidah
Jehoaddan
Jehoshabeath
Jehosheba
Jehudijah
Jemima
Jerioth
Jerusha
Jerushah
Jezebel
Joanna
Jochebed
Judith

Julia

Keren-happuch
Keturah
Kezia

Leah
Lois
Lo-ruhamah
Lydia

Maachah
Mahalah
Mahlah
Mara
Martha
Mary
Mary Magdalene
Matred
Mehetabel
Merab
Meshullemeth
Michaiah
Michal
Milcah
Miriam

Naamah
Narah
Naomi
Nehushta
Noadiah
Noah

Orpah

Peninnah
Persis
Phanuel
Phebe
Prisca
Priscilla
Puah

Rachel

Rahab
Rebecca
Rebekah
Reumah
Rhoda
Rizpah
Ruth

Salome
Sapphira
Sara
Sarah
Sarai
Serah
Shelomith
Sherah
Shimeath
Shimrith
Shiphrah
Shomer
Shua
Susanna
Syntyche

Tabitha
Tahpenes
Tamar
Taphath
Thamar
Timma
Tirzah
Tryphena
Tryphosa

Vashti

Zebudah
Zeresh
Zeruah
Zeruiah
Zibiah
Zillah
Zilpah
Zipporah

Men's Names

Aaron	Adonikam	Alphaeus	Areli
Abagtha	Adoniram	Alvah	Aretas
Abda	Adonizedek	Alvan	Argob
Abdeel	Adoram	Amal	Aridai
Abdi	Adrammelech	Amalek	Aridatha
Abdiel	Adriel	Amariah	Arieh
Abdon	Aeneas	Amasa	Ariel
Abednego	Agabus	Amasai	Arioch
Abel	Agag	Amashai	Arisai
Abia	Agee	Amasiah	Aristarchus
Abiah	Agrippa	Amaziah	Aristobulus
Abialbon	Agur	Ami	Armoni
Abiasaph	Ahab	Aminadab	Arnan
Abiathar	Aharah	Amittai	Arod
Abida	Aharhel	Ammiel	Arphaxad
Abidah	Ahasai	Ammihud	Artaxerxes
Abidan	Ahasbai	Amminadab	Artemas
Abiel	Ahasuerus	Amminadib	Arza
Abiezer	Ahaz	Ammishaddai	Asa
Abihail	Ahaziah	Ammizabad	Asahel
Abihu	Ahban	Ammon	Asahiah
Abihud	Aher	Amnon	Asaiah
Abijah	Ahi	Amok	Asaph
Abijam	Ahiah	Amon	Asareel
Abimael	Ahiam	Amos	Asarelah
Abimelech	Ahian	Amoz	Ashbea
Abinadab	Ahiezer	Amplias	Ashbel
Abinoam	Ahihud	Amram	Ashchenaz
Abiram	Ahijah	Amraphel	Asher
Abishai	Ahikam	Amzi	Ashkenaz
Abishalom	Ahilud	Anah	Ashpenaz
Abishua	Ahimaaz	Anaiah	Ashriel
Abishur	Ahiman	Anak	Ashur
Abitub	Ahimelech	Anan	Ashvath
Abiud	Ahimoth	Anani	Asiel
Abner	Ahinadab	Ananiah	Asnah
Abraham	Ahio	Ananias	Asnapper
Abram	Ahira	Anath	Aspatha
Absalom	Ahiram	Anathoth	Asriel
Achaicus	Ahisamach	Andrew	Asshur
Achan	Ahishahar	Andronicus	Asshurim
Achar	Ahishar	Aner	Assir
Achaz	Ahithophel	Aniam	Assur
Achbor	Ahitub	Annas	Asyncritus
Achim	Ahlai	Antipas	Ater
Achish	Ahoah	Antothijah	Athaiah
Adaiah	Aholah	Anub	Athaliah
Adalia	Aholiab	Apelles	Athlai
Adam	Aholibah	Aphiah	Attai
Adar	Aholibamah	Aphses	Augustus
Adbeel	Ahumai	Apollos	Azaliah
Addar	Ahuzam	Appaim	Azaniah
Addi	Ahuzzath	Aquila	Azarael
Ader	Aiah	Ara	Azareel
Adiel	Ajah	Arad	Azariah
Adin	Akan	Arah	Azaz
Adina	Akkub	Aram	Azaziah
Adino	Alameth	Aran	Azbuk
Adlai	Alemeth	Araunah	Azel
Admatha	Alexander	Arba	Azgad
Adna	Aliah	Archelaus	Aziel
Adnah	Alian	Archippus	Aziza
Adoni-bezek	Allon	Ard	Azmaveth
Adonijah	Almodad	Ardon	Azor

Azriel	Beri	Chushan-rishathaim	Eldaah
Azrikam	Beriah	Chuza	Eldad
Azur	Berodach-baladan	Cis	Elead
Azzan	Besai	Claudius	Eleasah
Azzur	Besodeiah	Clement	Eleazar
Baal	Beth-gader	Cleopas	Elhanan
Baal-hanan	Bethlehem	Cleophas	Eli
Baalis	Beth-rapha	Colhozeh	Eliab
Baana	Bethuel	Conaniah	Eliada
Baanah	Beth-zur	Coniah	Eliadah
Baaseiah	Bezai	Cononiah	Eliah
Baasha	Bezaleel	Core	Eliahba
Bakbakkar	Bezer	Cornelius	Eliakim
Bakbuk	Bichri	Cosam	Eliam
Bakbukiah	Bidkar	Coz	Elias
Balaam	Bigtha	Crescens	Eliasaph
Baladan	Bigthan	Crispus	Eliashib
Balac	Bigthana	Cush	Eliathah
Balak	Bigvai	Cushi	Elidad
Bani	Bildad	Cyrenius	Eliel
Barabbas	Bilgah	Cyrus	Elienai
Barachel	Bilgai	Dalaiah	Eliezer
Barak	Bilhan	Dalphon	Elihoenai
Bariah	Bilshan	Dan	Elihoreph
Bar-jesus	Bimhal	Daniel	Elihu
Barkos	Binea	Dara	Elijah
Barnabas	Binnui	Darda	Elika
Barsabas	Birsha	Darius	Elimelech
Barsabbas	Birzavith	Darkon	Elioenai
Bartholomew	Bishlam	Dathan	Eliphal
Bartimaeus	Biztha	David	Eliphalet
Baruch	Blastus	Debir	Eliphaz
Barzillai	Boaz	Dedan	Elipheleh
Bavai	Bocheru	Dekar	Eliphelet
Bazlith	Booz	Delaiah	Eliseus
Bazluth	Bukki	Demas	Elisha
Bealiah	Bukkiah	Dcmetrius	Elishah
Bebai	Bunah	Deuel	Elishama
Becher	Bunni	Diblaim	Elishaphat
Bechorath	Buz	Dibri	Elishua
Bedad	Buzi	Didymus	Eliud
Bedan	Caesar	Diklah	Elizaphan
Bedeiah	Caiaphas	Dionysius	Elizur
Beeliada	Cain	Diothephes	Elkanah
Beera	Cainan	Dishan	Elmodam
Beerah	Calcol	Dishon	Elnaam
Beeri	Caleb	Dodai	Elnathan
Bela	Canaan	Dodanim	Elon
Belah	Carcas	Dodavah	Elpaal
Belshazzar	Careah	Dodo	Elpalet
Belteshazzar	Carmi	Doeg	Eluzai
Benaiah	Carpus	Dumah	Elymas
Ben-Ammi	Carshena	Ebal	Elzabad
Ben-Hadad	Cephas	Ebed	Elzaphan
Ben-Hail	Chalcol	Ebed-melech	Emmor
Ben-Hanan	Chedorlaomer	Eber	Enan
Beninu	Chelluh	Ebiasaph	Enoch
Benjamin	Chelub	Eden	Enos
Beno	Chelubai	Eder	Enosh
Benoni	Chenaanah	Edom	Epaenetus
Ben-Zoheth	Chenani	Eglon	Epaphras
Beor	Chenaniah	Ehi	Epaphroditus
Bera	Cheran	Ehud	Ephah
Berachah	Chesed	Eker	Ephai
Berachiah	Chileab	Eladah	Epher
Beraiah	Chilion	Elah	Ephlal
Berechiah	Chimham	Elam	Ephod
Bered	Chislon	Elasah	Ephraim
			Ephron

Er
Eran
Erastus
Eri
Esaias
Esar-haddon
Esau
Eshbaal
Eshban
Eshcol
Eshek
Eshtemoa
Eshtemoh
Eshton
Esli
Esrom
Etam
Ethan
Ethbaal
Ethnan
Ethni
Eubulus
Eutychus
Evi
Evil-merodach
Ezar
Ezbai
Ezbon
Ezekias
Ezekiel
Ezer
Ezra
Ezri

Felix
Festus
Fortunatus

Gaal
Gabbai
Gad
Gaddi
Gaddiel
Gadi
Gaham
Gahar
Gaius
Galal
Gallio
Gamaliel
Gamul
Gareb
Gashmu
Gatam
Gazez
Gazzam
Geber
Gedaliah
Gedeon
Gedor
Gehazi
Gemalli
Gemariah
Genubath
Gera
Gershom
Gershon
Gesham
Geshem
Gether

Geuel
Gibbar
Gibea
Giddalti
Giddel
Gideon
Gideoni
Gilalai
Gilead
Ginath
Ginnetho
Gennethon
Gispa
Gog
Goliath
Gomer
Guni

Haahashtari
Habaiah
Habakkuk
Habaziniah
Hachaliah
Hachmoni
Hadad
Hadadezer
Hadarezer
Hadlai
Hadoram
Hagab
Hagaba
Hagabah
Haggai
Haggeri
Haggi
Haggiah
Hakkatan
Hakkoz
Hakupha
Hallohesh
Halohesh
Ham
Haman
Hammath
Hammedatha
Hammelech
Hamor
Hammuel
Hamuel
Hamul
Hanameel
Hanamel
Hanan
Hananeel
Hanani
Hananiah
Haniel
Hanniel
Hanoch
Hanun
Haran
Harbona
Harbonah
Hareph
Harhaiah
Harhas
Harhur
Harim
Hariph

Harnepher
Haroeh
Harum
Harumaph
Haruz
Hasadiah
Hasenuah
Hashabiah
Hashabnah
Hashabniah
Hashbadana
Hashem
Hashub
Hashubah
Hashum
Hashupha
Hasrah
Hassenaah
Hasshub
Hasupha
Hatach
Hathath
Hatipha
Hatita
Hattil
Hattush
Havilah
Hazael
Hazaiah
Hazarmaveth
Haziel
Hazo
Heber
Hebron
Hegai
Hege
Heldai
Heleb
Heled
Helek
Helem
Helez
Heli
Helkai
Helon
Hemam
Heman
Hemath
Hemdan
Hen
Hendad
Henoch
Hepher
Heresh
Hermas
Hermes
Hermogenes
Herod
Herodion
Hesed
Heth
Hezeki
Hezekiah
Hezion
Hezir
Hezrai
Hezro
Hezron
Hiddai

Hiel
Hilkiah
Hille
Hinnom
Hirah
Hiram
Hizkiah
Hizkijah
Hobab
Hod
Hodaiah
Hodaviah
Hodevah
Hodiah
Hodijah
Hoham
Homam
Hophni
Horam
Hori
Hosah
Hosea
Hoshaiah
Hoshama
Hoshea
Hotham
Hothan
Hothir
Hul
Hupham
Huppah
Huppim
Hur
Hurai
Huram
Huri
Hushah
Hushai
Husham
Hushim
Huz
Hymenaeus

Ibhar
Ibneiah
Ibnijah
Ibri
Ibzan
Ichabod
Idbash
Iddo
Igal
Igdaliah
Igeal
Ikkesh
Ilai
Imla
Imlah
Immer
Imma
Imnah
Imrah
Imri
Iphedeiah
Ir
Ira
Irad
Iram
Iri

Irijah	Jahdiel	Jehozabad	Joash
Irnahash	Jahdo	Jehozadak	Joatham
Iru	Jahleel	Jehu	Job
Isaac	Jahmai	Jehubbah	Jobab
Isaiah	Jahzeel	Jehucal	Joed
Ishbah	Jahzerah	Jehudi	Joel
Ishbak	Jahziel	Jehush	Joelah
Ishbi-benob	Jair	Jeiel	Joezer
Ishbosheth	Jairus	Jekameam	Jogli
Ishi	Jakan	Jekamiah	Joha
Ishiah	Jakeh	Jekuthiel	Johanan
Ishijah	Jakim	Jemuel	John
Ishma	Jalon	Jephthae	Joiada
Ishmael	Jambres	Jephthah	Joiakim
Ishmaiah	James	Jephunneh	Joiarib
Ishmerai	Jamin	Jerah	Jokim
Ishod	Jamlech	Jerahmeel	Jokshan
Ishpan	Janna	Jered	Joktan
Ishuah	Jannes	Jeremai	Jona
Ishuai	Japheth	Jeremiah	Jonadab
Ishui	Japhia	Jeremias	Jonah
Ismachiah	Japhlet	Jeremoth	Jonan
Ismaiah	Jarah	Jeremy	Jonas
Ispah	Jareb	Jeriah	Jonathan
Israel	Jared	Jeribai	Jorah
Isaachar	Jaresiah	Jeriel	Joram
Isshiah	Jarha	Jerijah	Jorim
Isuah	Jarib	Jerimoth	Jorkoam
Isui	Jaroah	Jeroboam	Josabad
Ithai	Jashen	Jeroham	Josaphat
Ithamar	Jashobeam	Jerubbaal	Jose
Ithiel	Jashub	Jerubbesheth	Josedech
Ithmah	Jashubi-lehem	Jesaiah	Joseph
Ithra	Jason	Jeshaiah	Joses
Ithran	Jathniel	Jesharelah	Joshah
Ithream	Javan	Jeshebeab	Joshaphat
Ittai	Jaziz	Jesher	Joshaviah
Izehar	Jeaterai	Jeshishai	Joshbekashah
Izhar	Jeberechiah	Jeshohaiah	Joshua
Izrahiah	Jecamiah	Jeshua	Josiah
Izri	Jechonias	Jeshuah	Josias
	Jeconiah	Jesiah	Josibiah
Jaakan	Jedaiah	Jesimiel	Josiphiah
Jaakobah	Jediael	Jese	Jotham
Jaala	Jedidiah	Jesui	Jozabad
Jaalah	Jeduthun	Jesus	Jozachar
Jaalam	Jeezer	Jether	Jozadak
Jaanai	Jehaleleel	Jetheth	Jubal
Jaare-oregim	Jehalelel	Jethro	Jucal
Jaasau	Jehdeiah	Jetur	Juda
Jaasiel	Jehezekel	Jeuel	Judah
Jaazaniah	Jehiah	Jeush	Judas
Jaaziah	Jehiel	Jeuz	Jude
Jaaziel	Jehieli	Jezaniah	Julius
Jabal	Jehizkiah	Jezer	Junia
Jabesh	Jehoadah	Jeziah	Jushab-hesed
Jabez	Jehoahaz	Jeziel	Justus
Jabin	Jehoash	Jezliah	
Jachan	Jehohanan	Jezoar	Kadmiel
Jachin	Jehoiachin	Jezrahiah	Kallai
Jacob	Jehoiada	Jezreel	Kareah
Jada	Jehoiakim	Jibsam	Kedar
Jadau	Jehoiarib	Jidlaph	Kedemah
Jaddua	Jehonadab	Jimna	Keilah
Jadon	Jehonathan	Jimnah	Kelaiah
Jahath	Jehoram	Joab	Kelita
Jahaziah	Jehoshaphat	Joah	Kemuel
Jahaziel	Jehoshua	Joahaz	Kanan
Jahdai	Jehoshuah	Joanna	Kenaz

Keros
Kirjath-jearim
Kish
Kishi
Kittim
Kohath
Kolaiah
Korah
Kore
Koz
Kushaiah

Laadah
Laadan
Laban
Lael
Lahad
Lahmi
Laish
Lamech
Lapidoth
Lazarus
Lebana
Lebanah
Lebbaeus
Lecah
Lehabim
Lemuel
Letushim
Leummim
Levi
Libni
Likhi
Linus
Lo-ammi
Lot
Lotan
Lucas
Lucifer
Lucius
Lud
Ludim
Luke
Lysanias
Lysias

Maacah
Maachah
Maadai
Maadiah
Maai
Maaseiah
Maasiai
Maath
Maaz
Maaziah
Machbanai
Machi
Machir
Machnadebai
Madai
Madmannah
Magbish
Magdiel
Magog
Magor-missabib
Magpiash
Mahalah
Mahalaleel
Mahali

Maharai
Mahath
Mahazioth
Maher-shalal-hash-baz
Mahlah
Mahli
Mahlon
Mahol
Malachi
Malcham
Malchiah
Malchiel
Malchijah
Malchiram
Malchi-shua
Malchus
Maleleel
Mallothi
Maluch
Mamre
Manaen
Manahath
Manasseh
Manasses
Manoah
Maoch
Maon
Marcus
Mareshah
Mark
Marsena
Mash
Massa
Mathusala
Matri
Mattan
Mattaniah
Mattatha
Mattathah
Mattathias
Mattenai
Matthan
Matthat
Matthew
Matthias
Mattithiah
Mebunnai
Medad
Medan
Mehetabeel
Mehetabel
Mehida
Mehir
Mehujael
Mehuman
Mehunim
Melatiah
Melchi
Melchiah
Melchisedec
Melchishua
Melchizedek
Melea
Melech
Melicu
Melzar
Memucan
Menahem
Menan

Meonothai
Mephibosheth
Meraiah
Meraioth
Merari
Mered
Meremoth
Meres
Merib-baal
Merodach-baladan
Mesech
Mesha
Meshach
Meshech
Meshelemiah
Meshezabeel
Meshillemith
Meshillemoth
Meshobab
Meshullam
Methusael
Methuselah
Meunim
Mezahab
Miamin
Mibhar
Mibsam
Mibzar
Micah
Micaiah
Micha
Michael
Michah
Michaiah
Michri
Midian
Mijamin
Mikloth
Mikneiah
Milalai
Miniamin
Mirma
Mishael
Misham
Mishma
Mishmannah
Mispereth
Mithredath
Mizpar
Mizraim
Mizzah
Mnason
Moab
Moadiah
Molid
Mordecai
Moses
Moza
Muppim
Mushi
Naam
Naaman
Naarai
Naashon
Naasson
Nabal
Naboth
Nachon

Nachor
Nadab
Nagge
Naham
Nahamani
Naharai
Nahari
Nahash
Nahath
Nahbi
Nahor
Nahshon
Nahum
Naphish
Naphtali
Narcissus
Nathan
Nathanael
Nathan-melech
Naum
Neariah
Nebai
Nebaioth
Nebajoth
Nebat
Nebo
Nebuchadnezzar
Nebuchadrezzar
Nebushasban
Nebuzar-adan
Necho
Nedabiah
Nehemiah
Nehum
Nekoda
Nemuel
Nepheg
Nephish
Nephthalim
Ner
Nereus
Nergal-sharezer
Neri
Neriah
Nethaneel
Nethaniah
Neziah
Nicanor
Nicodemus
Nicolas
Niger
Nimrod
Nimshi
Noadiah
Noah
Nobah
Nogah
Nohah
Non
Nun
Nymphas
Obadiah
Obal
Obed
Obed-edom
Obil
Ocran
Oded
Og

Ohad	Pharaoh	Rei	Shachia
Ohel	Pharaoh-hophra	Rekem	Shadrach
Olympas	Pharaoh-necho	Remaliah	Shage
Omar	Phares	Rephael	Shaharaim
Omri	Pharez	Rephah	Shallum
On	Pharosh	Rephaiah	Shallun
Onam	Phaseah	Resheph	Shalmai
Onan	Phichol	Reu	Shalman
Onesimus	Philemon	Reuben	Shalmaneser
Onesiphorus	Philetus	Reuel	Shama
Ophir	Philip	Rezia	Shamed
Ophrah	Philologus	Rezin	Shamer
Oreb	Phinehas	Rezon	Shamgar
Oren	Phlegon	Rhesa	Shamhuth
Ornan	Phurah	Ribai	Shamir
Osee	Phut	Rimmon	Shamma
Oshea	Phuvah	Riphath	Shammah
Othni	Phygellus	Roboam	Shammai
Othniel	Pilate	Rohgah	Shammoth
Ozem	Pildash	Romamti-ezer	Shammua
Ozias	Pileha	Rosh	Shammuah
Ozni	Piltai	Rufus	Shamsherai
	Pinon		Shapham
Paarai	Piram	Sabta	Shaphan
Padon	Pispah	Sabtah	Shaphat
Pagiel	Pithon	Sabtecha	Sharai
Pahath-moab	Pochereth	Sabtechah	Sharar
Palal	Poratha	Sacar	Sharezer
Pallu	Porcius	Sadoc	Shashai
Palti	Potiphar	Sala	Shashak
Paltiel	Poti-pherah	Salah	Shaul
Parmashta	Prochorus	Salathiel	Shavsha
Parmenas	Pua	Sallai	Sheal
Parnach	Puah	Salma	Shealtiel
Parosh	Publius	Salmon	Sheariah
Parshandatha	Pudens	Salu	Shear jashub
Paruah	Pul	Samgar-nebo	Sheba
Pasach	Put	Samlah	Shebaniah
Paseah	Putiel	Samson	Sheber
Pashur		Samuel	Shebna
Pathrusim	Quartus	Sanballat	Shebuel
Patrobas		Saph	Shecaniah
Paul	Raamah	Saraph	Shechaniah
Pedahel	Raamiah	Sargon	Shechem
Pedahzur	Rabmag	Sarsechim	Shedeur
Pedaiah	Rabsaris	Saruch	Shehariah
Pekah	Rabshakeh	Saul	Shelah
Pekahiah	Raddai	Sceva	Shelemiah
Pelaiah	Ragau	Seba	Sheleph
Pelaliah	Raguel	Secundus	Shelesh
Pelatiah	Raham	Segub	Shelomi
Peleg	Rakem	Seir	Shelomith
Pelet	Ram	Seled	Shelomoth
Peleth	Ramiah	Sem	Shelumiel
Peniel	Ramoth	Semachiah	Shem
Penuel	Rapha	Semei	Shema
Peresh	Raphah	Senaah	Shemaah
Perez	Raphu	Sennacherib	Shemaiah
Perida	Reaia	Senuah	Shemariah
Persis	Reaiah	Seorim	Shemember
Peter	Reba	Seraiah	Shemer
Pethahiah	Rechab	Sered	Shemida
Pethuel	Reelaiah	Sergius Paulus	Shemidah
Peulthai	Regem	Serug	Shemiramoth
Phalec	Regem-melech	Seth	Shemuel
Phallu	Rehabiah	Sethur	Shenazar
Phalti	Rehob	Shaaph	Shephatiah
Phaltiel	Rehoboam	Shaashgaz	Shephi
Phanuel	Rehoboth	Shabbethai	Shepho
	Rehum		

Shephupham
Shephuphan
Sherebiah
Sheresh
Sherezer
Sheshai
Sheshan
Sheshbazzar
Sheth
Shethar
Shetar-boznai
Sheva
Shilhi
Shillem
Shiloni
Shilshah
Shimea
Shimeah
Shimeam
Shimei
Shimeon
Shimhi
Shimi
Shimma
Shimon
Shimrath
Shimri
Shimrom
Shimron
Shimshai
Shinab
Shiphi
Shiphtan
Shisha
Shishak
Shitrai
Shiza
Shobab
Shobach
Shobai
Shobal
Shobek
Shobi
Shoham
Shomer
Shophach
Shua
Shuah
Shual
Shubael
Shuham
Shuni
Shupham
Shuppim
Shuthelah
Sia
Siaha
Sibbecai
Sibbechai
Sichem
Sidon
Sihon
SIlas
Silvanus
Simeon
Simon
Simri
Sippai
Sisamai

Sisera
So
Socho
Sodi
Solomon
Sopater
Sophereth
Sosipater
Sosthenes
Sotai
Stachys
Stephanas
Stephen
Suah
Susi
Sychar
Sychem
Tabbaoth
Tabeal
Tabeel
Tabrimon
Tahan
Tahath
Tahrea
Talmai
Talmon
Tamah
Tanhumeth
Tappuah
Tarah
Tarea
Tarshish
Tartan
Tatnai
Tebah
Tebaliah
Tehinnah
Tekoa
Telah
Telem
Tema
Teman
Temani
Temeni
Terah
Teresh
Tertius
Tertullus
Thaddaeus
Thahash
Thamah
Thara
Tharshish
Theophilus
Theudas
Thomas
Tiberius
Tibni
Tidal
Tiglath-pileser
Tikvah
Tikvath
Tilgath-pilneser
Tilon
Timaeus
Timna
Timnah
Timon

Timotheus
Timothy
Tiras
Tirhakah
Tirhanah
Tiria
Tirshatha
Titus
Toah
Tob-adonijah
Tobiah
Tobijah
Togarmah
Tohu
Toi
Tola
Tou
Trophimus
Tubal
Tubal-cain
Tychicus
Tyrannus

Ucal
Uel
Ulam
Ulla
Unni
Ur
Urbane
Uri
Uriah
Urias
Uriel
Urijah
Uthai
Uz
Uzai
Uzal
Uzza
Uzzah
Uzzi
Uzzia
Uzziah
Uzziel

Vajezatha
Vaniah
Vashni
Vophsi

Zaavan
Zavan
Zabad
Zabbai
Zabbud
Zabdi
Zabdiel
Zabud
Zaccai
Zacchaeus
Zacchur
Zaccur
Zachariah
Zacharias
Zacher
Zadok
Zaham
Zalaph
Zalmon
Zalmunna

Zanoah
Zaphnath-paaneah
Zaphon
Zara
Zarah
Zatthu
Zattu
Zaza
Zebadiah
Zebah
Zebedee
Zebina
Zebul
Zebulun
Zechariah
Zecher
Zedekiah
Zeeb
Zelek
Zelophehad
Zelotes
Zemira
Zenas
Zephaniah
Zephi
Zepho
Zephon
Zerah
Zerahiah
Zereth
Zeri
Zeror
Zerubbabel
Zetham
Zethan
Zethar
Zia
Ziba
Zibeon
Zibia
Zichri
Zidkijah
Zidon
Ziha
Zilthai
Zimmah
Zimran
Zimri
Zina
Ziph
Ziphah
Ziphion
Zippor
Zithri
Ziza
Zizah
Zohar
Zoheth
Zophah
Zophai
Zophar
Zorobabel
Zuar
Zuph
Zur
Zuriel
Zurishaddai

BIRTHSTONES & FLOWERS

January
Birthstone: Garnet
Flower: Carnation

February
Birthstone: Amethyst
Flower: Violet

March
Birthstone: Aquamarine
Flower: Jonquil

April
Birthstone: Diamond
Flower: Sweet Pea

May
Birthstone: Emerald
Flower: Lily of the Valley

June
Birthstone: Pearl
Flower: Rose

July
Birthstone: Ruby
Flower: Larkspur

August
Birthstone: Peridot
Flower: Gladiolus

September
Birthstone: Sapphire
Flower: Aster

October
Birthstone: Opal
Flower: Calendula

November
Birthstone: Topaz
Flower: Chrysanthemum

December
Birthstone: Turquoise
Flower: Narcissus

MOTHER'S
HERITAGE OF NAMES

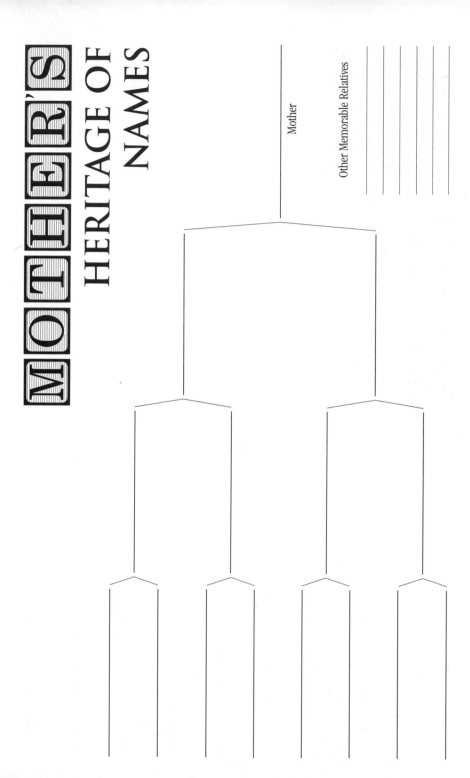

Mother

Other Memorable Relatives

FATHER'S
HERITAGE OF NAMES

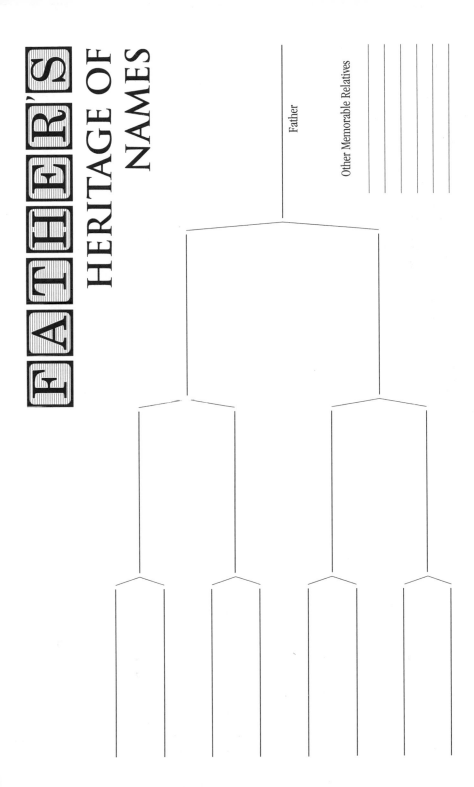

Father

Other Memorable Relatives

OUR FAVORITE
GIRL
NAMES

Rank   Mother's Choices

_____   _____

_____   _____

_____   _____

_____   _____

_____   _____

_____   _____

_____   _____

_____   _____

_____   _____

Rank   Father's Choices

_____   _____

_____   _____

_____   _____

_____   _____

_____   _____

_____   _____

_____   _____

_____   _____

_____   _____

OUR FAVORITE
🄱🄾🄨
NAMES

Rank   Mother's Choices

_____   _____

_____   _____

_____   _____

_____   _____

_____   _____

_____   _____

_____   _____

_____   _____

_____   _____

Rank   Father's Choices

_____   _____

_____   _____

_____   _____

_____   _____

_____   _____

_____   _____

_____   _____

_____   _____

_____   _____